THE NEW TESTAMENT APOCRYPHA

THE NEW TESTAMENT APOCRYPHA

As Compiled and Formatted by Derek A. Shaver

Shaver, Derek A.
THE NEW TESTAMENT APOCRYPHA

ISBN-13:
978-1480068209

ISBN-10:
1480068209

TABLE OF CONTENTS

THE NEW TESTAMENT APOCRYPHA

The *New Testament Apocrypha* are a number of writings by early
Christians that claim to be accounts of Jesus and his teachings, the
nature of God, or the teachings of his apostles and of their lives.
These writings often have links with books regarded as
"canonical". Not every branch of the Christian church agrees on
which writings should be regarded as "canonical" and which are
"apocryphal".

That some works are categorized as New Testament Apocrypha is
indicative of the wide range of responses that were engendered in
the interpretation of the message of Jesus of Nazareth. During the
first several centuries of the transmission of that message,
considerable debate turned on safeguarding its authenticity. Three
key methods of addressing this survive to the present day:
ordination, where groups authorize individuals as reliable teachers
of the message; creeds, where groups define the boundaries of
interpretation of the message; and canons, which list the primary
documents certain groups believe contain the message originally
taught by Jesus (in other words, the Bible).

The Source for these texts were largely comprised from;

"The Apocryphal New Testament"
M.R. James
Oxford: Clarendon Press, 1924

See; Apocrypha (page VII) for definitions of the term as derived
from *M.G. Easton M.A., D.D., Illustrated Bible Dictionary, Third
Edition, published by Thomas Nelson, 1897.*

II

INTRODUCTION
TO THE HOLY BIBLE

Bible, the English form of the Greek name "*Biblia*" , meaning "books," the name which in the fifth century began to be given to the entire collection of sacred books, the "Library of Divine Revelation." The name Bible was adopted by Wycliffe, and came gradually into use in our English language. The Bible consists of sixty-six different books, composed by many different writers, in three different languages, under different circumstances; writers of almost every social rank, statesmen and peasants, kings, herdsmen, fishermen, priests, tax-gatherers, tent-makers; educated and uneducated, Jews and Gentiles; most of them unknown to each other, and writing at various periods during the space of about 1600 years: and yet, after all, it is only one book dealing with only one subject in its numberless aspects and relations, the subject of man's redemption.

It is generally divided into the Old Testament, containing thirty-nine books, and the New Testament, containing twenty-seven books. The names given to the Old in the writings of the New are "the scriptures" (Matthew 21:42), "scripture" (2 Peter 1:20), "the holy scriptures" (Romans 1:2), "the law" (John 12:34), "the law of Moses, the prophets, and the psalms" (Luke 24:44), "the law and the prophets" (Matthew 5:17), "the old covenant" (2 Corinthians 3:14 , RSV).

The Old Testament is divided into three parts:,
1. The Law (Torah), consisting of the Pentateuch, or five books of Moses.
2. The Prophets, consisting of (1) the former, namely, Joshua, Judges, the Books of Samuel, and the Books of Kings; (2) the latter, namely, the greater prophets, Isaiah, Jeremiah, and Ezekiel, and the twelve "minor" prophets.
3. The Hagiographa, or holy writings, including the rest of the books. These were ranked in three divisions:, (1) The Psalms, Proverbs, and Job, distinguished by the Hebrew name, a word formed of the initial letters of these books, emeth , meaning truth. (2) Canticles, Ruth, Lamentations, Ecclesiastes, and Esther, called the five rolls, as being written for the synagogue use on five separate rolls. (3) Daniel, Ezra, Nehemiah, and 1 and 2 Chronicles. Between the Old and the New Testament no addition was believed by many traditions to be made to the revelation God had already given. The period of New Testament revelation, extending over a

century, began with the appearance of John the Baptist.

The New Testament consists of (1) the historical books, viz., the Gospels, and the Acts of the Apostles; (2) the Epistles; and (3) the book of prophecy, the Revelation.

The division of the Bible into chapters and verses is altogether of human invention, designed to facilitate reference to it. The ancient Jews divided the Old Testament into certain sections for use in the synagogue service, and then at a later period, in the ninth century A.D., into verses. Our modern system of chapters for all the books of the Bible was introduced by Cardinal Hugo about the middle of the thirteenth century (he died 1263). The system of verses for the New Testament was introduced by Stephens in 1551, and generally adopted, although neither Tyndale's nor Coverdale's English translation of the Bible has verses. The division is not always wisely made, yet it is very useful.

VERSIONS

Translations of the holy Scriptures. The word "version" is not found in the Bible, nevertheless, as frequent references are made in this work to various ancient as well as modern versions, it is fitting that some brief account should be given of the most important of these. These versions are important helps to the right interpretation of the Word.

1. The Targums

After the return from the Captivity, the Jews, no longer familiar with the old Hebrew, required that their Scriptures should be translated for them into the Chaldaic or Aramaic language and interpreted. These translations and paraphrases were at first oral, but they were afterwards reduced to writing, and thus targums, i.e., "versions" or "translations", have come down to us. The chief of these are,
The Onkelos Targum, i.e., the targum of Akelas=Aquila, a targum so called to give it greater popularity by comparing it with the Greek translation of Aquila mentioned below. This targum originated about the second century after Christ.
The targum of Jonathan ben Uzziel comes next to that of Onkelos in respect of age and value. It is more a paraphrase on the Prophets, however, than a translation. Both of these targums issued from the Jewish school which then flourished at Babylon.

IV

2. The Greek Versions

The oldest of these is the Septuagint, usually quoted as the LXX. The origin of this the most important of all the versions is involved in much obscurity. It derives its name from the popular notion that seventy-two translators were employed on it by the direction of Ptolemy Philadelphus, king of Egypt, and that it was accomplished in seventy-two days, for the use of the Jews residing in that country. There is no historical warrant for this notion. It is, however, an established fact that this version was made at Alexandria; that it was begun about 280 B.C., and finished about 200 or 150 B.C.; that it was the work of a number of translators who differed greatly both in their knowledge of Hebrew and of Greek; and that from the earliest times it has borne the name of "The Septuagint", i.e., The Seventy.

This version, with all its defects, must be of the greatest interest, (a) as preserving evidence for the text far more ancient than the oldest Hebrew manuscripts; (b) as the means by which the Greek Language was wedded to Hebrew thought; (c) as the source of the great majority of quotations from the Old Testament by writers of the New Testament.

The New Testament manuscripts fall into two divisions, Uncials, written in Greek capitals, with no distinction at all between the different words, and very little even between the different lines; and Cursives, in small Greek letters, and with divisions of words and lines. The change between the two kinds of Greek writing took place about the tenth century. Only five manuscripts of the New Testament approaching to completeness are more ancient than this dividing date. The first, numbered A, is the Alexandrian manuscript. Though brought to this country by Cyril Lucar, patriarch of Constantinople, as a present to Charles I., it is believed that it was written, not in that capital, but in Alexandria; whence its title. It is now dated in the fifth century A.D. The second, known as B, is the Vatican manuscript. The Third, C, or the Ephraem manuscript, was so called because it was written over the writings of Ephraem, a Syrian theological author, a practice very common in the days when writing materials were scarce and dear. It is believed that it belongs to the fifth century, and perhaps a slightly earlier period of it than the manuscript A. The fourth, D, or the manuscript of Beza, was so called because it belonged to the reformer Beza, who found it in the monastery of St. Irenaeus at

Lyons in 1562 A.D. It is imperfect, and is dated in the sixth century. The fifth (called Aleph) is the Sinaitic manuscript.

3. The Syriac Versions.

(2 Kings 18:26 ; Ezra 4:7 ; Daniel 2:4), more correctly rendered "Aramaic," including both the Syriac and the Chaldee languages. In the New Testament there are several Syriac words, such as "Eloi, Eloi, lama sabachthani?" (Mark 15:34 ; Matthew 27:46 gives the Heb. form, "Eli, Eli"), "Raca" (Matthew 5:22), "Ephphatha" (Mark 7:34), "Maran-atha" (1 Corinthians 16:22).

A Syriac version of the Old Testament, containing all the canonical books, along with some apocryphal books (called the Peshitto, i.e., simple translation, and not a paraphrase), was made early in the second century, and is therefore the first Christian translation of the Old Testament. It was made directly from the original, and not from the LXX. Version. The New Testament was also translated from Greek into Syriac about the same time. It is noticeable that this version does not contain the Second and Third Epistles of John, 2Peter, Jude, and the Apocalypse. These were, however, translated subsequently and placed in the version.

4. The Latin Versions.

A Latin version of the Scriptures, called the "Old Latin," which originated in North Africa, was in common use in the time of Tertullian (A.D. 150). Of this there appear to have been various copies or recensions made. That made in Italy, and called the Itala, was reckoned the most accurate. This translation of the Old Testament seems to have been made not from the original Hebrew but from the LXX.

This version became greatly corrupted by repeated transcription, and to remedy the evil Jerome (A.D. 329-420) was requested by Damasus, the bishop of Rome, to undertake a complete revision of it. It met with opposition at first, but was at length, in the seventh century, recognized as the "Vulgate" version. It appeared in a printed from about A.D. 1455, the first book that ever issued from the press. The Council of Trent (1546) declared it "authentic." It subsequently underwent various revisions, but that which was executed (1592) under the sanction of Pope Clement VIII. was adopted as the basis of all subsequent editions. It is regarded as the

sacred original in the Roman Catholic Church. All modern
European versions have been more or less influenced by the
Vulgate. This version reads ipsa_ instead of _ipse in Genesis 3:15 ,
"She shall bruise thy head."

5. Other Ancient Versions

There are several other ancient versions which are of importance
for Biblical critics, but which we need not mention particularly,
such as the Ethiopic, in the fourth century, from the LXX.; two
Egyptian versions, about the fourth century, the Memphitic,
circulated in Lower Egypt, and the Thebaic, designed for Upper
Egypt, both from the Greek; the Gothic, written in the German
language, but with the Greek alphabet, by Ulphilas (died A.D.
388), of which only fragments of the Old Testament remain; the
Armenian, about A.D. 400; and the Slavonic, in the ninth century,
for ancient Moravia. Other ancient versions, as the Arabic, the
Persian, and the Anglo-Saxon, may be mentioned.

6. The English Versions

The history of the English versions begins properly with Wycliffe.
Portions, however, of the Scriptures were rendered into Saxon (as
the Gospel according to John, by Bede, A.D. 735), and also into
English (by Orme, called the "Ormulum," a portion of the Gospels
and of the Acts in the form of a metrical paraphrase, toward the
close of the seventh century), long before Wycliffe; but it is to him
that the honour belongs of having first rendered the whole Bible
into English (A.D. 1380). This version was made from the Vulgate,
and renders Genesis 3:15 after that Version, "She shall trede thy
head."
   This was followed by Tyndale's translation (1525-1531); Miles
Coverdale's (1535-1553); Thomas Matthew's (1537), really,
however, the work of John Rogers, the first martyr under the reign
of Queen Mary. This was properly the first Authorized Version,
Henry VIII. having ordered a copy of it to be got for every church.
This took place in less than a year after Tyndale was martyred for
the crime of translating the Scriptures. In 1539 Richard Taverner
published a revised edition of Matthew's Bible. The Great Bible, so
called from its great size, called also Cranmer's Bible, was
published in 1539 and 1568. In the strict sense, the "Great Bible" is
"the only authorized version; for the Bishops' Bible and the present
Bible [the A.V.] never had the formal sanction of royal authority."
Next in order was the Geneva version (1557-1560); the Bishops'

Bible (1568); the Rheims and Douai versions, under Roman Catholic auspices (1582,1609); the Authorized Version (1611); and the Revised Version of the New Testament in 1880 and of the Old Testament in 1884.

CANON OF SCRIPTURE

The Canon of Scripture may be generally described as the "collection of books which form the original and authoritative written rule of the faith and practice of the Christian Church," i.e. the Old and New Testaments. The word canon , in classical Greek, is properly a straight rod , "a rule" in the widest sense, and especially in the phrases "the rule of the Church," "the rule of faith," "the rule of truth," The first direct application of the term canon to the Scriptures seems to be in the verses of Amphilochius (cir. 380 A.D.), where the word indicates the rule by which the contents of the Bible must be determined, and thus secondarily an index of the constituent books. The uncanonical books were described simply as "those without" or "those uncanonized." The canonical books were also called "books of the testament," and Jerome styled the whole collection by the striking name of "the holy library," which happily expresses the unity and variety of the Bible. After the Maccabean persecution the history of the formation of the Canon is merged in the history of its contents. The Old Testament appears from that time as a whole. The complete Canon of the New Testament, as commonly received at present, was ratified at the third Council of Carthage (A.D. 397), and from that time was accepted throughout the Latin Church. Respecting the books of which the Canon is composed.

THE APOCRYPHA

Meaning; *hidden*, or *spurious*. The name given to certain ancient books which found a place in the Greek Septuagint (LXX). and Latin Vulgate versions of the Old Testament, and were appended to all the great translations made from them in the sixteenth century.

The Old Testament Apocrypha *generally* consists of fourteen books, the chief of which are the Books of the Maccabees (q.v.), the Books of Esdras, the Book of Wisdom, the Book of Baruch, the Book of Esther, Ecclesiasticus, Tobit, Judith, etc.

The term apocrypha is used with various meanings, including "hidden", "esoteric", "spurious", "of questionable authenticity", ancient Chinese "revealed texts and objects" and "Christian texts that are not canonical".

The word is originally Greek (ἀπόκρυφα) and means "those hidden away". Specifically, ἀπόκρυφα is the neuter plural of ἀπόκρυφος, an adjective related to the verb ἀποκρύπτω [infinitive: ἀποκρύπτειν] (apocriptein), "to hide something away."[1]

The general term is usually applied to the books in the Roman Catholic Bible, and the Eastern Orthodox Bible, but not the Protestant Bible on their claim that it is not God's word. As such, it is misleading in this sense to refer to the Gospel according to the Hebrews or Gnostic writings as apocryphal, because they would not be classified in the same category by orthodox believers: they would be classified as a heretical subset of antilegomenae, to distinguish them from now-canonical ancient antilegomenae such as 2 Peter, 3 John and the Revelation of John, and non-canonical but non-heretical books which were quoted by the Early Fathers such as the pseudepigraphic Epistle of Barnabas, the Didache, or The Shepherd of Hermas. The gnostic writings are generally not accorded any status, not even a negative one: they are ignored, as they are incompatible with the accepted canon prima facie. Non-canonical books are texts of uncertain authenticity, or writings where the work is seriously questioned. Given that different denominations have different beliefs about what constitutes canonical scripture, there are several versions of the apocrypha.

During 16th-century controversies about the biblical canon, the word acquired a negative connotation, and has become a synonym for "spurious" or "false". This usage usually involves fictitious or legendary accounts that are plausible enough to be commonly considered true.

Greek Orthodox	Protestant Apocrypha	Roman Catholic
1 Esdras	1 Esdras	
	2 Esdras	
Tobit	Tobit	Tobit
Judith	Judith	Judith
Additions to Esther	Additions to Esther	Additions to Esther
Wisdom of Solomon	Wisdom of Solomon	Wisdom of Solomon
Ecclesiasticus	Ecclesiasticus	Ecclesiasticus
Baruch	Baruch	Baruch
Epistle of Jeremiah	Epistle of Jeremiah	Epistle of Jeremiah
Song of the Three	Song of the Three	Song of the Three
Story of Susanna	Story of Susanna	Story of Susanna
Bel and the Dragon	Bel and the Dragon	Bel and the Dragon
Prayer of Manasseh	Prayer of Manasseh	
1 Maccabees	1 Maccabees	
2 Maccabees	2 Maccabees	1 Maccabees
3 Maccabees		2 Maccabees
4 Maccabees		
Psalm 151		

PSEUDEPIGRAPHA

(from Ancient Greek pseudes "false", epigraphe = "inscription";
see the related epigraphy) are falsely attributed works, texts whose
claimed authorship is unfounded; a work, simply, "whose real
author attributed it to a figure of the past." For instance, few
Hebrew scholars would ascribe the Book of Enoch to the prophet
Enoch. Nevertheless, in some cases, especially for books
belonging to a religious canon, the question of whether a text is
pseudepigraphical or not elicits sensations of loyalty and can
become a matter of heavy dispute. The authenticity or value of the
work itself, which is a separate question for experienced readers,
often becomes sentimentally entangled in the association. Though
the inherent value of the text may not be called into question, the
weight of a revered or even apostolic author lends authority to a
text: in Antiquity pseudepigraphy was "an accepted and honored
custom practiced by students/admirers of a revered figure". This is
the essential motivation for pseudepigraphy in the first place.
Pseudepigraphy covers the false ascription of names of authors to
works, even to perfectly authentic works that make no such claim
within their text. Thus a widely accepted but incorrect attribution
of authorship may make a perfectly authentic text
pseudepigraphical. Assessing the actual writer of a text brings
questions of pseudepigraphical attributions within the discipline of
literary criticism. In a parallel case, forgers have been known to
improve the market value of a perfectly genuine 17th-century
Dutch painting by adding a painted signature Rembrandt fecit. On
a related note, a famous name assumed by the author of a work is
an allonym.

In Biblical studies, the Pseudepigrapha are Jewish religious works
written c 200 BC to 200 AD, not all of which are literally
pseudepigraphical. They are distinguished by Protestants from the
Deuterocanonica (Catholic and Orthodox) or Apocrypha
(Protestant), the books that appear in the Septuagint and Vulgate
but not in the Hebrew Bible or in Protestant Bibles. Catholics
distinguish only between the Deuterocanonica and all the other
books, that are called Apocrypha, name that is used also for the
Pseudepigrapha in the catholic usage.
In Biblical studies, pseudepigrapha refers particularly to works
which purport to be written by noted authorities in either the Old
and New Testaments or by persons involved in Jewish or Christian
religious study or history. These works can also be written about
Biblical matters, often in such a way that they appear to be as
authoritative as works which have been included in the many

versions of the Judeo-Christian scriptures. Eusebius of Caesarea indicates this usage dates back at least to Serapion, bishop of Antioch) whom Eusebius records as having said: "But those writings which are falsely inscribed with their name (ta pseudepigrapha), we as experienced persons reject...."
Many such works were also referred to as Apocrypha, which originally connoted "secret writings", those that were rejected for liturgical public reading. An example of a text that is both apocryphal and pseudepigraphical is the Odes of Solomon, pseudepigraphical because it was not actually written by Solomon but instead is a collection of early Christian (first to second century) hymns and poems, originally written not in Hebrew, and apocryphal because not accepted in either the Tanach or the New Testament.

But Protestants have also applied the word Apocrypha to texts found in the Roman Catholic and Orthodox scriptures which were not found in Hebrew manuscripts. Roman Catholics called those texts " deuterocanonical". Accordingly, there arose in some Protestant Biblical scholarship an extended use of the term pseudepigrapha for works that appeared as though they ought to be part of the Bibical canon, because of the authorship ascribed to them, but which stood outside both the Biblical canons recognized by Protestants and Catholics. These works were also outside the particular set of books that Roman Catholics called deuterocanonical and to which Protestants had generally applied the term Apocryphal. To confuse the matter even more, Orthodox Christians accept books as canonical that Roman Catholics and most Protestant denominations consider pseudepigraphical or at best of much less authority. There exist also churches that reject some of the books that Roman Catholics, Orthodox and Protestants accept. The same is true of some Jewish sects.

Examples of Old Testament pseudepigrapha are the Ethiopian Book of Enoch, Jubilees (both of which are canonical in the Abyssinian Church of Ethiopia); the Life of Adam and Eve and the Pseudo-Philo. Examples of New Testament pseudepigrapha (but in these cases also likely to be called New Testament Apocrypha) are the Gospel of Peter and the attribution of the Epistle to the Laodiceans to Paul. Further examples of New Testament pseudepigrapha include the aforementioned Gospel of Barnabas , and the Gospel of Judas, which begins by presenting itself as "the secret account of the revelation that Jesus spoke in conversation with Judas Iscariot".

THE NEW TESTAMENT APOCRYPHA

As Compiled and Formatted by Derek A. Shaver

THE GOSPEL OF THE BIRTH OF MARY

CHAPTER 1

1 The parentage of Mary. 7 Joachim her father, and Anna her mother, go to Jerusalem to the feast of the dedication. 9 Issachar the high priest reproaches Joachim for being childless.

THE blessed and ever glorious Virgin Mary, sprung from the royal race and family of David, was born in the city of Nazareth, and educated at Jerusalem, in the temple of the Lord.

2 Her father's name was Joachim, and her mother's Anna. The family of her father was of Galilee and the city of Nazareth. The family of her mother was of Bethlehem.

3 Their lives were plain and right in the sight of the Lord, pious and faultless before men. For they divided all their substance into three parts:

4 One of which they devoted to the temple and officers of the temple; another they distributed among strangers, and persons in poor circumstances; and the third they reserved for themselves and the uses of their own family.

5 In this manner they lived for about twenty years chastely, in the favour of God, and the esteem of men, without any children.

6 But they vowed, if God should favour them with any issue, they would devote it to the service of the Lord; on which account they went at every feast in the year to the temple of the Lord.

7 ¶ And it came to pass, that when the feast of the dedication drew near, Joachim, with some others of his tribe, went up to Jerusalem, and at that time, Issachar was high-priest;

8 Who, when he saw Joachim along with the rest of his neighbours, bringing his offering, despised both him and his offerings, and asked him,

9 Why he, who had no children, would presume to appear among those who had? Adding, that his offerings could never be acceptable to God, who was judged by him unworthy to have children; the Scripture having said, Cursed is every one who shall not beget a male in Israel.

10 He further said, that he ought first to be free from that curse by begetting some issue, and then come with his offerings into the presence of God.

11 But Joachim being much confounded with the shame of such reproach, retired to the shepherds, who were with the cattle in their pastures;

12 For he was not inclined to return home, lest his neighbours, who were present and heard all this from the high-priest, should publicly reproach him in the same manner.

CHAPTER 2

1 An angel appears to Joachim, 9 and informs him that Anna shall conceive and bring forth a daughter, who shall be called Mary, 11 be brought up in the temple, 12 and while yet a virgin, in a way unparalleled, bring forth the Son of God: 13 gives him a sign, 14 and departs.

BUT when he had been there for some time, on a certain day when he was alone, the angel of the Lord stood by him with a prodigious light.

2 To whom, being troubled at the appearance, the angel who had appeared to him, endeavouring to compose him said:

3 Be not afraid, Joachim, nor troubled at the sight of me, for I am an angel of the Lord sent by him to you, that I might inform you, that your prayers are heard, and your alms ascended in the sight of God.

4 For he hath surely seen your shame, and heard you unjustly reproached for not having children: for God is the avenger of sin, and not of nature;

5 And so when he shuts the womb of any person, he does it for this reason, that he may in a more wonderful manner again open it, and that which is born appear to be not the product of lust, but the gift of God.

6 For the first mother of your nation Sarah, was she not barren even till her eightieth year: And yet even in the end of her old age brought forth Isaac, in whom the promise was made a blessing to all nations.

7 Rachel also, so much in favour with God, and beloved so much by holy Jacob, continued barren for a long time, yet afterwards was the mot her of Joseph, who was not only governor of Egypt, but delivered many nations from perishing with hunger.

8 Who among the judges was more valiant than Samson, or more holy than Samuel? And yet both their mothers were barren.

9 But if reason will not convince you of the truth of my words, that there are frequent conceptions in advanced years, and that those who were barren have brought forth to their great surprise; therefore Anna your wife shall bring you a daughter, and you shall call her name Mary;

10 She shall, according to your vow, be devoted to the Lord from her infancy, and be filled with the Holy Ghost from her mother's womb;

11 She shall neither eat nor drink anything which is unclean, nor shall her conversation be without among the common people, but in the temple of the Lord; that so she may not fall under any slander or suspicion of what is bad.

12 So in the process of her years, as she shall be in a miraculous manner born of one that was barren, so she shall, while yet a virgin, in a way unparalleled, bring forth the Son of the most High God, who shall, be called Jesus, and, according to the signification of his name, be the Saviour of all nations.

13 And this shall be a sign to you of the things which I declare, namely, when you come to the golden gate of Jerusalem, you shall there meet your wife Anna, who being very much troubled that you returned no sooner, shall then rejoice to see you.

14 When the angel had said this he departed from him.

CHAPTER 3

1 The angel appears to Anna; 2 tells her a daughter shall be born unto her, 3 devoted to the service of the Lord in the temple, 5, who, being a virgin and not knowing man, shall bring forth the Lord, 6 and gives her a sign therefore. 8 Joachim and Anna meet and rejoice, 10 and praise the Lord. 11 Anna conceives, and brings forth a daughter called Mary.

AFTERWARDS the angel appeared to Anna his wife saying: Fear not, neither think that which you see is a spirit.

2 For I am that angel who hath offered up your prayers and alms before God, and am now sent to you, that I may inform you, that a daughter will be born unto you, who shall be called Mary, and shall be blessed above all women.

3 She shall be, immediately upon her birth, full of the grace of the Lord, and shall continue during the three years of her weaning in her father's house, and afterwards, being devoted to the service of the Lord, shall not depart from the temple, till she arrives to years of discretion.

4 In a word, she shall there serve the Lord night and day in fasting and prayer, shall abstain from every unclean thing, and never know any man;

5 But, being an unparalleled instance without any pollution or defilement, and a virgin not knowing any man, shall bring forth a son, and a maid shall bring forth the Lord, who both by his grace and name and works, shall be the Saviour of the world.

6 Arise therefore, and go up to Jerusalem, and when you shall come to that which is called the golden gate (because it is gilt with gold), as a sign of what I have told you, you shall meet your husband, for whose safety you have been so much concerned.

7 When therefore you find these things

thus accomplished, believe that all the rest which I have told you, shall also undoubtedly be accomplished.

8 ¶ According therefore to the command of the angel, both of them left the places where they were, and when they came to the place specified in the angel's prediction, they met each other.

9 Then, rejoicing at each other's vision, and being fully satisfied in the promise of a child, they gave due thanks to the Lord, who exalts the humble.

10 After having praised the Lord, they returned home, and lived in a cheerful and assured expectation of the promise of God.

11 ¶ So Anna conceived, and brought forth a daughter, and, according to the angel's command, the parents did call her name Mary.

CHAPTER 4

1 Mary brought to the temple at three years old. 6 Ascends the stairs of the temple by miracle. 8 Her parents sacrificed and returned home.

AND when three years were expired, and the time of her weaning complete, they brought the Virgin to the temple of the Lord with offerings.

2 And there were about the temple, according to the fifteen Psalms of degrees, fifteen stairs to ascend.

3 For the temple being built in a mountain, the altar of burnt-offering, which was without, could not be come near but by stairs;

4 The parents of the blessed Virgin and infant Mary put her upon one of these stairs;

5 But while they were putting off their clothes, in which they had travelled, and according to custom putting on some that were more neat and clean,

6 In the mean time the Virgin of the Lord in such a manner went up all the stairs one after another, without the help of any to lead or lift her, that any one would have judged from hence that she was of perfect age.

7 Thus the Lord did, in the infancy of his Virgin, work this extraordinary

work, and evidence by this miracle how great she was like to be hereafter.

8 But the parents having offered up their sacrifice, according to the custom of the law, and perfected their vow, left the Virgin with other virgins in the apartments of the temple, who were to be brought up there, and they returned home.

CHAPTER 5

2 Mary ministered unto by angels. 4 The high-priest orders all virgins of fourteen years old to quit the temple and endeavour to be married. 5 Mary refuses, 6 having vowed her virginity to the Lord. 7 The high-priest commands a meeting of the chief persons of Jerusalem, 11 who seek the Lord for counsel in the matter. 13 A voice from the mercy-seat. 15 The high priest obeys it by ordering all the unmarried men of the house of David to bring their rods to the altar, 17 that his rod which should flower, and on which the Spirit of God should sit, should betroth the Virgin.

BUT the Virgin of the Lord, as she advanced in fears, increased also in perfections, and according to the saying of the Psalmist, her father and mother forsook her, but the Lord took care of her.

2 For she every day had the conversation of angels, and every day received visitors from God, which preserved her from all sorts of evil, and caused her to abound with all good things;

3 So that when at length she arrived to her fourteenth year, as the wicked could not lay anything to her charge worthy of reproof, so all good persons, who were acquainted with her, admired her life and conversation.

4 At that time the high-priest made a public order. That all the virgins who had public settlements in the temple, and were come to this age, should return home, and, as they were now of a proper maturity, should, according to the custom of their country, endeavour

to be married.

5 To which command, though all the other virgins readily yielded obedience, Mary the Virgin of the Lord alone answered, that she could not comply with it.

6 Assigning these reasons, that both she and her parents had devoted her to the service of the Lord; and besides, that she had vowed virginity to the Lord, which vow she was resolved never to break through by lying with a man.

7 The high priest being hereby brought into a difficulty,

8 Seeing he durst neither on the one hand dissolve the vow, and disobey the Scripture, which says, Vow and pay,

9 Nor on the other hand introduce a custom, to which the people were strangers, commanded,

10 That at the approaching feast all the principal persons both of Jerusalem and the neighbouring places should meet together, that he might have their advice, how he had best proceed in so difficult a case.

11 When they were accordingly met, they unanimously agreed to seek the Lord, and ask counsel from him on this matter.

12 And when they were all engaged in prayer, the high-priest, according to the usual way, went to consult God.

13 And immediately there was a voice from the ark, and the mercy seat, which all present heard, that it must be inquired or sought out by a prophecy of Isaiah to whom the Virgin should be given and be betrothed;

14 For Isaiah saith, there shall come forth a rod out of the stem of Jesse, and a flower shall spring out of its root,

15 And the Spirit of the Lord shall rest upon him, the Spirit of Wisdom and Understanding, the Spirit of Counsel and Might, the Spirit of Knowledge and Piety, and the Spirit of the fear of the Lord shall fill him.

16 Then, according to this prophecy, he appointed, that all the men of the house and family of David, who were marriageable, and not married, should bring their several rods to the altar,

17 And out of whatsoever person's rod after it was brought, a flower should bud forth, and on the top of it the Spirit of the Lord should sit in the appearance of a dove, he should be the man to whom the Virgin should be given and be betrothed.

CHAPTER 6

1 Joseph draws back his rod. 5 The dove pitches on it. He betroths Mary and returns to Bethlehem. 7 Mary returns to her parents' house at Galilee.

AMONG the rest there was a man named Joseph, of the house and family of David, and a person very far advanced in years, who drew back his rod, when every one besides presented his.

2 So that when nothing appeared agreeable to the heavenly voice, the high-priest judged it proper to consult God again,

3 Who answered that he to whom the Virgin was to be betrothed was the only person of those who were brought together, who had not brought his rod.

4 Joseph therefore was betrayed.

5 For, when he did bring his rod, and a dove coming from Heaven pitched upon the top of it, every one plainly saw, that the Virgin was to be betrothed to him:

6 Accordingly, the usual ceremonies of betrothing being over, he returned to his own city of Bethlehem, to set his house in order, and make the needful for the marriage.

7 But the Virgin of the Lord, Mary, with seven other virgins of the same age, who had been weaned at the same time, and who had been appointed to attend her by the priest, returned to her parents' house in Galilee.

CHAPTER 7

7 The salutation of the Virgin by Gabriel, who explains to her that she shall conceive, without lying with a man, while a Virgin, by the Holy Ghost coming upon her without the heats of lust. 21 She submits.

NOW at this time of her first coming into Galilee, the angel Gabriel was sent to her from God, to declare to her the conception of our Saviour, and the manner and way of her conceiving him.

2 Accordingly going into her, he filled the chamber where she was with a prodigious light, and in a most courteous manner saluting her, he said,

3 Hail, Mary! Virgin of the Lord most acceptable! O Virgin full of Grace! The Lord is with you, you are blessed above all women, you are blessed above all men, that. have been hitherto born.

4 But the Virgin, who had before been well acquainted with the countenances of angels, and to whom such light from heaven was no uncommon thing,

5 Was neither terrified with the vision of the angel, nor astonished at the greatness of the light, but only troubled about the angel's words:

6 And began to consider what so extraordinary a salutation should mean, what it did portend, or what sort of end it would have.

7 To this thought the angel, divinely inspired, replies;

8 Fear not, Mary, as though I intended anything inconsistent with your chastity in this salutation:

9 For you have found favour with the Lord, because you made virginity your choice.

10 Therefore while you are a Virgin, you shall conceive without sin, and bring forth a son.

11 He shall be great, because he shall reign from sea to sea, and from the rivers to the ends of the earth.

12 And he shall be called the Son of the Highest; for he who is born in a mean state on earth reigns in an exalted one in heaven.

13 And the Lord shall give him the throne of his father David, and he shall reign over the house of Jacob for ever, and of his kingdom there shall be no end.

14 For he is the King of Kings, and Lord of Lords, and his throne is for ever and ever.

15 To this discourse of the angel the Virgin replied not, as though she were unbelieving, but willing to know the manner of it.

16 She said, How can that be? For seeing, according to my vow, I have never known any man, how can I bear a child without the addition of a man's seed?

17 To this the angel replied and said, Think not, Mary, that you shall conceive in the ordinary way.

18 For, without lying with a man, while a Virgin, you shall conceive; while a Virgin, you shall bring forth; and while a Virgin shall give suck.

19 For the Holy Ghost shall come upon you, and the power of the Most High shall overshadow you, without any of the heats of lust.

20 So that which shall be born of you shall be only holy, be. cause it only is conceived without sin, and being born, shall be called the Son of God.

21 Then Mary stretching forth her hands, and lifting her eyes to heaven, said, Behold the handmaid of the Lord! Let it be unto me according to thy word.

CHAPTER 8

1 Joseph returns to Galilee to marry the Virgin he had betrothed. 4 perceives she is with child, 5 is uneasy, 7 purposes to put her away privily, 8 is told by the angel of the Lord it is not the work of man but the Holy Ghost, 12 Marries her, but keeps chaste, 13 removes with her to Bethlehem, 15 where she brings forth Christ.

JOSEPH therefore went from Judæa to Galilee, with intention to marry the Virgin who was betrothed to him:

2 For it was now near three months since she was betrothed to him.

3 At length it plainly appeared she was with child, and it could not be hid from Joseph:

4 For going to the Virgin in a free manner, as one espoused, and talking familiarly with her, he perceived her to be with child.

5 And thereupon began to be uneasy and doubtful, not knowing what course it would be best to take;

6 For being a just man, he was not willing to expose her, nor defame her by the suspicion of being a whore, since he was a pious man.

7 He purposed therefore privately to put an end to their agreement, and as privately to put her away.

8 But while he was meditating these things, behold the angel of the Lord appeared to him in his sleep, and said Joseph, son of David, fear not;

9 Be not willing to entertain any suspicion of the Virgin's being guilty of fornication, or to think any thing amiss of her, neither be afraid to take her to wife;

10 For that which is begotten In her and now distresses your mind, is not the work of man, but the Holy Ghost.

11 For she of all women is that only Virgin who shall bring forth the Son of God, and you shall call his name Jesus, that is, Saviour: for he will save his people from their sins.

12 Joseph thereupon, according to the command of the angel, married the Virgin, and did not know her, but kept her in chastity.

13 And now the ninth month from her conception drew near, when Joseph took his wife and what other things were necessary to Bethlehem, the city from whence he came.

14 And it came to pass, while they were there, the days were fulfilled for her bringing forth.

15 And she brought forth her first-born son, as the holy Evangelists have taught, even our Lord Jesus Christ, who with the Father, Son, and Holy Ghost, lives and reigns to everlasting ages.

THE PROTEVANGELION

OR, AN HISTORICAL ACCOUNT OF THE BIRTH OF CHRIST, AND THE PERPETUAL VIRGIN MARY, HIS MOTHER

By James The Lesser, Cousin And Brother Of The Lord Jesus, Chief Apostle And First Bishop Of The Christians In Jerusalem.

CHAPTER 1

1 Joachim, a rich man, 2 offers to the Lord, 3 is opposed by Reuben the high-priest, because he has not begotten issue in Israel, 6 retires into the wilderness and fasts forty days and forty nights.

IN the history of the twelve tribes of Israel we read there was a certain person called Joachim, who being very rich, made double offerings to the Lord God, having made this resolution: my substance shall be for the benefit of the whole people, and that I may find mercy from the Lord God for the forgiveness of my sins.

2 But at a certain great feast of the Lord, when the children of Israel offered their gifts, and Joachim also offered his, Reuben the high-priest opposed him, saying it is not lawful for thee to offer thy gifts, seeing thou hast not begot any issue in Israel.

3 At this Joachim being concerned very much, went away to consult the registries of the twelve tribes, to see whether he was the only person who had begot no issue.

4 But upon inquiry he found that all the righteous had raised up seed in Israel:

5 Then he called to mind the patriarch Abraham, How that God in the end of

his life had given him his son Isaac;
upon which he was exceedingly
distressed, and would not be seen by his
wife:

6 But retired into the wilderness, and
fixed his tent there, and fasted forty
days and forty nights, saying to himself,
7 I will not go down either to eat or
drink, till the Lord my God shall look
down upon me, but prayer shall be my
meat and drink.

CHAPTER 2

*1 Anna, the wife of Joachim, mourns
her barrenness, is reproached with it by
Judith her maid, sits under a laurel tree
and prays to the Lord.*

IN the meantime his wife Anna was
distressed and perplexed on a double
account, and said I will mourn both for
my widowhood and my barrenness.
2 Then drew near a great feast of the
Lord, and Judith her maid said, How
long will you thus afflict your soul? The
feast of the Lord is now come, when it
is unlawful for any one to mourn.
3 Take therefore this hood which was
given by one who makes such things,
for it is not fit that I, who am a servant,
should wear it, but it well suits a person
of your greater character.
4 But Anna replied, Depart from me, I
am not used to such things; besides, the
Lord hath greatly humbled me.
5 I fear some ill-designing person hath
given thee this, and thou art come to
pollute me with my sin.
6 Then Judith her maid answered, What
evil shall I wish you when you will not
hearken to me?
7 I cannot wish you a greater curse than
you are under, in that God hath shut up
your womb, that you should not be a
mother in Israel.
8 At this Anna was exceedingly
troubled, and having on her wedding
garment, went about three o'clock in the
afternoon to walk in her garden.
9 And she saw a laurel-tree, and sat
under it, and prayed unto the Lord,
saying,
10 O God of my fathers, bless me and

regard my prayer as thou didst bless the
womb of Sarah, and gavest her a son
Isaac.

CHAPTER 3

*1 Anna perceiving a sparrow's nest in
the laurels bemoans her barrenness.*

AND as she was looking towards
heaven she perceived a sparrow's nest
in the laurel,
2 And mourning within herself, she
said, Woe is me, who begat me? and
what womb did bear me, that I should
be thus accursed before the children of
Israel, and that they should reproach
and deride me in the temple of my God:
Woe is me, to what can I be compared?
3 I am not comparable to the very
beasts of the earth, for even the beasts
of the earth are fruitful before thee, O
Lord! Woe is me, to what can I be
compared?
4 I am not comparable to the brute
animals, for even the brute animals are
fruitful before thee, O Lord! Woe is me,
to what am I comparable?
5 I cannot be compared to these waters,
for even the waters are fruitful before
thee, O Lord! Woe is me, to what can I
be compared?
6 I am not comparable to the waves of
the sea; for these, whether they are
calm, or in motion, with the fishes
which are in them, praise thee, O Lord!
Woe is me, to what can I be compared?
7 I am not comparable to the very earth,
for the earth produces its fruits, and
praises thee, O Lord!

CHAPTER 4

*1 An Angel appears to Anna and tells
her she shall conceive; two angels
appear to her on the same errand. 5
Joachim sacrifices. 8 Anna goes to
meet him, 9 rejoicing that she shall
conceive.*

THEN an angel of the Lord stood by
her and said, Anna, Anna, the Lord hath
heard thy prayer; thou shalt conceive
and bring forth, and thy progeny shall

be spoken of in all the world.

2 And Anna answered, As the Lord my God liveth, whatever I bring forth, whether it be male or female, I will devote it to the Lord my God, and it shall minister to him in holy things, during its whole life.

3 And behold there appeared two angels, saying unto her, Behold Joachim thy husband is coming with his shepherds.

4 For an angel of the Lord hath also come down to him, and said, The Lord God hath heard thy prayer, make haste and go hence, for behold Anna thy wife shall conceive.

5 And Joachim went down and called his shepherds, saying Bring me hither ten she-lambs without spot or blemish, and they shall be for the Lord my God.

6 And bring me twelve calves without blemish, and the twelve calves shall be for the priests and the elders.

7 Bring me also a hundred goats, and the hundred goats shall be for the whole people.

8 And Joachim went down with the shepherds, and Anna stood by the gate and saw Joachim coming with the shepherds.

9 And she ran, and hanging about his neck, said, Now I know that the Lord hath greatly blessed me:

10 For behold, I who was a widow am no longer a widow, and I who was barren shall conceive.

CHAPTER 5

1 Joachim abides the first day in his house, but sacrifices on the morrow. 2 consults the plate on the priest's forehead. 3 And is without sin. 6 Anna brings forth a daughter, 9 whom she calls Mary.

AND Joachim abode the first day in his house, but on the morrow he brought his offerings and said,

2 If the Lord be propitious to me let the plate which is on the priest's forehead make it manifest.

3 And he consulted the plate which the priest wore, and saw it, and behold sin

was not found in him.

4 And Joachim said, Now I know that the Lord is propitious to me, and hath taken away all my sins.

5 And he went down from the temple of the Lord justified, and he went to his own house.

6 And when nine months were fulfilled to Anna, she brought forth, and said to the midwife, What have I brought forth?

7 And she told her, a girl.

8 Then Anna said, the Lord hath this day magnified my soul; and she laid her in bed.

9 And when the days of her purification were accomplished, she gave suck to the child, and called her name Mary.

CHAPTER 6

1 Mary at nine months old, walks nine steps, 3 Anna keeps her holy, 4 When she is a year old, Joachim makes a great feast. 7 Anna gives her the breast, and sings a song to the Lord.

AND the child increased in strength every day, so that when she was nine months old, her mother put her upon the ground to try if she could stand; and when she had walked nine steps, she came again to her mother's lap.

2 Then her mother caught her up, and said, As the Lord my God liveth, thou shalt not walk again on this earth till I bring thee into the temple of the Lord.

3 Accordingly she made her chamber a holy place, and suffered nothing uncommon or unclean to come near her, but invited certain undefiled daughters of Israel, and they drew her aside.

4 But when the child was a year old, Joachim made a great feast, and invited the priests, scribes, elders, and all the people of Israel;

5 And Joachim then made an offering of the girl to the chief priests, and they blessed her, saying, The God of our fathers bless this girl, and give her a name famous and lasting through all generations. And all the people replied, So be it, Amen.

6 Then Joachim a second time offered

her to the priests, and they blessed her, saying, O most high God, regard this girl, and bless her with an everlasting blessing.

7 Upon this her mother took her up, and gave her the breast, and sung the following song to the Lord.

8 I will sing a new song unto the Lord my God, for he hath visited me, and taken away from me the reproach of mine enemies, and hath given me the fruit of his righteousness, that it may now be told the sons of Reuben, that Anna gives suck.

9 Then she put the child to rest in the room which she had consecrated, and she went out and ministered unto them.

10 And when the feast was ended, they went away rejoicing and praising the God of Israel.

CHAPTER 7

3 Mary being three years old, Joachim causes certain virgins to light each a lamp, and goes with her to the temple. 5 The high-priest places her on the third step of the altar, and she dances with her feet.

BUT the girl grew, and when she was two years old, Joachim said to Anna, Let us lead her to the temple of the Lord, that we may perform our vow, which we have vowed unto the Lord God, lest he should be angry with us, and our offering be unacceptable.

2 But Anna said, Let us wait the third year, lest she should be at a loss to know her father. And Joachim said, Let us then wait.

3 And when the child was three years old, Joachim said, Let us invite the daughters of the Hebrews, who are undefiled, and let them take each a lamp, and let them be lighted, that the child may not turn back again, and her mind be set against the temple of the Lord.

4 And they did thus till they ascended into the temple of the Lord. And the high-priest received her, and blessed her, and said, Mary, the Lord God hath magnified thy name to all generations,

and to the very end of time by thee will the Lord shew his redemption to the children of Israel,

5 And he placed her upon the third step of the altar, and the Lord gave unto her grace, and she danced with her feet, and all the house of Israel loved her.

CHAPTER 8

2 Mary fed in the temple by angels, 3 when twelve years old the priests consult what to do with her. 6 The angel of the Lord warns Zacharias to call together all the widowers, each bringing a rod. 7 The people meet by sound of trumpet. 8 Joseph throws away his hatchet, and goes to the meeting, 11 a dove comes forth from his rod, and alights on his head. 12 He is chosen to betroth the Virgin. 13 refuses because he is an old man, 15 is compelled, 16 takes her home, and goes to mind his trade of building.

AND her parents went away filled with wonder, and praising God, because the girl did not return back to them.

2 But Mary continued in the temple as a dove educated there, and received her food from the hand of an angel.

3 And when she was twelve years of age, the priests met in a council, and said, Behold, Mary is twelve years of age; what shall we do with her, for fear lest the holy place of the Lord our God should be defiled?

4 Then replied the priests to Zacharias the high-priest, Do you stand at the altar of the Lord, and enter into the holy place, and make petitions concerning her, and whatsoever the Lord shall manifest unto you, that do.

5 Then the high-priest entered into the Holy of Holies, and taking away with him the breastplate of judgment made prayers concerning her;

6 And behold the angel of the Lord came to him, and said, Zacharias, Zacharias, Go forth and call together all the widowers among the people, and let every one of them bring his rod, and he by whom the Lord shall shew a sign shall be the husband of Mary.

7 And the criers went out through all Judæa, and the trumpet of the Lord sounded, and all the people ran and met together.

8 ¶ Joseph also, throwing away the hatchet, went out to meet them; and when they were met, they went to the high-priest, taking every man his rod.

9 After the high-priest had received their rods, he went into the temple to pray;

10 And when he had finished his prayer, he took the rods, And went forth and distributed them, and there was no miracle attended them.

11 The last rod was taken by Joseph, and behold a dove proceeded out of the rod, and flew upon the head of Joseph.

12 And the high-priest said, Joseph, Thou art the person chosen to take the Virgin of the Lord, to keep her for him:

13 But Joseph refused, saying, I am an old man, and have children, but she is young, and I fear lest I should appear ridiculous in Israel.

14 Then the high-priest replied, Joseph, fear the Lord thy God, and remember how God dealt with Dathan, Korah, and Abiram, how the earth opened and swallowed them up, because of their contradiction.

15 Now therefore, Joseph, fear God, lest the like things should happen in your family.

16 Joseph then being afraid, took her unto his house, and Joseph said unto Mary, Behold, I have taken thee from the temple of the Lord, and now I will leave thee in my house; I must go to mind my trade of building. he Lord be with thee.

CHAPTER 9

1 The priests desire a new veil for the temple, 3 seven virgins cast lots for making different parts of it, 4 the lot to spin the true purple falls to Mary. 5 Zacharias, the high priest, becomes dumb. 7 Mary takes a pot to draw water, and hears a voice, 8 trembles and begins to work, 9 an angel appears, and salutes her, and tells her she shall conceive by the Holy Ghost,

17 she submits, 19 visits her cousin Elizabeth, whose child in her womb leaps.

AND it came to pass, in a council of the priests, it was said, Let us make a new veil for the temple.

2 And the high-priest said, Call together to me seven undefiled virgins of the tribe of David.

3 And the servants went and brought them into the temple of the Lord, and the high-priest said unto them Cast lots before me now, who of you shall spin the golden thread, who the blue, who the scarlet, who the fine linen, and who the true purple.

4 Then the high-priest knew Mary, that she was of the tribe of David; and he called her, and the true purple fell to her lot to spin, and she went away to her own house.

5 But from that time Zacharias the high-priest became dumb, and Samuel was placed in his room till Zacharias spoke again.

6 But Mary took the true purple, and did spin it.

7 ¶ And she took a pot, and went out to draw water, and heard a voice saying unto her, Hail thou who art full of grace, the Lord is with thee; thou art blessed among women.

8 And she looked round to the right and to the left (to see) whence that voice came, and then trembling went into her house, and laying down the water-pot she took the purple, and sat down in her seat to work it.

9 And behold the angel of the Lord stood by her, and said, Fear not, Mary, for thou hast found favour in the sight of God;

10 Which when she heard, she reasoned with herself what that sort of salutation meant.

11 And the angel said unto her, The Lord is with thee, and thou shalt conceive:

12 To which she replied, What! shall I conceive by the living God, and bring forth as all other women do?

13 But the angel returned answer, Not

so, O Mary, but the Holy Ghost shall come upon thee, and the power of the Most High shall overshadow thee;

14 Wherefore that which shall be born of thee shall be holy, and shall be called the Son of the Living God, and thou shalt call his name Jesus; for he shall save his people from their sins.

15 And behold thy cousin Elizabeth, she also hath conceived a son in her old age.

16 And this now is the sixth month with her, who was called barren; for nothing is impossible with God.

17 And Mary said, Behold the handmaid of the Lord; let it be unto me according to thy word.

18 ¶ And when she had wrought her purple, she carried it to the high-priest, and the high-priest blessed her, saying, Mary, the Lord God hath magnified thy name, and thou shalt be blessed in all the ages of the world.

19 Then Mary, filled with joy, went away to her cousin Elizabeth, and knocked at the door.

20 Which when Elizabeth heard, she ran and opened to her, and blessed her, and said, Whence is this to me, that the mother of my Lord should come unto me?

21 For lo! as soon as the voice of thy salutation reached my ears, that which is in me leaped and blessed thee.

22 But Mary, being ignorant of all those mysterious things which the archangel Gabriel had spoken to her, lifted up her eyes to heaven, and said, Lord! What am I, that all the generations of the earth should call me blessed?

23 But perceiving herself daily to grow big, and being afraid, she went home, and hid herself from the children of Israel; and was fourteen years old when all these things happened.

CHAPTER 10

1 Joseph returns from building houses, finds the Virgin grown big, being six months' gone with child, 2 is jealous and troubled, 8 reproaches her, 10 she affirms her innocence, 13 he leaves her, 16 determines to dismiss her privately,

17 is warned in a dream that Mary is with child by the Holy Ghost, 20 and glorifies God who hath shewn him such favour.

AND when her sixth month was come, Joseph returned from his building houses abroad, which was his trade, and entering into the house, found the Virgin grown big:

2 Then smiting upon his face, he said, With what face can I look up to the Lord my God? or, what shall I say concerning this young woman?

3 For I received her a Virgin out of the temple of the Lord my God, and have not preserved her such!

4 Who has thus deceived me? Who has committed this evil in my house, and seducing the Virgin from me, hath defiled her?

5 Is not the history of Adam exactly accomplished in me?

6 For in the very instant of his glory, the serpent came and found Eve alone, and seduced her.

7 Just after the same manner it has happened to me.

8 Then Joseph arising from the ground, called her, and said, O thou who hast been so much favoured by God, why hast thou done this?

9 Why hast thou thus debased thy soul, who wast educated in the Holy of Holies, and received thy food from the hand of angels?

10 But she, with a flood of tears, replied, I am innocent, and have known no man.

11 Then said Joseph, How comes it to pass you are with child?

12 Mary answered, As the Lord my God liveth, I know not by what means.

13 ¶ Then Joseph was exceedingly afraid, and went away from her, considering what he should do with her; and he thus reasoned with himself: 1

14 If I conceal her crime, I shall be found guilty by the law of the Lord;

15 And if I discover her to the children of Israel, I fear, lest she being with child by an angel, I shall be found to betray the life of an innocent person:

16 What therefore shall I do? I will privately dismiss her.

17 Then the night was come upon him, when behold an angel of the Lord appeared to him in a dream, and said,

18 Be not afraid to take that young woman, for that which is within her is of the Holy Ghost; .

19 And she shall bring forth a son, and thou shalt call his name Jesus, for he shall save his people from their sins.

20 Then Joseph arose from his sleep, and glorified the God of Israel, who had shown him such favour, and preserved the Virgin.

CHAPTER 11

3 Annas visits Joseph, perceives the Virgin big with child, 4 informs the high priest that Joseph had privately married her. 8 Joseph and Mary brought to trial on the charge. 17 Joseph drinks the water of the Lord as an ordeal, and receiving no harm, returns home.

THEN came Annas the scribe, and said to Joseph, Wherefore have we not seen you since your return?

2 And Joseph replied, Because I was weary after my journey, and rested the first day.

3 But Annas turning about perceived the Virgin big with child.

4 And went away to the priest, and told him, Joseph in whom you placed so much confidence, is guilty of a notorious crime, in that he hath defiled the Virgin whom he received out of the temple of the Lord, and hath privately married her, not discovering it to the children of Israel.

5 Then said the priest, Hath Joseph done this?

6 Annas replied, If you send any of your servants, you will find that she is with child.

7 And the servants went, and found it as he said.

8 Upon this both she and Joseph were brought to their trial, and the priest said unto her, Mary, what hast thou done?

9 Why hast thou debased thy soul, and forgot thy God, seeing thou wast brought up in the Holy of Holies, and didst receive thy food from the hands of angels, and heardest their songs?

10 Why hast thou done this?

11 To which with a flood of tears she answered, As the Lord my God liveth, I am innocent in his sight, seeing I know no man.

12 Then the priest said to Joseph, Why hast thou done this?

13 And Joseph answered, As the Lord my God liveth, I have not been concerned with her.

14 But the priest said, Lie not, but declare the truth; thou hast privately married her, and not discovered it to the children of Israel, and humbled thyself under the mighty hand (of God), that thy seed might be blessed.

15 And Joseph was silent.

16 Then said the priest (to Joseph), You must restore to the temple of the Lord the Virgin which you took thence.

17 But he wept bitterly, and the priest added, I will cause you both to drink the water of the Lord, which is for trial, and so your iniquity shall be laid open before you.

18 Then the priest took the water, and made Joseph drink, and sent him to a mountainous place.

19 And he returned perfectly well, and all the people wondered that his guilt was not discovered.

20 So the priest said, Since the Lord hath not made your sins evident, neither do I condemn you.

21 So he sent them away.

22 Then Joseph took Mary, and went to his house, rejoicing and praising the God of Israel.

CHAPTER 12

1 A decree from Augustus for taxing the Jews. 5 Joseph puts Mary on an ass, to return to Bethlehem, 6 she looks sorrowful, 7 she laughs, 8 Joseph inquires the cause of each, 9 she tells him she sees two persons, one mourning and the other rejoicing, 10 the delivery being near, he takes her from the ass, and places her in a cave.

AND it came to pass, that there went forth a decree from the Emperor Augustus, that all the Jews should be taxed, who were of Bethlehem in Judæa:

2 And Joseph said, I will take care that my children be taxed: but what shall I do with this young woman?

3 To have her taxed as my wife I am ashamed; and if I tax her as my daughter, all Israel knows she is not my daughter.

4 When the time of the Lord's appointment shall come, let him do as seems good to him.

5 And he saddled the ass, and put her upon it, and Joseph and Simon followed after her, and arrived at Bethlehem within three miles.

6 Then Joseph turning about saw Mary sorrowful, and said within himself, Perhaps she is in pain through that which is within her.

7 But when he turned about again he saw her laughing, and said to her,

8 Mary, how happens it, that I sometimes see sorrow, and sometimes laughter and joy in thy countenance?

9 And Mary replied to him, I see two people with mine eyes, the one weeping and mourning, the other laughing and rejoicing.

10 And he went again across the way, and Mary said to Joseph, Take me down from the ass, for that which is in me presses to come forth.

11 But Joseph replied, Whither shall I take thee? for the place is desert.

12 Then said Mary again to Joseph, take me down, for that which is within me mightily presses me.

13 And Joseph took her down.

14 And he found there a cave, and let her into it.

CHAPTER 13
1 Joseph seeks a Hebrew midwife, 2 perceives the fowls stopping in their flight, 3 the working people at their food not moving, 8 the sheep standing still, 9 the shepherd fixed and immoveable, 10 and kids with their mouths touching the water but not drinking.

AND leaving her and his sons in the cave, Joseph went forth to seek a Hebrew midwife in the village of Bethlehem.

2 But as I was going (said Joseph) I looked up into the air, and I saw the clouds astonished, and the fowls of the air stopping in the midst of their flight.

3 And I looked down towards the earth, and saw a table spread, and working people sitting around it, but their hands were upon the table, and they did not move to eat.

4 They who had meat in their mouths did not eat.

5 They who lifted their hands up to their heads did not draw them back:

6 And they who lifted them up to their mouths did not put anything in;

7 But all their faces were fixed upwards.

8 And I beheld the sheep dispersed, and yet the sheep stood still.

9 And the shepherd lifted up his hand to smite them, and his hand continued up.

10. And I looked unto a river, and saw the kids with their mouths close to the water, and touching it, but they did not drink.

CHAPTER 14
1 Joseph finds a midwife. 10 A bright cloud overshadows the care. 11 A great light in the cave, gradually increases until the infant is born. 13 The midwife goes out, and tells Salome that she has seen a virgin bring forth. 17 Salome doubts it. 20 her hand withers, 22 she supplicates the Lord, 28 is cured, 30 but warned not to declare what she had seen.

THEN I beheld a woman coming down from the mountains, and she said to me, Where art thou going, O man?

2 And I said to her, I go to inquire for a Hebrew midwife.

3 She replied to me, Where is the woman that is to be delivered?

4 And I answered, In the cave, and she is betrothed to me.

5 Then said the midwife, Is she not thy wife?

6 Joseph answered, It is Mary, who was educated in the Holy of Holies, in the house of the Lord, and she fell to my lot, and is not my wife, but has conceived by the Holy Ghost.

7 The midwife said, Is this true?

8 He answered, Come and see.

9 And the midwife went along with him, and stood in the cave.

10 Then a bright cloud overshadowed the cave, and the midwife said, This day my soul is magnified, for mine eyes have seen surprising things, and salvation is brought forth to Israel.

11 But on a sudden the cloud became a great light in the cave, so that their eyes could not bear it.

12 But the light gradually decreased, until the infant appeared, and sucked the breast of his mother Mary.

13 Then the midwife cried out, and said, How glorious a day is this, wherein mine eyes have seen this extraordinary sight!

14 And the midwife went out from the cave, and Salome met her.

15 And the midwife said to her, Salome, Salome, I will tell you a most surprising thing which I saw,

16 A virgin hath brought forth, which is a thing contrary to nature.

17 To which Salome replied, As the Lord my God liveth, unless I receive particular proof of this matter, I will not believe that a virgin hath brought forth.

18 ¶ Then Salome went in, and the midwife said, Mary, shew thyself, for a great controversy is risen concerning thee.

19 And Salome received satisfaction.

20 But her hand was withered, and she groaned bitterly.

21 And said, Woe to me, because of mine iniquity; for I have tempted the living God, and my hand is ready to drop off.

22 Then Salome made her supplication to the Lord, and said, O God of my fathers, remember me, for I am of the seed of Abraham, and Isaac, and Jacob.

23 Make me not a reproach among the children of Israel, but restore me sound to my parents.

24 For thou well knowest, O Lord, that I have performed many offices of charity in thy name, and have received my reward from thee.

25 Upon this an angel of the Lord stood by Salome, and said, The Lord God hath heard thy prayer, reach forth thy hand to the child, and carry him, and by that means thou shalt be restored.

26 Salome, filled with exceeding joy, went to the child, and said, I will touch him:

27 And she purposed to worship him, for she said, This is a great king which is born in Israel.

28 And straightway Salome was cured.

29 Then the midwife went out of the cave, being approved by God.

30 And lo! a voice came to Salome, Declare not the strange things which thou hast seen, till the child shall come to Jerusalem.

31 So Salome also departed, approved by God.

CHAPTER 15

1 Wise men come from the east. 3. Herod alarmed; 8 desires them if they find the child, to bring him word. 10 They visit the cave, and offer the child their treasure, 11 and being warned in a dream, do not return to Herod, but go home another way.

THEN Joseph was preparing to go away, because there arose a great disorder in Bethlehem by the coming of some wise men from the east,

2 Who said, Where is the king of the Jews born? For we have seen his star in the east, and are come to worship him.

3 When Herod heard this, he was exceedingly troubled, and sent messengers to the wise men, and to the priests, and inquired of them in the town-hall,

4 And said unto them, Where have you it written concerning Christ the king, or where should he be born?

5 Then they say unto him, In Bethlehem

of Judæa; for thus it is written: And thou Bethlehem in the land of Judah, art not the least among the princes of Judah, for out of thee shall come a ruler, who shall rule my people Israel.

6 And having sent away the chief priests, he inquired of the men in the town-hall, and said unto them, What sign was it ye saw concerning the king that is born?

7 They answered him, We saw an extraordinary large star shining among the stars of heaven, and so out-shined all the other stars, as that they became not visible, and we knew thereby that a great king was born in Israel, and therefore we are come to worship him.

8 Then said Herod to them, Go and make diligent inquiry; and if ye find the child, bring me word again, that I may come and worship him also.

9 So the wise men went forth, and behold, the star which they saw in the east went before them, till it came and stood over the cave where the young child was with Mary his mother.

10 Then they brought forth oat of their treasures, and offered unto him gold and frankincense, and myrrh.

11 And being warned in a dream by an angel, that they should not return to Herod through Judæa, they departed into their own country by another way.

CHAPTER 16

1 Herod enraged, orders the infants in Bethlehem to be slain. 2 Mary puts her infant in an ox manger. 3 Elizabeth flees with her son John to the mountains. 6 A mountain miraculously divides and receives them. 9 Herod incensed at the escape of John, causes Zacharias to be murdered at the altar, 23 the roofs of the temple rent, the body miraculously conveyed, and the blood petrified. 25 Israel mourns for him. 27 Simeon chosen his successor by lot.

THEN Herod perceiving that e he was mocked by the wise men, and being very angry, commanded certain men to go and to kill all the children that were in Bethlehem, from two years old and under.

2 But Mary hearing that the children were to be killed, being under much fear, took the child, and wrapped him up in swaddling clothes, and laid him in an ox-manger, because there was no room for them in the inn.

3 Elizabeth also, hearing that her son John was about to be searched for, took him and went up unto the mountains, and looked around for a place to hide him;

4 And there was no secret place to be found.

5 Then she groaned within herself, and said, O mountain of the Lord, receive the mother with the child.

6 For Elizabeth could not climb up.

7 And instantly the mountain was divided and received them.

8 And there appeared to them an angel of the Lord, to preserve them.

9 ¶ But Herod made search after John, and sent servants to Zacharias, when he was (ministering) at the altar, and said unto him, Where hast thou hid thy son?

10 He replied to them, I am a minister of God, and a servant at the altar; how should I know where my son is?

11 So the servants went back, and told Herod the whole; at which he was incensed, and said, Is not this son of his like to be king in Israel?

12 He sent therefore again his servants to Zacharias, saying, Tell us the truth, where is thy son, for you know that your life is in my hand.

13 So the servants went and told him all this:

14 But Zacharias replied to them, I am a martyr for God, and if he shed my blood, the Lord will receive my soul.

15 Besides know that ye shed innocent blood.

16 However Zacharias was murdered in the entrance of the temple and altar, and about the partition;

17 But the children of Israel knew not when he was killed.

18 ¶ Then at the hour of salutation the priests went into the temple, but Zacharias did not according to custom meet them and bless them;

19 Yet they still continued waiting for

him to salute them;

20 And when they found he did not in a long time come, one of them ventured into the holy place where the altar was, and he saw blood lying upon the ground congealed;

21 When, behold, a voice from heaven said, Zacharias is murdered, and his blood shall not be wiped away, until the revenger of his blood come.

22 But when he heard this, he was afraid, and went forth and told the priests what he had seen and heard; and they all went in, and saw the fact.

23 Then the roofs of the temple howled, and were rent from the top to the bottom:

24 And they could not find the body, but only blood made hard like stone.

25 And they went awry, and told the people, that Zacharias was murdered, and all the tribes of Israel heard thereof, and mourned for him, and lamented three days.

26 Then the priests took counsel together concerning a person to succeed him.

27 And Simeon and the other priests cast lots, and the lot fell upon Simeon.

28 For he had been assured by the Holy Spirit, that he should not die, till he had seen Christ come in the flesh.

¶ I James wrote this History in Jerusalem: and when the disturbance was I retired into a desert place, until the death of Herod. And the disturbance ceased at Jerusalem. That which remains is, that I glorify God that he hall; given me such wisdom to write unto you who are spiritual, and who love God: to whom (be ascribed) glory and dominion for ever and ever, Amen.

THE FIRST GOSPEL OF THE INFANCY OF JESUS CHRIST

CHAPTER 1

1 Caiaphas relates, that Jesus when in his cradle, informed his mother, that he was the Son. of God. 5 Joseph and Mary going to Bethlehem to be taxed, Mary's time of bringing forth arrives, and she goes into a cave. 8 Joseph fetches in a Hebrew woman, the cave filled with great lights. 11 The infant born, 17 cures the woman, 19 arrival of the shepherds.

THE following accounts we found in the book of Joseph the high-priest, called by some Caiaphas

2 He relates, that Jesus spake even when he was in the cradle, and said to his mother:

3 Mary, I am Jesus the Son of God, that word which thou didst bring forth according to the declaration of the angel Gabriel to thee, and my father hath sent me for the salvation of the world.

4 ¶ In the three hundred and ninth year of the æra of Alexander, Augustus published a decree that all persons should go to be taxed in their own country.

5 Joseph therefore arose, and with Mary his spouse he went to Jerusalem, and then came to Bethlehem, that he and his family might be taxed in the city of his fathers.

6 And when they came by the cave, Mary confessed to Joseph that her time of bringing forth was come, and she could not go on to the city, and said, Let us go into this cave.

7 At that time the sun was very near going down.

8 But Joseph hastened away, that he

might fetch her a midwife; and when he saw an old Hebrew woman who was of Jerusalem, he said to her, Pray come hither, good woman, and go into that cave, and you will there see a woman just ready to bring forth.

9 It was after sunset, when the old woman and Joseph with her reached the cave, and they both went into it.

10 And behold, it was all filled with lights, greater than the light of lamps and candles, and greater than the light of the sun itself.

11 The infant was then wrapped up in swaddling clothes, and sucking the breasts of his mother Mary.

12 When they both saw this light, they were surprised; the old woman asked Mary, Art thou the mother of this child?

13 Mary replied, She was.

14 On which the old woman said, Thou art very different from all other women.

15 Mary answered, As there is not any child like to my son, so neither is there any woman like to his mother.

16 The old woman answered, and said, O my Lady, I am come hither that I may obtain an everlasting reward.

17 Then our Lady, Mary, said to her, Lay thine hands upon the infant; which, when she had done, she became whole.

18 And as she was going forth, she said, From henceforth, all the days of my life, I will attend upon and be a servant of this infant.

19 After this, when the shepherds came, and had made a fire, and they were exceedingly rejoicing, the heavenly host appeared to them, praising and adoring the supreme God.

20 And as the shepherds were engaged in the same employment, the cave at that time seemed like a glorious temple, because both the tongues of angels and men united to adore and magnify God, on account of the birth of the Lord Christ.

21 But when the old Hebrew woman saw all these evident miracles, she gave praises to God, and said, I thank thee, O God, thou God of Israel, for that mine eyes have seen the birth of the Saviour of the world.

CHAPTER 2

1 The child circumcised in the cave, 2 and the old woman preserving his foreskin or navel-string in a box of spikenard, Mary afterwards anoints Christ with it. 5 Christ brought to the temple, 6 shines, 7 angels stand around him adoring. 8 Simeon praises Christ.

AND when the time of his circumcision was come, namely, the eighth day, on which the law commanded the child to be circumcised, they circumcised him in the cave.

2 And the old Hebrew woman took the foreskin (others say she took the navel-string), and preserved it in an alabaster-box of old oil of spikenard.

3 And she had a son who was a druggist, to whom she said, Take heed thou sell not this alabaster box of spikenard-ointment, although thou shouldst be offered three hundred pence for it.

4 Now this is that alabaster-box which Mary the sinner procured, and poured forth the ointment out of it upon the head and the feet of our Lord Jesus Christ, and wiped it off with the I hairs of her head.

5 Then after ten days they brought him to Jerusalem, and on the fortieth day from his birth they presented him in the temple before the Lord, making the proper offerings for him, according to the requirement of the law of Moses: namely, that every male which opens the womb shall be called holy unto God.

6 At that time old Simeon saw him shining as a pillar of light, when Mary the Virgin, his mother, carried him in her arms, and was filled with the greatest pleasure at the sight.

7 And the angels stood around him, adoring him, as a king's guards stand around him.

8 Then Simeon going near to Mary, and stretching forth his hands towards her, said to the Lord Christ, Now, O my Lord, thy servant shall depart in peace, according to thy word;

9 For mine eyes have seen thy mercy, which thou hast prepared for the salvation of all nations; a light to all people, and the glory of thy people Israel.

10 Hannah the prophetess was also present, and drawing near, she gave praises to God, and celebrated the happiness of Mary.

CHAPTER 3

1 The wise men visit Christ. Mary gives them one of his swaddling clothes. 3 An angel appears to them in the form of a star. They return and make a fire, and worship the swaddling cloth, and put it in the fire, where it remains unconsumed.

AND it came to pass, when the Lord Jesus was born at Bethlehem, a city of Judæa, in the time of Herod the King; the wise men came from the East to Jerusalem, according to the prophecy of Zoradascht, and brought with them offerings: namely, gold, frankincense, and myrrh, and worshipped him, and offered to him their gifts.

2 Then the Lady Mary took one of his swaddling clothes in which the infant was wrapped, and gave it to them instead of a blessing, which they received from her as a most noble present.

3 And at the same time there appeared to them an angel in the form of that star which had before been their guide in their journey; the light of which they followed till they returned into their own country.

4 On their return their kings and princes came to them inquiring, What they had seen and done? What sort of journey and return they had? What company they had on the road?

5 But they produced the swaddling cloth which Mary had given to them, on account whereof they kept a feast.

6 And having, according to the custom of their country, made a fire, they worshipped it.

7 And casting the swaddling cloth into it, the fire took it, and kept it.

8 And when the fire was put out, they took forth the swaddling cloth unhurt, as much as if the fire had not touched it.

9 Then they began to kiss it, and put it upon their heads and their eyes, saying, This is certainly an undoubted truth, and it is really surprising that the fire could not burn it, and consume it.

10 Then they took it, and with the greatest respect laid it up among their treasures.

CHAPTER 4

1 Herod intends to put Christ to death. 3 An angel warns Joseph to take the child and its mother into Egypt. 6 Consternation on their arrival. 13 The idols fall down. 15 Mary washes Christ's swaddling clothes, and hangs them to dry on a post. 16 A son of the chief priest puts one on his head, and being possessed of devils, they leave him.

NOW Herod, perceiving that the wise men did delay, and not return to him, called together the priests and wise men and said, Tell me in what place the Christ should be born?

2 And when they replied, in Bethlehem, a city of Judaea, he began to contrive in his own mind the death of the Lord Jesus Christ.

3 But an angel of the Lord appeared to Joseph in his sleep, and said, Arise, take the child and his mother, and go into Egypt as soon as the cock crows. So he arose, and went.

4 ¶ And as he was considering with himself about his journey, the morning came upon him.

5 In the length of the journey the girts of the saddle broke.

6 And now he drew near to a great city, in which there was an idol, to which the other idols and gods of Egypt brought their offerings and vows.

7 And there was by this idol a priest ministering to it, who, as often as Satan spoke out of that idol, related the things he said to the inhabitants of Egypt, and those countries.

8 This priest had a son three years old,

who was possessed with a great multitude of devils, who uttered many strange things, and when the devils seized him, walked about naked with his clothes torn, throwing stones at those whom he saw.

9 Near to that idol was the inn of the city, into which when Joseph and Mary were come, and had turned into that inn, all the inhabitants of the city were astonished.

10 And all the magistrates and priests of the idols assembled before that idol, and made inquiry there, saying, What means all this consternation, and dread, which has fallen upon all our country?

11 The idol answered them, The unknown God is come hither, who is truly God; nor is there any one besides him, who is worthy of divine worship; for he is truly the Son of God.

12 At the fame of him this country trembled, and at his coming it is under the present commotion and consternation; and we ourselves are affrighted by the greatness of his power.

13 And at the same instant this idol fell down, and at his fall all the inhabitants of Egypt, besides others, ran together.

14 ¶ But the son of the priest, when his usual disorder came upon him, going into the inn, found there Joseph and Mary, whom all the rest had left behind and forsook.

15 And when the Lady Mary had washed the swaddling clothes of the Lord Christ, and hanged them out to dry upon a post, the boy possessed with the devil took down one of them, and put it upon his head.

16 And presently the devils began to come out of his mouth, and fly away in the shape of crows and serpents.

17 From that time the boy was healed by the power of the Lord Christ, and he began to sing praises, and give thanks to the Lord who had healed him.

18 When his father saw him restored to his former state of health, he said, My son, what has happened to thee, and by what means wert thou cured?

19 The son answered, When the devils seized me, I went into the inn, and there found a very handsome woman with a boy, whose swaddling clothes she had just before washed, and hanged out upon a post.

20 One of these I took, and put it upon my head, and immediately the devils left me, and fled away.

21 At this the father exceedingly rejoiced, and said, My son, perhaps this boy is the son of the living God, who made the heavens and the earth.

22 For as soon as he came amongst us, the idol was broken, and all the gods fell down, and were destroyed by a greater power.

23 Then was fulfilled the prophecy which saith, Out of Egypt I have called my son.

CHAPTER 5

1 Joseph and Mary leave Egypt. 3 Go to the haunts of robbers, 4 Who, hearing a mighty noise as of a great army, flee away.

NOW Joseph and Mary, when they heard that the idol was fallen down and destroyed, were seized with fear and trembling, and said, When we were in the land of Israel, Herod, intending to kill Jesus, slew for that purpose all the infants at Bethlehem, and that neighbourhood.

2 And there is no doubt but the Egyptians if they come to hear that this idol is broken and fallen down, will burn us with fire.

3 They went therefore hence to the secret places of robbers, who robbed travellers as they pass by, of their carriages and their clothes, and carried them away bound.

4 These thieves upon their coming heard a great noise, such as the noise of a king with a great army and many horses, and the trumpets sounding at his Overture from his own city, at which they were so affrighted as to leave all their booty behind them, and fly away in haste.

5 Upon this the prisoners arose, and loosed each other's bonds, and taking each man his bags, they went away, and saw Joseph and Mary coming to wards

them, and inquired, Where is that king, the noise of whose approach the robbers heard, and left us, so that we are now come off safe?

6 Joseph answered, He will come after us.

CHAPTER 6

1 Mary looks on a woman in whom Satan had taken up his abode, and she becomes dispossessed. 5 Christ kissed by a bride made dumb by sorcerers, cures her, 11 miraculously cures a gentlewoman in whom Satan had taken up his abode. 16 A leprous girl cured by the water in which he was washed, and becomes the servant of Mary and Joseph. 20 The leprous son of a prince's wife cured in like manner. 37 His mother offers large gifts to Mary, and dismisses her.

THEN they went into another where there was a woman possessed with a devil, and in whom Satan, that cursed rebel, had taken up his abode.

2 One night, when she went to fetch water, she could neither endure her clothes, nor to be in any house; but as often as they tied her with chains or cords, she brake them, and went out into desert places, and sometimes standing where roads crossed, and in churchyards, would throw stones at men.

3 When Mary saw this woman, she pitied her; whereupon Satan presently left her, and fled away in the form of a young man, saying, Woe to me, because of thee, Mary, and thy son.

4 So the woman was delivered from her torment; but considering herself naked, she blushed, and avoided seeing any man, and having put on her clothes, went home, and gave au account of her case to her father and relations, who, as they were the best of the city, entertained Mary and Joseph with the greatest respect.

5 The next morning having received a sufficient supply of provisions for the road, they went from them, and about the evening of the day arrived at another town, where a marriage was then about to be solemnized; but by the arts of Satan and the practices of some sorcerers, the bride was become so dumb, that she could not so much as open her mouth.

6 But when this dumb bride saw the Lady Mary entering into the town, and carrying the Lord Christ in her arms, she stretched out her hands to the Lord Christ, and took him in her arms, and closely hugging him, very often kissed him, continually moving him and pressing him to her body.

7 Straightway the string of her tongue was loosed, and her ears were opened, and she began to sing praises unto God, who had restored her.

8 So there was great joy among the inhabitants of the town that night, who thought that God and his angels were come down among them.

9 ¶ In this place they abode three days, meeting with the greatest respect and most splendid entertainment.

10 And being then furnished by the people with provisions for the road, they departed and went to another city, in which they were inclined to lodge, because it was a famous place.

11 There was in this city a gentlewoman, who, as she went down one day to the river to bathe, behold cursed Satan leaped upon her in the form of a serpent,

12 And folded himself about her belly, and every night lay upon her.

13 This woman seeing the Lady Mary, and the Lord Christ the infant in her bosom, asked the Lady Mary, that she would give her the child to kiss, and carry in her arms.

14 When she had consented, and as soon as the woman had moved the child, Satan left her, and fled away, nor did the woman ever afterwards see him.

15 Hereupon all the neighbours praised the Supreme God, and the woman rewarded them with ample beneficence.

16 On the morrow the same woman brought perfumed water to wash the Lord Jesus; and when she had washed him, she preserved the water.

17 And there was a girl there, whose

THE FIRST GOSPEL OF THE INFANCY OF JESUS CHRIST

body was white with a leprosy, who being sprinkled with this water, and washed, was instantly cleansed from her leprosy.

18 The people therefore said Without doubt Joseph and Mary, and that boy are Gods, for they do not look like mortals.

19 And when they were making ready to go away, the girl, who had been troubled with the leprosy, came and desired they would permit her to go along with them; so they consented, and the girl went with them till. they came to a city, in which was the palace of a great king, and whose house was not far from the inn.

20 Here they staid, and when the girl went one day to the prince's wife, and found her in a sorrowful and mournful condition, she asked her the reason of her tears.

21 She replied, Wonder not at my groans, for I am under a great misfortune, of which I dare not tell any one.

22 But, says the girl, if you will entrust me with your private grievance, perhaps I may find you a remedy for it.

23 Thou, therefore, says the prince's wife, shalt keep the secret, and not discover it to any one alive!

24 I have been married to this prince, who rules as king over large dominions, and lived long with him, before he had any child by me.

25 At length I conceived by him, but alas! I brought forth a leprous son; which, when he saw, he would not own to be his, but said to me,

26 Either do thou kill him, or send him to some nurse in such a place, that he may be never heard of; and now take care of yourself; I will never see you more.

27 So here I pine, lamenting my wretched and miserable circumstances. Alas, my son! alas, my husband! Have I disclosed it to you?

28 The girl replied, I have found a remedy for your disease, which I promise you, for I also was leprous, but God hath cleansed me, even he who is called Jesus, the son of the Lady Mary.

29 The woman inquiring where that God was, whom she spake of, the girl answered He lodges with you here in the same house.

30 But how can this be? says she; where is he? Behold, replied the girl, Joseph and Mary; and the infant who is with them is called Jesus: and it is he who delivered me from my disease and torment.

31 But by what means, says she, were you cleansed from your leprosy? Will you not tell me that?

32 Why not? says the girl; I took the water with which his body had been washed, and poured it upon me, and my leprosy vanished.

33 The prince's wife then arose and entertained them, providing a great feast for Joseph among a large company of men.

34 And the next day took perfumed water to wash the Lord Jesus, and afterwards poured the same water upon her son, whom she had brought with her, and her son was instantly cleansed from his leprosy.

35 Then she sang thanks and praises unto God, and said, Blessed is the mother that bare thee, O Jesus!

36 Dost thou thus cure men of the same nature with thyself, with the water with which thy body is washed?

37 She then offered very large gifts to the Lady Mary, and sent her away with all imaginable respect.

CHAPTER 7

1 A man who could not enjoy his wife, freed from his disorder. 5 A young man who had been bewitched, and turned into a mule, miraculously cured by Christ being put on his back. 28 and is married to the girl who had been cured of leprosy.

THEY came afterwards to another city, and had a mind to lodge there.

2 Accordingly they went to a man's house, who was newly married, but by the influence of sorcerers could not enjoy his wife:

3 But they lodging at his house that

night, the man was freed of his disorder:

4 And when they were pre paring early in the morning to go forward on their journey, the new married person hindered them, and provided a noble entertainment for them?

5 But going forward on the morrow, they came to another city, and saw three women going from a certain grave with great weeping.

6 When Mary saw them, she spake to the girl who was their companion, saying, Go and inquire of them, what is the matter with them, and what misfortune has befallen them?

7 When the girl asked them, they made her no answer, but asked her again, Who are ye, and where are ye going? For the day is far spent, and the night is at hand.

8 We are travellers, saith the girl, and are seeking for an inn to lodge at.

9 They replied, Go along with us, and lodge with us.

10 They then followed them, and were introduced into a new house, well furnished with all sorts of furniture.

11 It was now winter-time, and the girl went into the parlour where these women were, and found them weeping and lamenting, as before.

12 By them stood a mule, covered over with silk, and an ebony collar hanging down from his neck, whom they kissed, and were feeding.

13 But when the girl said, How handsome, ladies, that mule is! they replied with tears, and said, This mule, which you see, was our brother, born of this same mother as we:

14 For when our father died, and left us a very large estate, and we had only this brother, and we endeavoured to procure him a suitable match, and thought he should be married as other men, some giddy and jealous woman bewitched him without our knowledge.

15 And we, one night, a little before day, while the doors of the house were all fast shut, saw this our brother was changed into a mule, such as you now see him to be:

16 And we, in the melancholy condition in which you see us, having no father to comfort us, have applied to all the wise men, magicians, and diviners in the world, but they have been of no service to us.

17 As often therefore as we find ourselves oppressed with grief, we rise and go with this our mother to our father's tomb, where, when we have cried sufficiently we return home.

18 When the girl had heard this, she said, Take courage, and cease your fears, for you have a remedy for your afflictions near at hand, even among you and in the midst of your house,

19 For I was also leprous; but when I saw this woman, and this little infant with her, whose name is Jesus, I sprinkled my body with the water with which his mother had washed him, and I was presently made well.

20 And I am certain that he is also capable of relieving you under your distress. Wherefore, arise, go to my mistress, Mary, and when you have brought her into your own parlour, disclose to her the secret, at the same time, earnestly beseeching her to compassionate your case.

21 As soon as the women had heard the girl's discourse, they hastened away to the Lady Mary, introduced themselves to her, and sitting down before her, they wept.

22 And said, O our Lady Mary, pity your handmaids, for we have no head of our family, no one older than us; no father, or brother to go in and out before us.

23 But this mule, which you see, was our brother, which some woman by witchcraft have brought into this condition which you see: we therefore entreat you to compassionate us.

24 Hereupon Mary was grieved at their case, and taking the Lord Jesus, put him upon the back of the mule.

25 And said to her son, O Jesus Christ, restore (or heal) according to thy extraordinary power this mule, and grant him to have again the shape of a man and a rational creature, as he had formerly.

26 This was scarce said by the Lady

Mary, but the mule immediately passed into a human form, and became a young man without any deformity.

27 Then he and his mother and the sisters worshipped the Lady Mary, and lifting the child upon their heads, they kissed him, and said, Blessed is thy mother, O Jesus, O Saviour of the world! Blessed are the eyes which are so happy as to see thee.

28 Then both the sisters told their mother, saying, Of a truth our brother is restored to his former shape by the help of the Lord Jesus Christ, and the kindness of that girl, who told us of Mary and her son.

29 And inasmuch as our brother is unmarried, it is fit that we marry him to this girl their servant.

30 When they had consulted Mary in this matter, and she had given her consent, they made a splendid wedding for this girl.

31 And so their sorrow being turned into gladness, and their mourning into mirth, they began to rejoice. and to make merry, and sing, being dressed in their richest attire, with bracelets.

32 Afterwards they glorified and praised God, saying, O Jesus son of David who changest sorrow into gladness, and mourning into mirth!

33 After this Joseph and Mary tarried there ten days, then went away, having received great respect from those people;

34 Who, when they took their leave of them, and returned home, cried,

35 But especially the girl.

CHAPTER 8

1 Joseph and Mary pass through a country infested by robbers, 3 Titus, a humane thief, offers Dumachus, his comrade, forty groats to let Joseph and Mary pass unmolested. 6 Jesus prophesies that the thieves, Dumachus and Titus, shall be crucified with him, and that Titus shall go before him into Paradise. 10 Christ causes a well to spring from a sycamore tree, and Mary washes his coat in it. 11 A balsam grows there from his sweat: They go to Memphis, where Christ works more miracles. Return to Judæa. 15 being warned, depart for Nazareth.

IN their journey from hence they came into a desert country, and were told it was infested with robbers; so Joseph and Mary prepared to pass through it in the night.

2 And as they were going along, behold they saw two robbers asleep in the road, and with them a great number of robbers, who were their confederates, also asleep.

3 The names of these two were Titus and Dumachus; and Titus said to Dumachus, I beseech thee let those persons go along quietly, that our company may not perceive anything of them:

4 But Dumachus refusing, Titus again said, I will give thee forty groats, and as a pledge take my girdle, which he gave him he had done speaking, that he might not open his mouth, or make a noise.

5 When the Lady Mary saw the kindness which this robber did shew them, she said to him, The Lord God will receive thee to his right hand, and grant thee pardon of thy sins.

6 Then the Lord Jesus answered, and said to his mother, When thirty years are expired, O mother, the Jews will crucify me at Jerusalem;

7 And these two thieves shall be with me at the same time upon the cross, Titus on my right hand, and Dumachus on my left, and from that time Titus shall go before me into paradise:

8 And when she had said, God forbid this should be thy lot, O my son, they went on to a city in which were several idols; which, as soon as they came near to it, was turned into hills of sand.

9 ¶ Hence they went to that sycamore tree, which is now called Matarea;

10 And in Matarea the Lord Jesus caused a well to spring forth, in which Mary washed his coat;

11 And a balsam is produced, or grows, in that country from the sweat which ran down there from the Lord Jesus.

12 Thence they proceeded to Memphis, and saw Pharaoh, and abode three years in Egypt.

13 And the Lord Jesus did very many miracles in Egypt, which are neither to be found in the Gospel of the Infancy nor in the Gospel of Perfection.

14 ¶ At the end of three years he returned out of Egypt, and when he came near to Judas, Joseph was afraid to enter;

15 For hearing that Herod was dead, and that Archelaus his son reigned in his stead, he was afraid;

16 And when he went to Judæa, an angel of God appeared to him, and said, O Joseph, go into the city Nazareth, and abide there.

17 It is strange indeed that he, who is the Lord of all countries, should be thus carried backward and forward through so many countries.

CHAPTER 9

2 Two sick children cured by water wherein Christ was washed.

WHEN they came afterwards into the city Bethlehem, they found there several very desperate distempers, which became so troublesome to children by seeing them, that most of them died.

2 There was there a woman who had a sick son, whom she brought, when he was at the point of death, to the Lady Mary, who saw her when she was washing Jesus Christ.

3 Then said the woman, O my Lady Mary, look down upon this my son, who is afflicted with most dreadful pains.

4. Mary hearing her, said, Take a little of that water with which I have washed my son, and sprinkle it upon him.

5 Then she took a little of that water, as Mary had commanded, and sprinkled it upon her son, who being wearied with his violent pains, had fallen asleep; and after he had slept a little, awaked perfectly well and recovered.

6 The mother being abundantly glad of this success, went again to Mary, and

Mary said to her, Give praise to God, who hath cured this thy son.

7 There was in the same place another woman, a neighbour of her, whose son was now cured.

8 This woman's son was afflicted with the same disease, and his eyes were now almost quite shut, and she was lamenting for him day and night.

9 The mother of the child which was cured, said to her, Why do you not bring your son to Mary, as I brought my son to her, when he was in the agonies of death; and he was cured by that water, with which the body of her son Jesus was washed?

10 When the woman heard her say this, she also went, and having procured the same water, washed her son with it, whereupon his body and his eyes were instantly restored to their former state.

11 And when she brought her son to Mary, and opened his case to her, she commanded her to give thanks to God for the recovery of her son's health, and tell no one what had happened.

CHAPTER 10

1 Two wives of one man, each have a son sick. 2 One of them, named Mary, and whose son's name was Caleb, presents the Virgin with a handsome carpet, and Caleb is cured; but the son of the other wife dies, 4 which occasions a difference between the women. 5 The other wife puts Caleb into a hot oven, and he is miraculously preserved; 9 she afterwards throws him into a well, and he is again preserved; 11 his mother appeals to the Virgin against the other wife, 12, whose downfall the Virgin prophesies, 13 and who accordingly falls into the well, 14 therein fulfilling a saying of old.

THERE were in the same city two wives of one man, who had each a son sick. One of them was called Mary and her son's name was Caleb.

2 She arose, and taking her son, went to the Lady Mary, the mother of Jesus, and offered her a very handsome carpet, saying, O my Lady Mary accept this

carpet of me, and instead of it give me a small swaddling cloth.

3 To this Mary agreed, and when the mother of Caleb was gone, she made a coat for her son of the swaddling cloth, put it on him, and his disease was cured; but the son of the other wife died.

4 ¶ Hereupon there arose between them, a difference in doing the business of the family by turns, each her week.

5 And when the turn of Mary the mother of Caleb came, and she was heating the oven to bake bread, and went away to fetch the meal, she left her son Caleb by the oven;

6 Whom, the other wife, her rival, seeing to be by himself, took and cast him into the oven, which was very hot, and then went away.

7 Mary on her return saw her son Caleb lying in the middle of the oven laughing, and the oven quite as cold as though it had not been before heated, and knew that her rival the other wife had thrown him into the fire.

8 When she took him out, she brought him to the Lady Mary, and told her the story, to whom she replied, Be quiet, I am concerned lest thou shouldest make this matter known.

9 After this her rival, the other wife, as she was drawing water at the well, and saw Caleb playing by the well, and that no one was near, took him, and threw him into the well.

10 And when some men came to fetch water from the well, they saw the boy sitting on the superficies of the water, and drew him out with ropes, and were exceedingly surprised at the child, and praised God.

11 Then came the mother and took him and carried him to the Lady Mary, lamenting and saying, O my Lady, see what my rival hath done to my son, and how she hath cast him into the well, and I do not question but one time or other she will be the occasion of his death.

12 Mary replied to her, God will vindicate your injured cause.

13 Accordingly a few days after, when the other wife came to the well to draw water, her foot was entangled in the rope, so that she fell headlong into the well, and they who ran to her assistance, found her skull broken, and bones bruised.

14 So she came to a bad end, and in her was fulfilled that saying of the author, They digged a well, and made it deep, but fell themselves into the pit which they prepared.

CHAPTER 11

1 Bartholomew, when a child and sick, miraculously restored by being laid on Christ's bed.

ANOTHER woman in that city had likewise two sons sick.

2 And when one was dead, the other, who lay at the point of death, she took in her arms to the Lady Mary, and in a flood of tears addressed herself to her, saying,

3 O my Lady, help and relieve me; for I had two sons, the one I have just now buried, the other I see is just at the point of death, behold how I (earnestly) seek favour from God, and pray to him.

4 Then she said, O Lord, thou art gracious, and merciful, and kind; thou hast given me two sons; one of them thou hast taken to thyself, O spare me this other.

5 Mary then perceiving the greatness of her sorrow, pitied her and said, Do thou place thy son in my son's bed, and cover him with his clothes.

6 And when she had placed him in the bed wherein Christ lay, at the moment when his eyes were just closed by death; as soon as ever the smell of the garments of the Lord Jesus Christ reached the boy, his eyes were opened, and calling with a loud voice to his mother, he asked for bread, and when he had received it, he sucked it.

7 Then his mother said, O Lady Mary, now I am assured that the powers of God do dwell in you, so that thy son can cure children who are of the same sort as himself, as soon as they touch his garments.

8 This boy who was thus cured, is the same who in the Gospel is called

Bartholomew.

CHAPTER 12

1 A leprous woman healed by Christ's washing water. 7 A princess healed by it and restored to her husband.

AGAIN there was a leprous woman who went to the Lady Mary, the mother of Jesus, and said, O my Lady, help me.

2 Mary replied, what help dost thou desire? Is it gold or silver, or that thy body be cured of its leprosy?

3 Who, says the woman, can grant me this?

4 Mary replied to her, Wait a little till I have washed my son Jesus, and put him to bed.

5 The woman waited, as she was commanded; and Mary when she had put Jesus in bed, giving her the water with which she had washed his body, said, Take some of the water, and pour it upon thy body;

6 Which when she had done, she instantly became clean, and praised God, and gave thanks to him.

7 ¶ Then she went away, after she had abode with her three days:

8 And going into the city, she saw a certain prince, who had married another prince's daughter;

9 But when he came to see her, he perceived between her eyes the signs of leprosy like a star, and thereupon declared the marriage dissolved and void.

10 When the woman saw these persons in this condition, exceedingly sorrowful, and shedding abundance of tears, she inquired of them the reason of their crying.

11 They replied, Inquire not into our circumstances; for we are net able to declare our misfortunes to any person whatsoever.

12 But still she pressed and desired them to communicate their case to her, intimating, that perhaps she might be able to direct them to a remedy.

13 So when they shewed the young woman to her, and the signs of the leprosy, which appeared between her eyes,

14 She said, I also, whom ye see in this place, was afflicted with the same distemper, and going on some business to Bethlehem, I went into a certain cave, and saw a woman named Mary, who had a son called Jesus.

15 She seeing me to be leprous, was concerned for me, and gave me some water with which she had washed her son's body; with that I sprinkled my body, and became clean.

16 Then said these women, Will you, Mistress, go along with us, and shew the Lady Mary to us?

17 To which she consenting, they arose and went to the Lady Mary, taking with them very noble presents.

18 And when they came in and offered their presents to her, they showed the leprous young woman what they brought with them to her.

19 Then said Mary, The mercy of the Lord Jesus Christ rest upon you;

20 And giving them a little of that water with which she had washed the body of Jesus Christ, she bade them wash the diseased person with it; which when they had done, she was presently cured;

21 So they, and all who were present, praised God; and being filled with joy, they went back to their own city, and gave praise to God on that account.

22 Then the prince hearing that his wife was cured, took her home and made a second marriage, giving thanks unto God for the recovery of his wife's health.

CHAPTER 13

1 A girl, whose blood Satan sucked, receives one of Christ's swaddling clothes from the Virgin. 14 Satan comes like a dragon, and she shews it to him; flames and burning coals proceed from it and fall upon him; 19 he is miraculously discomfited, and leaves the girl.

THERE was also a girl, who was afflicted by Satan;

2 For that cursed spirit did frequently appear to her in the shape of a dragon,

and was inclined to swallow her up, and had so sucked out all her blood, that she looked like a dead carcase.

3 As often as she came to herself, with her hands wringed about her head she would cry out, and say, Woe, Woe is me, that there is no one to be found who can deliver me from that impious dragon!

4 Her father and mother, and all who were about her and saw her, mourned and wept over her;

5 And all who were present would especially be under sorrow and in tears, when they heard her bewailing, and saying, My brethren and friends, is there no one who can deliver me from this murderer?

6 Then the prince's daughter, who had been cured of her leprosy, hearing the complaint of that girl, went upon the top of her castle, and saw her with her hands twisted about her head, pouring out a flood of tears, and all the people that were about her in sorrow.

7 Then she asked the husband of the possessed person, Whether his wife's mother was alive? He told her, That her father and mother were both alive.

8 Then she ordered her mother to be sent to her: to whom, when she saw her coming, she said, Is this possessed girl thy daughter? She moaning and bewailing said, Yes, madam, I bore her.

9 The prince's daughter answered, Disclose the secret of her case to me, for I confess to you that I was leprous, but the Lady Mary, the mother of Jesus Christ, healed me.

10 And if you desire your daughter to be restored to her former state, take her to Bethlehem, and inquire for Mary the mother of Jesus, and doubt not but your daughter will be cured; for I do not question but you will come home with great joy at your daughter's recovery.

11 As soon as ever she had done speaking, she arose and went with her daughter to the place appointed, and to Mary, and told her the case of her daughter.

12 When Mary had heard her story, she gave her a little of the water with which she had washed the body of her son Jesus, and bade her pour it upon the body of her daughter.

13 Likewise she gave her one of the swaddling cloths of the Lord Jesus, and said, Take this swaddling cloth and shew it to thine enemy as often as thou seest him; and she sent them away in peace.

14 ¶ After they had left that city and returned home, and the time was come in which Satan was wont to seize her, in the same moment this cursed spirit appeared to her in the shape of a huge dragon, and the girl seeing him was afraid.

15 The mother said to her, Be not afraid daughter; let him alone till he come nearer to thee! then shew him the swaddling cloth, which the Lady Mary gave us, and we shall see the event.

16 Satan then coming like a dreadful dragon, the body of the girl trembled for fear.

17 But as soon as she had put the swaddling cloth upon her head, and about her eyes, and shewed it to him, presently there issued forth from the swaddling cloth flames and burning coals, and fell upon the dragon.

18 Oh! how great a miracle was this, which was done: as soon as the dragon saw the swaddling cloth of the Lord Jesus, fire went forth and was scattered upon his head and eyes; so that he cried out with a loud voice, What have I to do with thee, Jesus, thou son of Mary, Whither shall I flee from thee?

19 So he drew back much affrighted, and left the girl.

20 And she was delivered from this trouble, and sang praises and thanks to God, and with her all who were present at the working of the miracle.

CHAPTER 14

1 Judas when a boy possessed by Satan, and brought by his parents to Jesus to be cured, whom he tries to bite, 7 but failing, strikes Jesus and makes him cry out. Whereupon Satan goes from Jesus in the shape of a dog.

ANOTHER woman likewise lived

there, whose son was possessed by Satan.

2 This boy, named Judas, as often as Satan seized him, was inclined to bite all that were present; and if he found no one else near him, he would bite his own hands and other parts.

3 But the mother of this miserable boy, hearing of Mary and her son Jesus, arose presently, and taking her son in her arms, brought him to the Lady Mary.

4 In the meantime, James and Joses had taken away the infant, the Lord Jesus, to play at a proper season with other children; and when they went forth, they sat down and the Lord Jesus with them.

5 Then Judas, who was possessed, came and sat down at the right hand of Jesus.

6 When Satan was acting upon him as usual, he went about to bite the Lord Jesus.

7 And because he could not do it, he struck Jesus on the right side, so that he cried out.

8 And in the same moment Satan went out of the boy, and ran away like a mad dog.

9 This same boy who struck Jesus, and out of whom Satan went in the form of a dog, was Judas Iscariot, who betrayed him to the Jews.

10 And that same side, on which Judas struck him, the Jews pierced with a spear.

CHAPTER 15

1 Jesus and other boys play together, and make day figures of animals. 4 Jesus causes them to walk, 6 also makes day birds, which he causes to fly, and eat and drink. 7 The children's parents alarmed, and take Jesus for a sorcerer. 8 He goes to a dyer's shop, and throws all the cloths into the furnace, and works a miracle therewith. 15 Whereupon the Jews praise God.

AND when the Lord Jesus was seven years of age, he was on a certain day with other boys his companions about the same age.

2 Who when they were at play, made clay into several shapes, namely, asses, oxen, birds, and other figures,

3 Each boasting of his work, and endeavouring to exceed the rest.

4 Then the Lord Jesus said to the boys, I will command these figures which I have made to walk.

5 And immediately they moved, and when he commanded them to return, they returned.

6 He had also made the figures of birds and sparrows, which, when he commanded to fly, did fly, and when he commanded to stand still, did stand still; and if he gave them meat and drink, they did eat and drink.

7 When at length the boys went away, and related these things to their parents, their fathers said to them, Take heed, children, for the future, of his company, for he is a sorcerer; shun and avoid him, and from henceforth never play with him.

8 ¶ On a certain day also, when the Lord Jesus was playing with the boys, and running about, he passed by a dyer's shop, whose name was Salem.

9 And there were in his shop many pieces of cloth belonging to the people of that city, which they designed to dye of several colours.

10 Then the Lord Jesus going into the dyer's shop, took all the cloths, and threw them into the furnace.

11 When Salem came home, and saw the cloths spoiled, he began to make a great noise, and to chide the Lord Jesus, saying,

12 What hast thou done to me, O thou Son of Mary? Thou hast injured both me and my neighbours; they all desired their cloths of a proper colour; but .thou hast come, and spoiled them all.

13 The Lord Jesus replied, I will change the colour of every cloth to what colour thou desirest;

14 And then he presently began to take the cloths out of the furnace, and they were all dyed of those same colours which the dyer desired.

15 And when the Jews saw this surprising miracle, they praised God

CHAPTER 16

1 Christ miraculously widens or contracts the gates, milk-pails, sieves, or bones, not properly made by Joseph, 4 he not being skilful at his carpenter's trade. 5 The King of Jerusalem gives Joseph an order for a throne. 6 Joseph works on it for two years in the king's palace, and makes it two spans too short. The king being angry with. him, 10 Jesus comforts him, 13 commands him to pull one side of the throne, while he pulls the other, and brings it to its proper dimensions. 14 Whereupon the bystanders praise God.

AND Joseph, wheresoever he went in the city, took the Lord Jesus with him, where he was sent for to work to make gates, or milk-pails, or sieves, or boxes; the Lord Jesus was with him wheresoever he went.

2 And as often as Joseph had anything in his work, to make longer or shorter, or wider, or narrower, the Lord Jesus would stretch his hand towards it.

3 And presently it became as Joseph would have it.

4 So that he had no need to finish anything with his own hands, for he was not very skilful at his carpenter's trade.

5 ¶ On a certain time the King of Jerusalem sent for him, and said, I would have thee make me a throne of the same dimensions with that place in which I commonly sit.

6 Joseph obeyed, and forthwith began the work, and continued two years in the king's palace before he finished it.

7 And when he came to fix it in its place, he found it wanted two spans on each side of the appointed measure.

8 Which, when the king saw, he was very angry with Joseph;

9 And Joseph afraid of the king's anger, went to bed without his supper, taking not any thing to eat.

10 Then the Lord Jesus asked him, What he was afraid of?

11 Joseph replied, Because I have lost my labour in the work which I have been about these two years.

12 Jesus said to him, Fear not, neither be cast down;

13 Do thou lay hold on one side of the throne, and I will the other, and we will bring it to its just dimensions.

14 And when Joseph had done as the Lord Jesus said, and each of them had with strength drawn his side, the throne obeyed, and was brought to the proper dimensions of the place:

15 Which miracle when they who stood by saw, they were astonished, and praised God.

16 The throne was made of the same wood, which was in being in Solomon's time, namely, wood adorned with various shapes and figures.

CHAPTER 17

1 Jesus plays with boys at hide and seek. 3 Some women put his playfellows in a furnace, 7 where they are transformed by Jesus into kids. 10 Jesus calls them to go and play, and they me restored to their former shape.

ON another day the Lord Jesus going out into the street, and seeing some boys who were met to play, joined himself to their company:

2 But when they saw him, they hid themselves, and left him to seek for them:

3 The Lord Jesus came to the gate of a certain house, and asked some women who were standing there, Where the boys were gone?

4 And when they answered, That there was no one there; the Lord Jesus said, Who are those whom ye see in the furnace?

5 They answered, They were kids of three years old.

6 Then Jesus cried out aloud, and said, Come out hither, O ye kids, to your shepherd;

7 And presently the boys came forth like kids, and leaped about him; which when the women saw, they were exceedingly amazed, and trembled.

8 Then they immediately worshipped the Lord Jesus, and beseeched him,

saying, O our Lord Jesus, son of Mary, thou art truly that good shepherd of Israel! have mercy on thy handmaids, who stand before thee, who do not doubt, but that thou, O Lord, art come to save, and not to destroy.

9 After that, when the Lord Jesus said, the children of Israel are like Ethiopians among the people; the women said, Thou, Lord, knowest all things, nor is any thing concealed from thee; but now we entreat thee, and beseech of thy mercy that thou wouldst restore those boys to their former state.

10 Then Jesus said, Come hither O boys, that we may go and play; and immediately, in the presence of these women, the kids were changed and returned into the shape of boys.

CHAPTER 18

1 Jesus becomes the king of his playfellows, and they crown him with flowers, 4 miraculously causes a serpent who had bitten Simon the Cananite, then a boy, to suck out all the poison again; 16 the serpent bursts, and Christ restores the boy to health.

IN the month Adar Jesus gathered together the boys, and ranked them as though he had been a king.

2 For they spread their garments on the ground for him to sit on; and having made a crown of flowers, put it upon his head, and stood on his right and left as the guards of a king.

3 And if any one happened to pass by, they took him by force, and said, Come hither, and worship the king, that you may have a prosperous journey.

4 ¶ In the mean time, while these things were doing, there came certain men, carrying a boy upon a couch;

5 For this boy having gone with his companions to the mountain to gather wood, and having found there a partridge's nest, and put his hand in to take out the eggs, was stung by a poisonous serpent, which leaped out of the nest; so that he was forced to cry out for the help of his companions: who, when they came, found him lying upon the earth like a dead person.

6 After which his neighbours came and carried him back into the city.

7 But when they came to the place where the Lord Jesus was sitting like a king, and the other boys stood around him like his ministers, the boys made haste to meet him, who was bitten by the serpent, and said to his neighbours, Come and pay your respects to the king;

8 But when, by reason of their sorrow, they refused to come, the boys drew them, and forced them against their wills to come.

9 And when they came to the Lord Jesus, he inquired, On what account they carried that boy?

10 And when they answered, that a serpent had bitten him, the Lord Jesus said to the boys, Let us go and kill that serpent.

11 But when the parents of the boy desired to be excused, because their son lay at the point of death; the boys made answer, and said, Did not ye hear what the king said? Let us go and kill the serpent; and will not ye obey him?

12 So they brought the couch back again, whether they would or not.

13 And when they were come to the nest, the Lord Jesus said to the boys, Is this the serpent's lurking place? They said, It was.

14 Then the Lord Jesus calling the serpent, it presently came forth and submitted to him; to whom he said, Go and suck out all the poison which thou hast infused into that boy;

15 So the serpent crept to the boy, and took away all its poison again.

16 Then the Lord Jesus cursed the serpent so that it immediately burst asunder, and died.

17 And he touched the boy with his hand to restore him to his former health;

18 And when he began to cry, the Lord Jesus said, Cease crying, for hereafter thou shalt be my disciple;

19 And this is that Simon the Canaanite, who is mentioned in the Gospel.

CHAPTER 19

THE FIRST GOSPEL OF THE INFANCY OF JESUS CHRIST

1 James being bitten by a viper, Jesus blows on the wound and cures him. 4. Jesus charged with throwing a boy from the roof of a house, 10 miraculously causes the dead boy to acquit Mm, 12 fetches water for his mother, breaks the pitcher and miraculously gathers the water in his mantle and brings it home, 16 makes fish-pools on the Sabbath, 20 causes a boy to die who broke them down, 22 another boy run against him, whom he also causes to die.

ON another day Joseph sent his son James to gather wood and the Lord Jesus went with him;

2 And when they came to the place where the wood was, and James began to gather it, behold, a venomous viper bit him, so that he began to cry, and make a noise.

3 The Lord Jesus seeing him in this condition, came to him, and blowed upon the place where the viper had bit him, and it was instantly well.

4 ¶ On a certain day the Lord Jesus was with some boys, who were playing on the housetop, and one of the boys fell down, and presently died.

5 Upon which the other boys all running away, the Lord Jesus was left alone on the house-top.

6 And the boy's relations came to him and said to the Lord Jesus, Thou didst throw our son down from the housetop.

7 But he denying it, they cried out, Our son is dead, and this is he who killed him.

8 The Lord Jesus replied to them, Do not charge me with a crime, of which you are not able to convict me, but let us go ask the boy himself, who will bring the truth to light.

9 Then the Lord Jesus going down stood over the head of the dead boy, and said with a loud voice, Zeinunus, Zeinunus, who threw thee down from the housetop?

10 Then the dead boy answered, thou didst not throw me down, but such a one did.

11 And when the Lord Jesus bade those who stood by to take notice of his words, all who were present praised God on account of that miracle.

12 ¶ On a certain time the Lady Mary had commanded the Lord Jesus to fetch her some water out of the well;

13 And when he had gone to fetch the water, the pitcher, when it was brought up full, brake.

14 But Jesus spreading his mantle gathered up the water again, and brought it in that to his mother.

15 Who, being astonished at this wonderful thing, laid up this, and all the other things which she had seen, in her memory.

16 ¶ Again on another day the Lord Jesus was with some boys by a river and they drew water out of the river by little channels, and made little fish-pools.

17 But the Lord Jesus had made twelve sparrows, and placed them about his pool on each side, three on a side.

18 But it was the Sabbath day, and the son of Hanani a Jew came by, and saw them making these things, and said, Do ye thus make figures of clay on the Sabbath? And he ran to them, and broke down their fish-pools.

19 But when the Lord Jesus clapped his hands over the sparrows which he had made, they fled away chirping.

20 At length the son of Hanani coming to the fish-pool of Jesus to destroy it, the water vanished away, and the Lord Jesus said to him,

21 In like manner as this water has vanished, so shall thy life vanish; and presently the boy died.

22 ¶ Another time, when the Lord Jesus was coming home in the evening with Joseph, he met a boy, who ran so hard against him, that he threw him down;

23 To whom the Lord Jesus said, As thou hast thrown me down, so shalt thou fall, nor ever rise.

24 And that moment the boy fell down and died.

CHAPTER 20

1 Sent to school to Zaccheus to learn his letters, and teaches Zaccheus. 13 Sent to another schoolmaster. 14

refuses to tell his letters, and the schoolmaster going to whip him his hand withers and he dies.

THERE was also at Jerusalem one named Zaccheus, who was a schoolmaster.

2 And he said to Joseph, Joseph, why dost thou not send Jesus to me, that he may learn his letters?

3 Joseph agreed, and told Mary;

4 So they brought him to that master; who, as soon as he saw him, wrote out an alphabet for him.

5 And he bade him say Aleph; and when he had said Aleph, the master bade him pronounce Beth.

6 Then the Lord Jesus said to him, Tell me first the meaning of the letter Aleph, and then I will pronounce Beth.

7 And when the master threatened to whip him, the Lord Jesus explained to him the meaning of the letters Aleph and Beth;

8 Also which were the straight figures of the letters, which the oblique, and what letters had double figures; which had points, and which had none; why one letter went before another; and many other things he began to tell him, and explain, of which the master himself had never heard, nor read in any book.

9 The Lord Jesus farther said to the master, Take notice how I say to thee; then he began clearly and distinctly to say Aleph, Beth, Gimel, Daleth, and so on to the end of the alphabet.

10 At this the master was so surprised, that he said, I believe this boy was born before Noah;

11 And turning to Joseph, he said, Thou hast brought a boy to me to be taught, who is more learned than any master.

12 He said also unto Mary, This your son has no need of any learning.

13 ¶ They brought him then to a more learned master, who, when he saw him, said, say Aleph.

14 And when he had said Aleph, the master bade him pronounce Beth; to which the Lord Jesus replied, Tell me first the meaning of the letter Aleph, and then I will pronounce Beth.

15 But this master, when he lift up his hand to whip him, had his hand presently withered, and he died.

16 Then said Joseph to Mary, henceforth we will not allow him to go out of the house; for every one who displeases him is killed.

CHAPTER 21

1 Disputes miraculously with the doctors in the temple, 7 on law, 9 on astronomy, 12 on physics and metaphysics, 21 is worshipped by a philosopher, 28 and fetched home by his mother.

AND when he was twelve years old, they brought him to Jerusalem to the feast; and when the feast was over, they returned.

2 But the Lord Jesus continued behind in the temple among the doctors and elders, and learned men of Israel; to whom he proposed several questions of learning, and also gave them answers:

3 For he said to them, Whose son is the Messiah? They answered, the son of David:

4 Why then, said he, does he in the spirit call him Lord? when he saith, The Lord said to my Lord, sit thou at my right hand, till I have made thine enemies thy footstool.

5 Then a certain principal Rabbi asked him, Hast thou read books?

6 Jesus answered, he had read both books, and the things which were contained in books.

7 And he explained to them the books of the law, and precepts, and statutes: and the mysteries which are contained in the books of the prophets; things which the mind of no creature could reach.

8 Then said that Rabbi, I never yet have seen or heard of such knowledge! What do you think that boy will be!

9 ¶ When a certain astronomer, who was present, asked the Lord Jesus, Whether he had studied astronomy?

10 The Lord Jesus replied, and told him the number of the spheres and heavenly

bodies, as also their triangular, square, and sextile aspect; their progressive and retrograde motion; their size and several prognostications; and other things which the reason of man had never discovered.

11 ¶ There was also among them a philosopher well skilled in physic and natural philosophy, who asked the Lord Jesus, Whether he had studied physic?

12 He replied, and explained to him physics and metaphysics.

13 Also those things which were above and below the power of nature;

14 The powers also of the body, its humours, and their effects.

15 Also the number of its members, and bones, veins, arteries, and nerves;

16 The several constitutions of body, hot and dry, cold and moist, and the tendencies of them;

17 How the soul operated upon the body;

18 What its various sensations and faculties were;

19 The faculty of speaking, anger, desire;

20 And lastly the manner of its composition and dissolution; and other things, which the understanding of no creature had ever reached.

21 Then that philosopher arose, and worshipped the Lord Jesus, and said, O Lord Jesus, from henceforth I will be thy disciple and servant.

22 ¶ While they were discoursing on these and such like things, the Lady Mary came in, having been three days walking about with Joseph, seeking for him.

23 And when she saw him sitting among the doctors, and in his turn proposing questions to them, and giving answers, she said to him, My son, why hast thou done thus by us? Behold I and thy father have been at much pains in seeking thee.

24 He replied, Why did ye seek me? Did ye not know that I ought to be employed in my father's house?

25 But they understood not the words which he said to them.

26 Then the doctors asked Mary, Whether this was her son? And when she said, He was, they said, O happy Mary, who hast borne such a son.

27 Then he returned with them to Nazareth, and obeyed them in all things.

28 And his mother kept all these things in her mind;

29 And the Lord Jesus grew in stature and wisdom, and favour with God and man.

CHAPTER 22
1 Conceals his miracles, 2 studies the law and is baptised.

NOW from this time Jesus began to conceal his miracles and secret works,

2 And he gave himself to the study of the law, till he arrived to the end of his thirtieth year;

3 At which time the Father publicly owned him at Jordan, sending down this voice from heaven, This is my beloved son, in whom I am well pleased;

4 The Holy Ghost being also present in the form of a dove.

5 This is he whom we worship with all reverence, because he gave us our life and being, and brought us from our mother's womb.

6 Who, for our sakes, took a human body, and hath redeemed us, so that he might so embrace us with everlasting mercy, and shew his free, large, bountiful grace and goodness to us.

7 To him be glory and praise, and power, and dominion, from henceforth and for evermore, Amen.

¶ The end of the whole Gospel of the Infancy, by the assistance of the Supreme God, according to what we found in the original.

THOMAS' GOSPEL OF THE INFANCY OF JESUS CHRIST

¶ An Account of the Actions and Miracles of our Lord and Saviour Jesus Christ in his Infancy.

CHAPTER 1
2 Jesus miraculously clears the water after rain. 4 plays with clay sparrows, which he animates on the sabbath day.

I THOMAS, an Israelite, judged it necessary to make known to our brethren among the Gentiles, the actions and miracles of Christ in his childhood, which our Lord and God Jesus Christ wrought after his birth in Bethlehem in our country, at which I myself was astonished; the beginning of which was as followeth.

2 ¶ When the child Jesus was five years of age and there had been a shower of rain, which was now over, Jesus was playing with other Hebrew boys by a running stream; and the water running over the banks, stood in little lakes;

3 But the water instantly became clear and useful again; he having smote them only by his word, they readily obeyed him.

4 Then he took from the bank of the stream some soft clay, and formed out of it twelve sparrows; and there were other boys playing with him.

5 But a certain Jew seeing the things which he was doing, namely, his forming clay into the figures of sparrows on the sabbath day, went presently away, and told his father Joseph, and said,

6 Behold, thy boy is playing by the river side, and has taken clay, and formed it into twelve sparrows, and profaneth the sabbath.

7 Then Joseph came to the place where he was, and when he saw him, called to him, and said, Why doest thou that which it is not lawful to do on the sabbath day?

8 Then Jesus clapping together the palms of his hands, called to the sparrows, and said to them: Go, fly away; and while ye live remember me.

9 So the sparrows fled away, making a noise.

10 The Jews seeing this, were astonished, and went away, and told their chief persons what a strange miracle they had seen wrought by Jesus.

CHAPTER 2
2 Causes a boy to wither who broke down his fish pools, 6 partly restores him, 7 dills another boy, 16 causes blindness to fall on his accusers, 18 for which Joseph pulls him by the ear.

BESIDES this, the son of Anna the scribe was standing there with Joseph, and took a bough of a willow tree, and scattered the waters which Jesus had gathered into lakes.

2 But the boy Jesus seeing what he had done, became angry, and said to him, Thou fool, what harm did the lake do thee, that thou shouldest scatter the water?

3 Behold, now thou shalt wither as a tree, and shalt not bring forth either leaves, or branches, or fruit.

4 And immediately he became withered all over.

5 Then Jesus went away home. But the parents of the boy who was withered, lamenting the misfortune of his youth, took and carried him to Joseph, accusing him, and said, Why dost thou keep a son who is guilty of such actions?

6 Then Jesus at the request of all who were present did heal him, leaving only some small member to continue withered, that they might take warning.

7 ¶ Another time Jesus went forth into the street, and a boy running by, rushed

upon his shoulder;

8 At which Jesus being angry, said to him, thou shalt go no farther.

9 And he instantly fell down dead:

10 Which when some persons saw, they said, Where was this boy born, that everything which he says presently cometh to pass?

11 Then the parents of the dead buy going to Joseph complained, saying, You are not fit to live with us, in our city, having such a boy as that:

12 Either teach him that he bless and not curse, or else depart hence with him, for he kills our children.

13 ¶ Then Joseph calling the boy Jesus by himself, instructed him saying, Why doest thou such things to injure the people so, that they hate us and prosecute us?

14 But Jesus replied, I know that what thou sayest is not of thyself, but for thy sake I will say nothing;

15 But they who have said these things to thee, shall suffer everlasting punishment.

16 And immediately they who had accused him became blind.

17 And all they who saw it were exceedingly afraid and confounded, and said concerning him, Whatsoever he saith, whether good or bad, immediately cometh to pass: and they were amazed.

18 And when they saw this action of Christ, Joseph arose, and plucked him by the ear, at which the boy was angry, and said to him, Be easy;

19 For if they seek for us, they shall not find us: thou hast done very imprudently.

20 Dost thou not know that I am thine? Trouble me no more.

CHAPTER 3

1 Astonishes his schoolmaster by his learning.

A CERTAIN schoolmaster named Zacchæus, standing in a certain place, heard Jesus speaking these things to his father.

2 And he was much surprised, that being a child, he should speak such things; and after a few days he came to Joseph, and said,

3 Thou hast a wise and sensible child, send him to me, that he may learn to read.

4 When he sat down to teach the letters to Jesus, he began with the first letter Aleph;

5 But Jesus pronounced the second letter Mpeth (Beth) Cghimel (Gimel), and said over all the letters to him to the end.

6 Then opening a book, he taught his master the prophets: but be was ashamed, and was at a loss to conceive how he came to know the letters.

7 And he arose and went home, wonderfully surprised at so strange a thing.

CHAPTER 4

1 Fragment of an adventure at a dyer's.

AS Jesus was passing by a certain shop, he saw a young man dipping (or dyeing) some cloths and stockings in a furnace, of a sad colour, doing them according to every person's particular order;

2 The boy Jesus going to the young man who was doing this, took also some of the cloths.

¶ Here endeth the Fragment of Thomas's Gospel of the Infancy of Jesus Christ.

THE INFANCY GOSPEL OF MATTHEW
CALLED ALSO, PSEUDO-MATTHEW

HERE beginneth the book of the Birth of the Blessed Mary and the Infancy of the Saviour. Written in Hebrew by the Blessed Evangelist Matthew, and

translated into Latin by the Blessed Presbyter Jerome.

To their well-beloved brother Jerome the Presbyter, Bishops Cromatius and Heliodorus in the Lord, greeting.The birth of the Virgin Mary, and the nativity and infancy of our Lord Jesus Christ, we find in apocryphal books. But considering that in them many things contrary to our faith are written, we have believed that they ought all to be rejected, lest perchance we should transfer the joy of Christ to Antichrist. While, therefore, we were considering these things, there came holy men, Parmenius and Varinus, who said that your Holiness had found a Hebrew volume, written by the hand of the most blessed Evangelist Matthew, in which also the birth of the virgin mother herself, and the infancy of our Saviour, were written. And accordingly we entreat your affection by our Lord Jesus Christ Himself, to render it from the Hebrew into Latin, not so much for the attainment of those things which are the insignia of Christ, as for the exclusion of the craft of heretics, who, in order to teach bad doctrine, have mingled their own lies with the excellent nativity of Christ, that by the sweetness of life they might hide the bitterness of death. It will therefore become your purest piety, either to listen to us as your brethren entreating, or to let us have as bishops exacting, the debt of affection which you may deem due.

REPLY TO THEIR LETTER BY JEROME.

To my lords the holy and most blessed Bishops Cromatius and Heliodorus, Jerome, a humble servant of Christ, in the Lord greeting.

He who digs in ground where he knows that there is gold, does not instantly snatch at whatever the uptorn trench may pour forth; but, before the stroke of the quivering spade raises aloft the glittering mass, he meanwhile lingers over the sods to turn them over and lift

them up, and especially he who has not added to his gains. An arduous task is enjoined upon me, since what your Blessedness has commanded me, the holy Apostle and Evangelist Matthew himself did not write for the purpose of publishing. For if he had not done it somewhat secretly, he would have added it also to his Gospel which he published. But he composed this book in Hebrew; and so little did he publish it, that at this day the book written in Hebrew by his own hand is in the possession of very religious men, to whom in successive periods of time it has been handed down by those that were before them. And this book they never at any time gave to any one to translate. And so it came to pass, that when it was published by a disciple of Manichaeus named Leucius, who also wrote the falsely styled Acts of the Apostles, this book afforded matter, not of edification, but of perdition; and the opinion of the Synod in regard to it was according to its deserts, that the ears of the Church should not be open to it. Let the snapping of those that bark against us now cease; for we do not add this little book to the canonical writings, but we translate what was written by an Apostle and Evangelist, that we may disclose the falsehood of heresy. In this work, then, we obey the commands of pious bishops as well as oppose impious heretics. It is the love of Christ, therefore, which we fulfil, believing that they will assist us by their prayers, who through our obedience attain to a knowledge of the holy infancy of our Saviour.

There is extant another letter to the same bishops, attributed to Jerome: --

You ask me to let you know what I think of a book held by some to be about the nativity of St. Mary. And so I wish you to know that there is much in it that is false. For one Seleucus, who wrote the Sufferings of the Apostles, composed this book. But, just as he wrote what was true about their powers, and the miracles they worked, but said a great deal that was false about their doctrine; so here too he has invented many untruths out of his own head. I shall take care to render it word for word, exactly as it is in the Hebrew, since it is asserted that it was composed by the holy Evangelist Matthew, and written in Hebrew, and set at the head of his Gospel. Whether this be true or not, I leave to the author of the preface and the trustworthiness of the writer: as for myself, I pronounce them doubtful; I do not affirm that they are clearly false. But this I say freely-- and I think none of the faithful will deny it -- that, whether these stories be true or inventions, the sacred nativity of St. Mary was preceded by great miracles, and succeeded by the greatest; and so by those who believe that God can do these things, they can be believed and read without damaging their faith or imperilling their souls. In short, so far as I can, following the sense rather than the words of the writer, and sometimes walking in the same path, though not in the same footsteps, sometimes digressing a little, but still keeping the same road, I shall in this way keep by the style of the narrative, and shall say nothing that is not either written there, or might, following the same train of thought, have been written.

CHAPTER 1

1 In those days there was a man in Jerusalem, Joachim by name, of the tribe of Judah. He was the shepherd of his own sheep, fearing the Lord in integrity and singleness of heart.

2 He had no other care than that of his herds, from the produce of which he supplied with food all that feared God, offering double gifts in the fear of God to all who laboured in doctrine, and who ministered unto Him.

3 Therefore his lambs, and his sheep, and his wool, and all things whatsoever he possessed, he used to divide into three portions: one he gave to the orphans, the widows, the strangers, and the poor; the second to those that worshipped God; and the third he kept

for himself and all his house.

4 And as he did so, the Lord multiplied to him his herds, so that there was no man like him in the people of Israel.

5 This now he began to do when he was fifteen years old. And at the age of twenty he took to wife Anna, the daughter of Achar, of his own tribe, that is, of the tribe of Judah, of the family of David.

6 And though they had lived together for twenty years, he had by her neither sons nor daughters.

CHAPTER 2

1 And it happened that, in the time of the feast, among those who were offering incense to the Lord, Joachim stood getting ready his gifts in the sight of the Lord.

2 And the priest, Ruben by name, coming to him, said: It is not lawful for thee to stand among those who are doing sacrifice to God, because God has not blessed thee so as to give thee seed in Israel.

3 Being therefore put to shame in the sight of the people, he retired from the temple of the Lord weeping, and did not return to his house, but went to his flocks, taking with him his shepherds into the mountains to a far country, so that for five months his wife Anna could hear no tidings of him.

4 And she prayed with tears, saying: O Lord, most mighty God of Israel, why hast Thou, seeing that already Thou hast not given me children, taken from me my husband also?

5 Behold, now five months that I have not seen my husband; and I know not where he is tarrying; nor, if I knew him to be dead, could I bury him.

6 And while she wept excessively, she entered into the court of His house; and she fell on her face in prayer, and poured out her supplications before the Lord.

7 After this, rising from her prayer, and lifting her eyes to God, she saw a sparrow's nest in a laurel tree, and uttered her voice to the Lord with groaning, and said:

8 Lord God Almighty, who hast given

offspring to every creature, to beasts wild and tame, to serpents, and birds, and fishes, and they all rejoice over their young ones, Thou hast shut out me alone from the gift of Thy benignity.

9 For Thou, O God, knowest my heart, that from the beginning of my married life I have vowed that, if Thou, O God, shouldst give me son or daughter, I would offer them to Thee in Thy holy temple.

10 And while she was thus speaking, suddenly an angel of the Lord appeared before her, saying:

11 Be not afraid, Anna, for there is seed for thee in the decree of God; and all generations even to the end shall wonder at that which shall be born of thee.

12 And when he had thus spoken, he vanished out of her sight.

13 But she, in fear and dread because she had seen such a sight, and heard such words, at length went into her bed-chamber, and threw herself on the bed as if dead.

14 And for a whole day and night she remained in great trembling and in prayer.

15 And after these things she called to her her servant, and said to her:

16 Dost thou see me deceived in my widowhood and in great perplexity, and hast thou been unwilling to come in to me?

17 Then she, with a slight murmur, thus answered and said:

18 If God hath shut up thy womb, and hath taken away thy husband from thee, what can I do for thee?

19 And when Anna heard this, she lifted up her voice, and wept aloud.

CHAPTER 3

1 At the same time there appeared a young man on the mountains to Joachim while he was feeding his flocks, and said to him: Why dost thou not return to thy wife?

2 And Joachim said: I have had her for twenty years, and it has not been the will of God to give me children by her.

3 I have been driven with shame and reproach from the temple of the Lord:

why should I go back to her, when I have been once cast off and utterly despised?

4 Here then will I remain with my sheep; and so long as in this life God is willing to grant me light, I shall willingly, by the hands of my servants, bestow their portions upon the poor, and the orphans, and those that fear God.

5 And when he had thus spoken, the young man said to him: I am an angel of the Lord, and I have to-day appeared to thy wife when she was weeping and praying, and have consoled her; and know that she has conceived a daughter from thy seed, and thou in thy ignorance of this hast left her.

6 She will be in the temple of God, and the Holy Spirit shall abide in her; and her blessedness shall be greater than that of all the holy women, so that no one can say that any before her has been like her, or that any after her in this world will be so.

7 Therefore go down from the mountains, and return to thy wife, whom thou wilt find with child. For God hath raised up seed in her, and for this thou wilt give God thanks; and her seed shall be blessed, and she herself shall be blessed, and shall be made the mother of eternal blessing.

8 Then Joachim adored the angel, and said to him: If I have found favour in thy sight, sit for a little in my tent, and bless thy servant.

9 And the angel said to him: Do not say servant, but fellow-servant; for we are the servants of one Master.

10 But my food is invisible, and my drink cannot be seen by a mortal.

11 Therefore thou oughtest not to ask me to enter thy tent; but if thou wast about to give me anything, offer it as a burnt-offering to the Lord.

12 Then Joachim took a lamb without spot, and said to the angel: I should not have dared to offer a burnt-offering to the Lord, unless thy command had given me the priest's right of offering.

13 And the angel said to him: I should not have invited thee to offer unless I had known the will of the Lord.

14 And when Joachim was offering the sacrifice to God, the angel and the odour of the sacrifice went together straight up to heaven with the smoke.

15 Then Joachim, throwing himself on his face, lay in prayer from the sixth hour of the day even until evening.

16 And his lads and hired servants who were with him saw him, and not knowing why he was lying down, thought that he was dead; and they came to him, and with difficulty raised him from the ground.

17 And when he recounted to them the vision of the angel, they were struck with great fear and wonder, and advised him to accomplish the vision of the angel without delay, and to go back with all haste to his wife.

18 And when Joachim was turning over in his mind whether he should go back or not, it happened that he was overpowered by a deep sleep; and, behold, the angel who had already appeared to him when awake, appeared to him in his sleep, saying:

19 I am the angel appointed by God as thy guardian: go down with confidence, and return to Anna, because the deeds of mercy which thou and thy wife Anna have done have been told in the presence of the Most High; and to you will God give such fruit as no prophet or saint has ever had from the beginning, or ever will have.

20 And when Joachim awoke out of his sleep, he called all his herdsmen to him, and told them his dream.

21 And they worshipped the Lord, and said to him: See that thou no further despise the words of the angel.

22 But rise and let us go hence, and return at a quiet pace, feeding our flocks.

23 And when, after thirty days occupied in going back, they were now near at hand, behold, the angel of the Lord appeared to Anna, who was standing and praying, and said:

24 Go to the gate which is called Golden, and meet thy husband in the way, for to-day he will come to thee.

25 She therefore went towards him in haste With her maidens, and, praying to the Lord, she stood a long time in the gate waiting for him.

26 And when she was wearied with long waiting, she lifted up her eyes and saw Joachim afar off coming with his flocks; and she ran to him and hung on his neck, giving thanks to God, and saying:

27 I was a widow, and behold now I am not so: I was barren, and behold I have now conceived.

28 And so they worshipped the Lord, and went into their own house. And when this was heard of, there was great joy among all their neighbours and acquaintances, so that the whole land of Israel congratulated them.

CHAPTER 4

1 After these things, her nine months being fulfilled, Anna brought forth a daughter, and called her Mary.

2 And having weaned her in her third year, Joachim, and Anna his wife, went together to the temple of the Lord to offer sacrifices to God, and placed the infant, Mary by name, in the community of virgins, in which the virgins remained day and night praising God.

3 And when she was put down before the doors of the temple, she went up the fifteen steps so swiftly, that she did not look back at all; nor did she, as children are wont to do, seek for her parents.

4 Whereupon her parents, each of them anxiously seeking for the child, were both alike astonished, until they found her in her temple, and the priests of the temple themselves wondered.

CHAPTER 5

1 Then Anna, filled with the Holy Spirit, said before them all:

2 The Lord Almighty, the God of Hosts, being mindful of His word, hath visited His people with a good and holy visitation, to bring down the hearts of the Gentiles who were rising against us, and turn them to Himself.

3 He hath opened His ears to our prayers:

4 He hath kept away from us the exulting of all our enemies.

5 The barren hath become a mother, and hath brought forth exultation and gladness to Israel.

6 Behold the gifts which I have brought to offer to my Lord, and mine enemies have not been able to hinder me.

7 For God hath turned their hearts to me, and Himself hath given me everlasting joy.

CHAPTER 6

1 And Mary was held in admiration by all the people of Israel; and when she was three years old, she walked with a step so mature, she spoke so perfectly, and spent her time so assiduously in the praises of God, that all were astonished at her, and wondered; and she was not reckoned a young infant, but as it were a grown-up person of thirty years old.

2 She was so constant in prayer, and her appearance was so beautiful and glorious, that scarcely any one could look into her face.

3 And she occupied herself constantly with her wool-work, so that she in her tender years could do all that old women were not able to do.

4 And this was the order that she had set for herself: From the morning to the third hour she remained in prayer; from the third to the ninth she was occupied with her weaving; and from the ninth she again applied herself to prayer.

5 She did not retire from praying until there appeared to her the angel of the Lord, from whose hand she used to receive food; and thus she became more and more perfect in the work of God.

6 Then, when the older virgins rested from the praises of God, she did not rest at all; so that in the praises and vigils of God none were found before her, no one more learned in the wisdom of the law of God, more lowly in humility, more elegant in singing, more perfect in all virtue.

7 She was indeed stedfast, immoveable, unchangeable, and daily advancing to perfection.

8 No one saw her angry, nor heard her speaking evil.

9 All her speech was so full of grace, that her God was acknowledged to be in her tongue.

10 She was always engaged in prayer and in searching the law, and she was anxious lest by any word of hers she should sin with regard to her companions.

11 Then she was afraid lest in her laughter, or the sound of her beautiful voice, she should commit any fault, or lest, being elated, she should display any wrong-doing or haughtiness to one of her equals.

12 She blessed God without intermission; and lest perchance, even in her salutation, she might cease from praising God; if any one saluted her, she used to answer by way of salutation: Thanks be to God.

13 And from her the custom first began of men saying, Thanks be to God, when they saluted each other.

14 She refreshed herself only with the food which she daily received from the hand of the angel; but the food which she obtained from the priests she divided among the poor.

15 The angels of God were often seen speaking with her, and they most diligently obeyed her.

16 If any one who was unwell touched her, the same hour he went home cured.

CHAPTER 7

1 Then Abiathar the priest offered gifts without end to the high priests, in order that he might obtain her as wife to his son. But Mary forbade them, saying:

2 It cannot be that I should know a man, or that a man should know me.

3 For all the priests and all her relations kept saying to her: God is worshipped in children and adored in posterity, as has always happened among the sons of Israel.

4 But Mary answered and said unto them: God is worshipped in chastity, as is proved first of all.

5 For before Abel there was none righteous among men, and he by his offerings pleased God, and was without mercy slain by him who displeased Him.

6 Two crowns, therefore, he received -- of oblation and of virginity, because in

his flesh there was no pollution.

7 Elias also, when he was in the flesh, was taken up in the flesh, because he kept his flesh unspotted.

8 Now I, from my infancy in the temple of God, have learned that virginity can be sufficiently dear to God.

9 And so, because I can offer what is dear to God, I have resolved in my heart that I should not know a man at all.

CHAPTER 8

1 Now it came to pass, when she was fourteen years old, and on this account there was occasion for the Pharisees' saying that it was now a custom that no woman of that age should abide in the temple of God, they fell upon the plan of sending a herald through all the tribes of Israel, that on the third day all should come together into the temple of the Lord.

2 And when all the people had come together, Abiathar the high priest rose, and mounted on a higher step, that he might be seen and heard by all the people; and when great silence had been obtained, he said:

3 Hear me, O sons of Israel, and receive my words into your ears.

4 Ever since this temple was built by Solomon, there have been in it virgins, the daughters of kings and the daughters of prophets, and of high priests and priests; and they were great, and worthy of admiration.

5 But when they came to the proper age they were given in marriage, and followed the course of their mothers before them, and were pleasing to God.

6 But a new order of life has been found out by Mary alone, who promises that she will remain a virgin to God.

7 Wherefore it seems to me, that through our inquiry and the answer of God we should try to ascertain to whose keeping she ought to be entrusted.

8 Then these words found favour with all the synagogue.

9 And the lot was east by the priests upon the twelve tribes, and the lot fell upon the tribe of Judah.

10 And the priest said: To-morrow let every one who has no wife come, and bring his rod in his hand.

11 Whence it happened that Joseph brought his rod along with the young men.

12 And the rods having been handed over to the high priest, he offered a sacrifice to the Lord God, and inquired of the Lord.

13 And the Lord said to him: Put all their rods into the holy of holies of God, and let them remain there, and order them to come to thee on the morrow to get back their rods; and the man from the point of whose rod a dove shall come forth, and fly towards heaven, and in whose hand the rod, when given back, shall exhibit this sign, to him let Mary be delivered to be kept.

14 On the following day, then, all having assembled early, and an incense-offering having been made, the high priest went into the holy of ho-lies, and brought forth the rods.

15 And when he had distributed the rods, and the dove came forth out of none of them, the high priest put on the twelve bells and the sacerdotal robe; and entering into the holy of holies, he there made a burnt-offering, and poured forth a prayer.

16 And the angel of the Lord appeared to him, saying:

17 There is here the shortest rod, of which thou hast made no account: thou didst bring it in with the rest, but didst not take it out with them.

18 When thou hast taken it out, and hast given it him whose it is, in it will appear the sign of which I spoke to thee.

19 Now that was Joseph's rod; and because he was an old man, he had been cast off, as it were, that he might not receive her, but neither did he himself wish to ask back his rod.

20 And when he was humbly standing last of all, the high priest cried out to him with a loud voice, saying: Come, Joseph, and receive thy rod; for we are waiting for thee.

21 And Joseph came up trembling, because the high priest had called him with a very loud voice.

22 But as soon as he stretched forth his

hand, and laid hold of his rod, immediately from the top of it came forth a dove whiter than snow, beautiful exceedingly, which, after long flying about the roofs of the temple, at length flew towards the heavens.

23 Then all the people congratulated the old man, saying: Thou hast been made blessed in thine old age, O father Joseph, seeing that God hath shown thee to be fit to receive Mary.

24 And the priests having said to him, Take her, because of all the tribe of Judah thou alone hast been chosen by God;

25 Joseph began bashfully to address them, saying: I am an old man, and have children; why do you hand over to me this infant, who is younger than my grandsons?

26 Then Abiathar the high priest said to him: Remember, Joseph, how Dathan and Abiron and Core perished, because they despised the will of God.

27 So will it happen to thee, if thou despise this which is commanded thee by God.

28 Joseph answered him: I indeed do not despise the will of God; but I shall be her guardian until I can ascertain concerning the will of God, as to which of my sons can have her as his wife.

29 Let some virgins of her companions, with whom she may meanwhile spend her time, be given for a consolation to her.

30 Abiathar the high priest answered and said:

31 Five virgins indeed shall be given her for consolation, until the appointed day come in which thou mayst receive her; for to no other can she be joined in marriage.

32 Then Joseph received Mary, with the other five virgins who were to be with her in Joseph's house.

33 These virgins were Rebecca, Sephora, Susanna, Abigea, and Cael; to whom the high priest gave the silk, and the blue, and the fine linen, and the scarlet, and the purple, and the fine flax.

34 For they cast lots among themselves what each virgin should do, and the purple for the veil of the temple of the Lord fell to the lot of Mary.

35 And when she had got it, those virgins said to her:

36 Since thou art the last, and humble, and younger than all, thou hast deserved to receive and obtain the purple.

37 And thus saying, as it were in words of annoyance, they began to call her queen of virgins.

38 While, however, they were so doing, the angel of the Lord appeared in the midst of them, saying: These words shall not have been uttered by way of annoyance, but prophesied as a prophecy most true.

39 They trembled, therefore, at the sight of the angel, and at his words, and asked her to pardon them, and pray for them.

CHAPTER 9

1 And on the second day, while Mary was at the fountain to fill her pitcher, the angel of the Lord appeared to her, saying:

2 Blessed art thou, Mary; for in thy womb thou hast prepared an habitation for the Lord.

3 For, lo, the light from heaven shall come and dwell in thee, and by means of thee will shine over the whole world.

4 Again, on the third day, while she was working at the purple with her fingers, there entered a young man of ineffable beauty.

5 And when Mary saw him, she exceedingly feared and trembled.

6 And he said to her: Hail, Mary, full of grace; the Lord is with thee: blessed art thou among women, and blessed is the fruit of thy womb.

7 And when she heard these words, she trembled, and was exceedingly afraid.

8 Then the angel of the Lord added: Fear not, Mary; for thou hast found favour with God:

9 Behold, thou shalt conceive in thy womb, and shalt bring forth a King, who fills not only the earth, but the heaven, and who reigns from generation to generation.

CHAPTER 10

1 While these things were doing,

Joseph was occupied with his work, house-building, in the districts by the sea-shore; for he was a carpenter.

2 And after nine months he came back to his house, and found Mary pregnant.

3 Wherefore, being in the utmost distress, he trembled and cried out, saying:

4 O Lord God, receive my spirit; for it is better for me to die than to live any longer.

5 And the virgins who were with Mary said to him: Joseph, what art thou saying?

6 We know that no man has touched her; we can testify that she is still a virgin, and untouched.

7 We have watched over her; always has she continued with us in prayer; daily do the angels of God speak with her; daily does she receive food from the hand of the Lord.

8 We know not how it is possible that there can be any sin in her.

9 But if thou wishest us to tell thee what we suspect, nobody but the angel of the Lord has made her pregnant.

10 Then said Joseph: Why do you mislead me, to believe that an angel of the Lord has made her pregnant?

11 But it is possible that some one has pretended to be an angel of the Lord, and has beguiled her. And thus speaking, he wept, and said:

12 With what face shall I look at the temple of the Lord, or with what face shall I see the priests of God? What am I to do?

13 And thus saying, he thought that he would flee, and send her away.

CHAPTER 11

1 And when he was thinking of rising up and hiding himself, and dwelling in secret, behold, on that very night, the angel of the Lord appeared to him in sleep, saying:

2 Joseph, thou son of David, fear not; receive Mary as thy wife: for that which is in her womb is of the Holy Spirit.

3 And she shall bring forth a son, and His name shall be called Jesus, for He will save His people from their sins.

4 And Joseph, rising from his sleep,

gave thanks to God, and spoke to Mary and the virgins who were with her, and told them his vision.

5 And he was comforted about Mary, saying: I have sinned, in that I suspected thee at all.

CHAPTER 12

1 After these things there arose a great report that Mary was with child.

2 And Joseph was seized by the officers of the temple, and brought along with Mary to the high priest.

3 And he with the priests began to reproach him, and to say:

4 Why hast thou beguiled so great and so glorious a virgin, who was fed like a dove in the temple by the angels of God, who never wished either to see or to have a man, who had the most excellent knowledge of the law of God?

5 If thou hadst not done violence to her, she would still have remained in her virginity.

6 And Joseph vowed, and swore that he had never touched her at all.

7 And Abiathar the high priest answered him:

8 As the Lord liveth, I will give thee to drink of the water of drinking of the Lord, and immediately thy sin will appear.

9 Then was assembled a multitude of people which could not be numbered, and Mary was brought to the temple.

10 And the priests, and her relatives, and her parents wept, and said to Mary: 11 Confess to the priests thy sin, thou that wast like a dove in the temple of God, and didst receive food from the hands of an angel.

12 And again Joseph was summoned to the altar, and the water of drinking of the Lord was given him to drink.

13 And when any one that had lied drank this water, and walked seven times round the altar, God used to show some sign in his face.

14 When, therefore, Joseph had drunk in safety, and had walked round the altar seven times, no sign of sin appeared in him.

15 Then all the priests, and the officers, and the people justified him, saying:

16 Blessed art thou, seeing that no charge has been found good against thee.

17 And they summoned Mary, and said: And what excuse canst thou have? or what greater sign can appear in thee than the conception of thy womb, which betrays thee?

18 This only we require of thee, that since Joseph is pure regarding thee, thou confess who it is that has beguiled thee.

19 For it is better that thy confession should betray thee, than that the wrath of God should set a mark on thy face, and expose thee in the midst of the people.

20 Then Mary said, stedfastly and without trembling:

21 O Lord God, King over all, who knowest all secrets, if there be any pollution in me, or any sin, or any evil desires, or unchastity, expose me in the sight of all the people, and make me an example of punishment to all.

22 Thus saying, she went up to the altar of the Lord boldly, and drank the water of drinking, and walked round the altar seven times, and no spot was found in her.

23 And when all the people were in the utmost astonishment, seeing that she was with child, and that no sign had appeared in her face, they began to be disturbed among themselves by conflicting statements: some said that she was holy and unspotted, others that she was wicked and defiled.

24 Then Mary, seeing that she was still suspected by the people, and that on that account she did not seem to them to be wholly cleared, said in the hearing of all, with a loud voice, As the Lord Adonai liveth, the Lord of Hosts before whom I stand, I have not known man; but I am known by Him to whom from my earliest years I have devoted myself.

25 And this vow I made to my God from my infancy, that I should remain unspotted in Him who created me, and I trust that I shall so live to Him alone, and serve Him alone; and in Him, as long as I shall live, will I remain unpolluted.

26 Then they all began to kiss her feet and to embrace her knees, asking her to pardon them for their wicked suspicions.

27 And she was led down to her house with exultation and joy by the people, and the priests, and all the virgins.

28 And they cried out, and said: Blessed be the name of the Lord for ever, because He hath manifested thy holiness to all His people Israel.

CHAPTER 13

1 And it came to pass some little time after, that an enrolment was made according to the edict of Caesar Augustus, that all the world was to be enrolled, each man in his native place.

2 This enrolment was made by Cyrinus, the governor of Syria, It was necessary, therefore, that Joseph should enrol with the blessed Mary in Bethlehem, because to it they belonged, being of the tribe of Judah, and of the house and family of David.

3 When, therefore, Joseph and the blessed Mary were going along the road which leads to Bethlehem, Mary said to Joseph:

4 I see two peoples before me, the one weeping, and the other rejoicing.

5 And Joseph answered: Sit still on thy beast, and do not speak superfluous words.

6 Then there appeared before them a beautiful boy, clothed in white raiment, who-said to Joseph:

7 Why didst thou say that the words which Mary spoke about the two peoples were superfluous?

8 For she saw the people of the Jews weeping, because they have departed from their God; and the people of the Gentiles rejoicing, because they have now been added and made near to the Lord, according to that which He promised to our fathers Abraham, Isaac, and Jacob: for the time is at hand when in the seed of Abraham all nations shall be blessed.

9 And when he had thus said, the angel ordered the beast to stand, for the time when she should bring forth was at hand; and he commanded the blessed

Mary to come down off the animal, and go into a recess under a cavern, in which there never was light, but always darkness, because the light of day could not reach it.

10 And when the blessed Mary had gone into it, it began to shine with as much brightness as if it were the sixth hour of the day.

11 The light from God so shone in the cave, that neither by day nor night was light wanting as long as the blessed Mary was there.

12 And there she brought forth a son, and the angels surrounded Him when He was being born.

13 And as soon as He was born, He stood upon His feet, and the angels adored Him, saying:

14 Glory to God in the highest, and on earth peace to men of good pleasure.

15 Now, when the birth of the Lord was at hand, Joseph had gone away to seek midwives.

16 And when he had found them, he returned to the cave, and found with Mary the infant which she had brought forth.

17 And Joseph said to the blessed Mary: I have brought thee two midwives--Zelomi and Salome; and they are standing outside before the entrance to the cave, not daring to come in hither, because of the exceeding brightness.

18 And when the blessed Mary heard this, she smiled; and Joseph said to her:

19 Do not smile; but prudently allow them to visit thee, in case thou shouldst require them for thy cure.

20 Then she ordered them to enter.

21 And when Zelomi had come in, Salome having stayed without, Zelomi said to Mary:

22 Allow me to touch thee. And when she had permitted her to make an examination, the midwife cried out with a loud voice, and said:

23 Lord, Lord Almighty, mercy on us! It has never been heard or thought of, that any one should have her breasts full of milk, and that the birth of a son should show his mother to be a virgin.

24 But there has been no spilling of blood in his birth, no pain in bringing him forth.

25 A virgin has conceived, a virgin has brought forth, and a virgin she remains.

26 And hearing these words, Salome said:

27 Allow me to handle thee, and prove whether Zelomi have spoken the truth.

28 And the blessed Mary allowed her to handle her.

29 And when she had withdrawn her hand from handling her, it dried up, and through excess of pain she began to weep bitterly, and to be in great distress, crying out, and saying:

30 O Lord God, Thou knowest that I have always feared Thee, and that without recompense I have cared for all the poor; I have taken nothing from the widow and the orphan, and the needy have I not sent empty away.

31 And, behold, I am made wretched because of mine unbelief, since without a cause I wished to try Thy virgin.

32 And while she was thus speaking, there stood by her a young man in shining garments, saying:

33 Go to the child, and adore Him, and touch Him with thy hand, and He will heal thee, because He is the Saviour of the world, and of all that hope in Him.

34 And she went to the child with haste, and adored Him, and touched the fringe of the cloths in which He was wrapped, and instantly her hand was cured.

35 And going forth, she began to cry aloud, and to tell the wonderful things which she had seen, and which she had suffered, and how she had been cured; so that many through her statements believed.

36 And some shepherds also affirmed that they had seen angels singing a hymn at midnight, praising and blessing the God of heaven, and saying:

37 There has been born the Saviour of all, who is Christ the Lord, in whom salvation shall be brought back to Israel.

38 Moreover, a great star, larger than any that had been seen since the beginning of the world, shone over the cave from the evening till the morning.

39 And the prophets who were in

Jerusalem said that this star pointed out the birth of Christ, who should restore the promise not only to Israel, but to all nations.

CHAPTER 14

1 And on the third day after the birth of our Lord Jesus Christ, the most blessed Mary went forth out of the cave, and entering a stable, placed the child in the stall, and the ox and the ass adored Him.

2 Then was fulfilled that which was said by Isaiah the prophet, saying:

3 The ox knoweth his owner, and the ass his master's crib.

4 The very animals, therefore, the ox and the ass, having Him in their midst, incessantly adored Him. Then was fulfilled that which was said by Abacuc the prophet, saying:

5 Between two animals thou art made manifest. In the same place Joseph remained with Mary three days.

CHAPTER 15

1 And on the sixth day they entered Bethlehem, where they spent the seventh day.

2 And on the eighth day they circumcised the child, and called His name Jesus; for so He was called by the angel before He was conceived in the womb.

3 Now, after the days of the purification of Mary were fulfilled according to the law of Moses, then Joseph took the infant to the temple of the Lord.

4 And when the infant had received parhithomus, --parhithomus, that is, circumcision--they offered for Him a pair of turtle-doves, or two young pigeons.

5 Now there was in the temple a man of God, perfect and just, whose name was Symeon, a hundred and twelve years old.

6 He had received the answer from the Lord, that he should not taste of death till he had seen Christ, the Son of God, living in the flesh.

7 And having seen the child, he cried out with a loud voice, saying:

8 God hath visited His people, and the Lord hath fulfilled His promise.

9 And he made haste, and adored Him.

10 And after this he took Him up into his cloak and kissed His feet, and said:

11 Lord, now lettest Thou Thy servant depart in peace, according to Thy word: for mine eyes have seen Thy salvation, which Thou hast prepared before the face of all peoples, to be a light to lighten the Gentiles, and the glory of Thy people Israel.

12 There was also in the temple of the Lord, Anna, a prophetess, the daughter of Phanuel, of the tribe of Asher, who had lived with her husband seven years from her virginity; and she had now been a widow eighty-four years.

13 And she never left the temple of the Lord, but spent her time in fasting and prayer. She also likewise adored the child, saying: In Him is the redemption of the world.

CHAPTER 16

1 And when the second year was past, Magi came from the east to Jerusalem, bringing great gifts.

2 And they made strict inquiry of the Jews, saying:

3 Where is the king who has been born to you? for we have seen his star in the east, and have come to worship him.

4 And word of this came to King Herod, and so alarmed him that he called together the scribes and the Pharisees, and the teachers of the people, asking of them where the prophets had foretold that Christ should be born.

5 And they said: In Bethlehem of Judah. For it is written: And thou Bethelehem, in the land of Judah, art by no means the least among the princes of Judah; for out of thee shall come forth a Leader who shall rule my people Israel.

6 Then King Herod summoned the magi to him, and strictly inquired of them when the star appeared to them.

7 Then, sending them to Bethlehem, he said:

8 Go and make strict inquiry about the child; and when ye have found him, bring me word again, that I may come and worship him also.

9 And while the magi were going on their way, there appeared to them the star, which was, as it were, a guide to them, going before them until they came to where the child was.

10 And when the magi saw the star, they rejoiced with great joy; and going into the house, they saw the child Jesus sitting in His mother's lap.

11 Then they opened their treasures, and presented great gifts to the blessed Mary and Joseph.

12 And to the child Himself they offered each of them a piece of gold.

13 And likewise one gave gold, another frankincense, and the third myrrh.

14 And when they were going to return to King Herod, they were warned by an angel in their sleep not to go back to Herod; and they returned to their own country by another road.

CHAPTER 17

1 And when Herod saw that he had been made sport of by the magi, his heart swelled with rage, and he sent through all the roads, wishing to seize them and put them to death.

2 But when he could not find them at all; he sent anew to Bethlehem and all its borders, and slew all the male children whom he found of two years old and under, according to the time that he had ascertained from the magi.

3 Now the day before this was done Joseph was warned in his sleep by the angel of the Lord, who said to him:

4 Take Mary and the child, and go into Egypt by the way of the desert.

5 And joseph went according to the saying of the angel.

CHAPTER 18

1 And having come to a certain cave, and wishing to rest in it, the blessed Mary dismounted from her beast, and sat down with the child Jesus in her bosom.

2 And there were with Joseph three boys, and with Mary a girl, going on the journey along with them.

3 And, lo, suddenly there came forth from the cave many dragons; and when the children saw them, they cried out in great terror.

4 Then Jesus went down from the bosom of His mother, and stood on His feet before the dragons; and they adored Jesus, and thereafter retired.

5 Then was fulfilled that which was said by David the prophet, saying: Praise the Lord from the earth, ye dragons; ye dragons, and all ye deeps.

6 And the young child Jesus, walking before them, commanded them to hurt no man.

7 But Mary and Joseph were very much afraid lest the child should be hurt by the dragons.

8 And Jesus said to them:

9 Do not be afraid, and do not consider me to be a little child; for I am and always have been perfect; and all the beasts of the forest must needs be tame before me.

CHAPTER 19

1 Lions and panthers adored Him likewise, and accompanied them in the desert.

2 Wherever Joseph and the blessed Mary went, they went before them showing them the way, and bowing their heads; and showing their submission by wagging their tails, they adored Him with great reverence.

3 Now at first, when Mary saw the lions and the panthers, and various kinds of wild beasts, coming about them, she was very much afraid.

4 But the infant Jesus looked into her face with a joyful countenance, and said:

5 Be not afraid, mother; for they come not to do thee harm, but they make haste to serve both thee and me.

6 With these words He drove all fear from her heart.

7 And the lions kept walking with them, and with the oxen, and the asses, and the beasts of burden which carried their baggage, and did not hurt a single one of them, though they kept beside them; but they were tame among the sheep and the rams which they had brought with them from Judaea, and which they had with them.

8 They walked among wolves, and

feared nothing; and no one of them was hurt by another.

9 Then was fulfilled that which was spoken by the prophet: Wolves shall feed with lambs; the lion and the ox shall eat straw together.

10 There were together two oxen drawing a waggon with provision for the journey, and the lions directed them in their path.

CHAPTER 20

1 And it came to pass on the third day of their journey, while they were walking, that the blessed Mary was fatigued by the excessive heat of the sun in the desert; and seeing a palm tree, she said to Joseph:

2 Let me rest a little under the shade of this tree.

3 Joseph therefore made haste, and led her to the palm, and made her come down from her beast.

4 And as the blessed Mary was sitting there, she looked up to the foliage of the palm, and saw it full of fruit, and said to Joseph:

5 I wish it were possible to get some of the fruit of this palm.

6 And Joseph said to her:

7 I wonder that thou sayest this, when thou seest how high the palm tree is; and that thou thinkest of eating of its fruit.

8 I am thinking more of the want of water, because the skins are now empty, and we have none wherewith to refresh ourselves and our cattle.

9 Then the child Jesus, with a joyful countenance, reposing in the bosom of His mother, said to the palm:

10 O tree, bend thy branches, and refresh my mother with thy fruit.

11 And immediately at these words the palm bent its top down to the very feet of the blessed Mary; and they gathered from it fruit, with which they were all refreshed.

12 And after they had gathered all its fruit, it remained bent down, waiting the order to rise from Him who bad commanded it to stoop.

13 Then Jesus said to it: Raise thyself, O palm tree, and be strong, and be the companion of my trees, which are in the paradise of my Father; and open from thy roots a vein of water which has been hid in the earth, and let the waters flow, so that we may be satisfied from thee.

14 And it rose up immediately, and at its root there began to come forth a spring of water exceedingly clear and cool and sparkling.

15 And when they saw the spring of water, they rejoiced with great joy, and were satisfied, themselves and all their cattle and their beasts. Wherefore they gave thanks to God.

CHAPTER 21

1 And on the day after, when they were setting out thence, and in the hour in which they began their journey, Jesus turned to the palm, and said:

2 This privilege I give thee, O palm tree, that one of thy branches be carried away by my angels, and planted in the paradise of my Father.

3 And this blessing I will confer upon thee, that it shall be said of all who conquer in any contest, You have attained the palm of victory.

4 And while He was thus speaking, behold, an angel of the Lord appeared, and stood upon the palm tree; and taking off one of its branches, flew to heaven with the branch in his hand.

5 And when they saw this, they fell on their faces, and became as it were dead.

6 And Jesus said to them: Why are your hearts possessed with fear?

7 Do you not know that this palm, which I have caused to be transferred to paradise, shall be prepared for all the saints in the place of delights, as it has been prepared for us in this place of the wilderness?

8 And they were filled with joy; and being strengthened, they all rose up.

CHAPTER 22

1 After this, while they were going on their journey, Joseph said to Jesus:

2 Lord, it is a boiling heat; if it please Thee, let us go by the sea-shore, that we may be able to rest in the cities on the coast.

3 Jesus said to him: Fear not, Joseph; I will shorten the way for you, so that what you would have taken thirty days to go over, you shall accomplish in this one day.

4 And while they were thus speaking, behold, they looked forward, and began to see the mountains and cities of Egypt.

5 And rejoicing and exulting, they came into the regions of Hermopolis, and entered into a certain city of Egypt which is called Sotinen; and because they knew no one there from whom they could ask hospitality, they went into a temple which was called the Capitol of Egypt.

6 And in this temple there had been set up three hundred and fifty-five idols, to each of which on its own day divine honours and sacred rites were paid.

7 For the Egyptians belonging to the same city entered the Capitol, in which the priests told them how many sacrifices were offered each day, according to the honour in which the god was held.

CHAPTER 23

1 And it came to pass, when the most blessed Mary went into the temple with the little child, that all the idols prostrated themselves on the ground, so that all of them were lying on their faces shattered and broken to pieces; and thus they plainly showed that they were nothing.

2 Then was fulfilled that which was said by the prophet Isaiah: Behold, the Lord will come upon a swift cloud, and will enter Egypt, and all the handiwork of the Egyptians shall be moved at His presence.

CHAPTER 24

1 Then Affrodosius, that governor of the city, when news of this was brought to him, went to the temple with all his army.

2 And the priests of the temple, when they saw Affrodosius with all his army coming into the temple, thought that he was making haste only to see vengeance taken on those on whose account the gods had fallen down.

3 But when he came into the temple, and saw all the gods lying prostrate on their faces, he went up to the blessed Mary, who was carrying the Lord in her bosom, and adored Him, and said to all his army and all his friends:

4 Unless this were the God of our gods, our gods would not have fallen on their faces before Him; nor would they be lying prostrate in His presence: wherefore they silently confess that He is their Lord.

5 Unless we, therefore, take care to do what we have seen our gods doing, we may run the risk of His anger, and all come to destruction, even as it happened to Pharaoh king of the Egyptians, who, not believing in powers so mighty, was drowned in the sea, with all his army.

6 Then all the people of that same city believed in the Lord God through Jesus Christ.

CHAPTER 25

1 After no long time the angel said to Joseph: Return to the land of Judah, for they are dead who sought the child's life.

CHAPTER 26

1 And it came to pass, after Jesus had returned out of Egypt, when He was in Galilee, and entering on the fourth year of His age, that on a Sabbath-day He was playing with some children at the bed of the Jordan.

2 And as He sat there, Jesus made to Himself seven pools of clay, and to each of them He made passages, through which at His command He brought water from the torrent into the pool, and took it back again.

3 Then one of those children, a son of the devil, moved with envy, shut the passages which supplied the pools with water, and overthrew what Jesus had built up.

4 Then said Jesus to him: Woe unto thee, thou son of death, thou son of Satan! Dost thou destroy the works which I have wrought?

5 And immediately he who had done

this died.

6 Then with great uproar the parents of the dead boy cried out against Mary and Joseph, saying to them:

7 Your son has cursed our son, and he is dead.

8 And when Joseph and Mary heard this, they came forthwith to Jesus, on account of the outcry of the parents of the boy, and the gathering together of the Jews.

9 But Joseph said privately to Mary: I dare not speak to Him; but do thou admonish Him, and say:

10 Why hast Thou raised against us the hatred of the people; and why must the troublesome hatred of men be borne by us?

11 And His mother having come to Him, asked Him, saying:

12 My Lord, what was it that he did to bring about his death?

13 And He said: He deserved death, because he scattered the works that I had made.

14 Then His mother asked Him, saying: Do not so, my Lord, because all men rise up against us.

15 But He, not wishing to grieve His mother, with His right foot kicked the hinder parts of the dead boy, and said to him:

16 Rise, thou son of iniquity for thou art not worthy to enter into the rest of my Father, because thou didst destroy the works which I had made.

17 Then he who had been dead rose up, and went away. And Jesus, by the word of His power, brought water into the pools by the aqueduct.

CHAPTER 27

1 And it came to pass, after these things, that in the sight of all Jesus took clay froth the pools which He had made, and of it made twelve sparrows.

2 And it was the Sabbath when Jesus did this, and there were very many children with Him.

3 When, therefore, one of the Jews had seen Him doing this, he said to Joseph:

4 Joseph, dost thou not see the child Jesus working on the Sabbath at what it is not lawful for him to do? for he has made twelve sparrows of clay.

5 And when Joseph heard this, he reproved him, saying:

6 Wherefore doest thou on the Sabbath such things as are not lawful for us to do?

7 And when Jesus heard Joseph, He struck His hands together, and said to His sparrows: Fly!

8 And at the voice of His command they began to fly.

9 And in the sight and hearing of all that stood by, He said to the birds:

10 Go and fly through the earth, and through all the world, and live.

11 And when those that were there saw such miracles, they were filled with great astonishment.

12 And some praised and admired Him, but others reviled Him.

13 And certain of them went away to the chief priests and the heads of the Pharisees, and reported to them that Jesus the son of Joseph had done great signs and miracles in the sight of all the people of Israel.

14 And this was reported in the twelve tribes of Israel.

CHAPTER 28

1 And again the son of Annas, a priest of the temple, who had come with Joseph, holding his rod in his hand in the sight of all, with great fury broke down the dams which Jesus had made with His own hands, and let out the water which He had collected in them from the torrent.

2 Moreover, he shut the aqueduct by which the water came in, and then broke it down.

3 And when Jesus saw this, He said to that boy who had destroyed His dams:

4 O most wicked seed of iniquity! O son of death! O workshop of Satan! verily the fruit of thy seed shall be without strength, and thy roots without moisture, and thy branches withered, bearing no fruit.

5 And immediately, in the sight of all, the boy withered away, and died.

CHAPTER 29

1 Then Joseph trembled, and took hold

of Jesus, and went with Him to his own house, and His mother with Him.

2 And, behold, suddenly from the opposite direction a boy, also a worker of iniquity, ran up and came against the shoulder of Jesus, wishing to make sport of Him, or to hurt Him, if he could.

3 And Jesus said to him: Thou shall not go back safe and sound from the way that thou goest.

4 And immediately he fell down, and died.

5 And the parents of the dead boy, who had seen what happened, cried out, saying:

6 Where does this child come from? It is manifest that every word that he says is true; and it is often accomplished before he speaks.

7 And the parents of the dead boy came to Joseph, and said to him:

8 Take away that Jesus from this place, for he cannot live with us in this town; or at least teach him to bless, and not to curse.

9 And Joseph came up to Jesus, and admonished Him, saying:

10 Why doest thou such things? For already many are in grief and against thee, and hate us on thy account, and we endure the reproaches of men because of thee.

11 And Jesus answered and said unto Joseph:

12 No one is a wise son but he whom his father hath taught, according to the knowledge of this time; and a father's curse can hurt none but evil-doers.

13 Then they came together against Jesus, and accused him to Joseph.

14 When Joseph saw this, he was in great terror, fearing the violence and uproar of the people of Israel.

15 And the same hour Jesus seized the dead boy by the ear, and lifted him up from the earth in the sight of all: and they saw Jesus speaking to him like a father to his son.

16 And his spirit came back to him, and he revived. And all of them wondered.

CHAPTER 30

1 Now a certain Jewish schoolmaster named Zachyas heard Jesus thus speaking; and seeing that He could not be overcome, from knowing the power that was in Him, he became angry, and began rudely and foolishly, and without fear, to speak against Joseph.

2 And he said: Dost thou not wish to entrust me with thy son, that he may be instructed in human learning and in reverence?

3 But I see that Mary and thyself have more regard for your son than for what the elders of the people of Israel say against him.

4 You should have given more honour to us, the elders of the whole church of Israel, both that he might be on terms of mutual affection with the children, and that among us he might be instructed in Jewish learning.

5 Joseph, on the other hand, said to him: And is there any one who can keep this child, and teach him

6 But if thou canst keep him and teach him, we by no means hinder him from being taught by thee those things which are learned by all.

7 And Jesus, having heard what Zachyas had said, answered and said unto him:

8 The precepts of the law which thou hast just spoken of, and all the things that thou hast named, must be kept by those who are instructed in human learning; but I am a stranger to your law-courts, because I have no father after the flesh.

9 Thou who readest the law, and art learned in it, abidest in the law; but I was before the law, But since thou thinkest that no one is equal to thee in learning, thou shalt be taught by me, that no other can teach anything but those things which thou hast named.

10 But he alone can who is worthy.

11 For when I shall be exalted on earth, I will cause to cease all mention of your genealogy.

12 For thou knowest not when thou wast born: I alone know when you were born, and how long your life on earth will be.

13 Then all who heard these words were struck with astonishment, and

cried out: Oh! oh! oh! this marvellously great and wonderful mystery.

14 Never have we heard the like! Never has it been heard from any one else, nor has it been said or at any time heard by the prophets, or the Pharisees, or the scribes.

15 We know whence he is sprung, and he is scarcely five years old; and whence does he speak these words?

16 The Pharisees answered: We have never heard such words spoken by any other child so young.

17 And Jesus answered and said unto them: At this do ye wonder, that such things are said by a child?

18 Why, then, do ye not believe me in those things which I have said to you?

19 And you all wonder because I said to you that I know when you were born.

20 I will tell you greater things, that you may wonder more.

21 I have seen Abraham, whom you call your father, and have spoken with him; and he has seen me.

22 And when they heard this they held their tongues, nor did any of them dare to speak.

23 And Jesus said to them: I have been among you with children, and you have not known me;

24 I have spoken to you as to wise men, and you have not understood my words; because you are younger than I am, and of little faith.

CHAPTER 31

1 A second time the master Zachyas, doctor of the law, said to Joseph and Mary:

2 Give me the boy, and I shall hand him over to master Levi, who shall teach him his letters and instruct him.

3 Then Joseph and Mary, soothing Jesus, took Him to the schools, that He might be taught His letters by old Levi.

4 And as soon as He went in He held His tongue.

5 And the master Levi said one letter to Jesus, and, beginning from the first letter Aleph, said to Him: Answer.

6 But Jesus was silent, and answered nothing.

7 Wherefore the preceptor Levi was angry, and seized his storax-tree rod, and struck Him on the head.

8 And Jesus said to the teacher Levi: Why dost thou strike me?

9 Thou shall know in truth, that He who is struck can teach him who strikes Him more than He can be taught by him.

10 For I can teach you those very things that yon are saying.

11 But all these are blind who speak and hear, like sounding brass or tinkling cymbal, in which there is no perception of those things which are meant by their sound.

12 And Jesus in addition said to Zachyas: Every letter from Aleph even to Thet is known by its arrangement.

13 Say thou first, therefore, what Thet is, and I will tell thee what Aleph is.

14 And again Jesus said to them: Those who do not know Aleph, how can they say Thet, the hypocrites?

15 Tell me what the first one, Aleph, is; and I shall then believe you when you have said Beth.

16 And Jesus began to ask the names of the letters one by one, and said:

17 Let the master of the law tell us what the first letter is, or why it has many triangles, gradate, subacute, mediate, obduced, produced, erect, prostrate, curvistrate.

18 And when Levi heard this, he was thunderstruck at such an arrangement of the names of the letters.

19 Then he began in the heating of all to cry out, and say:

20 Ought such a one to live on the earth? Yea, he ought to be hung on the great cross.

21 For he can put out fire, and make sport of other modes of punishment.

22 I think that he lived before the flood, and was born before the deluge.

23 For what womb bore him? or what mother brought him forth? or what breasts gave him suck?

24 I flee before him; I am not able to withstand the words from his mouth, but my heart is astounded to hear such words.

25 I do not think that any man can understand what he says, except God were with him.

26 Now I, unfortunate wretch, have given myself up to be a laughing- stock to him.

27 For when I thought I had a scholar, I, not knowing him, have found my master.

28 What shall I say? I cannot withstand the words of this child:

29 I shall now flee from this town, because I cannot understand them.

30 An old man like me has been beaten by a boy, because I can find neither beginning nor end of what he says.

31 For it is no easy matter to find a beginning of himself.

32 I tell you of a certainty, I am not lying, that to my eyes the proceedings of this boy, the commencement of his conversation, and the upshot of his intention, seem to have nothing in common with mortal man.

33 Here then I do not know whether he be a wizard or a god; or at least an angel of God speaks in him.

34 Whence he is, or where he comes from, or who he will turn out to be, I know not.

35 Then Jesus, smiling at him with a joyful countenance, said in a commanding voice to all the sons of Israel standing by and hearing:

36 Let the unfruitful bring forth fruit, and the blind see, and the lame walk right, and the poor enjoy the good things of this life, and the dead live, that each may return to his original state, and abide in Him who is the root of life and of perpetual sweetness.

37 And when the child Jesus had said this, forthwith all who had fallen under malignant diseases were restored.

38 And they did not dare to say anything more to Him, or to hear anything from Him.

CHAPTER 32

1 After these things, Joseph and Mary departed thence with Jesus into the city of Nazareth; and He remained there with His parents.

2 And on the first of the week, when Jesus was playing with the children on the roof of a certain house, it happened that one of the children pushed another down from the roof to the ground, and he was killed.

3 And the parents of the dead boy, who had not seen this, cried out against Joseph and Mary, saying:

4 Your son has thrown our son down to the ground, and he is dead.

5 But Jesus was silent, and answered them nothing.

6 And Joseph and Mary came in haste to Jesus.; and His mother asked Him, saying:

7 My lord, tell me if thou didst throw him down.

8 And immediately Jesus went down from the roof to the ground, and called the boy by his name, Zeno.

9 And he answered Him: My lord.

10 And Jesus said to him: Was it I that threw thee down from the roof to the ground?

11 And he said: No, my lord.

12 And the parents of the boy who had been dead wondered, and honoured Jesus for the miracle that had been wrought.

13 And Joseph and Mary departed thence with Jesus to Jericho.

CHAPTER 33

1 Now Jesus was six years old, and His mother sent Him with a pitcher to the fountain to draw water with the children.

2 And it came to pass, after He had drawn the water, that one of the children came against Him, and struck the pitcher, and broke it.

3 But Jesus stretched out the cloak which He had on, and took up in His cloak as much water as there had been in the pitcher, and carried it to His mother.

4 And when she saw it she wondered, and reflected within herself, and laid up all these things in her heart.

CHAPTER 34

1 Again, on a certain day, He went forth into the field, and took a little wheat from His mother's barn, and sowed it Himself.

2 And it sprang up, and grew, and multiplied exceedingly.

3 And at last it came to pass that He Himself reaped it, and gathered as the produce of it three kors, and gave it to His numerous acquaintances.

CHAPTER 35

1 There is a road going out of Jericho and leading to the river Jordan, to the place where the children of Israel crossed: and there the ark of the covenant is said to have rested.

2 And Jesus was eight years old, and He went out of Jericho, and went towards the Jordan.

3 And there was beside the road, near the bank of the Jordan, a cave where a lioness was nursing her cubs; and no one was safe to walk that way.

4 Jesus then, coming from Jericho, and knowing that in that cave the lioness bad brought forth her young, went into it in the sight of all.

5 And when the lions saw Jesus, they ran to meet Him, and adored Him.

6 And Jesus was sitting in the cavern, and the lion's cubs ran hither and thither round His feet, fawning upon Him, and sporting.

7 And the older lions, with their heads bowed down, stood at a distance, and adored Him, and fawned upon Him with their tails.

8 Then the people who were standing afar off, not seeing Jesus, said:

9 Unless he or his parents had committed grievous sins, he would not of his own accord have offered himself up to the lions.

10 And when the people were thus reflecting within themselves, and were lying under great sorrow, behold, on a sudden, in the sight of the people, Jesus came out of the cave, and the lions went before Him, and the lion's cubs played with each other before His feet.

11 And the parents of Jesus stood afar off, with their heads bowed down, and watched; likewise also the people stood at a distance, on account of the lions; for they did not dare to come close to them.

12 Then Jesus began to say to the people:

13 How much better are the beasts than you, seeing that they recognise their Lord, and glorify Him; while you men, who have been made after the image and likeness of God, do not know Him! 14 Beasts know me, and are tame; men see me, and do not acknowledge me.

CHAPTER 36

1 After these things Jesus crossed the Jordan, in the sight of them all, with the lions; and the water of the Jordan was divided on the right hand and on the left.

2 Then He said to the lions, in the hearing of all: Go in peace, and hurt no one; but neither let man injure you, until you return to the place whence you have come forth.

3 And they, bidding Him farewell, not only with their gestures but with their voices, went to their own place. But Jesus returned to His mother.

CHAPTER 37

1 Now Joseph was a carpenter, and used to make nothing else of wood but ox-yokes, and ploughs, and implements of husbandry, and wooden beds.

2 And it came to pass that a certain young man ordered him to make for him a couch six cubits long.

3 And Joseph commanded his servant to cut the wood with an iron saw, according to the measure which he had sent.

4 But he did not keep to the prescribed measure, but made one piece of wood shorter than the other.

5 And Joseph was in perplexity, and began to consider what he was to do about this.

6 And when Jesus saw him in this state of cogitation, seeing that it was a matter of impossibility to him, He addresses him with words of comfort, saying:

7 Come, let us take hold of the ends of the pieces of wood, and let us put them together, end to end, and let us fit them exactly to each other, and draw to us, for we shall be able to make them equal.

8 Then Joseph did what he was bid, for he knew that He could do whatever He wished.

9 And Joseph took hold of the ends of the pieces of wood, and brought them together against the wall next himself, and Jesus took hold of the other ends of the pieces of wood, and drew the shorter piece to Him, and made it of the same length as the longer one.

10 And He said to Joseph: Go and work, and do what thou hast promised to do.

11 And Joseph did what he had promised.

CHAPTER 38

1 And it came to pass a second time, that Joseph and Mary were asked by the people that Jesus should be taught His letters in school.

2 They did not refuse to do so; and according to the commandment of the elders, they took Him to a master to be instructed in human learning.

3 Then the master began to teach Him in an imperious tone, saying: Say Alpha.

4 And Jesus said to him: Do thou tell me first what Betha is, and I will tell thee what Alpha is.

5 And upon this the master got angry and struck Jesus; and no sooner had he struck Him, than he fell down dead.

6 And Jesus went home again to His mother. And Joseph, being afraid, called Mary to him, and said to her:

7 Know of a surety that my soul is sorrowful even unto death on account of this child.

8 For it is very likely that at some time or other some one will strike him in malice, and he will die.

9 But Mary answered and said: O man of God! do not believe that this is possible.

10 You may believe to a certainty that He who has sent him to be born among men will Himself guard him from all mischief, and will in His own name preserve him from evil.

CHAPTER 39

1 Again the Jews asked Mary and Joseph a third time to coax Him to go to another master to learn.

2 And Joseph and Mary, fearing the people, and the overbearing of the princes, and the threats of the priests, led Him again to school, knowing that He could learn nothing from man, because He had perfect knowledge from God only.

3 And when Jesus had entered the school, led by the Holy Spirit, He took the book out of the hand of the master who was teaching the law, and in the sight and hearing of all the people began to read, not indeed what was written in their book; but He spoke in the Spirit of the living God, as if a stream of water were gushing forth from a living fountain, and the fountain remained always full.

4 And with such power He taught the people the great things of the living God, that the master himself fell to the ground and adored Him.

5 And the heart of the people who sat and heard Him saying such things was turned into astonishment.

6 And when Joseph heard of this, he came running to Jesus, fearing that the master himself was dead.

7 And when the master saw him, he said to him:

8 Thou hast given me not a scholar, but a master; and who can withstand his words?

9 Then was fulfilled that which was spoken by the Psalmist: The river of God is full of water:

10 Thou hast prepared them corn, for so is the provision for it.

CHAPTER 40

1 After these things Joseph departed thence with Mary and Jesus to go into Capernaum by the sea-shore, on account of the malice of his adversaries.

2 And when Jesus was living in Capernaum, there was in the city a man named Joseph, exceedingly rich.

3 But he had wasted away under his infirmity, and died, and was lying dead in his couch.

4 And when Jesus heard them in the city mourning, and weeping, and lamenting over the dead man, He said to Joseph:

5 Why dost thou not afford the benefit

of thy favour to this man, seeing that he is called by thy name

6 And Joseph answered him: How have I any power or ability to afford him a benefit?

7 And Jesus said to him: Take the handkerchief which is upon thy head, and go and put it on the face of the dead man, and say to him: Christ heal thee; and immediately the dead man will be healed, and will rise from his couch.

8 And when Joseph heard this, he went away at the command of Jesus, and ran, and entered the house of the dead man, and put the handkerchief which he was wearing on his head upon the face of him who was lying in the couch, and said: Jesus heal thee.

9 And forthwith the dead man rose from his bed, and asked who Jesus was.

CHAPTER 41

1 And they went away from Capernaum into the city which is called Bethlehem; and Joseph lived with Mary in his own house, and Jesus with them.

2 And on a certain day Joseph called to him his first-born son James, and sent him into the vegetable garden to gather vegetables for the purpose of making broth.

3 And Jesus followed His brother James into the garden; but Joseph and Mary did not know this.

4 And while James was collecting the vegetables, a viper suddenly came out of a hole and struck his hand, and he began to cry out from excessive pain.

5 And, becoming exhausted, he said, with a bitter cry: Alas! alas! an accursed viper has struck my hand.

6 And Jesus, who was standing opposite to him, at the bitter cry ran up to James, and took hold of his hand; and all that He did was to blow on the hand of James, and cool it: and immediately James was healed, and the serpent died.

7 And Joseph and Mary did not know what had been done; but at the cry of James, and the command of Jesus, they ran to the garden, and found the serpent already dead, and James quite cured.

CHAPTER 42

1 And Joseph having come to a feast with his sons, James, Joseph, and Judah, and Simeon and his two daughters, Jesus met them, with Mary His mother, along with her sister Mary of Cleophas, whom the Lord God had given to her father Cleophas and her mother Anna, because they had offered Mary the mother of Jesus to the Lord.

2 And she was called by the same name, Mary, for the consolation of her parents.

3 And when they had come together, Jesus sanctified and blessed them, and He was the first to begin to eat and drink; for none of them dared to eat or drink, or to sit at table, or to break bread, until He had sanctified them, and first done so.

4 And if He happened to be absent, they used to wait until He should do this.

5 And when He did not wish to come for refreshment, neither Joseph nor Mary, nor the sons of Joseph, His brothers, came.

6 And, indeed, these brothers, keeping His life as a lamp before their eyes, observed Him, and feared Him.

7 And when Jesus slept, whether by day or by night, the brightness of God shone upon Him. To whom be all praise and glory for ever and ever. Amen, amen.

THE LIFE OF JOHN THE BAPTIST

1 With the assistance of God and His divine guidance we begin to write the life of the holy Man John the Baptist, son of Zacharias: may his intercession be with us. Amen!

2 There was an aged priest-Levite from the tribe of Judah, whose name was Zacharias.

3 He was a prophet who rose among the children of Israel in the days of Herod,

King of Judaea.

4 He had a God-loving wife, called Elizabeth, and she was from the daughters of Aaron, from the tribe of Levi.

5 She was barren and had no children, and she and her husband were advanced in years.

6 They were both righteous and pious people, guiding their steps by all the commandments and ordinances of God.

7 And Zacharias was officiating constantly in the Temple of the Lord. When it fell to him, during the turn of his division, to burn incense to the Lord, he entered the Temple according to his habit, at the time of the burning of the incense, and the angel of the Lord appeared to him immediately, standing on the right of the altar.

8 When Zacharias saw him he was frightened and startled.

9 But the angel said to him: "Do not be afraid, but rather rejoice, O Zacharias! God has heard your prayer, and your wife Elizabeth shall conceive and bear you a son, who shall be called John; you shall have joy and delight, and many shall rejoice over his birth.

10 He shall be great before the Lord, and he shall not drink any wine or strong drink, and he shall be filled with the Holy Spirit while still in the womb of his mother, and shall reconcile many of the children of Israel to the Lord their God.

11 He shall go before Him in the spirit and with the power of Elijah, in order to make ready for the Lord a people prepared for him."

12 Zacharias was astonished at these words, and doubt overtook him, because no child had been born to him. He did not remember Abraham, the head of the Patriarchs, to whom God gave Isaac, after he had reached the age of a hundred years, nor his wife Sarah who was also barren like his own wife.

13 Zacharias said, therefore, to the angel: "How can this happen to me while I am an old man, and my wife is advanced in years?"

14 And the angel answered and said to him: "I am the angel Gabriel. I have been sent to speak to you and bring you this news.

15 And from now you shall be silent and unable to speak until the day when this takes place, because you did not believe my words, which will be fulfilled in due course."

16 And he disappeared from his sight.

17 Meanwhile the people were waiting for Zacharias wondering at his remaining so long in the Temple. When he came out he was unable to speak to the people, and they perceived that he had seen a vision in the Temple, and he kept making signs to them. And as soon as his term of service was finished, he returned home.

18 And Elizabeth got information of the affair (from God).

19 In those days Elizabeth conceived, and lived in seclusion till the fifth month, because she felt somewhat ashamed.

20 She feared to appear in her old age while pregnant and milk dripping from her breasts.

21 She lived in a secluded room l of her own house, and Zacharias also lived likewise.

22 Between them stood a locked door, and they did not speak at all to anyone in all those days.

23 When she reached her sixth month the angel Gabriel was sent from God to a town in Galilee called Nazareth, to a virgin betrothed to a man named Joseph, from the house of David; and the name of the virgin was Mary.

24 When the angel came into her presence he said to her:

25 "Rejoice, O Mary, because you have been favoured with a grace from God. You shall be with child and shall give birth to a son, who shall be called Jesus.

26 He shall be great and shall be called Son of the Most High.'"

27 And Mary said to the angel: " How can this happen to me while I have not known any man? "

28 And the angel said to her: " The Holy Spirit shall descend upon you, and the power of the Most High shall overshadow you, because the child that is born of you is holy and shall be

called ' Son of God,' and lo Elizabeth who is related to you is also expecting a child in her old age, and it is now the sixth month with her who is called barren, because with God there is nothing impossible."

29 And she had no doubt on the matter but said to the head of the angels: "I am the servant of the Lord, let it be with me as you have said."

30 He then greeted her and disappeared.

31 Mary was astonished at the fact that Elizabeth was expecting a child, and kept saying in her heart: "

32 Thy acts are wonderful and great, O God Omnipotent, because Thou hast given descendants to an old and barren woman.

33 I shall not cease walking until I have met her and beheld the wonderful miracle which God has performed in our times: a virgin giving birth to a child," and a barren woman suckling."

34 In those days she rose up in haste and went into the hill-country, to the town of Judah, and she entered the house of Zacharias, and greeted Elizabeth.

35 The latter went to her with great joy and delight, and greeted her, saying: " Blessed are you among women and blessed is the fruit of your womb."

36 The holy and pious virgin embraced then the true turtle-dove, and the Word baptized John while still in the womb of his mother.

37 And David appeared in the middle and said: "Mercy and truth have met together, and righteousness and peace have kissed each other."

38 And immediately after John moved in the womb, as if wishing to come out and greet his master.

39 After they had finished their mutual greetings, the Virgin stayed with Elizabeth three months, until the latter's time was near, and then returned to her home.

40 When the holy Elizabeth gave birth (to her son) there was a great joy and delight in her house, and after eight days they went to circumcise him, and wished to call him Zacharias.

41 His mother, however, said: " No, call him John." And they said to her: "You have no relation of that name."

42 And she said to them: "Ask his father about his name." And he asked for a writing-tablet and wrote thus: "

43 His name is John." When he had written this he recovered the use of his tongue forthwith, and he glorified God who had granted him this great mercy, and uttered prophecies concerning his son John the Baptist, and was cognizant of the gift that he had received from God.

44 John grew up in a beautiful childhood and sucked his mother two years.

45 The grace of God was on his face, and he grew up fortified by the Spirit.

46 When Jesus Christ was born in Bethlehem of Judaea, behold magians came from the East saying:

47 "Where is he that is born, the King of the Jews? for we have seen his star in the East and are come to worship Him."

48 When Herod the king heard these words he was troubled by what he had heard from the magians that (that child) was the King of the Jews, and he immediately desired to kill him.

49 Then the angel of the Lord appeared forthwith to Joseph and said to him:

50 "Arise and take the child and his mother and flee into the land of Egypt, and be thou there until I bring thee word."

51 Then Herod sought the Master in order to destroy Him, but he did not find Him, and he began to kill all the children of Bethlehem.

52 And Elizabeth feared, 'that her son John might be killed like them, and she took him immediately to Zacharias in the Temple, and she said to him:

53 "My lord, let us go with our son John to some other countries, in order to save him from Herod the unbeliever, who is murdering children because of Jesus the Christ.

54 Mary and Joseph have already gone to the land of Egypt. Get up quickly that they may not kill our son, and change our joy into grief."

55 And Zacharias answered and said to her: "I must not leave the service of the

Temple of the Lord and go to a foreign land the inhabitants of which worship idols."

56 And she said to him: "What should I do in order to save my infant child?" And the old man answered and said to her : "

57 Arise and go to the wilderness of ' Ain Karim, and by the will of God you will be able to save your son. If they seek after him, they will shed -my blood instead of his."

58 How great was the amount of grief that occurred at that time when they separated from each other!

59 The holy Zacharias took the child to his bosom, blessed him, kissed him and said: " Woe is me, O my son John, O glory of my old age !

60 They have impeded me from having any access to your face which is full of grace."

61 He then took him and went into the Temple, and blessed him, saying: "May God protect you in your journey!"

62 Immediately after Gabriel, the head of the angels, came down to him from heaven holding a raiment and a leathern girdle, and said to him:

63 "O Zacharias, take these and put them on your son. God sent them to him from heaven.

64 This raiment is that of Elijah, and this girdle that of Elisha."

65 And the holy Zacharias took them from the angel, prayed over them and gave them to his son, and fastened on him the raiment which was of camel's hair with the leathern girdle.

66 He then brought him back to his mother and said to her: "Take him and bring him into the desert, because the hand of the Lord is with him.

67 I have learnt from God that he will stay in the desert till the day of his showing unto Israel."

68 The blessed Elizabeth took the child while weeping and Zacharias also was weeping, and the latter said:

69 "I know that I shall not see you again in the flesh. Go in peace. May God guide you."

70 Elizabeth walked then away with her son, and went into the wilderness of 'Ain Karim, and stayed there with him.

71 It happened that when King Herod sent troops to Jerusalem to kill its children, they came and began to kill children till the evening.

72 That day was the seventh of September. When they began to return to their king, behold, Satan came to them and said: " How did you leave the son of Zacharias without killing him?

73 He is hidden with his father in the Temple. Do not spare him but kill him in order that the king may not wax angry with you.

74 Go for him, and if you do not find the son, kill the father in his place."

75 The troops did what Satan taught them, and went to the Temple early in the morning, and found Zacharias standing and serving the Lord, and they said to him:

76 "Where is thy son whom thou hast hidden from us here?" And he answered them:

77 "I have no child here." They said to him: "You have a child whom you have hidden from the king."

78 And he answered and said: "O cruel ones whose king drinks blood like a lioness, how long will you shed the blood of innocent people?"

79 They said to him: Bring out your child so that we may kill him; if not, we shall kill you in his place."

80 And the prophet answered and said: "As to my son, he has gone with his mother to the wilderness, and I do not know his whereabouts."

81 Now when Zacharias has said goodbye to Elizabeth and his son John, he had blessed him and made him a priest, and afterwards delivered him to his mother, who said to him:

82 "Pray over me O my holy father, so that God may render my path in the wilderness easy."

83 And he said to her: "May He who made us beget our child in our old age, direct your path."

84 Then she took the child and went into the wilderness in which no soul lived.

85 "O blessed Elizabeth, your story is truly wonderful and praiseworthy.

86 You did not ask for an adult to accompany you, and you knew neither the way nor a hiding place.

87 You did not care to provide food nor a little drinking water for the child.

88 You did not say to his father Zacharias: 'To whom are you sending me in the wilderness?'

89 At that time there was neither a monastery in the desert nor a congregation of monks so that you may say:

90 'I shall go and stay with them with my son.' Tell me, O blessed Elizabeth: whom did you trust, inasmuch as the evangelist testifies to the fact that you were advanced in years without having had any child, and now you have been suckling this child of yours for three years?"

91 Listen now to the answer of the blessed Elizabeth:

92 "Why are you astonished at me that I am going alone into the wilderness? What should I fear while a kinsman of God is in my arms?

93 Behold Gabriel is accompanying me and paving the way for me."

94 And she said: "I have confidence in the kiss that Mary, His mother, gave me, because when I greeted her the babe leaped with joy in my womb, and I heard both babes embracing each other in our wombs."

95 And Elizabeth added: " I went and put on my son a raiment of camel's hair and a leathern girdle in order that the mountain of the holy wilderness may (in future) be inhabited, and in order that monasteries and congregations of monks may increase in it and that sacrifice may be offered in it in the name of the Lord Jesus Christ.

96 If God assisted Hagar and her son when they wandered in the desert, and they were only slaves, how will He not apply to us the precedent that He has himself established beforehand? "

97 In the above words we have described to you the merits of the holy Elizabeth. Let us now proceed and commemorate the holy Zacharias, the martyr, and relate to you a few of his numerous merits:

98 " I should wish to praise your true life, but I fear to hear a reproof from you, similar to that you made to the blessed Elizabeth.

99 I am full of admiration for you, O pious Zacharias! In the time when the soldiers of Herod came to you and asked you saying:

100 "Where is your infant son, the child of your old age?" You did not deny the fact and say: "I have no knowledge of such a child," but you simply answered:

101 "His mother took him into the desert."

102 And when Zacharias uttered these words to the soldiers concerning his son, they killed him inside the Temple, and the priests shrouded his body and placed it near that of his father Berechiah in a hidden cemetery, from fear of the wicked (king) ; and his blood boiled on the earth for fifty years, until Titus son of Vespasian, the Emperor of the Romans, came and destroyed Jerusalem and killed the Jewish priests for the blood of Zacharias, as the Lord ordered him.

103 As to the blessed John he wandered in the desert with his mother, and God prepared for him locusts and wild honey as food, in accordance with what his mother was told about him not to let any unclean food enter his mouth.

104 After five years the pious and blessed old mother Elizabeth passed away, and the holy John sat weeping over her, as he did not know how to shroud her and bury her, because on the day of her death he was only seven years and six months old.

105 And Herod also died the same day as the blessed Elizabeth.

106 The Lord Jesus Christ who with His eyes sees heaven and earth saw His kinsman John sitting and weeping near his mother, and He also began to weep for a long time, without anyone knowing the cause of His weeping.

107 When the mother of Jesus saw Him weeping, she said to Him: "Why are you weeping? Did the old man Joseph or any other one chide you ? "

108 And the mouth that was full of life answered: "No, O my mother, the real

reason is that your kinswoman, the old Elizabeth, has left my beloved John an orphan. He is now weeping over her body which is lying in the mountain."

109 When the Virgin heard this she began to weep over her kinswoman, and Jesus said to her: "Do not weep, O my virgin mother, you will see her in this very hour."

110 And while he was still speaking with his mother, behold a luminous cloud came down and placed itself between them.

111 And Jesus said: " Call Salome and let us take her with us." And they mounted the cloud which flew with them to the wilderness of 'Ain Karim and to the spot where lay the body of the blessed Elizabeth, and where the holy John was sitting.

112 The Saviour said then to the cloud: "Leave us here at this side of the spot."

113 And it immediately went, reached that spot, and departed. Its noise, however, reached the ears of Mar John, who, seized with fear, left the body of his mother.

114 A voice reached him immediately and said to him: "Do not be afraid, O John. I am Jesus Christ, your master. I am your kinsman Jesus, and I came to you with my beloved mother in order to attend to the business of the burial of the blessed Elizabeth, your happy mother, because she is my mother's kinswoman."

115 When the blessed and holy John heard this, he turned back, and Christ the Lord and His virgin mother embraced him. Then the Saviour said to His virgin mother: "Arise, you and Salome, and wash the body."

116 And they washed the body of the blessed Elizabeth in the spring from which she used to draw water for herself and her son.

117 Then the holy virgin Mart Mary got hold of the blessed (John) and wept over him, and cursed Herod on account of the numerous crimes which he had committed.

118 Then Michael and Gabriel came down from heaven and dug a grave; and the Saviour said to them:

119 "Go and bring the soul of Zacharias, and the soul of the priest Simeon, in order that they may sing while you bury the body."

120 And Michael brought immediately the souls of Zacharias and Simeon, who shrouded the body of Elizabeth and sang for a long time over it.

121 And the mother of Jesus and Salome wept, and the two priests made the sign of the cross on the body and prayed over it three times before they laid it to rest in the grave; then they buried it, and sealed the grave with the sign of the cross, and went back to their own places in peace.

122 And Jesus Christ and His mother stayed near the blessed and the holy John seven days, and consoled with him at the death of his mother, and taught him how to live in the desert. And the day of the death of the blessed Elizabeth was the 15th of February.

123 Then Jesus Christ said to His mother; "Let us now go to the place where I may proceed with my work."

124 The Virgin Mary wept immediately over the loneliness of John, who was very young and said: "We will take him with us, since he is an orphan without anyone."

125 But Jesus said to her: "This is not the will of My Father who is in the heavens.

126 He shall remain in the wilderness till the day of his showing unto Israel.

127 Instead of a desert full of wild beasts, he will walk in a desert full of angels and prophets, as if they were multitudes of people.

128 Here is also Gabriel, the head of the angels, whom I have appointed to protect him and to grant to him power from heaven.

129 Further, I shall render the water of this spring of water as sweet and delicious to him as the milk he sucked from his mother.

130 Who took care of him in his childhood? Is it not I, O my mother, who love him more than all the world?

131 Zacharias also loved him, and I have ordered him to come to him and inquire after him, because although his

body is buried in the earth, his soul is alive.

132 "As to Elizabeth his mother, she will constantly visit him and comfort him, as if she was not dead at all.

133 Blessed is she, O my mother, because she bore my beloved.

134 Her mouth will never suffer putrefaction, because she kissed your pure lips ; and her tongue will not be dismembered in the earth, because she prophesied concerning you and said:

135 'Happy is she who believed that the promise that she received from the Lord would be fulfilled'; nor will her womb decay in the earth, because her body, like her soul, shall suffer no putrefaction.

136 And my beloved John will last forever, and he will see us and be comforted."

137 These words the Christ our Lord spoke to his mother, while John was in the desert.

138 And they mounted the cloud, and John looked at them and wept, and Mart Mary wept also bitterly over him, saying: "Woe is me, O John, because you are alone in the desert without anyone.'

139 Where is Zacharias, your father, and where is Elizabeth, your mother? Let them come and weep with me to-day."

140 And Jesus Christ said to her: "Do not weep over this child, O my mother. I shall not forget him."

141 And while he was uttering these word, behold the clouds lifted them up and brought them to Nazareth. And He fulfilled there everything pertaining to humanity except sin.

142 And John dwelt in the desert, and God and His angels were with him. He lived in great asceticism and devotion. His only food was grass and wild honey. He prayed constantly, fasted much and was in expectation of the salvation of Israel.

143 And Herod the Younger who reigned over Judea, lived with his brother's wife, in the second year of his reign.

144 He did not marry her openly, but he used to find an opportune moment to send after her and usher her in his bedchamber which was full of corruption, and there perpetrate their abomination.'

145 At that time Gabriel, head of the angels, taught John in the desert to say:

146 "O King, you have no right to live with the wife of your brother, while he is still alive." And he repeated this, crying in the desert, as the angel had taught him.

147 In the night people could hear his voice, and Herodias used to light a lamp and search the bedchamber, believing that somebody may have intruded into it, but found nobody, and only heard the voice.

148 The two began then to have misgivings on account of this happening , and Herodias said to Herod: "Arise and despatch troops to the desert of 'Am Karim, in order that they may kill John, because the voice we hear is his."

149 God, however, was with the lad, and delivered him from their hands.

150 When she ascertained that through him there would be no peace for her in her (iniquitous) act, she persuaded the wicked king who gave her the following promise:

151 "If we happen to hear this voice again, we shall summon the magicians and inform them to take hold of John and kill him secretly."

152 And the voice did not cease to worry them.

153 And the wicked Herodias said: "How can this John, a wanderer in the desert and in the wilderness, a man whose body is not fit to wear the clothing of men, but a raiment of camel's hair, rebuke the king of his own country, whose authority extends to his own region?"

154 Then Herodias said to the king: "What pleases you to do, do it openly, and do not believe that anyone in this region will blame you for it, except John, and when opportunity offers itself we shall get rid of him."

155 It is in this way that the adulteress set the heart of Herod on their sin, and

persuaded him to deliver his brother to death, and to marry her openly.

156 And John did not cease to rebuke Herod every day in the desert until he was thirty years old.

157 As to Jesus, He increased in wisdom, stature, and grace with God and men, and did not show any deeds of His Divinity, but acted with humility towards all men.

158 And when He was twelve years old, He began to rebuke the Teachers and deceivers of the people. And in the fifteenth year of the reign of Tiberius Caesar, who reigned after Augustus, when Herod was tetrarch of Galilee, and when Annas and Caiaphas were high priests, in that year the word of God came unto John, son of Zacharias, in the wilderness. He came into the countries that surround the Jordan preaching and

159 saying: "Repent ye for the kingdom of Heaven is at hand." And people from all the region of Judaea and Jerusalem went out to him and were baptized by him in the Jordan confessing their sins.

160 In those days the Saviour came to him from Galilee to the Jordan and said to him: "Baptize me."

161 When John saw God standing before him and wishing to be baptized by him, he was seized with great fright and said to him:

162 "He who made the children of Israel walk in the Red Sea and drink sweet water from a solid rock, stands before His servant who is in need to be baptized with His Divine hands, and says ' Baptize me'"! And he began to turn away from Him. But (Jesus) said to him: "Stop now; it is thus that we must fulfill all righteousness."

163 Then both of them went down into the water, and the holy John baptized Him, saying:

164 "I baptize the One Whom the Father has sent to establish a great sacrament."

165 And immediately after the heavens opened and the Holy Spirit descended upon Him, like a dove.

166 And John saw it face to face, and the Father cried saying: "This is my beloved Son in whom I delight, obey Him."

167 And our Saviour came out of the water and went forthwith into the desert. As to John, he remained near the Jordan, baptizing all those who came to him.

168 In that rime Herod rose against Philip his brother and intrigued against him with the Emperor Caesar, saying:

169 "The one whom you have appointed to be the ruler of Trachoniris, who is Philip, has misgoverned your region, and said:

170 "I shall not pay tribute to the king because I am also a king."

171 Caesar waxed greatly angry and ordered Herod to dispossess him of his region and to confiscate all his estate and his house, and not to have any pity, not even on his soul.

172 Herod acted on the orders of the Emperor and plundered the region of his brother Philip with his house and all his possessions, and reigned over his region.

173 And Philip had a wife called Herodias, who had a daughter by the same Philip, called Arcostiana. The mother was even more adulteress than the daughter.

174 When Philip became poorer than anybody else, Herodias hated him greatly, and said to him:

175 "I shall not remain with you any more, but shall go to your new lord Herod who is better than you."

176 Then she wrote immediately to Herod saying: " Herodias writes to Herod as follows:

177 'Now that you have all Syria under your sway and you reign over all the earth, you have not taken me as your wife. I am very beautiful and better than all the women of Judaea. I have also a daughter the like of whom I have never seen in all the world for beauty and stature. I wish to be your wife. I hated your brother very much in order to strengthen your kingdom.' "

178 When these cunning words reached the wicked (king), he was pleased with them, and he immediately gave orders that she and her daughter be taken out

of the house of Philip.

179 When Philip saw that his wife was being taken from him by force, he wept bitterly and said to his daughter:

180 "You stay with your father in case your mother is taken from me."

181 But the adulteress said to him: "I shall not stay with you, but shall accompany my mother wherever she goes."

182 They were, therefore, taken both of them and presented to Herod, who was greatly pleased with them, because he was an adulterer.

183 They performed marvels of diabolical cunning, and the wicked king lived daily with both of them in adultery. Some people, however, brought their story to the knowledge of John the Baptist on behalf of Philip, Herodias' husband. Now John was considered by all as a prophet, and everybody praised him because he was teaching the people and saying:

184 "Bring forth fruits meet for repentance, because every tree which bringeth not forth good fruit is hewn down and cast into the fire."

185 When John heard the news from Philip he was much afflicted at the perdition of Herod and Herodias, and he immediately sent a message to Herod and said to him:

186 "John the Baptist, son of Zacharias, tells you, O Herod, that you have no right to marry the wife of your brother, while he is still alive."

187 When Herod heard these words he was much frightened and perplexed, and he went to Herodias and said to her: "O Herodias, what shall we do?

188 It is the end of our sinful union as it has been brought to the knowledge of John the Baptist, and behold he has rebuked me.

189 Woe to us, because our sins have increased greatly and reached the ears of the prophets."

190 The wicked woman said then to him: "Long live you, O king! Who is John, the wearer of camel's hair, to contradict and rebuke a mighty monarch like you?

191 He surely deserves that somebody should pull out and cut off his tongue." And he said to her: "What can we do? We cannot bear the rebuke of that great (prophet)."

192 And she answered and said to him: "Summon him here and I will kill him, and we shall continue our mutual relations in peace."

193 And she performed before him obscene acts and immoral artifices, and Satan filled his heart against the holy and just man Mar John the Baptist, and he dispatched soldiers against him, who seized him and cast him in prison.

194 Then Herodias summoned him out of prison to her presence and said to him:

195 "What is your business with me, O chaste man, that you wish to separate me from the king? I conjure you by the God of your father not to do this with me again.

196 To tell you the truth, if you are silent concerning me and do not rebuke me another time, I shall deliver you from prison and bestow great favours upon you."

197 And the holy Mar John the Baptist said to her: "I say to you, O Herodias, not to live with Herod while your husband Philip is alive."

198 When the wicked woman heard this, she was incensed with anger against him and said to him: "You will surely die at my hands, and I shall put the hair of your head in the pillow on which I lay my head with Herod, and I shall bury your head in the place where I wash after having enjoyed myself with the king."

199 John then said to her: "The Lord will allow you to kill me but my head you will not see.

200 It will remain after me, and proclaim your iniquity and shame to all the world. Woe to you for my unjust murder, because your end is at hand."

201 She then said to his keepers: "Take him and keep him in prison with fetters, and if he escapes, you shall lose your souls."

202 And the soldiers took him and kept him in prison with chains.

203 And Herodias tried to induce Herod

to kill him, but he said to her:

204 "I cannot kill him in this way. People will rise against me, drive me out, and bring accusation against me to the Emperor, who will take my kingdom from me as he took that of my brother Philip."

205 And he said to her: "Show me a better method of doing away with him."

206 And she said to him: "I will tell you a word, and if you listen to it, you will have an opportunity of killing him."

207 And he said to her: "Tell it to me."

208 And she said to him: "Behold the envoys of the king are with you, arise and prepare a dinner for them, to which you will invite all your high officials; and your birthday falls also in these days.

209 When people become hilarious and begin to get drunk with wine, I shall send in my daughter dressed in her best clothes, and she will dance before you, O king, with her sweet face.

210 When she has done this ask her, saying, 'Desire of me whatever you like,' and you will swear to her by the life of the Emperor that you will give her whatever she wishes. She will then ask for the head of John, and you will have an opportune moment to cut off his head."

211 Herod was circumvented by the reasoning of the adulteress, and began to fulfill her desires, as he loved her because of her beauty and diabolical artifices.

212 In that very day he prepared the dinner, and the messengers of the Emperor were sitting next to him.

213 When they began to get drunk the accursed Uxoriana entered the room, and on her were strings of gold and silver, perfumes and jewellery of high value, and presented herself to all the company.

214 She danced with a diabolical passion, and Satan filled the hearts of the guests with evil and passion through her iniquitous artfulness.

215 All were pleased with her, and Herod was proud and said to her: "Ask me for whatever you like, and by the life of the Emperor Tiberius Caesar, I will give it to you, even if it be the half of my kingdom and my possessions."

216 And she said what she was taught by her mother:

217 "I wish here to have the head of John the Baptist, on a dish." The king began to be very sad, on account of the oath he had taken by the life of the Emperor, and he owned to the guests that he was unable to break his oath.

218 He therefore dispatched an executioner, who went to the prison and there cut off John's head on a dish, on the second of the month of September, and he brought it to Herod, who handed it to the girl, and the girl handed it to her mother.

219 Now, before the messengers of the king and the executioner had gone to him, to behead him, John had said to his disciples:

220 "Behold the king has sent men to cut off my head. They have already left with unsheathed swords in their hands, and with lanterns, lamps, and weapons."

221 What is happening in this hour will happen in the night in which Christ will be betrayed. As to me, my head will be cut off and be shown on a dish, but the Christ will be lifted up on the cross, in order that He may purify all with His pure blood; as to me I am going to my place, but woe to the king who ordered my head to be cut off; many calamities will befall him, and the people of Israel will be scattered because of him.

222 As to you, do not be afraid, because no one will be able to do you any harm."

223 He then opened his mouth and blessed and glorified God for his incomprehensible gifts, saying: "I bless Thee and praise Thee, O invisible Father, O visible Son, and O comforting Holy Spirit."

224 Let us now proceed to describe the story of the head of the blessed Mar John the Baptist.

225 When it was brought before Herodias, the eyes of the holy John were open and his ears were hearing as in his lifetime.

226 The adulteress spoke then with ire before the head as follows: "O accursed one, who were not ashamed to look at the king in the face and answer him, I shall put out your eyes with my hands and place them on a dish, and I shall cut off the tongue which used to say to the king that it was unlawful for him to marry Herodias, his brother's wife.

227 As to the hair of your head and of your beard I shall pluck it and place it under the feet of my bedstead."

228 She said all this with malice and wickedness, and she stretched her hand to hold the head of Mar John the Baptist and do with it what she had said.

229 But immediately after the head of the blessed John let the locks of its hair rise from the dish, and it flew to the middle of the convivial room before the king and his high officials.

230 In that very moment the roof of the house was opened and the head of John flew in the air.

231 As to Herodias her eyes were put out and fell on the floor and the roof of her room fell upon her, and the earth opened her mouth and swallowed her up to her neck, and she went alive to the depth of hell.

232 As to her daughter she became mad and broke all the utensils of the dinner party. In her madness she went to the icy pond and danced on it, and by order of the Lord the ice broke under her and she sank to her neck. In vain did the soldiers endeavour to pull her up, because the Lord did not wish her deliverance.

233 Then they cut off her head with the very sword that was used to kill John the Baptist. Then a fish cast her out of the pond, dead. May God not have mercy upon her!

234 In that moment Herod also had a sudden stroke before his guests.

235 When his agent noticed these great miracles, he repaired quickly to the prison, took the body of the saint and gave it to his disciples, who took it to the town of Sebaste where they buried it, near the body of the prophet Elisha.

236 As to his head, it flew over Jerusalem, and cried for three years to the town, saying: "It is not lawful for you, O Herod, to marry the wife of your brother while he is still alive."

237 After it had cried for three years, it went to all the world shouting and proclaiming the horrible crime of Herod, and repeating the words: "It is not lawful for you, O Herod, to marry the wife of your brother while he is still alive."

238 Fifteen years after it had been cut off it ceased proclaiming, and rested on the town of Horns.

239 The faithful who were in that town took it and buried it with great pomp. A long time after, a church was built on it, which is still standing in our time.

240 And the head of the holy John the Baptist was buried there fifteen years after the resurrection of Christ, the Lord, and it remained there down to our own days.

241 As to the body of the holy John the Baptist, the saint whose feast we are celebrating to-day, it remained in Sebaste which is Nabulus of Samaria for four hundred years.

242 Then a pagan king, whose name was Julian, reigned over the world. He had been a Christian at the beginning of his reign, but after that Satan filled his heart and he forsook the faith of our Lord the Christ and worshipped fire.

243 He ordered temples and places of worship to be built in every place where idols could be worshipped, and intimated that such a temple should be erected in the town of Sebaste where lay the body of the holy Baptist. People, however, were unable to comply with the order and to worship idols in that place, on account of the (holy) bodies that were buried there.

244 They, therefore, assembled and informed the Emperor that as bodies of holy men were buried there, they had been delayed in their building of the temples. Then he said to them: "Go and burn (the bodies) with fire."

245 The Lord, however, did not allow the fire to come near the place where lay the coffins of the prophets, but the same fire consumed a great number of the pagans who had kindled it, and

great treasures were brought to light there. Above one of the coffins was seen a vessel containing a leathern girdle, a raiment of camel's hair, a frock, and two leathern belts.

246 The faithful who were in that place understood immediately that the coffins belonged to John the Baptist and to the prophet Elisha, and they wished to remove them from there, but from fear of the wicked Emperor they were not able to do so.

247 When, however, God destroyed him with a death more wretched than that of any other, pious men assembled there and carried the two coffins to the sea with the intention of bringing them to Alexandria, to the holy Father, the Patriarch Athanasius, because they said:

248 'There is in these days no one in the world worthy to take care of these except Father Athanasius, the Patriarch of Alexandria."

249 When they reached the sea they found a boat bound for Alexandria, and they boarded it with the coffins.

250 They journeyed on the sea and landed on the shores of Alexandria, but as they were unable to disclose their affair to any one because the time was not convenient for that, they went direct to the Patriarch and related to him all that had occurred, and how they were moved by the Holy Spirit to bring the coffins to him.

251 He was greatly pleased with them and went by night to the boat with his brother, and they took the remains in a kerchief and brought them with them, and (the Patriarch) placed them with him in a place in his dwelling, and he did not disclose their whereabouts to anyone.

252 And this Father wished to build a church to John the Baptist, and he was not able to do so because of the troubles caused by the wicked ones.

253 The bodies remained therefore hidden in the place in which Father Athanasius had secretly placed them, until the time of his death. After his death he was succeeded by Father Peter, whose throne was occupied after his death by Father Timothy, who ordained

my humble self, your Father Serapion, to this see, without merits on my part.

254 After his death, he was succeeded by Father Theophilus who is now sitting on the (Patriarchal) see, In his time the grace of God increased, and the faith was strengthened through the pious Theodosius and God united the Emperor and the Patriarch with ties of love.

255 The former threw open the temples in which were treasures, and especially the great temple of Alexandria, in which there was great quantity of gold and silver.

256 And the pious Theodosius honoured the Patriarch, made him superintendent of all the treasures, and said to him:

257 "O Father Theophilus, take these and enrich the churches with them, from this town to Aswan, for the glory of God and His saints."

258 After this he began to build churches. The first church to be built was one under the name of the holy Mar John the Baptist in the great city of Alexandria.

259 He adorned it and made it a great church and wished to place in it the body of the holy Mar John the Baptist. When he had finished it completely, he thought of consecrating it, and he sent immediately to all the bishops under his jurisdiction to congregate for the consecration of the church.

260 The invitation was also sent to my weakness, and I went with the rest of the bishops to the Pope, the Father Theophilus of Alexandria. When it came to his knowledge that all the bishops were nearing the city of Alexandria, he was pleased with us, like one who had found much booty. He came out to meet us accompanied by all the (clergy) who were in the city. We entered the city and stayed some days with him. After this he began to consecrate the church, and he took us and showed it to us, and we found in it wonderful buildings, and he said to us : " O my children, this is the place designated for the purpose by Athanasius, whom time did not favour."

261 And Father Theophilus added: "I was walking with them while I was a simple acolyte at that time and serving him. And when he came to this place, he said to me:

262 "O my son, Theophilus, if you can find opportunity, build in this place a church to Mar John the Baptist and place his bones in it, and after I had built this place, I remembered the saying of the man of God, the Father Athanasius, especially when I bethought me that my Father was like the prophet David, who wished to build a house to God, but was not favoured with it, on account of wars in which he was continually engaged, and God said to him:

263 "Thou shalt not build a house for me, but the one who comes out of thy loins shall build it for me," and this was Solomon.

264 Since I have finished with the wars against the pagans, I considered myself worthy of building this church which is under the name of the holy Mar John the Baptist, the morning star."

265 When the second of the month of June came, he took us to the place where the body was placed, and we did not know the right spot, but after praying nocturns God showed it to him.

266 And when he brought it out, he called all the inhabitants of the town and they assembled to him with many lanterns and lamps so that the night shone like day.

267 He let the bishops carry the coffin on their heads and the Patriarch preceded them, and the deacons were singing with majesty and splendour, until we brought the coffin to the church in great pomp.

268 When we entered the church, the Patriarch took hold of the coffin, embraced it, and allowed all the people to be blessed by the holy body, which he placed afterwards inside the church on a chair at a corner of the altar.

269 He then prepared to consecrate the church in that day, and we said mass, and all of us received the sacrament from the Patriarch, and it was the second day of the month Baouna?

270 After this the Patriarch said goodbye to us, and we left the town, each one of us going to his own country, in the peace of God. Amen.

271 And the body of the holy Mar John the Baptist wrought miracles, prodigies, and wonders of healings in the people of the Lord Jesus Christ. The miracles (which we will mention below) will bear witness to this.

272 Praise, glory, and power are due to you, O Father, Son, and Holy Spirit who is one in nature, now, always, and forever and ever.

THE GOSPEL OF THOMAS

These are the hidden words which the Living Jesus spoke and Didymos Judas Thomas wrote down.

1 Jesus said; Whoever finds the meaning of these words, [he] will not taste of death.

2 Jesus Said; Let He who seeks, continue to seek until he finds. And when he finds he will be troubled; and if he should be troubled he will become amazed; and then [he] will become king over everything.

3 Jesus said; If those who lead you should speak to you and say; Behold the kingdom is in the sky. Then the birds will become first before you of the sky. If they should speak to you and say; The kingdom is in the sea, then the fish will become first before you. Rather the kingdom, is inside [of] you and is [before] your eyes.
When you should know yourselves then they will know you and you will realize that you are the sons of the Father who lives. If however, you will not know yourselves then you exist in (a) poverty and you are the poverty.

4 Jesus said; the man of age will not delay, in his days, to ask a little boy (Lit. small son) he being of seven days, about the place of (the) Life and he will

live. For many (who are) first will become last and they will become one alone. (Be as one)

5 Jesus Said; Know that which is in the presence of your face and that which is hidden from you will be revealed forth to you. (For) [there is] Nothing hidden [that] will appear forth not. {Alt. Not be made manifest}

6 And Jesus' disciples asked him these things, saying; Do you want (us to) [Lit. that we] fast? And what is the way (manner) that we will (should) pray? Shall we give alms? And shall we abstain from what [certain] foods? And Jesus said this; Do not tell lies and do not do that which you hate, for all these things are revealed outwardly in the presence of the heavens (for) [there is] nothing hidden [that] will not appear forth, and nothing covered will remain unrevealed.

7 Jesus Said; Blessed is the lion, [the one] which the man will eat and the lion becomes man. And cursed is the man which the lion will eat and the lion will become man.

8 And He said, Man is comparable to a fisherman (who is) wise. the one who cast his net to the sea; he drew up the net from the sea, being full of little fish, from below. Among them he found a large fish that was good. The wise fisherman cast all of the little fish away [back] down [in]to the sea. He chose the great fish [over them all] without trouble. He who has an ear of him to hear let him hear.

9 Jesus Said, Behold he who sows filled his hand (with seeds) and he cast. Some indeed fell onto the road and the birds they gathered them. some others they fell onto the rock and they didn't send roots down to the earth, and they didn't send sheaves up to the sky. And some others they fell onto thorns and they choked the seeds and the worms ate them. And some others fall upon the earth that is good and he gave fruit up to the sky well and became sixty per measure and one hundred and twenty per measure.

10 Jesus Said, I have cast a fire upon the world and behold, I watch over that fire until it (Lit. he) burns.

11 Jesus said, This sky will pass away and that which is above it will [also] pass away. And those who are dead, they live not, and those who live, they will not die. In the days you were eating, he who is dead, you were making him he who lives. When you should come to be in the light what is it you will do? On the day you were one you made the two, when, however, you should come to be two what is it you will do?

12 The disciples said to Jesus We know that you will go from our hand. (or, Away from us) Who is he who will become great up over us? (or, Become our leader?) And Jesus said to them, the place you have come there you will be going. Up to Jacob [Greek= James. Literal = Jacob] the Righteous, the one the sky and the earth has come into being because of him.

13 Jesus said to his disciples, Compare me and tell me this; whom do I resemble ? And Simon Peter said, You resemble an Angel who is Righteous. Matthew said to him You resemble a man of philosophy who is wise. Thomas said to him, Master wholly my mouth will not accept that I (should) speak this; (who you resemble.) Jesus Said I am not your Master because You drank and got drunk out of the spring which bubbles (up), the one I have measured. And he took him (Thomas Didymos) and withdrew. He spoke to him three words. When Thomas, however, returned to his companions they asked him, What did Jesus speak to you? And Thomas said to them, If I should speak one of the words he has spoken to me you will take (up) stones and cast them at me and a fire will come out of the stones and burn you all.

14 Jesus Said to them, If you should fast you will beget to yourselves a sin and if you should pray they will condemn you. And if you should give alms you will be making an evil to your spirits. And if you should go to any land and you walk in the districts, what they will put under you, eat it; Heal the sick

among them. For what will go in your mouth it will not defile you. Rather, what comes out of your mouth, [it] is what will defile you.

15 Jesus said, When you should look upon he who was not begotten out of the woman,

prostrate yourselves [bow] onto your faces and worship him, [for he]who is there is your Father.

16 Jesus said, Perhaps men are thinking that I have come to cast peace upon the world and they know not that I have come to cast divisions upon the earth; Fire, Sword, and war. For five will [be] in a house, three will be against two, and two against three. the father against the son and the son against the father. And they will stand alone to their feet being alone. [as one]

17 Jesus Said; I will give you what no eye has looked upon, what no ear has heard and what no mind has touched, and what has not come up on the mind of man.

18 The Disciples said to Jesus; speak to us and tell us our end. Which way will it be? Jesus said, Have you revealed forth the beginning so that you will be seeking after the end? For in the place where the beginning is, there the end will be. Blessed is he who will stand in the beginning, he will know the end, and he will taste not of death.

19 Jesus said, Blessed is he who is from the beginning before he came to be. If you should be to me disciples and listen to my words these stones will become servants to you. For you have five trees in paradise which move not, summer nor winter, and their leaves do not fall down. He who will know them, he will not taste of death.

20 The disciples said to Jesus, Speak to us this, The Kingdom of Heaven what is it comparable to? He said unto them, She is comparable to a grain of mustard. Small. More so than all of the other seeds. When however, she should fall onto the tilled earth, he sends out a great branch and it comes to be shelter for the birds of the sky.

21 Mary asked Jesus, Whom are your disciples like? and he said; They are like small children dwelling in a field which is not theirs. When the lords of the field should come they will speak and say; Give our field back to us and they will undress (Lit. strip naked) in their presence that they give the field back to them.

Therefore I say to you if the lord of the house knows that a thief is coming he will keep watch before he comes and not permit him to tunnel into the house of his kingdom to take his goods. You however, keep watch from the beginning of the world. Gird up your loins (Lit. Bind [up] your loins) in great power so that the thieves do not fall on a road to come up to you. For the help which you look outward for will fall on them.

Let there be among you a man of understanding. When the fruit ripened (Lit. split open) he came with great haste with his sickle in his hand and reaped it. He that has an ear let him hear.

22 Jesus saw some infants being suckled and said to his disciples; These little ones who are being suckled are like those who enter into the Kingdom. And they said to him; Shall we, as infants, enter the Kingdom? And Jesus said to them When you should make the two [as] one, and if you should make the inside like the outside and the outer like the inner, and the utmost like the least (Lit. the side above like the side below).

So too will I be making man and woman one. So that neither shall man be male nor the woman, female.

When you should make eyes in the place of an eye and a hand to the place of a hand, and a foot in the place of a foot, an image in the place of an image then you shall enter into the Kingdom.

23 Jesus said I will choose you one out of a thousand and two out of ten thousand and they shall stand together as one. (Lit. stand to their feet as a single one.)

24 The Disciples said to Jesus; Show us to the place, which you are (there), because to us it is necessary that we seek (after) it. Jesus said to them; He

who has an ear let him hear: Light exists inside a man of light and he becomes light to all of the world. If he doesn't become light, a darkness is he.

25 Jesus said love your brother like your soul and guard him like the pupil of your eye.

26 Jesus said; the mote which is in the eye of your brother, you do see but the Beam, however, which is in your [own] eye, you see it not. When you should cast the beam out of your [own] eye then you will [be able] to see outward[ly] to cast the mote out of the eye of your brother.

27 [Jesus said] If you do not fast from [Resist] the world you will not find (Lit. fall not to) the Kingdom. If you do not keep the Sabbath as the Sabbath, you will not look upon the Father.

28 Jesus said; I stood to my feet in the midst of the world and I appeared outwardly to them in [the] flesh; I found (Lit. fell upon) all of them drunken; I did find anyone among them thirsting and my soul was pained (Lit. did give pain) over the sons of men. for blind men they are in their mind and they look not outward for they have come to the world empty, they seek also that they come out of the world empty. But now they are drunk when they should cast off their wine. Then will they repent.

29 Jesus said; If the flesh came to be because of the spirit, a wonder it is. If Spirit (however) because of the body a wondrous wonder it is. Rather I myself become amazed at this, that how this great richness was placed in this poverty.

30 Jesus said; The place which has three gods (there), in God they are; the place which has two or one, I myself, exist with him [them?].

31 Jesus said; No prophet is accepted in his own village; No physician heals those who know him.

32 Jesus said; A city they are building upon a mountain raised up, it being fortified, no way that it will fall, nor can it be hidden.

33 Jesus said; He who you will hear in your ear (and in the other ear) preach

him [that] upon your housetops. For no one burns a lamp and puts it under his ear and he does not put it in a place that is hidden. Rather does he put it upon a lamp stand so that anyone who goes in and who comes out, [even] they may look to his light.

34 Jesus said; If a blind man should lead before him a blind man, they both (Lit. The two of them.) [will] fall down into a pit.

35 Jesus said; (Lit. no way can one) [No one can] go in to the house of the strong and take it by force unless he bind his hands. Then he will move [him?] out of his house.

36 Jesus said; Do not take care from morning unto evening and from evening unto morning for what it is you will put upon yourselves.

37 The disciples said [to Jesus]; Which day will you appear forth to us? And which day will we look upon you? And Jesus said; When you should strip yourselves naked without being ashamed and take your garments and put them under the ground of your feet, like those little small children and you trample them, then you will look upon the Son of He Who Lives and you will not [be] afraid. (Lit. You will become afraid not)

38 Jesus said; Many times did you become desirous to listen to these words that I speak to you and you did not have another one to hear them from his hand. There are some days [that] will come to be, [that] you will seek after me [but] you will not find me. (Lit. Will fall not upon me.)

39 Jesus said; The Pharisees and the scribes, they took the keys of Knowledge [and] they hid them; They didn't go in and those who desire to go in they did not let them. You (However) Come to be, [and] become cunning like serpents, and [the] innocent like doves.

40 Jesus said; [If] a vine of grapes [were] planted outside the Father, and not fortified, it will be pulled up by the root and it will be destroyed.

41 Jesus said; He who has [he] in his hand it will be given to him, and he who has not [he] the [other] little bit

which he has will be taken from his hand.

42 Jesus said; Come into being as you pass away

{Alt. Jesus said; become as one Passing away}

{Alt. Jesus said; Become [as] Passers by}

43 The Disciples said to him [Jesus]; Who are you that you should speak these things to us? You do not realize who I am from the [words] which I speak to you. (Rather) you have come to be like those Judeans, for they love their tree and hate its fruit, [for] they love their fruit and hate its tree.

44 Jesus Said; He who blasphemes against the Father, it will be forgiven and he who blasphemes against the Son, it will be forgiven; But he who blasphemes against the Holy Spirit, it will not be forgiven him neither in the earth nor in heaven.

45 Jesus said; They do not harvest grapes out of thorns (and) they do not gather figs out of thistles (for) they do not give fruit--- A good man brings good things out of his treasure. An evil man brings evil things out of his treasure which is wicked, which is in his mind. And he speaks of evil things (for) out of the excess of the mind he brings out evil things.

46 Jesus said; From Adam up to John the Baptist, among the begotten of women, no one is greater than (Lit. raised up above) John the Baptist so that his eyes [should not be] lowered. However, I have said this; He who will come to be among you, he being a little one. He will know the Kingdom and he will be greater than (Lit. raised up above) John.

47 Jesus said; No man can climb onto two horses or (lit. and) stretch two bows and no man can serve two Lords or he will honor the one and despise the other one.

No man drinks old wine and immediately desires to drink new wine. And they don't pour new wine into old wine skins so that [or] they will split open.

And they don't pour old wine into new wineskins so that it destroys it.

They do not sew old patches on new garments, because there a split [will] come to be.

48 Jesus said; "Should two make peace with each other in [this] one house, they will speak to the mountain and say 'Move away' and it will move.

49 Jesus said; "Blessed are the solitary and the chosen, for you will find the Kingdom. For you came out of it, [and] again to it you will be going."

50 Jesus said; If they say to you: 'Where have you come from?', say unto them 'We have come out of the light. That place where the light came to be, and appeared by his own hand; He stood to his feet and manifested in their image.

If they should speak to you and say 'Are you him?', say unto them "We are his sons, and we are the chosen of the Father who lives. [Lit. The Living Father]

If they should ask you saying: 'What is the sign of your Father which is in you?' then say to them; 'It is a movement and a repose.'

51 The Disciples asked him; "When will the repose of those who are dead [resurrection] come to be? and when will the new world come?"

He [Jesus] answered them and said :

That which you look outwardly for has already come. But you have not known it.

52 The Disciples said to him; "Twenty four prophets spoke in Israel and all of them spoke in you. (Lit. they spoke, all of them, down in you.)

And he said to them; You have left He who lives in your presence, and have spoken about those who are dead.

53 The Disciples asked him; "Is circumcision beneficial to us or not?" and He said to them; If it were beneficial, their fathers would beget them out of their mother already circumcised. Rather, True circumcision [is] in the Spirit, and it is found profitable [in] all things.

54 Jesus said; Blessed are the poor for yours is the Kingdom of the Heavens.

55 Jesus said; Whoever hates not his

father and his mother, he can be no disciple to me. And if he does not hate his brothers and his sisters and does not take his cross in my way, he will come to be undeserving to me.

56 Jesus said; Whoever has known the world has found a corpse, and whoever has found [the world to be] a corpse, the world is not worthy of him.

57 Jesus said; The Kingdom of the Father is like a man who had good seed and his enemy came in the night and sowed a weed upon the seed which was good. The Man did not permit them to pull up the weed. And he said to them; Lest you go to pull up the weed and pull up the grain with it. For on the day of the harvest, the weeds will appear forth and they will pull them up and burn them.

58 Jesus said; Blessed is the man who has been troubled; [For] he has found the Life.

59 Jesus said; Look after [He Who Lives] while you are living, lest you should die and you seek to see him and you cannot find the power.

60 <They saw> a Samaritan taking a lamb and going into Judea and he[Jesus] said to his disciples; That one is like the lamb. And his disciples said to him "[He is going] so that he might kill it and eat it." And he[Jesus] said to them; "While living, he will not eat him; Rather, if he should kill him and he becomes a corpse." And his Disciples said; "He can do it no other way." And he said to them; "You, also, seek after a place to yourselves of rest so that you will not become corpses and they eat you."

61 Jesus said; "There are two who will rest on a bed, the one will die, the other one will live. And Salome said; " Who are you? Man born of another (man). [Because] You sleep [on my bed] (Lit. have climbed onto my bed) , and you eat with me." (Lit. ate from off of my table.)

And Jesus said to her; "I am He who exists out of He who is just (Lit. equal), they gave [those things] to me out of that [which is] of my Father.

<Salome says?> "I am your disciple"

<Jesus says?> "Because of this (saying) I say (unto you); when he should come to be destroyed, he will be full of light; when, however, he should come to be divided, he will be full of darkness.

62 Jesus said; I speak my mysteries to those who are worthy of my mysteries. That which your right will do, let not your left realize what it is [doing].

63 Jesus said; There was a man of wealth who had many riches. And he said; "I will make use of my riches, so that I might sow and reap and plant, and fill my storehouse (Lit. treasure house) with fruit so that I will not need anything." These were his thoughts about [these things] in his mind. And that night he died. He who has an ear let him hear.

64 Jesus said; A man was having some visitors and when he had prepared dinner he sent his servant so he might call the visitors. He went to the first and said to him, "My lord calls you." and the man answered the servant and said "I have some money for some traders who are coming this evening, I must go and place orders with them. I beg you excuse me from the dinner. The Servant went up to another and said to him; "Did my lord call you?" And the man answered and said; "I have bought a house and they require of me a days time and I will not have time to rest." The Servant went to another and said to him; "My lord calls you." and the man answered him and said; "My friend is getting married and I am making the [wedding] dinner and cannot come. I beg you excuse me from [your lord's] dinner."

The Servant went to another man and said to him; "My lord calls you." And the man answered and said; "I have bought a farm and I am going to pay the taxes and I cannot come. I beg you excuse me."

So the servant returned and spoke to his lord and said; "Those who you have called to the dinner have asked that they be excused." And the lord said to his servant; "Go outside to the roads; those who you will find bring them so that they may dine.

[Jesus said;] The buyers and the traders, they may not go in to the places of my Father.

65 <Jesus> said; A just man had a vineyard; he [leased] it to some tenant [farmers] so they might work it and he might collect the fruits from them. He sent his servant so that the tenants might give him the fruit of the vineyard. They grabbed his servant and they beat him. Had it been another little while, they would have killed him. The Servant went and he spoke to his lord. And the lord [of the vineyard] said; Perhaps he didn't know them. He sent another servant and the tenant farmers beat him also. Then the lord [of the vineyard] send his son. He said; Perhaps they will be ashamed before my son. And the tenants, who were there, knew that he was to inherit the vineyard, so they seized him and killed him. He who has an ear let him hear.

66 Jesus said; Show me the stone, the one, the builders have rejected; He is the cornerstone.

67 Jesus said; If he who knows everything, needs himself, he [also] needs the place of all of it.

68 Jesus said; Blessed are you when they hate you and persecute you. They (those who persecute you) will find no place in the place where they persecuted you [down?] in him.

69 Jesus said; Blessed are they who have been persecuted [down?] in their minds. [Those who are] They have known the Father in truth. Blessed are those who are hungry, so they may satisfy the belly of he (they?) who desires.

70 Jesus said; When you should beget [Lit. "that one"] in yourselves, [the one] which you have begotten, he will save you; If you have not that one in you, the one which you have not in you, will kill you.

71 Jesus said; I will destroy [this house] and no one can build it [Lit. "him"] [again].

72 A man said, <to Jesus>; "Speak to my brothers so they may divide the belongings of my father with me." And he <Jesus> answered and said; "O

man, who is he [that has] made me a divider? [Jesus] turned to his disciples and said; "truly, Do I exist as a divider?"

73 Jesus said; The harvest indeed is plentiful, the laborers, however, are few; [but] pray to the Lord so he might send laborers out to the harvest.

74 Jesus said; "Lord, There are many (around) the fountain, but nothing in the well."

75 Jesus said; There are many standing at the door; Rather, the single ones are those who will go in to the place of marriage.

76 Jesus said; The Kingdom of the Father is comparable to a merchant who had [much] [merchandise to sell for someone else](Lit. Consignment) and [in the merchandise] he found a pearl. The merchant was wise, [so] he gave the merchandise back and bought the pearl for himself. Just that pearl alone. You also; seek after the treasure that does not perish; that endures where no moth approaches it to eat nor the worms [can] destroy.

77 Jesus said; I am the Light, the one which is above all of them. I am everything; everything has come out of me, and everything has been opened (Lit. Split/reach up) to me. Split open a timber, I am there; take up the stone and you will find me there.

78 Jesus said; Because of what did you come out to the field? To see a reed moving about by means of the wind? And to see a man having soft garments on him like your kings and your powerful ones? These [are] garments (Lit. in-garments?) which are soft upon them, and they can not know the truth.

79 A woman in the crowd said to him <Jesus> "blessed is she, the womb which bore you and the breasts which nursed you. And he <Jesus> said; Blessed are they who have listened to the Word of the Father, they have watched over him in truth.{Alt. They have kept it in truth} For there are days that will come to be when you will say "Blessed is the womb that didn't conceive, and the breasts which didn't

give milk.

80 Jesus said; Whoever has (truly) known the world has found the body. However, Whoever has found this body, the world is not worthy of him.

81 Jesus said; Whoever has become rich, let him become king, and he who has power let him renounce [it].

82 Jesus said; He who is close to me, he is close to the fire, and he who is far from me, he is far from the Kingdom.

83 Jesus said; The images, they are revealed to man, and the light which is in them is hidden in the image of the light of the Father. It will be revealed, and his image hidden away, by means of his light.

84 Jesus said; The days you look upon your resemblance; you rejoice. When, however, you should look upon your images, which came to be upon your beginning -that neither die nor do they appear forth- How much will you [be able] to bear?

85 Jesus said; Adam has come to be out of a great power and a great richness, and he didn't come to be worthy of you. For had they been deserving he would have tasted not of The Death.

86 Jesus said; the foxes have their dens, and the birds they have their nest(s), The Son of Man, however, has not a place to lay his head and rest himself.

87 Jesus said; Wretched is the body which clings to a body, and wretched is the soul which clings to these two.

88 Jesus said; the angels come to you with the prophets and they will give to you those [things] which you have [for them]. And you, yourselves, give to them those [things] which are of you and say to yourselves; "Which day is [it] which they [will] come and take that which is theirs?"

89 Jesus said; Because of what do you wash the outside of the cup? Do you not understand that whoever created the inside, he is also he who created the outside?

90 Jesus said; Come unto me for just is my yoke and my Lordship, a gentle man is she, and you will find repose (or, rest) for yourselves.

91 They said to him <Jesus>; "Tell us who you are, so we may believe in you." And he said to them; "You read the face of the sky and the earth and you did not know he, who was in your presence, and this time you know now (how) to read it."

92 Jesus said; Seek and you will find. But those things you asked me about in those days; I did not tell them to you in that day. Now, it pleases me to tell them, and you seek not after them.

93 <Jesus said;> Do not give that which is (Lit. He who is) Holy to the dogs, so that they cast them not onto the dung-heap; Do not cast pearls to swine, so that it (might) not be [made] [.......................]

*[[***NOTE**** Line 569 contains one of the few lacuna [.........] in the manuscript and has yet to be satisfactorily resolved. However, one can refer to a parallel saying taken from the Gospel of Matthew Chapter 7 Verse 6;*

"Give not that which is holy unto the dogs, neither cast ye your pearls before swine, <u>lest they trample them under their feet, and turn again and rend you.</u>"

It is interesting to note that translators may, or may not have, rendered the Matthew saying into a more palatable rendition by leaving out any reference to dung. Although it is a fairly common fact that pigs do, in fact, "trample" in their own waste and anything "cast" to them would eventually find itself trampled into it.

In the same instance I have noticed many people quoting this passage usually also forget, or leave off, the ending of this famous passage "Lest they turn again and rend you". Trampling something of yours is one thing but to be "rent" by a feral pig is quite another but I digress.]]

94 Jesus said; He who seeks, he will find, and he who calls [in], it will be opened to him.

95 Jesus said; If you have money, do not give it at interest. Rather, give to him who you will [Lit. not take from his hand.]

(or, give to him who has nothing to give you)

{Alt. give to him who you would not take anything from}

96 Jesus said; The kingdom of the Father, it is like [Lit. comparable to] a woman who took a little bit of leaven and hid it in some dough; she made it into some large (loaves of) bread [Lit. some great (large) breads].

He who has an ear, let him hear.

97 Jesus said; The kingdom of the Father, it is comparable to a woman carrying [Lit. bearing under] a jar full of meal; walking on a road (from) far away. (Then) the jar broke [Lit. the ear of the jar broke] and the meal emptied out behind her on the road. She did not know (that it was broken) (nor did) she realize the problem. When she arrived at her house, she put the jar down and she found it to be empty.

98 Jesus said; The kingdom of the Father, it is comparable to a man wanting to kill a(nother) powerful man. He drew his sword in his own house and stuck it into the wall, so that he might realize that his hand will be strong enough [Lit. Strong inwardly]. then he slew the powerful one.

99 The Disciples said to him <Jesus>: "Your brothers and your mother, they are standing outside. and he said to them; "Those, in these places, who do the will of my Father, these are my brothers and my mother. It is they who will go into the Kingdom of my Father.

100 They showed Jesus a gold piece and said to him; "Those who are from Ceasar, they demand of us the taxes." He said to them; "Give the things of Ceasar to Ceasar; Give to God the things of God; and that which is mine give it to me."

101 <....> Whoever hates not his father and his mother, in my way, he can not become a disciple to me; and whoever loves not his father and his mother, in my way, he can not become a disciple to me. For my mother she

[........................]

[.........................] my mother, however, true, she gave to me the Life.

[[*NOTE*** Lines 607-608 contain one of the few lacunae not yet satisfactorily resolved. Paterson Brown suggests [gave birth to me] similar to a proposal of Styze van der Laan; [Begot me]. however, the issue remains unresolved.]]

102 Jesus said; Woe to them, the Pharisees, for they resemble a dog resting upon the manger of some oxen, for he eats not (and) he permits not the oxen to eat.

103 Jesus said; Blessed is the man, the one, who knows [where] the thieves are coming in, so he may arise and gather his kingdom, and bind himself upon his loins from the beginning, before they come in.

104 They said to Jesus; "Come pray today and fast". And Jesus said; "What is the sin I have commited [Lit. done], or in what have they won over me? Rather, when the bridegroom should come out of the bridal chamber, then let them fast and let them pray.

105 Jesus said; He who will know the Father and the Mother, they will refer to him as the 'son of (the) harlot.

106 Jesus said; When you should make the two (into) one, you will come to be the Sons of Man, and if you should speak and say "mountain, move away" it will move.

107 Jesus said; the Kingdom it is comparable to a Shepherd [Lit. A man sheep-herding], who had (there) a hundred sheep. (then) one of them -the largest- went astray leaving the ninety-nine. He sought after that one until he found him; having been troubled, he said to the sheep; " I love you and want you more than the ninety-nine."

108 Jesus said; Whoever drinks out of my mouth, he will come to be in my way; {Alt. Whoever accepts the Word that I speak will come to be part of me and my way (i.e The Way) } I also, will come to be as he is, and those {things} which [or, who] are hidden will appear

to him.

109 Jesus said; the Kingdom is comparable to a man who had a treasure in his field buried [Lit. hiding], he being (ignorant) (about it); And after his death, he left the field to his son. The Son knew not. He took the field which was there and gave it away, and whoever bought it, he came (and began) plowing and He found the treasure. (With it) he began to give money (at interest) {Alt. Loan money, etc.} to those he loved.

110 Jesus said; whoever has found the world and become rich, let him renounce the world.

111 Jesus said; The Heavens and the Earth will be rolled up in your presence and he who lives out of He Who Lives, he will look not on death. {Alt. He will not see death} because Jesus says; Whoever finds [it] himself, the world is not worthy of him.

112 Jesus said; Woe to the flesh, the one who clings to the soul; (&) Woe to the soul the one who clings to the flesh.

113 His Disciples said unto him <Jesus>; The kingdom is coming on what day? <.....> "It is not coming (that you should) look outward (and see it). They will not say; "Behold that way [Lit. side]" or, "behold there (it is)". Rather, the Kingdom of the Father is pread out upon the earth and men cannot look upon it. {Alt. Cannot see it}

114 Simon who is called Peter said to them; "Let Mary go out from (among) us. For women (are) not worthy of The Life." and Jesus said; "Behold, I myself will lead her, so that I might make her male, so she might come to be a living spirit resembling you males. For any woman making herself male, she will go in to the Kingdom of (the) Heaven(s)."

THE GOSPEL OF THE HOLY TWELVE

Here beginneth the Gospel of the Perfect Life of Jesu-Maria, the Christ, the offspring of David through Joseph and Mary after the flesh, and the Son of God, through Divine Love and Wisdom, after the Spirit.

CHAPTER 1
The Parentage And Conception Of John The Baptist

1 THERE was in the days of Herod, the King of Judea, a certain priest named Zacharias, of the course of Abia; and his wife was of the daughters of Aaron, and her name was Elisabeth.

2 And they were both righteous before God, walking in all the commandments and ordinances of the Lord blameless. And they had no child, because that Elisabeth was barren, and they both were now well stricken in years.

3 And it came to pass, that while he executed the priest's office before God in the order of his course, according to the custom of the priest's office, his lot was to burn incense when he went into the temple IOVA. And the whole multitude of the people were praying without at the time of the offering of incense.

4 And there appeared unto him an angel of the Lord standing over the altar of incense. And when Zacharias saw, he was troubled, and fear fell upon him. But the angel said unto him, Fear not, Zacharias, for thy prayer is heard; and thy wife Elisabeth, shall bear thee a son, and thou shalt call his name John.

5 And thou shalt have joy and gladness; and many shall rejoice at his birth; for he shall be great in the sight of the Lord, and shall neither eat flesh meats,

nor drink strong drink; and he shall be filled with the Holy Spirit, even from his mother's womb.

6 And many of the children of Israel shall he turn to the Lord their God; And he shall go before him in the spirit and power of Elias, to turn the hearts of the fathers to the children, and the disobedient to the wisdom of the just; to make ready a people prepared for the Lord.

7 And Zacharias said unto the angel, Whereby shall I know this? for I am an old man, and my wife is well stricken in years. And the angel answering said unto him, I am Gabriel, that stand in the presence of God; and am sent to speak unto thee, and to announce unto thee these glad tidings.

8 And, behold, thou art dumb, and not able to speak, until the day that these things shall be performed, then shall thy tongue be loosed that thou mayest believe my words which shall be fulfilled in their season.

9 And the people waited for Zacharias, and marvelled that he tarried so long in the temple. And when he came out, he could not speak unto them; and they perceived that he had seen a vision in the temple; for he made signs unto them, and remained speechless.

10 And it came to pass, that, as soon as the days of his ministration were accomplished, he departed to his own house. And after those days, his wife Elisabeth, conceived, and hid herself five months saying, Thus hath the Lord dealt with me in the days wherein he looked on me, to take away my reproach among men.

CHAPTER 1.1 The opening paragraph of this Gospel was evidently before the eyes, or in the mind of St. Paul when he wrote Romans 1-4 (See Luke 1:5) This is only one of several instances where this Gospel, or the words of Jesus recorded in it, are used subsequently, without specially indicating the fact (as shewn further on), being well-known to his hearers at that time.

CHAPTER 2

The Immaculate Conception Of Jesus The Christ

1 AND in the sixth month the angel Gabriel was sent from God, unto a city of Galilee, named Nazareth, to a virgin espoused to a man whose name was Joseph, of the house of David; and the virgin's name was Mary.

2 Now Joseph was a just and rational Mind, and he was skilled in all manner of work in wood and in stone. And Mary was a tender and discerning Soul, and she wrought veils for the temple. And they were both pure before God; and of them both was Jesu-Maria who is called the Christ.

3 And the angel came in unto her and said, Hail, Mary, thou that art highly favoured, for the Mother of God is with thee: blessed art thou among women and blessed be the fruit of thy womb.

4 And when she saw him, she was troubled at his saying, and cast in her mind what manner of salutation this should be. And the angel said unto her, Fear not, Mary, for thou hast found favour with God and, behold, thou shalt conceive in thy womb and bring forth a child, and He shall be great and shalt be called a Son of the Highest.

5 And the Lord God shall give unto him the throne of his father David: and he shall reign over the house of Jacob forever; and of his kingdom there shall be no end.

6 Then said Mary unto the angel, How shall this be, seeing I know not a man? And the angel answered and said unto her The Holy Spirit shall come upon Joseph thy Spouse, and the power of the Highest shall overshadow thee, O Mary, therefore also that holy thing which shall be born of thee shall be called the Christ, the Child of God, and his Name on earth shalt be called Jesu-Maria, for he shall save the people from their sins, whosoever shall repent and obey his Law.

7 Therefore ye shall eat no flesh, nor drink strong drink, for the child shall be consecrated unto God from its mother's womb, and neither flesh nor strong drink shall he take, nor shall razor touch his head.

8 And, behold, thy cousin Elisabeth, she hath also conceived a son in her old age: and this is the sixth month with her, who was called barren. For with God no thing shall be impossible. And Mary said, Behold the handmaid of the Lord; be it unto me according to thy word. And the angel departed from her.

9 And in the same day the angel Gabriel appeared unto Joseph in a dream and said unto him, Hail, Joseph, thou that art highly favoured, for the Fatherhood of God is with thee. Blessed art thou among men and blessed be the fruit of thy loins.

10 And as Joseph thought upon these words he was troubled, and the angel of the Lord said unto him, Fear not, Joseph, thou Son of David, for thou hast found favour with God, and behold thou shalt beget a child, and thou shalt call his name Jesu-Maria for he shall save his people from their sins.

11 Now all this was done that it might be fulfilled which was written in the prophets saying, Behold a Maiden shall conceive and be with child and shall bring forth a son, and shall call his name Emmanuel, which being interpreted is, God Within Us.

12 Then Joseph being raised from sleep did as the angel had bidden him, and went in unto Mary, his espoused bride, and she conceived in her womb the Holy One.

13 AND Mary arose in those days and went into the hill country with haste, into a city of Judea and entered into the house of Zacharias, and saluted Elisabeth.

14 And it came to pass, that, when Elisabeth heard the salutation of Mary, the babe leaped in her womb; and Elisabeth was filled with the power of the Spirit and spake, with a clear voice and said, Blessed art thou among women and blessed is the fruit of thy womb.

15 Whence is this to me, that the mother of my Lord should come to me? For, lo, as soon as the voice of thy salutation sounded in my ears, the babe leaped for joy. And blessed is she that believed: for there shall. be a performance of those things which were told her from the Holy One.

16 And Mary said: My soul doth magnify Thee, the Eternal, and my spirit doth rejoice in God my Saviour. For thou hast regarded the low estate of thy handmaiden; for, behold, from henceforth all generations shall call me blessed.

17 For Thou that art mighty hast done to me great things; and holy is Thy Name. And Thy mercy is on them that fear Thee from generation to generation.

18 Thou hast shewed strength with Thy arm; thou hast scattered the proud in the imagination of their hearts.

19 Thou hast put down the mighty from their seats and exalted the humble and the meek. Thou hast fill the hungry with good things and the rich Thou dost send empty away.

20 Thou dost help thy servant Israel, in remembrance of thy mercy: as Thou spakest to our ancestors to Abraham and to his seed for ever. And Mary abode with her about three months and returned to her own house.

21 And these are the words that Joseph spake,, saying: Blessed be the God of our fathers and our mothers in Israel: for in an acceptable time Thou hast heard me, and in the day of salvation hast Thou helped me.

22 For Thou saids't I will preserve and make thee a covenant of the people to renew the face of the earth: and to cause the desolate places to be redeemed from the hands of the spoiler.

23 That thou mayest say to the captives, Go ye forth and be free; and to them that are in darkness, Show yourselves in the light. And they shall feed in the ways of pleasantness; and they shall no more hunt nor worry the creatures which I have made to rejoice before me.

24 They shall not hunger nor thirst any more neither shall the heat smite them nor the cold destroy them. And I will make on all My mountains a way for travellers; and My high places shall be exalted.

25 Sing ye heavens and rejoice thou earth; O ye deserts break forth with

song: for Thou O God dost comfort Thy people; and console them that have suffered wrong.

CHAPTER 2 10- "Joseph begat (of Mary the Virgin, his wife) Jesus, who is called the Christ."-Curetonian and Lewis's Syriac, MS. ; and several of the oldest Latin MSS., in Matt. I.16, A.V. CHAPTER 2 21-25-The canticle of Joseph here given is very similar to a certain portion of the book of Isaiah; indeed, appears to be taken from it, as John borrowed from the Old Testament prophets. It has been omitted in all other Gospels extant. It is of singular beauty, and appropriate for use at Matins, as Magnificat is for Vesper, the Song of Zacharias finding an equally appropriate place at Nocturns.

CHAPTER 3
The Nativity Of John The Baptist
1 NOW Elisabeth's full time came that she should be delivered; and she brought forth a son. And her neighbours and her cousins heard how the Lord had shewed great mercy upon her; and they rejoiced with her.

2 And it came to pass, that on the eighth day they came to circumcise the child; and they called him Zacharias, after the name of his father. And his mother answered and said, Not so; but he shall be called John. And they said unto her, There is none of thy kindred that is called by thy name.

3 And they made signs to his father, how he would have him called. And he asked for a writing table, and wrote, saying, his name is John. And they all marvelled, for his mouth was opened immediately, and his tongue loosed, and he spake, and praised God.

4 And great awe came on all that dwelt round about them; and all these came on all that dwelt round about them; and all these sayings were made known abroad throughout all the hilly country of Judea. And all they that heard them laid them up in their hearts, saying, What manner of child shall this be! And the hand of Jova was with him.

5 And his father Zacharias was filled with the holy Spirit, and prophesied, saying, Blessed be thou, O God of Israel; for thou hast visited and redeemed thy people. And hast raised up an horn of salvation for us in the house of thy servant David. As thou spakest by the mouth of thy holy prophets, which have been since the world began.

6 That we should be saved from our enemies, and from the hand of all that hate us. To perform the mercy promised to our ancestors, and to remember thy holy covenant.

7 The oath which thou did'st sware to our father Abraham, that thou wouldest grant unto us, that we being delivered out of the hand of our enemies might serve thee without fear, in holiness and righteousness before thee all the days of our life.

8 And this child shalt be called the Prophet of the Highest: for he shalt go before Thy face, O God, to prepare Thy ways; to give knowledge of salvation unto Thy people by the remission of their sins.

9 Through the tender mercy of our God, whereby the dayspring from on high hath visited us; to give light to them that sit in darkness and in the shadow of death, to guide our feet into the way of peace.

10 And the child grew, and waxed strong in spirit, and his mission was hidden till the day of his shewing forth unto Israel.

CHAPTER 4
Nativity of Jesus the Christ
1 NOW the birth of Jesu-Maria the Christ was on this wise. It came to pass in those days, that there went out a decree from Caesar Augustus, that all the world should be taxed. And all the people of Syria went to be taxed, every one into his own city, and it was midwinter.

2 And Joseph with Mary also went up from Galilee, out of the city of Nazareth into Judea, unto the city of David, which is called Bethlehem (because they were of the house and lineage of David), to be taxed with Mary his

espoused wife, who was great with child.

3 And so it was, that, while they were there, the days were accomplished that she should be delivered. And she brought forth her firstborn child in a Cave, and wrapped him in swaddling clothes, and laid him in a manger, which was in the cave; because there was no room for them in the inn. And behold it was filled with many lights, on either side Twelve, bright as the Sun in his glory.

4 And there were in the same cave an ox, and a horse, and an ass, and a sheep, and beneath the manger was a cat with her little ones, and there were doves also, overhead, and each had its mate after its kind, the male with the female.

5 Thus it came to pass that he was born in the midst of the animals which, through the redemption of man from ignorance and selfishness, he came to redeem from their sufferings, by the manifestation or the sons and the daughters of God.

6 And there were in the same country, shepherds abiding in the field, keeping watch over their flock by night. And when they came, lo, the angel of God came upon them, and the glory of the Highest shone round about them; and they were sore afraid.

7 And the angel said unto them, Fear not: for, behold, I bring you good tidings of great joy, which shall be to all people, for unto you is born this day in the city of David a saviour, which is Christ, the Holy One of God. And this shall be a sign unto you; Ye shall find the babe wrapped in swaddling clothes lying in a manger.

8 And suddenly there was with the angel a multitude of the heavenly host praising God and saying, Glory to God in the highest, and on earth peace toward men of goodwill.

9 And it came to pass, as the angels were gone away from them into heaven, the shepherds said to one another, Let us now go even unto Bethlehem, and see this thing which is come to pass, which our God hath made known unto us.

10 And they came with haste, and found Mary and Joseph in the cave, and the Babe lying in a manger. And when they had seen these things, they made known abroad the saying which was told them concerning the child.

11 And all they that heard it, wondered at those things told them by the shepherds; but Mary kept all these things, and pondered them in her heart. And the shepherds returned, glorifying and praising God for all the things that they had heard and seen.

12 AND when eight days were accomplished for the circumcising of the child, his name was called Jesu-Maria, as was spoken by the angel before he was conceived in the womb. And when the days of her purification according to the law of Moses were accomplished, they brought the child to Jerusalem, to present it unto God (as it is written in the law of Moses, every male that openeth the womb shall be called holy to the Lord).

13 And, behold, there was a man in Jerusalem, whose name was Simeon; and the same man was just and devout, waiting for the consolation of Israel; and the Holy Spirit was upon him. And it was revealed unto him that he should not see death, before he had seen the Christ of God.

14 And he came by the Spirit into the temple; and when the parents brought in the child Jesus, to do for him after the custom of the law, he perceived the child as it were a Pillar of light. Then took he him "up in his arms, and blessed God, and said:

15 Now lettest thou thy servant depart in peace, according to thy word. For mine eyes have seen thy salvation, which thou has prepared before the face of all people; to be a light to lighten the Gentiles, and to be the glory of thy people Israel. And his parents marvelled at those things which were spoken of him.

16 And Simeon blessed them, and said unto Mary his mother, Behold, this child is set for the falling and rising again of many in Israel; and for a Sign which shall be spoken against (yea, a

sword shall pierce through thy own soul also), that the thoughts of many hearts may be revealed.

17 And there was one Anna, a prophetess, the daughter of Phanuel of the tribe of Aser, of a great age, who departed not from the temple, but served God with fastings and prayers night and day.

18 And she coming in that instant gave thanks likewise unto God, and spake of him to all them that looked for redemption in Jerusalem. And when they had performed all things according to the law they returned into Galilee, to their own city Nazareth.

CHAPTER 4 1 -The accepted date of the birth of Christ as corrected in the A. V. is A.M. 4000, or A.D. 1 This being so, his second visit to the Temple A.M. 4012, and after that his travels about A.M. 4018-4030; his Baptism A.M. 4031 ; His Transfiguration on the Mount, 4042 ; and his Crucifixion A.M. 4049, leaving eighteen years for his public ministry ; and his numerous teachings, which S. John declares would fill a vast number of books, more than could be contained (comprehended by the world).

CHAPTER 4 4 - The animals here mentioned are sacred to the Deity in various countries and religions, the Cat and the Dove being specially honored and protected in Egypt (the most ancient centre of civilization, religion, philosophy and true science), as the symbols of Isis, the foreshadower of the "Divine Mother" of Christianity. Egypt (with her Trinity of Father, Mother, Child) gave refuge and sanctuary to the Infant Christ, Who came forth from thence to redeem humanity. The cat is not wilfully a "cruel animal," as falsely alleged by the ignorant, no more than the babe which torments it in ignorance of the pain it gives. Far more cruel are human beings, who torture and destroy millions of innocent creatures to gratify a depraved appetite or to minister to their vanity, or their lust for cruel experiment. The cat truly, as alleged by occultists, both ancient and modern,

"the most human of all animals," and it is probable it was for this reason that it appears as the favourite animal of Jesus who was ever the friend of the despised, maligned and neglected although the most loving, gentle and graceful of all animals, rather than the more self assertive dog, especilly as taught by man to hunt and to worry. CHAPTER 4 12-Iesu Maria is the complete name. Jesus, he shall save, Maria, his people. Jesus is only the first part of the Holy Name, He saves His people, not at once, the entire human race, but those of goodwill - homines bonce voluntatis - men and women of peace, and obedient to the divine law; and by these, their brethren through the ages, who will to be saved. The first part of the sacred Name seems to be generally used in the Gospel, as indicating that only the first part of his mission is now. When all men and women are gathered in, then will Christ be manifest as the complete Saviour, Jesu-Maria.

CHAPTER 5

The Manifestation of Jesus to the Magi

1 Now when Jesus was born in Bethlehem of Judea, in the days of Herod the king, behold, there came certain Magi men from the east to Jerusalem, who had purified themselves and tasted not of flesh nor of strong drink, that they might find the Christ whom they sought. And they said, Where is he that is born King of the Jews? for we in the East have seen his Star, and are come to worship him.

2 When Herod the king had heard these things he was troubled, and all Jerusalem with him. And when he had gathered all the chief priests and scribes of the people together, he demanded of them where the Christ should be born.

3 And they said unto him, Bethlehem of Judea; for thus it is written by the prophet, and thou Bethlehem, in the land of Judea, art not the least among the princes of Judah; for out of thee shall come forth a Governor, that shall rule my people Israel.

4 Then Herod, when he had privily

called the Magi, enquired of them diligently what time the Star appeared. And he sent them to Bethlehem, and said, Go and search diligently for the young child; and when ye have found him, bring me word again, that I may come and worship him also.

5 When they had heard the king, they departed; and, lo, the Star which the Magi of the East saw, and the angel of the Star went before them, till it came and stood over the place where the young child was, and the Star had the appearance of six rays.

6 And as they went on their way with their camels and asses laden with gifts, and were intent on the heavens seeking the child by the Star, they forgot for a little, their weary beasts who had borne thee burden and heat of the day, and were thirsty and fainting, and the Star was hidden from their sight.

7 In vain they stood and gazed, and looked one upon the other in their trouble. Then they bethought them of their camels and asses, and hastened to undo their burdens that they might have rest.

8 Now there was near Bethlehem a well by the way, And as they stooped down to draw water for their beasts, lo, the Star which they had lost appeared to them, being reflected in the stillness of the water.

9 And when they saw it they rejoiced with exceeding great joy.

10 And they praised God who had shewn his mercy unto them even as they shewed mercy unto their thirsty beasts.

11 And when they were come into the house, they saw the young child with Mary his mother, and fell down, and worshipped him: and when they had opened their treasures, they presented unto him gifts; gold, and frankincense, and myrrh.

12 And being warned of God in a dream that they should not return to Herod, they departed into their own country another way. And they kindled a fire according to their custom and worshipped God in the Flame.

13 And when they were departed,

behold the angel of God appeared to Joseph in a dream, saying, Arise, and take the young child and his mother, and flee into Egypt, and there remain until I bring thee word, for Herod will seek to destroy him.

14 AND when he arose, he took the young child and his mother by night, and departed into Egypt, and was there for about seven years until the death of Herod, that it might be fulfilled which was spoken of God by the prophet, saying, Out of Egypt have I called my son.

15 Elizabeth too when she heard it, took her infant son and went up into a mountain and hid him. And Herod sent his officers to Zacharias in the temple and said to him, Where is thy child? And he answered I am a minister of God and am continually in the temple. I know not where he is.

16 And he sent again, saying, Tell me truly where is thy son, Dost thou not know thy life is in my hand? And Zacharias answered, The Lord is witness if thou shed my blood, my spirit will God receive, for thou sheddest the blood of the innocent.

17 And they slew Zacharias in the Temple between the holy place and the altar; and the people knew it, for a voice was heard, Zacharias is slain, and his blood shall not be washed out until the avenger shall come. And after a time the priests cast lots, and the lot fell upon Simeon, and he filled his place.

18 Then Herod, when he saw that he was mocked of the wise men, was exceedingly wroth, and sent forth, and slew all the children that were in Bethlehem, and in all the coasts thereof, from two years old and under, according to the time which he had diligently enquired of the wise men.

19 Then was fulfilled that which was spoken by Jeremy the prophet, saying, In Rama was there a voice heard, lamentation, and weeping, and great mourning, Rachel weeping for her children, and would not be comforted, because they are not.

20 BUT when Herod was dead, behold, an angel of God appeared in a dream to

Joseph in Egypt. Saying, Arise, and take the young child and his mother, and return into the land of Israel: for they are dead which sought the young child's life.

21 And he arose, and took the young child and his mother and came into the land of Israel. And they came and dwelt in a city called Nazareth; and he was called the Nazarene.

CHAPTER 5 9 -Note the beautiful lesson taught by these words. They look in vain for the signs of God who forget the needs of the poorer brethren and their beasts under their care. To look upon the needs of these who cannot speak (in human tongue) is to find the bright light they lose who only look upwards.

CHAPTER 5 16 -Alluding to 2 Chron. xxiv. 20, in the Jerusalem Talmud, and also in the Babylonish, is an account of a priest named Zacharias, who was slain in the court of the priests near the altar, and whose blood never ceased to bubble from the earth, till a great number of priests and rabbins were slaughtered (Talmud Hierosal, fol. 69). In the Protevangelium attributed to James, the first Bishop or Angel of the Church in Jerusalem is introduced the present story of Zacharias, and that Herod who slew the infants in Bethlehem slew also Zacharias the priest in the Temple when he said that he knew not where his infant son John was hidden. It is this story, and not the incident in Chronicles, that most probably is referred to in a latter part of the Gospel by Jesus, being fresh in the memories of that generation, and so more likely to fasten attention.

CHAPTER 6
The Childhood And Youth Of Jesus the Christ.
He Delivereth A Lion From The Hunters

1 NOW, Joseph and Mary, his parents, went up to Jerusalem every year at the Feast of the Passover and they observed the feast after the manner of their brethren, who abstained from bloodshed and the eating of flesh and from strong drink. And when he was twelve years old, he went to Jerusalem with them after the custom of the feast.

2 And when they had fulfilled the days, as they returned, the child Jesus tarried behind in Jerusalem; and his parents knew not of it. But they, supposing him to have been in the company, went a day's Journey and they sought him among their kinsfolk and acquaintance. And when they found him not, turned back to Jerusalem, seeking him.

3 And it came to pass, that after three days they found him in the temple, sitting in the midst of the doctors, both hearing them, and asking them questions. And all that heard him were astonished at his understanding and answers.

4 And when they saw him, they were amazed; and his mother said unto him, Son, why hast thou thus dealt with us? Behold, thy father and I have sought thee sorrowing. And he said unto them, How is it that ye sought me? Wist ye not that I must be in my Parents' House. And they understood not the saying which he spake unto them. But his mother kept all these sayings in her heart.

5 And a certain prophet seeing him, said unto him, Behold the Love and the Wisdom of God are one in thee, therefore in the age to come shalt thou be called Jesu-Maria, for by the Christ shall God save mankind, which now is verily as the bitterness of the sea, but it shall yet be turned into sweetness, but to this generation the Bride shall not be manifest, nor yet to the age to come.

6 And he went down with them, and came to Nazareth, and was subject unto them. And he made wheels, and yokes, and tables also, with great skill. And Jesus increased in stature, and in favour with God and man.

7 AND on a certain day the child Jesus came to a place where a snare was set for birds, and there were some boys there. And Jesus said to them, who hath set this snare for the innocent creatures of God? Behold in a snare shall they in like manner be caught. And he beheld

twelve sparrows as it were dead.

8 And he moved his hands over them, and said to them, Go, fly away, and while ye live remember me. And they arose and fled away making a noise. And the Jews, seeing this, were astonished and told it unto the priests.

9 And other wonders did the child, and flowers were seen to spring up beneath his feet, where there had been naught but barren ground before. And his companions stood in awe of him.

10 AND in the eighteenth year of his age, Jesus was espoused unto Miriam, a virgin of the tribe of Judah with whom he lived seven years, and she died, for God took her, that he might go on to the higher things which he had to do, and to suffer for the sons and daughters of men.

11 And Jesus, after that he had finished his study of the law, went down again into Egypt that he might learn of the wisdom of the Egyptians, even as Moses did. And going into the desert, he meditated and fasted and prayed, and obtained the power of the Holy Name, by which he wrought many miracles.

12 And for seven years he conversed with God face to face, and he learned the language of birds and of beasts, and the healing powers of trees, and of herbs, and of flowers, and the hidden secrets of precious stones, and he learned the motions of the Sun and the Moon and the stars, and the powers of the letters, and mysteries of the Square and the Circle and the Transmutation of things, and of forms, and of numbers, and of signs. From thence he returned to Nazareth to visit his parents, and he taught there and in Jerusalem as an accepted Rabbi, even in the temple, none hindering him.

13 AND after a time he went into Assyria and India and into Persia and into the land of the Chaldeans. And he visited their temples and conversed with their priests, and their wise men for many years, doing many wonderful works, healing the sick as he passed through their countries.

14 And the beasts of the field had respect unto him and the birds of the air were in no fear of him, for he made them not afraid, yea even the wild beasts of the desert perceived the power of God in him, and did him service bearing him from place to place.

15 For the Spirit of Divine Humanity filling him, filled all things around him, and made all things subject unto him, and thus shall yet be fulfilled the words of the prophets, The lion shall lie down with the calf, and the leopard with the kid, and the wolf with the lamb, and the bear with the ass, and the with the dove. And a child shall lead them.

16 And none shall hurt or destroy in my holy mountain, for the earth shall be full of the knowledge of the Holy One even as the waters cover the bed of the sea. And in that day I will make again a covenant with the beasts of the earth and the fowls of the air, and the fishes of the sea and with all created things. And will break the bow and the sword and all the instruments of warfare will I banish from the earth, and will make them to lie down in safety, and to live without fear.

17 And I will betroth thee unto me for ever in righteousness and in peace and in loving kindness, and thou shalt know thy God, and the earth shalt bring forth the corn the wine and the oil, and I will say unto them which were not my people, Thou art my people; and they shall say unto me, Thou art our God.

18 And on a certain day as he was passing by a mountain side nigh unto the desert, there met him a lion and many men were pursuing him with stones and javelins to slay him.

19 But Jesus rebuked them, saying, Why hunt ye these creatures of God, which are more noble than you? By the cruelties of many generations they were made the enemies of man who should have been his friends.

20 If the power of God is shown in them, so also is shown his long suffering and compassion. Cease ye to persecute this creature who desireth not to harm you, see ye not how he fleeth from you, and is terrified by your violence?

21 And the lion came and lay at the feet

of Jesus, and shewed love to him; and the people were astonish, and said, Lo, this man loveth all creatures and hath power to command even these beasts from the desert, and they obey him.

CHAPTER 6 5 -In what way this prediction is to be fulfilled is not as yet made manifest - whether Jesus shall yet be manifest and received by his people as the Two-in-One, the All-gentle as well as the All-powerful, or whether He shall assume the feminine form, or whether He shall be manifest with His counterpart. Many false Christs shall come with signs and lying wonders. CHAPTER 6 10 -Iosephus mentions a section of the Essenes, or Iessenes, who, unlike the great majority of them, lived in "honourable marriage," observing their rules and customs in all other matters, such as abstinence from blood sacrifices, flesh eating, etc. Some consider it most probable, therefore, that at this period Jesus married, according to the usual custom of the Iews, and in his case especially, that he might have full experience of human life, and thus be a perfect Example for all, knowing the joys and sorrows of all,-and that it was just before his further travels preparatory to his entrance into the Ministry that he lost by death the wedded partner of his youth. He was " in all things like as we are, yet without sin"

CHAPTER 7
The Preaching Of John The Baptist
1 NOW in the fifteenth year of the reign of Tiberius Caesar, Pontius Pilate being governor of Judea, and Herod being tetrarch of Galilee (Caiaphas being the high priest, and Annas chief of the Sanhedrim) the word of God came unto John the son of Zacharias, in the wilderness.
2 And he came into all the country about Jordan, preaching the baptism of repentance for the remission of sins. As it is written in the prophets, Behold I send my messenger before thy face, who shall prepare thy way before thee; the voice of one crying in the wilderness, Prepare ye the way of the Holy One, make straight the paths of the Anointed.
3 Every valley shall be filled, and every mountain and hill shall be brought low; and the crooked shall be made straight, and the rough ways shall be made smooth. And all flesh shall see the salvation of God.
4 And the same John had his raiment of camel's hair, and a girdle of the same about his loins, and his meat was the fruit of the locust tree and wild honey. Then went out to him Jerusalem, and all Judea, and all the region round about Jordan, and were baptized of him in the Jordan confessing their sins.
5 And he said to the multitude that came forth to be baptized of him, O generation of disobedient ones, who hath warned you to flee from the wrath to come? Bring forth therefore fruits worthy of repentance and begin not to say within yourselves, We have Abraham to our father.
6 For I say unto you, that God is able of these stones to raise up children unto Abraham. And now also the axe is laid unto the root of the trees: every tree therefore which bringeth not forth good fruit is hewn down, and cast into the fire.
7 And the wealthier people asked him, saying, What shall we do then? He answereth and saith unto them, He that hath two coats, let him impart to him that hath none; and he that hath food let him do likewise.
8 Then came also certain taxgatherers to be baptised and said unto him, Master, what shall we do? And he said unto them, Exact no more than that which is appointed you, and be merciful after your power.
9 And the soldiers likewise demanded of him, saying, And what shall we do? And he said unto them, Do violence to no man, neither accuse any falsely; and be content with sufficient wages.
10 And to all he spake, saying, Keep yourselves from blood and things strangled and from dead bodies of birds and beasts, and from all deeds of cruelty, and from all that is gotten of

wrong; Think ye the blood of beasts and birds will wash away sin! I tell you Nay, Speak the Truth. Be just, Be merciful to one another and to all creatures that live, and walk humbly with your God.

11 And as the people were in expectation, and all men mused in their hearts of John, whether he were the Christ or not, John answered; saying unto them all, I indeed baptize you with water; but One mightier than I cometh, the latchet of whose shoes I am not worthy to unloose.

12 He shall also baptize you with water and with fire. Whose fan is in his hand, and he will thoroughly purge his floor, and will gather the wheat into his garner; but the chaff he will burn with fire unquenchable. And many other things in his exortation preached he unto the people.

CHAPTER 7 4-The fruit of the Carob tree ("S. John's Bread") ; not the insect of that name, as is supposed by the people in general.
CHAPTER 7 10,-As noticed before, the Essenes did not frequent the blood sacrifices of the Temple. John and Jesus acted accordingly.

CHAPTER 8
The Baptism of Iesu Maria The Christ
1 AND it was in the midst of the summer, the tenth month. Then cometh Jesus from Galilee to Jordan unto John, to be baptized of him. But John forbade him, saying, I have need to be baptized of thee, and comest thou to me? And Jesus answering said unto him, Suffer it to be so now, for thus it becometh us to fulfil all righteousness. Then he suffered him.

2 And Jesus, when he was baptized, went up straightway out of the water; and, lo, the heavens were opened unto him, and a bright cloud stood over him, and from behind the cloud Twelve Rays of light, and thence in the form of a Dove, the Spirit of God descending and lighting upon him. And, lo, a voice from heaven saying, This is my beloved Son, in whom I am well pleased; this day have I begotten thee.

3 And John bare witness of him ,saying, This was he of whom I spake, He that cometh after me is preferred before me, for he was before me. And of his fulness have all we received, and grace for grace. For the law was in part given by Moses, but grace and truth cometh in fulness by Jesus Christ.

4 No man hath seen God at any time. The only begotten which cometh from the bosom of the Eternal in the same is God revealed. And this is the record of John, when the Jews sent priests and Levites from Jerusalem to ask him, Who art I thou ? And he deified not, but confessed I am not the Christ.

5 And they asked him, What then? Art thou Elias? And he saith, I am not, Art thou that prophet of whom Moses spake? And he answered, No. Then said they unto him, Who art thou ? that we may give an answer to them that sent us. What sayest thou of thyself? And he said, I am the voice of one crying in the wilderness, Make straight the way of the Holy One, as said the Prophet Esaias.

6 And they which were sent were of the Pharisees, and they asked him and said unto him, Why baptizest thou then, if thou be not that Christ, nor Elias, neither that prophet of whom Moses spake?

7 John answered them, saying, I baptize with water; but there standeth One among you, whom ye know not, He shall baptize with water and with fire. He it is who coming after me is preferred before me, whose shoe's latchet I am not worthy to unloose.

8 These things were done in Bethabara, beyond Jordan, where John was baptizing. And Jesus began at this time to be thirty years of age, being after the flesh indeed the Son of Joseph and Mary; but after the Spirit. the Christ, the Son of God, the Father and Mother Eternal, as was declared by the Spirit of holiness with power.

9 AND Joseph was the son of Jacob and Elisheba, and Mary was the daughter of Eli (called Joachim) and Anna, who were the children of David and

Bathsheba, of Judah and Shela, of Jacob and Leah, of Isaac and Rebecca, of Abraham and Sarah, of Seth and Maat, of Adam and Eve, who were the children of God.

CHAPTER 8 2 -This "bright light" at his baptism is mentioned in the "Gospel of the Hebrews," which is undoubtedly the original Gospel of S. Matthew, and the one used in the primitive Church of Jerusalem, and identical with this. Iustin Martyn quotes this Gospel as the original Gospel of Matthew, and endeavours to explain away the supposed "heresy" in the words, "This day have I begotten thee," which shows that the present Gospel of Matthew could not have been extant in his time, else he would have quoted it with gladness as omitting these words.
v. 7-The earthly ministry of Jesus, beginning at thirty years of age, complete and continuing till his death at the age of forty-nine, must therefore have lasted much longer than is generally supposed, even eighteen years. During the latter part of it, the Iews who knew him attested that he was then " not fifty years old."

CHAPTER 9
The Four Temptations
1 THEN was Jesus led up of the spirit into the wilderness to be tempted of the Devil. And the wild beasts of the desert were around him, and became subject unto him. And when he had fasted forty days and forty nights he was afterwards an hungered.
2 And when the tempter came to him, he said, If thou be the Son of God, command that these stones be made bread, for it is written, I will feed thee with the finest of wheat and with honey, out of the rock will I satisfy thee.
3 But he answered and said, It is written, Man shall not live by bread alone, but by every word that proceeded out of the mouth of God.
4 Then the Devil placeth before him a woman, of exceeding beauty and comeliness and of subtle wit, and a ready understanding withal, and he said

unto him. Take her as thou wilt, for her desire is unto thee, and thou shalt have love and happiness and comfort all thy life, and see thy children's children, yea is it not written, It is not good for man that he should be alone?
5 And Jesu-Maria said, Get thee behind me, for it is written, Be not led away by the beauty of woman, yea, all flesh is as grass and the flower of the field; the grass withereth and the flower fadeth away, but the Word of the Eternal endureth for ever. My work is to teach and to heal the children of men, and he that is born of God keepeth his seed within him.
6 And the Devil taketh him up into the holy city, and setteth him on a pinnacle of the Temple. And saith unto him, If thou be the Son of God, cast thyself down; for it is written, He shall give his angels charge concerning thee; and in their hands they shall bear thee up lest at any time thou dash thy foot against a stone.
7 And Jesus said unto him, It is written again, Thou shalt not tempt the Lord thy God.
8 Then the Devil took him up into an exceeding high mountain in the midst of a great plain and, round about, twelve cities and their peoples, and shown from thence he shown unto him all the kingdoms of the world in a moment of time. And the Devil said unto him, All this power will I give thee, and the glory of them: for that is delivered unto me; and to whomsoever I will, I give it: for it is written, thou shalt have dominion from sea to sea, so thou shalt judge thy people with righteousness and thy poor with mercy, and. make a full end of oppression. If thou therefore wilt worship me, all shall be thine.
9 And Jesu-Maria answered and said unto him, get thee behind me, Satan; for it is written, Thou shalt worship thy God, and Him only shalt thou serve. Without the power of God, the end of evil cannot come.
10 Then the Devil having ended all the temptations leaveth him and departed for a season. And behold, angels of God

came and ministered unto him.

CHAPTER 9 1 -The Essenes or Nazarenes, somewhat like the Indian Yogi, sought to attain divine union by solitary meditation in unfrequented places. In the monastery of our Lord on the summit of Quarantania, a cell is shown with rude frescoes of the event. This mountain is about 18,000 feet high, in a barren and desolate region east of Jerusalem, north of the road to Jericho, overlooking the valley of the Iordan.

v. 2-9 -Observe, the temptations are addressed to the fourfold nature of man, as recognised by the ancient Egyptians. 1st.-To the outer body, with its physical needs. 2nd. -To the inner body, the seat of the senses and desires. 3rd.-To the soul, the seat of the intellect.

CHAPTER 9 3 -In all the ancient initiations woman was one of the temptations placed in the way of the aspirant. That this was not omitted in the trial of the "Perfect Man" we may be certain, and we are expressly told in the Epistle to the Hebrews that "he was in all points tempted even as we are." Why then the writers of the Canonical Gospels omitted this trial, or whether it was dropped out of the original by accident we cannot say, but here we have it restored in its place. It is evidently inculcated by Jesus in this second temptation (what has always been known to the wise) that adepts should store up their physical strength for work on a higher plane, and this Jesus did for the work of the ministry as an example for all who would follow him and heal the bodies and souls of others.

Here we have one of the many passages which show that the words attributed to the writers of the Epistles are quotations from this Gospel, and that such portions at least were extant in their time.-e.g., I. John iii. 9 (A. V.).

CHAPTER 10
Joseph And Mary Make A Feast Unto Jesus.

Andrew And Peter Find Jesus.

1 AND when he had returned from the wilderness, the same day, his parents made him a feast, and they gave unto him the gifts which the Magi had presented to him in his infancy. And Mary said, These things have we kept for thee even to this day, and she gave unto him the gold and the frankincense and the myrrh. And he took of the frankincense, but of the gold he gave unto his parents for the poor, and of the myrrh he gave unto Mary who is called Magdalene.

2 Now this Mary was of the city of Magdala in Galilee. And she was a great sinner, and had seduced many by her beauty and comeliness. And the same came unto Jesus by night and confessed her sins, and he put forth his hand and healed her, and cast out of her seven demons, and he said unto her, Go in peace, thy sins are forgiven thee. And she arose and left all and followed him, and ministered unto him of her substance, during the days of his ministry in Israel.

3 THE next day John saw Jesus coming unto him, and said, Behold the Lamb of God, which by righteousness taketh away the sin of the world. This is he of whom I said, He was before me; and I knew him not; but that he should be made manifest to Israel; therefore am I come baptizing with water.

4 And John bare record, saying, I saw the Spirit descending from heaven like a Dove, and it abode upon him. And I knew him not, but he that sent me to baptize with water, the same said unto me, Upon whom thou shalt see the Spirit descending, and remaining on him, the same is he which baptized with water and with fire, even the Spirit. And I saw, and bare record that this was the Son of God.

5 THE day after, John stood by the Jordan and two of his disciples. And looking upon Jesus as he walked, he saith, Behold the Christ, the Lamb of God! And the two disciples heard him speak, and they followed Jesus.

6 Then Jesus turned and saw them following and saith unto them, What

seek ye? They said unto him, Rabbi (which is, being interpreted, Master), where dwellest thou? He saith unto them, Come and see. They came and saw where he dwelt, and abode with him that day: for it was about the tenth hour.

7 One of the two which heard John speak and followed him was Andrew, Simon Peter's brother. He first findeth his own brother Simon and said unto him, We have found the Messias, which is, being interpreted the Christ. And he brought him to Jesus And when Jesus beheld him, he said, Thou art Simon Bar Jona: thou shalt be called Kephas (which is, by interpretation, a rock).

8 THE day following, Jesus goeth forth into Galilee, and findeth Philip, and saith unto him, Follow me. Now Philip was of Bethsaida, the city of Andrew and Peter. Philip findeth Nathanael, who is called Bar Tholmai, and saith unto him, We have found him, Of whom Moses in the law and the Prophets did write, Jesus of Nazareth, the son of Joseph and Mary, And Nathanael said unto him, Can there any good thing come out of Nazareth ? Philip said unto him, Come and see.

9 Jesus saw Nathanael coming to him and saith of him, Behold an Israelite indeed, in whom is no guile! Nathanael saith unto him, Whence knowest thou me? Jesus answered and said unto him, Before that Philip called thee, when thou wast under the Fig tree, I saw thee. Nathanael answered and saith unto him, Rabbi, thou art the Son of God. thou art the King of Israel. Yea, under the Fig tree did I find thee.

10 Jesus answered and said unto him, Nathanael Bar Tholmai, because I said unto thee, I saw thee under the Fig tree, believest thou ? thou shalt see greater things than these. And he saith unto him, Verily, verily, I say unto you, hereafter ye shall see heaven open, and the angels of God ascending and descending upon the Son of man.

CHAPTER 11
The Anointing By Mary Magdalene
1 AND one of the Pharisees desired him that he would eat with him. And he went into the Pharisee's house and sat down to eat.

2 And behold a certain woman of Magdala, who was reputed to be a sinner, was in the city, and when she knew that Jesus sat at meat in the Pharisee's house, she brought an Alabaster box of ointment, and stood at his feet behind him, weeping, and washed His feet with tears, and did wipe them with the hairs of her head and kissed his feet, and anointed them with ointment.

3 Now when the Pharisee which had bidden him saw it, he thought within himself, saying, This man, if he were a prophet, would have known who and what manner of woman this is that toucheth him: for she is a sinner.

4 And Jesus answering said unto him, Simon, I have somewhat to say unto thee. And he saith, Master, say on.

5 There was a certain creditor which had two debtors: the one owed five hundred pence and the other fifty. And when they had nothing to pay, he frankly forgave them both. Tell me, therefore, which of them will love him most.

6 Simon answered and said, I suppose that he to whom he forgave most. And he said unto him, Thou hast rightly judged.

7 And he said unto Simon, Seest thou this woman? I entered into thine house, thou gavest me no water for my feet; but she hath washed my feet with tears and wiped them with the hairs of her head. Thou gavest me no kiss: but this woman since the time I came in hath not ceased to kiss my feet. My head with oil thou didst not anoint: but this woman hath anointed my feet with ointment.

8 Wherefore I say unto thee, man but also beast and birds of the air, yea, even the fishes of the sea; but to whom little is forgiven, the same loveth little. Her sins, which are many, are forgiven, for she loved much, not only man but also beast and birds of the air, yea, even the fishes of the sea; but to whom little is forgiven, the same loveth little.

9 And he said unto her, Thy sins are forgiven, and they who sat at the table began to say within themselves, who is this that forgiveth sins also?

10 Though he had said not, I forgive thee, but Thy sins are forgiven thee, for he discerned true faith and penitence in her heart. And Jesus needed not that any should testify of any man, for he himself knew what was in man.

CHAPTER 11 1-2-There are two anointings by Mary Magdalene recorded. The first was to his prophetical ministry, the last preparatory to his self-oblation unto death on the cross in the upper room, and his subsequent murder by the Roman authorities and the Iewish priests.

CHAPTER 12
The Marriage In Cana
The Healing of the Nobleman's Son
1 AND the next day there was a marriage in Cana of Galilee; and the mother of Jesus was there: And both Jesus and Mary Magdalene were there, and his disciples came to the marriage.

2 And when they wanted wine the mother of Jesus saith unto him, They have no wine. Jesus saith unto her, Woman, what is that to thee and to me ? mine hour is not yet come. His mother saith unto the servants, Whatsoever he saith unto you, do it.

3 And there were set there six waterpots of stone, after the manner of the purifying of the Jews, containing two or three firkins apiece. And Jesus saith unto them, Fill the waterpots with water. And they filled them up to the brim. And he said unto them, Draw out now, and bear unto the governor of the feast. And they bare it.

4 When the ruler of the feast had tasted the water that was made wine to them, and knew not whence it was; the governor of the feast called the bridegroom, and saith unto him. Every man at the beginning doth set forth good wine and when men have well drunk, then that which is worse; but thou hast kept the good wine until now.

5 This beginning of miracles did Jesus in Cana of Galilee, and manifested forth his glory; and many disciples believed on him.

6 After this he went down to Capernaum, he, and his mother, with Mary Magdalene, and his brethren, and his disciples: and they continued there for many.

7 And there arose a question between some of John's disciples and the Jews about purifying. And they came unto John, and said unto him, Rabbi, he that was with thee beyond Jordan, to whom thou bearest wittness, behold, the same baptizeth, and all do come to him.

8 John answered and said, A man can receive nothing, except it be given him from heaven. Ye yourselves bear me witness, that I said, I am not the Christ, but that I am sent before him.

9 He that hath the bride is the bridegroom; but the friend of the bridegroom, which standeth and heareth him, rejoiceth greatly because of the bridegroom's voice; this my joy therefore is fulfilled. He must increase; but I must decrease. He that is of the earth is earthly, and speaketh of the earth: he that cometh from heaven is above all.

10 AND certain of the Pharisees came and questioned Jesus, and said unto him, how sayest thou that God will condemn the world ? And Jesus answered, saying, God so loveth the world, that the only begotten Son is given, and cometh into the world, that whosoever believeth in him may not perish, but have everlasting life. God sendeth not the Son into the world to condemn the world; but that the world through him may be saved.

11 They who believe on him are not condemned: but they that believe not are condemned already, because they have not believed in the name of the only begotten of God. And this is the condemnation, that the light is come into the world, and men love darkness rather than light, because their deeds are evil .

12 For all they that do evil hate the light, neither come they to the light, lest

THE GOSPEL OF THE HOLY TWELVE

their deeds may be condemned. But they that do righteousness come to the light, that their deeds may be made manifest, that they are wrought in God. 13 AND there was a certain nobleman, whose son was sick at Capernaum. When he heard that Jesus was come into Galilee, he went unto him, and besought him that he would come down, and heal his son; for he was at the point of death.
14 Then said Jesus unto him, Except ye see signs and wonders, ye will not believe. The nobleman saith unto him, Sir, come down ere my child die.
15 Jesus saith unto him, Go thy way; thy son liveth. And the man believed the word that Jesus had spoken unto him, and he went his way. And as, he was now going down, his servants met him, and told him, saying, Thy son liveth.
16 Then enquired he of them the hour when he began to amend. And they said unto him, Yesterday of the seventh hour the fever left him. So the father knew that it was at the same hour, in the which Jesus said unto him, Thy son liveth. And himself believed, and his whole house.

CHAPTER 12 3-4-Jesus being a Yessene (Essene) could not drink intoxicating wine, and it is to be remarked here, that he did not provide it. He poured water into jars, and they tasted it as wine unfermented, or, if fermented, with four times or least twice its volume of water, which makes what is termed all through the Gospel the "fruit of the vine." It is impossible that Jesus could sanction drunkenness, though his enemies slandered him as a "wine-bibber."
v. 16-Two modes of reckoning time were in use. The Roman, from 12 midnight to 12 midnight. The Jewish from 6 a.m. (mean time is here spoken of) in the even to 6 p.m. of next even. The Jewish hours, adopted from the Temple in the Christian Church in her devotions, were as follows:
6 p.m. 1st watch, Vespers. Ferial.
9 p.m. 2nd watch. Nightfall

("Compline" Lat. use).
12 midnight 3rd watch. Nocturms.
3 a.m. 4th watch. Daybreak. (Lauds).
5-6 p.m. Seventh or last hour of the night.
6 a.m. Matins (or "Prime" Lat. use). First hour.
9 a.m. Terce. Third hour.
12 midday. Sext. Sixth hour.
3 p.m. Nones. Ninth hour.
5-6 p.m. Eleventh or last hour of the day. Vespers. Festal. Really "Compline" in its true sense.
The "seventh hour," in this place is therefore 1 p.m. of our reckoning; whether by Jewish or Roman time-13th hour in some countries.

CHAPTER 13
The First Sermon In The Synagogue Of Nazareth
1 AND Jesus came to Nazareth, where he had been brought up: and, as his custom was, he went into the synagogue on the sabbath day, and stood up for to read. And there was delivered unto him the roll of the prophet Esaias.
2 And when he had opened the roll, he found the place where it was written. The Spirit of the Lord Is upon me, because he hath anointed me to preach the gospel to the poor; he hath sent me to heal the brokenhearted, to preach deliverance to the captives and recovering of sight to the blind, to set at liberty them that are bound. To preach the acceptable year of the Lord.
3 And he closed the roll, and gave it again to the minister, and sat down, And the eyes of all them that were in the synagogue were fastened on him. And he began saying unto them. This day is this scripture fulfilled in your ears. And all bare him witness, and wondered at the gracious words which proceeded out of his mouth. And they said, Is not this Joseph's son?
4 And some brought unto him a blind man to test his power, and said, Rabbi, here is a son of Abraham blind from birth. Heal him as thou hast healed Gentiles in Egypt. And he, looking upon him, perceived his unbelief and

the unbelief of those that brought him, and their desire to ensnare him. And he could do no mighty work in that place because of their unbelief.

5 And they said unto him, Whatsoever we have heard done in Egypt, do also here in thy own country. And he said, Verily I say unto you, No prophet is accepted in his own home or in his own country, neither doth a physician work cures upon them that know him.

6 And I tell you of a truth, many widows were in Israel in the days of Elias, when the heaven was shut up three years and six months, when great famine was throughout all the land. But unto none of them was Elias sent, save unto Sarepta, a city of Sidon, unto a woman that was a widow.

7 And many lepers were in Israel in the time of Eliseus the prophet; and none of them was cleansed, saving Naaman the Syrian.

8 And all they in the synagogue, when they heard these things, were filled with wrath. And rose up, and thrust him out of the city, and led him unto the brow of the hill whereon their city was built, that they might cast him down headlong. But he, passing through the midst of them, went his way and escaped them.

CHAPTER 13 5 -The effects of his education in Egypt and his travels in other countries and knowledge of their religion and mysteries are here clearly seen in the largeness of the heart of Jesus, and his sympathy with all men. He is the true Catholic, who excludes none from his love whose hearts are unto righteousness, while he pities those that are not, knowing the terrible fate that awaits them.

CHAPTER 14
*The Calling Of Andrew And Peter
The Teaching of Cruelty in Animals
The Two Rich Men*
1 NOW Herod the tetrarch, being reproved by John the Baptist for Herodias his brother Philip's wife, and for all the evils which he had done, added yet this above all, that he shut up

John in prison.

2 And Jesus began to preach, and to say, Repent; for the kingdom of heaven is at hand. And as he was walking by the sea of Galilee, he saw Simon called Peter, and Andrew his brother, casting a net in the sea; for they were fishers. And he saith unto them, Follow me, and I will make you fishers of men. And they straightway forsook their nets, and followed him.

3 And going on from thence, he saw other two brethren, James the son of Zebedee, and John his brother, in a ship with Zebedee their father, mending their nets; and he called them. And they immediately left their nets, and the ship, and their father, and followed him.

4 And Jesus went about all Galilee, teaching in, their synagogues, and preaching the gospel of the kingdom, and healing all manner of sickness and all manner of disease among the people. And the fame of his miracles went throughout all Syria, and they brought unto him many sick people that were taken with divers diseases and torments, and those which were lunatick, and those that had the palsy, and he healed them.

5 And there followed him great multitudes of people from Galilee, and from Decapolis, and from Jerusalem, and from Judea, and from beyond Jordan.

6 AND as Jesus was going with some of his disciples he met with a certain man who trained dogs to hunt other creatures. And he said to the man, Why doest thou thus? and the man said, By this I live and what profit is there to any in these creatures? these creatures are weak, but the dogs they are strong. And Jesus said, Thou lackest wisdom and love. Lo, every creature which God hath made hath its end, and purpose, and who can say what good is there in it? or what profit to thyself, or mankind?

7 And, for thy living, behold the fields yielding their increase, and the fruit-bearing trees and the herbs; what needest thou more than these which honest work of thy hands will not give

to thee? Woe to the strong who misuse their strength, Woe to the hunters for they shall be hunted.

8 And the man marvelled, and left off training the dogs to hunt, and taught them to save life rather than destroy, And he learned of the doctrines of Jesus and became his disciple.

9* AND behold there came to him two rich men, and one said, Good Master. But he said, Call me not good, for One alone is the All good, and that is God.

10 And the other said to him, Master, what good thing shall I do and live? Jesus said, Perform the Law and the prophets. He answered, I have performed them. Jesus answered, Go, sell all thou hast and divide with the poor, and follow me. But this saying pleased him not.

11 And the Lord said unto him, How sayest thou that thou hast performed the Law and the prophets? Behold many of thy brethren are clad with filthy rags, dying from hunger and thy house is full of much goods, and there goeth from it nought unto them.

12 And he said unto Simon, It is hard for the rich to enter the kingdom of heaven, for the rich care for themselves, and despise them that have not.

CHAPTER 14 4 -Miracles are not violations of the laws of nature, but rather suspensions of lower by higher laws- wonders wrought by using wisely the subtle forces of nature, (whether by seen or unseen agencies) unknown to the science of the day, and in advance of the knowledge of the people. Many are the spiritual agencies, the knowledge of which we are now recovering, but which have existed and acted all through the ages. Occult phenomena also appear to have been used by religious teachers in all ages in the East, to attract the attention of the listless and thoughtless, and having roused and secured their interest, to teach them spiritual truths or give them higher revelations; just as in the West. in modern times, they Bound a bell, or sing an " invitatory" or a hymn to "call the people."

CHAPTER 15
Healing Of The Leper And The Man With Palsy
The Deaf Man who Denied that Others could Hear

1 AND it came to pass, when he was in a certain city, behold a man full of leprosy, who, seeing Jesus, fell toward the earth, and besought him, saying, Lord if thou wilt, thou canst make me clean. And he put forth his hand, and touched him, saying, Blessed be thou who believest; I will, be thou clean. And immediately the leprosy departed from him.

2 And he charged him saying, Tell no man: but go, and shew thyself to the priest, and offer for thy cleansing, according as Moses commanded, for a testimony unto them. But so much the more went there a fame abroad of him; and great multitudes came together to hear, and to be healed by him of their infirmities. And he withdrew himself into the wilderness, and prayed.

3 AND it came to pass on a certain day, as he was teaching, that there were Pharisees and doctors of the law sitting by, to see them which were come out of every town, of Galilee, and Judea, and Jerusalem, and the power of God was present to heal them.

4 AND, behold, they brought in a bed a man who was taken with a palsy: and they sought means to bring him in, and to lay him before him. And when they could not find by what way they might bring him in because of the multitude, they went upon the housetop, and let him down through the tiling with his couch into the midst before Jesus. And when he saw their faith, he said unto him, Man, thy sins are forgiven thee.

5 And the scribes and the pharisees began to reason, saying, Who is this which speaketh blasphemies? Who can forgive sins, but God alone? But when Jesus perceived their thoughts, he answering said unto them, What reason ye in your hearts? Can even God forgive sins, if man repent not? Who said, I forgive thee thy sins? Said I not rather, Thy sins are forgiven thee?

6 Whether is easier to say. Thy sins be forgiven thee; or to say, Rise up and walk? But that ye may know that the Son of Man hath power upon earth to discern, and declare the forgiveness of sins (he said unto the sick of the palsy), I say unto thee, Arise, and take up thy couch, and go to thine house.

7 And immediately he arose up before them, and took up that whereon he lay, and departed to his own house, glorifying God. And they were all amazed, and they glorified God, and were filled with the Spirit of reverence, saying, We have seen strange things to day.

8 AND as Jesus was going into a certain village there met him a man who was deaf from his birth. And he believed not in the sound of the rushing wind, or the thunder, or the cries of the beasts, or the birds which complained of their hunger or their hurt, nor that others heard them.

9 And Jesus breathed into his ears, and they were opened, and he heard. And he rejoiced with exceeding joy in the sounds he before denied. And he said, Now hear all things.

10 But Jesus said unto him. How sayest thou, I hear all things? Canst thou hear the sighing of the prisoner, or the language of the birds or the beasts when they commune with each other, or the voice of angels and spirits? Think how much thou canst not hear, and be humble in thy lack of knowledge.

CHAPTER 15 4 -The houses in Palestine were constructed with flat roofs, and entrance was easily made into the court below without entering by the door below.

CHAPTER 16
Calling of Matthew
Parable of the New Wine in the Old Bottles

1 AND after these things he went forth, and saw a tax gatherer, named Levi, sitting at the receipt of custom: and he said unto him, Follow me. And he left all, rose up, and followed him.

2 And Levi made him a great feast in his own house: and there was a great company of taxgatherers and of others that sat down with them. But the Scribes and Pharisees murmured against his disciples, saying, Why do ye eat and drink with publicans and sinners?

3 And Jesus answering said unto them, They that are whole need not a physician; but they that are sick. I came not to call the righteous, but sinners to repentance.

4 And they said unto him, Why do the disciples of John fast often, and make prayers, and likewise the disciples of the Pharisees; but thine do eat and drink?

5 And he said unto them, Wherewith shall I liken the men of this generation, and to what are they like? They are like unto children, sitting in the market place and calling one to another and saying, We have piped unto you, and ye have not danced, we have mourned to you and ye have not lamented.

6 For John the Baptist came neither eating nor drinking, and ye say, He hath a devil, The Son of Man cometh eating and drinking the fruits of the earth, and the milk of the flock, and the fruit of the vine, and ye say, Behold a glutton and wine bibber, a friend of publicans and sinners.

7 Can ye make the children of the bridechamber fast, while the bridegroom is with them? But the days will come, when the bridegroom shall be taken away from them, and then shall they fast in those days.

8 AND he spake also this parable unto them, saying, No man putteth a piece of new cloth on an old garment; for then the new agreeth not with the old, and the garment is made worse.

9 And no one putteth new wine into old bottles; else the new wine will burst the bottles, and be spilled, and the bottles shall perish. But new wine must be put into new bottles, and both are preserved.

10 None also having drunk old wine, straightway desire new: for they say, The old is better. But the time cometh when the new shall wax old, and then

the new shall be desired by them. For as one changeth old garments for new ones, so do they also change the body of death for the body of life, and that which is past for that which is coming.

CHAPTER 16 1 -"Levi" is by tradition identified with Matthew, the writer of the second of the four Gospels (as received by the Church), Mark being the first of the four Evangelists, though placed second in the A. V.
v. 9 -It was the custom in Palestine to use the skins of animals to hold wine as we do glass bottles, and such leathern bottles when filled with new wine were liable to burst by reason of the fermentation of the wine within them.

CHAPTER 17
Jesus Sendeth Forth The Twelve and their Fellows
1 AND Jesus went up into a mountain to pray. And when he had called unto him his twelve disciples, he gave them power against unclean spirits to cast them out and to heal all manner of sickness and all manner of disease. Now the names of the twelve apostles are these who stood for the twelve tribes of Israel:
2 Peter, called Cephas, for the tribe of Reuben James, for the tribe of Naphtali; Thomas, called Dydimus, for the tribe of Zabulon; Matthew, called Levi for the tribe of Gad; John, for the tribe of Ephraim Simon, for the tribe of Issachar.
3 Andrew, for the tribe of Joseph; Nathanael, for the tribe of Simeon; Thaddeus, for the tribe of Zabulon; Jacob, for the tribe of Benjamin; Jude, for the tribe of Dan; Philip, for the tribe of Asher. And Judas Iscariot, a Levite, who betrayed him, was also among them (but he was not of them). And Matthia and Barsabbas were also present with them.
4 Then he called in like manner twelve others to be Prophets, men of light to be with the Apostle and shew unto them the hidden things of God. And their names were Hermes, Aristobulus, Selenius, Nereus, Apollos, and Barsabbas; Andronicus, Lucius, Apelles, Zachaeus, Urbanus, and Clementos. And then he called twelve who should be Evangelists, and twelve who should be Pastors. A fourfold twelve did he call that he might send them forth to the twelve tribes of Israel, unto each, four.
5 And they stood around the Master, clad in white linen raiment, called to be a holy priesthood unto God for the service of the twelve tribes whereunto they should be sent.
6 These fourfold Twelve Jesus sent forth and charged them, saying, I will that ye be my Twelve Apostle with your companions, for a testimony into Israel. Go ye into the cities of Israel and to the lost sheep of the House of Israel. And as ye go, preach, saying, The kingdom of heaven is at hand. As I have baptized you in wader, so baptize ye them who believe.
7 Anoint and heal the sick, cleanse the lepers, raise the dead, cast out devils, freely ye have received, freely give. Provide neither gold, nor silver, nor brass in your purses. Nor scrip for your journey, neither two coats, neither shoes, nor yet staves; for the workman is worthy of his food; and eat that which is set before you, but of that which is gotten by taking of life, touch not, for it is not lawful to you.
8 And into whatsoever city or town ye shall enter, enquire who in it is worthy; and there abide till ye go thence. And when ye come into an house, salute it. And if the house be worthy, let your peace come upon it: but if it be not worthy, let your peace return to you.
9 Be ye wise as serpents and harmless as doves. Be ye innocent and undefiled. The Son of Man is: not come to destroy but to save, neither to take life, but to give life, to body and soul.
10 And fear not them which kill the body but are not able to kill the soul; but rather fear him who is able to destroy both soul and body in Gehenna.

11 Are not two sparrows sold for a farthing? and one of them shall not fall on the ground without permission of the

All Holy. Yea, the very hairs of your head are all numbered. Fear yet not therefore, if God careth for the sparrow, shall he not care for you!

12 It is enough for disciples that they be as their master, and the servants as their lord. If they have called the master of the house Beelzebub, how much more shall they call them of his household? Fear them not therefore, for there is nothing covered, that shall not be revealed; or hid, that shall not be known.

13 What I tell you in darkness, that speak ye in light when the time cometh: and what ye hear in the ear, that preach ye upon the housetops. Whosoever therefore shall confess the truth before men, them will I confess also before my Parent Who is in heaven. But whosoever shall deny the truth before men, them will I also deny before my Parent Who is in heaven.

14 Verily I am come to send peace upon earth, but when I speak, behold a sword followeth. I am come to unite, but, behold, a man shall be at variance with his father, and the daughter with her mother, and the daughter-in-law with her mother-in-law. And a man's foes shall be they of his own household. For the unjust cannot mate with them that are just.

15 They who take not their cross and follow after me are not worthy of me. He that findeth his life shall lose it; and he that loseth his life for my sake, shall find it.

CHAPTER 17 3 -Judas Iscariot is here called a Levite. It may be symbolical of the fact, that the older priesthood was the bitter enemy of Jesus, the Prophets and the Priest of the newer Christian Dispensation.

v. 2-5 -Here we have a flood of light thrown on an obscure passage in Ephesians iv. 11, referring to an event of which there is no record whatever in the A. V. or in any other version of the Gospels which has come down to us. Plain enough is the passage in Ephesians as it stands, but obscure in its reference; and the only body of

Christians who have in later times restored this ancient fourfold ministry is the "Catholic Apostolic Church," but with this difference, that what Jesus intended to be a permanent order, they have made only a lifetime institution, dying with the men that fill the office, at present the one left being removed by death. Under Jesus, the High Priest, or chief Shepherd and Bishop of the Universal Church, while the two and seventy afterward sent forth were the deacons in the higher ministry, altogether making the full number a hundred and twenty.

v. 6-9 -These words leave no doubt that the organization which Jesus first established was based on the older organization of the Yessenes (similar to that of the Buddhists), and from which have come the monasteries, friaries, and sisterhoods of the Christian Church, which have always been popular with the poor, and befriended them in times of trouble, and set them an example of Godly living; the corruptions and abuses, which set in now and then, being no argument against the use. They were a continual protest against the ways of the world, its vices and luxury and evil pursuits. "Leave all and follow me," was the continual call of the master, to those who could receive it.

CHAPTER 18
The Sendeth Forth Of The Two and Seventy

1 AFTER these things the Lord appointed two and seventy also, and sent them two and two before his face into every city and place of the tribes whither he himself would come.

2 Therefore said he unto them, The harvest truly is great, but the labourers are few, pray ye therefore the Lord of the harvest that he would send forth labourers into the harvest.

3 Go your ways, behold I send you forth as lambs among wolves. Carry neither purse, nor scrip, nor shoes, and salute no man by the way.

4 And into whatsoever house ye enter, first say, Peace be to this house. And if

the spirit of peace be there your peace shall rest upon it, if not it shall turn to you again.

5 And into whatsoever city ye enter, and they receive you, eat such things as are set before you without taking of life.

And heal the sick that are therein, and say unto them, The kingdom of God is come nigh unto you.

6 And in the same house remain, eating and drinking such things as they give without shedding of blood, for the labourer is worthy of his hire. Go not from house to house.

7 But into whatsoever city ye enter and they receive you not, go your ways out into the streets of the same and say, Even the very dust of your city, which cleaveth on us, we do wipe off against you, notwithstanding be ye sure of this, that the kingdom of God is come nigh unto you.

8 Woe unto thee, Chorazin! woe unto thee, Bethsaida! for if the mighty works had been done in Tyre and Sidon, which have been done in you, they had a great while ago repented, sitting in sackcloth and ashes. But it shall be more tolerable for them in the judgement than for you.

9 And thou, Capernaum, which art exalted to heaven shalt be thrust down to hades. They that hear you, hear also me; and they that despise you, despise also me; and they that despise me, despise Him that sent me. But let all be persuaded in their own minds.

10 AND again Jesus said unto them: Be merciful, so shall ye obtain mercy. Forgive others, so shall ye be forgiven. With what measure ye mete, with the same shall it be meted unto you again.

11 As ye do unto others, so shall it be done you. As ye give, so shall it be given unto you. As ye judge others, so shall ye be judged. As ye serve others, so. shall ye be served.

12 For God is just, and rewardeth every one according to their works. That which they sow they shall also reap.

CHAPTER 18 1 -This number (seventy-two), symbolizing amongst the Jews the Nations of the Earth, and late-denoting the Diaconate of the Church Universal

(in priestly orders), was afterwards selected by the Christian Church as the complete number of its cardinals, as it had been before the number of members of the Jewish Sanhedrim.

CHAPTER 19
Jesus Teacheth how to Pray
Error even in Prophets

1 As Jesus was praying in a certain place on a mountain, some of his disciples came unto him, and one of then said, Lord teach us how to pray. And Jesus said unto them, When thou prayest enter into thy secret chamber, and when thou hast closed the door, pray to Abba Amma Who is above and within thee, and thy Father-Mother Who seest all that is secret shall answer thee openly.

2 But when ye are gathered together, and pray in common, use not vain repetitions, for your heavenly Parent knoweth what things ye have need of before ye ask them. After this manner therefore pray ye:

3 Our Father-Mother Who art above and within: Hallowed be Thy Name in twofold Trinity. In Wisdom, Love and Equity Thy Kingdom come to all. Thy will be done, As in Heaven so in Earth. Give us day by day to partake of Thy holy Bread, and the fruit of the living Vine. As Thou dost forgive us our trespasses, so may we forgive others who trespass against us. Shew upon us Thy goodness, that to others we may shew the same. In the hour of temptation, deliver us from evil.

4 Shew upon us Thy goodness, that to others we may shew the same. In the hour of temptation, deliver us from evil.

5 And wheresoever there are seven gathered together in My Name there am I in the midst of them; yea, if only there be three or two; and where there is but one who prayeth in secret, I am with that one.

6 Raise the Stone, and there thou shall find me. Cleave the wood, and there am I. For in the fire and in the water even as in every living form, God is manifest as it's Life and it's Substance.

7 AND the Lord said, If thy brother hath sinned in word seven times a day, and seven times a day hath made amendment, receive him. Simon said to him, Seven times a day ?

8 The Lord answered and said to him, I tell thee also unto seventy times seven, for even in the Prophets, after they were anointed by the Spirits utterance of sin was found.

9 Be ye therefore considerate, be tender, be ye pitiful, be ye kind, not to your own kind alone, but to every creature which is within your care, for ye are to them as gods, to whom they look in their need. Be ye slow to anger for many sin in anger which they repented of, when their anger was past.

10 AND there was a man whose hand was withered and he came to Jesus and said, Lord, I was a mason seeking sustenance by my hands, I beseech thee restore to me my health that I may not beg for food with shame. And Jesus healed him, saying There is a house made without hands, seek that thou mayest dwell therein.

CHAPTER 19 2 -There are two versions given of the Lord's Prayer, this one, the fullest, being given to the Twelve and their companions, and a shorter form afterwards to the people in his Sermon on the Mount.

v. 5, 6 -An ancient saying, long lost to the Church. The all-pervading nature of Deity seems plainly taught, which, in a recently recovered fragment, is obscure.

CHAPTER 20

The Return of the Two and Seventy

1 AND after a season the two and seventy returned again with joy, saying, Lord, even the demons are subject unto us through thy name.

2 And he said unto them, I beheld Satan as lightning fall from heaven.

3 Behold I give unto you power to tread on serpents and scorpions, and over all the power of the enemy; and nothing shall by any means hurt you. Notwithstanding in this, rejoice not, that the spirits are subject unto you; but rather rejoice, because your names are written in Heaven.

4 In that hour Jesus rejoiced in spirit, and said I thank thee, Holy Parent of heaven and earth, that thou hast hid these things from the wise and prudent, and hast revealed them unto babes: even so, All Holy, for so it seemed good in thy sight.

5 All things are delivered to me of the All-Parent: and no man knoweth the Son who is the Daughter, but the All Parent; nor who the All-Parent is, but the Son even the Daughter, and they to whom the Son and the Daughter will reveal it.

6 And he turned him unto his disciples, and said privately, Blessed are the eyes which see the things that ye see. For I tell you, that many prophets and kings have desired to see those things which ye see, and have not seen them; and to hear those things which ye hear, and have not heard them.

7 Blessed are ye of the inner circle who hear my word and to whom mysteries are revealed, who give to no innocent creature the pain of prison or of death, but seek the good of all, for to such is everlasting life.

8 Blessed are ye who abstain from all things gotten by bloodshed and death, and fulfill all righteousness: Blessed are ye, for ye shall attain to "beatitudes of Christ"

CHAPTER 20 9 -There is no trace of the events between CHAPTERs 18 and 20 other than this giving of the form of Prayer as a model for all time.

CHAPTER 21

Jesus Rebuketh Cruelty to a Horse. Condemneth the Service of Mammon.

1 AND it came to pass that the Lord departed from the City and went over the mountains with this disciples. And they came to a mountain whose ways were steep and there they found a man with a beast of burden.

2 But the horse had fallen down, for it was over laden, and he struck it till the blood flowed. And Jesus went to him and said: "Son of cruelty, why strikest thou thy beast? Seest thou not that it is

too weak for its burden, and knowest thou not that it suffereth?"

3 But the man answered and said: "What hast thou to do therewith? I may strike it as much as it pleaseth me, for it is mine own, and I bought it with a goodly sum of money. Ask them who are with thee, for they are of mine acquaintance and know thereof."

4 And some of the disciples answered and said: Yea, Lord, it is as he saith, We have seen when he bought it. And the Lord said again "See ye not then how it bleedeth, and hear ye not also how it waileth and lamenteth ?" But they answered and said: "Nay, Lord, we hear not that it waileth and lamenteth? "

5 And the Lord was sorrowful, and said: "Woe unto you because of the dullness of your hearts, ye hear not how it lamenteth and crieth unto the heavenly Creator for mercy, but thrice woe unto him against whom it crieth and waileth in its pain."

6 And he went forward and touched it, and the horse stood up, and its wounds were healed. But to the man he said: "Go now thy way and strike it henceforth no more, if thou also desireth to find mercy."

7 AND seeing the people come unto him, Jesus, said unto his disciples, Because of the sick I am sick; because of the hungry I am hungry; because of the thirsty I am athirst.

8 He also said, I am come to end the sacrifices and feasts of blood, and if ye cease not offering and eating of flesh and blood, the wrath of God shall not cease from you, even as it came to your fathers in the wilderness, who lusted for flesh, and they eat to their content, and were filled with rottenness, and the plague consumed them.

9 And I say unto you, Though ye be gathered together in my bosom, if ye keep not my commandments I will cast you forth. For if ye keep not the lesser mysteries, who shall give you the greater.

10 He that is faithful in that which is least is faithful also in much: and he that is unjust in the least is unjust also in much.

11 If therefore ye have not been faithful in the mammon of unrighteousness, who will commit to your trust the true riches? And if ye have not been faithful in that which is another man's, who shall give you that which is your own ?

12 No servant can serve two masters: for either he will hate the one, and love the other; or else he will hold to the one and despise the other. Ye cannot serve God and mammon. And the Pharisees also, who were covetous, heard all these things, and they derided him.

13 And he said unto them, Ye are they which justify yourselves before men; but God knoweth your hearts: for that which is highly esteemed among men is abomination in the sight of God.

14 The law and the prophets were until John; since that time the kingdom of God is preached, and every man presseth into it. But it is easier for heaven and earth to pass away, than one title of the law to fail.

15 Then there came some women to him and brought their infants unto him, to whom they yet gave suck at their breasts, that he should bless them; and some said, Why trouble ye the master? 16 But Jesus rebuked them, and said, Of such will come forth those who shall yet confess me before men. And he took them up in his arms and blessed them.

CHAPTER 21 2-6 -This touching incident is to be found also in a very ancient Coptic fragment of the Life of Jesus- others of a like nature also recorded in their places in this Gospel, show how he, the Divine Saviour of the world, regarded the ill-treatment of the "lower" animals as a grievous sin.
v. 12 -The divine love of Jesus for all God's creatures is everywhere evidenced by this Gospel, and his belief that all life is one, is abundantly justified by the teaching of true modern science, physical and occult.

CHAPTER 22
The Restoration Of lairus' Daughter
1 AND behold there cometh one of the rulers of the synagogue, Iairus by name; and when he saw him, he fell at his feet,

and he besought him greatly, saying, My little daughter lieth at the point of death; I pray thee, come and lay thy hands on her, that she may be healed, and she shall live. And Jesus went with him, and much people followed him and thronged him.

2 AND a certain woman, which had an issue of blood twelve years, and had suffered many things of many physicians, and had spent all that she had, and was nothing bettered, but rather grew worse.

3 When she had heard of Jesus, she came in the press behind and touched his garments For she said, If I may touch but his garment, I shall be whole. find straightway the fountain of her blood was dried up; and she felt in her body that she was healed of that plague.

4 And Jesus, immediately knowing in himself that virtue had gone out of him, turned him about in the press and said, Who touched my vesture? And his disciples said unto him, Thou seest the multitude thronging thee and sayeth thou, Who touched me?

5 And he looked round about to see her that had done this thing. But the woman, fearing and trembling, knowing what was done in her, came and fell down before him and told him all the truth. And he said unto her, Daughter, thy faith hath made thee whole; go in peace and be whole of thy plague.

6 WHILE he yet spake, there came from the ruler of the synagogue's house certain which said, Thy daughter is dead: why troublest thou the Master any further ?

7 As soon as Jesus heard the word that was spoken, he saith unto the ruler of the synagogue, Be not afraid, only believe. And he suffered no man to follow him save Peter and James and John the brother of James.

8 And he cometh to the house of the ruler of the synagogue, and seeth the tumult and the minstrels, and them that lamented and wailed greatly.

9 And when he was come in he said unto him, Why make ye this ado and weep? The damsel is not dead but sleepeth. And they laughed him to scorn, for they thought she was dead, and believed him not. But when he had put them all out, he taketh two of his disciples with him, and entered in where the damsel was lying.

10 And he took the damsel by the hand and said unto her, Talitha cumi; which is, being interpreted, Damsel, I say unto thee arise.

11 And straightway the damsel arose and walked. And she was of the age of twelve years. And they were astonished with a great astonishment.

12 And he charged them straightly that no man should make it known, and commanded that something should be given to her to eat.

CHAPTER 22 -The daily increasing discoveries in modern times of cases of trance or of suspended animation, in which those carried to burial certified as dead by medical men have revived, suggest the thought how much more numerous must have been such cases in days when medical science knew little or nothing of the symptoms of real death. When it is now ascertained that five per thousand on an average are restored to life who have been certified dead or carried to burial, how many more such cases must have occurred in those times when true physicians and magnetic healers were looked upon almost as gods?

CHAPTER 23
Jesus And The Samaritan Woman

1 THEN cometh Jesus to a city of Samaria, which is called Sychar, near to the parcel of ground that Jacob gave to his son Joseph.

2 Now Jacob's well was there. Jesus therefore, being wearied with his journey, sat alone on the edge of the well, and it was about the sixth hour.

3 And there cometh a woman of Samaria to draw water; Jesus saith unto her, Give me to drink. (For his disciples were gone away unto the city to buy food).

4 Then saith the woman of Samaria unto him, How is it that thou being a

Jew, asketh drink of me, who am a woman of Samaria? (for the Jews have no dealings with the Samaritans.)

5 Jesus answered and said unto her, If thou knewest the gift of God and who it is that saith to thee, Give me drink, thou wouldest have asked of God, who would have given thee living water.

6 The woman saith unto him, Sir, thou hast nothing to draw with, and the well is deep, from whence hast thou that living water. Art thou greater than our father Jacob, who gave us the well and drank thereof, himself and his children and his camels and oxen and sheep.

7 Jesus answered and said unto her, Whosoever drinketh of this water shall thirst again, but whosoever drinketh of the water that I shall give him shall never thirst; but the water that I shall give him shall be in him a well of water springing up into everlasting life.

8 The woman saith unto him, Sir, give me this water, that I thirst not, neither come hither to draw. Jesus saith unto her, Go, call thy husband and come hither. The woman answered and said, I have no husband.

9 Jesus looking upon her, answered and said unto her, Thou hast well said, I have no husband. For thou hast had five husbands and he whom thou now hast is not called thy husband, in that saidst thou truly.

10 The woman saith unto him, Sir, I perceive that thou art a prophet. Our fathers worshipped in this mountain and ye say that in Jerusalem is the place where men ought to worship.

11 Jesus saith unto her, Woman, believe me, the hour cometh, when ye shall neither in this mountain nor yet at Jerusalem worship God. Ye worship ye know not what; we know what we worship; for salvation is of Israel.

12 But the hour cometh and now is, when the true worshippers shall worship the All-Parent in spirit and in truth; for such worshippers the All-Holy seeketh. God is a Spirit and they that worship, must worship in spirit and in truth.

13 The woman saith unto him, I know that Messiah cometh who is called the Christ: when he is come he will tell us all things. Jesus saith unto her, I am he Who speaketh unto thee.

14 And upon this came his disciples and marveled that he talked with the woman, yet no man said, What seekest thou ? or, Why talkest thou with her?

15 The woman then left her waterpot, and went her way into the city and saith unto the men, Come, see a man which told me all things that ever I did: is not this the Christ?

16 Then they went out of the city and came unto him, and many of the Samaritans believed on him, and they besought him that he would tarry with them; and he abode there two days.

CHAPTER 23 1-13 -A similar event is recorded in the life of Buddha, where he asks water of a woman, and receives it from a woman of lower caste, who asks how he, of a higher caste, a Brahmin, comes to ask water of one so much lower. It should cast no doubt on this passage.

CHAPTER 24
Jesus Denounces Cruelty
He Healeth the Sick

1 As Jesus passed through a certain village he saw a crowd of idlers of the baser sort, and they were tormenting a cat which they had found and shamefully treating it. And Jesus commanded them to desist and began to reason with them, but they would have none of his words, and reviled him.

2 Then he made a whip of knotted cords and drove them away, saying, This earth which my Father-Mother made for joy and gladness, ye have made into the lowest hell with your deeds of violence and cruelty; And they fled before his face.

3 But one more vile than the rest returned and defied him. And Jesus put forth his hand, and the young man's arm weathered, and great fear came upon all; and one said, He is a sorcerer.

4 And the next day the mother of the young man came unto Jesus, praying that he would restore the withered arm. And Jesus spake unto them of the law

of love and the unity of all life in the one family of God. And he also said, As ye do in this life to your fellow creatures, so shall it be done to you in the life to come.

5 And the young man believed and confessed his sins, and Jesus stretched forth his hand, and his withered arm became whole even as the other, And the people glorified God who had given such power unto man.

6 AND when Jesus departed thence, two blind men followed him, crying and saying, Thou son of David, have mercy on us. And when he was come into the house the blind men came to him, and Jesus saith unto them, Believe ye that I am able to do this?

7 They said unto him, Yea, Lord. Then touched he their eyes, saying, According to your faith be it unto you. And their eyes were opened, and Jesus straitly charged them, saying, See that ye tell no man, But they, when they were departed, spread abroad his fame in all that country.

8 As they went forth, behold, they brought to him a dumb man possessed with a demon. And when the demon was cast out the dumb spake, and the multitude marvelled, saying, It was never so seen in Israel. But the Pharisees said, He casteth out demons through the prince of the demons.

9 AND Jesus went about all the cities and villages, teaching in their synagogues and preaching the gospel of the kingdom and healing every sickness and every disease among the people.

10 But when he saw the multitudes he was moved with compassion on them, because they fainted and were scattered abroad, as sheep having no shepherd.

11 Then said he unto his disciples, The harvest truly is plentiful, but the labourers are few; pray ye therefore the Lord of the harvest, that he will send forth labourers into his harvest.

12 AND his disciples brought him two small baskets with bread and fruit, and a pitcher of water. And Jesus set the bread and the fruit before them and also the water. And they did eat and drink and were filled.

13 And they marvelled, for each had enough and to spare, and there were four thousand. And they departed blessing God for what they had heard and seen.

CHAPTER 24 1-5 -The cat was an ancient symbol of Deity, on account of its seeing in the dark and otter attributes. More than one instance is given of Jesus' protection of these beautiful animals which in Iudea were, as they are even now in some places, unjustly despised and regarded with disfavour. He, the Friend of all things that suffered, cast his protection round these innocent creatures, teaching men and women to do likewise, and to feel for all the weak and oppressed. This beautiful and much maligned animal was a native of Egypt. But there is no difficulty here, for Egyptian families visited Palestine, and would naturally bring their venerated animals with them, not leave them to neglect or worse, as some "Christians" who ought to know better.

CHAPTER 25
The Sermon On The Mount (Part I)
1 Jesus seeing the multitudes, went up into a mountain: and when he was seated, the twelve came unto him, and he lifted up his eyes on his disciples and said:

2 Blessed in spirit are the poor, for theirs is the kingdom of heaven. Blessed are they that mourn: for they shall be comforted. Blessed are the meek; for they shall inherit the earth. Blessed are they who do hunger and thirst after righteousness: for they shall be filled.

3 Blessed are the merciful: for they shall obtain mercy. Blessed are the pure in heart: for they shall see God. Blessed are the peacemakers: for they shall be called the children of God. Blessed are they which are persecuted for righteousness sake: for theirs is the kingdom of God.

4 Yea, blessed are ye, when men shall hate you' and when they shall separate you from their company, and shall

reproach you, and cast out your name as evil, for the Son of man's sake. Rejoice ye in that day, and leap for joy: for, behold, your reward is great in heaven; for in the like manner did their fathers unto the prophets.

5 Woe unto you that are rich! for ye have received in this life your consolation. Woe unto you that are full! for ye shall hunger. Woe unto you that laugh now! for ye shall mourn and weep. Woe unto you when all men shall speak well of you' for so did their fathers to the false prophets.

6 Ye are the salt of the earth, for every sacrifice must be salted with salt, but if the salt have lost its savour, wherewith shall it be salted? it is thenceforth good for nothing, but to be cast out, and to be trodden under foot.

7 Ye are the light of the world. A city that is built on a hill cannot be hid. Neither do men light a candle, and put it under a bushel, but on a candlestick; and it giveth light unto all that are in the house. Let your light so shine before men, that they may see your good works, and glorify your Parent who is in heaven.

8 Think not that I am come to destroy the law, or the prophets: I am not come to destroy, but to fulfill. For verily I say unto you, Till heaven and earth pass, one jot or one tittle shall in no way pass from the law or the prophets till all be fulfilled. But behold One greater than Moses is here. and he will give you the higher law, even the perfect Law, and this Law shall ye obey.

9 Whosoever therefore shall break one of these commandments which he shall give, and shall teach men so, they shall be called the least in the kingdom; but whosoever shall do, and teach them, the same shall be called great in the kingdom of Heaven.

10 Verily they who believe and obey shall save their souls, and they who obey not shall lose them. For I say unto you, That except your righteousness shall, exceed the righteousness of the scribes and Pharisees ye shall not enter the kingdom of Heaven.

11 Therefore if thou bring thy gift to the altar and there rememberest that thy brother hath aught against thee, leave there thy gift before the altar, and go thy way; first be reconciled to thy brother, and then come and offer thy gift.

12 Agree with thine adversary quickly, while thou art in the way with him; lest at any time thy adversary deliver thee to the Judge, and the judge deliver thee to the officer, and thou be cast into prison. Verily I say unto thee. Thou shalt by no means come out thence till thou hast paid the uttermost farthing.

13 Ye have heard that it hath been said, Thou shalt love thy neighbour and hate thine enemy. But I say unto you which hear, Love your enemies, do good to them which hate you.

14 Bless them that curse you, and pray for them which despitefully use you. That ye may be the children of your Parent Who maketh the sun to rise on the evil and the good, and sendeth rain on the Just and on the unjust.

15 For if ye love them which love you what thank have ye? for sinners also love those that love them. And if ye do good to them which do good to you, what thank have ye? for sinners even do the same. And if ye salute your brethren only, what do ye more than others? do not even so the taxgatherers?

16 And if a desire be unto thee as thy life, and it turn thee from the truth, cast it out from thee, for it is better to enter life possessing truth, than losing it, to be cast into outer darkness.

17 And if that seem desirable to thee which costs another pain or sorrow, cast it out of thine heart; so shalt thou attain to peace. Better it is to endure sorrow, than to inflict it, on those who are weaker.

18 Be ye therefore perfect, even as your Parent Who is in heaven is perfect.

CHAPTER 25 2 -It is remarkable how persistent has been the false rendering of these words in the received Gospels. It is too evident to need any comment. It is not poverty of spirit that Christ commended, but the spiritual effects of literal poverty (not pauperism), which are more frequent than those of abundant riches.

v. 6-7 -Suggestive is this passage of the custom of the Christian Church in building their monasteries and convents generally on high places, the bands of holy men and women therein being truly, in the Dark Ages, the salt of the earth, the light on a hill, without which society would have rotted to the core, and been universally corrupt. The occasional abuses argue nothing against their more blessed influences. Without them our Scriptures would not have been preserved, even in their present condition, and civilization would have been extinct. To the monks of S. Basil and S. Benedict are due the remains of Christianity that have been handed down to us, and by such institutions rationally conducted will Christianity be revived in a higher and purer form, and the Scriptures restored to their original purity, as well as the ancient worship of God. The laxity of some modern monasteries is to be regretted in the matter of flesh-eating, under the plea of health, there being really no such necessity with the abundance of food from the vegetable world as well as animal products. The Carthusian and other monasteries stand as a noble testimony to the healthfulness of the rule when observed in strictness and unabated rigour.

CHAPTER 26

The Sermon On The Mount (Part II)
1 TAKE heed that ye do not your alms before men, to be seen of them: otherwise ye have no reward of your Parent who is in heaven. Therefore when thou doest thine alms, do not sound a trumpet before thee, as the hypocrites do in the synagogues and in the streets, that they may have glory of men. Verily I say unto you, they have their reward.

2 But when thou givest alms, let not thy left hand know what thy right hand doeth, and take heed that thine alms may be in secret; and the Secret One which seest in secret shall approve then openly.

3 And when thou prayest, thou shalt not be as the hypocrites are: for they love to pray standing in the synagogues and on the corners of the streets that they may be seen of men. Verily I say unto you, They have their reward.

4 But thou, when thou prayest enter into thy chamber and when thou hast shut thy door pray to thy Father-Mother who is in secret; and the secret One that seeth in secret shall approve thee openly.

5 And when ye pray in common, use not vain petitions, as the heathen do: for they think that they shall be heard for their much speaking. Be not ye therefore like unto them: for your heavenly Parent knoweth what things ye have need of, before ye ask After this manner therefore pray ye, when ye are gathered together:

6 Our Parent Who art in heaven: Hallowed be Thy Name. Thy kingdom come. Thy will be done; in earth as it is in heaven. Give us day by day our daily bread, and the fruit of the living Vine. As Thou forgivest us our trespasses, so may we forgive the trespasses of others. Leave us not in temptation. Deliver us from evil. Amen.

7 For if ye forgive men their trespasses, your heavenly Parent will also forgive you: but if ye forgive not men their trespasses, neither will your Parent in heaven forgive you your trespasses.

8 Moreover when ye fast, be not, as the hypocrites, of a sad countenance; for they disfigure their faces, that they may appear unto men to fast. Verily I say unto you, they have their reward.

9 And I say unto you, Except ye fast from the world and its evil ways, ye shall in no wise find the Kingdom; and except ye keep the Sabbath and cease your haste to gather riches, ye shall not see the Father-Mother in heaven. But thou, when thou fastest, anoint thine head and wash thy face, that thou appear not unto men to fast, and the Holy One who seeth in secret will approve thee openly.

10 Likewise also do ye, when ye mourn for the dead and are sad, for your loss in their gain. Be not as those who mourn

before men and make loud lamentation and rend their garments, that they may be seen of men to mourn. For all souls are in the hands of God, and they who have done good, do rest with your ancestors in the bosom of the Eternal.

11 Pray ye rather for their rest and advancement, and consider that they are in the land of rest, which the Eternal hath prepared for them, and have the just reward of their deeds, and murmur not as those without hope.

12 Lay not up for yourselves treasures upon earth, where moth and rust doth corrupt, and where thieves break through and steal; but lay up for yourselves treasures in heaven, where neither moth not rust doth corrupt and where thieves do not break through nor steal. For where your treasure is, there will your heart be also.

13 The lamps of the body are the eyes: if therefore thy sight be clear, thy whole body shall be full of light. But if thine eyes be dim or lacking, thy whole body shall be full of darkness. If therefore the light that is in thee be darkness, how great is that darkness!

14 No man can serve two masters; for either he will hate the one and love the other; or else he will hold to the one and despise the other. Ye cannot serve God and mammon.

15 Therefore I say unto you, Be not over anxious for your life what ye shall eat, or what ye shall drink; nor yet for your body, what ye shall put on. Is not the life more than meat and the body than raiment? And what shall it profit a man if he gain the whole world and lose his life ?

16 Behold the fowls of the air; for they sow not, neither do they reap, nor gather into barns; yet your heavenly Parent feedeth them. Are ye not much better cared for than they? Which of you by taking thought can add one cubit unto his stature? And why spend all your thought for raiment ? Consider the lilies of the field, how they grow; they toil not, neither do they spin. And yet I say unto you, Solomon in all his glory was not arrayed like one of these.

17 Wherefore shall not God who clothes the grass of the field, which to day is, and tomorrow is cast into the oven, much more clothe you, O ye of little faith?

18 Therefore be not over anxious, saying, What shall we eat? or, What shall we drink? or, Wherewithal shall we be clothed? (all Which things do the Gentiles seek). For your heavenly Parent knoweth that ye have need of all these things. But seek ye first the kingdom of God and its righteousness and all these things shall be added unto you. Meet not in advance the evils of the morrow; sufficient unto the day is the evil thereof.

CHAPTER 26 9 -Meaning; that if the vision be set on one single object and no other, great is the clearness of vision; while, if the eyes be set on number of other objects, the clearness will be diminished with regard to that one.

CHAPTER 27
The Sermon On The Mount (Part III)
1 JUDGE not, that ye be not judged. For with what judgment ye judge, ye shall be judged: and with what measure ye mete, it shall be measured to you again; and as ye do unto others, so shall it be done unto you.

2 And why beholdest thou the mote that is in thy brother's eye, but considerest not the beam that is in thine own eye? Or how wilt thou say to thy brother, Let me pull the mote out of thine eye; and behold a beam is in thine own eye? Thou hypocrite, first cast the beam out of thine own eye; and then shall thou see clearly to cast the mote out of thy brother's eye.

3 Give not that which is holy unto the dogs' neither cast ye your pearls before swine; lest they trample them under their feet and turn again and rend you.

4 Ask and it shall be given you; seek, and ye shall find; knock, and it shall be opened unto you: for everyone that asketh receiveth, and he that seeketh findeth, and to them that knock it shall be opened.

5 What man is there of you who, if his

child ask bread, will give it a stone? Or, if it ask a fish, will give it a serpent? If ye then, being evil, know how to give good gifts unto your children, how much more shall your Parent Who is in heaven give good things to them that ask?

6 Therefore all things whatsoever ye would that men should do to you, do ye even so to them. And what ye would not that men should do unto you, do ye not so unto them; for this is the Law and the prophets.

7 Enter ye in at the strait gate, for strait is the way and narrow the gate that leadeth unto life, and few there be that find it. But wide is the gate and broad is the way that leadeth to destruction, and many there be who go in thereat.

8 Beware of false prophets, which come to you in sheep's clothing, but inwardly are ravening wolves. Ye shall know them by their fruits. Do men gather grapes of thorns, or figs of thistles?

9 Even so, every good tree bringeth forth good fruit, but a corrupt tree bringeth forth evil fruit. Every tree that bringeth not forth good fruit is only fit to be hewn down and cast into the fire. Wherefore by their fruits ye shall know the good from the evil.

10 Not every one that saith unto me, Lord, Lord, shall enter into the kingdom of heaven; but he that doeth the will of my Father-Mother Who is in heaven. Many will say to me in that day, Lord, Lord, have we not prophesied in thy Name? and in thy Name have cast out devils? and in thy Name done many wonderful works? And then will I say unto them, I never knew you: depart from me, ye that work iniquity.

11 Therefore whosoever heareth these sayings of mine, and doeth them, I will liken him unto a wise man who built his house foursquare upon a rock. And the rain descended, and the floods came, and the winds blew upon that house; and it fell not, for it was founded upon a rock.

12 And everyone that heareth these sayings of mine, and doeth them not, shall be likened unto a foolish man, who built his house upon the sand, and

the rain descended, and the floods came and the winds blew and beat upon that house, and it fell, and great was the fall of it. But a city which is built foursquare, enclosed in a circle or on the top of a hill, and established on a rock, can neither fall nor be hidden.

13 And it came to pass, when Jesus had ended these sayings, the people were astonished at his doctrine. For he taught them as one appealing to the reason and the heart, and not as the scribes who taught rather by authority.

CHAPTER 27 2 -The sin of hypocrisy is most loathsome, and the most difficult for those to see who are vitiated by it. To condemn in others the sins we practice ourselves is a common sin of society, which Christ ever reprobates. CHAPTER 27 12 -Note the importance which these symbols (including the equilateral triangle) possessed in the eyes of Jesus as illustrations of Eternal truths. The slight mention of these shows the Gospel was written, or addressed to people well acquainted with the mysteries they represent.

CHAPTER 28
Jesus Releases The Rabbits And Pigeons

1 IT came to pass one day as Jesus had finished his discourse, in a place near Tiberias where there are seven wells, a certain young man brought live rabbits and pigeons, that he might have to eat with his disciples.

2 And Jesus looked on the young man with love and said to him, Thou hast a good heart and God shall give thee light, but knowest thou not that God in the beginning gave to man the fruits of the earth for food, and did not make him lower than the ox, or the horse, or the sheep, that he should kill and eat the flesh and blood of his fellow creatures.

3 Ye believe that Moses indeed commanded such creatures to be slain and offered in sacrifice and eaten, and so do ye in the Temple, but behold a greater than Moses is herein and he cometh to put away the bloody sacrifices of the law, and the feasts on

them, and to restore to you the pure oblation and unbloody sacrifice as in the beginning, even the grains and fruits of the earth.

4 Of that which ye offer undo God in purity shall ye eat, but of that kind which ye offer not in purity shall ye not eat, for the hour cometh when your sacrifices and feasts of blood shall cease, and ye shall worship God with a holy worship and a pure Oblation.

5 Let these creatures therefore go free, that they may rejoice in God and bring no guilt to man. And the young man set them free, and Jesus break their cages and their bonds.

6 But lo, they feared lest they should again be taken captive, and they went not away from him, but he spake unto them and dismissed them, and they obeyed his word, and departed in gladness.

7 AT that time as they sat by the well, which was in the midst of the six Jesus stood up and cried out, If any are thirsty, let them come unto me and drink, for I will give to them of the waters of life.

8 They who believe in me, out of their hearts shall flow rivers of water, and that which is given unto them shall they speak with power, and their doctrine shall be as living water.

9 (This he spake of the Spirit, which they that believed on him should receive, for the fullness of the Spirit was not yet given because that Jesus was not yet glorified).

10 Whosoever drinketh of the water that I shall give shall never thirst, but the water which cometh from God shall be in them a well of water, springing up unto everlasting life.

11 AND at that time John sent two of his disciples, saying, Art thou he that should come, or look we for another? and in that same hour he cured many of their infirmities and plagues, and of evil spirits, and unto many blind, he gave sight.

12 Then Jesus answering said unto them, Go your way, and tell John what things ye have seen and heard; how that the blind see, the lame walk, the lepers are cleansed, the deaf hear, the dead are raised, to the poor the gospel is preached. And blessed is he, whosoever shall not be offended in me.

13 And when the messengers of John were departed, he began to speak unto the people concerning John, What went ye out into the wilderness for to see? A reed shaken with the wind, or a man clothed in soft raiment? Behold, they which are georgeously apparelled, and live delicately, are in kings' courts.

14 But what went ye out for to see? A prophet Yea, I say unto you, and the greatest of prophets.

15 This is he, of whom it is written, Behold, I send my messenger before thy face, which shall prepare thy way before thee. For I say unto you, Among those that are born of women, there is not a greater prophet than John the Baptist.

16 And all the people that heard him, and the taxgatherers, justified God, being baptized with the baptism of John. But the Pharisees and lawyers rejected the counsel of God against themselves, being not baptized of him.

CHAPTER 28 1-5 -It is easy to see how this would have horrified the mind of Jesus had he lived in these semi-heathen times.
CHAPTER 28 16 -To exalt unduly the Christian Sacrament of Baptism, certain words have been interpolated in the A.V. The context shows that such was not the intended meaning, for immediately after, they "justified God by being baptized with John's Baptism."

CHAPTER 29
The feeding of the Five Thousand With Six Loaves and Seven Clusters Of Grapes.
Healing Of The Sick

1 AND the Feast of the Passover drew nigh, and the Apostles and their fellows gathered themselves together unto Jesus and told him all things, both what they had done and what they had taught. And he said unto them, Come ye yourselves apart into a desert place and rest a while: for there were many coming and

going, and they had no leisure so much as to eat.

2 And they departed into a desert place by ship privately. And the people saw them departing, and many knew him, and ran afoot thither out of all cities, and outwent them, and came together unto him.

3 And Jesus, when he came forth, saw much people and was moved with compassion towards them, because they were as sheep having not a shepherd.

4 And the day was far spent, and his disciples came unto him and said, This is a desert place, and now the time is far passed. Send them away, that they may go into the country round about into the villages, and buy themselves bread, for they have nothing to eat.

5 He answered and said unto them, Give ye them to eat. And they say unto him, Shall we go and buy two hundred pennyworth of bread, and give them to eat ?

6 He saith unto them, How many loaves have ye? go and see. And when they knew, they said, Six loaves and seven clusters of grapes. And he commanded them to make all sit down by companies of fifty upon the grass. And they sat down in ranks by hundreds and by fifties.

7 And when he had taken the six loaves and the seven clusters of grapes, he looked up to heaven, and blessed and brake the loaves, and the grapes also and gave them to his disciples to set before them and they divided them among them all.

8 And they did all eat and were filled. And they took up twelve baskets full of the fragments that were left. And they that did eat of the loaves and of the fruit were about five thousand men, women and children, and he taught them many things.

9 And when the people had seen and heard, they were filled with gladness and said, Truly this is that Prophet that should come into the world. And when he perceived that they would take him by force to make him a king, he straightway constrained his disciples to get into the ship, and to go to the other side before him unto Bethsaida, while he sent away the people.

10 And when he had sent them away he departed into a mountain to pray. And when even was come, he was there alone, but the ship was now in the midst of the sea, tossed with waves, for the wind was contrary.

11 The third watch of the night Jesus went unto them, walking on the sea. And when the disciples saw him walking on the sea, they were troubled, saying, It is a spirit; and they cried out for fear. But straightway Jesus spake unto them, saying. Be of good cheer; it is I; be not afraid.

12 And Peter answered him and said, Lord, if it be thou, bid me come unto thee on the water. And he said, Come. And when Peter was come down out of the ship, he walked on the water, to go to Jesus. But when he saw the wind boisterous, he was afraid, and beginning to sink, he cried, saying, Lord, save me.

13 And immediately Jesus stretched forth his hand, and caught him, and said unto him, O thou of little faith, wherefore didst thou doubt? For did I not call thee ?

14 And he went up unto them into the ship, and the wind ceased, and they were sore amazed in themselves beyond measure and wondered. For they considered not the miracle of the loaves and the fruit, for their heart was hardened.

15 And when they were come into the ship there was a great calm. Then they that were in the ship came and worshipped him, saying, Of a truth thou art a Son of God.

16 And when they had passed over, they came unto the land of Gennesaret and drew to the shore And when they were come out of the ship straightway they knew him. And ran through that whole region round about, and began to carry about in beds, those that were sick, where they heard he was.

17 And withersoever he entered, into villages, or cities, or country, they laid the sick in the streets, and besought him that they might touch if it were but the

border of his garment, and as many as touched him were made whole.

18 After these things Jesus came with his disciples into Judea, and there he tarried and baptized many who came unto him and received his doctrine.

CHAPTER 29 -The feeding of five thousand with five loaves and seven clusters of grapes has a deep mystical significance, which space forbids to enter on here, but the wise will understand. The two numbers, e.g, symbolize Matter and Spirit, Bread and Wine, Substance and Life.

CHAPTER 30

The Bread Of Life And The Living Vine

1 THE day following, the people which stood on the other side of the sea, saw that there had been no other boat there, save the one whereinto his disciples had entered and that Jesus went not with his disciples into the boat, but that his disciples were gone alone. And when the people therefore saw that Jesus was not there, neither his disciples, they also took ship and came to Capernaum, seeking for Jesus.

2 And when they had found him on the other side of the sea, they said unto him, Rabbi, how camest thou hither? Yeshua answered them and said, Verily, verily, I say unto you, ye seek me, not because ye saw the miracles, but because ye did eat of the loaves and the fruit, and were filled. Labour not for the meat which perisheth, but for that meat which endureth unto everlasting life, which the Son of Man, Who is also the Child of God, shall give unto you, for him hath God the All Parent sealed.

3 Then said they unto him, What shall we do that we may work the works of God? Jesus answered and said unto them, This is the work of God, that ye believe the truth, in me who am, and who giveth unto you, the Truth and the Life.

4 They said therefore unto him, What sign shewest thou then that we may see and believe thee? What dost thou work? Our fathers did eat manna in the desert; as it is written, He gave them bread from heaven to eat.

5 Then Jesus said unto them, Verily, verily, I say unto you, Moses gave you not the true bread from heaven, but my Parent giveth you the true bread from heaven and the fruit of the living vine. For the food of God is that which cometh down from heaven, and giveth life unto the world.

6 Then said they unto him, Lord, evermore give us this bread, and this fruit. And Jesus said unto them, I am the true Bread, I am the living Vine, they that come to me shall never hunger; and they that believe on me shall never thirst. And verily I say unto you, Except ye eat the flesh and drink the blood of God, ye have no life in you. But ye have seen me and believe not.

7 All that my Parent hath given to me shall come to me and they that come to me I will in no wise cast out. For I came down from heaven, not to do mine own will, but the will of God who sent me. And this is the will of God who hath sent me, that of all which are given unto me I should lose none, but should raise them up again at the last day.

8 The Jews then murmured at him, because he said I am the bread which cometh down from heaven. And they said, Is not this Jesus, the son of Joseph and Mary whose parentage we know? how is it then that he saith, I came down from heaven?

9 Jesus therefore answered and said unto them, Murmur ye not among yourselves. None can come to me except holy Love and Wisdom draw them, and these shall rise at the last day. It is written in the prophets, They shall be all taught of God. Every man therefore that hath heard and hath learned of the Truth, cometh unto me.

10 Not that anyone hath seen the Holiest at any time, save they which are of the Holiest, they alone, see the Holiest. Verily, verily, I say unto you, They who believe the Truth, have everlasting life.

CHAPTER 30 8 -The original Gospels

know nothing of the modern doctrine of the Anglican Church. Jesus was "the son of Mary and Joseph, whose parentage we know." This does not contradict, but rather suggests (to reconcile with Church doctrine), the Immaculate Conception of both parents to which the Church is now tending.

CHAPTER 31

The Bread of Life And The Living Vine. Jesus Rebuketh The Thoughtless Driver.

1 AGAIN Jesus said, I am the true Bread and the living Vine. Your fathers did eat manna in the wilderness and are dead. This is the food of God which cometh down from heaven, that whosoever eat thereof shall not die. I am the living food which came down from heaven, if any eat of this food they shall live for ever; and the bread that I will give is My truth and the wine which I will give is my life.

2 And the Jews strove amongst themselves, saying, How can this man give us himself for food? Then Jesus said, Think ye that I speak of the eating of flesh, which ye ignorantly do in the Temple of God?

3 Verily my body is the substance of God, and this is meat indeed, and my blood is the life of God and this is drink indeed. Not as your ancestors, who craved for flesh, and God gave them flesh in his wrath, and they ate of corruption till it stank in their nostrils, and their carcases fell by the thousand in the wilderness by reason of the plague.

4 Of such it is written, They shall wander nine and forty years in the wilderness till they are purified from their lusts, ere they enter into the land of rest, yea, seven times seven years shall they wander because they have not known My ways, neither obeyed My laws.

5 But They who eat this flesh and drink this blood dwell in me and I in them. As the Father- Mother of life hath sent me, and by Whom I live, so they that eat of me who am the truth and the life, even they shall live by me.

6 This is that living bread which coming down from heaven giveth life to the world. Not as your ancestors did eat manna and are dead. They that eat of this bread and this fruit, shall live for ever. These things said he in the synagogue, as he taught in Capernaum. Many therefore of his disciples, when they heard this, said, This is an hard saying, who can receive it?

7 When Jesus knew in himself that his disciples murmured at it, he said unto them, Doth this offend you? What and if ye shall see the Son and Daughter of man ascend to where they were before? It is the spirit that quickeneth, the flesh and blood profiteth nothing. The words that I speak unto you, they are spirit and they are life.

8 But there are some of you that believe not, For Jesus knew from the beginning who they were who should believe not, and who should betray him. Therefore said he unto them. No one can come unto me, except it were given from above.

9 From that time many of his disciples went back and walked no more with him. Then said Jesus unto the twelve, Will ye also go away ?

10 Then Simon Peter answered him, Lord to whom shall we go? thou hast the words of eternal life. And we believe and we are sure that thou art that Christ, a Son of the living God.

11 Jesus answered them, Have not I chosen you Twelve, and one also who is a traitor ? He spake of Judas Iscariot son of Simon the Levite, for it was that should betray him.

12 AND Jesus was travelling to Jerusalem, and there came a camel heavy laden with wood. and the camel could not drag it up the hill whither he went for the weight thereof, and the driver beat him and cruelly ill-treated him, but he could make him go no further.

13 And Jesus seeing this, said unto him, Wherefore beatest thou thy brother? And the man answered, I wot not that he is my brother, is he not a beast of burden and made to serve me?

14 And Jesus said, Hath not the same God made of the same substance the

camel and thy children who serve thee, and have ye not one breath of life which ye have both received from God ?

15 And the man marvelled much at this saying, and he ceased from beating the camel, and took off some of the burden and the camel walked up the hill as Jesus went before him, and stopped no more till he ended his journey.

16 And the camel knew Jesus, having felt of the love of God in him. And the man inquired further of the doctrine, and Jesus taught him gladly and he became his disciple.

CHAPTER 31 4 -Jesus quoted from a more ancient version than we now possess.

CHAPTER 32
God the Food and Drink of All.
1 AND it came to pass as he sat at supper with his disciples one of them said unto him: Master, how sayest thou that thou wilt give thy flesh to eat and thy blood to drink, for it is a hard saying unto many?

2 And Jesus answered and said: The words which I spake unto you are Spirit and they are Life. To the ignorant and the carnally minded they savour of bloodshed and death, but blessed are they who understand.

3 Behold the corn which groweth up into ripeness and is cut down, and ground in the mill, and baked with fire into bread! of this bread is my body made, which ye see: and lo the grapes which grow on the vine unto ripeness, and are plucked and crushed in the winepress and yield the fruit of the vine! of this fruit of the vine and of water is made my blood.

4 For of the fruits of the trees and the seeds of the herbs alone do I partake, and these are changed by the Spirit into my flesh and my blood. Of these alone and their like shall ye eat who believe in me, and are my disciples, for of these, in the Spirit come life and health and healing unto man.

5 Verily shall my Presence be with you in the Substance and Life of God, manifested in this body, and this blood;

and of these shall ye all eat and drink who believe in me.

6 For in all places I shall be lifted up for the life of the world, as it is written in the prophets; From the rising up of the sun unto the going down of the same, in every place a pure Oblation with incense shall be offered unto my Name.

7 As in the natural so in the spiritual. My doctrine and my life shall be meat and drink unto you, —the Bread of Life and the Wine of Salvation.

8 As the corn and the grapes are transmuted into flesh and blood, so must your natural minds be changed into spiritual. Seek ye the Transmutation of the natural into the Spiritual.

9 Verily I say unto you, in the beginning, all creatures of God did find their sustenance in the herbs and the fruits of the earth alone, till the ignorance and the selfishness of man turned many of them from the use which God had given them to that which was contrary to their original use, but even these shall yet return to their natural food, as it is written in the prophets, and their words shall not fail.

10 Verily God ever giveth of the Eternal Life and Substance to renew the forms of the universe. It is therefore of the flesh and blood, even the Substance and Life of the Eternal, that ye are partakers unto life, and my words are spirit and they are life.

11 And if ye keep My commandments and live the life of the righteous, happy shall ye be in this life, and in that which is to come. Marvel not therefore that I said unto you, Except ye eat of the flesh and drink the blood of God, ye have no life in you.

12 And the disciples answered saying: Lord, evermore give us to eat of this bread, and to drink of this cup, for thy words are meat and drink indeed;. By thy Life and by thy Substance may we live forever.

CHAPTER 32 4,5, 8 -The true significance of the bread and the wine in the Holy Eucharist is here taught by anticipation -the substance and life of the Eternal One given and shed for the sustenance of the universe, and this does not exclude, but contains, all other mystical significations which piety suggests, as good, beautiful, and true -each in its place.

CHAPTER 33
By The Shedding Of Blood Of Others Is No Remission Of Sins.

1 IESUS was teaching his disciples in the outer court of the Temple and one of them said unto him: Master, it is said by the priests that without shedding of blood there is no remission. Can then the blood offering of the law take away sin?

2 And Jesus answered: No blood offering, of beast or bird, or man, can take away sin, for how can the conscience be purged from sin by the shedding of innocent blood? Nay, it will increase the condemnation.

3 The priests indeed receive such offering as a reconciliation of the worshippers for the trespasses against the law of Moses, but for sins against the Law of God there can be no remission, save by repentance and amendment.

4 Is it not written in the prophets, Put your blood sacrifices to your burnt offerings, and away with them, and cease ye from the eating of flesh, for I spake not to your fathers nor commanded them, when I brought them out of Egypt, concerning these things? But this thing I commanded saying:

5, Obey my voice and walk in the ways that I have commanded you, and ye shall be my people, and it shall be well with you. But they hearkened not, nor inclined their ear.

6 And what doth the Eternal command you but to do justice, love mercy and walk humbly with your God? Is it not written that in the beginning God ordained the fruits of the trees and the seeds and the herbs to be food for all flesh?

7 But they have made the House of Prayer a den of thieves, and for the pure Oblation with Incense, they have polluted my altars with blood, and eaten of the flesh of the slain.

8 But I say unto you: Shed no innocent blood nor eat ye flesh. Walk uprightly, love mercy, and do justly, and your days shall be long in the land.

9 The corn that groweth from the earth with the other grain, is it not transmuted by the Spirit into my flesh? The grapes of the vineyard, with the other fruits are they not transmuted by the Spirit into my blood? Let these, with your bodies and souls be your Memorial to the Eternal.

10 In these is the presence of God manifest as the Substance and as the Life of the world. Of these shall ye eat and drink for the remission of sins, and for eternal life, to all who obey my words.

11 Now there is at Jerusalem by the sheep market, a pool which is called Bethesda, having five porches. In these lay a great multitude of impotent folk, of blind, halt, withered, waiting for the moving of the waters.

12 For at a certain season, an angel went down into the pool and troubled the waters; whosoever went first into the waters was made whole of whatever disease he had. And a man impotent from his birth was there.

13 And Jesus said unto him. Bring not the waters healing? He said unto him. Yea, Lord, but I have no man when the water is troubled to put me in, and while I am trying to come another steppeth down before me. And Jesus said to him, Arise, take up thy bed and walk. And immediately he rose and walked. And on the same day was the Sabbath.

14 The Jews therefore said to him, It is the Sabbath it is not lawful for thee to carry thy bed. And he that was healed wist not that it was Jesus. And Jesus had conveyed himself away, a multitude being in that place.

CHAPTER 33 4 -Here is given the true significance of Ier. vii. 22, or as it should be rendered in that place, " Ye add burnt sacrifice to burnt offering and ye eat flesh. But I spake not to your fathers nor commanded them concerning these things," etc. Else, as translated in the A. V. it is inimical to the sense, see Numbers xi.

CHAPTER 34
Love of Jesus for All Creatures.

1 WHEN Jesus knew how the Pharisees had murmured and complained because he made and baptized more disciples than John, he left Judea, and departed unto Galilee.

2 AND Jesus came to a certain Tree and abode beneath it many days. And there came Mary Magdalene and other women and ministered unto him of their substance, and he taught daily all that came unto him.

3 And the birds gathered around him, and welcomed him with their song, and other living creatures came unto his feet, and he fed them, and they ate out of his hands.

4 And when he departed he blessed the women who shewed love unto him, and turning to the fig tree, he blessed it also, saying. Thou hast given me shelter and shade from the burning heat, and withal thou hast given me food also.

5 Blessed be thou, increase and be fruitful, and let all who come to thee, find rest and shade and food, and let the birds of the air rejoice in thy branches.

6 And behold the tree grew and flourished exceedingly, and its branches took root downward, and sent shoots upward, and it spread mightily, so that no tree was like unto it for its size and beauty, and the abundance and goodness of its fruit.

7 AND as Jesus entered into a certain village he saw a young cat which had none to care for her, and she was hungry and cried unto him, and he took her up, and put her inside his garment, and she lay in his bosom.

8 And when he came into the village he set food and drink before the cat, and she ate and drank, and shewed thanks unto him. And he gave her unto one of his disciples, who was a widow, whose name was Lorenza, and she took care of her.

9 And some of the people said, This man careth for all creatures, are they his brothers and sisters that he should love them ? And he said unto them, Verily these are your fellow creatures of the great Household of God, yea, they are your brethren and sisters, having the same breath of life in the Eternal.

10 And whosoever careth for one of the least of these, and giveth it to eat and drink in its need, the same doeth it unto me, and whoso willingly suffereth one of these to be in want, and defendeth it not when evilly entreated, suffereth the evil as done unto me; for as ye have done in this life, so shall it be done unto you in the life to come.

CHAPTER 34 2 -This beautiful incident does not stand alone in history, a similar story is related of Buddha, the Enlightener of India, the "Light of the East"; nor is it by any means irreverent to suppose that similar things should happen to persons of similar minds.

CHAPTER 35
The Good Law. -Mary And Martha.

1 AND behold a certain lawyer stood up and tempted him, saying, Master, what shall I do to gain eternal life? He said unto him, What is written in the law ? how readest thou ?

2 And he answering, said, Thou shalt not do unto others, as thou wouldst not that they should do unto thee. Thou shalt love thy God with all thy heart and all thy soul and all thy mind. Thou shalt do unto others, as thou wouldst that they should do unto thee.

3 And he said unto him, Thou hast answered right, this do and thou shalt live; on these three commandments hang all the law and the prophets, for who loveth God, loveth his Neighbour also.

4 But he, willing to justify himself, said unto Jesus, And who is my neighbour? And Jesus answering said, A certain man went down from Jesusalem to Jericho, and fell among, thieves, which stripped him of his raiment and wounded him and departed leaving him half dead.

5 And by chance there came down a certain priest that way, and when he

saw him he passed by on the one side. And likewise a Levite also came and looked on him, and passed by on the other side.

6 But a certain Samaritan, as he journeyed, came where he was, and when he saw him he had compassion on him. And went to him and bound up his wounds, pouring in oil and wine, and set him on his own beast, and brought him to an inn and took care of him.

7 And on the morrow when he departed he took out two pence, and gave them to the host, and said, Take care of him and whatsoever thou spendest more, when I come again, I will repay thee.

8 Which now of these three, thinkest thou, was neighbour unto him that fell among thieves? And he said. He that shewed mercy on him. Then said Jesus unto him, Go, and do thou likewise.

9 Now it came to pass, as they went, that he entered into a certain village, and a woman named Martha received him into her house. And she had a sister called Mary, who also sat at Jesus, feet, and heard his word.

10 But Martha was cumbered about much serving and came to him saying, Lord, dost thou not care that my sister hath left me to serve alone? bid her therefore that she may help me.

11 And Jesus answered and said unto her, Martha, Martha, thou art careful and troubled about many things, but one thing is needful, and Mary hath chosen that good part, which shall not be taken away from her.

12 AGAIN, as Jesus sat at supper with his disciples in a certain city, he said unto them, As a Table set upon twelve pillars, so am I in the midst of you.

13 Verily I say unto you, Wisdom buildeth her house and heweth out her twelve pillars. She doth prepare her bread and her oil, and mingle her wine. She doth furnish her table.

14 And she standeth upon the high places of the city, and crieth to the sons and the daughters of men! Whosoever will, let them turn in hither, let them eat of my bread and take of my oil, and drink of my wine.

15 Forsake the foolish and live, and go in the way of understanding. The veneration of God is the beginning of wisdom, and the knowledge of the holy One is understanding. By me shall your days be multiplied, and the years of your life shall he increased.

CHAPTER 35 2 -Although these words do not occur as they stand verbatim in any version of the Law of Moses as commonly received, the spirit of them certainly is there to be found, and in the original copy of the law (the best portion of which has been recovered by spiritual revelation) the very words also. And this original version was doubtless known to this young lawyer, as it evidently was to Jesus, when afterwards he gave the new law to his disciples on the holy Mount when he was transfigured before them in the company of Moses and Elias, the representatives of the old law, which was itself transfigured into the New. v. 9 -" But one thing is needful " has been interpreted by some, not without reason or probability, as meaning that there were flesh and non-flesh food at the feast, and so he said to Martha, " but one thing (dishes or food) is needful, and Mary hath chosen the better portion." Meaning also, in the spiritual plane, the pure food of heavenly wisdom for the soul. It may have been spoken against luxurious multiplicity of dishes in general.

CHAPTER 36
The Woman Taken In Adultery.
1 ON a certain day, early in the morning, Jesus came again into the temple, and all the people came unto him, and he sat down and taught them.

2 And the scribes and Pharisees brought unto him a woman taken in adultery, and when they had set her in the midst, they said unto him, Master, this woman was taken in adultery, in the very acts. Now Moses in the law commanded us that such should be stoned, but what sayest thou?

3 This they said, tempting him, that they might have to accuse him. But Jesus stooped down, and with his finger

wrote on the ground, as though he heard them not.

4 So when they continued asking him, he lifted up himself, and said unto them, He that is without sin among you, let him cast the first stone at her.

5 And again he stooped down and wrote on the ground. And they which heard it, being convicted by their own conscience, went out one by one, beginning at the eldest, even unto the last; and Jesus was left alone, and the woman standing in the midst.

6 When Jesus had lifted up himself, and saw none but the woman, he said unto her, Woman, where are those thine accusers? hath no man condemned thee? She said unto him, No man, Lord. And Jesus said unto her, Neither do I condemn thee. From henceforth sin no more; go in peace.

7 AND he spake this parable unto certain which trusted in themselves that they were righteous, and despised others: Two men went up into the Temple to pray; the one a rich Pharisee, learned in the law, and the other a taxgatherer, who was a sinner.

8 The Pharisee stood and prayed thus with himself; God, I thank thee, that I am not as other men are, extortioners, unjust, adulterers, or even as this taxgatherer. I fast twice in the week, I give tithes of all that I possess,

9 And the taxgatherer, standing afar off, would not lift up so much as his eyes unto heaven, but smote upon his breath, saying, God be merciful to me a sinner.

10 I tell you, this man went down to his house justified rather than the other; for every one that exalteth himself shall be abased; and he that humbleth himself shall be exalted.

CHAPTER 36 2-6 -This beautiful story, so characteristic of Jesus, has been most unjustifiably pronounced by modern revisers as an interpolation. It is a parable of human life, ever true, never old. "Let him who is without sin amongst you cast the first stone."

CHAPTER 37
The Re-generation Of The Soul.

1 IESUS sat in the porch of the Temple, and some came to learn his doctrine, and one said unto him, Master, what teachest thou concerning life?

2 And he said unto them, Blessed are they who suffer many experiences, for they shall be made perfect through suffering: they shall be as the angels of God in Heaven and shall die no more, neither shall they be born any more, for death and birth have no more dominion over them.

3 They who have suffered and overcome shall be made Pillars in the Temple of my God, and they shall go out no more. Verily I say unto you, except ye be born again of water and of fire, ye cannot see the kingdom of God.

4 And a certain Rabbi (Nicodemus) came unto him by night for fear of the Jews, and said unto him. How can a man be born again when he is old? can he enter a second time into his mother's womb and be born again ?

5 Jesus answered, Verily I say unto you except a man be born again of flesh and of spirit, he cannot enter into the kingdom of God. The wind bloweth where it listeth, and ye hear the sound thereof, but cannot tell whence it cometh or whither it goeth.

6 The light shineth from the East even unto the West; out of the darkness, the Sun ariseth and goeth down into darkness again; so is it with man, from the ages unto the ages.

7 When it cometh from the darkness, it is that he hath lived before, and when it goeth down again into darkness, it is that he may rest for a little, and thereafter again exist.

8 So through many changes must ye be made perfect, as it is written in the book of Job, I am a wanderer, changing place after place and house after house, until I come unto the City and Mansion which is eternal.

9 And Nicodemus said unto him, How can these things be? And Jesus answered and said unto him, Art thou a teacher in Israel, and understandeth not these things? Verily we speak that which we do know, and bear witness to that which we have seen, and ye receive

not our witness.

10 If I have told you of earthly things and ye believe not, how shall ye believe if I tell you of Heavenly things? No man hath ascended into Heaven, but he that descended out of Heaven, even the Son-Daughter of man which is in Heaven.

CHAPTER 37 8 -That our Lord spoke here primarily of a physical rebirth as the great aid of the spiritual re-birth, there can be no doubt, for he distinctly declares he had been telling Nicodemus of "earthly things" in the preceding words, albeit as the analogies and correspondences of spiritual things, as his usual method was. To interpret this dialogue, even as in the A. V., exclusively of the spiritual re-birth, is contrary to the plain meaning of the words.

CHAPTER 38

Jesus Condemneth the Ill-Treatment Of Animals.

1 AND some of his disciples came and told him of a certain Egyptian, a son of Belial, who taught that it was lawful to torment animals, if their sufferings brought any profit to men.

2 And Jesus said unto them, Verily I say unto you, they who partake of benefits which are gotten by wronging one of God's creatures, cannot be righteous: nor can they touch holy things, or teach the mysteries of the kingdom, whose hands are stained With blood, or whose mouths are defiled with flesh.

3 God giveth the grains and the fruits of the earth for food: and for righteous man truly there is no other lawful sustenance for the body.

4 The robber who breaketh into the house made by man is guilty, but they who break into the house made by God, even of the least of these are the greater sinners. Wherefore I say unto all who desire to be my disciples, keep your hands from bloodshed and let no flesh meat enter your mouths, for God is just and bountiful, who ordaineth that man shall live by the fruits and seeds of the earth alone.

5 But if any animal suffer greatly, and if its life be a misery unto it. or if it be dangerous to you, release it from its life quickly, and with as little pain as you can, Send it forth in love and mercy, but torment it not, and God the Father-Mother will shew mercy unto you, as ye have shown mercy unto those given into your hands.

6 And whatsoever ye do unto the Cast of these my children, ye do it unto me. For I am in them and they are in me, Yea, I am in all creatures and all creatures are in me. In all their joys I rejoice, in all their afflictions I am afflicted. Wherefore I say unto you: Be ye kind one to another, and to all the creatures of God.

7 AND it came to pass the day after, that he came into a city called Nain; and many of his disciples went with him, and much people.

8 Now when he came nigh to the gate of the city, behold there was a dead man carried out the only son of his mother, and she was a widow: and much people of the city was with her.

9 And when the Lord saw her, he had compassion on her, and said unto her, Weep not, thy son sleepeth. And he came and touched the bier: and they that bare him stood still. And he said, Young man, I say unto thee, Arise.

10 And he that was esteemed dead sat up, and began to speak. And he delivered him to his mother. And there came an awe upon all: and they glorified God, saying, A great prophet is risen up among us; and God hath visited his people.

CHAPTER 38 -"Death" here, as in other cases, is a state of trance or suspended animation, not easily distinguishable from death even by the physician. A circumstance often leading to the revolting fact of burial alive -a fate, however, not so utterly hopeless in the East, where the dead are buried earth to earth in their shrouds, as in the countries of the West, with the modern and barbarous custom of closed coffins, with covers fastened down, and seven feet of earth over them. It is now ascertained by the more advanced and enlightened medical men, and others, and their official reports, that five per 1,000 must, in these English countries, come to this terrible fate, as there are yet no efforts made to prevent it, as in France, Holland, and other countries, where more rational and civilized practices prevail, and where it is found that five per 1,000 come to life, before actual interment, or show signs of premature burial after, when exhumed.

CHAPTER 39
Seven Parables of the The Kingdom of Heaven.

1 AGAIN Jesus was sitting under the Fig tree, and his disciples gathered round him, and, round them came a multitude of people to hear him, and said unto them, Whereunto shall I liken the Kingdom of Heaven ?

2 AND he spake this parable, saying. The kingdom of Heaven is like to a certain seed, small among seeds, which a man taketh and soweth in his field, but when it is grown it becometh a great tree which sendeth forth its branches all around, which again, shooting downward into the earth take root and grow upward, till the field is covered by the tree, so that the birds of the air come and lodge in the branches thereof and the creatures of the earth find shelter beneath it.

3 ANOTHER parable put he forth unto them, saying, The kingdom of Heaven is like unto a great treasure hid in a field, the which when a man findeth he hideth it, and for joy thereof goeth and selleth all that he hath and buyeth that field, knowing how great will be the wealth therefrom,

4 AGAIN is the kingdom of Heaven like to one pearl of great price, which is found by a merchant seeking goodly pearls, and the merchant finding it, selleth all that he hath and buyeth it knowing how many more times it is worth than that which he gave for it.

5 AGAIN, the Kingdom of Heaven is like unto a woman who taketh of the incorruptible leaven and hideth it in three measures of meal, till the whole is leavened, and being baked by fire, becometh one loaf. Or, again, to one who taketh a measure of pure wine, and poureth it into two or four measures of water, till the whole being mingled becometh the fruit of the vine.

6 AGAIN, the Kingdom of Heaven is like unto a City built foursquare on the top of a high hill, and established on a rock, and strong in its surrounding wall, and its towers and its gates, which lie to the north, and to the south, and to the east, and to the west. Such a city falleth not, neither can it be hidden, and its gates are open unto all, who, having the keys, will enter therein.

7 AND he spake another parable, saying: The Kingdom of Heaven is like unto good seed that man sowed in his field, but in the night, while men slept, his enemy came and sowed tares also among the wheat, and went his way. But when the blade sprung up and brought forth fruit in the ear, there appeared the tares also.

8 And the servants of the householder came unto him and said, Sir, didst thou not sow good seed in thy field, whence then hath it tares? And he said unto them, An enemy hath done this.

9 And the servants said unto him, Wilt thou then that we go and gather them up ? But he said, Nay, lest haply while ye gather up the tares, ye root up the good wheat with them.

10 Let both grow together until the harvest, and in the time of the harvest I will say to the reapers,
Gather up first the tares and bind them in bundles to burn them and enrich the soil, but gather the wheat into my barn.

11 AND again he spake, saying, The kingdom of Heaven is like unto the sowing of seed. Behold a sower went forth to sow, and as he sowed, some seeds fell by the wayside, and the fowls of the air came and devoured them.

12 And others fell upon rocky places without much earth, and straightway they sprang up because they had no deepness of earth, and when the sun was risen they were scorched, and because they had no root they whithered away.

13 And others fell among thorns, and the thorns grew up and choked them. And others fell upon good ground, ready prepared, and yielded fruit, some a hundredfold, some sixty, some thirty. They who have ears to hear let them hear.

CHAPTER 40
Jesus Expounds His Inner Teaching To The Twelve.

1 AND the disciples came and said unto him, Why speakest thou unto the multitude in parables? He answered and said unto them, Because it is given unto you to know the mysteries of the kingdom of Heaven, but to them it is not given.

2 For whosoever hath to him shall be given and he shall have more abundance; but whosoever hath not, from him shall be taken away even that which he seemeth to have.

3 Therefore speak I to them in parables because they seeing see not, and hearing they hear not, neither do they understand.

4 For in them is fulfilled the prophecy of Esaias. which saith, Hearing ye shall hear and shall not understand and seeing ye shall see and shall not perceive; for this people's heart is waxed gross, and their ears are dull of hearing and their eyes they have closed, lest at any time they should see with their eyes, and hear with their ears, and should understand with their heart, and should be converted and I should heal them.

5 But blessed are your eyes for they see, and your ears for they hear, and your hearts for they understand. For verily I say unto you, That many prophets and righteous men have desired to see those things which ye See, and have not seen them, and hear those things which ye hear, and have not heard them.

6 THEN Jesus sent the multitude away and his disciples came unto him, saying, Declare unto us the parable of the field; and he answered and said unto them, He that soweth the good seed Is the Son of man; the field is the world, the good seed are the children of the kingdom, but the tares are the children of the wicked one. The enemy that sowed them is the devil, the harvest is the end of the world, and the reapers are the angels.

7 As therefore the tares are gathered and burned in the fire so shall it be in the end of this world. The Son of man shall send forth his angels, and they shall gather out of his kingdom all things that offend, and them which do iniquity, and shall cast them into a furnace of fire, and they who will not be purified shall be utterly consumed. Then shall the righteous shine forth as the Sun in the kingdom of Heaven.

8 HEAR ye also the parable of the sower. The seed that fell by the wayside is like as when any hear the word of the kingdom, and understand it not, then cometh the wicked one and catcheth away that which was sown in their heart. These are they which received seed by the wayside.

9 And they that received the seed into stony places, the same are they that hear the Word and anon with joy receive it. Yet have they not root in themselves but endure only a while, for when tribulation or persecution ariseth because of the Word, by and by they are offended.

10 They also that received seed among the thorns are they that hear the Word, and the cares of this world and the deceitfulness of riches choke the Word, and they become unfruitful.

11 But they that receive the seed into the good ground, are they that hear the Word and understand it, who also bear fruit and bring forth, some thirty, some sixty, some a hundred fold.

12 These things I declare unto you of the inner circle; but to those of the outer in parables. Let them hear who have ears to hear.

CHAPTER 41
Jesus setteth free the Caged Birds.
The Blind Man who denied that others saw.

1 AND as Jesus was going to Jericho there met him a man with a cage full of birds which he had caught and some

young doves. And he saw how they were in misery having lost their liberty, and moreover being tormented with hunger and thirst.

2 And he said unto the man, What doest thou with these? And the man answered, I go to make my living by selling these birds which I have taken.

3 And Jesus said, What thinkest thou, if another, stronger than thou or with greater craft, were to catch thee and bind thee, or thy wife, or thy children, and cast thee into a prison, in order to sell thee into captivity for his own profit, and to make a living?

4 Are not these thy fellow creatures, only weaker than thou? And doth not the same God our Father-Mother care for them as for thee? Let these thy little brethren and sisters go forth into freedom and see that thou do this thing no more, but provide honestly for thy living.

5 And the man marvelled at these words and at his authority, and he let the birds go free. So when the birds came forth they flew unto Jesus and stood on his shoulder and sang unto him.

6 And the man inquired further of his doctrine, and he went his way, and learnt the craft of making baskets, and by this craft he earned his bread, and afterwards he brake his cages and his traps, and became a disciple of Jesus.

7 AND Jesus beheld a man working on the Sabbath, and he said unto him, Man, if thou knowest not the law in the spirit; but if thou knowest not, thou art accursed and a transgresor of the law.

8 And again Jesus said unto his disciples, what shall be done unto these servants who, knowing their Lord's will, prepare not themselves for his coming, neither do according to his will?

9 Verily I say unto you, They that know their Master's will, and do it not, shall be beaten with many stripes. But they who not knowing their Master's will, do it not, shall be beaten with but few stripes. To whomsoever much is given, of them is much required. And to whom little is given from them is required but little.

10 AND there was a certain man who was blind from his birth. And he denied that there were such things as Sun, Moon, and Stars, or that colour existed. And they tried in vain to persuade him that other people saw them; and they led him to Jesus, and he anointed his eyes and made him to see.

11 And he greatly rejoiced with wonder and fear, and confessed that before he was blind. And now after this, he said, I see all, I know everything, I am god.

12 And Jesus again said unto him, How canst thou know all? Thou canst not see through the walls of thine house, nor read the thoughts of thy fellow men, nor understand the language of birds, or of beasts. Thou canst not even recall the events of thy former life, conception, or birth.

13 Remember with humility how much remains unknown to thee, yea, unseen, and doing so, thou mayest see more clearly.

CHAPTER 41 11-13 -Very applicable to the present age also.

CHAPTER 42
Jesus Teacheth Concerning Marriage The Blessing of Children

1 AND it came to pass that when Jesus had finished these sayings, he departed from Galilee and came into the coasts of Judea beyond Jordan; and great multitudes followed him and he healed them there.

2 The Pharisees also came unto him, tempting him and saying unto him, Is it lawful for a man to put away a wife for every cause?

3 And he answered and said unto them, In some nations, one man hath many wives, and putteth away whom he will for a just cause; and in some, a woman hath many husbands, and putteth away whom she will for a just cause; and in others, one man is joined to one woman, in mutual love, and this is the first and the better way.

4 For have ye not read that God who made them at the beginning, made them male and female, and said, For this cause shall a man or a woman leave

father and mother, and shall cleave to his wife or her husband, and they twain shall be one flesh.

5 Wherefore they are no more twain, but one flesh. What therefore God have joined together, let not man put asunder.

6 They said unto him, Why did Moses then command to give a writing of divorcement? He saith unto them, Moses because of the hardness of your hearts suffered you to put away your wives. even as he permitted you to eat flesh, for many causes, but from the beginning it was not so.

7 And I say unto you, Whosoever shall put away a wife, except it be for a just cause, and shall marry another in her place, committeth adultery. His disciples say unto him, If the case of the man be so with his wife it is not good to marry.

8 But he said unto them All cannot receive this saying, save they to whom it is given. For there are some, celibates who were so born from their mother's womb, and there are some, which were made celibates of men, and there be some, who have made themselves celibates for the kingdom of Heaven's sake. He that is able to receive it, let him receive it.

9 THEN there came unto him little children that he should put his hands on them and bless them, and the disciples rebuked them.

10 But Jesus said, Suffer little children to come unto me and forbid them not, for of such is the kingdom of Heaven. And he laid his hands on them and blessed them.

11 AND as he entered into a certain village, there met him ten men that were lepers, which stood afar off. And they lifted up their voices, and said, Jesus Master, have mercy on us.

12 And when he saw them, he said unto them Go, shew yourselves unto the priests. And it came to pass, that, as they went, they were cleansed. And one of them, when he saw that he was healed, turned back, and with a loud voice glorified God and fell down on his face at his feet, giving him thanks: and he was a Samaritan.

13 And Jesus answering said, Were there not ten cleansed? but where are the nine? There are not found that returned to give glory to God, save this stranger. And he said unto him, Arise, go thy way: thy faith hath made thee whole.

CHAPTER 43

Jesus Teacheth Concerning the Riches of this World and the Washing of Hands and Eating Of Unclean Meats

1 AND, behold, one came and said unto him. Good Master, what good thing shall I do, that I may have eternal life? And he said unto him, Why callest thou me good? there is none good but one, that is, God; but if thou wilt enter into life, keep the commandments. He saith unto him, which be they?

2 Jesus said, What teacheth Moses? Thou shalt not kill, thou shalt not commit adultery, thou shalt not steal, thou shalt not bear false witness, honor thy father and thy mother and thou shalt love thy neighbour as thyself. The young man saith unto him, All these things have I kept from my youth up; what lack I yet?

3 Jesus said unto him, If thou wilt be perfect go and sell that thou hast in abundance, and give to those who have not, and thou shalt have treasure in heaven; and come and follow me.

4 But when the young man heard that saying, he went away sorrowful, for he had great possessions, yea, more than satisfied his needs.

5 Then said Jesus unto his disciple, Verily I say unto you, that the rich man shall hardly enter into the kingdom of Heaven. And again I say unto you, It is easier for a camel to go through the 'gate of the needle's eye" than for a rich person to enter into the kingdom of God.

6 When his disciples heard it, they were exceedingly amazed, saying, Who then can be saved? But Jesus beheld them, and said unto them, For the carnal mind this is impossible, but with the spiritual mind all things are possible.

7 And I say. unto you, Make not to yourselves friends of the Mammon of

unrighteousness that when ye fail they may receive you into their earthly habitations; but rather of the true riches, even the Wisdom of God, that so ye may be received into everlasting mansions which fade not away.

8 Then Peter, said unto him, Behold we have forsaken all and followed thee. And Jesus said unto them, Verily I say unto you, that ye which have followed me, in the regeneration, when the Son of man shall sit in the throne of his glory, ye also shall sit upon twelve thrones, judging the twelve tribes of Israel, but the things of this world it is not mine to give.

9 And everyone that hath forsaken riches, houses, friends, for the kingdom of Heaven's sake and its righteousness, shall receive a hundred fold in the age to come and shall inherit everlasting life. But many that are first shall be last, and many that are last shall be first.

10 AND there came unto him certain of the Scribes and Pharisees who had seen one of his disciples eat with unwashed hands.

11 And they found fault, for the Jews eat not except they have first washen their hands and many other things observe they, in the washing of Cups and of vessels and of tables.

12 And they said, Why, walk not all thy disciples after the tradition of the elders, for we saw one who did eat with unwashed hands?

13 And Jesus said, Well hath Moses commanded you to be clean, and to keep your bodies clean, and your vessels clean, but ye have added things which ofttimes cannot be observed by every one at all times and in all places.

14 Hearken unto me therefore, not only unclean things entering into the body of man defile the man, but much more do evil thoughts and unclean, which pour from the heart of man, defile the inner man and defile others also. Therefore take heed to your thoughts and cleanse your hearts and let your food be pure.

15 These things ought ye to do, and not to leave the others undone. Whoso breaketh the law of purification of necessity, are blameless, for they do it not of their own will, neither despising the law which is just and good. For cleanliness in all things is great gain.

16 Be ye not followers of evil fashions of the world even in appearance; for many are led into evil by the outward seeming, and the likeness of evil.

CHAPTER 44
The Confession of the Twelve.

1 AGAIN Jesus sat near the sea, in a circle of twelve palm trees, where he oft resorted, and the Twelve and their fellows came unto him, and they sat under the shade of the trees, and the holy One' taught them sitting in their midst.

2 And Jesus said unto them, Ye have heard what men in the world say concerning me, but whom do ye say that I am? Peter rose up with Andrew his brother and said, Thou art the Christ, the Son of the living God, who descendeth from heaven and dwelleth in the hearts of them who believe and obey unto righteousness. And the rest rose up and said, each after his own manner, These words are true, so we believe.

3 And Jesus answered them saying, Blessed are ye my twelve who believe, for flesh and blood hath not revealed this unto you, but the spirit of God which dwelleth in you. I indeed am the way, the Truth and the Life; and the Truth understandeth all things.

4 All truth is in God, and I bear witness unto the truth. I am the true Rock, and on this Rock do I build my Church, and the gates of Hades shall not prevail against it, and out of this Rock shall flow rivers of living water to give life to the peoples of the earth.

5 Ye are my chosen twelve. In me, the Head and Corner stone, are the twelve foundations of my house builded on the rock, and on you in me shall my Church be built, and in truth and righteousness shall my Church be established.

6 And ye shall sit on twelve thrones and send forth light and truth to all the twelve tribes of Israel after the Spirit, and I will be with you, even unto the end of the world.

7 But there shall arise after you, men of perverse minds who shall through ignorance or through craft, suppress many things which I have spoken unto you, and lay to me things which I never taught, sowing tares among the good wheat which I have given you to sow in the world.

8 Then shall the truth of God endure the contradiction of sinners, for thus it hath been, and thus it will be. But the time cometh when the things which they have hidden shall be revealed and made known, and the truth shall make free those which were bound.

9 One is your Master, all ye are brethren, and one is not greater than another in the place which I have given unto you, for ye have one Master, even Christ, who is over you and with you and in you, and there is no inequality among my twelve, or their fellows.

10 All are equally near unto me. Strive ye not therefore for the first place, for ye are all first, because ye are the foundation stones and pillars of the Church, built on the truth which is in me and in you, and the truth and the law shall ye establish for all, as shall be given unto you.

11 Verily when ye and your fellows agree together touching anything in my Name, I am in the midst of you and with you.

12 Woe is the time when the spirit of the world entereth into the Church, and my doctrines and precepts are made void through the corruption of men and of women. Woe is the world when the Light is hidden. Woe is the world when these things shall be.

13 AT that time Jesus lifted his voice and said, I thank thee, O most righteous Parent, Creator of Heaven and Earth, that though these things are hidden from the wise and the prudent, they are nevertheless revealed unto babes.

14 No one knoweth thee, save the Son, who is the Daughter of man. None do know the Daughter or the Son save they to whom the Christ is revealed, who is the Two in One.

15 Come unto me all ye that labour and are heavy laden, and I will give you rest. Take my yoke upon you and learn of me, for I am meek and lowly in heart, and ye shall find rest unto your souls. For my yoke is equal and it is easy, my burden is light and presseth not unequally.

CHAPTER 44 4 -In the Syrian Paschito, accepted by all Christians, in the Aramaic, the very language spoken by the Lord while on earth, the passage reads thus -"Thou art Kepha (rock), and on this rock I will build my Church, and the gates of Sheol shall not prevail against her." In the Aramaic original there is but one word for rock or stone, not two petros and petra, as in the Greek -on which anti-Catholic controversialists found their views. Rather do these words, "petros" and "petra," being simply the masculine and feminine forms, denote a duality, viz. Intuition and Intellects conjoined in the one human Individual; or in philosophy, the inductive and the deductive methods, the one of Plato, the other of Aristotle.

CHAPTER 45
Seeking For Signs - The Unclean Spirit.
1 THEN certain of the Scribes and of the Pharisees answered saying, Master we would see a sign from thee. But he answered and said unto them, An evil and adulterous generation seeketh after a sign and there shall no sign be given to it, but the sign of the prophet Jonas.

2 Yea, as Jonas was three days and three nights in the whale's belly, so shall the Son of Man be three days and three nights in the heart of the earth, and after he shall rise again.

3 The men of Nineveh shall rise in judgment with this generation and shall condemn it, because they repented at the preaching of Jonas, and behold a greater than Jonas is here.

4 The Queen of the South shall rise up in the judgment with this generation, and shall condemn it; for she came from the uttermost parts of the earth to hear the wisdom of Solomon, and behold, a greater than Solomon is here.

5 AGAIN he said: When the unclean

spirit is gone out of any, he walketh through dry places seeking rest, and finding none it saith, I will return into my house from whence I came out. And when he is come he findeth it empty, swept and garnished, for they asked not the Good Spirit to dwell within them, and be their eternal Guest.

6 Then he goeth and taketh with him seven other spirits more wicked than himself, and they enter in and dwell there, and the last state of all such is worse than the first. Even so shall it be also unto this wicked generation, which refuseth entrance to the Spirit of God.

7 For I say unto you, whosoever blasphemeth the Son of Man, it shall be forgiven them; but whoso blasphemeth the Holy Spirit it shall not be forgiven them either in this age, or in the next, for they resist the Light of God, by the false traditions of men.

8 WHILE, he yet talked to the people, behold his parents and his brethren and his sisters stood without, desiring to speak with him. Then one said unto him, Behold thy father and thy mother, and thy brethren and thy sisters stand without, desiring to speak with thee.

9 But he answered and said unto him that told him; Who is my father and who is my mother? and who are my brethren and my sisters?

10 And he stretched forth his hand towards his disciples and said, Behold my father and my mother, my brethren and sisters, and my children! For whosoever shall do the will Of my Parent Who is in Heaven the same is my father and my mother, my brother and my sister, my son and my daughter.

11 AND there were some Pharisees, who were covetous and proud of their riches, and he said unto them, Take heed unto yourselves, and beware of covetousness, for a man's life consisteth not in the abundance of things which he possesseth.

12 And he spake a parable unto them, saying, The ground of a certain rich man brought forth plentifully; and he thought within himself, saying, What shall I do, because I have no room where to bestow my fruits?

13 And he said, This will I do; I will pull down my barns, and build greater; and there will I bestow all my fruits and my goods.

14 And I will say to my soul, thou hast much goods laid up for many years, take thine ease, drink and be merry.

15 But God said unto him, Thou fool, this night thy life shall be required of thee; then whose shall those things be, which thou hast provided?

16 So are they that lay up treasures for themselves, and are not rich in good works to them that need, and are in want.

CHAPTER 45 7 -The word "Blasphemy" is derived from the Greek , "blapto" to hinder, retard, obstruct (progress) and "pheme" to speak, thus signifying what is usually known as that conservatism which injures progress and obstructs it. Such a mind is held in bonds by too great deference to authority, or customs, or fashions, or traditions, and closes itself against fresh truths, or the restatement or development of old truths, and thus resists the light which may come through a divine messenger, and commits the "sin against the Holy Spirit" by closing eyes and ears against the higher teaching of God's truth. Such cannot be forgiven i.e. obtain release in this age (incarnation} or the succeeding. For the effects of persistent resistance are age enduring, like a prison house of the mind, and it cannot break the strong walls of prejudice and come forth, being fast bound, and needing, it may be ages, for its emancipation from error long cherished.

CHAPTER 45 10 -Without slighting any believer's love to the B.V.M., these words clearly shew how Jesus regarded Righteousness as relating all true believers to him more than any blood relationship could possibly do.

CHAPTER 46
The Transfiguration on the Mount.
The Giving of the Law.
1 AFTER six days, when the Feast of

Tabernacles was nigh at hand, Jesus taketh the twelve and bringeth them up into a high mountain apart, and as he was praying the fashion of his countenance was changed, and he was transfigured before them, and his face did shine as the sun, and his raiment was white as the light.

2 And, behold, there appeared unto them Moses and Elias talking with him and spake of the Law, and of his decease which he should accomplish at Jerusalem.

3. And Moses spake, saying, This is he of whom I foretold, saying, A prophet from the midst of thy brethren, like unto me shall the Eternal send unto you, and that which the Eternal speaketh unto him, shall he speak unto you, and unto him shall ye hearken, and whoso will not obey shall bring upon themselves their own destruction.

4 Then Peter said unto Jesus, Lord, it is good for us to be here; if thou wilt let us make here three tabernacles; one for thee, and one for Moses, and one for Elias.

5 While he yet spake, behold a bright cloud overshadowed them, and twelve rays as of the sun issued from behind the cloud, and a voice came out of the cloud, which said, This is my beloved Son, in whom I am well pleased; hear ye him.

6 And when the disciples heard it, they fell on their faces and were sore amazed, and Jesus came and touched them and said, Arise and be not afraid. And when they had lifted up their eyes, they saw no man, save Jesus only. And the six glories were seen upon him.

7 AND Jesus said unto them, Behold a new law I give unto you, which is not new but old. Even as Moses gave the Ten Commandments to Israel after the flesh, so also I give unto you the Twelve for the Kingdom of Israel after the Spirit.

8 For who are the Israel of God ? Even they of every nation and tribe who work righteousness, love mercy and keep my commandments, these are the true Israel of God. And standing upon his feet, Jesus spake, saying:

9 Hear O Israel, JOVA, thy God is One; many are My seers, and My prophets. In Me all live and move, and have subsistence.

10 Ye shall not take away the life of any creature for your pleasure, nor for your profit. nor yet torment it.

11 Ye shall not steal the goods of any, nor gather lands and riches to yourselves, beyond your need or use.

12 Ye shall not eat the flesh, nor drink the blood of any slaughtered creature, nor yet any thing which bringeth disorder to your health or senses.

13 Ye shall not make impure marriages, where love and health are not, nor yet corrupt yourselves, or any creature made pure by the Holy.

14 Ye shall not bear false witness against any, nor wilfully deceive any by a lie to hurt them.

15 Ye shall not do unto others, as ye would not that others should do unto you.

16 Ye shall worship One Eternal, the Father-Mother in Heaven, of Whom are all things, and reverence the holy Name.

17 Ye shall revere your fathers and your mothers on earth, whose care is for you, and all the Teachers of Righteousness.

18 Ye shall cherish and protect the weak, and those who are oppressed, and all creatures that suffer wrong.

19 Ye shall work with your hands the things that are good and seemly; so shalt ye eat the fruits Of the earth, and live long in the land.

20 Ye shall purify yourselves daily and rest the Seventh Day from labour, keeping holy the Sabbaths and the Festival of your God.

21 Ye shall do unto others as ye would that others should do unto you.

22 And when the disciples heard these words, they smote upon their breasts, saying: Wherein we have offended. O God forgive us: and may thy wisdom, love and truth within us incline our hearts to love and keen this Holy Law.

23 And Jesus said unto them, My yoke is equal and my burden light, if ye will to bear it, to you it will be easy. Lay no other burden on those that enter into the

kingdom, but only these necessary things.

24 This is the new Law unto the Israel of God, and the Law is within, for it is the Law of Love, and it is not new but old. Take heed that ye add nothing to this law, neither take anything from it. Verily I say unto you, they who believe and obey this law shall be saved, and they who know and obey it not, shall be lost.

25 But as in Adam all die so in Christ shall all be made alive. And the disobedient shall be purged through many fires; and they who persist shall descend and shall perish eternally.

26 And as they came down from the mountain, Jesus charged them, saying, Tell the vision to no man, until the Son of man be risen again from the dead.

27 His disciples asked him, saying, Why then say the scribes that Elias must first come? And Jesus answered and said unto them, Elias truly shall first come and restore all things.

28 But I say unto you, that Elias is come already, and they knew him not, but have done unto him whatsoever they listed. Likewise shall also the Son of man suffer of them. Then the disciples understood that he spake unto them of John the Baptist.

CHAPTER 46 2-7 -The appearance of Moses, to hand over, as it were, the Law and the Dispensation to Jesus, throws a light on the reason of the Transfiguration, which is lost in the accepted version. Elias also appears, so as to make, with Moses, the "two witnesses" required by the law. They recognize Jesus, and witness to him as the great Prophet whom God should raise to succeed and take the place of Moses as the Legislator of the New Dispensation.

The "six glories" may have reference to the six precepts In each table of the law as now given, or more probably to the six attributes of each of the two aspects of the Christ, six feminine and six masculine, as inherent in the Two in One -the " Father-Mother of the age to come." They are referred to in one of

the most ancient gospels.

CHAPTER 46 10-12 -Compare this with the Law as given by Moses in the "Book of the Going Forth of Israel," p. 35, all chiefly negative precepts. In the law given by Christ there are six negative and six positive. The negative is the external Way, in which certain actions are forbidden. The positive the interior way, in which certain duties are enjoined. As the prohibitions are summed up in the negative form of the Golden Rule, so the commands are summed up in the positive form. Had this law been faithfully observed by all Christians, there would have been no divisions or war as now, and this earth would have been a paradise for all. The allegations brought against Christianity and Christ as the cause of strife and bloodshed, are therefore baseless. It is the spirit of selfishness, of perversity, in direct opposition to the Law of Christ, which has been the root of all the evils laid to the charge of Christianity, as he said, "Behold I come to bring peace upon earth, but what if a sword cometh?" Besides the loss of life by wars and intemperance of all kinds, the amount of material wealth wasted yearly in Christian countries, is not only needless, but injurious things, forbidden by the Laws of Christ, is simply appalling.

v. 12 -" Slaughtered " is the truer rendering which has in former editions been wrongly translated "living."

CHAPTER 46 24.-The law as given through Moses "by the ministry of angels," and as the Church of Israel (the typical nation) received it through their Interpreters and Scribes, had no precept forbidding cruelty, oppression, flesh eating, drunkenness, the worship of mammon, impure marriages for money or position, and other vices and crimes which are the cause of nearly all the misery which now afflicts men and women " called to be happy sons and daughters of God Almighty , and which are visited by the holy Law on the children to the third and fourth generation of them that despise it, shewing mercy to all who love it." Nor yet did it include that mutual consideration for each other (positively and negatively) which is summed up in the one commandment of Christ " Love ye one another," not excluding therefrom the creatures which God hath given to be our earth mates and companions.

CHAPTER 47
The Spirit Giveth Life.
The Rich Man and the Beggar.

1 AND when they were come down from the Mount one of his disciples asked him, Master, if a man keep not all these commandments shall he enter into Life? And he said, the Law is good in the letter without the spirit is dead, but the spirit maketh the letter alive.

2 Take ye heed that ye obey from the heart, and in the spirit of love, all the Commandments which I have given unto you.

3 It hath been written, Thou shalt not kill, but I say unto you, if any hate and desire to slay, they are guilty of the law, yea, if they cause hurt or torture to any Innocent Creature they are guilty, But if they kill to put an end to suffering which cannot be healed, they are not guilty, if they do it quickly and in love.

4 It hath been said, Thou shalt not steal, but I say unto you, if any, not content with that which they have, desire and seek after that which is another's or if they withhold that which is just from the worker, they have stolen in their heart already, and their guilt is greater than that of one who stealeth a loaf in necessity, to satisfy his hunger.

5 Again ye have been told, Thou shalt not commit adultery, but I say unto you, if man or woman join together in marriage with unhealthy bodies, and beget unhealthy offspring, they are guilty, even though they have not taken their neighbour's spouse: and if any have not taken a woman who belongeth to another, but desire in their heart and seek after her, they have committed adultery already in spirit.

6 And again I say unto you, if any desire and seek to possess the body of any creature for food, or for pleasure, or for profit, they defile themselves thereby.

7 Yea, and if a man telleth the truth to his neighbour in such wise as to lead him into evil, even thought it be true in the letter, he is guilty.

8 Walk ye in the spirit, and thus shall ye fulfill the law and be meet for the kingdom. Let the Law be within your own hearts rather than on tables of memorial; which things nevertheless ye ought to do and not to leave the other undone for the Law which I have given unto you is holy, just and good, and blessed are all they who obey and walk therein.

9 God is Spirit, and they who worship God must worship in spirit and in truth, at all times, and in all places.

10 AND he spake this parable unto them who were rich, saying, There was a certain rich man, which was clothed in purple, and fine linen, and fared sumptuously every day.

11 And there was a certain beggar named Lazarus, which was laid at his gate, full of sores. And desiring to be fed with the crumbs which fell from the rich man's table; moreover the dogs came and licked his sores.

12 And it came to pass, that the beggar died, and was carried by the angels into Abraham's bosom; the rich man also died, and was buried with great pomp. And in Hades he lift up his eyes, being in torments, and seeth Abraham afar off, and Lazarus in his bosom.

13 And he cried and said, Father Abraham, have mercy on me, and send Lazarus, that he may dip the tip of his finger in water, and cool my tongue, for I am tormented in this place.

14 But Abraham said, Son, remember that thou in thy lifetime receivedst thy good things, and likewise Lazarus evil things: but now he is comforted, and thou art tormented. And thus are the changes of life for the perfecting of souls. And beside all this, between us and you there is a great gulf fixed, so that they which would pass from hence to you cannot; neither can they pass to us, that would come from thence, till their time be accomplished.

15 Then he said, I pray thee therefore, father, that thou wouldest send him to my Father's house; for I have five brethren, that he may testify unto them, lest they also came into this place of torment.

16 Abraham saith unto him, They have Moses and the prophets; let them hear them. And he said, Nay, father Abraham; but if one went unto them from the dead, they will repent.

17 And Abraham said unto him, if they hear not Moses and the prophets, neither will they be persuaded, though one rose from the dead.

CHAPTER 47 2-7 -There is hardly a law that has been given by man or by God, but has been abused and turned into an instrument of oppression by the perversity of man, evading the spirit and insisting on the letter alone.
vv. 10-16 -This parable of Dives and Lazarus is pregnant with deepest teaching, utterly setting aside the narrow dogmas of the sects which have been founded on the traditional interpretation of it in the A. V.

CHAPTER 48
Jesus Feedeth One Thousand with Five Melons.
Heals the Withered Hand On The Sabbath Day.

1 AND it came to pass as Jesus had been teaching the multitudes, and they were hungry and faint by reason of the heat of the day, that there passed by that way a woman on a camel laden with melons and other fruits.

2 And Jesus lifted up his voice and cried, O ye that thirst, seek ye the living water which cometh from Heaven, for this is the water of life, which whoso drinketh thirsteth not again.

3 And he took of the fruit, five melons and divided them among the people, and they eat, and their thirst was quenched, and he said unto them, If God maketh the sun to shine, and the water to fill out these fruits of the earth, shall not the Same be the Sun of your souls, and fill you with the water of life?

4 Seek ye the truth and let your souls be satisfied. The truth of God is that water which cometh from heaven, without money and without price, and they who drink shall be satisfied. And those whom he fed were one thousand men, women and children—and none of them went home a hungered or athirst; and many that had fever were healed.

5 At that time Jesus went on the Sabbath day through the cornfields, and his disciples were an hungered, and began to pluck the ears of corn, and to eat.

6 But when the Pharisees saw it, they said unto him, Behold, thy disciples do that which is not lawful to do upon the Sabbath day.

7 And he said unto them, Have ye not read what David did, when he was an hungered and they that were with him; how he entered into the house of God and did eat the shewbread, which was not lawful for him to eat, neither for them which were with him, but only for the priests?

8 Or have yet not read in the law, how that on the Sabbath days the priests in the Temple do work on the Sabbath and are blameless? But I say unto you, That in this place is One greater than the Temple.

9 But if ye had known what this meaneth, I will have mercy and not sacrifice, ye would not have condemned the guiltless. For the Son of man is Lord even of the Sabbath.

10 AND when he was departed thence, he went into their synagogue. And, behold, there was a man which had his hand withered. And they asked him, saying, is it lawful to heal on the Sabbath days? that they might accuse him.

11 And he said unto them, What man shall there be among you that shall have but one sheep, and if it fall into a pit on the Sabbath day will he not lay hold on it and lift it out? And if ye give help to a sheep, shall ye not also to a man that needeth?

12 Wherefore it is lawful to do well on the Sabbath day. Then saith he to the man, Stretch forth thine hand. And he

stretched it forth, and it was restored whole, like as the other.

13 Then the Pharisees went out and held a council against him, how they might destroy him. But when Jesus knew it, he withdrew himself from thence; and great multitudes followed him, and he healed their sick and infirm, and charged them that they should not make it known.

14 So it was fulfilled, which was spoken by Esaias the prophet, saying, Behold my servant, whom I have chosen; my beloved, in whom my soul is well pleased; I will put my spirit upon him and he shall shew judgment to the Gentiles.

15 He shall not strive nor cry, neither shall any man hear his voice in the streets. A bruised reed shall he not break, and smoking flax shall he not quench till he send forth judgment unto victory. And in his Name shall the Gentiles trust.

CHAPTER 48 l-3 -The feeding of one thousand with five melons is another instance of the love of Jesus to the hungry and thirsty thousand who came to his ministry. He first feeds the body, then instructs the soul. Too often it is the reverse of this among his followers. Hence, "The lack of love causeth many to wax cold."

CHAPTER 49
The True Temple of God

1 AND the Feast of the Passover was at hand. And it came to pass that some of the disciples being masons, were set to repair one of the chambers Of the Temple. And Jesus was passing by, and they said unto him, Master, Sees't thou these great buildings and what manner of stones are here, and how beautiful is the work of our ancestors?

2 And Jesus said, Yea, it is beautiful and well wrought are the stones, but the time cometh when not one stone shall be left on another, for the enemy shall overthrow both the city and the Temple.

3 But the true Temple is the body of man in which God dwelleth by the Spirit, and when this Temple is destroyed, in three days, God raiseth up a more glorious temple, which the eye of the natural man perceiveth not.

4 Know ye not that ye are the temples of the holy spirit? and whoso destroyeth one of these temples the same shall be himself destroyed.

5 AND some or the scribes, hearing him, sought to entangle him in his talk and said, If thou wouldst put away the sacrifices of sheep and oxen and birds, to what purpose was this Temple built for God by Solomon, which has been now forty and six years in restoring?

6 And Jesus answered and said, It is written in the prophets, My house shall be called a house of prayer for all nations, for the sacrifice of praise and thanksgiving. But ye have made it a house of slaughter and filled it with abominations.

7 Again it is written, From the rising of the sun unto the setting of the same, my Name shall be great among the Gentiles, and incense with a pure Offering shall be offered unto me. But ye have made it a desolation with your offerings of blood and used the sweet incense only to cover the ill savor thereof. I am come not to destroy the law but to fulfill it.

8 Know ye not what is written? Obedience is better than sacrifice and to hearken than the fat of rams. I, the Lord, am weary of your burnt offerings, and vain oblations, your hands are full of blood.

9 And is it not written, what is the true sacrifice? Wash you and make you clean and put away the evil from before mine eyes, cease to do evil, learn to do well. Do justice for the fatherless and the widow and all that are oppressed. So doing ye shall fulfill the law.

10 The day cometh when all that which is in the outer court, which pertaineth to blood offerings, shall be taken away and pure worshippers shall worship the Eternal in purity and in truth.

11 And they said, Who art thou that seekest to do away with the sacrifices, and despiseth the seed of Abraham? From the Greeks and the Egyptians hast thou learnt this blasphemy?

12 And Jesus said, Before Abraham was, I Am. And they refused to listen and some said, he is inspired by a demon, and others said, he is mad; and they went their way and told these things to the priests and elders. And they were wrath, saying, He hath spoken blasphemy.

CHAPTER 49 7 -Jesus here disclaims the sacrifices of bleeding victims as being by part of true religion, but rather contrary thereto, adding to the guilt of the offerers. How often religion, so called, is put before morality, and dogma before loving-kindness and mercy.

CHAPTER 50
Christ the Light of the World.
1 THEN spake Jesus again unto them, saying, I am the Light of the world: he that followeth me shall not walk in darkness, but shall have the light of life.
2 The Pharisees therefore said unto him, Thou bearest record of thyself thy record is not true.
3 Jesus answered and said unto them, Though I bear record of myself, yet my record is true: for I know whence I came, and whither I go: but ye cannot tell whence I come, and whither I go.
4 Ye judge after the flesh; I judge no man. And yet if I judge, my judgment is true: for I am not alone, but I come from the Father-Mother who sent me.
5 It is also written in your law, that the testimony of two men is true. I am one that bear witness of myself, John bore witness of me, and he is a prophet, and the Spirit of truth that sent me bareth witness of me.
6 Then said they unto him, Where is thy Father and thy Mother? Jesus answered, Ye neither know me, nor my Parent: if ye had known me, ye should have known my Father and my Mother also.
7 And one said, shew us the Father, shew us the Mother, and we will believe thee. And he answered saying, if thou hast seen thy brother and felt his love, thou hast seen the Father, if thou hast seen thy sister and felt her love thou hast seen the Mother.

8 Far and near, the All Holy knoweth Their own, yea, in each of you, the Fatherhood and the Motherhood may be seen, for the Father and the Mother are One in God.
9 These words spake Jesus in the treasury, as he taught in the temple. And no man laid hands on him; for his hour was not yet come. Then said Jesus again unto them, I go my way, and ye shall seek me, and shall die in your sins; whither I go, ye cannot come.
10 Then said the Jews, Will he kill himself? because he said, Whither I go, ye cannot come. And he said unto them, Ye are from beneath; I am from above; ye are of this world; I am not of this world.
11 I said therefore unto you, that ye shall die in your sins; for if ye believe not that I Am of God, ye shall die in your sins.
12 Then said they unto him, Who art thou? And Jesus said unto them, Even the Same that I said unto you from the beginning.
13 I have many things to say which shall judge you: but the Holy One that sent me is true; and I speak to the world those things which I have heard from above.
14 Then said Jesus unto them, When ye have lifted up the Son of man, then shall ye know that I am sent of God, and that I do nothing of myself; but as the All Holy hath taught me, I speak these things. Who sent me is with me: the All Holy hath not left me alone; for I do always those things that please the Eternal.
15 As he spake these words, many believed on him, for they said, He is a Prophet sent from God. Him let us hear.

CHAPTER 51
The Truth Maketh Free
1 THEN said Jesus to those Jews which believed on him, If ye continue in my word, then are ye my disciples indeed; And ye shall know the truth, and the truth shall make you free.
2 They answered him, We be Abraham's seed, and were never in bondage to any man: how sayest thou,

Ye shall be made free? Jesus answered them Verily, verily, I say unto you, Whosoever committeth sin is the servant of sin. And the servant abideth not in the house for ever: but the Son even the Daughter abideth ever.

3 If the Son therefore shall make you free, ye shall be free indeed. I know that ye are Abraham's seed after the flesh; but ye seek to kill me, because my word hath no place in you.

4 I speak that which I have seen with my Parent and ye do that which ye have seen with your parent. They answered and said unto him, Abraham is our father. Jesus said unto them, If ye were Abraham's children, ye would do the works of Abraham.

5 But now ye seek to kill me, a man that hath told you the truth, which I have heard of God: this did not Abraham. YE do the deeds of your father. Then said they to him, We be not born of fornication; we have one Father, even God.

6 Jesus said unto them, If God were your Parent, ye would love me: for I proceeded forth and came from God; neither came I of myself, but the All Holy sent me. Why do ye not understand my speech? even because ye cannot hear my word.

7 Ye are of your father the devil, and the lusts of your father ye will do. He was a murderer from the beginning, and abode not in the truth, because there is no truth in him.

8 When he speaketh a lie, he speaketh of his own; for he is a liar, and the father of it. And because I tell you the truth, ye believe me not.

9 As Moses lifted up the Serpent in the wilderness, so must the Son and Daughter of man be lifted up, that whosoever gazeth, believing should not perish, but have everlasting life.

10 Which of you convicteth me of sin ? And if I say, the truth, why do ye not believe me? He that is of God heareth God's words: ye therefore hear them not, because ye are not of God.

11 Then answered the Jews, and said unto him, Say we not well that thou art a Samaritan, and hath a demon ? Jesus answered, I have not a demon; but I honour the All Holy, and ye do dishonour me. And I seek not mine own glory, but the glory of God. But there is One who judgeth.

12 And certain of the Elders and Scribes from the Temple came unto him saying, Why do thy disciples teach men that it is unlawful to eat the flesh of beasts though they be offered in sacrifice as by Moses ordained.

13 For it is written, God said to Noah, The fear and the dread of you shall be upon every beast of the field, and every bird of the air, and every fish of the sea, into your hand they are delivered.

14 And Jesus said unto them, Ye hypocrites, well did Esaias speak of you, and your forefathers, sayings This people draweth nigh unto Me, with their mouths, and honour me with their lips, but their heart is far from me, for in vain do they worship Me teaching and believing, and teaching for divine doctrines, the commandments of men in my name but to satisfy their own lusts.

15 As also Jeremiah bear witness when he saith, concerning blood offerings and sacrifices I the Lord God commanded none of these things in the day that ye came out of Egypt, but only this I commanded you to do, righteousness, walk in the ancient paths, do justice, love mercy, and walk humbly with thy God.

16 But ye did not hearken to Me, Who in the beginning gave you all manner of seed, and fruit of the trees and seed having been for the food and healing of man and beast. And they said, Thou speakest against the law.

17 And he said against Moses indeed I do not speak nor against the law, but against them who corrupted his law, which he permitted for the hardness of your hearts.

18 But, behold, a greater than Moses is here! and they were wrath and took up stones to cast at him. And Jesus passed through their midst and was hidden from their violence.

CHAPTER 51 2 -Many people think that perfect freedom is the power to do

wrong as well as right. Such is not
Christ's teaching. Freedom is the power
to do moral good, nothing else : the
other is not freedom, but slavery to the
evil nature. This is the teaching of
Rosmini and of the Franciscans, and is
evidently the teaching of Christ. Other
animals than man have the freedom
essential to their nature, which, if they
are allowed to follow, is a kind of moral
good. In a true state of nature, the other
animals are found innocent, till
corrupted by the cruelty of man.

CHAPTER 52
He Declareth His Pre-Existence.
1 ANOTHER time Jesus said, Verily,
verily, I say unto you, If a man keep my
saying, he shall never see death. Then
said the Jews unto him, Now we know
that thou hast a demon.
2 Abraham is dead, and the prophets;
and thou sayest, If a man keep my
saying, he shall never taste of death. Art
thou greater than our father Abraham,
which is dead ? and the Prophets are
dead: whom makest thou thyself ?
3 Jesus answered, If I honour myself,
my honour is nothing: it is my Father
that honoureth me; of whom ye say, that
he is your God: Yet ye have not known
him; but I now him: and if I should say
I know him not I shall be a liar like unto
you; but I know the All Holy and am
known of the Eternal.
4 Your father Abraham rejoiced to see
my day; and he saw it, and was glad.
Then said the Jews unto him, Thou art
not yet forty five years old, and hast
thou seen Abraham?
5 Jesus said unto them, Verily, verily, I
say unto you, Before Abraham was, I
AM.
6 And he said unto them, The All Holy
hath sent you many prophets, but ye
rose against them that were contrary to
your lusts, reviling some and slaying
others.
7 Then took they up stones to cast at
him: but Jesus was hidden, and went
out of the temple, through the midst of
them, and so again passed unseen by
them.
8 Again when his disciples were with

him in a place apart, one of them asked
him concerning the kingdom, and he
said unto them:
9 As it is above, so it is below. As it is
within, so it is without. As on the right
hand, so on the left. As it is before, so it
is behind. As with the great so with the
small. As with the male, so with the
female. When these things shall be
seen, then ye shall see the kingdom of
God.
10 For in me there is neither Male nor
Female, but both are One in the All
perfect. The woman is not without the
man, nor is the man without the
woman.
11 Wisdom is not without love, nor is
love without wisdom. The head is not
without the heart, nor is the heart
without the head, in the Christ who
atoneth all things. For God hath made
all things by number, by weight, and by
measure, corresponding, the one with
the other.
12 These things are for them that
understand, to believe. If they
understand not, they are not for them.
For to believe is to understand, and to
believe not, is not to understand.

CHAPTER 52 4 -The testimony of those
who saw and knew Jesus as to his age,
has been strangely ignored by writers
of Biblical history and by the Church in
general. This matter is briefly discussed
elsewhere in these Notes, and deserves
the attention of every student and
thoughtful person.

CHAPTER 53
Jesus Healeth The Blind On The
Sabbath.
1 AND at another time as Jesus passed
by, he saw a man which was blind from
his birth. And his disciples asked him
saying, Master, who did sin, this man,
or his parents, that he was born blind?
2 Jesus answered, To what purport is it,
whether this man sinned, or his parents,
so that the works of God are made
manifest in him? I must work the works
of my Parent who sent me, while it is
day; the night cometh, when no man
can work. As long as I am in the world,

I am the Light of the world.

3 When he had thus spoken, he spat on the ground, and mingled clay with the spittle, and he anointed the eyes of the blind man with the clay And said unto him, Go, wash in the pool of Siloam (this meaneth by interpretation, Sent.) He went his way therefore, and washed, and came seeing.

4 The neighbours therefore, and they which before had seen him that he was blind, said, Is not this he that sat and begged? Some said, This is he: others said, He is like him: but he said, I am he.

5 Therefore said they unto him, How were thine eyes opened? He answered and said, A man that is called Jesus made clay, and anointed mine eyes, and said unto me, Go to the pool of Siloam, and wash: and I went and washed, and I received sight.

6 Then said they unto him, Where is he? He said, I know not where he is, that made me whole.

7 Then came to Him certain of the Sadducces, who deny that there is a resurrection, and they asked him saying, Master, Moses wrote unto us, if any man's brother die having a wife and leaving no children, that his brother should take his wife and raise up seed to his brother.

8 Now there were six brethren, and the first took a wife and he died childless: And the second took her to wife and he died childless: And the third, even unto the sixth, and they died also leaving no children Last of all the woman died also.

9 Now in the resurrection, whose of them is she, for the six had her to wife.

10 And Jesus answered them saying, whether a woman with six husbands, or a man with six wives, the case is the same. For the children of this world marry and are given in marriage.

11 But they, which being worthy, attain to the resurrection from the dead, neither marry, nor are given in marriage, neither can they die any more, for they are equal to the angels and are the children of God, being the children of the resurrection.

12 Now that the dead are raised even Moses shewed at the bush, when he called the Lord, the God Abraham, Isaac and Jacob, for he is not the God of the dead, but of the living, for all live unto Him.

CHAPTER 53 3 -The healing of the blind by means of clay mingled with saliva is mentioned by ancient physicians. Vespasian is said to have cured by this means. This shows that Jesus did not hesitate to employ natural remedies, when they were likely to effect their purpose.

CHAPTER 54
The Examination of Him Who was Born Blind.

1 THEN they brought to the Pharisees him that aforetime was blind. And it was the Sabbath day when Jesus made the clay, and opened his eyes.

2 Then again the Pharisees also asked him how he had received his sight. He said unto them, He put clay upon mine eyes, and I washed, and do see.

3 Therefore said some of the Pharisees, This man is not of God, because he keepeth not the Sabbath day. Others said, how can a man that is a sinner do such miracles? And there was a division among them.

4 They say unto the blind man again, What sayest thou of him, that he hath opened thine eyes? He said, He is a prophet.

5 But the Jews did not believe concerning him, that he had been blind, and received his sight, until they called the parents of him that had received his sight.

6 And they asked them, saying, Is this your son, who ye say was born blind? how then doth he now see? His parents answered them and said, We know that this is our son, and that he was born blind; but by what means he now seeth we know not; nor who hath opened his eyes; he is of age; ask him, he shall speak for himself.

7 These words spake his parents, because they feared the Jews; for the Jews had agreed already, that if any

man did confess that he was the Christ he should be put out of the synagogue. Therefore said his parents, He is of age? ask him.

8 Then again called they the man that was blind, and said unto him, Give God the praise: we know that this man is a sinner. He answered and said, Whether he be a sinner or no, I know not; one thing I know, that, whereas I was blind, now I see.

9 Then said they to him again, What did he to thee? how opened he thine eyes? He answered them, I have told you already, and ye did not hear: wherefore would ye hear it again? will ye also be his disciples?

10 Then they reviled him, and said, Thou art his disciple; but we are Moses' disciples. We know that God spake unto Moses: as for this fellow, we know not from whence he is.

11 The man answered and said unto them, Why herein is a marvellous thing, that ye know not from whence he is, and yet he hath opened mine eyes. Now we know that God heareth not sinners;

12 But if any man be a worshipper of God, and doeth his will, him he heareth. Since the world began was it not heard that any man opened the eyes of one that was born blind. If this man were not of God, he could do nothing.

13 They answered and said unto him, Thou wast altogether born in sins, and dost thou teach us? And they cast him out.

14 Jesus heard that they had cast him out; and when he had found him, he said unto him, Dost thou believe on the Son of God ? He answered and said, Who is he, Lord, that I might believe on him.

15 And Jesus said unto him, Thou hast both seen him, and it is he that talketh with thee. And he said, Lord, I believe. And he worshipped him.

16 And Jesus said, For judgment I am come into this world, that they which see not might see; and that they which see might be made blind. And some of the Pharisees which were with him heard these words, and said unto him, Are we blind also?

17 AND Jesus, when he came to a certain place where seven palm trees grew, gathered his disciples around him, and to each he gave a number and a name which he only knew who received it. And he said unto them, Stand ye as pillars in the House of God, and shew forth the order according to your numbers which ye have received.

18 And they stood around him, and they made a body four square, and they counted the number, and could not. And they said unto him, Lord we cannot. And Jesus said, Let him who is greatest among you be even as the least, and the symbol of that which is first be as the symbol of that which is last.

19 And they did so, and in every way was there equality, and yet each bore a different number and the one side was as the other and the upper was as the lower, and the inner as the outer. And the Lord said, It is enough. Such is the House of the wise Master Builder. Foursquare it is, and perfect. Many are the Chambers, but the House is One.

20 Again consider the Body of man, which is a Temple of the Spirit. For the body is one, united to its head, which with it is one body. And it has many members, yet, all are one body and the one Spirit ruleth and worketh in all; so also in the kingdom.

21 And the head doth not say to the bosom, I have no need of thee, nor the right hand to the left, I have no need of thee, nor the left foot to the right, I have no need of thee; neither the eyes to the ears, we have no need of you, nor the mouth to the nose, I have no need for thee. For God hath set in the one body every member as is fitting.

22 If the whole were the head, where were the breasts? If the whole were the belly, where were the feet? yea, those members which some affirm are less honourable, upon them hath God bestowed the more honour.

23 And those parts which some call uncomely, upon them hath been bestowed more abundant comeliness, that they may care one for the other; so, if one member suffers, all members suffer with it, and if one member is

honoured all members rejoice.

24 Now ye are my Body; and each one of you is a member in particular, and to each one of you do I give the fitting place, and one Head over all, and one Heart the centre of all, that there be no lack nor schism, that so with your bodies, your souls and your spirits ye may glorify the All Parent through the Divine Spirit which worketh in all and through all.

CHAPTER 54 1-13 -The wrangling of the Pharisees over this case of healing has its parallels in our times in the Churches which assign to the devil all that they cannot comprehend, and cut out the Healer as a sinner and a heretic, denying the power of God in Man.

CHAPTER 54 14 -This is one of those "parables and dark sayings" of him who spake as never man spake. The words taken literally suggest to the mind a perfect crystal sphere, and by correspondence, a perfect man or woman- in modern phrase "an all rounder," one who views things not from one side only, but from every side. There are many who keep the law in one or more points, but neglect all the rest; or keep it in all points but the one which is against their own particular failing -who "compound for sins they are inclined to, by damming those they have no mind to."

CHAPTER 54 17-20 -The meaning of these words and this action is very obscure, but if we describe the magic square of 7, it seems to make it intelligible as the mystic symbol of him who regarded everything by number and by measure, and which seems to have reference to the period of his mortal life, 49 years, as well as the number of the Council, Cardinals and Priests of the Church universal, 48, presided over by its Head, 49, which the action of Jesus seemed to symbolize, and in a way, foreshadow.

CHAPTER 54 21-24 -Here we have the original words of Christ, from which Paul adopted his simile in Rom. xii., and In 1 Cor. xii.

CHAPTER 55

Christ The Good Shepherd. One With the Father.

1 AT that time there passed by the way a shepherd leading his flock to the fold; and Jesus took up one of the young lambs in his arms and talked to it lovingly and pressed it to his bosom. And he spake to his disciples saying:

2 I am the good shepherd and know my sheep and am known of mine. As the Parent of all knoweth me, even so know I my sheep, and lay down my life for the sheep. And other sheep I have, which are not of this fold; them also must I bring, and they shall hear my voice, and there shall be one flock and one shepherd.

3 I lay down my life, that I may take it again. No man taketh it from me, but I lay it down of myself. I have power to lay my body down and I have power to take it up again.

4 I am the good shepherd; the good shepherd feedeth his flock, he gathereth his lambs in his arms and carrieth them in his bosom and gently leadeth those that are with young, yea the good shepherd giveth his life for the sheep.

5 But he that is an hireling, and not the shepherd, whose own the sheep are not, seeth the wolf coming and leaveth the sheep and fleeth, and the wolf catcheth them and scattereth the sheep. The hireling fleeth because he is an hireling and careth not for the sheep.

6 I am the door: by me all who enter shall be safe, and shall go in and out and find pasture. The evil one cometh not but for to steal and to kill and destroy; I am come that they might have life, and that they might have it more abundantly.

7 He that entereth in by the door, is the shepherd of the sheep, to whom the porter openeth, and the sheep hear his voice, and he calleth his sheep by name, and leadeth them out, and he knoweth the number.

8 And when he putteth forth his sheep he goeth before them and the sheep follow him for they know his voice. And a stranger will they not follow, but

will flee from him, for they know not the voice of strangers.

9 This parable spake Jesus unto them, but they understood not what things they were which he spake unto them. Then said Jesus unto them again, My sheep hear my voice, and I know them, and they follow me and I give unto them eternal life and they shall never perish, neither shall any man pluck them out of my hand.

10 My Parent who gave them me, is greater than all and no man is able to pluck them out of my Parent's hand. I and my Parent are One.

11 Then the Jews took up stones again to stone him. Jesus answered them, Many good works have I shewed you from my Parent, for which of those works do ye stone me?

12 The Jews answered him, saying, For a good work we stone thee not, but for blasphemy, because that thou being a man maketh thyself equal with God. Jesus answered them, Said I that I was equal to God? nay, but I am one with God. Is it not written in the Scripture, I said, Ye are gods?

13 If he called them gods, unto whom the word of God came, and the Scripture cannot be broken, say ye of him, whom the Parent of all hath sanctified and sent into the world. Thou blasphemest; because I said I am the Son of God, and therefore One with the All Parent?

14 If I do not the works of my Parent believe me not, but if I do, though ye believe not me, believe the works, that ye may know and believe that the Spirit of the great Parent is in me, and I in my Parent.

15 Therefore they sought again to take him, but he escaped out of their hands and went away again beyond Jordan, into the place where John at first baptized and there he abode.

16 And many resorted unto him, and said, John, indeed did not miracle, He is the Prophet that should come. And many believed on him.

CHAPTER 55 1 -This beautiful parable bas been sadly mangled in the A.V., and shorn of the opening incident which led to the discourse.

CHAPTER 56
The Raising of Lazarus.

1 Now a certain man was sick, named Lazarus of Bethany, the town of Mary and her sister Martha. (It was that Mary who anointed the Lord with ointment and wiped his feet with her hair, whose brother Lazarus was sick).

2 Therefore his sisters sent unto him saying, Lord, behold he whom thou lovest is sick. When Jesus heard that, he said, This sickness is not unto death, but that the glory of God might be manifest in him. Now Jesus loved Mary and her sister and Lazarus.

3 When he heard that he was sick, he abode two days still in the same place where he was. Then after that, saith he to his disciples, Let us go into Judea again.

4 His disciples said unto him, Master, the Jews of late sought to stone thee and goest thou thither again? Jesus answered, Are there not twelve hours in the day? If any man walketh in the day he stumbleth not, because he seeth the light of this world.

5 But if a man walk in the night, he stumbleth, because there is no light in him. These things said he, and after that he saith unto them, Our friend Lazarus sleepeth, but I go that I may awake him out of sleep.

6 Then said his disciples, Lord if he sleep, he shall do well. And a messenger came unto him saying, Lazarus is dead.

7 Now when Jesus came, he found that he had lain in the grave four days already (Bethany was nigh unto Jerusalem, about fifteen furlongs off). And many of the Jews came to Martha and Mary to comfort them concerning their brother.

8 Then Martha, as soon as she heard that Jesus was coming, went and met him, but Mary sat still in the house. Then said Martha unto Jesus, Lord if thou hadst been here my brother had not died. But I know that even now, whatsoever thou wilt ask of God, God

will give it thee.

9 Jesus saith unto her, Thy brother sleepeth, and he shall rise again. Martha said unto him, I know that he shall rise again, at the resurrection at the last day.

10 Jesus said unto her, I am the resurrection and the life, he that believeth in me, though he were dead yet shall he live. I am the Way, the Truth and the Life, and whosoever liveth and believeth in me shall never die.

11 She saith unto him, Yea, Lord : I believe that thou art the Christ, the Son of God, which should come into the world. And when she had so said she went her way and called Mary her sister secretly saying, The Master is come and calleth for thee. As soon as she heard that she arose quickly and came unto him.

12 Now Jesus was not yet come into the town, but was in that place where Martha met him. The Jews then which were with her in the house and comforted her, when they saw Mary that she arose up hastily and went out, followed her saying, She goeth unto the grave to weep there.

13 Then when Mary was come to where Jesus was, and saw him she fell down at his feet, saying unto him, Lord if thou hadst been here my brother had not died. When Jesus therefore saw her weeping and the Jews also weeping that came with her, he groaned in the spirit and was troubled. And said, Where have ye laid him? They said unto him, Lord, come and see, and Jesus wept.

14 Then said the Jews, Behold, how he loved him! And some of them said, Could not this man which opened the eyes of the blind, have caused that even this man should not have died? Jesus therefore groaning again in himself (for he feared that he might be already dead) cometh to the grave. It was a cave and a stone lay upon it.

15 Jesus said, Take ye away the stone. Martha, the sister of him supposed to be dead, saith unto him, Lord by this time he stinketh, for he hath been dead four days. Jesus saith unto her, Said I not unto thee, that if thou wouldest believe

thou shouldst see the glory of God? Then they took away the stone from the place where Lazarus was laid.

16 And Jesus lifted up his eyes and chanting, invoked the great Name, and said, My Parent, I thank Thee that thou has heard me. And I know that Thou hearest me always, but because of the people which stand by I call upon Thee that they may believe that Thou hast sent me. And when he had thus spoken he cried with a loud voice, Lazarus come forth.

17 And he that was as dead came forth bound hand and foot with graveclothes, and his face was: bound about with a napkin.

18 Jesus said unto them, Loose him and let him go. When the thread of life is cut indeed, it cometh not again, but when it is whole there is hope. Then many of the Jews which came to Mary and had seen the things which Jesus did, believed on him.

CHAPTER 56 -This touching account of the raising of Lazarus is here given as it took place. The verses 13-16 in the Authorized Version are an evident interpolation to magnify the occasion, for, being omitted, the narrative is unbroken and complete without them. As with the daughter of Lazarus, so with Lazarus, he was carried to his burial in a state of trance, indistinguishable from death, and by his friends believed to be dead. At the present time in countries where there are mortuaries or waiting rooms for the dead, it is found that five per thousand recover on their way to burial who otherwise would have been buried alive.

CHAPTER 57
Concerning little Children.
The Forgiveness of Those Who Trespass.
Parable of the Fishes.

1 AT the same time came the disciples unto Jesus, saying, who is the greatest in the kingdom of Heaven? And Jesus called a little child unto him and set him in the midst of them and said, Verily I

say unto you, except ye be converted and become innocent and teachable as little children, ye shall not enter into the kingdom of Heaven.

2 Whosoever therefore shall humble himself as this little child, the same is the greatest in the kingdom of Heaven. And whoso shall receive one such little child in my name receiveth me.

3 Woe unto the world because of offenses! for it must needs be that offences come, but woe to that man by whom the offence cometh. Wherefore if thy lust, or thy pleasure do offend others, cut them off and cast them from thee, it is better for thee to enter into life without, rather than having that which will be cast into everlasting fire.

4 Take heed that ye neglect not one of these little ones, for I say unto you, That in heaven their angels do always behold the Face of God. For the Son of man is come to save that which was lost.

5 How think ye? if a man have a hundred sheep, and one of them be gone astray, doth he not leave the ninety and nine and go into the mountains and seek that which is gone astray? And if so be that he find it, verily I say unto you, he rejoiceth more over that sheep than over the ninety and nine which went not astray.

6 Even so it is not the will of your Parent, Who is in heaven, that one of these little one should perish.

7 AND there were certain men of doubtful mind, came unto Jesus, and said unto him: Thou tellest us that our life and being is from God, but we have never seen God, nor do we know of any God. Canst thou shew us Whom thou callest the Father-Mother, one God? We know not if there be a God.

8 Jesus answered them, saying, Hear ye this parable of the fishes. The fishes of a certain river communed with one another, saying, They tell us that our life and being is from water, but we have never seen water, we know not what water is. Then some among them, wiser than the rest, said: We have heard there dwelleth in the sea a wise and learned Fish, who knoweth all things.

Let us journey to him, and ask him to shew us what water is.

9 So several of them set out to find this great and wise Fish and they came at last to the sea wherein the wise Fish dwelt, and they asked of him.

10 And when he heard them he said unto them, O ye foolish fish that consider not! Wise are ye, the few, who seek. In the water ye live, and move, and have your being; from the water ye came, to the water ye return. Ye live in the water, yet ye know it not. In like manner, ye live in God, and yet ye ask of me, "Shew us God." God is in all things, and all things are in God.

11 AGAIN Jesus said unto them, If thy brother or sister shall trespass against thee, go and declare the fault between thee and thy brother or sister alone; if they shall hear thee, thou hast gained them. But if they will not hear thee, then take with thee one or two more, that in the mouth of two or three witnesses every word may be established.

12 And if they shall neglect to hear them, tell it unto the church, but if they neglect to hear them, tell it unto the church, but if they neglect to hear the church, let them be unto thee as those that are outside the church. Verily I say unto you, Whatsoever ye shall justly bind on earth, shall be bound in heaven, and whatsoever ye shall justly loose in earth, shall be loosed in heaven.

13 Again I say unto you, That if seven, or even if three of you shall agree on earth as touching anything that they ask, it shall be done for them of my Father-Mother Who is in heaven. For where even three are gathered together in my name there I am in the midst of them, and if there be but one, I am in the heart of that one.

14 THEN came Peter to him and said, Lord, how oft shall my brother sin against me and I forgive him? till seven times? Jesus saith unto him, I say not unto thee, Until seven times, but until seventy times seven. For in the Prophets likewise unrighteousness was found, even after they were anointed by the Holy Spirit.

15 And he spake this parable, saying, There was a certain king who would take account of his servants, and when he had begun to reckon, one was brought unto him which owed him ten thousand talents. But forasmuch as he had not to pay, his lord commanded him to be sold, and his wife and children and all that he had, and payment to be made.

16 The servant therefore, fell down and worshipped him, saying, Lord, have patience with me and I will pay thee all. Then the lord of that servant was moved with compassion and loosed him, and forgave him his debt.

17 But the same servant went out and found one of his fellow-servants which owed him a hundred pence, and he laid hands on him and took him by the throat, saying, Pay me that thou owest. 18 And his fellow-servant fell down at his feet and besought him, saying, Have patience with me and I will pay thee all. And he would not, but went and cast him into prison till he should pay the debt.

19 So when his fellow-servants saw what he had done they were very sorry, and came and told unto their lord all that was done.

20 Then his lord, after he had called him, said unto him, O thou wicked servant, I forgave thee all that debt because thou desiredst me; shouldst not thou also have had compassion on thy fellow-servant, even as I had pity on thee. And his lord was wroth, and delivered him to the tormentors, till he should pay all that was due unto him.

21 So likewise shall the heavenly Parent judge you, if ye from your hearts forgive not every one, his brother or sister, their trespasses. Nevertheless, let every man see that he pay that which he oweth, for God loveth the just.

CHAPTER 57 4 -The doctrine of guardian angels receives full support from these words. But the Churches of the so-called Reformation have flung away this consoling and helpful belief, with other doctrines of the Christian Church in all ages, the truth of which
science and occultism are now showing.

CHAPTER 58
Divine Love To The Repentant.

1 Jesus said unto the disciples and to the multitude around them, Who is the son of God? Who is the daughter of God? Even the company of them who turn from all evil and do righteousness, love mercy and walk reverently with their God. These are the sons and the daughters of man who come up out of Egypt, to whom it is given that they should be called the sons and the daughters of God.

2 And they are gathered from all tribes and nations and peoples and tongues, and they come from the East and the West and the North and the South, and they dwell on Mount Zion, and they eat bread and they drink of the fruit of the vine at the table of God, and they see God face to face.

3 Then drew near unto him all the taxgatherers and sinners for to hear him. And the Pharisees and Scribes murmured, saying, This man receiveth sinners and eateth with them.

4 AND he spake this parable unto them, saying, What man of you having an hundred sheep, if he lose one of them doth not leave the ninety and nine in the wilderness, and go after that which is lost, until he find it? And when he hath found it he layeth it on his shoulders, rejoicing.

5 And when he cometh home, he calleth together his friends and neighbours, saying unto them, Rejoice with me, for I have found my sheep which was lost. I say unto you, that likewise joy shall be in heaven over one sinner that repenteth, more than over ninety and nine just persons which need no repentance.

6 Either what woman having ten pieces of silver, if she lose one piece doth not light a candle and seek diligently till she find it? And when she hath found it she calleth her friends and her neighbours together, saying, Rejoice with me, for I have found the piece of silver which I had lost. Likewise, I say

unto you, there is joy in the presence of the angels of God over one sinner that repenteth.

7 AND he also spake this parable, A certain man had two sons, and the younger of them said to his parents, Give me the portion of goods that falleth to me. And they divided unto him their living. And not many days after the younger son gathered all together and took his journey into a fair country, and there wasted his substance with riotous living.

8 And when he had spent all, there arose a mighty famine in that land, and he began to be in want. And he went and joined himself to a citizen of that country, and he sent him into his fields to feed swine. And he would fain have filled his body with the husks that the swine did eat, and no man gave unto him.

9 And when he came to himself he said, How many hired servants of my father's have bread enough and to spare, and I perish with hunger! I will arise and go to my father and mother, and will say unto them. My father and my mother, I have sinned against Heaven and before you, and am no more worthy to be called your son, make me as one of your hired servants.

10 And he arose and came to his parents. But when he was a great way off, his mother and his father saw him and had compassion, and ran and fell on his neck and kissed him. And the son said unto them, My father and my mother, I have sinned against Heaven and in your sight, and am no more worthy to be called your son.

11 But the father said to his servants, Bring forth the best robe, and put it on him, and put a ring on his hand and shoes on his feet, and bring hither the best ripe fruits, and the bread and the oil and the wine, and let us eat and be merry; for this my son was dead and is alive again, he was lost and is found. And they began to be merry.

12 Now his elder son was in the field, and as he came and drew nigh to the house he heard music and dancing. And he called one of the servants and asked what these things meant. And he said unto him, Thy brother who was lost is come back, and thy father and thy mother have prepared the bread and the oil and the wine and the best ripe fruits, because they have received him safe and sound.

13 And he was angry and would not go in, therefore came his father out and entreated him. And he answering, said to his father, Lo, these many years have I served thee, neither transgressed I at any time thy commandments, and yet thou never gavest me such goodly feast that I may make merry with my friends.

14 But as soon as this thy son is come, which hath devoured thy living with harlots, thou preparest for him a feast of the best that thou hast.

15 And his father said unto him, Son, thou art ever with me, and all that I have is thine. It was meet, therefore, that we should be merry and be glad, for this thy brother was dead and is alive again, and was lost and is found.

CHAPTER 58 2 -The charity and comprehensiveness of the true doctrine of Jesus here manifests themselves. It is not a mere narrow creed or belief, but true repentance which merits the forgiveness of God.

CHAPTER 59
Jesus Forewarneth His Disciples. He Findeth Zaccheus.

1 AND Jesus went up into a mountain and there he sat with his disciples and taught them, and he said unto them, Fear not, little flock, for it is your Father's good pleasure to give you the kingdom.

2 Sell that ye have and do that which is good, for them which have not; provide yourselves bags which wax not old, a treasure in the heavens that faileth not, where no thief approacheth, neither moth corrupteth. For where your treasure is, there will your heart be also.

3 Let your loins be girded about, and your lights burning, and ye yourselves like unto men that wait for their lord, when he will return from the wedding that when he cometh and knocketh they

may open unto him immediately.

4 Blessed are those servants whom the lord, when he cometh, shall find watching; verily I say unto you that he shall gird himself and make them to sit down at his table, and will come forth and serve them.

5 And if he shall come in the second watch, or come in the third watch and find them so, blessed rare those servants.

6 And this know, that the guardian of the house not knowing what hour the thief would come, would have watched and not have suffered his house to have been broken through. Be ye therefore ready also, for the Son of man cometh at an hour when ye think not.

7 Then Peter said unto him, Lord, speakest thou this parable unto us, or even to all? And the Lord said, Who then is that faithful and wise steward, whom his lord shall make ruler over his household, to give them who serve their portion in due season?

8 Blessed is that servant whom his lord when he cometh shall find so doing. Of a truth I say unto you, that he will make him ruler over all that he hath.

9 But and if that servant say in his heart, My lord delayeth his coming and shall begin to beat the menservants and maidservants and to eat and drink and to be drunken, the lord of that servant will come in a day when he looketh not for him, and at an hour when he is not aware and will appoint him his portion with the unfaithful.

10 And that servant which knew his lord's will and prepared not himself, neither did according to his will, shall be beaten with many stripes. But he that knew not, and did commit things worthy of stripes, shall be beaten with few stripes. For unto whomsoever much is given, of him shall they much require the less.

11 For they who know the Godhead, and have found in the way of Life the mysteries of light and then have fallen into sin, shall be punished with greater chastisements than they who have not known the way of Life.

12 Such shall return when their cycle is completed and to them will be given space to consider, and amend their lives, and learning the mysteries, enter into the kingdom of light.

13 AND Jesus entered and passed through Jericho. And, behold, there was a man named Zaccheus, which was the chief among the collectors of tribute, and he was rich.

14 And he sought to see Jesus who he was; and could not for the press, because he was little of stature. And he ran before, and climbed up into a sycamore tree to see him: for he was to pass that way.

15 And when Jesus came to the place, he looked up, and saw him, and said unto him, Zacheus, make haste, and come down; for to day I must abide at thy house. And he made haste and came down, and received him joyfully.

16 And when they saw it, they all murmured, saying, That he was gone to be guest with a man that is a sinner.

17 And Zachaeus stood, and said unto the Lord, Behold, Lord, the half of my goods I give to the poor; and if I have taken anything from any man by false accusation, I restore him fourfold.

18 And Jesus said unto him, This day is salvation come to thine house, forsomuch as thou art a just man, thou also art a son of Abraham. For the Son of man is come to seek and to save that which ye deem to be lost.

CHAPTER 59 11-12 -The teaching of our Lord as to cycles, and the unity of life, in many existences, has been suppressed for long ages, but now sees the light, at the end of the cycle.

CHAPTER 60

Jesus Rebuketh Hypocrisy.

1 THEN spake Jesus to the multitude, and to his disciples, saying. The scribes and the Pharisees sit in Moses's seat. All therefore whatsoever they bid you observe, that observe and do; but do not ye after their works: for they say and do not. For they bind heavy burdens and grievous to be borne, and lay them on men's shoulders; but they themselves will not move them with one of their

fingers.

2 But all their works they do for to be seen of men; they make broad their phylacteries, and enlarge the borders of their garments, and love the uppermost rooms at feasts, and the chief seats in the synagogues, and greetings in the markets, and to be called of men, Rabbi, Rabbi.

3 But desire not ye to be called Rabbi: for one is your Rabbi, even Christ; and all ye are brethren. And call not any one father on earth, for on earth are fathers in the flesh only; but in Heaven there is One Who is your Father and your Mother, Who hath the Spirit of truth, Whom the world cannot receive.

4 Neither desire ye to be called masters, for one is your Master, even Christ. But they that are greatest among you shall be your servants. And whosoever shall exalt themselves shall be abased; and they that are humble in themselves shall be exalted.

5 Woe unto you, scribes and Pharisees, hypocrites! for ye shut up the kingdom of Heaven against men: for ye neither go in yourselves neither suffer ye them that are entering, to go in,

6 Woe unto you, scribes and Pharisees, hypocrites" for ye devour widows' houses, and for a pretence make long prayer; therefore ye shall receive the greater damnation.

7 Woe unto you, scribes and Pharisees, hypocrites! for ye compass sea and land to make one proselyte; and when he is made, ye make him twofold more the child of hell than yourselves.

8 Woe unto you, ye blind guides, who say, Whosoever shall swear by the Temple, it is nothing, but whosoever shall swear by the gold of the Temple, he is a debtor! Ye fools and blind; for whether is greater, the gold, or the Temple that sanctifieth the gold?

9 And, Whosoever shall swear by the altar, it is nothing; but whosoever sweareth by the gift that is upon it, he is guilty. Ye fools and blind: for whether is greater, the gift, or the altar, that sanctifieth the gift?

10 Whoso therefore shall swear by the altar, sweareth by it, and by all things

thereon. And whoso shall swear by the Temple, sweareth by it, and by him that dwelleth therein. And he that shall swear by Heaven sweareth by the throne of God, and by the Holy One that sitteth thereon.

11 Woe unto you, scribes and Pharisees, hypocrites! for ye pay tithe of mint and anise and cummin, and have omitted the weightier matters of the law, judgment, mercy, and faith: these ought ye to have done, and not to leave the other undone. Ye blind guides! for ye strain out a gnat, and swallow a camel.

12 Woe unto you, scribes and Pharisees, hypocrites! for ye make clean the outside of the cup and of the platter, but within they are full of extortion and excess. Thou blind Pharisee, cleanse first that which is within the cup and platter, then the outside of them that they may be clean also.

13 Woe unto you, scribes and Pharisees, hypocrites! for ye are like unto whited sepulchres, which indeed appear beautiful outward, but are within full of the bones of the dead and of all uncleanness. Even so ye also outwardly appear righteous unto men, but within ye are full of hypocrisy and make believe.

14 Woe unto you, scribes and Pharisees, hypocrites! because ye build the tombs of the prophets, and garnish the sepulchres of the righteous, and say, If we had been in the days of our fathers, we would not have been partakers with them in the blood of the prophets.

15 Wherefore ye be witness unto yourselves, that ye do as the children of them which killed the prophets. Fill ye up then the measure of your fathers.

16 Wherefore saith holy Wisdom, behold I send unto you prophets, and wise men, and scribes: and some of them ye shall kill and crucify; and some of them shall ye scourge in your synagogues, and persecute them from city to city. And upon you shall come all the righteous blood shed upon the earth, from the blood of righteous Abel unto the blood of Zacharias son of Barachias, who was slain between the temple and the altar. Verily I say unto

you, All these things shall come upon this generation.

17 O Jerusalem, Jerusalem, thou that killest the prophets, and stonest them which are sent unto thee, how often would I have gathered thy children together, even as a hen gathereth her chickens under her wings, and ye would not!

18 Behold, now your house is left unto you desolate. For I say unto you, Ye shall not see me henceforth, till ye shall say, Holy, Holy, Holy, Blessed are they who come in the Name of the Just One.

CHAPTER 60 16 -The same Zaccharias who is mentioned in the beginning as the father of John the Baptist, also the Proto Evangelism attributed to James, the Bishop of Jerusalem.

CHAPTER 61
Jesus Foretells The End Of The Cycle.

1 AND as Jesus sat upon the Mount of Olives, the disciples came unto him privately, saying, Tell us, when shall these things be? and what shall be the sign of thy coming, and of the end of the world? And Jesus answered and said unto them, Take heed that no man deceive you. For many shall come in my Name, saying, I am Christ; and shall deceive many.

2 And ye shall hear of wars and rumours of wars; see that ye be not troubled; for all these things must come to pass, but the end is not yet. For nation shall rise against nation, and kingdom against kingdom; and there shall be famines, and pestilences, and earthquakes, in divers places. All these are the beginning of sorrows.

3 And in those days those that have power shall gather to themselves the lands and riches of the earth for their own lusts, and shall oppress the many who lack and hold them in bondage, and use them to increase their riches, and they shall oppress even the beasts of the field, setting up the abominable thing. But God shall send them his messenger and they shall proclaim his laws, which men have hidden by their traditions, and those that transgress shall die.

4 Then shall they deliver you up to be afflicted, and shall kill you; and ye shall be hated of all nations for my Name's sake. And then shall many be offended, and shall betray one another, and shall hate one another. And many false prophets shall rise, and shall deceive many.

5 And because iniquity shall abound, the love of many shall wax cold. But he that shall endure unto the end, the same shall be saved. And this gospel of the kingdom shall be preached in all the world for a witness unto all nations; and then shall the end come.

6 When ye therefore shall see the abomination of desolation, spoken of by Daniel the prophet, stand in the holy place, (whoso readeth, let him understand) then let them which be in Judea flee to the mountains. Let them which are on the housetop not come down to take anything out of the house; neither let them who are in the field return back to take their clothes.

7 And woe unto them that are with child, and to them that give suck in those days! But pray ye that your fight be not in the winter, neither on the Sabbath day; for there shall be great tribulation, such as was not since the beginning of the world to this time, no, nor ever shall be. And except those days be shortened, there should no flesh be saved; but for the elect's sake those days shall be shortened.

8 Then if any man shall say unto you, Lo, here is Christ, or there; haste not to believe. For there shall arise false Christs, and false prophets, who shall shew great signs and wonders; insomuch that, if it were possible, they shall deceive the very elect. Behold, I have told you before.

9 Wherefore if they shall say unto you, Behold, he is in the desert; go not forth: behold, he is in the secret chambers; haste not to believe. For as the lightening cometh out of the east, and shineth even unto the west; so shall also the coming of the Son of man be. For wheresoever the carcass is, there will the eagles be gathered together.

10 Immediately after the tribulation of those days shall the sun be darkened, and the moon shall not give her light, and the stars shall fall from Heaven, and the powers of the Heavens shall be shaken.

11 And then shall appear the sign of the Son of man in Heaven; and then shall all the tribes of the earth mourn, and they shall see the Son of man coming in the clouds of Heaven with power and great glory. And he shall send his angels with a great sound as of a trumpet, and they shall gather together his elect from the four winds, from one end of Heaven to the other.

12 Now learn a parable of the fig tree; When its branch is yet tender, and putteth forth leaves, ye know that summer is nigh. So likewise ye, when ye shall see all these things, know that it is near, even at the doors. Verily I say unto you, this generation shall not pass till all these things be fulfilled. Heaven and earth shall pass away, but my words shall not pass away.

13 But of that day and hour knoweth no man, no, not the angels of Heaven, but the All Parent only. For as the days of Noe were, so shall also the coming of the Son of man be.

14 For as in the days that were before the flood, they were eating and drinking, marrying and giving in marriage, until the day that Noe entered into the ark and knew not until the flood came, and took them all away; so shall also the coming of the Son of man be.

15 Then shall two be in the field; the one shall be taken, and the other left. Two women shall be grinding at the mill; the one shall be taken, and the other left. Watch therefore: for ye know not what hour your Lord doth come.

16 But know this, that if the guardian of the house had known in what watch the thief would come, he would have watched, and would not have suffered his house to be broken up. Therefore be ye also ready: for in such an hour as ye think not, the Son of man cometh.

17 Who then is a faithful and wise servant, whom his lord hath made ruler over his household, to give them meat in due season?

18 Blessed be that servant, whom his lord when he cometh shall find so doing. Verily I say unto you, That he shall make him ruler over all his goods.

19 But and if that evil servant shall say in his heart, My lord delayeth his coming, and shall begin to smite his fellow servants, and to eat with the glutton, and drink with the drunken.

20 The lord of that servant shall come in a day when he looketh not for him, and in an hour that he is not aware of. And shall appoint him his portion with the hypocrites in the outer darkness with the cruel, and them that have no love, no pity: there shall be weeping and gnashing of teeth.

CHAPTER 61 -All through this chapter the language is highly symbolical, but will present little difficulty to the initiated. v. 12

CHAPTER 62
The Parable Of The Ten Virgins.

1 THEN shall the kingdom of Heaven be like unto ten virgins, which took their lamps, and went forth to meet the bridegroom. And five of them were wise, and five were foolish.

2 They that were foolish took their lamps, and took no oil with them: But the wise took oil in their vessels with their lamps.

3 While the bridegroom tarried, they all slumbered and slept. And at midnight there was a great cry made, Behold, the bridegroom cometh; go ye out to meet him. Then all those virgins arose, and trimmed their lamps.

4 And the foolish said unto the wise, Give us of your oil; for our lamps are gone out. But the wise answered, saying, Not so, lest there be not enough for us and you: but go ye rather to them that sell, and buy for yourselves.

5 And while they went to buy, the bridegroom came; and they that were ready went in with him to the marriage: and the door was shut.

6 Afterwards came also the other virgins, saying Lord, Lord, open to us. But he answered and said, Verily I say

unto you. I know you not.

7 Watch therefore, for ye know neither the day nor the hour wherein the Son of man cometh. Keep your lamps burning.

CHAPTER 62 1 -*This parable of the ten virgins most accurately indicates the oblivion and indifference which shall come on Christians in the last days of the Christian Church -the days of Laodicean indifference, the Seventh or last age.*

CHAPTER 63
Parable Of The Talents

1 He also said: The kingdom of Heaven is as a man traveling into a far country, who called his own servants, and delivered unto them his goods. And unto one he gave five talents, to another two, and to another one; to every man according to his several ability; and straightway took his journey.

2 Then he that had received the five talents went and traded with the same, and made them other five talents. And likewise he that had received two, he also gained other two. But he that had received one went and digged in the earth, and hid his lord's money.

3 After a long time, the lord of those servants cometh, and reckoneth with them. And so he that had received five talents came and brought other five talents, saying, Lord, thou deliveredst unto me five talents; behold, I have gained beside them five talents more. His lord said unto him, Well done, thou good and faithful servant: thou hast been faithful over a few things, I will make thee ruler over many things; enter thou into the joy of thy lord.

4 He also that had received two talents came and said, Lord, thou deliveredst unto me two talents; behold, I have gained two other talents beside them. His lord said unto him, Well done, good and faithful servant; thou hast been faithful over a few things, will make thee ruler over many things; enter thou into the joy of thy lord.

5 Then he which had received the one talent came and said, Lord, I knew thee that thou art an hard man, reaping where thou hast not sown, and gathering where thou hast not strawed. And I was afraid, and went and hid thy talent in the earth; lo, there thou hast that is thine.

6 His lord answered and said unto him, Thou wicked and slothful servant, dost thou tell me that I reap where I sowed not, and gather where I have not strawed? Thou oughtest therefore to have put thy talents to use, with profit, and then at my coming I should have received mine own with usury.

7 Take therefore the talent from him, and give it unto him who hath two talents. For unto every one that hath improved shall be given, and he shall have abundance, but from him that hath not improved, shall be taken away, even that which he hath. And cast yet out the unprofitable servant into outer darkness, for that is the portion he hath chosen.

8 Jesus also said unto his disciples, Be ye approved money-changers of the kingdom, rejecting the bad and the false, and retaining the good and the true.

9 AND Jesus sat over against the Treasury and beheld how the people cast money into the Treasury.

10 And there came a certain poor widow and she threw in two mites, which make a farthing.

11 And He called His disciples unto him and said, Verily I say unto you, that this poor widow hath cast more in than all they which have cast into the Treasure.

12 For all they did cast in of their abundance, but she of her poverty did cast in all that she had, even all her living.

CHAPTER 63 8 -*These words are one of the "last sayings" of Jesus and vividly describe the duty of a Christian Council, so oft neglected.*

CHAPTER 64
Jesus Teacheth In The Palm Circle.

1 JESUS came to a certain fountain near Bethany, around which grew twelve palm trees, where he often went

with his disciples to teach them of the mysteries of the kingdom, and there he sat beneath the shade of the trees and his disciples with him.

2 And one of them said, Master, it is written of old, The Alohim made man in Their own image, male and female created They them. How sayest thou then that God is one? And Jesus said unto them, Verily, I said unto you, In God there is neither male nor female and yet both are one, and God is the Two in One. He is She and She is He. The Alohim—our God—is perfect, Infinite, and One.

3 As in the man, the Father is manifest, and the Mother hidden; so in the woman, the Mother is manifest, and the Father hidden. Therefore shall the name of the Father and the Mother be equally hallowed, for They are the great Powers of God, and the one is not without the other, in the One God.

4 Adore ye God, above you, beneath you, on the right hand, on the left hand before you, behind you, within you, around you. Verily, there is but One God, Who is All in All, and in Whom all things do consist, the Fount of all Life and all Substance, without beginning and without end.

5 The things which are seen and pass away are The manifestations of the unseen which are eternal, that from the visible things of Nature ye may reach to the invisible things of the Godhead; and by that which is natural, attain to that which is spiritual.

6 Verily, the Alohim created man in the divine image male and female, and all nature is in the Image of God, therefore is God both male and female, not divided, but the Two in One, Undivided and Eternal, by Whom and in Whom are all things, visible and invisible.

7 From the Eternal they flow, to the Eternal they return. The spirit to Spirit, soul to Soul, mind to Mind, sense to Sense, life to Life, form to Form, dust to Dust.

8 In the beginning God willed and there came forth the beloved Son, the divine Love, and the beloved Daughter, the holy Wisdom, equally proceeding from the One Eternal Fount; and of these are the generations of the Spirits of God, the Sons and Daughters of the Eternal.

9 And These descend to earth, and dwell with men and teach them the ways of God, to love the laws of the Eternal, and obey them, that in them they may find salvation.

10 Many nations have seen their day. Under divers names have they been revealed to them, and they have rejoiced in their light; and even now they come again unto you, but Israel receiveth them not.

11 Verily I say unto you, my twelve whom I have chosen, that which hath been taught by them of old time is true —though corrupted by the foolish imaginations of men.

12 Again, Jesus spake unto Mary Magdalene saying, It is written in the law, Whoso leaveth father or mother, let him die the death. Now the law speaketh not of the parents in this life, but of the Indweller of light which is in us unto this day.

13 Whoso therefore forsaketh Christ the Saviour, the Holy law, and the body of the Elect, let them die the death. Yea, let them be lost in the outer darkness, for so they willed and none can hinder.

CHAPTER 64 -The occult teaching, in this discourse, of Jesus to his twelve has been handed down in spirit through the ages, but the world is blind and perceives not. See the same teaching in "New Light on Old Truths," founded on this Scripture.

CHAPTER 64 8 -Beneath this profound saying of the Ghost Physician, the student cannot fail to notice the intimate and correct knowledge of the human frame, underlying the spiritual truth, which he enunciated. This knowledge has been claimed by science only some centuries later. The inner self- "alternate sex," in every man and woman, which occasionally manifests itself in the dream state, seems to be no mystery to him.

CHAPTER 65
The Last Anointing by Mary

Magdalene.

1 NOW, on the evening of the Sabbath before the Passover, as Jesus was in Bethany he went to the house of Simon the leper, and there they made him a supper, and Martha served while Lazarus was one of them that sat at table with him.

2 And there came Mary called Magdalene, having an alabaster box of ointment of spikenard, very precious and costly, and she opened the box and poured the ointment on the head of Jesus, and anointed his feet, and wiped them with the hair of her head

3 Then said one among his disciples, Judas Iscariot, who was to betray him, Why is this waste of ointment which might have been sold for three hundred pence and given to the poor? And this he said not that he cared for the poor but because he was filled with jealousy and greed, and had the bag, and bare what was put therein. And they murmured against her.

4 And Jesus said, Let her alone, why trouble ye her? for she hath done all she could; yea, she hath wrought a good work on me. For ye have the poor always with you, but me ye have not always. She hath anointed my body for the day of my burial.

5 And verily, I say unto you, wheresoever this Gospel shall be preached in the whole world there shall also be told this that she hath done for a memorial of her.

6 Then entered Satan into the heart of Judas Iscariot and he went his way and communed with the chief priests and captains how he might betray him. And they were glad and covenanted with him for thirty pieces of silver, the price of a slave, and he promised them, and after that sought opportunity to betray him.

7 And at that time Jesus said to his disciples Preach ye unto all the world, saying, Strive to receive the mysteries of Light, and enter into the Kingdom of Light, for now is the accepted time and now is the day of Salvation.

8 Put ye not off from day to day, and from cycle to cycle and eon to eon, in the belief, that when ye return to this world ye will succeed in gaining the mysteries, and entering into the Kingdom of Light.

9 For ye know not when the number of perfected souls shall be filled up, and then will be shut the gates of the Kingdom of Light, and from hence none will be able to come in thereby, nor will any go forth.

10 Strive ye that ye may enter while the calls is made, until the number of perfected souls shall be sealed and complete, and the door is shut.

CHAPTER 65 2 -It has been supposed by some, and not without some reason from the words of the Gospel, that envy and jealousy, and not greed of money, were the cause of Judas' treachery, because he desired Mary Magdalene, and she had given all her love and devotion to her Master. This inner feeling seems to be concealed beneath the cloak of zeal for the poor. "From that hour he sought to betray him." It is as probable that all three motives urged him, as they do the multitudes nowadays, who grudge magnificence of architecture, music, etc., under the cloak of "unity." "These things ought ye to have done and not left the other undone." But such show their hypocrisy by their reckless contributions to war, and to all manner of pleasures and amusements and luxuries which minister to self. By the spirit of Judas Iscariot are all such led and dominated.

CHAPTER 66

Jesus Again Teacheth His Disciples

1 AGAIN Jesus taught them saying, God hath raised up witnesses to the truth in every nation and every age, that all might know the will of the Eternal and do it, and after that, enter into the kingdom, to be rulers and workers with the Eternal,

2 God is Power, Love and Wisdom, and these three are One. God is Truth, Goodness and Beauty, and these three are One.

3 God is Justice, Knowledge and Purity, and these three are One. God is

Splendour, Compassion and Holiness, and these three are One.

4 And these four Trinities are One in the hidden Deity, the Perfect, the Infinite, the Onely.

5 Likewise in every man who is perfected, there are three persons, that of the son, that of the spouse. and that of the father, and these three are one.

6 So in every woman who is Perfected are there three persons, that of the daughter, that of the bride, and that of the mother and these three are one; and the man and the woman are one, even as God is One

7 Thus it is with God the Father-Mother, in Whom is neither male nor female and in Whom is both, and each is threefold, and all are One in the hidden Unity.

8 Marvel not at this, for as it is above so it is below, and as it is below so it is above, and that which is on earth is so, because it is so in Heaven.

9 Again I say unto you, I and My Bride are one, even as Maria Magdalena, whom I have chosen and sanctified unto Myself as a type, is one with Me; I and My Church are One. And the Church is the elect of humanity for the salvation of all.

10 The Church of the first born is the Maria of God. Thus saith the Eternal, She is My Mother and she hath ever conceived Me, and brought Me forth as Her Son in every age and clime. She is My Bride, ever one in Holy Union with Me her Spouse. She is My Daughter, for she hath ever issued and proceeded from Me her Father, rejoicing in Me.

11 And these two Trinities are One in the Eternal, and are strewn forth in each man and woman who are made perfect, ever being born of God, and rejoicing in light, ever being lifted up and made one with God, ever conceiving and bringing forth God for the salvation of the many.

12 This is the Mystery of the Trinity in Humanity, and moreover in every individual child of man must be accomplished the mystery of God, ever witnessing to the light, suffering for the truth, ascending into Heaven, and sending forth the Spirit of Truth And

this is the path of salvation, for the kingdom of God is within.

13 And one said unto him, Master, when shall the kingdom come? And he answered and said, When that which is without shall be as that which is within, and that which is within shall be as that which is without, and, the male with the female, neither male nor female, but the two in One. They who have ears to hear, let them hear.

CHAPTER 67

Entry Into Jerusalem

1 NOW on the first day of the week when they came nigh to Jerusalem, unto Bethage and Bethany, at the Mount of Olives, he sendeth forth two of his disciples, and saith unto them, Go your way into the village over against you, and as soon as you be entered into it, ye shalt find an ass tied, whereon never man sat, loose him and bring him.

2 And if any say unto you, Why do ye this? say ye that the Lord hath need of him, and straightway they will send him hither.

3 And they went their way and found the ass tied without in a place where two ways met, and they loosed him. And certain of them that stood there said unto them, What do ye, loosing the colt? And they said unto them, even as Jesus had commanded. And they let them go.

4 And they brought the ass to Jesus, and cast their garments upon him, and he sat upon the ass. And many spread their garments in the way, and others cut down branches off the trees and strewed them in the way.

5 And they that went before, and they that followed cried, saying, Hosanna, Blessed art thou who comest in the name of Jova: Blessed be the Kingdom of our ancestor David, and blessed be thou that comest in the name of the Highest: Hosanna in the highest.

6 AND Jesus entered into Jerusalem and into the Temple, and when he had looked round about upon all things, he spake this parable unto them, saying—

7 When the Son of man shall come in his glory and all the holy angels with

him, then shall he sit upon the throne of his glory. And before him shall be gathered all nations, and he shall separate them one from another, as a shepherd divideth his sheep from the goats. And he shall set the sheep on his right hand, but the goats on the left.

8 Then shall the King say unto them on his right hand, Come ye blessed of my Parent, inherit the kingdom prepared for you from the foundation of the world. For I was an hungered and ye gave me food. was thirsty and ye gave me drink. I was a stranger anal ye took me in. Naked and ye clothed me. I was sick and ye visited me. I was in prison and ye came unto me.

9 Then shall the righteous answer him, saying, Lord, when saw we thee an hungered and fed thee? Or thirsty and gave thee drink? when saw we thee a stranger and took thee in? or naked and clothed thee? Or when saw we thee sick, or in prison and came unto thee ?

10 And the King shall answer and say unto them, Behold, I manifest myself unto you, in all created forms; and verily I say unto you, Inasmuch as ye have done it unto the least of these my brethren, ye have done it unto me.

11 Then shall he say also unto them on his left hand, Depart from me ye evil souls into the eternal fires which ye have prepared for yourselves, till ye are purified seven times and cleansed from your sins.

12 For I was an hungered and ye gave me no food, I was thirsty and ye gave me no drink. I was a stranger and ye took me not in, naked and ye clothed me not, sick and in prison and ye visited me not.

13 Then shall they also answer him, saying, Lord, when saw we thee an hungered, or athirst, or a stranger, or naked, or in prison, and did not minister unto thee ?

14 Then shall he answer them, saying, Behold I manifest myself unto you, in all created forms, and Verily I say unto you, Inasmuch as ye did it not to the least of these, my brethren, ye did it not unto me.

15 And the cruel and the loveless shall go away into chastisement for ages, and if they repent not, be utterly destroyed; but the righteous and the merciful, shall go into life and peace everlasting.

CHAPTER 68
The Householder And The Husbandmen.
Order Out Of Disorder.

1 AND Jesus said, Hear another parable: There was a certain householder, who planted a vineyard, and hedged it round about and digged a winepress in it, and built a tower, and let it out to husbandmen and went into a far country.

2 And when the time of the ripe fruits drew near, he sent his servants to the husbandmen that they might receive the fruits of it. And the husbandmen took his servants and beat one, and stoned another, and killed another.

3 Again he sent other servants, more honourable than the first, and they did unto them likewise. But last of all he sent unto them his son, saying, They will reverence my son.

4 But when the husbandmen saw the son, they said among themselves. This is the heir, come let us kill him, and let us seize on his inheritance. And they caught him and cast him out of the vineyard and slew him.

5 When the lord of the vineyard cometh what will he do unto those husbandmen? They say unto him, He will miserably destroy those wicked men and will let out his vineyard to other husbandmen, which shall render him the fruits in their seasons.

6 Jesus saith unto them, Did ye never read in the scriptures, The Stone which the builders rejected, the same is become the head of the Pyramid? this is the Lord's doing and it is marvellous in our eyes?

7 Therefore say I unto you, The kingdom of God shall be taken from you and given to a nation bringing forth the fruits thereof. And whosoever shall fall on this Stone shall be broken, but on whomsoever it shall fall, it will grind them to powder.

8 And when the chief priests and

Pharisees had heard his parables, they perceived that he spake of them. But when they sought to lay hands on him they feared the multitude, because they took him for a prophet.

9 And the disciples asked him afterwards the meaning of this parable, and he said unto them, The vineyard is the world, the husbandmen are your priests, and the messengers are the servants of the good Law, and the Prophets.

10 When the fruits of their labour are demanded of the priests, none are given, but they evilly treat the messengers who teach the truth of God, even as they have done from the beginning.

11 And when the Son of Man cometh, even the Christ of God, they gather together against the Holy One, and slay him, and cast him out of the vineyard, for they have not wrought the things of the Spirit, but sought their own pleasure and gain, rejecting the holy Law.

12 Had they accepted the Anointed One, who is the corner stone and the head, it would have been well with them, and the Building would have stood, even as the Temple of God inhabited by the Spirit.

13 But the day will come when the Law which they reject shall become the head stone, seen of all, and they who stumble on it shall be broken, but they who persist in disobedience shall he ground to pieces.

14 For to some of the angels God gave dominion over the course of this world, charging them to rule in wisdom. in justice and in love. But they have neglected the commands of the Most High, and rebelled against the good order of God. Thus cruelty and suffering and sorrow have entered the world, till the time the Master returns, and taketh possession of all things, and calleth his servants to account.

15 AND he spake another parable, saying: A certain man had two sons, and he came to the first and said, Son, go work today in my vineyard, and he answered and said, I will not, but afterwards he repented and went. And he came to the second and said likewise, and he answered and said, I go, sir, and went not. Whether of them twain did the will of his father?

16 They say unto him, The first, and Jesus saith unto them, Verily I say unto you, That the publicans and harlots go into the kingdom of God before you. For John came unto you in the way of righteousness and ye believed him not, but the taxgatherers and the harlots believed him, and ye, when ye had seen it, repented not afterwards, that ye might believe him.

17 AND the Lord gathered together all his disciples in a certain place. And he said unto them, Can ye make perfection to appear out of that which is imperfect? Can ye bring order out of disorder? And they said, Lord, we cannot.

18 And he placed them according to the number of each in a four-square order, each side lacking one of twelve (and this he did, knowing who should betray him, who should be counted one of them by man, but was not of them)

19 The first in the seventh rank from above in the middle, and the last in the seventh from below, and him that was neither first nor last did he make the Centre of all, and the rest according to a Divine order did he place them, each finding his own place, so those which were above, were even as those which were below, and the left side was equal to the right side, and the right side to the left, according to the sum of their numbers.

20 An he said, See you how ye stand? I say unto you, In like manner is the order of the kingdom, and the One who ruleth all is in your midst, and he is the centre, and with him are the hundred and twenty, the elect of Israel, and after them cometh the hundred and forty and four thousand, the elect of the Gentiles, who are their brethren.

CHAPTER 68 -Again, studying these "dark sayings" so difficult to understand, recourse has been had to certain figures known to the early Gnostics. The Magic Square of 11 has been found wonderfully to explicate, symbolically at least, to the mystical, the meaning of the passage. The form exactly illustrates what the Lord in symbol taught to his disciples of the bringing forth of order out of disorder, perfection out of imperfection, and out of deficiency fulness. Compare the Magic Square given below with the natural square which anyone can form by writing the numbers in consecutive order; the result is at once seen, and may help to arrive at the meaning of this very mystical passage.

CHAPTER 69
The Christ Within, The Resurrection And The Life.

1 As Jesus sat by the west of the Temple with his disciples, behold there passed some carrying one that was dead to burial, and a certain one said unto him, Master, if a man die, shall he live again?

2 And he answered and said, I am the resurrection and the life, I am the Good, the Beautiful, the True, if a man believe in me he shall not die, but live eternally. As in Adam all die, so in the Christ shall all be made alive. Blessed are the dead who die in me, and are made perfect in my image and likeness, for they rest from their labours and their works do follow them. They have overcome evil, and are made Pillars in the Temple of my God, and they go out no more, for they rest in the Eternal.

3 For them that have done evil there is no rest, but they go out and in, and suffer correction for ages, till they are made perfect. But for them that have done good and attained unto perfection, there is endless rest and they go into life everlasting. They rest in the Eternal.

4 Over them the repeated death and birth have no power, for them the wheel of the Eternal revolves no more, for they have attained unto the Centre, where is eternal rest, and the centre of all things is God.

5 AND one of the disciples asked him, How shall a man enter into the Kingdom? And he answered and said, If ye make not the below as the above,

and the left as the right, and the behind as the before, entering into the Centre and passing into the Spirit, ye shall not enter into the Kingdom of God.

6 And he also said, Believe ye not that any man is wholly without error for even among the prophets. and those who have keen initiated into the Christhood, the word of error has been found. But there are a multitude of error which are covered by love.

7 AND now when the eventide was come, he went out unto Bethany with the twelve. For there abode Lazarus and Mary and Martha whom he loved.

8 And Salome came unto him, and asked him, saying, Lord, how long shall death hold sway? And he answered, So long as ye men inflict burdens and ye woman bring forth, and for this purpose I am come, to end the works of the heedless..

9 And Salome saith unto him, Then I have done well in not bringing forth. And the Lord answered and said Eat of every pasture which is good, but of that which hath the bitterness of death, eat not.

10 And when Salome asked when those things of which she enquired should be known, the Lord said, When ye shall tread upon the vesture of shame and rise above desire; when the two shall be one, and the male with the female shall be neither male nor female.

11 And again, to another disciple who asked, When shall all obey the law? Jesus said, When the Spirit of God shall fill the whole earth and every heart of man and of woman.

12 I cast the law into the earth and it took root and bore in due time twelve fruits for the nourishment of all. I cast the law into the water and it was cleansed from all defilements of evil. I cast the law into the fire, and the gold was purged from all dross. I cast the law into the air, and it was made alive by the Spirit of the Living One that filleth all things and dwelleth in every heart.

13 And many other like sakings he spake unto them who had ears to hear, and an understanding mind. But to the

multitude they were dark sayings.

CHAPTER 69 8, 9 -This saying of Jesus is very difficult to the popular mind, as apparently reversing the original injunction in Gen.1-3, "Be ye fruitful and multiply." To understand this, it must be borne in mind that the promise of a Messiah to redeem the world, has, from the earliest times, begotten in the woman of the Hebrew nation, to whom it was specially given, that insatiable desire for offspring, each woman thinking of herself as the possible mother of Him who was to come and save. Jesus, the true Prophet, seeing the tendency to the propagation of the unfit (as we now see) to bring want, misery, squalor, vice and crime, through the inability of most parents to bring them up as they should be, owing to the curse of competition and greed, here proclaimed to Salome, in answer to her query, that he would reverse all this tendency among his followers, and through them, extend this reversal to mankind at large, for He, the desire and hope of nations, having come, there was no longer any supposed necessity or reason for such increase, of which He, the Prophet of God, fully foresaw the evil, in the ages to come, as we now fully experience it.

CHAPTER 70

Jesus Rebukes Peter For His Haste.
1 NOW on the morrow as they were coming from Bethany, Peter was hungry, and perceiving a fig tree afar off having leaves thereon, he came if happily he might find fruit thereon, and when he came he found nothing but leaves, for the time of figs was not yet.
2 And Peter was angry and said unto it, Accursed tree, no man eat fruit of thee hereafter for ever. And some of the disciples heard of it.
3 And the next day as Jesus and his disciples passed by, Peter said unto Jesus, Master, behold, the fig tree which I cursed is green and flourishing, wherefore did not my word prevail?
4 Jesus said unto Peter, Thou knowest not what spirit thou art of. Wherefore

didst thou curse that which God hath not cursed? And Peter said, Behold Lord I was a hungered, and finding leaves and no fruit, I was angry, and I cursed the tree.
5 And Jesus said, Son of Jonas knewest thou not that the time of figs was not yet? Behold the corn which is in the field which groweth according to its nature first the green shoot, then the stalk, then the ear—would thou be angry if thou camest at the time of the tender shoot or the stalk, and didst not find the corn in the ear? And wouldst thou curse the tree which, full of buds and blossoms, had not yet ripe fruit?
6 Verily Peter I say unto thee, one of my twelve will deny me thrice in his fear and anger with curses, and swear that he knows me not, and the rest will forsake me for a season.
7 But ye shall repent and grieve bitterly, because in your heart ye love me, and ye shall be as an Altar of twelve hewn stones, and a witness to my Name, and ye shall be as the Servants of servants, and the keys of the Church will I give unto you, and ye shall feed my sheep and my lambs and ye shall be my vice-gerents upon earth.
8 But there shall arise men amongst them that succeed you, of whom some shall indeed love me even as thou, who being hotheaded and unwise, and void of patience, shall curse those whom God hath not cursed, and persecute them in their ignorance, because they cannot yet find in them the fruits they seek.
9 And others being lovers of themselves shall make alliance with the kings and rulers of the world, and seek earthly power, and riches, and domination, and put to death by fire and sword those who seek the truth, and therefore are truly my disciples.
10 And in their days I Jesus shall be crucified afresh and put to open shame, for they will profess to do these things in my Name. And Peter said, Be it far from thee Lord.
11 And Jesus answered, As I shall be nailed to the cross, so also shall my Church in those days, for she is my

Bride and one with me. But the day shall come when this darkness shall pass away, and true Light shall shine.

12 And one shall sit on my throne, who shall be a Man of Truth and Goodness and Power, and he shall be filled with love and wisdom beyond all others, and shall rule my Church by a fourfold twelve and by two and seventy as of old, and that only which is true shall he teach.

13 And my Church shall be filled with Light, and give Light unto all nations of the earth, and there shall be one Pontiff sitting on his throne as a King and a Priest.

14 And my Spirit shall be upon him and his throne shall endure and not be shaken, for it shall be founded on love and truth and equity, and light shall come to it, and go forth from it, to all the nations of the earth, and the Truth shall make them free.

CHAPTER 70 1-5 -Long has Jesus suffered reproach, for those words so falsely attributed to him, in place of the impulsive Peter, who spoke them, and with whose character they were in full harmony.

CHAPTER 71

The Cleansing Of The Temple

1 AND the Jews' Passover was at hand, and Jesus went up again from Bethany into Jerusalem. And he found in the temple those that sold oxen and sheep and doves, and the changers of money sitting.

2 And when he had made a scourge of seven cords, he drove them all out of the temple and loosed the sheep and the oxen, and the doves, and poured out the changers' money, and overthrew the tables;

3 And said unto them, Take these things hence; make not my Father's House an House of merchandise. Is it not written, My House is a House of prayer, for all nations? but ye have made it a den of thieves, and filled it with all manner of abominations.

4 And he would not suffer that any man should carry any vessel of blood through the temple, or that any animals should be slain. And the disciples remembered that it was written, Zeal for thine house hath eaten me up.

5 Then answered the Jews, and said unto him, What sign shewest thou unto us, seeing that thou doest these things? Jesus answered and said unto them, Again I say unto you, Destroy this temple, and in three days I will raise it up.

6 Then said the Jews, Forty and six years was this temple in building and wilt thou rear it up in three days? But he spake of the temple of his Body.

7 When therefore he was risen from the dead, his disciples remembered that he had said this unto them; and believed the scripture and the word which Jesus had said.

8 But the scribes and the priests saw and heard, and were astonished and sought how they might destroy him, for they feared him, seeing that all the people were attentive to his doctrines.

9 And when even was come he went out of the city. For by day he taught in the Temple and at night he went out and abode on the Mount of Olives, and the people came early in the morning to hear him in the Temple courts.

10 Now when he was in Jerusalem at the passover, many believed in his Name, when they saw the miracles which he did.

11 But Jesus did not commit himself unto them, because he knew all men. And needed not that any should testify of man; for he knew what was in man.

12 And Jesus seeing the passover night was at hand, sent two of his disciples, that they should prepare the upper room where he desired to eat with his twelve, and buy such things as were needful for the feast which he purposed thereafter.

CHAPTER 71 3 - Often translated as slaughterhouse in text having the characteristics of language past and not surviving chiefly on behalf of the revisionists alone.

CHAPTER 71 1-4 -Twice the Lord is said to have performed this symbolic act. Surely, at his return, it will be his first work! For since the first ages till now the spirit of the world ruleth, and mammon is dominant, and every kind of wickedness in the name of religion, zeal for purity, etc.

CHAPTER 72
The Many Mansions In The One House

1 AND as Jesus sat with his disciples in the Garden of Gethsemane he said unto them: Let not your heart be troubled; ye believe in God, believe also in me. In my parent's house are many mansions: if it were not so, I would have told you. I go to prepare a place for you. And if I go and prepare a place for you, I will come again, and receive you unto myself; that where I am, there ye may be also. And whither I go ye know, and the way ye know.

2 Thomas said unto him, Lord, we know not whither thou goest; and how can we know the way? Jesus saith unto him, I am the Way, the Truth, and the Life: no man cometh unto the All Parent but by me, If ye had known me, ye should have known my Parent also: and from henceforth ye know and have seen my Parent.

3 Philip saith unto him, Lord, shew US the All-Parent and it sufficeth us. Jesus saith unto him, Have I been so long time with you, and yet hast thou not known me, Philip? he that hath seen me hath seen the All-Parent; and how sayest thou then, Shew us the All-Parent? Believest thou not that I am in the All-Parent, and the All-Parent in me? the words that I speak unto you I speak not of myself: but the All-Parent who dwelleth in me doeth the works.

4 Believe me, that I am in the All-Parent and the All-Parent in me: or else, believe me for the very works' sake. Verily, verily, I say unto you, They who believe on me, the works that I do shall they do also; and greater works than these shall they do; because I go unto my Parent.

5 And whatsoever ye shall ask in my Name, that will I do, that the All-Parent may be glorified in the Son and Daughter of Man. If ye shall ask anything in my Name, I will do it.

6 If ye love me, keep my commandments. And I will pray the All-Parent, Who shall give you another Comforter, to abide with you for ever; even the Spirit of truth. whom the world cannot receive, because it seeth not, neither knoweth, but ye know; for the Spirit dwelleth with you, and shall be in you.

7 They who have my commandments, and keep them, these are they who love me; and they that love me shall be loved of my Parent, and I will love them and will manifest myself to them.

9 Judas saith unto him, Lord, how is it that thou wilt manifest thyself unto us, and not unto the world? Jesus answered and said unto him, If any love me, they will keep my words: and the Holy One will love them and we will come unto them, and make our abode with them.

10 They that love me not keep not my sayings: and the word which ye hear is not mine, but the All-Parent's who sent me. These things have I spoken unto you, being yet present with you. But the Comforter, who is my Mother, Holy Wisdom, whom the Father will send in my name, she shall teach you all things, and bring all things to your remembrance, whatsoever I have said unto you.

11 Peace I leave with you, my peace I give unto you: not as the world giveth, give I unto you. Let not your heart be troubled, neither let it be afraid. Ye have heard how I said unto you, I go away, and come again unto you. If ye loved me ye would rejoice, because I said, I go unto the All-Parent: for the All-Parent is greater than I.

12 And now I have told you before it come to pass, that, when it is come to pass, ye may believe. Hereafter I will not talk much with you; for the prince of this world cometh, and hath nothing in me.

13 But that the world may know that I love the All-Parent; as the All-Parent gave me commandment, even so I do. Even unto the end.

CHAPTER 72 1 -In the language of the Churches of this day, there is but one mansion in the Father's house, and that is claimed by each of over 300 different sects as its own, and all outside are damned, not for their evil deeds, but because they cannot see as their rulers profess to see.

CHAPTER 73
The True Vine

1 AFTER these things Jesus spake saying unto them: I am the true vine, and my Parent is the vinedresser. Every branch in me that beareth not fruit is taken away: and every branch that beareth fruit, is purged that it may bring forth more fruit.

2 Abide in me, and I in you. As the branch cannot bear fruit of itself, except it abide in the vine; no more can ye, except ye abide in me. I am the tree, ye are the branches: Whoso abide in me and I in them, the same bring forth much fruit; for without me ye do nothing.

3 If any abide not in me, they are cast forth as useless branches, and they wither away; and men gather them, and cast them into the fire, and they are burned. If ye abide in me, and my words abide in you, ye shall ask what ye will, and it will be done unto you.

4 Verily, I am the true Bread which cometh down out of Heaven, even the Substance of God which is one with the Life of God. And, as many grains are in one bread, so are ye, who believe, and do the will of my Parent, one in me. Not as your ancestors did eat manna and are dead; but they who eat this Bread shall live for ever.

5 As the wheat is separated from the chaff, so must ye be separated from the falsities of the world; yet must ye not go out of the world, but live separate in the world, for the life of the world.

6 Verily, verily, the wheat is parched by fire, so must ye my disciples pass through tribulations. But rejoice ye: for having suffered with me as one body ye shall reign with me in one body, and give life to the world.

7 Herein is my Parent glorified, that ye bear much fruit; so shall ye be my disciples. As the All-Parent hath loved me, so have I loved you: continue ye in my love. If ye keep my commandments, ye shall abide in my love; even as I have kept my Parent's commandments, and abide in the spirit of love.

8 These things have I spoken unto you, that my joy might remain in you, and that your joy might be full. This is my commandment, That ye love one another, as I have loved you. Greater love hath no man than this, that a man lay down his life for his friend Ye are my friends, if ye do whatsoever I command you.

9 Henceforth I call you not servants; for the servant knoweth not what his lord doeth: but I have called you friends; for all things that I have heard of my Parent I have made known unto you. Ye have not chosen me, but I have chosen you, and ordained you, that ye should remain: that whatsoever ye shall ask of the All-Parent in my Name, ye may receive.

10 These things I command you, that ye love one another and all the creatures of God. If the world hate you, ye know that it hated me before it hated you. If ye were of the world, the world would love its own: but because ye are not of the world, but I have chosen you out of the world' therefore the world hateth you.

11 Remember the word that I said unto you, The servant is not greater than his lord. If they have persecuted me, they will also persecute you; if they have kept my saying, they will keep yours also. But all these things will they do unto you for my Name's sake, because they know not him that sent me.

12 If I had not come and spoken unto them, they had not had sin: but now they have no cloke for their sin. He that hateth me hateth my Parent also. If I had not done among them the works which none other man did, they had not had sin: but now have they, have seen and hated both me and my Parent. But this cometh to pass, that the word might be fulfilled that is written in their law, They hated me without a cause.

13 But when the Comforter is come, Whom I will send unto you from the All

Parent, even the Spirit of truth, which proceedeth from the Father and the Mother the same shall testify of me: And ye also shall bear witness, because ye have been with me from the beginning.

CHAPTER 73 1-6 -"I am the true Vine, ye are the branches" -in unity with the stem by the continual possession of the One Life, not by mere external unity, valuable as this is, and certainly not by a dead uniformity of opinion in all things. "Tot homines tut sententice."

CHAPTER 74
Jesus Foretelleth Persecutions
1 THESE things have I spoken unto you that ye should be forewarned, They shall put you out of the synagogues; yea, the time cometh, that whosoever killeth you will think that they do God's service. And these things will they do unto you, because they have not known the All Parent, nor me.
2 But these things have I told you, that when the time shall come, ye may remember that I told you of them. And these things I said not unto you at the beginning, because I was with you. But now I go my way to my Parent that sent me; and none of you asketh me, Whither goest thou? But because I have said these thing unto you, sorrow hath filled your heart.
3 Nevertheless I tell you the truth; It is expedient for you that I go away; for if I go not away, the Comforter will not come unto you; but if I depart, I will send my Spirit unto you. And when the Spirit is come, the world shall be reproved of sin and of righteousness, and of judgement.
4 Of sin, because they believe not on me; of righteousness, because I go to my Father, and ye see me no more; of judgement, because the prince of this world is judged.
5 I have yet many things to say unto you, but ye cannot bear them now. Howbeit when the Spirit of Truth is come, she will guide you into all truth: and the same will shew you things to come and shall glorify me: for the same

shall receive of mine, and shall shew it unto you.
6 All things that my Parent hath are mine: therefore said I, that the Comforter shall take of mine and shall shew it unto you. A little while, and ye shall not see me: and again, a little while, and ye shall see me, because I go to the All-Parent. Then said some of his disciples among themselves, What is that he saith unto us, A little while, and ye shall not see me: and again, a little while, and ye shall see me; and, Because I go to the All-Parent?
7 Now Jesus knew that they were desirous to ask him, and said unto them, Do ye enquire among yourselves of that I Said, A little while, and ye shall see me? Verily, verily, I say unto you, That ye shall weep and lament, but the world shall rejoice: and ye shall be sorrowful, but your sorrow shall be turned into joy.
8 A woman when she is in travail hath sorrow, because her hour is come: but as soon as she is delivered of the child, she remembereth no more the anguish, for joy that a man is born into the world. And ye now therefore have sorrow; but I will see you again, and your heart shall rejoice, and your joy no man taketh from you.
9 And in that day ye shall ask me nothing. Verily, verily, I say unto you, Whatsoever ye shall ask my Parent in my name, ye will receive. Hitherto have ye asked nothing in my name: ask and ye shall receiveth that your joy may be full. These things have I spoken unto you in proverbs; but the time cometh, when I shall no more speak unto you in a mystery, but I shall shew you plainly of the All-Parent.
10 At that day ye shall ask in my name: and I say not unto you, that I will pray my Parent for you; For the All-Parent in truth loveth you, because ye have loved me, and have believed that I came out from God. I came forth from God, and am come into the world; again, I leave the world, and go unto my God.
11 His disciples said unto him, Lo, now speakest thou plainly, and speakest no mystery. Now are we sure that thou knowest all things, and needest not that

any man should ask thee: by this we believe that thou comest forth from God.

12 Jesus answered them, Do ye now believe? Be hold, the hour cometh, yea, is now come, that ye shall be scattered, every man to his own home, and shall leave me alone: and yet I am not alone, because the Father is with me.

13 These things I have spoken unto you, that in me ye might have peace. In the world ye shall have tribulation: but be of good cheer; I have overcome the world. Arise, let us go hence.

CHAPTER 75
The Last Paschal Supper

1 AND at evening the Master cometh into the house, and there are gathered with him the Twelve and their fellows; Peter and Jacob and Thomas and John and Simon and Matthew and Andrew and Nathanael and James and Thaddeus and Jude and Philip and their companions (and there was also Judas Iscariote, who by men was numbered with the twelve, till the time when he should be manifested).

2 And they were all clad in garments of white linen, pure and clear, for linen is the righteousness of the saints; and each had the colour of his tribe. But the Master was clad in his pure white robe, over all, without seam or spot.

3 And there arose contention among them as to which of them should be esteemed the greatest, wherefore he said unto them, He that is greatest among you let him be as he that doth serve.

4 And Jesus said, With desire have I desired to eat this Passover with you before I suffer. and to institute the Memorial of my Oblation for the service and salvation of all. For behold the hour cometh when the Son of man shall be betrayed into the hands of sinners.

5 And one of the twelve said unto him, Lord, is it I ? And he answered, He to whom I give the sop the same is he.

6 And Iscariot said unto him, Master, behold the unleaven bread, the mingled wine and the oil and the herbs, but where is the lamb that Moses commanded? (for Judas had bought the lamb, but Jesus had forbidden that it should be killed).

7 And John spake in the Spirit, saying, Behold the Lamb of God, the good Shepherd which giveth his life for the sheep. And Judas was troubled at these words, for he knew that he should betray him. But again Judas said, Master, is it not written in the law that a lamb must be slain for the passover within the gates?

8 And Jesus answered, If I am lifted up on the cross then indeed shall the lamb be slain; but woe unto him by whom it is delivered into the hands of the slayers; it were better of him had he not been born.

9 Verily I say unto you, for this end have I come into the world, that I may put away all blood offerings and the eating of the flesh of the beasts and the birds that are slain by men.

10 In the beginning, God gave to all, the fruits of the trees, and the seeds, and the herbs, for food; but those who loved themselves more than God, or their fellows, corrupted their ways, and brought diseases into their bodies, and filled the earth with lust and violence.

11 Not by shedding innocent blood, therefore, but by living a righteous life, shall ye find the peace of God. Ye call me the Christ of God and ye say well, for I am the Way, the Truth and the Life.

12 Walk ye in the Way, and ye shall find God. Seek ye the Truth, and the Truth shall make you free. Live in the Life, and ye shall see no death. All things are alive in God, and the Spirit of God filleth all things.

13 Keep ye the commandments. Love thy God with all thy heart, and love thy neighbour as thyself. On these hang all the law and the prophets. And the sum of the law is this—Do not ye unto others as ye would not that others should do unto you. Do ye unto others, as ye would that others should do unto you.

14 Blessed are they who keep this law, for God is manifested in all creatures.

All creatures live in God, and God is hid in them.

15 After these things, Jesus dipped the sop and gave it to Judas Iscariot, saying, What thou doest, do quickly. He then, having received the sop, went out immediately, and it was light.

16 And when Judas Iscariot had gone out, Jesus said, Now is the Son of man glorified among his twelve, and God is glorified in him. And verily I say unto you, they who receive you receive me, and they who receive me receive the Father-Mother Who sent me, and ye who have been faithful unto the truth shall sit upon twelve thrones, judging the twelve tribes of Israel.

17 And one said unto him, Lord, wilt thou at this time restore the kingdom unto Israel? And Jesus said, My kingdom is not of this world, neither are all Israel which are called Israel.

18 They in every nation who defile not themselves with cruelty, who do righteousness, love mercy, and reverence all the works of God, who give succour to all that are weak and oppressed—the same are the Israel of God.

CHAPTER 75 1 -Jacob is the same as James -called "the great." Nathanael is Bartholomew. There is no proof that Jude was the same with Thaddeus, as is alleged by some. The number at first seems to have been twelve exclusive, or thirteen (to the world's eye) including Judas Iscariot, till he should manifest his falsity by his treachery, when he went out directly before the holy supper, leaving Jesus with the twelve -the complete number of Apostleship, which, being even, admitted of no one among them being "Master," save Jesus, who was over them.

v. 2 -Whether the appearance of the Master and his disciples in symbolic festal garb may not have been seen only by the spiritual eye of some of the disciples or not, the lesson is the same. Reverence and love of beauty and order are to be seen in God's House -symbols of the glorious garments of that Being Who is the Eternal Mystery and Beauty

manifest in all things.

vv. 15, 16 -That Twelve is the complete number of the Apostleship and that Jesus sat down "with his twelve" at the holy supper before his crucifixion, seems evident from the received gospels, and still more so, from the fragments lately brought to light. Judas Iscariot appears then to have been among the twelve but not of them, therefore before the Eucharistic rite is celebrated "he goes out." If there were any ill omen at all about the number thirteen it would therefore be thirteen as the number of Apostles present, exclusive of the Master and Head. But to thirteen, inclusive of the presiding host, no ill omen could attach, but the reverse.

CHAPTER 76
The Washing Of Feet.
New Commandment.
The Eucharistic Oblation.

1 AND the Paschal Supper being ended, the lights were kindled, for it was even. And Jesus arose from the table and laid aside his garment, and girded himself with a towel, and pouring water into a basin, washed the feet of each of the fourfold Twelve, and wiped them with the towel with which he was girded.

2 And one of them said, Lord, thou shalt not wash my feet. And Jesus said, If I wash thee not thou hast no part with me. And he answered, Lord, wash not my feet only, but my head and my hands.

3 And he said unto him, They who have come out of the bath, need not but to wash their feet, and they are clean every whit.

4 AND then putting on the overgarment of pure white linen without spot or seam, he sat at the table and said unto them, Know ye what I have done unto you? Ye call me Lord and Master, and if then your Lord and Master have washed your feet, ye ought also to wash one another's feet. For I have given this example, that as I have done unto you, so also should ye do unto others.

5 A new commandment I give unto you, that ye love one another and all the

creatures of God. Love is the fulfilling of the law. Love is of God, and God is love. Whoso loveth not, knoweth not God.

6 Now ye are clean through the word which I have spoken unto you. By this shall all men know that ye are my disciples if ye have love one to another and shew mercy and love to all creatures of God, especially to those that are weak and oppressed and suffer wrong. For the whole earth is filled with dark places of cruelty, and with pain and sorrow, by the selfishness and ignorance of man.

7 I say unto you, Love your enemies, bless them that curse you, and give them light for their darkness and let the spirit of love dwell within your hearts, and abound unto all. And again I say unto you, Love one another, and all the creation of God And when he had finished, they said, Blessed be God.

8 Then he lifted up his voice, and they joined him, saying, As the hart panteth after the water brooks, so panteth my soul after thee, O God. And when they had ended, one brought unto him a censer full of live coals, and he cast frankincense thereon even the frankincense which his mother had given him in the day of his manifestation, and the sweetness of the odour filled the room.

9 Then Jesus, placing before him the platter, and behind it the chalice, and lifting up his eyes to heaven, gave thanks for the goodness of God in all things and unto all, and after that he took in his hands the unleavened bread, and blessed it; the wine likewise mingled with water and blessed it; chanting the Invocation of the Holy Name the Sevenfold, calling upon the thrice Holy Father-Mother in Heaven to send down the Holy Spirit and make the bread to be his body, even the Body of the Christ, and the fruit of the vine to be his Blood, even the Blood of the Christ, for the remission of sins and everlasting life, to all who obey the gospel.

10 Then lifting up the Oblation towards heaven, he said, The Son who is also the Daughter of man is lifted up from the earth, and I shall draw all men unto me; then it shall be known of the people that I am sent from God.

11 These things being done, Jesus spake these words, lifting his eyes to heaven. Abba Amma, the hour is come, Glorify thy Son that Thy Son may be glorified in thee.

12 Yea, Thou hast glorified me, Thou hast filled my heart with fire, Thou hast set lamps on my right hand and on my left, so that no part of my being should be without light. Thy Love shineth on my right hand and on my left, so that no part of my being should be without light. Thy Love shineth on my right hand, and Thy Wisdom on my left. Thy Love, Thy Wisdom, Thy Power are manifest in me.

13 I have glorified Thee on earth, I have finished the work Thou gavest me to do. Holy One, keep through Thy Name the Twelve and their fellows whom Thou hast given me, that they may be One even as we are One. Whilst I was with them in the world I kept them in Thy Name, and none of them is lost, for he who went out from us, was not of us, nevertheless, I pray for him that he may be restored. Father-Mother, forgive him, for he knoweth not what he doeth.

14 And now come I to Thee, and these things I speak in the world that they may have my joy fulfilled in themselves. I give them Thy word, and the world hath them, because they are not of the world, even as I am not of the world.

15 I pray not that Thou shouldst take them out of the world, but that Thou shouldst keep them from evil, whilst yet in the world, Sanctify them through Thy truth. Thy word is Truth. As thou sendest me into the world, so also I send them into the world, and for their sakes I sanctify myself, that they also may be sanctified through the Truth.

16 Neither pray I for these alone, but for all that shall be added to their number, and for the Two and Seventy also whom I sent forth, yea, and for all that shall believe in the Truth through Thy word, that they also may be one as Thou Most Holy art in me and I in

Thee, that they may also be one in Thee, that the world may know that Thou hast sent me.

17 Holy Parent, I will also, that they whom Thou hast given me, yea all who live, be with me where I am, that they may partake of my glory which thou givest me, for Thou lovest me in all, and all in me, from before the foundations of the world.

18 The world hath not known Thee in Thy righteousness, but I know Thee, and these know that Thou hast sent me.

19 And I have declared unto them Thy Name that the love wherewith Thou hast loved me may be in them, and that from them it may abound, even unto all Thy creatures, yea, even unto all These words being ended, they all lifted up their voices with him, and prayed as he taught them, saying:

20 Our Father-Mother: Who art above and within. Hallowed be Thy sacred Name, in Biune Trinity. In Wisdom, Love and Equity Thy Kingdom come to all. Thy holy Will be done always, as in Heaven, so on Earth. Give us day by day to partake of Thy holy Bread, and the fruit of Thy living Vine. As we seek to perfect others, so perfect us in Thy Christ. Shew upon us Thy goodness, that to others we many shew the same. In the hour of trial, deliver us from evil.

21 For Thine are the Kingdom, the Power and the Glory: From the Ages of ages, Now, and to the Ages of ages. Amen.

22 THEN our Master taketh the holy Bread and breaketh it, and the Fruit of the Vine also, and mingleth it, and having blessed and hallowed both, and casting a fragment of the Bread into the Cup, he blessed the holy Union.

23 Then he giveth the bread which he had hallowed to his disciples saying, Eat ye, for this is my Body, even the Body of the Christ, which is given for the Salvation of the body and the soul.

24 Likewise he giveth unto them the fruit of the Vine which he had blessed saying unto them, Drink ye, for this is my Blood, even the Blood of the Christ which is shed for you and for many, for the Salvation of the Soul and the Body.

25 And when all had partaken, he said unto them, As oft as ye assemble together in my Name, make this Oblation for a Memorial of me, even the Bread of everlasting life and the Wine of eternal salvation' and eat and drink thereof with pure heart, and ye shall receive of the Substance and the Life of God, which dwelleth in me.

26 And when they had sung a hymn, Jesus stood up in the midst of his apostles, and going to him who was their Centre, as in a solemn dance, they rejoiced in him. And then he went out to the Mount of Olives, and his disciples followed him.

27 Now Judas Iscariot had gone to the house of Caiaphas and said unto him, Behold he has celebrated the Passover, within the gates, with the Mazza in place of the lamb. I indeed bought a lamb, but he forbade that it should be killed, and lo, the man of whom I bought it is witness.

28 And Caiaphas rent his clothes and said, Truly this is a Passover of the law of Moses. He hath done the deed which is worthy of death, for it is a weighty transgression of the law. What need of further witness? Yea, even now two robbers have broken into the Temple and stolen the book of the law, and this is the end of his teaching. Let us tell these things to the people who follow him, for they will fear the authority of the law.

29 And one that was standing by as Judas came out, said unto him, Thinkest thou that they will put him to death?

30 And Judas said, Nay, for he will do some mighty work to deliver himself out of their hands, even as when they of the synagogue in Capernaum rose up against him, and brought him to the brow of the hill that they might throw him down headlong, and did he not pass safely through their midst? He will surely escape them now also, and proclaim himself openly and set up the Kingdom whereof he spake.

CHAPTER 76 4 -There are two other alternative versions of these circumstances of the last supper in the

A. V.-First, that of St. John who, in the received version, expressly affirms that Jesus was crucified on the very day of the Passover and consequently the Eucharist was instituted the day before and not on the feast day Itself' and the Passover was on the morrow after the trial on the day of the crucifixion. Secondly, that of the three other gospels, which all affirm that the Eucharist was Instituted on the Passover the pascal lamb was slain. If the latter, it must be remembered that the Essenes (of whom Jesus was apparently one), were by Jewish regulation allowed a separate table at which no lamb or other flesh-meat was eaten, as they were vowed abstainers from blood sacrifices and the eating of flesh. If the former it was not the Passover at all, and Jesus was not bound as a Jew to eat of a lamb. In neither of these cases, therefore, was Jesus under the alleged necessity of killing a lamb and eating of flesh-meat in order to fulfill the law. In any case the causing of an innocent lamb to be killed and the eating of such is contrary to all that is known of the character of Jesus the Christ, whose tender love extends to all creatures. If Jesus was not an Essene, then nothing can be said against the accuracy of this version of the holy supper, and the charges brought against him in the account of the trial as now given by the Spirit.

v. 9 -"Bread," i.e. unleavened cakes of pure meal such as in use at the Passover. "Wine," here and through the Gospels, as used by Jesus and His disciples, means "the fruit of the Vine." which is pure wine mingled with four or two parts of pure water, the latter mystically representing the humanity, and the former the Divine Spirit. The strong fermented wine of modem use was never used on such festive occasions, nor even generally, except thus mingled with water. It is to be noted that the Saviour consecrated the Eucharist by Invocation of the Holy Spirit, and this has been faithfully followed by all Churches of the East, the words of institution being merely

recited before, as a historical preamble, giving the authority for the action, and in no case as the words of consecration, according to the corrupt use of the West.

v. 13 -In the received Gospel Judas is consigned to eternal perdition, but it appears rather that he who was all compassion and prayed for his murderers, prayed also for the man who was overmastered by his passions, blinded by envy, jealousy, greed of money, or, as some say, by desire to push matters to their conclusion, and procure some decisive miracle that would establish the claim of his Master to set up a temporal kingdom.

v. 26 -It is not stated whether there was any musical accompaniment, as is usual in the religious dances and processions of the East, but if so it was probably of the simplest, such as the Pipe, used on such occasions.

v. 27 -The Mazza, or unleavened cake, to which may the word "Mass" be traced as applied to the Eucharist, or "Breaking of Bread" -but preferable perhaps is the interpretation of "ite missa est " -the oblation (= prayer) is gone, "sent up."

v. 30 -Here was perhaps more probably the sole motive actuating Judas -his ambition- the desire to see a miracle, and the early sovereignty set up before the time.

CHAPTER 77

The Agony In The Garden

1 AND as they went to the Mount of Olives, Jesus said unto them, All ye shall be offended because of me this night; for it is written, I will smite the shepherd, and the sheep of the flock shall be scattered abroad. But after I am risen again, I will go before you into Galilee.

2 Simon answered and said unto him, Though all men shall be offended because of thee, yet will I never be offended. And the Lord said, Simon, Simon, behold Satan hath desired to have you, that he may sift you as wheat. But I have prayed for thee that thy faith fail not; and when thou art converted,

strengthen thy brethren.

3 And he said unto him, Lord, I am ready to go with thee, both unto prison and unto death. And Jesus said, I tell thee, Simon, the cock shall not crow this night, before that thou shalt thrice deny that thou knowest me.

4 Then cometh Jesus with them, having crossed the brook Kedron, unto the garden called Gethsemane, and saith unto the disciples, Sit ye here while I go and pray yonder. (Judas also, which betrayed him, knew the place, for Jesus ofttimes resorted thither with his disciples.)

5 Then saith he unto them, My soul is exceeding sorrowful, even unto death; tarry ye here, and watch with me.

6 And he went little farther and fell on his face and prayed, saying, O my Father-Mother, if it be possible, let this cup pass from me; nevertheless not as I will, but as Thou wilt.

7 And there appeared an angel unto him, from heaven strengthening him. And he cometh unto the disciples and finding them asleep, saith unto Peter, What, could ye not watch with me one hour?

8 Watch and pray that ye enter not into temptation: the spirit indeed is willing, but the flesh is weak.

9 He went away again a second time and prayed, saying, O my Father-Mother, if this cup may not pass away from me, except I drink it, Thy will be done.

10 And being in an agony he prayed more earnestly: and his sweat was as it were great drops of blood falling to the ground.

11 And he came and found them asleep again, for their eyes were heavy.

12 And he left them and went away again and prayed a third time, saying, O my Father-Mother, not my will but Thine be done, in earth as it is in heaven.

13 Then cometh he unto his disciples and saith unto them, Sleep on now, and take your rest; behold, the hour is at hand, and the Son of man is betrayed into the hands of sinners. Rise, let us be going: behold, he is at hand that doth betray me.

CHAPTER 77 2 - Here the Lord addresses Simon, not Peter. In the A. V. confusion has arisen owing to the same name being given to two Apostles, and Peter is made to reply. It does not seem likely that one who thrice betrayed the Lord should by him have been placed in the highest authority, as it subsequently appears that Peter was.

CHAPTER 78
The Betrayal by Judas Iscariot

1 AND it came to pass while Jesus yet spake, behold there came a multitude, and Judas that was called Iscariot went before them. For Judas, having received a band of men and officers from the chief priests and Pharisees, came thither with lanterns and torches and weapons.

2 Jesus therefore, knowing all things that should a come upon him, went forth and said unto them, Whom seek ye? They answered him, Jesus of Nazareth. Jesus saith unto them, I am he.

3 As soon then as he had said unto them, I am he, they went backward and fell to the ground. And when they arose, then asked he them again, Whom seek ye? And they said, Jesus of Nazareth. And Jesus answered, I have told you, I am he; if therefore ye seek me let these go their way.

4 Now he that betrayeth him gave them a sign, saying, Whomsoever I shall kiss, that same is he: hold him fast.

5 And forthwith he came to Jesus and said, Hail, Master; and kissed him. And Jesus said unto him. Friend, wherefore art thou come? Is it with a kiss that thou betrayest the Son of man?

6 Then Jesus said unto the chief priests and captains of the temple and the elders, which were come to him, Why ye come out as against a thief, with swords and staves? When I was daily with you in the temple, ye stretched forth no hands against me; but this is your hour, and the power of darkness.

7 Then came they and laid hands on Jesus. And Simon Peter stretched forth his hand, and drew his sword and struck

a servant of the high priest's and smote off his ear.

8 Then said Jesus unto him, Put up again thy sword into its place; all they that take the sword shall perish by the sword. And Jesus touched his ear and healed him.

9 And he said unto Peter, Thinkest thou that I cannot now pray to my Parent, and He shall presently give me more than twelve legions of angels? But how then shall the scriptures be fulfilled, that thus it must be?

10 Then all the disciples forsook him and fled. And they that had laid hands on Jesus led him away to Caiaphas, the high priest. But they brought him to Annas first because he was father-in-law to Caiaphas, who was the high priest for that same year.

11 Now Caiaphas was he who gave council to the Jews that it was expedient that one man should die for the sins of the people.

12 And the scribes and the elders were assembled together, but Peter and John and Simon and Jude followed far off unto the high priest's palace, and they went in and sat with the servants to see the end.

13 And they had kindled a fire in the midst of the hall, and when they were set down together, Peter sat down among them and warmed himself, and Simon also sat by him.

14 But a certain maid beheld him as he sat by the fire, and earnestly looked upon him and said, This man was also with him. And he denied him, saying, Woman, I know him not.

15 And after a little while, another saw him and said, Thou art also of them. And Simon said, Man, I am not.

16 And about the space of one hour another confidently affirmed, saying, Of a truth this fellow was with Jesus of Nazareth for his speech betrayeth him.

17 And Simon denied the third time with an oath, saying, I know not the man. And immediately, while he yet spake, the cock crew.

18 And the Lord turned and looked upon Simon. And Simon remembered the word of the Lord, how he had said unto him, Before the cock crow this day thou shalt deny me thrice. And Simon went out and wept bitterly.

CHAPTER 78 12-18 -The belief that Peter denied his Master is probably owing to two of the Apostles bearing the same name, Simon Peter and Simon the Canaanite. Here we are given the right version. The error is one that might have been easily made. It is worthy of notice, that this ancient Gospel attributes to Simon (not to Simon Peter) the thrice denial of Jesus, and his fully exonerates Peter from the baseness generally attributed to him, and to which there is no allusion in his writings, but rather the reverse in the accepted gospel, where he was first to draw the sword in defense of his Master.

CHAPTER 79
The Hebrew Trial Before Caiaphas.

1 THE high priest then asked Jesus of his disciples and of his doctrine, saying, How old art thou? Art thou he that said that our father Abraham saw thy day?

2 And Jesus answered, Verily before Abraham was I am. And the high priest said, Thou are not yet fifty years old. How sayest thou that thou hast seen Abraham? Who art thou? Whom makest thou thyself to be? What dost thou teach?

3 And Jesus answered him, I spake openly to the world; I even taught in the synagogue and in the temple, whither the Jews always resort; and in secret have I said nothing. Why asketh thou me? Ask them which heard me, what I have said unto them; behold, they know what I said.

4 And when he had thus spoken, one of the officers which stood by, struck Jesus with the palm of his hand, saying, Answerest thou the high priest so? Jesus answered him, If I have spoken evil, bear witness of the evil, but if well why smitest thou me?

5 Now the chief priests and elders, and all the council sought false witnesses against Jesus to put him to death; but found none; yea, many false witnesses

came, yet they agreed not together.

6 At the last came two false witnesses. And one of them said, This fellow said, I am able to destroy the temple of God and to build it in three days. And the other said, This man said I will destroy this temple and build up another.

7 And the high priests arose and said unto him, Answerest thou nothing? What is it which these witnesses speak against thee? But Jesus held his peace. Now it was unlawful among the Hebrews to try a man by night.

8 And they said unto him, Art thou the Christ? tell us. And he said unto them, If I tell you, ye will not believe; and if I also ask you, ye will not answer me, nor let me go.

9 And they asked him further saying, Dost thou abolish the sacrifices of the law, and the eating of flesh as Moses commanded? And he answered, Behold, a greater than Moses is here.

10 And the high priest answered and said unto him, I adjure thee by the living God, that thou tell us whether thou be the Christ, the Son of God. Jesus saith unto him, thou hast said; and I say unto you, Hereafter shall ye see the Son of man sitting on the right hand of power and coming in the clouds of Heaven.

11 Then the high priest rent his clothes, saying, He hath spoken blasphemy; what further need have we of witnesses? Behold, now ye have heard his blasphemy. What think ye? They answered and said, He is worthy of death.

12 Then did they spit in his face and buffeted him; and others smote him with the palms of their hands, saying, Prophesy unto us, thou Christ, Who is he that smote thee?

13 Now when morning was come all the chief priests and the elders of the people, even the whole council held a consultation, and took council against Jesus to put him to death.

14 And they gave forth their sentence against Jesus, that he was worthy of death, and that he should be bound and carried away, and delivered unto Pilate.

CHAPTER 79 2 -In a preceding CHAPTER (LII.) the Jews at that time adjudged him then to be forty-five, and here Caiaphas, who must certainly have known his age, declared him to be "not yet 50," ie. about 49 This is borne out by the A. V. and by the testimony of S. Irenaeus, A.D. 120-22, and the testimony of S. John the Apostle and his immediate disciples.

CHAPTER 80
The Penance Of Judas.

1 NOW Judas, who had betrayed him, when he saw that he was condemned, repented himself, and brought again the thirty pieces of silver to the chief priests and elders, saying, I have sinned in that I have betrayed the innocent blood.

2 And they said, What is that to us? See thou to that. And he cast down the pieces of silver in the temple and departed and went out and hanged himself.

3 And the chief priests took the pieces of silver and said, It is not lawful for to put them into the treasury, because it is the price of blood.

4 And they took council and bought with them the potter's field, to bury strangers in. Wherefore that field was called Aceldama, that is, the field of blood, unto this day.

5 Then was fulfilled that which was spoken by Zachariah, the prophet, saying, They weighed for my price thirty pieces of silver. And they took the thirty pieces of silver, the price of him that was valued, whom they of the children of Israel did value, and gave them for the potteries field, and cast them to the potter in the House of the Lord.

6 Now, Jesus had said to his disciples, Woe unto the man who receiveth the mysteries, and falleth into sin thereafter.

7 For such there is no place of repentance in this cycle, seeing they have crucified afresh the Divine Offspring of God and man, and put the Christ within them to an open shame.

8 Such are worse than the beasts, whom ye ignorantly affirm to perish, for in your Scriptures it is written, That which

befalleth the beast befalleth the sons of men.

9 All live by one breath, as the one dieth so dieth the other, so that a man hath no preeminence over a beast, for all go to the same place—all come from the dust and return to the dust together.

10 These things spake Jesus concerning them which were not regenerate, not having received the Spirit of Divine Love, who, once having received the Light, crucified the Son of God afresh, putting him to an open shame.

CHAPTER 80 1 -The heading of this CHAPTER in the A. V. is most misleading. "Penance," implying reparation of some kind (even though not of the right kind), is the more correct description of the act.

CHAPTER 81

The Roman Trial Before Pilate

1 THEN led they Jesus from Caiaphas unto the hall of judgment, to Pontius Pilate, the Governor, and it was early, and they themselves went not into the judgment hall, lest they should be defiled; but that they might keep the feast.

2 Pilate therefore went out unto them and said, What accusation bring ye against this man? They answered and said unto him, If he were not a malefactor, we would not have delivered him up unto thee. We have a law and by our law he ought to die, because he would change the customs and rites which Moses delivered unto us, yea, he made himself the Son of God.

3 Then said Pilate unto them, Take ye him, and Judge him according to your law. For he knew that for envy they had delivered him.

4 The Jews therefore said unto him, It is not lawful for us to put any man to death. So the saying of Jesus was fulfilled, which he spake, signifying what death he should die.

5 And they further accused him saying, We found this fellow perverting the nation, and forbidding to give tribute to Caesar, saying that he himself is Christ a King.

6 Then Pilate entered into the judgment hall again and called Jesus and said unto him, Art thou the King of the Jews? Jesus answered him, Sayest thou this thing of thyself, or did others tell it thee of me?

7 Pilate answered, Am I a Jew ? Thine own nation and the chief priests have delivered thee unto me; what hast thou done? Jesus answered, My kingdom is not of this world, if my kingdom were of this world, then would my servants fight, that I should not be delivered to the Jews; but now is my kingdom not from hence.

8 Pilate therefore said unto him, Art thou a King then? Jesus answered, Thou sayest that I am, yea, a King I am. To this end was I born and for this cause came I unto the world, that I should bear witness unto the truth. Every one that is of the truth heareth my voice.

9 Pilate said unto him, What is truth? Jesus said, Truth is from heaven. Pilate said, Then truth is not on earth. Jesus said unto Pilate, Believe thou, that truth is on earth amongst those who receive and obey it. They are of the truth who judge righteously.

10 And when he had heard this, he went out again unto the Jews and saith unto them, I find in him no fault at all. And when he was accused of the chief priests and elders he answered them nothing.

11 Then said Pilate unto him, Hearest thou not, how many things they witness against thee?

12 And he answered him never a word, insomuch that the governor marveled greatly, and again he said unto them, I find no fault in this man.

13 And they waxed the more fierce saying, He stirreth up the people, teaching throughout all Jewry, beginning from Galilee to this place. When Pilate heard of Galilee he asked, whether the man were a Galilean.

14 AND as soon as he knew that he belonged unto Herod's jurisdiction, he sent him to Herod, who himself also, was at Jerusalem at the time.

15 And when Herod saw Jesus he was

exceedingly glad, for he was desirous to see him of a long season, because he had heard many things of him, and he hoped to have seen some miracle done by him.

16 Then he questioned with him in many words, but he answered him nothing. And the chief priests and scribes stood and vehemently accused him, and many false witnesses rose up against him, and laid to his charge things that he knew not.

17 And Herod with his men of war set him at nought, and mocked him, and arrayed him in a gorgeous robe and sent him again to Pilate. And the same day Pilate and Herod were made friends together, for before they were at enmity between themselves.

18 And Pilate went again into the Judgment Hall and saith unto Jesus, Whence art thou? But Jesus gave him no answer. Then saith Pilate unto him, Speakest thou not unto me? knowest thou not that I have power to crucify thee, and have power to release thee?

19 Jesus answered, Thou couldest have no power at all against me, except it were given thee from above, therefore he that delivered me unto thee hath the greater sin.

20 And from thenceforth Pilate sought to release him; but the Jews cried out, saying, If thou let this man go thou art no Caesar's friend, whosoever maketh himself a king speaketh against Caesar.

21 And Pilate called together the chief priests and rulers of the people. When he was set down on the judgement seat his wife sent unto him, saying. Have thou nothing to do with that just man, for I have suffered many things this day in a dream, because of him.

22 And Pilate said unto them, Ye have brought this man unto me, as one that perverteth the people, and behold I have examined him before you, and have found no fault in this man touching those things: whereof ye accuse him. No, nor yet Herod, for I sent you to him, and lo nothing worthy of death was found in him.

23 But ye have a custom that I should release unto you one at the Passover,

will ye therefore that I release unto you the King of the Jews?

24 Then cried they all again, saying, Not this man, but Barabbas. Now Barabbas was a robber. And, for sedition made in the city, and for murder, was cast into prison.

25 Pilate therefore, willing to release Jesus, spake again to them. Whether of the twain will ye that I release unto you; Jesus Barabbas, or Jesus which is called the Christ? They said, Barabbas

26 Pilate said unto them, What then shall I do with Jesus which is called the Christ? They all say unto him, Let him be crucified.

27 And the Governor said, Why what evil hath he done? But they cried out all the more saying, Crucify him, crucify him.

28 Pilate therefore went forth again and said unto him, Behold, again, I bring him forth to you, that ye may know that I find no fault in him, and again they cried out, Crucify him, crucify him.

29 And Pilate said unto them, the third time, Why, what evil hath he done? I have found no cause of death in him: I will therefore chastise him, and let him go.

30 And they were instant with loud voices, requiring that he might be crucified. And the voices of them and of the chief priests prevailed.

31 When Pilate saw that he could prevail nothing, but that rather a tumult was made, he took water, and washed his hands before the multitude, saying, I am innocent of the blood of this just person: see ye to it.

32 Then answered all the people, and said, His blood be on us and on our children. And Pilate gave sentence that it should be as they required. And he delivered Jesus to their will.

CHAPTER 81 2 -This verse, suppressed by corruption of the Gospel, doubtless refers to the keeping the Passover within the gates without the slaying of So lamb, a capital offence by the law (See " New Aspects of Religion," by Dr. H. Pratt), or it might refer to keeping Passover the day before. There is much

uncertainty on this point, the Gospels in the A. V. setting forth two different views, mutually contradicting each other, but neither of them implying necessarily the eating of a lamb by Jesus and his Apostles.
CHAPTER 81 9 -These words, or the substance of them, are also to be found in one of the gnostic Gospels, which record many genuine sayings of the Master.

CHAPTER 82
The Crucifixion

1 THEN released he Barabbas unto them, and when he had scourged Jesus he delivered him to be crucified. Then the soldiers of the governor took Jesus to the common hall and gathered unto him the whole band of soldiers.

2 And they stripped him and put on him a purple robe. And when they had plaited a crown of thorns they put it upon his head and a reed in his right hand, and they bowed the knee before him and mocked him, saying, Hail, King of the Jews!

3 Then came Jesus forth, wearing the crown of thorns, and the purple robe. And Pilate saith unto them, Behold the man!

4 When the chief priests therefore and officers saw him, they cried out, saying, Crucify him, crucify him. And Pilate saith unto them, Take ye him and crucify him, for I find no fault in him.

5 And they spit upon him, and took the reed and smote him on the head. And after that they had mocked him they took the robe off from him, and put his own raiment on him, and led him away to crucify him.

6 And as they led him away, they laid hold upon one Simon, a Cyrenian, coming out of the county, and on him they laid the cross that he might bear it after Jesus. And there followed him a great company of people and of women, which also bewailed and lamented him.

7 But Jesus, turning unto them, said, Daughters of Jerusalem, weep not for me, but weep for yourselves and for your children. For behold the days are coming in which they shall say, Blessed are the barren, and the wombs that never bare, and the paps which never gave suck.

8 Then shall they begin to say to the mountains, Fall on us; and to the hills, Cover us. For it they do these things in a green tree, what shall be done in the dry.

9 And there were also two other malefactors led with him to be put to death. And when they were come unto a place called Calvary, and Golgotha, that is to say a place of a skull, there they crucified him; and the malefactors, one on the right hand, and other on the left.

10 And it was the third hour when they crucified him, and they gave him vinegar to drink mingled with gall, and when he had tasted thereof, he would not drink. And Jesus said, Abba Amma, forgive them, for they know not what they do.

11 Then the soldiers, when they had crucified Jesus, took his raiment and made four parts, to every soldier a part; and also his vesture. Now the vesture was without seam, woven from the top throughout. They said therefore among themselves, Let us not rend it, but cast lots for it, whose it shall be.

12 That the scripture might be fulfilled, which saith, They parted my raiment among them, and for my vesture they did cast lots. These things therefore the soldiers did. And sitting down they watched him there.

13 And a superscription was also written over him in letters of Greek, and Latin, and Hebrew, This is the King of the Jews.

14 This title then read many of the Jews, for the place where Jesus was crucified was nigh to the city, and it was written in Hebrew and Greek and Latin. then said the chief priests of the Jews to Pilate, Write not, The King of the Jews, but that, he said, I am the King of the Jews. Pilate answered, What I have written, I have written.

15 And one of the malefactors which were hanged railed on him, saying, If thou be the Christ, save thy self and us. But the other answering rebuked him, saying, Dost not thou fear God, seeing

thou art in the same condemnation? And we indeed justly, for we receive the due reward of our deeds, but this man hath done nothing amiss.

16 And he said unto Jesus, Lord remember me when thou comest into thy kingdom. And Jesus said unto him, Verily I say unto thee, to day shalt thou be with me in Paradise.

17 And they that passed by reviled him, wagging heir heads and saying, Thou that wouldst destroy the temple, and build it in three days, save thyself. If thou be the Son of God, come down from the Cross.

18 Likewise also the chief priests mocking him, while the scribes and elders said, He saved a lamb, himself he cannot save. If he be the King of Israel, let him now come down from the cross and we will believe him. He trusted in God, let Him deliver him now, if He will have him, for he said, I am the Son of God.

19 The usurers and the dealers in beasts and birds also cast the like things into his teeth, saying, Thou who drivest from the temple the traders in oxen and sheep and doves, art thyself but a sheep that is sacrificed.

20 Now from the Sixth hour there was darkness over all the land unto the Ninth hour, and some standing around, lighted their torches, for the darkness was very great. And about the Sixth hour Jesus cried with a loud voice, Eli, Eli, lame sabachthani? that, is to say, My God, My God, why hast Thou forsaken me ?

21 Some of them that stood there, when they heard that, said, This man calleth for Elias; others said, He calleth on the Sun. The rest said, Let be, let us see whether Elias will come to save him.

22 Now there stood by the cross of Jesus his mother and his mother's sister, Mary, the wife of Cleophas, and Mary Magdalene.

23 When Jesus therefore saw his mother, and the disciple standing by whom he loved, he saith unto his mother, Woman, behold thy son! And he said to the disciple, Behold thy mother! And from that hour that

disciple took her into his own home.

24 After this, Jesus knowing that all things were now accomplished, that the scripture might be fulfilled, saith, I am athirst. And from a vessel they filled a sponge with vinegar and put it upon hyssop and put it to his mouth.

25 And Jesus cried with a loud voice, saying, Abba Amma, into Thy hand I commend my spirit.

26 When Jesus had therefore received the vinegar, he cried aloud, It is finished; and he bowed his head and gave up the ghost. And it was the ninth hour.

27 And behold there was great thunder and lightning, and the partition wall of the Holy place, from which hung the veil, fell down, and was rent in twain, and the earth did quake, and the rocks also were rent.

28 Now when the centurion and they that were with him watching Jesus, saw the earthquake and those things that were done, they feared greatly, saying, Truly this was a Son of God.

29 And many women were there, which followed from Galilee, ministering unto them, and among them were Mary the mother of James and Joses, and the mother of Zebedee's children and they lamented, saying, The light of the world is hid from our eyes, the Lord our Love is crucified.

30 Then the Jews, because it was the preparation, that the bodies should not remain upon the cross on the Sabbath, for that was a Paschal Sabbath, besought Pilate that their legs might be broken, and that they might be taken away.

31 Then came the soldiers, and brake the legs of the two who were crucified with him. But when they came to Jesus, and saw that he was dead already, they brake not his legs, but one of the soldiers with a spear pierced his heart and forthwith came there out blood and water.

32 And he that saw it bare record and his record is true, and he knoweth that he saith true, that ye might believe. For these things were done that the Scriptures might be fulfilled—A bone

of him shall not be broken, and again—In the midst of the week the Messiah shall be cut off.

CHAPTER 82 10-12 -Eli Reclus, a French writer, has some interesting remarks on the rite of human sacrifice as practised among the Khonds from time immemorial. The coincidences in the details are very striking, shewing the similarity of superstitious ideas in all countries and tribes of the primitive world-ideas which survive even in our own times " civilized ., as we boast them to be, but in reality savages when the skin deep "civilization" and culture are suddenly brushed away by some violent popular outburst, as in England, against the peaceful peoples of the Transvaal by which she brought herself to the lowest depths of infamy, and unwittingly clothed herself in the colour symbolic of dirt and mire.

v. 20 -In the Gospel attributed to Peter there is mention of the same circumstance. And to bring to mind, by symbolical art, this awful scene, among other reasons, the dark unbleached candles are lighted on the Altar on the day and at the hour when the Church commemorates the crucifixion of the Redeemer by an ingrate priesthood and people, when the light of the sun is shut out or obscured, and the chancels are draped in black.

v. 30 -It should be observed that in this Gospel, the mystically central organ of the Sacred Body, the "Heart" is emphasized rather than "his side," as in the A. V. on which last reading the strange custom of having a side entrance or porch to Churches is alleged to have been founded. The traditonal but corrupt reading of Gen. vi.16 has doubtless originated the error. v. 31 -They pierced his Sacred Heart with a spear, and this is symbolised in Christian Churches (which are generally cruciform either externally or internally where they are not circular), where the choir (Cor.) is in the intersection of nave and transept, and the altar of incense is (ought to be) in the midst under the great dome,

symbolizing that the Sacred Heart of the Crucified is venerated from the centre to the extreme limits of Christendom-the Heart of God which embraces all creatures in its boundless love.

CHAPTER 83
The Burial Of Jesus

1 NOW, when the even was come, Joseph of Arimathea, an honourable councillor, who also waited for the Kingdom of God, came and went in boldly unto Pilate and craved the body of Jesus. (He was a good man and just, and had not consented to the council and deed of them).

2 And Pilate marvelled if he were already dead, and calling unto him the centurion, he asked him whether he had been any while dead. And when he knew it of the centurion, he gave the body to Joseph. He came therefore, and took the body of Jesus.

3 And there came also Nicodemus, who at the first came to Jesus by night, and brought a mixture of myrrh and aloes, about an hundred weight. Then took they the body of Jesus and wound it in linen clothes with the spices, as the manner of the Jews is to bury.

4 Now in the place where he was crucified there was a garden, and in the garden a new sepulchre, wherein was never man yet laid. There laid they Jesus therefore, and it was about the beginning of the second watch when they buried him, because of the Jews' preparation day, for the sepulchre was nigh at hand.

5 And Mary Magdalene and the other Mary, and Mary the mother of Joses beheld where he was laid. There at the tomb they kept watch for three days and three nights.

6 And the women also, who came with him from Galilee, followed after, bearing lamps in their hands and beheld the sepulchre and how his body was laid, and they made lamentation over him.

7 And they returned and rested the next clay, being a high day, and on the day following they bought and prepared

spices and ointments and waited for the end of the Sabbath.

8 Now the next day that followed, the chief priests and Pharisees came together unto Pilate, saying, Sir we remember that deceiver said, while he was yet alive, After three days I will rise again.

9 Command therefore that the sepulchre be made sure until the third day be past, lest his disciples come by night and steal him away, and say unto the people, He is risen from the dead, so the last error shall be worse than the first.

10 Pilate said unto them, Ye have a watch, go your way, make it as sure as you can. So they went and made the sepulchre sure, sealing the stone and setting a watch till the third day should be past.

CHAPTER 83 5 -It has been maintained by some with no small degree of reason and probability, that the day of Crucifixion was not Friday, the day now observed by Christendom, but Wednesday (mid-week), by which date alone would be truly fulfilled the prophecy of Daniel, and the only sign of the truth of His mission which he would give to his generation. There shall no sign be given it, but the sign of the prophet Ionas, for as Ionas was three days and three nights in the whale's belly, so shall the Son of man be three days and three nights In the heart of the earth." Against this plain testimony there is of course the canonical record as we now have it including the frequent explanatory notes which may have been incorporated in very early times from the margin into the text, or interpolated in ignorance of the original script, which no man living has ever Been from this to the 10th century when all manuscripts were in the hands of the religious orders of the Church, and from them proceeded. If these words of Jesus be a genuine portion of the Gospel, as all admit they are, those notes of time, in the present accepted Gospels must be spurious, or the work of scribes who sought with honest and pious intent to harmonise the words of Scripture with the existent beliefs and observances of their age. In the gospel as now given there is absolutely nothing to militate against either of these views except the words of Jesus above cited, which cast the weight in favour of this chronological arrangement which interferes with nothing of Christian doctrine. Sunday, as now the day of his public entry into Jerusalem, preceded by the last anointing by Mary Magdalene on the eve before it. Monday, the day of evil counsel. Tuesday, the day of the Pascal feast of Christ. Wednesday, the day of the crucifixion, if not of the actual Jewish Passover. Thursday, Friday, Sabbath days of watch, of mourning and vigil. Sunday the day of the Resurrection, midnight or 8 a.m., early dawn " (after three days and three nights were fulfilled) and of the rising of many who slept and of their appearance in the holy City."

CHAPTER 84

The Resurrection Of Jesus

1 NOW after the Sabbath was ended and it began to dawn, on the first day of the week, came Mary Magdalene to the sepulchre, bearing the spices which she had prepared, and there were others with her.

2 And as they were going, they said among themselves, who shall roll away the stone from the door of the sepulchre? For it was great. And when they came to the place and looked, they saw that the stone was rolled away.

3 For behold there was a great earthquake; and the angel of the Lord descended from heaven, and rolled back the stone from the door, and sat upon it. His countenance was like lighting and his raiment white as snow: And for fear of him the keepers did shake and became as dead men.

4 And the angel answered and said unto the women, Fear not ye, for I know that ye seek Jesus, which was crucified. He is not here: for he is risen, as he said.

5 Come, see the place where the Lord lay. And go quickly and tell his

disciples that he is risen from the dead; and, behold he goeth before you into Galilee; there shall ye see him; lo, I have told you.

6 And they entered in and found not the body of Jesus. Then she ran and came to Simon Peter and the other disciple whom Jesus loved, and said unto them, They have taken away the Lord out of the sepulchre, and we know not where they have laid him.

7 And they ran and came to the scpulchre, and looking in, they saw the linen clothes lying, and the napkin that had been about his head not lying with the linen clothes, but wrapped up in a place by itself.

8 And it came to pass as they were much perplexed, behold, two angels stood by them in glistening garments of white, and said unto them, Why seek ye the living among the dead? He is not here, he is risen, and, behold, he goeth before you into Galilee, there shall we see him.

9 Remember ye not how he spake unto you, when he was yet in Galilee, that the Son of Man should be crucified and that he would rise again after the third day? And they remembered his words. And they went out quickly and fled from the sepulchre, for they trembled with amazement, and they were afraid.

10 NOW at the time of the earthquake, the graves were opened; and many of the saints which slept arose, and came out of the graves after his resurrection, and went into the city and appeared unto many.

11 But Mary stood without at the sepulchre weeping, and as she wept she again stooped down, and looked into the sepulchre and saw two angels in white garments, the one at the head, and the other at the feet, where the body of Jesus had lain. And they said unto her, Woman, why weepest thou?

12 She saith unto them, Because they have taken away my Lord, and I know not where they have laid him. And when she had thus said, she turned herself back, and saw Jesus standing, and knew not that it was Jesus.

13 Jesus saith unto her, Woman, why weepest thou? Whom seekest thou? She, supposing him to be the gardener, saith unto him, Sir, if thou have borne him hence, tell me where thou hast laid him, and I will take him away. Jesus said unto her, Mary, She turned herself and saith unto him, Rabboni; which is to say, Master.

14 Jesus saith unto her, Touch me not, for I am not yet ascended to my Father One with my Mother, but go to my brethren, and say unto them, I ascend unto my Parent and your Parent; to my God and your God.

15 And Mary Magdalene came and told the disciples that she had seen the Lord, and that he had spoken these things unto her, and commanded her to announce his resurrection from the dead.

CHAPTER 84 6 - On this passage the celebrated writer M. Renan, bases his assertion that "but for Mary Magdalene Christianity would never have existed." It was she who first proclaimed the central fact -the Resurrection of the Lord. There is a true and a false side to his words.

CHAPTER 85
Jesus Risen Again Appears To Two At Emmaus

1 AND behold, two of them went that same day to a village called Emmaus, which was from Jerusalem about threescore furlongs. And they talked together of all these things which had happened.

2 And it came to pass, that, while they communed together and reasoned, Jesus himself drew near, and went with them. But their eyes were holden that they should not know him.

3 And he said unto them, What manner of communications are these that ye have one with another, as ye walk and are sad?

4 And the one of them, whose name was Cleophas, answering, said unto him, Art thou only a stranger in Jerusalem and hast not known the things which are come to pass there in these days? And he said unto them,

What things?

5 And they said unto him, Concerning Jesus of Nazareth who was a Prophet mighty in deed and word before God and all the people; and how the chief priests and our rulers delivered him to be condemned to death, and have crucified him. But we trusted that it had been he which should have redeemed Israel; and beside all this three days have passed since these things were done.

6 Yea, and certain women also of our company made us astonished, which were early at the sepulchre; and when they found not his body, they came saying, that they had also seen a vision of angels, who said that he was alive.

7 And certain of them who were with us went to the sepulchre, and found it even so as the women had said; but him they saw not.

8 Then he said unto them, O fools and slow of heart to believe all that the prophets have spoken; Ought not Christ to have suffered these things, and then to enter into his glory?

9 And beginning at Moses and all the prophets, he expounded unto them in all the scriptures, the things concerning himself.

10 And they drew nigh unto the village whither they went; and he made as though he would have gone further. But they constrained him, saying, Abide, with us, for it is toward evening, and the day is far spent. And he went in to tarry with them.

11 And it came to pass as he sat at table with them, he took bread and the fruit of the vine, and gave thanks, blessed, and brake, and gave to them. And their eyes were opened, and they knew him; and he vanished out of their sight.

12 And they said one to another, Did not our hearts burn within us while he talked with us by the way, and while he opened to us the scriptures? And they rose up the same hour and returned to Jerusalem, and found the twelve gathered together, and them that were with them, saying, The Lord is risen indeed, and hath appeared to Simon.

13 And they told what things were done in the way and how he was known of them in breaking of bread.

14 Now while they had been going to Emmaus, some of the watch came into the city, and showed unto Caiaphas what things had been done.

15 And they assembled with the elders and took council and said, Behold, while the soldiers slept, some of his disciples came and took his body away; and is not Joseph of Arimathea one if his disciples?

16 For this cause then did he beg the body from Pilate that he might bury it in his garden in his own tomb. Let us therefore give money to the soldiers, saying, say ye, His disciples came by night and stole him away while we slept. And if this come to the ears of the governor we will persuade him, and secure you.

CHAPTER 85 15 -These words though not fully given in the A. V. have been made the basis of an attempted explanation by M. Renan, who could not receive the alternative view that the body of Jesus was dematerialized, rose, and then appeared in spiritual form, which view is held by believers of modern manifestations

CHAPTER 86

Jesus Appears In The Temple and Blood Sacrifices Cease

1 THE same day, at the time of sacrifice in the Temple there appeared among the dealers in beasts and in birds, One clothed in white raiment, bright as light, and in his hand a whip of seven cords.

2 And at the sight of him, those who sold and bought fled in terror, and some of them fell as dead men, for they remembered how before his death Jesus had driven them away from the Temple enclosure, in like manner.

3 And some declared that they had seen a spirit. And others that they had seen him who was crucified and that he had risen from the dead.

4 And the sacrifices ceased that day in the Temple, for all were in fear, and none could be had to sell or to buy, but, rather, they let their captives go free.

5 And the priests and elders caused a report to be spread, That they who had seen it were drunken, and had seen nothing. But many affirmed that they had seen him with their own eyes, and felt on their backs the scourge, but were powerless to resist, for when some of the bolder among them put forth their hands, they could not seize the form which they beheld, nor grasp the whip which chastised them.

6 And from that time, these believed in Jesus, that he was sent from God, to deliver the oppressed, and free those that were bound. And they turned from their ways and sinned no longer.

7 To others he also appeared in love and mercy and healed them by his touch, and delivered them from the hands of the persecutor. And many like things were reported of him, and many said, Of a truth the Kingdom is come.

8 And some of those who had slept and risen, when Jesus rose from the dead appeared, and were seen by many in the holy City, and great fear fell upon the wicked, but light and gladness came to the righteous in heart.

CHAPTER 86 4 -"The sacrifices ceased that day" -here is not meant for any permanence (as generally believed) for they went on, we are told, for forty years, till the destruction of the Temple by the Romans.

CHAPTER 87
Jesus Appeareth To His Disciples.
1 THEN the same day at evening, being the first day of the week, when the doors were shut where the disciples were assembled for fear of the Jews, came Jesus and stood in the midst, and saith unto them, Peace be unto you. But they were affrighted and supposed that they had seen a spirit.

2 And he said unto them, Behold, it is I myself, like as ye have seen me aforetime. A spirit can in deed appear in flesh and bones as ye see me have. Behold my hands and my feet, handle and see.

3 And when he had so said, he shewed unto them his hands and his Heart.

Then were the disciples glad, when they saw the Lord.

4 For Thomas, called Didymus, one of the disciples, had said unto them, Except I shall see in his hands the print of the nails, and thrust my hand into his heart, I will not believe. Then saith he to Thomas, Behold my hands, my heart, and my feet; reach hither thy hands, and be not faithless but believing.

5 And Thomas answered and said unto him, My Lord and my God! And Jesus saith unto him, Thomas, because thou hast seen me, thou hast believed; blessed are they that have not seen and yet have believed.

6 Then saith Jesus unto them again, Peace be unto you, as Abba Amma hath sent me, even so send I you. And when he had said this he breathed on them and said unto them, Receive ye the Holy Ghost; preach the Gospel, and anounce ye unto all nations; the resurrection of the Son of Man.

7 Teach ye the holy law of love which I have delivered unto you. And whosoever forsake their sins, they are remitted unto them, and whosoever continue in their sins they are retained unto them.

8 Baptise them who believe and repent, bless and anoint them, and offer ye the pure Oblation of the fruits of the earth, which I have appointed unto you for a Memorial of me.

9 Lo, I have given my body and my blood to be offered on the Cross, for the redemption of the world from the sin against love, and from the bloody sacrifices and feasts of the past.

10 And ye shall offer the Bread of life, and the Wine of salvation, for a pure Oblation with incense, as it is written of me, and ye shall eat and drink thereof for a memorial, that I have delivered all who believe in me from the ancient bondage of your ancestors.

11 For they, making a god of their belly, sacrificed unto their god the innocent creatures of the earth, in place of the carnal nature within themselves.

12 And eating of their flesh and drinking of their blood to their own destruction, corrupted their bodies and

shortened their days, even as the Gentiles who knew not the truth, or who knowing it, have changed it into a lie.

13 As I send you, so send ye others also, to do these things in my Name, and he laid his hands upon them.

14 In the like manner as the Apostles, so also be ordained Prophets and Evangelists and Pastors, a Holy Priesthood, and afterwards he laid his hand upon those whom they chose for Deacons, one for each of the fourfold twelve.

15 And these are for the rule and guidance of the Church Universal, that all may be perfected in their places in the Unity of the Body of the Christ.

CHAPTER 87 1 -The power to come in, or to go out through closed doors, has been shown in modern times to be no impossibility, but a proven fact in psychological phenomena. The words here do not necessarily imply that such manifestation took place. It is not said, "they were locked," but the power of the Spirit to materialize, and dematerialize, Bond appear in human form (under certain conditions) is too well known to be denied." Report of Dialectical Society on Spiritual Phenomena," etc. CHAPTER 87 2 -The contradiction in the A.V. is here no longer seen. That a spirit can appear in flesh and bones has been testified over by thousands of competent witnesses in this as well as other ages. There is no death, and the returning spirit can appear in any form. Of these things we are witnesses. v. 8-A similar passage to this occurs in the "Pistis Sophia," an ancient gnostic Gospel.

CHAPTER 88

The Eighth Day After The Resurrection

1 AND after seven days again, his disciples were within the Upper Room; then came Jesus, the doors being shut, and stood in their midst and said, Peace be unto you, and he was known unto them in the holy Memorial.

2 And he said unto them. Love ye one another and all the creatures of God. Yet

I say unto you, not all are men, who are in the form of man. Are they men or women in the image of God whose ways are ways of violence, of oppression and wrong, who choose a lie rather than the truth?

3 Nay, verily, till they are born again, and receive the Spirit of Love and Wisdom within their hearts. Then only are they sons and daughters of Israel, and being of Israel they are children of God, And for this cause came I into the world, and for this I have suffered at the hands of sinners.

4 These are the words which I spake unto you, while I was yet with you, that all things must be fulfilled which were written in the law of Moses and in the prophets, and in the psalms, concerning me.

5 And Jesus said, I stood in the midst of the world, and in the flesh was I seen and heard, and I found all men glutted with their own pleasures, and drunk with their own follies, and none found I hungry or athirst for the wisdom which is of God. My soul grieveth over the sons and daughters of men because they are blind in their heart, and in their soul are they deaf and hear not my voice.

6 Then opened he their understanding, that they might understand the scriptures. And said unto them, Thus it is written, and thus it behooved the Christ to suffer, and to rise from the dead after the third day. And that repentance and remission of sins should be preached in my name among all nations, beginning at Jerusalem. And ye are witnesses of these things.

7 And, behold, I send the promice of my Parent upon you, even of my Father One with my Mother, Whom ye have not seen on the earth. For I say unto you of a truth, as the whole world have been ruined by the sin and vanity of woman, so by the simplicity and truth of woman shall it be saved, even by you shall it be saved.

8 Rejoice therefore and be ye glad, for ye are more blessed than all who are on earth, for it is ye, my twelve thousand who shall save the whole world.

9 Again I say unto you when the great

tyrant and all the seven tyrants began to fight in vain against the Light, they knew not with Whom or What they fought.

10 For they saw nothing beyond a dazzling Light, and when they fought they expended their strength one against another, and so it is.

11 For this cause I took a fourth part of their strength, so that they might not have such power, and prevail in their evil deeds.

12 For by involution and evolution shall the salvation of all the world be accomplished: by the Descent of Spirit into matter, and the Ascent of matter into Spirit, through the ages.

CHAPTER 88 5 -Most affecting is this, the experience of all who in this world of madness and unreason attempt to declare the whole counsel of God. It broke the heart of Jesus, it crushes the heart of every prophet or apostle worker for good, filled with his spirit- " Jerusalem, Jerusalem I would - but ye would not."

CHAPTER 89

Jesus Appeareth At The Sea Of Tiberias
1 AFTER these things Jesus shewed himself again to the disciples at the sea of Tiberias, and on this wise shewed he himself. There were together Simon, Peter, and Thomas, called Didymus, and Nathanael of Cana in Galilee, and James and John and two other of his disciples.

2 And Peter saith unto them, I go a fishing. They say unto him, We also go with thee. They went forth and entered into a ship immediately, and that night they caught nothing. And when the morning was now come, Jesus stood on the shore, but the disciples knew not that it was Jesus.

3 Then Jesus said unto them, Children, have ye any meat? They answered him, Nay, Lord, not enough for all; there is naught but a small loaf, a little oil, and a few dried fruits. And he said unto them, Let these suffice; come and dine.

4 And he blessed them, and they ate and were filled, and there was a pitcher of water also, and he blessed it likewise, and lo, it was the fruit of the vine.

5 And they marvelled, and said. It is the Lord. And none of the disciples dost ask him. Who art thou? knowing it was the Lord.

6 This is now the sixth time that Jesus shewed himself to his disciples, after that he was risen from the dead. So when they had dined, Jesus saith to Peter, son of Jonas, lovest thou me more than these? He saith unto him, Yea, Lord, thou knowest that I love thee. He saith unto him, Feed my lambs. He saith unto him again the second time, Peter, son of Jonas, lovest thou me? He saith unto him, Yea, Lord thou knowest that I love thee. He said unto him. Feed my sheep.

7 He saith unto him the third time, Peter, son of Jonas, lovest thou me? Peter was grieved because he said unto him the third time, Lovest thou me ? And he said unto him, Lord, thou knowest all things; thou knowest that I love thee.

8 Jesus saith unto him, Feed my Flock. Verily verily, I say unto thee, thou art a rock from the Rock, and on this rock will I build my Church, and I will raise thee above my twelve to be my vicegerent upon earth for a centre of Unity to the twelve, and another shall be called and chosen to fill thy place among the twelve, and thou shalt be the Servant of servants and shalt feed my rams, my sheep and my lambs.

9 And yet another shall arise and he shall teach many things which I have taught you already, and he shall spread the Gospel among the Gentiles with great zeal. But the keys of the Kingdom will I give to those who succeed thee in my Spirit and obeying my law.

10 And again I say unto thee. When thou wast young thou girdedst thyself and walketh whither thou wouldst, but when thou shalt be old, thou shalt stretch forth thy hands and another shall gird thee and carry thee whither thou wouldst not. This spake he, signifying by what death he should glorify God.

11 And when he had spoken this he saith unto him, Follow me. Then Peter,

turning about, seeth the disciple whom Jesus loved following. Peter seeing him, saith to Jesus, Lord and what shall this man do? Jesus saith unto him, If I will that he tarry till I come, what is that to thee? follow thou me.

12 Then went this saying abroad among the brethren that disciple should not die: yet Jesus said not unto him, He shall not die, but, if I will that he tarry till I come, what is that to thee.

CHAPTER 89 2 -"That night they caught nothing" -henceforth their labours were to be in the Spiritual Kingdom to save souls -not destroy them- by bringing them within the Church of Christianity, from barbarism and darkness to reason and light and love.

CHAPTER 90
What Is Truth?

1 AGAIN the twelve were gathered together in the Circle of palm trees, and one of them even Thomas said to the other, What is Truth? for the same things appear different to different minds, and even to the same mind at different times. What, then, is Truth?

2 And as they were speaking Jesus appeared in their midst and said, Truth, one and absolute, is in God alone, for no man, neither any body of men, knoweth that which God alone knoweth, who is the All in All.. To men is Truth revealed, according to their capacity to understand and receive.

3 The One Truth hath many sides, and one seeth one side only, another seeth another, and some see more than others, according as it is given to them.

4 Behold this crystal: how the one light its manifest in twelve faces, yea four times twelve, and each face reflecteth one ray of light, and one regardeth one face, and another another, but it is the one crystal and the one light that shineth in all.

5 Behold again, When one climbeth a mountain and attaining one height, he saith, This is the top of the mountain, let us reach it, and when they have reached that height, lo, they see another beyond it until they come to that height from which no other height is to be seen, if so be they can attain it.

6 So it is with Truth. I am the Truth and the Way and the Life, and have given to you the Truth I have received from above. And that which is seen and received by one, is not seen and received by another. That which appeareth true to some, seemeth not true to others. They who are in the valley see not as they who are on the hill top.

7 But to each, it is the Truth as the one mind seeth it, and for that time, till a higher Truth shall be revealed unto the same: and to the soul which receiveth higher light, shall be given more light. Wherefore condemn not others, that ye be not condemned.

8 As ye keep the holy Law of Love, which I have given unto you, so shall the Truth be revealed more and more unto you, and the Spirit of Truth which cometh from above shall guide you, albeit through many wanderings, into all Truth, even as the fiery cloud guided the children of Israel through the wilderness.

9 Be faithful to the light ye have, till a higher light is given to you. Seek more light, and ye shall have abundantly; rest not, till ye find.

10 God giveth you all Truth, as a ladder with many steps, for the salvation and perfection of the soul, and the truth which seemeth to day, ye will abandon for the higher truth of the morrow. Press ye unto Perfection.

11 Whoso keepeth the holy Law which I have given, the same shall save their souls, however differently they may see the truths which I have given.

12 Many shall say unto me, Lord, Lord, we have been zealous for thy Truth. But I shall say unto them, Nay, but, that others may see as ye see, and none other truth beside. Faith without charity is dead. Love is the fulfilling of the Law.

13 How shall faith in what they receive profit them that hold it in unrighteousness? They who have love have all things, and without love there

is nothing worth. Let each hold what they see to be the truth in love, knowing that where love is not, truth is a dead letter and profiteth nothing.

14 There abide Goodness, and Truth, and Beauty, but the greatest of these is Goodness. If any have hatred to their fellows, and harden their hearts to the creatures of God's hands, how can they see Truth unto salvation, seeing their eyes are blinded and their hearts are hardened to God's creation?

15 As I have reveived the Truth, so have I given it to you. Let each receive it according to their light and ability to understand, and persecute not those who receive it after a different interpretation.

16 For Truth is the Might of God, and it shall prevail in the end over all errors. But the holy Law which I have given is plain for all, and just and good. Let all observe it for the salvation of their souls.

CHAPTER 90 4 -The art of cutting and polishing glass and stone was well known in Phoenicia and Egypt, before the Christian era, and in Pompeii numbers of such crystals were found in great variety. It is a beautiful symbol appealing to the mind.

CHAPTER 90 12 -Our Lord never damned or blamed those who could not see the divine truths, which he taught, and receive them. He had patience with them, as being without the fold, without light, and not admissible to the Kingdom, so long as they remained in their darkness and impenitence and self-doomed to eternal death if they persisted.

CHAPTER 91
The Order of the Kingdom. (Part I.)
1 In that time after Jesus had risen from the dead he tarried ninety days with Mary his mother and Mary Magdalene, who anointed his body, and Mary Cleophas and the twelve, and their fellows, instructing them and answering questions concerning the kingdom of God.

2 And as they sat at supper—when it was even— Mary Magdalene asked him, saying, Master, wilt thou now declare unto us the Order of the Kingdom?

3 And Jesus answered and said, Verily I say unto thee, O Mary, and to each of any disciples, The kingdom of Heaven is within you. But the time cometh when that which is within shall be made manifest in the without, for the sake of the world.

4 Order indeed is good, and needful, but before all things is love. Love ye one another and all the creatures of God, and by this shall all men know that ye are my disciples.

5 AND one asked him saying, Master, wilt thou that infants be received into the congregation in like manner as Moses commanded by circumcision? And Jesus answered, For those who are in Christ there is no cutting of the flesh, nor shedding of blood.

6 Let the infant of eight clays be Presented unto the Father-Mother, who is in Heaven, with prayer and thanksgiving, and let a name be given to it by its parents, and let the presbyter sprinkle pure water upon it, according to that which is written in the prophets, and let its parents see to it that it is brought up in the ways of righteousness, neither eating flesh, nor drinking strong drink, nor hurting the creatures which God hath given into the hands of man to protect .

7 AGAIN one said unto him, Master, how wilt thou when they grow up? And Jesus said, After seven years, or when they begin to know the evil from the good, and learn to choose the good, let them come unto me and receive the blessing at the hands of the presbyter or the angel of the church with prayer and thanksgiving, and let them be admonished to keep from flesh eating and strong drink, and from hunting the innocent creatures of God, for shall they be lower than the horse or the sheep to whom these things are against nature?

8 And again he said, If there come to us any that eat flesh and drink strong drink, shall we receive them? And Jesus said unto him, Let such abide in the

outer court till they cleanse themselves from these grosser evils; for till they perceive, and repent of these, they are not fit to receive the higher mysteries.

9 AND another asked him saying, When wilt thou that they receive Baptism? And Jesus answered, After another seven years, or when they know the doctrine, and do that which is good, and learn to work with their own hands, and choose a craft whereby they may live, and are stedfastly set on the right way. Then let them ask for initiation, and let the angel or presbyter of the church examine them and see if they are worthy, and let him offer thanksgiving and prayer, and bury them in the waters of separation, that they may rise to newness of life, confessing God as their Father and Mother, vowing to obey the Holy Law, and keep themselves separate from the evil in the world.

10 AND another asked him, Master, at what time shall they receive the Anointing? And Jesus answered, When they have reached the age of maturity, and manifested in themselves the sevenfold gifts of the Spirit, then let the angel offer prayer and thanksgiving and seal them with the seal of the Chrism. It is good that all be tried in each degree seven years. Nevertheless let it be unto each according to their growth in the love, and the wisdom of God.

CHAPTER 91 5 -The idea of baptizing unconscious infants seems never to have entered the mind of Jesus. He blessed them, but he also blessed other animals, and things that had no sentient life. Baptism implies belief and confession of faith and repentance from evil works and ways.

CHAPTER 91 6 -Over 2,000 years before Christ there existed on the shores of Lake Meeris, in Egypt, a labyrinth of seven circular wall-enclosed winding paths, represented by Boticelli in one of his engravings, which we here reproduce adapted for Christian rites. This was used by the Egyptians in their initiations as a symbol of life, and the wanderings of the soul in the flesh, till "seven times

seven" times purified and meet to appear before God.

CHAPTER 91 7-8 -In the Editor's former work "Palingenesia, or Earth's New Birth," 1884, incorporating some Ideas from this Gospel (part of which he had then received) these two rites referred to, by some oversight were transposed. Here, as in" Church of the Future" 1896, by the same Editor, the correct order is given. It is at present out of print.

CHAPTER 92

The Order of the Kingdom. (Part II.)

1 AND another asked him saying, Master, wilt thou that there be marriages among us as it is among the nations of earth? And Jesus answered, saying, Among some it is the custom that one woman may marry several men, who shall say unto her, Be thou our wife and take away our reproach. Among others it is the custom, that one man may marry several women, and who shall say unto him, Be thou our husband and take away our reproach, for they who love feel it is a reproach to be unloved.

2 But unto you my disciples, I shew a better and more perfect way, even this, that marriage should be between one man and one woman, who by perfect love and sympathy are united, and that while love and life do last, howbeit in perfect freedom. But let them see to it that they have perfect health, and that they truly love each other in all purity, and not for worldly advantage only, and then let them plight their troth one to another before witnesses.

3 Then, when the time is come, let the angel or presbyter offer prayer and thanksgiving and bind them with the scarlet cord, if ye will, and crown them, and lead them thrice around the altar and let them eat of one bread and drink of one cup. Then holding their hands together, let him say to them in this wise, Be ye two in one, blessed be the holy union, you whom God doth join together let no man put asunder, so long as life and love do last.

4 And if they bear children, let them do

so with discretion and prudence according to their ability to maintain them. Nevertheless to those who would be perfect and to whom it is given, I say, let them be as the angels of God in Heaven, who neither marry nor are given in marriage, nor have children, nor care for the morrow, but are free from bonds, even as I am, and keep and store up the power of God within, for their ministry, and for works of healing, even as I have done. But the many cannot receive this saying, only they to whom it is given.

5 AND another asked him saying, Master, in what manner shall we offer the Holy Oblation? And Jesus answered, saying, The oblation which God loveth in secret is a pure heart. But for a Memorial of worship offer ye unleavened bread, mingled wine, oil and incense. When ye come together in one place to offer the Holy Oblation, the lamps being lighted, let him who presideth, even the angel of the church, or the presbyter, having clean hands and a pure heart, take from the things offered, unleavened bread and mingled wine with incense.

6 And let him give thanks over them and bless them, calling upon the Father-Mother in Heaven to send their Holy Spirit that it may come upon and make them to be the Body and Blood, even the Substance and Life of the Eternal, which is ever being broken and shed for all.

7 And let him lift it up toward Heaven and pray for all, even for those who are gone before, for those who are yet alive, and for those who are yet to come As I have taught you, so pray ye, and after this let him break the bread and put a fragment in the cup, and then bless the holy union, and then let him give unto the faithful, saying after this manner, This is the body of the Christ even the substance of God (ever being broken and shed, for you and for all), unto eternal life. As ye have seen me do, so do ye also, in the spirit of love, for the words I speak unto you, they are spirit and they are life.

CHAPTER 92 4 -Here we have further proof, if any were needed, that Jesus was brought up in the tenets and customs of the Essenes. See "Christianity and Buddhism" (a remarkable book by Arthur Lillie) for the full discussion of the subject.
v. 6 -Similar were the rites of Mithra. From the days of Noah and Melchizedek these pure mysteries were celebrated -though not in the fulness of the light of Christ.

CHAPTER 93
The Order of the Kingdom. (Part III.)
1 AND another spake, saying, Master, if one have committed a sin, can a man remit or retain his sin? And Jesus said, God forgiveth all sin to those who repent, but as ye sow, so also must ye reap; Neither God nor man can remit the sins of those who repent nor nor forsake their sins; nor yet retain the sins of those who forsake them. But if one being in the spirit seeth clearly that any repent and forsake their sins, such may truly say unto the penitent, Thy sins are forgiven thee, for All sin is remitted by repentance and amendment and they are loosed from it, who forsake it and bound to it, who continue it.

2 Nevertheless the fruits of the sin must continue for a season, for as we sew so must we reap, for God is not mocked, and they who sow to the flesh shall reap corruption, they who sow to the spirit shall reap life, everlasting. Wherefore if any forsake their sins and confess them, let the presbyter say unto such in this wise, May God forgive thee thy sins, and bring thee to everlasting life. All sin against God is forgiven by God, and sin against man by man.

3 AND another asked him, saying, If any be sick among us, shall we have power to heal even as thou dost? And Jesus answered, This power cometh of perfect chastity and of faith. They who are born of God keep their seed within them.

4 Nevertheless if any be sick among you, let them send for the presbyters of the church that they may anoint them with oil of olive in the Name of de

Lord, and the prayer of faith, and the going out of power, with the voice of thanksgiving, shall raise them up, if they are not detained by sin, of this, or a former life.

5 AND another asked him saying, Master, how shall the holy assembly be ordered and who shall minister therein? And Jesus answered. When my disciples are gathered in my name let them choose from among themselves true and faithful men and women, who shall be ministers and counsellors in temporal things and provide for the necessities of the poor, and those who cannot work, and let these look to the ordering of the goods of the church, and assist at the Oblation, and let these be your deacons, with their helps.

6 And when these have given proof, of their ministry, let them choose from them, those who have spiritual gifts, whether of guidance, or of prophecy, or of preaching and of teaching and healing, that they may edify the flock, offer the holy Oblation and minister the mysteries of God and let these be your presbyter, and their helps.

7 And from these who have served well in their degree let one be chosen who is counted most worthy, and let him preside over all and he shall be your Angel. And let the Angel ordain the deacons and consecrate the presbyters —anoint them and laying their hands upon them and breathing upon them that they may receive the Holy Spirit for the office to which they are called. And as for the Angel let one of the higher ministry anoint and consecrate him, even one of the Supreme Council.

8 For as I send Apostles and Prophets so also I send Evangelists And Pastors —the eight and forty pillars of the tabernacle—that by the ministry of the four I may build up and perfect my Church. and they shall sit in Jerusalem a holy congregation, each with his helper and deacon, and to them shall the scattered congregations refer in all matters pertaining to the Church. And as light cometh so shall they rule and guide and edify and teach my holy Church. They shall receive light from all, and to all shall they give more light.

9 And forget not with your prayers and supplications intercessions and giving of thanks, to offer the incense, as it is written in the last of your prophets, saying, From the rising of the sun unto the setting of the same incense shall be offered unto My Name in all places with a pure oblation, for My Name shall be great among the Gentiles.

10 For verily I say unto you, incense is the memorial of the intercession of the saints within the veil, with words that cannot be uttered.

CHAPTER 94

The Order of the Kingdom. (Part IV.)

1 AND another asked him, saying, Master, how wilt thou that we bury our dead? And Jesus answered, Seek ye council of the deacons in this matter, for it concerneth the body only. Verily, I say, unto you there is no death to those who believe in the life to come. Death, as ye deemed it, is the door to life, and the grave is the gate to resurrection, for those who believe and obey. Mourn ye not, nor weep for them that have left you, but rather rejoice for their entrance into life.

2 As all creatures come forth from the unseen into this world, so they return to the unseen, and so will they come again till they be purified. Let the bodies of them that depart be committed to the elements, and the Father-Mother, who reneweth all things, shall give the angels charge over them, and let the presbyter pray that their bodies may rest in peace, and their souls awake to a joyful resurrection.

3 There is a resurrection from the body, and there is a resurrection in the body. There is a raising out of the life of the flesh, and there is a falling into the life of the flesh. Let prayer be made For those who are gone before, and For those that are alive, and For those that are yet to come, for all are One family in God. In God they live and move and have their being.

4 The body that ye lay in the grave, or that is consumed by fire, is not the body that shall be, but they who come shall

receive other bodies, yet their own, and as they have sown in one life, so shall they reap in another. Blessed are they who have worked righteousness in this life, for they shall receive the crown of life.

5 AND another asked him, saying, Master, under the law Moses clad the priests with garments of beauty for their ministration in the Temple. Shall we also clothe them to whom we commit the ministry of sacred things as thou hast taught us? And Jesus answered, White linen is the righteousness of the Saints, but the time truly cometh when Zion shall be desolate, and after the time of her affliction is past, she shall arise and put on her beautiful garments as it is written.

6 But seek ye first the kingdom of righteousness, and all these things shall be added unto you. In all things seek simplicity, and give not occasion to vain glory. Seek ye first to be clothed with charity, and the garment of salvation and the robe of righteousness.

7 For what doth it profit if ye have not these? As the sound of brass and tinkling of cymbal are ye, if ye have not love. Seek ye righteousness and love and peace, and all things of beauty shall be added to you.

8 AND yet another asked him, saying, Master, how many of the rich and mighty will enter into life and join us who are poor and despised. How, then, shall we carry on the work of God in the regeneration of mankind? And Jesus said, This also is a matter for the deacons of the church in council with the elders.

9 But when my disciples are come together on the Sabbath, at even, or in the morning of the first day of the week, let them each bring an offering of a tithe, or the tithe of a tithe of their increase, as God doth prosper them, and put it in the treasury, for the maintenance of the church and the ministry, and the works thereof. For I say unto you, it is more blessed to give than to receive.

10 So shall all things be done, decently and in order, And the rest will the Spirit set in order who proceedeth from the Father-Mother in heaven. I have instructed you now in first principles, and, lo, I am with you always, even unto the end of the Age.

CHAPTER 94 7 -From this, as from other words of the Master on previous occasions, it is evident that his servant Paul borrowed from him many of the ideas, and similes and wise sayings scattered through his Epistles, and not Paul only, but also the other Apostles. (See also verse 9).

v. 10 -It has been alleged that the laying down of rites and ordinances for Christianity has been the cause of division and strife in all countries. Nay, rather have not these divisions and dissensions been caused by the omission of the directions given by the One Head acknowledged by all during the period between his resurrection and ascension and the generation immediately after, and the handling of them down by that tradition so liable to corruption in place of the written record. But much more were these divisions and dissensions caused by the interpolation of dogmas not making for goodness and unity, by the suppression from the records of the vital essence in the holy law given by Jesus on the Mount, which, had it been preached and known and obeyed by all, would have made the earth a paradise in place of a hen for the weak and the helpless.

CHAPTER 95
The Ascension.

1 AND Jesus after he had shewed himself alive to his disciples after his resurrection, and sojourned with them for ninety days, teaching and speaking of the Kingdom, and the things pertaining to the Kingdom of God, and had finished all things that he had to do, led forth the twelve with Mary Magdalene, and Joseph his father and Mary his mother, and the other holy women as far as Bethany to a mountain called Olivet, where he had appointed them.

2 And when they saw him as he stood in the midst of them, they worshipped him, but some doubted. And Jesus spake unto them, saying, Behold, I have chosen you from among men, and have given you the Law, and the Word of truth.

3 I have set you as the light of the world, and as a city that cannot be hid. But the time cometh when darkness shall cover the earth, and gross darkness the people, and the enemies of truth and righteousness shall rule in my Name, and set up a kingdom of this world, and oppress the peoples, and cause the enemy to blaspheme, putting for my doctrines the opinions of men, and teaching in my Name that which I have not taught, and darkening much that I have taught by their traditions.

4 But be of good cheer, for the time will also come when the truth they have hidden shall be manifested, and the light shall shine, and the darkness shall pass away, and the true kingdom shall be established which shall be in the world, but not of it, and the Word of righteousness and love shall go forth from the Centre, even the holy city of Mount Zion, and the Mount which is in the land of Egypt shall be known as an altar of witness unto the Lord.

5 And now I go to my Parent and your Parent, my God and your God. But ye, tarry in Jerusalem, and abide in prayer, and after seven days ye shall receive power from on high, and the promise of the Holy Spirit shall be fulfilled unto you, and ye shall go forth from Jerusalem unto all the tribes of Israel, and to the uttermost parts of the earth.

6 And having said these things, he lifted up his pure and holy hands and blessed them. And it came to pass that while he blessed them, he was parted from them, and a cloud, as the sun in brightness, received him out of their sight, and as he went up some held him by the feet and others worshipped him, falling to the earth on their faces.

7 And while they gazed steadfastly into heaven, behold two stood by them in white apparel, and said, Ye men of Israel, why stand ye gazing into thee, heaven; this same Jesus who is taken from you in a cloud, and as ye have seen him go into heaven, so shall he come again to the earth.

8 Then returned they unto Jerusalem from the Mount of Olives, which is from the city a Sabbath day's journey. And as they returned they missed Mary Magdalene, and they looked for her, but found her not. And some of the disciples said, The Master hath taken her, and they marvelled and were in great awe.

9 Now it was midsummer when Jesus ascended into heaven, and he had not yet attained his fiftieth year, for it was needful that seven times seven years should be fulfilled in his life.

10 Yea, that he might be perfected by the suffering of all experiences, and be an example unto all, to children and parents, to the married and the celibates, to youth and those of full age, yea, and unto all ages and conditions of mortal life.

CHAPTER 95 5 -There is no doubt that the "power" here referred to means the spiritual power which we read of as exercised by the followers of Jesus and other great prophets in all ages more or less. Taking the various accounts in the Gospel and ecclesiastical history as correct, miracles (i.e., wondrous works wrought by the exercise of faith and will power and often by the uses of subtle forces of nature, quite natural, but seemingly supernatural to those in ignorance of these forces) were of frequent occurrences in those days, even as they are in these days, but better understood, false miracles being no proof of the non-existence of true ones. Often they would be the effect exercised on the minds and imaginations of vast numbers of the poor and afflicted, the diseased and suffering of humanity by faith in some great champions of the oppressed, themselves destroyed by the oppressor, yet realised by faith, if not by actual knowledge as still living and acting, with hands outstretched to heal and bless those who invoked their aid.

v. 9 -From the testimony of the Jews, John viii. 57, A. V., it appears that Jesus at that time was not far from fifty years of age, and this is supported by S. Irenmus, 120-200 A.D., who appeals to the gospel as received by those of his day and to all the elders as testifying the same," those who were conversant in Asia with John, the disciple of the Lord, affirming that John conveyed to them this tradition." "Some of them," he says again, "not only saw John but the other Apostles also, and heard the very same tradition from them. Bond bear testimony to the truth of the statement." The Editor of this Gospel has been credibly informed by an esteemed friend of his, "a Syrian Bishop," and a relative of the late learned Pope Pius IX., that he frequently (in private) assured him that he firmly held this (as a private opinion), the present time (1870) not being yet ripe for a public declaration on this and similar subjects, now introduced into the notes to this and other publications of the O.A.

CHAPTER 95 8 -Mary Magdalene was chosen by our Lord as a type of the Church, in her fallen condition, redeemed by His love, and would be fitly one of the first fruits taken to be with her Lord, as Joseph and Mary were after. She was the constant companion of Jesus' Ministry, to him she ministered of her substance, she anointed him for his Ministry, and for his Burial. She was the last at the Cross, and the first at the Tomb, and to her alone He gave the commission, " Go tell Peter," and wheresoever the Gospel was to be preached, her love and devotion to her Master were to be declared.

CHAPTER 96

The Pouring Out Of The Spirit.

1 AND as the disciples were gathered together in the upper room when they returned from the Mount, they all continued with one accord in prayer and supplication, and their number was about one hundred and twenty.

2 And in that day James stood up and said; Men and brethren, it is known unto you how the Lord, before he left us, chose Peter to preside over us and watch over us in his Name; and how it must needs be that one of those who have been with us and a witness to his resurrection be chosen and appointed to take his place.

3 And they chose two called Barsabas and Matthias, and they prayed and said, Thou lord, who knowest the hearts of all men, shew which of these two thou hast chosen to take part in this Apostleship from which thou dost raise thy servant Peter to preside over us.

4 And they gave forth their lots, and the lot fell upon Matthias, and the Twelve received him, and he was numbered among the Apostles.

5 Then John and James separated Peter from their number by laying on of hands, that he might preside over them in the Name of the Lord, saying, Brother be thou as a hewn stone, sixsquared. Even thou, Petros, which art Petra, bearing witness to the Truth on every side.

6 And to the Apostles were given staves to guide their steps in the ways of truth, and crowns of glory withal; and to the Prophets burning lamps to shew light on the path and censers with fire; and to the Evangelists the book of the holy law to recall the people to the first principles; and to the Pastors were given the cup and platter to feed and nourish the flock.

7 But to none was given aught that was not given to all, for all were one priesthood under the Christ as their Master Great High Priest in the Temple of God; and to the Deacons were given baskets that they might carry therein the things needful for the holy worship. And the number was about one hundred and twenty, Peter presiding over them.

8 AND when the third day had fully come they were all with one accord in the one place, and as they prayed there came a sound from heaven as of a rushing mighty wind, and the room in which they were assembled was shaken, and it filled the place.

9 And there appeared cloven tongues of

flame like fire, and sat upon the head of each of them. And they were all filled with the Holy Spirit and began to speak with tongues as the Spirit gave them utterance. And Peter stood up and preached the Law of Christ unto the multitude of all nations and tongues who were gathered together by the report of what had been seen and heard, each man hearing in his own tongue wherein he was born.

10 And of them that listened there were gathered unto the Church that day, three thousand souls, and they received the Holy Law, repented of their sins, and were baptized and continued stedfastly in the Apostles' fellowship and worship, and the Oblation and prayers.

11 And they who believed gave up their possessions, and had all things in common and abode together in one place, shewing the love and the goodness of God to their brothers and sisters and to all creatures, and working with their hands for the common weal.

12 And from these there were called twelve to be Prophets with the Apostles, and twelve to be Evangelists and twelve to be Pastors, and their Helps were added unto them, and Deacons of the Church Universal, and they numbered one hundred and twenty. And thus was the Tabernacle of David set up, with living men filled with goodness, even as the Master had shewn unto them.

13 And to the Church in Jerusalem was given James the Lord's brother for its president and Angel, and under him four and twenty priests in a fourfold ministry, and helpers and deacons also. And after six days many came together, and there were added six thousand men and women who received the holy Law of Love, and they received the word with gladness.

14 AND as they gathered together on the Lord's Day after the Sabbath was past, and were offering the holy Oblation, they missed Mary and Joseph, the parents of Jesus. And they made search but found them not.

15 And some of them said, Surely the Lord hath taken them away, as he did Magdalene. And they were filled with awe, and sung praises to God.

16 And the Spirit of God came upon the Apostles and the Prophets with them and, remembering what the Lord had taught them, with one voice they confessed and praised God, saying.

17 We believe in One God: the Infinite, the Secret Fount, the Eternal Parent: Of Whom are all things invisible and visible. The ALL in all, through all around all. The holy Twain, in whom all things consist; Who hath been, Who is, Who shall be.

18 We believe in one Lord our Lady, the perfect holy Christ: God of God, Light of light begotten. Our Lord, the Father, Spouse and Son. Our Lady, the Mother, Bride and Daughter. Three Modes in one Essence undivided: One Biune Trinity. That God may be manifest as the Father, Spouse and Son of every soul: and that every soul may be perfected as the Mother, Bride and Daughter of God

19 And this by ascent of the soul into the spirit and the descent of the spirit into the soul. Who cometh from heaven, and is incarnate of the Virgin ever blessed, in Jesu-Maria and every Christ of God: and is born and teacheth the way of life and suffereth under the world rulers, and is crucified, and is buried and descendeth into Hell. Who riseth again and ascendeth into glory; from thence giving light and life to all.

20 We believe in the Sevenfold Spirit of God, the Life-Giver: Who proceedeth from the holy Twain. Who cometh upon Jesu-Maria and all that are faithful to the light within: Who dwelleth in the Church, the Israel elect of God. Who cometh ever into the world and lighteth every soul that seeks. Who giveth the Law which judgeth the living and the dead, Who speaketh by the Prophets of every age and clime.

21 We believe in One Holy Universal and Apostolic Church: the Witness to all truth, the Receiver and Giver of the same. Begotten of the Spirit and Fire of God: Nourished by the waters, seeds and fruits of earth. Who by the Spirit of Life, her twelve Books and Sacraments, her holy words and works: knitteth

together the elect in one mystical communion and atoneth humanity with God. Making us partakers of the Divine Life and Substance: betokening the same in holy Symbols.

22 And we look for the coming of the Universal Christ: and the Kingdom of Heaven wherein dwelleth righteousness. And the holy City whose gates are Twelve: wherein are the Temple and Altar of God. Whence proceed three Orders in fourfold ministry: to teach all truth and offer the daily sacrifice of praise.

23 As in the inner so in the outer: as in the great so in the small. As above, so below: as in heaven so in earth. We believe in the Purification of the soul: through many births and experiences. The Resurrection from the dead: and the Life everlasting of the just. The Ages of Ages: and Rest in God for ever. —Amen.

24 And as the smoke of the incense arose, there was heard the sound as of many bells, and a multitude of the heavenly host praising God and saying: 25 Glory, honour, praise and worship be to God; the Father,, Spouse, and Son: One with the Mother, Bride and Maid: From Whom proceedeth the Eternal Spirit: By whom are all created things. From the Ages of Ages. Now: and to the Ages of Ages—Amen—Alleluia, Alleluia, Alleluia.

26 And if any man take from, or add, to the words of this Gospel, or hide, as under a bushel, the light thereof, which is given by the Spirit through us, the twelve witnesses chosen of God, for the enlightenment of the world unto salvation: Let him be Anathema Maranatha, until the coming of Christ Jesu-Maria, our Saviour, with all the Holy Saints.

27 For them that believe, these things are true. For them that believe not, they are as an idle tale. But to those with perceiving minds and hearts, regarding the spirit rather than the letter which killeth, they are spiritual verities.

28 For the things that are written are true, not because they are written, but rather they are written because they are true, and these are written that ye may believe with your hearts, and proclaim with your mouths to the salvation of many. Amen.

Here endeth the Holy Gospel of the Perfect Life of Jesu-Maria, the Christ, the Son of David after the Flesh, the Son of God after the Spirit. Glory be to God by Whose power and help it has been written.

CHAPTER 96 1 -This number, 120, has many mystic significances, and was foreshadowed by the number of souls saved in the Ark at the Flood, which included 48 (i.e., double 7 + 34) + 72, a number of deep mystic significance. v. 2 -The manifestations described here have been repeated in modern times. What God does in one age, whether by angels, spirits, or adepts in the flesh, the same unchanging God repeats in another. Whether the miracle respecting the preaching of Peter took place in the persons of the Apostles, or in their hearers, we have no means of ascertaining, but the fact remains. Most probably in the hearing of the hearers, so that each was enabled spiritually to understand. or else all were moved to speak and to hear in a tongue common to all.

THE GOSPEL OF NICODEMUS

CHAPTER 1

1 Christ accused to Pilate by the Jews of healing on the sabbath, 9 summoned before Pilate by a messenger who does him honour, 20 worshipped by the standards bowing down to him.

ANNAS and Caiaphas, and Summas, and Datam, Gamaliel, Judas, Levi, Nepthalim, Alexander, Cyrus, and other Jews, went to Pilate about Jesus, accusing him with many bad crimes.

2 And said, We are assured that Jesus is the son of Joseph the carpenter, land born of Mary, and that he declares himself the Son of God, and a king; and not only so, but attempts the dissolution of the sabbath, and the laws of our fathers.

3 Pilate replied; What is it which he declares? and what is it which he attempts dissolving?

4 The Jews told him, We have a law which forbids doing cures on the sabbath day; but he cures both the lame and the deaf, those afflicted with the palsy, the blind, and lepers, and demoniacs, on that day by wicked methods.

5 Pilate replied, How can he do this by wicked methods? They answered, He is a conjurer, and casts out devils by the prince of the devils; and so all things become subject to him.

6 Then said Pilate, Casting out devils seems not to be the work of an unclean spirit, but to proceed from the power of God.

7 The Jews replied to Pilate, We entreat your highness to summon him to appear before your tribunal, and hear him yourself.

8 Then Pilate called a messenger and said to him, By what means will Christ be brought hither?

9 Then went the messenger forth, and knowing Christ, worshipped him; and having spread the cloak which he had in his hand upon the ground, he said, Lord, walk upon this, and go in, for the governor calls thee.

10 When the Jews perceived what the messenger had done they exclaimed (against him) to Pilate, and said, Why did you not give him his summons by a beadle, and not by a messenger?—For the messenger, when he saw him, worshipped him, and spread the cloak which he had in his hand upon the ground before him, and said to him, Lord, the governor calls thee.

11 Then Pilate called the messenger, and said, Why hast thou done thus?

12 The messenger replied, When thou sentest me from Jerusalem to Alexander, I saw Jesus sitting in a mean figure upon a she-ass, and the children of the Hebrews cried out, Hosannah, holding boughs of trees in their hands.

13 Others spread their garments in the way, and said, Save us, thou who art in heaven; blessed is he who cometh in the name of the Lord.

14 Then the Jews cried out, against the messenger, and said, The children of the Hebrews made their acclamations in the Hebrew language; and how couldst thou, who art a Greek, understand the Hebrew?

15 The messenger answered them and said, I asked one of the Jews and said, What is this which the children do cry out in the Hebrew language?

16 And he explained it to me, saying, they cry out Hosannah, which being interpreted, is, O, Lord, save me; or, O Lord, save.

17 Pilate then said to them, Why do you yourselves testify to the words spoken by the children, namely, by your silence? In what has the messenger done amiss? And they were silent.

18 Then the governor said unto the messenger, Go forth and endeavour by any means to bring him in.

19 But the messenger went forth, and did as before; and said, Lord, come in, for the governor calleth thee.

20 And as Jesus was going in by the ensigns, who carried the standards, the tops of them bowed down and worshipped Jesus.

21 Whereupon the Jews exclaimed more vehemently against the ensigns.

22 But Pilate said to the Jews, I know it is not pleasing to you that the tops of the standards did of themselves bow and worship Jesus; but why do ye exclaim against the ensigns, as if they had bowed and worshipped?

23 They replied to Pilate, We saw the ensigns themselves bowing and worshipping Jesus.

24 Then the governor called the ensigns and said unto them, Why did you do thus?

25 The ensigns said to Pilate, We are all Pagans and worship the gods in temples; and how should we think anything about worshipping him? We

only held the standards in our hands and they bowed themselves and worshipped him.

26 Then said Pilate to the rulers of the synagogue, Do ye yourselves choose some strong men, and let them hold the standards, and we shall see whether they will then bend of themselves.

27 So the elders of the Jews sought out twelve of the most strong and able old men, and made them hold the standards and they stood in the presence of the governor.

28 Then Pilate said to the messenger, Take Jesus out, and by some means bring him in again. And Jesus and the messenger went out of the hall.

29 And Pilate called the ensigns who before had borne the standards, and swore to them, that if they had not borne the standards in that manner when Jesus before entered in, he would cut off their heads.

30 Then the governor commanded Jesus to come in again.

31 And the messenger did as he had done before, and very much entreated Jesus that he would go upon his cloak, and walk on it, and he did walk upon it, and went in.

32 And when Jesus went in, the standards bowed themselves as before, and worshipped him.

CHAPTER 2

2 Is compassionated by Pilate's wife, 7 charged with being born in fornication. 12 Testimony to the betrothing of his parents. Hatred of the Jews to him.

NOW when Pilate saw this, he was afraid, and was about to rise from his seat.

2 But while he thought to rise, his own wife who stood at a distance, sent to him, saying Have thou nothing to do with that just man; for I have suffered much concerning him in a vision this night. 1

3 When the Jews heard this they said to Pilate, Did we not say unto thee, He is a conjuror? Behold, he hath caused thy wife to dream.

4 Pilate then calling Jesus, said, thou hast heard what they testify against thee, and makest no answer?

5 Jesus replied, If they had not a power of speaking, they could not have spoke; but because every one has the command of his own tongue, to speak both good and bad, let him look to it.

6 But the elders of the Jews answered, and said to Jesus, What shall we look to?

7 In the first place, we know this concerning thee, that thou wast born through fornication; secondly, that upon the account of thy birth the infants were slain in Bethlehem; thirdly, that thy father and mother Mary fled into Egypt, because they could not trust their own people.

8 Some of the Jews who stood by spake more favourably, We cannot say that he was born through fornication; but we know that his mother Mary was betrothed to Joseph, and so he was not born through fornication.

9 Then said Pilate to the Jews who affirmed him to be born through fornication, This your account is not true, seeing there was a betrothment, as they testify who are of your own nation.

10 Annas and Caiaphas spake to Pilate, All this multitude of people is to be regarded, who cry out, that he was born through fornication, and is a conjuror; but they who deny him to be born through fornication, are his proselytes and disciples.

11 Pilate answered Annas and Caiaphas, Who are the proselytes? They answered, They are those who are the children of Pagans, and are not become Jews, but followers of him.

12 Then replied Eleazer, and Asterius, and Antonius, and James, Caras and Samuel, Isaac and Phinees, Crispus and Agrippa, Annas and Judas, We are not proselytes, but children of Jews, and speak the truth, and were present when Mary was betrothed.

13 Then Pilate addressing himself to the twelve men who spake this, said to them, I conjure you by the life of Cæsar, that ye faithfully declare whether he was born through

fornication, and those things be true which ye have related.

14 They answered Pilate, We have a law, whereby we are forbid to swear, it being a sin: Let them swear by the life of Cæsar that it is not as we have said, and we will be contented to be put to death.

15 Then said Annas and Caiaphas to Pilate, Those twelve men will not believe that we know him to be basely born, and to be a conjuror, although he pretends that he is the son of God, and a king: which we are so far from believing, that we tremble to hear.

16 Then Pilate commanded every one to go out except the twelve men who said he was not born through fornication, and Jesus to withdraw to a distance, and said to them, Why have the Jews a mind to kill Jesus?

17 They answered him, They are angry because he wrought cures on the Sabbath day. Pilate said, Will they kill him for good work? They say unto him, Yes, Sir.

CHAPTER 3

1 Is exonerated by Pilate. 11 Disputes with Pilate concerning Truth.

THEN Pilate, filled with anger, went out of the hall, and said to the Jews, I call the whole world to witness that I find no fault in that man.

2 The Jews replied to Pilate, If he had not been a wicked person, we had not brought him before thee.

3 Pilate said to them, Do ye take him and try him by your law.

4 Then the Jews said, It is not lawful for us to put any one to death.

5 Pilate said to the Jews, The command, therefore thou shalt not kill, belongs to you, but not to me.

6 And he went again into the hall, and called Jesus by himself, and said to him, Art thou the king of the Jews?

7 And Jesus answering, said to Pilate, Dost thou speak this of thyself, or did the Jews tell it thee concerning me?

8 Pilate answering, said to Jesus, Am I a Jew? The whole nation and rulers of the Jews have delivered thee up to me. What hast thou done?

9 Jesus answering, said, My kingdom is not of this world: if my kingdom were of this world, then would my servants fight, and I should not have been delivered to the Jews; but now my kingdom is not from hence.

10 Pilate said, Art thou a king then? Jesus answered, Thou sayest that I am a king: to this end was I born, and for this end came I into the world; and for this purpose I came, that I should bear witness to the truth; and every one who is of the truth, heareth my voice.

11 Pilate saith to him, What is truth?

12 Jesus said, Truth is from heaven.

13 Pilate said, Therefore truth is not on earth.

14 Jesus said to Pilate, Believe that truth is on earth among those, who when they have the power of judgment, are governed by truth, and form right judgment.

CHAPTER 4

1 Pilate finds no fault in Jesus. 16 The Jews demand his crucifixion.

THEN Pilate left Jesus in the hall, and went out to the Jews, and said, I find not any one fault in Jesus.

2 The Jews say unto him, But he said, I can destroy the temple of God, and in three days build it up again.

3 Pilate saith unto them, What sort of temple is that of which he speaketh?

4 The Jews say unto him, That which Solomon was forty-six years in building, he said he would destroy, and in three days build up.

5 Pilate said to them again, I am innocent from the blood of that man; do ye look to it. 5

6 The Jews say to him, His blood be upon us and our children. Then Pilate calling together the elders and scribes, priests and Levites, saith to them privately, Do not act thus; I have found nothing in your charge (against him) concerning his curing sick persons, and breaking the sabbath, worthy of death.

7 The Priests and Levites replied to

Pilate, By the life of Cæsar, if any one be a blasphemer, he is worthy of death; but this man hath blasphemed against the Lord.

8 Then the governor again commanded the Jews to depart out of the hall; and calling Jesus, said to him, What shall I do with thee?

9 Jesus answered him, Do according as it is written.

10 Pilate said to him, How is it written?

11 Jesus saith to him, Moses and the prophets have prophesied concerning my suffering and resurrection.

12 The Jews hearing this, were provoked, and said to Pilate, Why wilt thou any longer hear the blasphemy of that man?

13 Pilate saith to them, If these words seem to you blasphemy, do ye take him, bring him to your court, and try him according to your law.

14 The Jews reply to Pilate, Our law saith, he shall be obliged to receive nine and thirty stripes, but if after this manner he shall blaspheme against the Lord, he shall be stoned.

15 Pilate saith unto them, If that speech of his was blasphemy, do ye try him according to your law.

16 The Jews say to Pilate, Our law commands us not to put any one to death: we desire that he may be crucified, because he deserves the death of the cross.

17 Pilate saith to them, It is not fit he should be crucified: let him be only whipped and sent away. 3

18 But when the governor looked upon the people that were present and the Jews, he saw many of the Jews in tears, and said to the chief priests of the Jews, All the people do not desire his death.

19 The elders of the Jews answered to Pilate, We and all the people came hither for this very purpose, that he should die.

20 Pilate saith to them, Why should he die?

21 They said to him, Because he declares himself to be the Son of God, and a King.

CHAPTER 5

1 Nicodemus speaks in defence of Christ, and relates his miracles. 12 Another Jew, 26 with Veronica, 34 Centurio, and others, testify of other miracles.

BUT Nicodemus, a certain Jew, stood before the governor, and said, I entreat thee, O righteous judge, that thou wouldst favour me with the liberty of speaking a few words.

2 Pilate said to him, Speak on.

3 Nicodemus said, I spake to the elders of the Jews, and the scribes, and priests and Levites, and all the multitude of the Jews, in their assembly; What is it ye would do with this man?

4 He is a man who hath wrought many useful and glorious miracles, such as no man on earth ever wrought before, nor will ever work. Let him go, and do him no harm; if he cometh from God, his miracles, (his miraculous cures) will continue; but if from men, they will come to nought. 2

5 Thus Moses, when he was sent by God into Egypt, wrought the miracles which God commanded him, before Pharaoh king of Egypt; and though the magicians of that country, Jannes and Jambres, wrought by their magic the same miracles which Moses did, yet they could not work all which he did; 4

6 And the miracles which the magicians wrought, were not of God, as ye know, O Scribes and Pharisees; but they who wrought them perished, and all who believed them. 5

7 And now let this man go; because the very miracles for which ye accuse him, are from God; and he is not worthy of death.

8 The Jews then said to Nicodemus, Art thou become his disciple, and making speeches in his favour?

9 Nicodemus said to them, Is the governor become his disciple also, and does he make speeches for him? Did not Cæsar place him in that high post?

10 When the Jews heard this they trembled, and gnashed their teeth at Nicodemus, and said to him, Mayest

thou receive his doctrine for truth, and have thy lot with Christ!

11 Nicodemus replied, Amen; I will receive his doctrine, and my lot with him, as ye have said.

12 ¶ Then another certain Jew rose up, and desired leave of the governor to hear him a few words.

13 And the governor said, Speak what thou hast a mind.

14 And he said, I lay for thirty-eight years by the sheep-pool at Jerusalem, labouring under a great infirmity, and waiting for a cure which should be wrought by the coming of an angel, who at a certain time troubled the water; and whosoever first after the troubling of the water stepped in, was made whole of whatsoever disease he had.

15 And when Jesus saw me languishing there, he said to me, Wilt thou be made whole? And I answered, Sir, I have no man, when the water is troubled, to put me into the pool.

16 And he said unto me, Rise, take up thy bed and walk. And I was immediately made whole, and took up my bed and walked.

17 The Jews then said to Pilate, Our Lord Governor, pray ask him what day it was on which he was cured of his infirmity.

18 The infirm person replied, It was on the sabbath.

19 The Jews said to Pilate, Did we not say that he wrought his cures on the sabbath, and cast out devils by the prince of devils?

20 Then another certain Jew came forth, and said, I was blind, could hear sounds, but could not see any one; and as Jesus was going along, I heard the multitude passing by, and I asked what was there?

21 They told me that Jesus was passing by: then I cried out, saying, Jesus, Son of David, have mercy on me. And he stood still, and commanded that I should be brought to him, and said to me, What wilt thou?

22 I said, Lord, that I may receive my sight.

23 He said to me, Receive thy sight: and presently I saw, and followed him, rejoicing and giving thanks.

24 Another Jew also came forth, and said, I was a leper, and he cured me by his word only, saying, I will, be thou clean; and presently I was cleansed from my leprosy.

25 And another Jew came forth, and said, I was crooked, and he made me straight by his word.

26 ¶ And a certain woman named Veronica, said, I was afflicted with an issue of blood twelve years, and I touched the hem of his garments, and presently the issue of my blood stopped.

27 The Jews then said, We have a law, that a woman shall not be allowed as an evidence.

28 And, after other things, another Jew said, I saw Jesus invited to a wedding with his disciples, and there was a want of wine in Cana of Galilee;

29 And when the wine was all drank, he commanded the servants that they should fill six pots which were there with water, and they filled them up to the brim, and he blessed them, and turned the water into wine, and all the people drank, being surprised at this miracle.

30 And another Jew stood forth, and said, I saw Jesus teaching in the synagogue at Capernaum; and there was in the synagogue a certain man who had a devil; and he cried out, saying, let me alone; what have we to do with thee, Jesus of Nazareth? Art thou come to destroy us? I know that thou art the Holy One of God.

31 And Jesus rebuked him, saying, Hold thy peace, unclean spirit, and come out of the man; and presently he came out of him, and did not at all hurt him.

32 The following things were also said by a Pharisee; I saw that a great company came to Jesus from Galilee and Judaea, and the sea-coast, and many countries about Jordan, and many infirm persons came to him, and he healed them all. 6

33 And I heard the unclean spirits crying out, and saying, Thou art the Son

of God. And Jesus strictly charged them, that they should not make him known.

34 ¶ After this another person, whose name was Centurio, said, I saw Jesus in Capernaum, and I entreated him, saying, Lord, my servant lieth at home sick of the palsy.

35 And Jesus said to me, I will come and cure him.

36 But I said, Lord, I am not worthy that thou shouldst come under my roof; but only speak the word, and my servant shall be healed.

37 And Jesus said unto me, Go thy way; and as thou hast believed, so be it done unto thee. And my servant was healed from that same hour.

38 Then a certain nobleman said, I had a son in Capernaum, who lay at the point of death; and when I heard that Jesus was come into Galilee, I went and besought him that he would come down to my house, and heal my son, for he was at the point of death.

39 He said to me, Go thy way, thy son liveth.

40 And my son was cured from that hour.

41 Besides these, also many others of the Jews, both men and women, cried out and said, He is truly the Son of God, who cures all diseases only by his word, and to whom the devils are altogether subject.

42 Some of them farther said,, This power can proceed fro none but God.

43 Pilate said to the Jews Why are not the devils subject your doctors?

44 Seine of them said, The power of subjecting devils can not proceed but from God.

45 But others said to Pilate That he had raised Lazarus from the dead, after he had been four days in his grave.

46 The governor hearing this, trembling said to the multitude of the Jews, What will it profit you to shed innocent blood?

CHAPTER 6

1 Pilate dismayed by the turbulence of the Jews, who demand Barabbas to be released, and Christ to be crucified, 9 Pilate warmly expostulates with them, 20 washes his hands of Christ's blood, 23 and sentences him to be whipped and crucified.

THEN Pilate having called together Nicodemus, and the fifteen men who said that Jesus was not born through fornication, said to them, What shall I do, seeing there is like to be a tumult among the people.

2 They said unto him, We know not; let them look to it who raise the tumult.

3 Pilate then called the multitude again, and said to them, Ye know that ye have a custom, that I should release to you one prisoner at the feast of the passover;

4 I have a noted prisoner, a murderer, who is called Barabbas, and Jesus who is called Christ, in whom I find nothing that deserves death; which of them therefore have you a mind that I should release to you?

5 They all cry out, and say, Release to us Barabbas.

6 Pilate saith to them, What then shall I do with Jesus who, is called Christ?

7 They all answer, Let him be crucified.

8 Again they cry out and say to Pilate, You are not the friend of Cæsar, if you release this man? for he hath declared that he is the Son of God, and a king. But are you inclined that he should be king, and not Cæsar?

9 Then Pilate filled with anger said to them, Your nation hath always been seditious, and you are always against those who have been serviceable to you?

10 The Jews replied, Who are those who have been serviceable to us?

11 Pilate answered them, Your God who delivered you from the hard bondage of the Egyptians, and brought you over the Red Sea as though it had been dry land, and fed you in the wilderness with manna and the flesh of quails, and brought water out of the rock, and gave you a law from heaven:

12 Ye provoked him all ways, and desired for yourselves a molten calf,

and worshipped it, and sacrificed to it, and said, These are Thy Gods, O Israel, which brought thee out of the land of Egypt

13 On account of which your God was inclined to destroy you; but Moses interceded for you, and your God heard him, and forgave your iniquity.

14 Afterwards ye were enraged against, and would have killed your prophets, Moses and Aaron, when they fled to the tabernacle, and ye were always murmuring against God and his prophets.

15 And arising from his judgment seat, he would have gone out; but the Jews all cried out, We acknowledge Cæsar to be king, and not Jesus.

16 Whereas this person, as soon as he was born, the wise men came and offered gifts unto him; which when Herod heard, he was exceedingly troubled, and would have killed him.

17 When his father knew this, he fled with him and his mother Mary into Egypt. Herod, when he heard he was born, would have slain him; and accordingly sent and slew all the children which were in Bethlehem, and in all the coasts thereof, from two years old and under.

18 When Pilate heard this account, he was afraid; and commanding silence among the people, who made a noise, he said to Jesus, Art thou therefore a king?

19 All the Jews replied to Pilate, he is the very person whom Herod sought to have slain.

20 Then Pilate taking water, washed his hands before the people and said, I am innocent of the blood of this just person; look ye to it.

21 The Jews answered and said, His blood be upon us and our children.

22 Then Pilate commanded Jesus to be brought before him, and spake to him in the following words:

23 Thy own nation hath charged thee as making thyself a king; wherefore I, Pilate, sentence thee to be whipped according to the laws of former governors; and that thou be first bound, then hanged upon a cross in that place

where thou art now a prisoner; and also two criminals with thee, whose names are Dimas and Gestas.

CHAPTER 7
1 Manner of Christ's crucifixion with the two thieves.

THEN Jesus went out of the hall, and the two thieves with him.

2 And when they came to the place which is called Golgotha, they stript him of his raiment, and girt him about with a linen cloth, and put a crown of thorns upon his head, and put a reed in his hand.

3 And in like manner did they to the two thieves who were crucified with him, Dimas on his right hand and Gestas on his left.

4 But Jesus said, My Father, forgive them; For they know not what they do.

5 And they divided his garments, and upon his vesture they cast lots.

6 The people in the mean time stood by, and the chief priests and elders of the Jews mocked him, saying, he saved others, let him now save himself if he can; if he be the son of God, let him now come down from the cross.

7 The soldiers also mocked him, and taking vinegar and gall offered it to him to drink, and said to him, If thou art king of the Jews deliver thyself.

8 Then Longinus, a certain soldier, taking a spear, pierced his side, and presently there came forth blood and water.

9 And Pilate wrote the title upon the cross in Hebrew, Latin, and Greek letters, viz. This is the king of the Jews.

10 But one of the two thieves who were crucified with Jesus, whose name was Gestas, said to Jesus, If thou art the Christ, deliver thyself and us.

11 But the thief who was crucified on his right hand, whose name was Dimas, answering, rebuked him, and said, Dost not thou fear God, who art condemned to this punishment? We indeed receive rightly and justly the demerit of our actions; but this Jesus, what evil hath he done?

12 After this groaning, he said to Jesus, Lord, remember me when thou comest into thy kingdom.

13 Jesus answering, said to him, Verily I say unto thee, that this day thou shalt be with me in Paradise.

CHAPTER 8

1 Miraculous appearance at his death. 10 The Jews say the eclipse was natural. 12 Joseph of Arimathæa embalms Christ's body and buries it.

AND it was about the sixth hour, and darkness was upon the face of the whole earth until the ninth hour.

2 And while the sun was eclipsed, behold the vail of the temple was rent from the top to the bottom; and the rocks also were rent, and the graves opened, and many bodies of saints, which slept, arose.

3 And about the ninth hour Jesus cried out with a loud voice, saying, Hely, Hely, lama zabacthani? which being interpreted, is, My God, My God, why hast thou forsaken me?

4 And after these things, Jesus said, Father, into thy hands I commend my spirit; and having said this, he gave up the ghost.

5 But when the centurion saw that Jesus thus crying out gave up the ghost, he glorified God, and said, Of a truth this was a just man.

6 And all the people who stood by, were exceedingly troubled at the sight; and reflecting upon what had passed, smote upon their breasts, and then returned to the city of Jerusalem.

7 The centurion went to the governor, and related to him all that had passed;

8 And when he had heard all these things, he was exceeding sorrowful;

9 And calling the Jews together, said to them, Have ye seen the miracle of the sun's eclipse, and the other things which came to pass, while Jesus was dying?

10 Which when the Jews heard, they answered to the governor, The eclipse of the sun happened according to its usual custom.

11 But all those who were the acquaintance of Christ, stood at a distance, as did the women who had followed Jesus from Galilee, observing all these things.

12 And behold a certain man of Arimathæa, named Joseph, who also was a disciple of Jesus, but not openly so, for fear of the Jews, came to the governor, and entreated the governor that he would give him leave to take away the body of Jesus from the cross.

13 And the governor gave him leave.

14 And Nicodemus came, bringing with him a mixture of myrrh and aloes about a hundred pound weight; and they took down Jesus from the cross with tears, and bound him with linen cloths with spices, according to the custom of burying among the Jews,

15 And placed him in a new tomb, which Joseph had built, and caused to be cut out of a rock, in which never any man had been put; and they rolled a great stone to the door of the sepulchre.

CHAPTER 9

1 The Jews angry with Nicodemus; 5 and with Joseph of Arimathæa, 7 whom they imprison.

WHEN the unjust Jews heard that Joseph had begged and buried the body of Jesus, they sought after Nicodemus; and those fifteen men who had testified before the Governor, that Jesus was not born through fornication, and other good persons who had shewn any good actions towards him.

2 But when they all concealed themselves through fear of the Jews, Nicodemus alone shewed himself to them, and said, How can such persons as these enter into the synagogue?

3 The Jews answered him, But how durst thou enter into the synagogue who wast a confederate with Christ? Let thy lot be along with him in the other world.

4 Nicodemus answered, Amen; so may it be, that I may have my lot with him in his kingdom.

5 In like manner Joseph, when he came to the Jews, said to them Why are ye

angry with me for desiring the body of Jesus of Pilate? Behold, I have put him in my tomb, and wrapped him up in clean linen, and put a stone at the door of the sepulchre:

6 I have acted rightly towards him; but ye have acted unjustly aghast that just person, in crucifying him, giving him vinegar to drink, crowning him with thorns, tearing his body with whips, and prayed down the guilt of his blood upon you.

7 The Jews at the hearing of this were disquieted, and troubled; and they seized Joseph, and commanded him to be put in custody before the sabbath, and kept there till the sabbath was over.

8 And they said to him, Make confession; for at this time it is not lawful to do thee any harm, till the first day of the week come. But we know that thou wilt not be thought worthy of a burial; but we will give thy flesh to the birds of the air, and the beasts of the earth.

9 Joseph answered, That speech is like the speech of proud Goliath, who reproached the living God in speaking against David. But ye scribes and doctors know that God saith by the prophet, Vengeance is mine, and I will repay to you evil equal to that which ye have threatened to me.

10 The God whom you have hanged upon the cross, is able to deliver me out of your hands. All your wickedness will return upon you.

11 For the governor, when he washed his hands, said, I am clear from the blood of this just person. But ye answered and cried out, His blood be upon us and our children. According as ye have said, may ye perish for ever.

12 The elders of the Jews hearing these words, were exceedingly enraged; and seizing Joseph, they put him into a chamber where there was no window; they fastened the door, and put a seal upon the lock;

13 And Annas and Caiaphas placed a guard upon it, and took counsel with the priests and Levites, that they should all meet after the sabbath, and they contrived to what death they should put Joseph.

14 When they had done this, the rulers, Annas and Caiaphas, ordered Joseph to be brought forth.

¶ In this place there is a portion of the Gospel lost or omitted, which cannot be supplied.

CHAPTER 10

1 Joseph's escape. 2 The soldiers relate Christ's resurrection. 18 Christ is seen preaching in Galilee. 21 The Jews repent of their cruelty to him.

WHEN all the assembly heard this, they admired and were astonished, because they found the same seal upon the lock of the chamber, and could not find Joseph.

2 Then Annas and Caiaphas went forth, and while they were all admiring at Joseph's being gone, behold one of the soldiers, who kept the sepulchre of Jesus, spake in the assembly.

3 That while they were guarding the sepulchre of Jesus, there was an earthquake; and we saw an angel of God roll away the stone of the sepulchre and sit upon it;

4 And his countenance was like lightning and his garment like snow; and we became through fear like persons dead.

5 And we heard an angel saying to the women at the sepulchre of Jesus, Do not fear; I know that you seek Jesus who was crucified; he is risen as he foretold.

6 Come and see the place where he was laid; and go presently, and tell his disciples that he is risen from the dead, and he will go before you into Galilee; there ye shall see him as he told you.

7 Then the Jews called together all the soldiers who kept the sepulchre of Jesus, and said to them, Who are those women, to whom the angel spoke? Why did ye not seize them?

8 The soldiers answered and said, We know not whom the women were; besides we became as dead persons through fear, and how could we seize those women?

9 The Jews said to them, As the Lord liveth we do not believe you.

10 The soldiers answering said to the Jews, when ye saw and heard Jesus working so many miracles, and did not believe him, how should ye believe us? Ye well said, As the Lord liveth, for the Lord truly does live.

11 We have heard that ye shut up Joseph, who buried the body of Jesus, in a chamber, under a lock which was sealed; and when ye opened it, found him not there.

12 Do ye then produce Joseph whom ye put under guard in the chamber, and we will produce Jesus whom we guarded in the sepulchre.

13 The Jews answered and said, We will produce Joseph, do ye produce Jesus. But Joseph is in his own city of Arimathæa.

14 The soldiers replied, If Joseph be in Arimathæa, and Jesus in Galilee, we heard the angel inform the women.

15 The Jews hearing this, were afraid, and said among themselves, If by any means these things should become public, then every body will believe in Jesus.

16 Then they gathered a large sum of money, and gave it to the soldiers, saying, Do ye tell the people that the disciples of Jesus came in the night when ye were asleep and stole away the body of Jesus; and if Pilate the governor should hear of this, we will satisfy him and secure you.

17 The soldiers accordingly took the money, and said as they were instructed by the Jews; and their report was spread abroad among the people.

18 ¶ But a certain priest Phinees, Ada a schoolmaster, and a Levite, named Ageus, they three came from Galilee to Jerusalem, and told the chief priests and all who were in the synagogues, saying,

19 We have seen Jesus, whom ye crucified, talking with his eleven disciples, and sitting in the midst of them in Mount Olivet, and saying to them, 1

20 Go forth into the whole world, preach the Gospel to all nations, baptizing them in the name of the Father, and the Son, and the Holy Ghost; and whosoever shall believe and be baptized, shall be saved.

21 And when he had said these things to his disciples, we saw him ascending up to heaven.

22 When the chief priests, and elders, and Levites heard these things, they said to these three men, Give glory to the God of Israel, and make confession to him, whether those things are true, which ye say ye have seen and heard.

23 They answering said, As the Lord of our fathers liveth, the God of Abraham, and the God of Isaac, and the God of Jacob, according as we heard Jesus talking with his disciples, and according as we saw him ascending up to heaven, so we have related the truth to you.

24 And the three men farther answered, and said, adding these words, If we should not own the words which we heard Jesus speak, and that we saw him ascending into heaven, we should be guilty of sin.

25 Then the chief priests immediately rose up, and holding the book of the law in their hands, conjured these men, saying, Ye shall no more hereafter declare those things which ye have spoke concerning Jesus.

26 And they gave them a large sum of money, and sent other persons along with them, who should conduct them to their own country, that they might not by any means make any stay at Jerusalem.

27 Then the Jews did assemble all together, and having expressed the most lamentable concern, said, What is this extraordinary thing which is come to pass in Jerusalem?

28 But Annas and Caiaphas comforted them, saying, Why should we believe the soldiers who guarded the sepulchre of Jesus, in telling us, that an angel rolled away the stone from the door of the sepulchre?

29 Perhaps his own disciples told them this, and gave them money that they should say so, and they themselves took away the body of Jesus.

30 Besides, consider this, that there is no credit to be given to foreigners,

because they also took a large sum of us, and they have declared to us according to the instructions which we gave them. They must either be faithful to us, or to the disciples of Jesus.

CHAPTER 11

1 Nicodemus counsels the Jews. 6 Joseph found. 11 Invited by the Jews to return. 19 Relates the manner of his miraculous escape.

THEN Nicodemus arose, and said, Ye say right, O sons of Israel, ye have heard what those three men have sworn by the Law of God, who said, We have seen Jesus speaking with his disciples upon Mount Olivet, and we saw him ascending up to heaven.

2 And the scripture teacheth us that the blessed prophet Elijah was taken up to heaven; and Elisha being asked by the sons of the prophets, Where is our father Elijah? He said to them, that he is taken up to heaven.

3 And the sons of the prophets said to him, Perhaps the spirit hath carried him into one of the mountains of Israel, there perhaps we shall find him. And they besought Elisha, and he walked about with them three days, and they could not find him.

4 And now hear me, O sons of Israel, and let us send men into the mountains of Israel, lest perhaps the spirit hath carried away Jesus, and there perhaps we shall find him, and be satisfied.

5 And the counsel of Nicodemus pleased all the people; and they sent forth men who sought for Jesus, but could not find him: and they returning, said, We went all about, but could not find Jesus, but we have found Joseph in his city of Arimathæa.

6 The rulers hearing this, and all the people, were glad, and praised the God of Israel, because Joseph was found, whom they had shut up in a chamber, and could not find.

7 And when they had formed a large assembly, the chief priests said, By what means shall we bring Joseph to us to speak with him?

8 And taking a piece of paper, they wrote to him, and said, Peace be with thee, and all thy family. We know that we have offended against God and thee. Be pleased to give a visit to us your fathers, for we were perfectly surprised at your escape from prison.

9 We know that it was malicious counsel which we took against thee, and that the Lord took care of thee, and the Lord himself delivered thee from our designs. Peace be unto thee, Joseph, who art honourable among all the people.

10 And they chose seven of Joseph's friends, and said to them, When ye come to Joseph, salute him in peace, and give him this letter.

11 Accordingly, when the men came to Joseph, they did salute him in peace, and gave him the letter.

12 And when Joseph had read it, he said, Blessed be the Lord God, who didst deliver me from the Israelites, that they could not shed my blood. Blessed be God, who has protected me under thy wings.

13 And Joseph kissed them, and took them into his house. And on the morrow, Joseph mounted his ass, and went along with them to Jerusalem.

14 And when all the Jews heard these things, they went out to meet him, and cried out, saying, Peace attend thy coming hither, father Joseph.

15 To which he answered, Prosperity from the Lord attend all the people.

16 And they all kissed him; and Nicodemus took him to his house, having prepared a large entertainment.

17 But on the morrow, being a preparation-day, Annas, and Caiaphas, and Nicodemus, said to Joseph, Make confession to the God of Israel, and answer to us all those questions which we shall ask thee;

18 For we have been very much troubled, that thou didst bury the body of Jesus; and that' when we had locked thee in a chamber, we could not find thee; and we have been afraid ever since, till this time of thy appearing among us. Tell us therefore before God,

all that came to pass.

19 Then Joseph answering, said, Ye did indeed put me under confinement, on the day of preparation, till the morning.

20 But while I was standing at prayer in the middle of the night, the house was surrounded with four angels; and I saw Jesus as the brightness of the sun, and fell down upon the earth for fear.

21 But Jesus laying hold on my hand, lifted me from the ground, and the dew was then sprinkled upon me; but he, wiping my face, kissed me, and said unto me, Fear not, Joseph; look upon me, for it is I.

22 Then I looked upon him, and said, Rabboni Elias! He answered me, I am not Elias, but Jesus of Nazareth, whose body thou didst bury.

23 I said to him, Shew me the tomb in which I laid thee.

24 Then Jesus, taking me by the hand, led me unto the place where I laid him, and shewed me the linen clothes, and napkin which I put round his head. Then I knew that it was Jesus, and worshipped him, and said, Blessed be he who cometh in the name of the Lord.

25 Jesus again taking me by the hand, led me to Arimathæa to my own house, and said to me, Peace be to thee; but go not out of thy house till the fortieth day; but I must go to my disciples.

CHAPTER 12

1 The Jews astonished and confounded. 17 Simeon's two sons, Charinus and Lenthius, rise from the dead at Christ's crucifixion. 19 Joseph proposes to get them to relate the mysteries of their resurrection. 21 They are sought and found, 22 brought to the synagogue, 23 privately sworn to secrecy, 25 and undertake to write what they had seen.

WHEN the chief priests and heard all these things, they were astonished, and fell down with their faces on the ground as dead men, and crying out to one another said, What is this extraordinary sign which is come to pass in Jerusalem? We know the father and mother of Jesus.

2 And a certain Levite said, I know many of his relations, religious persons, who are wont to offer sacrifices and burnt-offerings to the God of Israel, in the temple, with prayers.

3 And when the high priest Simeon took him up in his arms. he said to him, Lord, now lettest thou thy servant depart in peace, according to thy word; for mine eyes have seen thy salvation, which thou hast prepared before the face of all people: a light to enlighten the Gentiles, and the glory of thy people Israel.

4 Simeon in like manner blessed Mary the mother of Jesus, and said to her, I declare to thee concerning that child; He is appointed for the fall and rising again of many, and for a sign which shall be spoken against.

5 Yea, a sword shall pierce through thine own soul also, and the thoughts of many hearts shall be revealed.

6 Then said all the Jews, Let us send to those three men, who said they saw him talking with his disciples in Mount Olivet.

7 After this, they asked them what they had seen; who answered with one accord, In the presence of the God of Israel we affirm, that we plainly saw Jesus talking with his disciples in Mount Olivet, and ascending up to heaven.

8 Then Annas and Caiaphas took them into separate places, and examined them separately; who unanimously confessed the truth, and said, they had seen Jesus.

9 Then Annas and Caiaphas said "Our law saith, By the mouth of two or three witnesses every word shall be established." 2

10 But what have we said? The blessed Enoch pleased God, and was translated by the word of God; and the burying-place of the blessed Moses is known.

11 But Jesus was delivered to Pilate, whipped, crowned with thorns, spit upon, pierced with a spear, crucified, died upon the cross, and was buried, and his body the honorable Joseph buried in a new sepulchre, and he testifies that he saw him alive.

12 And besides these men have declared, that they saw him talking with his disciples in Mount Olivet, and ascending up to heaven.

13 ¶ Then Joseph rising up. said to Annas and Caiaphas, Ye may be justly under a great surprise, that you have been told, that Jesus is alive, and gone up to heaven.

14 It is indeed a thing really surprising, that he should not only himself arise from the dead, but also raise others from their graves, who have been seen by many in Jerusalem. 3

15 And now hear me a little: We all knew the blessed Simeon, the high-priest, who took Jesus when an infant into his arms in the temple.

16 This same Simeon had two sons of his own, and we were all present at their death and funeral.

17 Go therefore and see their tombs, for these are open, and they are risen: and behold, they are in the city of Arimathæa, spending their time together in offices of devotion.

18 Some, indeed, have heard the sound of their voices in prayer, but they will not discourse with any one, but they continue as mute as dead men.

19 But come, let us go to them, and behave ourselves towards them with all due respect and caution. And if we can bring them to swear, perhaps they will tell us some of the mysteries of their resurrection.

20 When the Jews heard this, they were exceedingly rejoiced.

21 Then Annas and Caiaphas, Nicodemus, Joseph, and Gamaliel, went to Arimathæa, but did not find them in their graves; but walking about the city, they bound them on their bended knees at their devotions:

22 Then saluting them with all respect and deference to God, they brought them to the synagogue at Jerusalem: and having shut the gates, they took the book of the law of the Lord,

23 And putting it in their hands, swore them by God Adonai, and the God of Israel, who spake to our fathers by the law and the prophets, saying, If ye believe him who raised you from the dead, to be Jesus, tell us what ye have seen, and how ye were raised from the dead.

24 Charinus and Lenthius, the two sons of Simeon, trembled when they heard these things, and were disturbed, and groaned; and at the same time looking up to heaven, they made the sign of the cross with their fingers on their tongues.

25 And immediately they spake, and said, Give each of us some paper, and we will write down for you all those things which we have seen. And they each sat down and wrote, saying,

CHAPTER 13

1 The narrative of Charinus and Lenthius commences. 3 A great light in hell. 7 Simeon arrives, and announces the coming of Christ.

O LORD Jesus and Father, who art God, also the resurrection and life of the dead, give us leave to declare thy mysteries, which we saw after death, belonging to thy cross; for we are sworn by thy name.

2 For thou hast forbid thy servants to declare the secret things, which were wrought by thy divine power in hell.

3 ¶ When we were placed with our fathers in the depth of hell, in the blackness of darkness, on a sudden there appeared the colour of the sun like gold, and a substantial purple-coloured light enlightening the place.

4 Presently upon this, Adam, the father of all mankind, with all the patriarchs and prophets, rejoiced and said, That light is the author of everlasting light, who hath promised to translate us to everlasting light.

5 Then Isaiah the prophet cried out, and said, This is the light of the Father, and the Son of God, according to my prophecy, when I was alive upon earth.

6 The land of Zabulon, and the land of Nephthalim beyond Jordan, a people who walked in darkness, saw a great light; and to them who dwelled in the region of the shadow of death, light is arisen. And now he is

come, and hath enlightened us who sat in death.

7 And while we were all rejoicing in the light which shone upon us, our father Simeon came among us, and congratulating all the company, said, Glorify the Lord Jesus Christ the Son of God.

8 Whom I took up in my arms when an infant in the temple, and being moved by the Holy Ghost, said to him, and acknowledged, That now mine eyes have seen thy salvation, which thou hast prepared before the face of all people, a light to enlighten the Gentiles and the glory of thy people Israel.

9 All the saints who were in the depth of hell, hearing this, rejoiced the more.

10 Afterwards there came forth one like a little hermit, and was asked by every one, Who art thou?

11 To which he replied, I am the voice of one crying in the wilderness, John the Baptist, and the prophet of the Most High, who went before his coming to prepare his way, to give the knowledge of salvation to his people for the forgiveness of sins.

12 And I John, when I saw Jesus coming to me, being moved by the Holy Ghost, I said, Behold the Lamb of God, behold him who takes away the sins of the world.

13 And I baptized him in the river Jordan, and saw the Holy Ghost descending upon him in the form of a dove, and heard a voice from heaven, saying, This is my beloved Son, in whom I am well pleased.

14 And now while I was going before him, I came down hither to acquaint you, that the Son of God will next visit us, and, as the day-spring from on high, will come to us, who are in darkness and the shadow of death.

CHAPTER 14

1 Adam causes Seth to relate what he heard from Michael the archangel, when he sent him to Paradise to entreat God to anoint his head in his sickness.

BUT when the first man our father

Adam heard these things, that Jesus was baptized in Jordan, he called out to his son, Seth, and said,

2 Declare to your sons, the patriarchs and prophets, all those things, which thou didst hear from Michael, the archangel, when I sent thee to the gates of Paradise, to entreat God that he would anoint my head when I was sick.

3 Then Seth, coming near to the patriarchs and prophets, said, I Seth, when I was praying to God at the gates of Paradise, beheld the angel of the Lord, Michael appear unto me saying, I am sent unto thee from the Lord; I am appointed to preside over human bodies.

4 I tell thee Seth, do not pray to God in tears, and entreat him for the oil of the tree of mercy wherewith to anoint thy father Adam for his head-ache;

5 Because thou canst not by any means obtain it till the last day and times, namely, till five thousand and five hundred years be past.

6 Then will Christ, the most merciful Son of God, come on earth to raise again the human body of Adam, and at the same time to raise the bodies of the dead, and when he cometh he will be baptized in Jordan:

7 Then with the oil of his mercy he will anoint all those who believe on him; and the oil of his mercy will continue to future generations, for those who shall be born of the water and the Holy Ghost unto eternal life.

8 And when at that time the most merciful Son of God, Christ Jesus, shall come down on earth, he will introduce our father Adam into Paradise, to the tree of mercy.

9 When all the patriarchs and prophets heard all these things from Seth, they rejoiced more.

CHAPTER 15

1 Quarrel between Satan and the prince of hell concerning the expected arrival of Christ in hell.

WHILE all the saints were vv rejoicing, behold Satan, the prince and captain of death, said to the prince of hell, 1

2 Prepare to receive Jesus of Nazareth himself, who boasted that he was the Son of God, and yet was a man afraid of death, and said, My soul is sorrowful even to death.

3 Besides he did many injuries to me and to many others; for those whom I made blind and lame and those also whom I tormented with several devils, he cured by his word; yea, and those whom I brought dead to thee, he by force takes away from thee.

4 To this the prince of hell replied to Satan, Who is that so-powerful prince, and yet a man who is afraid of death?

5 For all the potentates of the earth are subject to my power, whom thou broughtest to subjection by thy power.

6 But if be be so powerful in his human nature, I affirm to thee for truth, that he is almighty in his divine nature, and no man can resist his power.

7 When therefore he said be was afraid of death, he designed to ensnare thee, and unhappy it will be to thee for everlasting ages.

8 Then Satan replying, said to the prince of hell, Why didst thou express a doubt, and wast afraid to receive that Jesus of Nazareth, both thy adversary and mine?

9 As for me, I tempted him and stirred up my old people the Jews with zeal and anger against him?

10 I sharpened the spear for his suffering; I mixed the gall and vinegar, and commanded that he should drink it; I prepared the cross to crucify him, and the nails to pierce through Ibis hands and feet; and now his death is near at hand, I will bring him hither, subject both to thee and me.

11 Then the prince of hell answering, said, Thou saidst to me just now, that he took away the dead from me by force.

12 They who have been kept here till they should live again upon earth, were taken away hence, not by their own power, but by prayers made to God, and their almighty God took them from me.

13 Who then is that Jesus of Nazareth that by his word hath taken away the dead from me without prayer to God?

14 Perhaps it is the same who took away from me Lazarus, after he had been four days dead, and did both stink and was rotten, and of whom I had possession as a dead person, yet he brought him to life again by his power.

15 Satan answering, replied to the prince of hell, It is the very same person, Jesus of Nazareth.

16 Which when the prince of hell heard, he said to him, I adjure thee by the powers which belong to thee and me, that thou bring him not to me.

17 For when I heard of the power of his word, I trembled for fear, and all my impious company were at the same time disturbed;

18 And we were not able to detain Lazarus, but he gave himself a shake, and with all the signs of malice, he immediately went away from us; and the very earth, in which the dead body of Lazarus was lodged, presently turned him out alive.

19 And I know now that he is Almighty God who could perform such things, who is mighty in his dominion, and mighty in his human nature, who is the Saviour of mankind.

20 Bring not therefore this person hither, for he will set at liberty all those whom I hold in prison under unbelief, and bound with the fetters of their sins, and will conduct them to everlasting life.

CHAPTER 16

1 Christ's arrival at hell-gates; the confusion thereupon. 10 He descends into hell.

AND while Satan and the prince of hell were discoursing thus to each other, on a sudden there was a voice as of thunder and the rushing of winds, saying, Lift up your gates, O ye princes; and be ye lift up, O everlasting gates, and the King of Glory shall come in.

2 When the prince of hell heard this, he said to Satan, Depart from me, and begone out of my habitations; if thou art a powerful warrior, fight with the King of Glory. But what hast thou to do

with him?

3 And he cast him forth from his habitations.

4 And the prince said to his impious officers, Shut the brass gates of cruelty, and make them fast with iron bars, and fight courageously, lest we be taken captives.

5 But when all the company of the saints heard this they spake with a loud voice of anger to the prince of hell:

6 Open thy gates that the King of Glory may come in.

7 And the divine prophet David, cried out saying, Did not I when on earth truly prophesy and say, O that men would praise the Lord for his goodness, and for his wonderful works to the children of men.

8 For he hath broken the gates of brass, and cut the bars of iron in sunder. He hath taken them because of their iniquity, and because of their unrighteousness they are afflicted.

9 After this another prophet, namely, holy Isaiah, spake in like manner to all the saints, did not

I rightly prophesy to you when I was alive on earth?

10 The dead men shall live, and they shall rise again who are in their graves, and they shall rejoice who are in earth; for the dew which is from the Lord shall bring deliverance to them.

11 And I said in another place, O death, where is thy victory? O death, where is thy sting?

12 When all the saints heard these things spoken by Isaiah, they said to the prince of hell, Open now thy gates, and take away thine iron bars; for thou wilt now be bound, and have no power.

13 Then there was a great voice, as of the sound of thunder saying, Lift up your gates, O princes; and be ye lifted up, ye gates of hell, and the King of Glory will enter in.

14 The prince of hell perceiving the same voice repeated, cried out as though he had been ignorant, Who is that King of Glory?

15 David replied to the prince of hell, and said, I understand the words of that voice, because I spake them by his spirit. And now, as I have above said, I say unto thee, the Lord strong and powerful, the Lord mighty in battle: he is the King of Glory, and he is the Lord in heaven and in earth;

16 He hath looked down to hear the groans of the prisoners, and to set loose those that are appointed to death. 2

17 And now, thou filthy and stinking prince of hell, open thy gates, that the King of Glory may enter in; for he is the Lord of heaven and earth.

18 While David was saying this, the mighty Lord appeared in the form of a man, and enlightened those places which had ever before been in darkness,

19 And broke asunder the fetters which before could not be broken; and with his invincible power visited those who sate in the deep darkness by iniquity, and the shadow of death by sin. 3

CHAPTER 17

1 Death and the devils in great horror at Christ's coming. 13 He tramples on death, seizes the prince of hell, and takes Adam with him to heaven.

IMPIOUS Death and her cruel officers hearing these things, were seized with fear in their several kingdoms, when they saw the clearness of the light,

2 And Christ himself on a sudden appearing in their habitations; they cried out therefore, and said, We are bound by thee; thou seemest to intend our confusion before the Lord.

3 Who art thou, who hast no sign of corruption, but that bright appearance which is a full proof of thy greatness, of which yet thou seemest to take no notice?

4 Who art thou, so powerful and so weak, so great and so little, a mean and yet a soldier of the first rank, who can command in the form of a servant as a common soldier?

5 The King of Glory, dead and alive, though once slain upon the cross?

6 Who layest dead in the grave, and art come down alive to us, and in thy death all the creatures trembled, and all the stars were moved, and now hast thou

thy liberty among the dead, and givest disturbance to our legions?

7 Who art thou, who dost release the captives that were held in chains by original sin, and bringest them into their former liberty

8 Who art thou, who dost spread so glorious and divine a light over those who were made blind by the darkness of sin?

9 In like manner all the legions of devils were seized with the like horror, and with the most submissive fear cried out, and said,

10 Whence comes it, O thou Jesus Christ, that thou art a man so powerful and glorious in majesty, so bright as to have no spot, and so pure as to have no crime? For that lower world of earth, which was ever till now subject to us, and from whence we received tribute, never sent us such a dead man before, never sent us such presents as these to the princes of hell.

11 Who therefore art thou, who with such courage enterest among our abodes, and art not only not afraid to threaten us with the greatest punishments, but also endeavourest to rescue all others from the chains in which we hold them?

12 Perhaps thou art that Jesus, of whom Satan just now spoke to our prince, that by the death of the cross thou wert about to receive the power of death.

13 Then the King of Glory trampling upon death, seized the prince of hell, deprived him of all his power, and took our earthly father Adam with him to his glory.

CHAPTER 18

1 Beelzebub, prince of hell, vehemently upbraids Satan for persecuting Christ and bringing him to hell. 4. Christ gives Beelzebub dominion over Satan for ever, as a recompense for taking away Adam and his sons.

THEN the prince of hell took Satan, and with great indication said to him, O thou prince of destruction, author of Beelzebub's defeat and banishment, the scorn of God's angels and loathed by all righteous persons! What inclined thee to act thus?

2 Thou wouldst crucify the King of Glory, and by his destruction, hast made us promises of very large advantages, but as a fool wert ignorant of what thou wast about.

3 For behold now that Jesus of Nazareth, with the brightness of his glorious divinity, puts to flight all the horrid powers of darkness and death;

4 He has broke down our prisons from top to bottom, dismissed all the captives, released all who were bound, and all who were wont formerly to groan under the weight of their torments have now insulted us, and we are like to be defeated by their prayers.

5 Our impious dominions are subdued, and no part of mankind is now left in our subjection, but on the other hand, they all boldly defy us;

6 Though, before, the dead never durst behave themselves insolently towards us, nor, being prisoners, could ever on any occasion be merry.

7 ¶ O Satan, thou prince of all the wicked, father of the impious and abandoned, why wouldest thou attempt this exploit, seeing our prisoners were hitherto always without the least hopes of salvation and life?

8 But now there is not one of them does ever groan, nor is there the least appearance of a tear in any of their faces.

9 O prince Satan, thou great keeper of the infernal regions, all thy advantages which thou didst acquire by the forbidden tree, and the loss of Paradise, thou hast now lost by the wood of the cross;

10 And thy happiness all then expired, when thou didst crucify Jesus Christ the King of Glory.

11 Thou hast acted against thine own interest and mine, as thou wilt presently perceive by those large torments and infinite punishments which thou art about to suffer.

12 O Satan, prince of all evil, author of death, and source of all pride, thou shouldest first have inquired into the

evil crimes of Jesus of Nazareth, and then thou wouldest have found that he was guilty of no fault worthy of death.

13 Why didst thou venture, without either reason or justice, to crucify him, and hast brought down to our regions a person innocent and righteous, and thereby hast lost all the sinners, impious and unrighteous persons in the whole world?

14 While the prince of hell was thus speaking to Satan, the King of Glory said to Beelzebub, the prince of hell, Satan, the prince shall be subject to thy dominion for ever, in the room of Adam and his righteous sons, who are mine.

CHAPTER 19

1 Christ takes Adam by the hand, the rest of the saints join hands, and they all ascend with him to Paradise.

THEN Jesus stretched forth his hand, and said, Come to me, all ye my saints, who were created in my image, who were condemned by the tree of forbidden fruit, and by the devil and death;

2 Live now by the wood of my cross; the devil, the prince of this world, is overcome, and death is conquered.

3 Then presently all the saints were joined together under the hand of the most high God; and the Lord Jesus laid hold on Adam's hand and said to him, Peace be to thee, and all thy righteous posterity, which is mine.

4 Then Adam, casting himself at the feet of Jesus, addressed himself to him, with tears, in humble language, and a loud voice, saying, 1

5 I will extol thee, O Lord, for thou hast lifted me up, and hast not made my foes to rejoice over me. O Lord my God, I cried unto thee, and thou hast healed me.

6 O Lord thou hast brought up my soul from the grave; thou hast kept me alive, that I should not go down to the pit.

7 Sing unto the Lord, all ye saints of his, and give thanks at the remembrance of his holiness. For his anger endureth but for a moment; in his favour is life.

8 In like manner all the saints, prostrate at the feet of Jesus, said with one voice, Thou art come, O Redeemer of the world, and hast actually accomplished all things, which thou didst foretell by the law and thy holy prophets.

9 Thou hast redeemed the living by thy cross, and art come down to us, that by the death of the cross thou mightest deliver us from hell, and by thy power from death.

10 O, Lord, as thou hast put the ensigns of thy glory in heaven, and hast set up the sign of thy redemption, even thy cross on earth! so, Lord, set the sign of the victory of thy cross in hell, that death may have do minion no longer.

11 Then the Lord stretching forth his hand, made the sign of the cross upon Adam, and upon all his saints.

12 And taking hold of Adam by his right hand, he ascended from hell, and all the saints of God followed him.

13 Then the royal prophet David boldly cried, and said, O sing unto the Lord a new song, for he hath done marvellous things; his right hand and his holy arm have gotten him the victory.

14 The Lord hath made known his salvation, his righteousness hath he openly shewn in the sight of the heathen.

15 And the whole multitude of saints answered, saying, This honour have all his saints, Amen, Praise ye the Lord.

16 Afterwards, the prophet Habakkuk cried out, and said, Thou wentest forth for the salvation of thy people, even for the salvation of thy people.

17 And all the saints said, Blessed is he who cometh in the name of the Lord; for the Lord hath enlightened us. This is our God for ever and ever; he shall reign over us to everlasting ages, Amen.

18 In like manner all the prophets spake the sacred things of his praise, and followed the Lord.

CHAPTER 20

1 Christ delivers Adam to Michael the archangel. 3. They meet Enoch and Elijah in heaven, 5 and also the blessed thief, who relates how he cares to

Paradise.

THEN the Lord holding Adam by the hand, delivered him to Michael the archangel; and he led them into Paradise, filled with mercy and glory;

2 And two very ancient men met them, and were asked by the saints, Who are ye, who have not yet been with us in hell, and have had your bodies placed in Paradise?

3 One of them answering, said, I am Enoch, who was translated by the word of God: and this man who is with me, is Elijah the Tishbite, who was translated in a fiery chariot.

4 Here we have hitherto been, and have not tasted death, but are now about to return at the coming of Antichrist, being armed with divine signs and miracles, to engage with him in battle, and to be slain by him at Jerusalem, and to be taken up alive again into the clouds, after three days and a half.

5 ¶ And while the holy Enoch and Elias were relating this, behold there came another man in a miserable figure carrying the sign of the cross upon his shoulders.

6 And when all the saints saw him, they said to him, Who art thou? For thy countenance is like a thief's; and why dost thou carry a cross upon thy shoulders?

7 To which he answering, said, Ye say right, for I was a thief who committed all sorts of wickedness upon earth.

8 And the Jews crucified me with Jesus; and I observed the surprising things which happened in the creation at the crucifixion of the Lord Jesus.

9 And I believed him to be the Creator of all things, and the Almighty King; and I prayed to him, saying, Lord, remember me, when thou comest into thy kingdom.

10 He presently regarded my supplication, and said to me, Verily I say unto thee, this day thou shalt be with me in Paradise.

11 And he gave me this sign of the cross saying, Carry this, and go to Paradise; and if the angel who is the guard of Paradise will not admit thee, shew him the sign of the cross, and say unto him: Jesus Christ who is now crucified, hath sent me hither to thee.

12 When I did this, and told the angel who is the guard of Paradise all these things, and he heard them, he presently opened the gates, introduced me, and placed me on the right-hand in Paradise,

13 Saying, Stay here a little time, till Adam, the father of all mankind, shall enter in, with all his sons, who are the holy and righteous servants of Jesus Christ, who was crucified.

14 When they heard all this account from the thief, all the patriarchs said with one voice, Blessed be thou, O Almighty God, the Father of everlasting goodness, and the Father of mercies, who hast shewn such favour to those who were sinners against him, and hast brought them to the mercy of Paradise, and hast placed them amidst thy large and spiritual provisions, in a spiritual and holy life. Amen.

CHAPTER 21

1 Charinus and Lenthius being only allowed three days to remain on earth, 7 deliver in their narratives, which miraculously correspond; they vanish, 13 and Pilate records these transactions.

THESE are the divine and sacred mysteries which we saw and heard. I, Charinus and Lenthius are not allowed to declare the other mysteries of God, as the archangel Michael ordered us,

2 Saying, ye shall go with my brethren to Jerusalem, and shall continue in prayers, declaring and glorifying the resurrection of Jesus Christ, seeing he hath raised you from the dead at the same time with himself.

3 And ye shall not talk with any man, but sit as dumb persons till the time come when the Lord will allow you to relate the mysteries of his divinity.

4 The archangel Michael farther commanded us to go beyond Jordan, to an excellent and fat country, where there are many who rose from the dead

along with us for the proof of the resurrection of Christ.

5 For we have only three days allowed us from the dead, who arose to celebrate the passover of our Lord with our parents, and to bear our testimony for Christ the Lord, and we have been baptized in the holy river of Jordan. And now they are not seen by any one.

6 This is as much as God allowed us to relate to you; give ye therefore praise and honour to him, and repent, and he will have mercy upon you. Peace be to you from the Lord God Jesus Christ, and the Saviour of us all. Amen, Amen, Amen.

7 And after they had made an end of writing and had wrote in two distinct pieces of paper, Charinus gave what he wrote into the hands of Annas, and Caiaphas, and Gamaliel.

8 Lenthius likewise gave what he wrote into the hands of Nicodemus and Joseph; and immediately they were changed into exceeding white forms and were seen no more.

9 But what they had wrote was found perfectly to agree, the one not containing one letter more or less than the other.

10 When all the assembly of the Jews heard all these surprising relations of Charinus and Lenthius, they said to each other, Truly all these things were wrought by God, and blessed be the Lord Jesus for ever and ever, Amen.

11 And they went about with great concern, and fear, and trembling, and smote upon their breasts and went away every one to his home.

12 But immediately all these things which were related by the Jews in their synagogues concerning Jesus, were presently told by Joseph and Nicodemus to the governor.

13 And Pilate wrote down all these transactions, and placed all these accounts in the public records of his hall.

CHAPTER 22

1 Pilate goes to the temple; calls together the rulers, and scribes, and doctors. 2 Commands the gates to be shut; orders the book of the Scripture; and causes the Jews to relate what they really knew concerning Christ. 14 They declare that they crucified Christ in ignorance, and that they now know him to be the Son of God, according to the testimony of the Scriptures; which, after they put him to death, they are examined.

AFTER these things Pilate went to the temple of the Jews, and called together all the rulers and scribes, and doctors of the law, and went with them into a chapel of the temple.

2 And commanding that all the gates should be shut, said to them, I have heard that ye have a certain large book in this temple; I desire you therefore, that it may be brought before me.

3 And when the great book, carried by four ministers of the temple, and adorned with gold and precious stones, was brought, Pilate said to them all, I adjure you by the God of your Fathers, who made and commanded this temple to be built, that ye conceal not the truth from me.

4 Ye know all the things which are written in that book; tell me therefore now, if ye in the Scriptures have found any thing of that Jesus whom ye crucified, and at what time of the world he ought to have come: shew it me.

5 Then having sworn Annas and Caiaphas, they commanded all the rest who were with them to go out of the chapel.

6 And they shut the gates of the temple and of the chapel, and said to Pilate, Thou hast made us to swear, O judge, by the building of this temple, to declare to thee that which is true and right.

7 After we had crucified Jesus, not knowing that he was the Son of God, but supposing he wrought his miracles by some magical arts, we summoned a large assembly in this temple.

8 And when we were deliberating among one another about the miracles which Jesus had wrought,

we found many witnesses of our own country, who declared that they had seen him alive after his death, and that they heard him discoursing with his disciples, and saw him ascending unto the height of the heavens, and entering into them;

9 And we saw two witnesses, whose bodies Jesus raised from the dead, who told us of many strange things which Jesus did among the dead, of which we have a written account in our hands.

10 And it is our custom annually to open this holy book before an assembly, and to search there for the counsel of God.

11 And we found in the first of the seventy books, where Michael the archangel is speaking to the third son of Adam the first man, an account that after five thousand five hundred years, Christ the most beloved Son of God was come on earth,

12 And we further considered, that perhaps he was the very God of Israel who spoke to Moses, Thou shalt make the ark of the testimony; two cubits and a half shall be the length thereof, and a cubit and a half the breadth thereof, and a cubit and a half the height thereof.

13 By these five cubits and a half for the building of the ark of the Old Testament, we perceived and knew that in five thousand years and a half (one thousand) years, Jesus Christ was to come in the ark or tabernacle of a body;

14 And so our scriptures testify that he is the son of God, and the Lord and King of Israel.

15 And because after his suffering, our chief priests were surprised at the signs which were wrought by his means, we opened that book to search all the generations down to the generation of Joseph and Mary the mother of Jesus, supposing him to be of the seed of David;

16 And we found the account of the creation, and at what time he made the heaven and the earth and the first man Adam, and that from thence to the flood, were two thousand, two hundred and twelve years.

17 And from the flood to Abraham, nine hundred and twelve. And from Abraham to Moses, four hundred and thirty. And from Moses to David the king, five hundred and ten.

18 And from David to the Babylonish captivity, five hundred years. And from the Babylonish captivity to the incarnation of Christ, four hundred years.

19 The sum of all which amounts to five thousand and half (a thousand).

20 And so it appears, that Jesus whom we crucified, is Jesus Christ the Son of God, and true and Almighty God. Amen.

In the name of the Holy Trinity, thus end the Acts of our Saviour Jesus Christ, which the Emperor Theodosius the Great found at Jerusalem, in the hall of Pontius Pilate among the public records; the things were acted in the nineteenth year of Tiberius Cæsar, Emperor of the Romans, and in the seventeenth year of the government of Herod the son of Herod king of Galilee, on the eighth of the calends of April, which is the twenty-third day of the month of March, in the CCIId Olympiad, when Joseph and Caiaphas were Rulers of the Jews; being a History written in Hebrew by Nicodemus, of what happened after our Saviour's crucifixion.

THE GOSPEL OF PETER

[[Large portions of this text are missing.
It begins...]]

1 But of the Jews none washed his hands, neither Herod nor one of his judges. And since they did not desire to wash, Pilate stood up.

2 And then Herod the king orders the Lord to be taken away, having said to them, 'What I ordered you to do, do.'

3 But Joseph, the friend of Pilate and of

THE GOSPEL OF PETER

the Lord, had been standing there; and knowing they were about to crucify him, he came before Pilate and requested the body of the Lord for burial.

4 And Pilate, having sent to Herod, requested his body.

5 And Herod said: 'Brother Pilate, even if no one had requested him, we would have buried him, since indeed Sabbath is dawning. For in the Law it has been written: The sun is not to set on one put to death.'

And he gave him over to the people before the first day of their feast of the Unleavened Bread.

6 But having taken the Lord, running, they were pushing him and saying, 'Let us drag along the Son of God now that we have power over him.'

7 And they clothed him with purple and sat him on a chair of judgment, saying: 'Judge justly, King of Israel.'

8 And a certain one of them, having brought a thorny crown, put it on the head of the Lord.

9 And others who were standing there were spitting in his face, and others slapped his cheeks. Others were jabbing him with a reed; and some scourged him, saying, 'With such honor let us honor the Son of God.'

10 And they brought two wrongdoers and crucified the Lord in the middle of them. But he was silent as having no pain.

11 And when they had set the cross upright, they inscribed that THIS IS THE KING OF ISRAEL.

12 And having put his garments before him, they divided them up and threw as a gamble for them.

13 But a certain one of those wrongdoers reviled them, saying: 'We have been made suffer thus because of the wrong that we have done; but this one, having become Savior of men, what injustice had he done to you?'

14 And having become irritated at him, they ordered that there be no leg-breaking, so that he might die tormented.

15 But is was midday, and darkness held fast all Judea; and they were distressed and anxious lest the sun had set, since he was still living. For it is written for them: Let not the sun set on one put to death.

16 And someone of them said: 'Give him to drink gall with vinegary wine.' And having made a mixture, they gave to drink.

17 And they fulfilled all things and completed the sins on their own head.

18 But many went around with lamps, thinking that it was night, and they fell.

19 And the Lord screamed out, saying: 'My power, O power, you have forsaken me.' And having said this, he was taken up.

20 And at the same hour the veil of the Jerusalem sanctuary was torn into two.

21 And they drew out the nails from the hands of the Lord and placed him on the earth; and all the earth was shaken, and a great fear came about.

22 Then the sun shone, and it was found to be the ninth hour.

23 And the Jews rejoiced and gave his body to Joseph that he might bury it, since he was one who had seen the many good things he did.

24 And having taken the Lord, he washed and tied him with a linen cloth and brought him into his own sepulcher, called the Garden of Joseph.

25 Then the Jews and the elders and the priests, having come to know how much wrong they had done themselves, began to beat themselves and say: 'Woe to our sins. The judgment has approached and the end of Jerusalem.'

26 But I with the companions was sorrowful; and having been wounded in spirit, we were in hiding, for we were sought after by them as wrongdoers and as wishing to set fire to the sanctuary.

27 In addition to all these things we were fasting; and we were sitting mourning and weeping night and day until the Sabbath.

28 But the scribes and Pharisees and elders, having gathered together with one another, having heard that all the people were murmuring and beating their breasts, saying that 'If at his death these very great signs happened, behold how just he was,'

29 feared (especially the elders) and came before Pilate, begging him and saying,

30 'Give over soldiers to us in order that we may safeguard his burial place for three days, lest, having come, his disciples steal him, and the people accept that he is risen from the death, and they do us wrong.'

31 But Pilate gave over to them Petronius the centurion with soldiers to safeguard the sepulcher. And with these the elders and scribes came to the burial place.

32 And having rolled a large stone, all who were there, together with the centurion and the soldiers, placed it against the door of the burial place.

33 And they marked it with seven wax seals; and having pitched a tent there, they safeguarded it.

34 But early when the Sabbath was dawning, a crowd came from Jerusalem and the surrounding area in order that they might see the sealed tomb.

35 But in the night in which the Lord's day dawned, when the soldiers were safeguarding it two by two in every watch, there was a loud voice in heaven;

36 And they saw that the heavens were opened and that two males who had much radiance had come down from there and come near the sepulcher.

37 But that stone which had been thrust against the door, having rolled by itself, went a distance off the side; and the sepulcher opened, and both the young men entered.

38 And so those soldiers, having seen, awakened the centurion and the elders (for they too were present, safeguarding).

39 And while they were relating what they had seen, again they see three males who have come out from they sepulcher, with the two supporting the other one, and a cross following them,

40 and the head of the two reaching unto heaven, but that of the one being led out by a hand by them going beyond the heavens.

41 And they were hearing a voice from the heavens saying, 'Have you made proclamation to the fallen-asleep?'

42 And an obeisance was heard from the cross, 'Yes.'

43 And so those people were seeking a common perspective to go off and make these clear to Pilate;

44 and while they were still considering it through, there appear again the opened heavens and a certain man having come down and entered into the burial place.

45 Having seen these things, those around the centurion hastened at night before Pilate (having left the sepulcher which they were safeguarding) and described all the things that they indeed had seen, agonizing greatly and saying: 'Truly he was God's Son.'

46 In answer Pilate said: 'I am clean of the blood of the Son of God, but it was to you that this seemed the thing to do.'

47 Then all, having come forward, were begging and exhorting him to command the centurion and the soldiers to say to no one what they had seen.

48 'For,' they said, 'it is better for us to owe the debt of the greatest sin in the sight of God than to fall into the hands of the Jewish people and be stoned.'

49 And so Pilate ordered the centurion and the soldiers to say nothing.

50 Now at the dawn of the Lord's Day Mary Magdalene, a female disciple of the Lord (who, afraid because of the Jews since they were inflamed with anger, had not done at the tomb of the Lord what women were accustomed to do for the dead beloved by them),

51 Having taken with her women friends, came to the tomb where he had been placed.

52 And they were afraid lest the Jews should see them and were saying, 'If indeed on that day on which he was crucified we could not weep and beat ourselves, yet now at his tomb we may do these things.

53 But who will roll away for us even the stone placed against the door of the tomb in order that, having entered, we may sit beside him and do the expected things?

54 For the stone was large, and we were afraid lest anyone see us. And if we are

unable, let is throw against the door what we bring in memory of him; let us weep and beat ourselves until we come to our homes.'

55 And having gone off, they found the sepulcher opened. And having come forward, they bent down there and saw there a certain young man seated in the middle of the sepulcher, comely and clothed with a splendid robe, who said to them:

56 'Why have you come? Whom do you seek? Not that one who was crucified? He is risen and gone away. But if you do not believe, bend down and see the place where he lay, because he is not here. For he is risen and gone away to there whence he was sent.'

57 Then the women fled frightened.

58 Now it was the final day of the Unleavened Bread; and many went out returning to their home since the feast was over.

59 But we twelve disciples of the Lord were weeping and sorrowful; and each one, sorrowful because of what had come to pass, departed to his home.

60 But I, Simon Peter, and my brother Andrew, having taken our nets, went off to the sea. And there was with us Levi of Alphaeus whom the Lord ...

So ends the found texts of the Gospel of Peter

THE GOSPEL ACCORDING TO MARY MAGDALENE
OR, THE GOSPEL OF MARY

[[Pages 1 to 6 of the manuscript, containing chapters 1 - 3, are lost. The extant text starts on page 7...]]

CHAPTER 4

[. . .]Will matter then be destroyed or not?

[.........................]

22 The Savior said, All nature, all formations, all creatures exist in and with one another, and they will be resolved again into their own roots.

23 For the nature of matter is resolved into the roots of its own nature alone.

24 He who has ears to hear, let him hear.

25 Peter said to him, Since you have explained everything to us, tell us this also: What is the sin of the world?

26 The Savior said There is no sin, but it is you who make sin when you do the things that are like the nature of adultery, which is called sin.

27 That is why the Good came into your midst, to the essence of every nature in order to restore it to its root.

28 Then He continued and said, That is why you become sick and die, for you are deprived of the one who can heal you.

29 He who has a mind to understand, let him understand.

30 Matter gave birth to a passion that has no equal, which proceeded from something contrary to nature. Then there arises a disturbance in its whole body.

31 That is why I said to you, Be of good courage, and if you are discouraged be encouraged in the presence of the different forms of nature.

32 He who has ears to hear, let him hear.

33 When the Blessed One had said this, He greeted them all,saying, Peace be with you. Receive my peace unto yourselves.

34 Beware that no one lead you astray saying Lo here or lo there! For the Son of Man is within you.

35 Follow after Him!

36 Those who seek Him will find Him.

37 Go then and preach the gospel of the Kingdom.

38 Do not lay down any rules beyond what I appointed you, and do not give a law like the lawgiver lest you be constrained by it.

39 When He said this He departed.

CHAPTER 5

1 But they were grieved. They wept greatly, saying, How shall we go to the Gentiles and preach the gospel of the Kingdom of the Son of Man? If they did not spare Him, how will they spare us?

2 Then Mary stood up, greeted them all, and said to her brethren, Do not weep and do not grieve nor be irresolute, for His grace will be entirely with you and will protect you.

3 But rather, let us praise His greatness, for He has prepared us and made us into Men.

4 When Mary said this, she turned their hearts to the Good, and they began to discuss the words of the Savior.

5 Peter said to Mary, Sister we know that the Savior loved you more than the rest of woman.

6 Tell us the words of the Savior which you remember which you know, but we do not, nor have we heard them.

7 Mary answered and said, What is hidden from you I will proclaim to you.

8 And she began to speak to them these words: I, she said, I saw the Lord in a vision and I said to Him, Lord I saw you today in a vision. He answered and said to me,

9 Blessed are you that you did not waver at the sight of Me. For where the mind is there is the treasure.

10 I said to Him, Lord, how does he who sees the vision see it, through the soul or through the spirit?

11 The Savior answered and said, He does not see through the soul nor through the spirit, but the mind that is between the two that is what sees the vision and it is [...]

[[(pages 11 - 14 are missing from the manuscript)]]

CHAPTER 8

[..............]

10 And desire said, I did not see you descending, but now I see you ascending. Why do you lie since you

belong to me?

11 The soul answered and said, I saw you. You did not see me nor recognize me. I served you as a garment and you did not know me.

12 When it said this, it (the soul) went away rejoicing greatly.

13 Again it came to the third power, which is called ignorance.

14 The power questioned the soul, saying, Where are you going? In wickedness are you bound. But you are bound; do not judge!

15 And the soul said, Why do you judge me, although I have not judged?

16 I was bound, though I have not bound.

17 I was not recognized. But I have recognized that the All is being dissolved, both the earthly things and the heavenly.

18 When the soul had overcome the third power, it went upwards and saw the fourth power, which took seven forms.

19 The first form is darkness, the second desire, the third ignorance, the fourth is the excitement of death, the fifth is the kingdom of the flesh, the sixth is the foolish wisdom of flesh, the seventh is the wrathful wisdom. These are the seven powers of wrath.

20 They asked the soul, Whence do you come slayer of men, or where are you going, conqueror of space?

21 The soul answered and said, What binds me has been slain, and what turns me about has been overcome,

22 and my desire has been ended, and ignorance has died.

23 In a aeon I was released from a world, and in a Type from a type, and from the fetter of oblivion which is transient.

24 From this time on will I attain to the rest of the time, of the season, of the aeon, in silence.

CHAPTER 9

1 When Mary had said this, she fell silent, since it was to this point that the Savior had spoken with her.

2 But Andrew answered and said to the

brethren, Say what you wish to say about what she has said. I at least do not believe that the Savior said this. For certainly these teachings are strange ideas.

3 Peter answered and spoke concerning these same things.

4 He questioned them about the Savior: Did He really speak privately with a woman and not openly to us? Are we to turn about and all listen to her? Did He prefer her to us?

5 Then Mary wept and said to Peter, My brother Peter, what do you think? Do you think that I have thought this up myself in my heart, or that I am lying about the Savior?

6 Levi answered and said to Peter, Peter you have always been hot tempered.

7 Now I see you contending against the woman like the adversaries.

8 But if the Savior made her worthy, who are you indeed to reject her? Surely the Savior knows her very well.

9 That is why He loved her more than us. Rather let us be ashamed and put on the perfect Man, and separate as He commanded us and preach the gospel, not laying down any other rule or other law beyond what the Savior said.

10 And when they heard this they began to go forth to proclaim and to preach.

THE GOSPEL OF BARTHOLOMEW

[[(the opening 3 verses are given from each of the three texts)]]

CHAPTER 1

[[Greek.]]

1 After the resurrection from the dead of our Lord Jesus Christ, Bartholomew came unto the Lord and questioned him, saying: Lord, reveal unto me the mysteries of the heavens.

2 Jesus answered and said unto him: If I put off the body of the flesh, I shall not be able to tell them unto thee.

3 Om.

[[Slavonic.]]

1 Before the resurrection of our Lord Jesus Christ from the dead, the apostles said: Let us question the Lord: Lord, reveal unto us the wonders.

2 And Jesus said unto them: If I put off the body of the flesh, I cannot tell them unto you.

3 But when he was buried and risen again, they all durst not question him, because it was not to look upon him, but the fullness of his Godhead was seen.

4 But Bartholomew...*[[, &c.]]*

[[Latin 2.]]

1 At that time, before the Lord Jesus Christ suffered, all the disciples were gathered together, questioning him and saying: Lord, show us the mystery in the heavens.

2 But Jesus answered and said unto them: If I put not off the body of flesh I cannot tell you.

3 But after that he had suffered and risen again, all the apostles, looking upon him, durst not question him, because his countenance was not as it had been aforetime, but showed forth the fullness of power.

[[Greek.]]

4 Bartholomew therefore drew near unto the Lord and said: I have a word to speak unto thee, Lord.

5 And Jesus said to him: I know what thou art about to say; say then what thou wilt, and I will answer thee.

6 And Bartholomew said: Lord, when thou wentest to be hanged upon the cross, I followed thee afar off and saw thee hung upon the cross, and the angels coming down from heaven and worshipping thee. And when there came darkness,

7 I beheld, and I saw thee that thou wast vanished away from the cross and I

heard only a voice in the parts under the earth, and great wailing and gnashing of teeth on a sudden. Tell me, Lord, whither wentest thou from the cross?

8 And Jesus answered and said: Blessed art thou, Bartholomew, my beloved, because thou sawest this mystery, and now will I tell thee all things whatsoever thou askest me.

9 For when I vanished away from the cross, then went I down into Hades that I might bring up Adam and all them that were with him, according to the supplication of Michael the archangel.

10 Then said Bartholomew: Lord, what was the voice which was heard?

11 Jesus saith unto him: Hades said unto Beliar: As I perceive, a God cometh hither.

[[Slavonic and latin 2 continue:]]

And the angels cried unto the powers, saying: Remove your gates, ye princes, remove the everlasting doors, for behold the King of glory cometh down.

12 Hades said: Who is the King of glory, that cometh down from heaven unto us?

13 And when I had descended five hundred steps, Hades was troubled, saying: I hear the breathing of the Most High, and I cannot endure it. (latin 2. He cometh with great fragrance and I cannot bear it.)

14 But the devil answered and said: Submit not thyself, O Hades, but be strong: for God himself hath not descended upon the earth.

15 But when I had descended yet five hundred steps, the angels and the powers cried out: Take hold, remove the doors, for behold the King of glory cometh down. And Hades said: O, woe unto me, for I hear the breath of God.]

[[Greek.]]

16-17 And Beliar said unto Hades: Look carefully who it is that , for it is Elias, or Enoch, or one of the prophets that this man seemeth to me to be. But Hades answered Death and said: Not yet are six thousand years

accomplished. And whence are these, O Beliar; for the sum of the number is in mine hands.

[[Slavonic.]]

16 And the devil said unto Hades: Why affrightest thou me, Hades? it is a prophet, and he hath made himself like unto God: this prophet will we take and bring him hither unto those that think to ascend into heaven.

17 And Hades said: Which of the prophets is it? Show me: Is it Enoch the scribe of righteousness? But God hath not suffered him to come down upon the earth before the end of the six thousand years. Sayest thou that it is Elias, the avenger? But before he cometh not down. What shall I do, whereas the destruction is of God: for surely our end is at hand? For I have the number (of the years) in mine hands.]

[[Greek.]]

18 : Be not troubled, make safe thy gates and strengthen thy bars: consider, God cometh not down upon the earth.

19 Hades saith unto him: These be no good words that I hear from thee: my belly is rent, and mine inward parts are pained: it cannot be but that God cometh hither. Alas, whither shall I flee before the face of the power of the great king? Suffer me to enter into myself (thyself, Latin): for before (of, latin) thee was I formed.

20 Then did I enter in and scourged him and bound him with chains that cannot be loosed, and brought forth thence all the patriarchs and came again unto the cross.

21 Bartholomew saith unto him: [latin 2, I saw thee again, hanging upon the cross, and all the dead arising and worshipping thee, and going up again into their sepulchres.] Tell me, Lord, who was he whom the angels bare up in their hands, even that man that was very great of stature? [Slav., Latin. 2, And what spakest thou unto him that he sighed so sore?]

22 Jesus answered and said unto him: It was Adam the first-formed, for whose sake I came down from heaven upon

earth. And I said unto him: I was hung upon the cross for thee and for thy children's sake. And he, when he heard it, groaned and said: So was thy good pleasure, O Lord.

23 Again Bartholomew said: Lord, I saw the angels ascending before Adam and singing praises.

24 But one of the angels which was very great, above the rest, would not ascend up with them: and there was in his hand a sword of fire, and he was looking steadfastly upon thee only.

[[Slavonic.]]

25 And all the angels besought him that he would go up with them, but he would not. But when thou didst command him to go up, I beheld a flame of fire issuing out of his hands and going even unto the city of Jerusalem.

26 And Jesus said unto him: Blessed art thou, Bartholomew my beloved because thou sawest these mysteries. This was one of the angels of vengeance which stand before my Father's throne: and this angel sent he unto me.

27 And for this cause he would not ascend up, because he desired to destroy all the powers of the world. But when I commanded him to ascend up, there went a flame out of his hand and rent asunder the veil of the temple, and parted it in two pieces for a witness unto the children of Israel for my passion because they crucified me. (Lat. 1. But the flame which thou sawest issuing out of his hands smote the house of the synagogue of the Jews, for a testimony of me wherein they crucified me.)].

[[Greek.]]

28 And when he had thus spoken, he said unto the apostles: Tarry for me in this place, for today a sacrifice is offered in paradise.

29 And Bartholomew answered and said unto Jesus: Lord, what is the sacrifice which is offered in paradise? And Jesus said: There be souls of the righteous which to-day have departed out of the body and go unto paradise,

and unless I be present they cannot enter into paradise.

30 And Bartholomew said: Lord, how many souls depart out of the world daily? Jesus saith unto him: Thirty thousand.

31 Bartholomew saith unto him: Lord, when thou wast with us teaching the word, didst thou receive the sacrifices in paradise? Jesus answered and said unto him: Verily I say unto thee, my beloved, that I both taught the word with you and continually sat with my Father, and received the sacrifices in paradise everyday.

32 Bartholomew answered and said unto him: Lord, if thirty thousand souls depart out of the world every day, how many souls out of them are found righteous? Jesus saith unto him: Hardly fifty [three] my beloved.

33 Again Bartholomew saith: And how do three only enter into paradise? Jesus saith unto him: The [fifty] three enter into paradise or are laid up in Abraham's bosom: but the others go into the place of the resurrection, for the three are not like unto the fifty.

34 Bartholomew saith unto him: Lord, how many souls above the number are born into the world daily? Jesus saith unto him: One soul only is born above the number of them that depart.

[[30, &c., Latin

1. Bartholomew said: How many are the souls which depart out of the body every day? Jesus said: Verily I say unto thee, twelve (thousand) eight hundred, four score and three souls depart out of the body every day.]]

35 And when he had said this he gave them the peace, and vanished away from them.

CHAPTER 2

1 Now the apostles were in the place [Cherubim, Cheltoura, Chritir] with Mary.

2 And Bartholomew came and said unto Peter and Andrew and John: Let us ask her that is highly favoured how she conceived the incomprehensible, or

how she bare him that cannot be carried, or how she brought forth so much greatness. But they doubted to ask her.

3 Bartholomew therefore said unto Peter: Thou that art the chief, and my teacher, draw near and ask her. But Peter said to John: Thou art a virgin and undefiled (and beloved) and thou must ask her.

4 And as they all doubted and disputed, Bartholomew came near unto her with a cheerful countenance and said to her: Thou that art highly favoured, the tabernacle of the Most High, unblemished we, even all the apostles, ask thee (or All the apostles have sent me to ask thee) to tell us how thou didst conceive the incomprehensible, or how thou didst bear him that cannot be carried, or how thou didst bring forth so much greatness.

5 But Mary said unto them: Ask me not (or Do ye indeed ask me) concerning this mystery. If I should begin to tell you, fire will issue forth out of my mouth and consume all the world.

6 But they continued yet the more to ask her. And she, for she could not refuse to hear the apostles, said: Let us stand up in prayer.

7 And the apostles stood behind Mary: but she said unto Peter: Peter, thou chief, thou great pillar, standest thou behind us? Said not our Lord: the head of the man is Christ ? now therefore stand ye before me and pray.

8 But they said unto her: In thee did the Lord set his tabernacle, and it was his good pleasure that thou shouldest contain him, and thou oughtest to be the leader in the prayer (al. to go with us to).

9 But she said unto them: Ye are shining stars, and as the prophet said, 'I did lift up mine eyes unto the hills, from whence shall come mine help'; ye, therefore, are the hills, and it behoveth you to pray.

10 The apostles say unto her: Thou oughtest to pray, thou art the mother of the heavenly king.

11 Mary saith unto them: In your likeness did God form the sparrows, and sent them forth into the four corners of the world.

12 But they say unto her: He that is scarce contained by the seven heavens was pleased to be contained in thee.

13 Then Mary stood up before them and spread out her hands toward the heaven and began to speak thus: Elphue Zarethra Charboum Nemioth Melitho Thraboutha Mephnounos Chemiath Aroura Maridon Elison Marmiadon Seption Hesaboutha Ennouna Saktinos Athoor Belelam Opheoth Abo Chrasar

[[(this is the reading of one Greek copy: the others and the Slavonic have many differences as in all such cases: but as the original words-assuming them to have once had a meaning-are hopelessly corrupted, the matter is not of importance), which is in the Greek tongue(Hebrew, Slav.):]]

O God the exceeding great and all-wise and king of the worlds (ages), that art not to be described, the ineffable, that didst establish the greatness of the heavens and all things by a word, that out of darkness (or the unknown) didst constitute and fasten together the poles of heaven in harmony, didst bring into shape the matter that was in confusion, didst bring into order the things that were without order, didst part the misty darkness from the light, didst establish in one place the foundations of the waters, thou that makest the beings of the air to tremble, and art the fear of them that are on (or under) the earth, that didst settle the earth and not suffer it to perish, and filledst it, which is the nourisher of all things, with showers of blessing: (Son of) the Father, thou whom the seven heavens hardly contained, but who wast well-pleased to be contained without pain in me, thou that art thyself the full word of the Father in whom all things came to be: give glory to thine exceeding great name, and bid me to speak before thy holy apostles .

14 And when she had ended the prayer she began to say unto them: Let us sit down upon the ground; and come thou,

THE GOSPEL OF BARTHOLOMEW

Peter the chief, and sit on my right hand and put thy left hand beneath mine armpit; and thou, Andrew, do so on my left hand; and thou, John, the virgin, hold together my bosom; and thou, Bartholomew, set thy knees against my back and hold my shoulders, lest when I begin to speak my bones be loosed one from another.

15 And when they had so done she began to say: When I abode in the temple of God and received my food from an angel, on a certain day there appeared unto me one in the likeness of an angel, but his face was incomprehensible, and he had not in his hand bread or a cup, as did the angel which came to me aforetime.

16 And straightway the robe (veil) of the temple was rent and there was a very great earthquake, and I fell upon the earth, for I was not able to endure the sight of him.

17 But he put his hand beneath me and raised me up, and I looked up into heaven and there came a cloud of dew and sprinkled me from the head to the feet, and he wiped me with his robe.

18 And said unto me: Hail, thou that art highly favoured, the chosen vessel, grace inexhaustible. And he smote his garment upon the right hand and there came a very great loaf, and he set it upon the altar of the temple and did eat of it first himself, and gave unto me also.

19 And again he smote his garment upon the left hand and there came a very great cup full of wine: and he set it upon the altar of the temple and did drink of it first himself, and gave also unto me. And I beheld and saw the bread and the cup whole as they were.

20 And he said unto me: Yet three years, and I will send my word unto thee and then shalt conceive my (or a) son, and through him shall the whole creation be saved. Peace be unto thee, my beloved, and my peace shall be with thee continually.

21 And when he had so said he vanished away from mine eyes, and the temple was restored as it had been before.

22 And as she was saying this, fire issued out of her mouth; and the world was at the point to come to an end: but Jesus appeared quickly (lat. 2, and laid his hand upon her mouth) and said unto Mary: Utter not this mystery, or this day my whole creation will come to an end (Lat. 2, and the flame from her mouth ceased). And the apostles were taken with fear lest haply the Lord should be wroth with them.

CHAPTER 3

1 And he departed with them unto the mount Mauria (Lat., Mambre), and sat in the midst of them.

2 But they doubted to question him, being afraid.

3 And Jesus answered and said unto them: Ask me what ye will that I should teach you, and I will show it you. For yet seven days, and I ascend unto my Father, and I shall no more be seen of you in this likeness.

4 But they, yet doubting, said unto him: Lord, show us the deep (abyss) according unto thy promise.

5 And Jesus said unto them: It is not good (Lat., is good) for you to see the deep: notwithstanding, if ye desire it, according to my promise, come, follow me and behold.

6 And he led them away into a place that is called Cherubim (Cherukt Slav., Chairoudee Gr., Lat. 2 omits), that is the place of truth.

7 And he beckoned unto the angels of the West and the earth was rolled up like a volume of a book and the deep was revealed unto them.

8 And when the apostles saw it they fell on their faces upon the earth.

9 But Jesus raised them up, saying: Said I not unto you, 'It is not good for you to see the deep'. And again he beckoned unto the angels, and the deep was covered up.

CHAPTER 4

1 And he took them and brought them again unto the Mount of olives.

2 And Peter said unto Mary: Thou that art highly favoured, entreat the Lord that he would reveal unto us the things

that are in the heavens.

3 And Mary said unto Peter: O stone hewn out of the rock, did not the Lord build his church upon thee? Go thou therefore first and ask him.

4 Peter saith again: O tabernacle that art spread abroad .

5 Mary saith: Thou art the image of Adam: was not he first formed and then Eve? Look upon the sun, that according to the likeness of Adam it is bright. and upon the moon, that because of the transgression of Eve it is full of clay. For God did place Adam in the east and Eve in the west, and appointed the lights that the sun should shine on the earth unto Adam in the east in his fiery chariots, and the moon in the west should give light unto Eve with a countenance like milk. And she defiled the commandment of the Lord. Therefore was the moon stained with clay (Lat. 2, is cloudy) and her light is not bright. Thou therefore, since thou art the likeness of Adam, oughtest to ask him: but in me was he contained that I might recover the strength of the female.

6 Now when they came up to the top of the mount, and the Master was withdrawn from them a little space, Peter saith unto Mary: Thou art she that hast brought to nought the transgression of Eve, changing it from shame into joy; it is lawful, therefore, for thee to ask.

7 When Jesus appeared again, Bartholomew saith unto him: Lord, show us the adversary of men that we may behold him, of what fashion he is, and what is his work, and whence he cometh forth, and what power he hath that he spared not even thee, but caused thee to be hanged upon the tree.

8 But Jesus looked upon him and said: Thou bold heart! thou askest for that which thou art not able to look upon.

9 But Bartholomew was troubled and fell at Jesus' feet and began to speak thus: O lamp that cannot be quenched, Lord Jesu Christ, maker of the eternal light that hast given unto them that love thee the grace that beautifieth all, and hast given us the eternal light by thy

coming into the world, that hast accomplished the work of the Father, hast turned the shame-facedness of Adam into mirth, hast done away the sorrow of Eve with a cheerful countenance by thy birth from a virgin: remember not evil against me but grant me the word of mine asking.

[[(Lat. 2, who didst come down into the world, who hast confirmed the eternal word of the Father, who hast called the sadness of joy, who hast made the shame of Eve glad, and restored her by vouchsafing to be contained in the womb.)]]

10 And as he thus spake, Jesus raised him up and said unto him: Bartholomew, wilt thou see the adversary of men? I tell thee that when thou beholdest him, not thou only but the rest of the apostles and Mary will fall on your faces and become as dead corpses.

11 But they all said unto him: Lord, let us behold him.

12 And he led them down from the Mount of Olives and looked wrathfully upon the angels that keep hell (Tartarus), and beckoned unto Michael to sound the trumpet in the height of the heavens. And Michael sounded, and the earth shook, and Beliar came up, being held by 660 (560 Gr., 6,064 Lat. 1, 6,060 Lat. 2) angels and bound with fiery chains.

13 And the length of him was 1,600 cubits and his breadth 40 (Lat. 1, 300, Slav. 17) cubits (Lat. 2, his length 1,900 cubits, his breadth 700, one wing of him 80), and his face was like a lightning of fire and his eyes full of darkness (like sparks, Slav.). And out of his nostrils came a stinking smoke; and his mouth was as the gulf of a precipice, and the one of his wings was four-score cubits.

14 And straightway when the apostles saw him, they fell to the earth on their faces and became as dead. 15 But Jesus came near and raised the apostles and gave them a spirit of power, and he saith unto Bartholomew: Come near,

Bartholomew, and trample with thy feet on his neck, and he will tell thee his work, what it is, and how he deceiveth men.

16 And Jesus stood afar off with the rest of the apostles.

17 And Barthololmew feared, and raised his voice and said: Blessed be the name of thine immortal kingdom from henceforth even for ever. And when he had spoken, Jesus permitted him, saying: Go and tread upon the neck of Beliar: and Bartholomew ran quickly upon him and trode upon his neck: and Beliar trembled. (For this verse the Vienna MS. has: And Bartholomew raised his voice and said thus: O womb more spacious than a city, wider than the spreading of the heavens, that contained him whom the seven heavens contain not, but thou without pain didst contain sanctified in thy bosom, &c.: evidently out of place. Latin 1 has only: Then did Antichrist tremble and was filled with fury.)

18 And Bartholomew was afraid, and fled, and said unto Jesus: Lord, give me an hem of thy garments (Lat. 2, the kerchief (?) from thy shoulders) that I may have courage to draw near unto him.

19 But Jesus said unto him: Thou canst not take an hem of my garments, for these are not my garments which I wore before I was crucified.

20 And Bartholomew said: Lord, I fear lest, like as he spared not thine angels, he swallow me up also.

21 Jesus saith unto him: Were not all things made by my word, and by the will of my Father the spirits were made subject unto Solomon? thou, therefore, being commanded by my word, go in my name and ask him what thou wilt. (lat. 2 omits 20.)

22 [And Bartholomew made the sign of the cross and prayed unto Jesus and went behind him. And Jesus said to him: Draw near. And as Bartholomew drew near, fire was kindled on every side, so that his garments appeared fiery. Jesus saith to Bartholomew: As I said unto thee, tread upon his neck and ask him what is his power.] And

Bartholomew went and trode upon his neck, and pressed down his face into the earth as far as his ears.

23 And Bartholomew saith unto him: Tell me who thou art and what is thy name. And he said to him: Lighten me a little, and I will tell thee who I am and how I came hither, and what my work is and what my power is.

24 And he lightened him and saith to him: Say all that thou hast done and all that thou doest.

25 And Beliar answered and said: If thou wilt know my name, at the first I was called Satanael, which is interpreted a messenger of God, but when I rejected the image of God my name was called Satanas, that is, an angel that keepeth hell (Tartarus).

26 And again Bartholomew saith unto him: Reveal unto me all things and hide nothing from me.

27 And he said unto him: I swear unto thee by the power of the glory of God that even if I would hide aught I cannot, for he is near that would convict me. For if I were able I would have destroyed you like one of them that were before you.

28 For, indeed, I was formed (al. called) the first angel: for when God made the heavens, he took a handful of fire and formed me first, Michael second

[[Vienna MS. here has these sentences: for he had his Son before the heavens and the earth and we were formed (for when he took thought to create all things, his Son spake a word), so that we also were created by the will of the Son and the consent of the Father. He formed, I say, first me, next Michael the chief captain of the hosts that are above]],

Gabriel third, Uriel fourth, Raphael fifth, Nathanael sixth, and other angels of whom I cannot tell the names.

[[Jerusalem MS., Michael, Gabriel, Raphael, Uriel, Xathanael, and other 6,000 angels. Lat. 1, Michael the honour of power, third Raphael, fourth

Gabriel, and other seven. Lat. 2,
Raphael third, Gabriel fourth, Uriel
fifth, Zathael sixth, and other six.]]
(29)
For they are the rod-bearers (lictors) of
God, and they smite me with their rods
and pursue me seven times in the night
and seven times in the day, and leave
me not at all and break in pieces all my
power. These are the (twelve, lat. 2)
angels of vengeance which stand before
the throne of God: these are the angels
that were first formed.

30 And after them were formed all the
angels. In the first heaven are an
hundred myriads, and in the second an
hundred myriads, and in the third an
hundred myriads, and in the fourth an
hundred myriads, and in the fifth an
hundred myriads, and in the sixth an
hundred myriads, and in the seventh (an
hundred myriads, and outside the seven
heavens, Jerusalem MS.) is the first
firmament (flat surface) wherein are the
powers which work upon men.

31 For there are four other angels set
over the winds. The first angel is over
the north, and he is called Chairoum
(. . . broil, Jerusalem MS.; lat. 2, angel
of the north, Mauch), and hath in his
hand a rod of fire, and restraineth the
super-fluity of moisture that the earth
be not overmuch wet.

32 And the angel that is over the north
is called Oertha (Lat. 2, Alfatha): he
hath a torch of fire and putteth it to his
sides, and they warm the great coldness
of him that he freeze not the world.

33 And the angel that is over the south
is called Kerkoutha (Lat. 2, Cedar) and
they break his fierceness that he shake
not the earth.

34 And the angel that is over the south-
west is called Naoutha, and he hath a
rod of snow in his hand and putteth it
into his mouth, and quencheth the fire
that cometh out of his mouth. And if the
angel quenched it not at his mouth it
would set all the world on fire.

35 And there is another angel over the
sea which maketh it rough with the
waves thereof.

36 But the rest I will not tell thee, for he
that standeth by suffereth me not.

37 Bartholomew saith unto him: Flow
chastisest thou the souls of men?

38 Beliar saith unto him: Wilt thou that
I declare unto thee the punishment of
the hypocrites, of the back-biters, of the
jesters, of the idolaters, and the
covetous, and the adulterers, and the
wizards, and the diviners, and of them
that believe in us, and of all whom I
look upon (deceive?)?

[38 Lat.] : When I will show any
illusion by them. But they that do these
things, and they that consent unto them
or follow them, do perish with me.

39 Bartholomew said unto him: Declare
quickly how thou persuadest men not to
follow God and thine evil arts, that are
slippery and dark, that they should
leave the straight and shining paths of
the Lord.) [*Lat. 39] Bartholomew saith*
unto him: I will that thou declare it in
few words.

40 And he smote his teeth together,
gnashing them, and there came up out
of the bottomless pit a wheel having a
sword flashing with fire, and in the
sword were pipes.

41 And I (he) asked him, saying: What
is this sword?

42 And he said: This sword is the sword
of the gluttonous: for into this pipe are
sent they that through their gluttony
devise all manner of sin; into the
second pipe are sent the backbiters
which backbite their neighbour secretly;
into the third pipe are sent the
hypocrites and the rest whom I
overthrow by my contrivance.

[Lat.:40] And Antichrist said: I will tell
thee. And a wheel came up out of the
abyss, having seven fiery knives. The
first knife hath twelve pipes (canales).. .
.

42 Antichrist answered: The pipe of fire
in the first knife, in it are put the casters
of lots and diviners and enchanters, and
they that believe in them or have sought
them, because in the iniquity of their
heart they have invented false
divinations. In the second pipe of fire
are first the blasphemers ... suicides ...
idolaters.... In the rest are first
perjurers . . .

THE GOSPEL OF BARTHOLOMEW

[[(long enumeration)]]

43 And Bartholomew said: Dost thou then do these things by thyself alone?
44 And Satan said: If I were able to go forth by myself, I would have destroyed the whole world in three days: but neither I nor any of the six hundred go forth. For we have other swift ministers whom we command, and we furnish them with an hook of many points and send them forth to hunt, and they catch for us souls of men, enticing them with sweetness of divers baits, that is by drunkenness and laughter, by backbiting, hypocrisy, pleasures, fornication, and the rest of the trifles that come out of their treasures.

[[(Lat. 2 amplifies enormously.)]]

45 And I will tell thee also the rest of the names of the angels. The angel of the hail is called Mermeoth, and he holdeth the hail upon his head, and my ministers do adjure him and send him whither they will. And other angels are there over the snow, and other over the thunder, and other over the lightning, and when any spirit of us would go forth either by land or by sea, these angels send forth fiery stones and set our limbs on fire.

[[(Lat. 2 enumerates all the transgressions of Israel and all possible sins in two whole pages.)]]

46 Bartholomew saith: Be still (be muzzled) thou dragon of the pit.
47 And Beliar said: Many things will I tell thee of the angels. They that run together throughout the heavenly places and the earthly are these: Mermeoth, Onomatath, Douth, Melioth, Charouth, Graphathas, Oethra, Nephonos, Chalkatoura. With them do fly (are administered?) the things that are in heaven and on earth and under the earth.
48 Bartholomew saith unto him: Be still (be muzzled) and be faint, that I may entreat my Lord.

49 And Bartholomew fell upon his face and cast earth upon his head and began to say: O Lord Jesu Christ, the great and glorious name. All the choirs of the angels praise thee, O Master, and I that am unworthy with my lips . . . do praise thee, O Master. Hearken unto me thy servant, and as thou didst choose me from the receipt of custom and didst not suffer me to have my conversation unto the end in my former deeds, O Lord Jesu Christ, hearken unto me and have mercy upon the sinners.
50 And when he had so said, the Lord saith unto him: Rise up, suffer him that groaneth to arise: I will declare the rest unto thee.
51 And Bartholomew raised up Satan and said unto him: Go unto thy place, with thine angels, but the Lord hath mercy upon all his world.

[[(50, 51, again enormously amplified in lat. 2. Satan complains that he has been tricked into telling his secrets before the time. The interpolation is to some extent dated by this sentence: ' Simon Magus and Zaroes and Arfaxir and Jannes and Mambres are my brothers.' Zaroes and Arfaxatare wizards who figure in the Latin Acts of Matthew and of Simon and Jude (see below). 49 follows 51 in this text.)]]

52 But the devil said: Suffer me, and I will tell thee how I was cast down into this place and how the Lord did make man.
53 I was going to and fro in the world, and God said unto Michael: Bring me a clod from the four corners of the earth, and water out of the four rivers of paradise. And when Michael brought them God formed Adam in the regions of the east, and shaped the clod which was shapeless, and stretched sinews and veins upon it and established it with Joints; and he worshipped him, himself for his own sake first, because he was the image of God, therefore he worshipped him.
54 And when I came from the ends of the earth Michael said: Worship thou the image of God, which he hath made

233

according to his likeness. But I said: I am fire of fire, I was the first angel formed, and shall worship clay and matter?

55 And Michael saith to me: Worship, lest God be wroth with thee. But I said to him: God will not be wroth with me; but I will set my throne over against his throne, and I will be as he is. Then was God wroth with me and cast me down, having commanded the windows of heaven to be opened.

56 And when I was cast down, he asked also the six hundred that were under me, if they would worship: but they said: Like as we have seen the first angel do, neither will we worship him that is less than ourselves. Then were the six hundred also cast down by him with me.

57 And when we were cast down upon the earth we were senseless for forty years, and when the sun shone forth seven times brighter than fire, suddenly I awaked; and I looked about and saw the six hundred that were under me senseless.

58 And I awaked my son Salpsan and took him to counsel how I might deceive the man on whose account I was cast out of the heavens.

59 And thus did I contrive it. I took a vial in mine hand and scraped the sweat from off my breast and the hair of mine armpits, and washed myself...

[[(Lat. 2, I took fig leaves in my hands and wiped the sweat from my bosom and below mine arms and cast it down beside the streams of waters. 69 is greatly prolonged in this text)]]

...in the springs of the waters whence the four rivers flow out, and Eve drank of it and desire came upon her: for if she had not drunk of that water I should not have been able to deceive her.

60 Then Bartholomew commanded him to go into hell.

61 And Bartholomew came and fell at Jesus' feet and began with tears to say thus: Abba, Father, that art past finding out by us, Word of the Father, whom the seven heavens hardly contained, but who wast pleased to be contained easily and without pain within the body of the Virgin: whom the Virgin knew not that she bare: thou by thy thought hast ordained all things to be: thou givest us that which we need before thou art entreated.

62 Thou that didst wear a crown of thorns that thou mightest prepare for us that repent the precious crown from heaven; that didst hang upon the tree, that (a clause gone): (lat. 2, that thou mightest turn from us the tree of lust and concupiscence (etc., etc.). The verse is prolonged for over 40 lines) (that didst drink wine mingled with gall) that thou mightest give us to drink of the wine of compunction, and wast pierced n the side with a spear that thou mightest fill us with thy body and thy blood:

63 Thou that gavest names unto the four rivers: to the first Phison, because of the faith (pistis) which thou didst appear in the world to preach; to the second Geon, for that man was made of earth (ge); to the third Tigris, because by thee was revealed unto us the consubstantial Trinity in the heavens (to make anything of this we must read Trigis); to the fourth Euphrates, because by thy presence in the world thou madest every soul to rejoice (euphranai) through the word of immortality.

64 My God, and Father, the greatest, my King: save, Lord, the sinners.

65 When he had thus prayed Jesus said unto him: Bartholomew, my Father did name me Christ, that I might come down upon earth and anoint every man that cometh unto me with the oil of life: and he did call me Jesus that I might heal every sin of them that know not . . . and give unto men (several corrupt words: the Latin has) the truth of God.

66-(67) And again Bartholomew saith unto him: Lord, is it lawful for me to reveal these mysteries unto every man? Jesus saith unto him: Bartholomew, my beloved, as many as are faithful and are able to keep them unto themselves, to them mayest thou entrust these things. For some there are that be worthy of them, but there are also other some unto whom it is not fit to entrust them: for they are vain (swaggerers), drunkards, proud, unmerciful, partakers in idolatry, authors of fornication, slanderers, teachers of foolishness, and doing all works that are of the devil, and therefore are they not worthy that these should be entrusted to them.

68 And also they are secret, because of those that cannot contain them; for as many as can contain them shall have a part in them. Herein (Hitherto?) therefore, my beloved, have I spoken unto thee, for blessed art thou and all thy kindred which of their choice have this word entrusted unto them; for all they that can contain it shall receive whatsoever they will in the of my judgement.

69 Then I, Bartholomew, which wrote these things in mine heart, took hold on the hand of the lord the lover of men and began to rejoice and to speak thus: *Glory be to thee, O Lord Jesus Christ, that givest unto all thy grace which all we have perceived. Alleluia.*
Glory be to thee, O Lord, the life of sinners.
Glory be to thee, O Lord, death is put to shame.
Glory be to thee, O Lord, the treasure of righteousness.
For unto God do we sing.

70 And as Bartholomew thus spake again, Jesus put off his mantle and took a kerchief from the neck of Bartholomew and began to rejoice and say...

[70 lat.] , Then Jesus took a kerchief (?) I and said: I am good: mild and gracious and merciful, strong and righteous, wonderful and holy):

I am good. Alleluia. I am meek and gentle. Alleluia. Glory be to thee, O Lord: for I give gifts unto all them that desire me. Alleluia.
Glory be to thee, O Lord, world without end. Amen. Alleluia.

71 And when he had ceased, the apostles kissed him, and he gave them the peace of love.

CHAPTER 5

1 Bartholomew saith unto him: Declare unto us, Lord what sin is heavier than all sins?

2 Jesus saith unto him: Verily I say unto thee that hypocrisy and backbiting is heavier than all sins: for because of them, the prophet said in the psalm, that 'the ungodly shall not rise in the judgement, neither sinners in the council of the righteous', neither the ungodly in the judgement of my Father. Verily, verily, I say unto you, that every sin shall be forgiven unto every man, but the sin against the Holy Ghost shall not be forgiven.

3 And Bartholomew saith unto him: What is the sin against the Holy Ghost?

4 Jesus saith unto him: Whosoever shall decree against any man that hath served my holy Father hath blasphemed against the Holy Ghost: For every man that serveth God worshipfully is worthy of the Holy Ghost, and he that speaketh anything evil against him shall not be forgiven.

5 Woe unto him that sweareth by the head of God, yea woe (?) to him that sweareth falsely by him truly. For there are twelve heads of God the most high: for he is the truth, and in him is no lie, neither forswearing.

6 Ye, therefore, go ye and preach unto all the world the word of truth, and thou, Bartholomew, preach this word unto every one that desireth it; and as many as believe thereon shall have eternal life.

7 Bartholomew saith: O Lord, and if any sin with sin of the body, what is their reward?

8 And Jesus said: It is good if he that is baptized present his baptism blameless: but the pleasure of the flesh will become a lover. For a single marriage belongeth to sobriety: for verily I say unto thee, he that sinneth after the third marriage (wife) is unworthy of God.

[[8 Lat.] 2 is to this effect: . . . But if the lust of the flesh come upon him, he

ought to be the husband of one wife. The married, if they are good and pay tithes, will receive a hundredfold. A second marriage is lawful, on condition of the diligent performance of good works, and due payment of tithes: but a third marriage is reprobated: and virginity is best.)]]

9 But ye, preach ye unto every man that they keep themselves from such things: for I depart not from you and I do supply you with the Holy Ghost.

[[(lat. 2, At the end of 9, Jesus ascends in the clouds, and two angels appear and say: 'Ye men of Galilee', and the rest)]]

10 And Bartholomew worshipped him with the apostles, and glorified God earnestly, saying: Glory be to thee, Holy Father, Sun unquenchable, incomprehensible, full of light. Unto thee be glory, unto thee honour and adoration, world without end. Amen.

[[(Lat., End of the questioning of the most blessed Bartholomew and (or) the other apostles with the Lord Jesus Christ.)]]

THE BOOK OF THE RESURRECTION OF CHRIST
BY BARTHOLOMEW THE APOSTLE

[[The book was addressed by Bartholomew to his son Thaddaeus]]

[[It begins with Christ is on the cross, but his side has been pierced, and he is dead.

A man in the crowd named Ananias, of Bethlehem, rushes to the cross and embraces and salutes the body breast to breast, hand to hand, and denounces the Jews.

A voice comes from the body of Jesus and blesses Ananias, promising him incorruption and the name of ' the firstfruits of the immortal fruit '.

The priests decide to stone Ananias: he utters words of exultation.

The stoning produces no effect.

They cast him into a furnace where he remains till Jesus has risen.

At last they pierce him with a spear.

The Saviour takes his soul to heaven, and blesses him.

[[There can be but little matter lost between this and the opening of the British Museum MS., in the first lines of which the taking of Ananias' soul to heaven is mentioned.

We now take up the British Museum MS. as our basis. Certain passages of it are preserved in Paris fragments which partly overlap each other, and so three different texts exist for some parts: but it will not be important for our purpose to note many of the variations.]]

1 Joseph of Arimathaea buried the body of Jesus. Death came into Amente (the underworld), asking who the new arrival was, for he detected a disturbance.

2 He came to the tomb of Jesus with his six sons in the form of serpents. Jesus lay there (it was the second day, i. e. the Saturday) with his face and head covered with napkins.

3 Death addressed his son the Pestilence, and described the commotion which had taken place in his domain.

4 Then he spoke to the body of Jesus and asked, 'Who art thou?'

5 Jesus removed the napkin that was on his face and looked in the face of Death and laughed at him.

6 Death and his sons fled. Then they approached again, and the same thing happened.

7 He addressed Jesus again at some length, suspecting, but not certain, who he was.

8 Then Jesus rose and mounted into the chariot of the Cherubim.

9 He wrought havoc in Hell, breaking the doors, binding the demons Beliar and Melkir (cf. Melkira in the Ascension of Isaiah), and delivered Adam and the holy souls.

10 Then he turned to Judas Iscariot and uttered a long rebuke, and described the sufferings which he must endure.

11 Thirty names of sins are given, which are the snakes which were sent to devour him.

12 Jesus rose from the dead, and Abbaton (Death) and Pestilence came back to Amente to protect it, but they found it wholly desolate, only three souls were left in it (those of Herod, Cain, and Judas, says the Paris MS.).

13 Meanwhile the angels were singing the hymn which the Seraphim sing at dawn on the Lord's day over his body and his blood.

14 Early in the morning of the Lord's day the women went to the tomb.

15 They were Mary Magdalene, Mary the mother of James whom Jesus delivered out of the hand of Satan, Salome who tempted him, Mary who ministered to him and Martha her sister, Joanna (al. Susanna) the wife of Chuza who had renounced the marriage bed, Berenice who was healed of an issue of blood in Capernaum, Lia (Leah) the widow whose son he raised at Nain, and the woman to whom he said, 'Thy sins which are many are forgiven thee'.

16 These were all in the garden of Philogenes, whose son Simeon Jesus healed when he came down from the Mount of Olives with the apostles (probably the lunatic boy at the Mount of Transfiguration).

17 Mary said to Philogenes: If thou art indeed he, I know thee.

18 Philogenes said: Thou art Mary the mother of Thalkamarimath, which means joy, blessing, and gladness.

19 Mary said: If thou have borne him away, tell me where thou hast laid him and I will take him away: fear not.

20 Philogenes told how the Jews sought a safe tomb for Jesus that the body might not be stolen, and he offered to place it in a tomb in his own garden and watch over it: and they sealed it and departed.

21 At midnight he rose and went out and found all the orders of angels: Cherubim, Seraphim, Powers, and (Virgins?).

22 Heaven opened, and the Father raised Jesus. Peter, too, was there and supported Philogenes, or he would have died.

23 The Saviour then appeared to them on the chariot of the Father and said to Mary: Mari Khar Mariath (Mary the mother of the Son of God).

24 Mary answered: Rabbouni Kathiathari Mioth (The Son of God the Almighty, my Lord, and my Son.).

[[A long address to Mary from Jesus follows, in the course of which he bids her tell his brethren, 'I ascend unto my Father and your Father', &c.]]

25 Mary says: If indeed I am not permitted to touch thee, at least bless my body in which thou didst deign to dwell.

26 Believe me, my brethren the holy apostles, I, Bartholomew beheld the Son of God on the chariot of the Cherubim.

27 All the heavenly hosts were about him. He blessed the body of Mary.

28 She went and gave the message to the apostles, and Peter blessed her, and they rejoiced.

29 Jesus and the redeemed souls ascended into Heaven, and the Father crowned him.

[[The glory of this scene Bartholomew could not describe. It is here that he enjoins his son Thaddaeus not to let this book fall into the hands of the impure...

30 'Do not let this book come into the hand of any man who is an unbeliever and a heretic. Behold this is the seventh time that I have commanded thee, O my son Thaddaeus, concerning these mysteries. Reveal not thou them to any impure man, but keep them safely. '

31 Then follows a series of hymns sung in heaven, eight in all, which accompany the reception of Adam and the other holy souls into glory.
32 Adam was eighty cubits high and Eve fifty.
33 They were brought to the Father by Michael. Bartholomew had never seen anything to compare with the beauty and Glory of Adam, save that of Jesus.
34 Adam was forgiven, and all the angels and saints rejoiced and saluted him, and departed each to their place.
35 Adam was set at the gate of life to greet all the righteous as they enter, and Eve was set over all the women who had done the will of God, to greet them as they come into the city of Christ.
36 As for me, Bartholomew, I remained many days without food or drink, nourished by the glory of the vision.
37 The apostles thanked and blessed Bartholomew for what he had told them: he should be called the apostle of the mysteries of God.
38 But he protested: I am the least of you all, a humble workman.
39 Will not the people of the city say when they see me, 'Is not this Bartholomew the man of Italy, the gardener the dealer in vegetables?
40 Is not this the man that dwelleth in the garden of Hierocrates the governor of our city? How has he attained this greatness?

[[The next words introduce a new section.]]

1 At the time when Jesus took us up into the Mount of Olives he spoke to us in an unknown tongue, which he revealed to us, saying:
2 Anetharath (or Atharath Thaurath).
3 The heavens were opened and we all went up into the seventh heaven.

[[(so the London MS.: in the Paris copy only Jesus went up, and the apostles gazed after him)]].

4 He prayed the Father to bless us.
5 The Father, with the Son and the Holy Ghost, laid His hand on the head of Peter (and made him archbishop of the wholeworld: Paris B). All that is bound or loosed by him on earth shall be so in heaven; none who is not ordained by him shall be accepted.
6 Each of the apostles was separately blessed (there are omissions of single names in one or other of the three texts). Andrew, James, John, Philip (the cross will precede him wherever he goes), Thomas, Bartholomew (he will be the depositary of the mysteries of the Son), Matthew (his shadow will heal the sick) James son of Alphaeus, Simon Zelotes, Judas of James, Thaddeus, Matthias who was rich and left all to follow Jesus).
7 And now, my brethren the apostles, forgive me: I, Bartholomew, am not a man to be honoured.
8 The apostles kissed and blessed him. And then, with Mary, they offered the Eucharist.
9 The Father sent the Son down into Galilee to console the apostles and Mary: and he came and blessed them and showed them his wounds, and committed them to the care of Peter, and gave them their commission to preach.
10 They kissed his side and sealed themselves with the blood that flowed thence. He went up to heaven.
11 Thomas was not with them, for he had departed to his city, hearing that his son Siophanes (Theophanes?) was dead: it was the seventh day since the death when he arrived.
12 He went to the tomb and raised him in the name of Jesus.
13 Siophanes told him of the taking of his soul by Michael: how it sprang from his body and lighted on the hand of Michael, who wrapped it in a fine linen cloth: how he crossed the river of fire and it seemed to him as water, and was washed thrice in the Acherusian lake: how in heaven he saw the twelve splendid thrones of the apostles, and was not permitted to sit on his father's throne.

14 Thomas[......] and he went into the city to the consternation of all who saw them.

15 He, Siophanes, addressed the people and told his story: and Thomas baptized 12,000 of them, founded a church, and made Siophanes its bishop.

16 Then Thomas mounted on a cloud and it took him to the Mount of Olives and to the apostles, who told him of the visit of Jesus: and he would not believe.

17 Bartholomew admonished him. Then Jesus appeared, and made Thomas touch his wounds: and departed into heaven.

18 This is the second time that he showed himself to his disciples after that he had risen from the dead.

19 This is the Book of the Resurrection of Jesus the Christ, our Lord, in joy and gladness. In peace. Amen.

20 Peter said to the apostles: Let us offer the offering before we separate. They prepared the bread, the cup, and incense.

21 Peter stood by the sacrifice and the others round the Table. They waited

[[(break in the text: Budge and others suppose an appearance of Christ, but I do not think this is correct: 4 1/2 lines are gone then there are broken words):]]

....table . . . their hearts rejoiced . . . worshipped the Son of God.

22 He took his seat . . . his Father (probably, who sitteth at the right hand of the Father).

23 His Body (The Bread) was on the Table about which they were assembled; and they divided it.

24 They saw (A vision) of the blood of Jesus pouring out as living blood down into the cup.

25 Peter said: God hath loved us more than all, in letting us see these great honours: and our Lord Jesus Christ hath allowed us to behold and hath revealed to us the glory of his body and his divine blood.

26 They partook of the bread and cup- and then they separated and preached the word.

THE LOST CHAPTER OF ACTS
CHAPTER TWENTY NINE

1 And Paul, full of the blessings of Christ, and abounding in spirit, departed from Rome, determining to go to Spain, for he had proposed to go there for a long time, and also from there to Britain.

2 For he had heard in Phoenicia that some of the children of Israel, about the time of the Assyerian captivity, had escaped by sea to "the Isles afar off" as spoken by the prophet , and called by the Romans, Britain.

3 And the LORD commanded the gospel to be preached to all the nations of the gentiles, and to the lost sheep of the house of Israel.

4 And no man hindered Paul; for he testified boldly of Jesus before the tribunes and among the people.

5 He took with him certain brethren which were with him at Rome, and they boarded a ship at Ostrium and having the winds fair were brought safely to a heaven of Spain.

6 And many people were gathered together from the towns and villages, and the hill country; for they had heard of the conversion of the apostle, and his many miracles.

7 And Paul preached mightily in Spain and great multitudes were converted, for they perceived that he was an apostle sent by God.

8 And when leaving Spain, and Paul and his company found a ship in Armorica, which was sailing to Britain, they sailed along the south coast until they reached a port called Raphinus.

9 Now when it was known that the apostle had landed on their coast, great multitudes of the inhabitants met him, and they treated Paul courteously and

he entered in at the east gate of their city, and stayed in the house of a Hebrew, one of his own nation.

10 The next day he came to mount Lud and the people thronged the gate, and assembled in the Broadway, and he preached Christ to them, and they believed the word and the testimony of Jesus.

11 At the even the Holy Spirit fell upon Paul, and he prophesied saying behold, in the last days the God of peace shall dwell in the cities, and the inhabitants thereof shall be numbered.

12 In the seventh numbering of the people, their eyes shall be opened, and the glory of their inheritance shine forth before them.

13 The nations shall come up to worship on the mount that testifies of the patience and long suffering of the servant of the Lord.

14 And in the latter days new things of the gospel shall issue forth out of Jerusalem, and the hearts of the people shall rejoice, and behold the fountains shall be opened, and their shall be no more plague.

15 In those days there shall be wars and rumors of war; and a king shall raise up, and his sword, shall be for the healing of the nations, and his peace making shall abide, and the glory of his kingdom a wonder among the princes.

16 And it shall come to pass that certain of the Druids came to Paul privately, and showed by their rites and ceremonies they were descended from the Jews which escaped from bondage in the land of Egypt, and the apostle believed these things, and gave them the kiss of peace.

17 And Paul abode in his lodgings three months confirming in the faith and preaching Christ continually.

18 After these things Paul and his brethren departed from Raphinus and sailed to Atium in Gaul. Paul preached to the Roman garrison and among the people, exhorting all men to repent and confess their sins.

19 And certain of the Belgae came to inquire of him and of the new doctrine, and of the man Jesus.

20 Paul opened his heart unto them and told them all things that had befallen him, and how Christ Jesus came into the world to save sinners; and they departed pondering among themselves upon the things which they had heard.

21 And after much preaching and toil, Paul and his fellow laborers passed into Helvetia, and came to Mount Pontius Pilate, where he who condemned the Lord Jesus dashed himself down headlong, and so miserably perished.

22 And immediately a torrent gushed out of the mountain and washed his body, broken in pieces, into a lake.

23 And Paul stretched forth his hands upon the water, and prayed unto the Lord, saying O Lord God, give a sign unto all nations that here Pontius Pilate which condemned your only-begotten Son, plunged down headlong into the pit.

24 And while Paul was yet speaking, behold there came a great earthquake, and the face of the waters was changed, and the form of the lake like unto the Son of Man hanging in agony upon the cross.

25 And there came a voice out of heaven saying even Pilate has escaped the wrath to come, for he washed his hands before the multitude at the blood-shedding of our Lord Jesus Christ.

26 When, therefore, Paul and those who were with him saw the earthquake, and heard the voice of the angel, they glorified God, and were mightily strengthened in the spirit.

27 And they journeyed and came to Mount Julius where stood two pillars, one on the right hand and one on the left hand, erected by Caesar Augustus.

28 Paul, filled with the Holy Spirit, stood up between the two pillars, saying, "Men and brethren these stones which you see this day shall testify of my journey here.

29 Truly I say, they shall remain until the out pouring of the spirit upon all nations, neither shall the way be hindered throughout all generations."

30 Then they traveled to Illtricum, intending to go by Macedonia into Asia, and grace was found in all the churches,

and they prospered in peace. Amen.

THE ACTS OF JOHN

[[Text Missing]]

18 Now John was hastening to Ephesus, moved thereto by a vision. Damonicus therefore, and Aristodemus his kinsman, and a certain very rich man Cleobius, and the wife of Marcellus, hardly prevailed to keep him for one day in Miletus, reposing themselves with him. And when very early in the morning they had set forth, and already about four miles of the journey were accomplished, a voice came from heaven in the hearing of all of us, saying: John, thou art about to give glory to thy Lord in Ephesus, whereof thou shalt know, thou and all the brethren that are with thee, and certain of them that are there, which shall believe by thy means. John therefore pondered, rejoicing in himself, what it should be that should befall (meet) him at Ephesus, and said: Lord, behold I go according to thy will: let that be done which thou desirest.

19 And as we drew near to the city, Lycomedes the praetor of the Ephesians, a man of large substance, met us, and falling at John's feet besought him, saying: Is thy name John? the God whom thou preachest hath sent thee to do good unto my wife, who hath been smitten with palsy now these seven days and lieth incurable. But glorify thou thy God by healing her, and have compassion on us. For as I was considering with myself what resolve to take in this matter, one stood by me and said: Lycomedes, cease from this thought which warreth against thee, for it is evil (hard): submit not thyself unto it. For I have compassion upon mine handmaid Cleopatra, and have sent from Miletus a man named John who shall raise her up and restore her to

thee whole. Tarry not, therefore, thou servant of the God who hath manifested himself unto me, but hasten unto my wife who hath no more than breath. And straightway John went from the gate, with the brethren that were with him and Lycomedes, unto his house. But Cleobius said to his young men: Go ye to my kinsman Callippus and receive of him comfortable entertainment -for I am come hither with his son- that we may find all things decent.

20 Now when Lycomedes came with John into the house wherein his wife lay, he caught hold again of his feet and said: See, lord, the withering of the beauty, see the youth, see the renowned flower of my poor wife, whereat all Ephesus was wont to marvel: wretched me, I have suffered envy, I have been humbled, the eye of mine enemies hath smitten me: I have never wronged any, though I might have injured many, for I looked before to this very thing, and took care, lest I should see any evil or any such ill fortune as this. What profit, then, hath Cleopatra from my anxiety? what have I gained by being known for a pious man until this day? nay, I suffer more than the impious, in that I see thee, Cleopatra, lying in such plight. The sun in his course shall no more see me conversing with thee: I will go before thee, Cleopatra, and rid myself of life: I will not spare mine own safety though it be yet young. I will defend myself before Justice, that I have rightly deserted, for I may indict her as judging unrighteously. I will be avenged on her when I come before her as a ghost of life. I will say to her: Thou didst force me to leave the light when thou didst rob me of Cleopatra: thou didst cause me to become a corpse when thou sentest me this ill fortune: thou didst compel me to insult Providence, by cutting off my joy in life (my con- fidence).

21 And with yet more words Lycomedes addressing Cleopatra came near to the bed and cried aloud and lamented: but John pulled him away, and said: Cease from these lamentations and from thine unfitting words: thou

must not disobey him that appeared unto thee: for know that thou shalt receive thy consort again. Stand, therefore, with us that have come hither on her account and pray to the God whom thou sawest manifesting himself unto thee in dreams. What, then, is it, Lycomedes? Awake, thou also, and open thy soul. Cast off the heavy sleep from thee: beseech the Lord, entreat him for thy wife, and he will raise her up. But he fell upon the floor and lamented, fainting.

[[It is evident from what follows that Lycomedes died: but the text does not say so; some words may have fallen out.]]

John therefore said with tears: Alas for the fresh (new) betraying of my vision! for the new temptation that is prepared for me! for the new device of him that contriveth against me! the voice from heaven that was borne unto me in the way, hath it devised this for me? was it this that it foreshowed me should come to pass here, betraying me to this great multitude of the citizens because of Lycomedes? the man lieth without breath, and I know well that they will not suffer me to go out of the house alive. Why tarriest thou, Lord (or, what wilt thou do)? why hast thou shut off from us thy good promise? Do not, I beseech thee, Lord, do not give him cause to exult who rejoiceth in the suffering of others; give him not cause to dance who alway derideth us; but let thy holy name and thy mercy make haste. Raise up these two dead whose death is against me.

22 And even as John thus cried out, the city of the Ephesians ran together to the house of Lycomedes, hearing that he was dead. And John, beholding the great multitude that was come, said unto the Lord: Now is the time of refreshment and of confidence toward thee, O Christ; now is the time for us who are sick to have the help that is of thee, O physician who healest freely; keep thou mine entering in hither safe from derision. I beseech thee, Jesu,

succour this great multitude that it may come to thee who art Lord of all things: behold the affliction, behold them that lie here. Do thou prepare, even from them that are assembled for that end, holy vessels for thy service, when they behold thy gift. For thyself hast said, O Christ, 'Ask, and it shall be given you'. We ask therefore of thee, O king, not gold, not silver, not substance, not possessions, nor aught of what is on earth and perisheth, but two souls, by whom thou shalt convert them that are here unto thy way, unto thy teaching, unto thy liberty (confidence), unto thy most excellent (or unfailing) promise: for when they perceive thy power in that those that have died are raised, they will be saved, some of them. Do thou thyself, therefore, give them hope in thee: and so go I unto Cleopatra and say: Arise in the name of Jesus Christ. 23 And he came to her and touched her face and said: Cleopatra, He saith, whom every ruler feareth, and every creature and every power, the abyss and all darkness, and unsmiling death, and the height of heaven, and the circles of hell [and the resurrection of the dead, and the sight of the blind], and the whole power of the prince of this world, and the pride of the ruler: Arise, and be not an occasion unto many that desire not to believe, or an affliction unto souls that are able to hope and to be saved. And Cleopatra straightway cried with a loud voice: I arise, master: save thou thine handmaid.

Now when she had arisen seven days, the city of the Ephesians was moved at the unlooked -for sight. And Cleopatra asked concerning her husband Lycomedes, but John said to her: Cleopatra, if thou keep thy soul unmoved and steadfast, thou shalt forthwith have Lycomedes thine husband standing here beside thee, if at least thou be not disturbed nor moved at that which hath befallen, having believed on my God, who by my means shall grant him unto thee alive. Come therefore with me into thine other bedchamber, and thou shalt behold him, a dead corpse indeed, but raised again by the power of my God.

24 And Cleopatra going with John into her bedchamber, and seeing Lycomedes dead for her sake, had no power to speak (suffered in her voice), and ground her teeth and bit her tongue, and closed her eyes, raining down tears: and with calmness gave heed to the apostle. But John had compassion on Cleopatra when he saw that she neither raged nor was beside herself, and called upon the perfect and condescending mercy, saying: Lord Jesus Christ, thou seest the pressure of sorrow, thou seest the need; thou seest Cleopatra shrieking her soul out in silence, for she constraineth within her the frenzy that cannot be borne; and I know that for Lycomedes' sake she also will die upon his body. And she said quietly to John: That have I in mind, master, and nought else.

And the apostle went to the couch whereon Lycomedes lay, and taking Cleopatra's hand he said: Cleopatra, because of the multitude that is present, and thy kinsfolk that have come in, with strong crying, say thou to thine husband: Arise and glorify the name of God, for he giveth back the dead to the dead. And she went to her husband and said to him according as she was taught, and forthwith raised him up. And he, when he arose, fell on the floor and kissed John's feet, but he raised him, saying: O man, kiss not my feet but the feet of God by whose power ye are both arisen.

25 But Lycomedes said to John: I entreat and adjure thee by the God in whose name thou hast raised us, to abide with us, together with all them that are with thee. Likewise Cleopatra also caught his feet and said the same. And John said to them: For tomorrow I will be with you. And they said to him again: We shall have no hope in thy God, but shall have been raised to no purpose, if thou abide not with us. And Cleobius with Aristodemus and Damonicus were touched in the soul and said to John: Let us abide with them, that they continue without offence towards the Lord. So he continued there with the brethren.

26 There came together therefore a gathering of a great multitude on John's account; and as he discoursed to them that were there, Lycomedes, who had a friend who was a skilful painter, went hastily to him and said to him: You see me in a great hurry to come to you: come quickly to my house and paint the man whom I show you without his knowing it. And the painter, giving some one the necessary implements and colours, said to Lycomedes: Show him to me, and for the rest have no anxiety. And Lycomedes pointed out John to the painter, and brought him near him, and shut him up in a room from which the apostle of Christ could be seen. And Lycomedes was with the blessed man, feasting on the faith and the knowledge of our God, and rejoiced yet more in the thought that he should possess him in a portrait.

27 The painter, then, on the first day made an outline of him and went away. And on the next he painted him in with his colours, and so delivered the portrait to Lycomedes to his great joy. And lie took it and set it up in his own bedehamber and hung it with garlands: so that later John, when he perceived it, said to him: My beloved child, what is it that thou always doest when thou comest in from the bath into thy bedchamber alone? do not I pray with thee and the rest of the brethren? or is there something thou art hiding from us? And as he said this and talked jestingly with him, he went into the bedchamber, and saw the portrait of an old man crowned with garlands, and lamps and altars set before it. And he called him and said: Lycomedes, what meanest thou by this matter of the portrait? can it be one of thy gods that is painted here? for I see that thou art still living in heathen fashion. And Lycomedes answered him: My only God is he who raised me up from death with my wife: but if, next to that God, it be right that the men who have benefited us should be called gods -it is thou, father, whom I have had painted in that portrait, whom I crown and love and reverence as having become my

good guide.

28 And John who had never at any time seen his own face said to him: Thou mockest me, child: am I like that in form, thy Lord? how canst thou persuade me that the portrait is like me? And Lycomedes brought him a mirror. And when he had seen himself in the mirror and looked earnestly at the portrait, he said: As the Lord Jesus Christ liveth, the portrait is like me: yet not like me, child, but like my fleshly image; for if this painter, who hath imitated this my face, desireth to draw me in a portrait, he will be at a loss, the colours that are now given to thee, and boards and plaster (?) and glue (?), and the position of my shape, and old age and youth and all things that are seen with the eye.

29 But do thou become for me a good painter, Lycomedes. Thou hast colours which he giveth thee through me, who painteth all of us for himself, even Jesus, who knoweth the shapes and appearances and postures and dispositions and types of our souls. And the colours wherewith I bid thee paint are these: faith in God, knowledge, godly fear, friendship, communion, meekness, kindness, brotherly love, purity, simplicity, tranquillity, fearlessness, griefiessness, sobriety, and the whole band of colours that painteth the likeness of thy soul, and even now raiseth up thy members that were cast down, and levelleth them that were lifted up, and tendeth thy bruises, and healeth thy wounds, and ordereth thine hair that was disarranged, and washeth thy face, and chasteneth thine eyes, and purgeth thy bowels, and emptieth thy belly, and cutteth off that which is beneath it; and in a word, when the whole company and mingling of such colours is come together, into thy soul, it shall present it to our Lord Jesus Christ undaunted, whole (unsmoothed), and firm of shape. But this that thou hast now done is childish and imperfect: thou hast drawn a dead likeness of the dead.

There need be no portion of text lost at this point: but possibly some few sentences have been omitted. The transition is abrupt and the new episode has not, as elsewhere, a title of its own.

30 And he commanded Verus (Berus), the brother that ministered to him, to gather the aged women that were in all Ephesus, and made ready, he and Cleopatra and Lycomedes, all things for the care of them. Verus, then, came to John, saying: Of the aged women that are here over threescore years old I have found four only sound in body, and of the rest some . . . . (a word gone) and some palsied and others sick. And when he heard that, John kept silence for a long time, and rubbed his face and said: O the slackness (weakness) of them that dwell in Ephesus! O the state of dissolution, and the weakness toward God! O devil, that hast so long mocked the faithful in Ephesus! Jesus, who giveth me grace and the gift to have my confidence in him, saith to me in silence: Send after the old women that are sick and come (be) with them into the theatre, and through me heal them: for there are some of them that will come unto this spectacle whom by these healings I will convert and make them useful for some end.

31 Now when all the multitude was come together to Lycomedes, he dismissed them on John's behalf, saying: Tomorrow come ye to the theatre, as many as desire to see the power of God. And the multitude, on the morrow, while it was yet night, came to the theatre: so that the proconsul also heard of it and hasted and took his sent with all the people. And a certain praetor, Andromeus, who was the first of the Ephesians at that time, put it about that John had promised things impossible and incredible: But if, said he, he is able to do any such thing as I hear, let him come into the public theatre, when it is open, naked, and holding nothing in his hands, neither let him name that magical name which I have heard him utter.

32 John therefore, having heard this and being moved by. these words, commanded the aged women to be

brought into the theatre: and when they were all brought into the midst, some of them upon beds and others lying in a deep sleep, and all the city had run together, and a great silence was made, John opened his mouth and began to say:

33 Ye men of Ephesus, learn first of all wherefore I am visiting in your city, or what is this great confidence which I have towards you, so that it may become manifest to this general assembly and to all of you (or, so that I manifest myself to). I have been sent, then, upon a mission which is not of man's ordering, and not upon any vain journey; neither am I a merchant that make bargains or exchanges; but Jesus Christ whom I preach, being compassionate and kind, desireth by my means to convert all of you who are held in unbelief and sold unto evil lusts, and to deliver you from error; and by his power will I confound even the unbelief of your praetor, by raising up them that lie before you, whom ye all behold, in what plight and in what sicknesses they are. And to do this (to confound Andronicus) is not possible for me if they perish: therefore shall they be healed.

34 But this first I have desired to sow in your ears, even that ye should take care for your souls -on which account I am come unto you- and not expect that this time will be for ever, for it is but a moment, and not lay up treasures upon the earth where all things do fade. Neither think that when ye have gotten children ye can rest upon them (?), and try not for their sakes to defraud and overreach. Neither, ye poor, be vexed if ye have not wherewith to minister unto pleasures; for men of substance when they are diseased call you happy. Neither, ye rich, rejoice that ye have much money, for by possessing these things ye provide for yourselves grief that ye cannot be rid of when ye lose them; and besides, while it is with you, ye are afraid lest some one attack you on account of it.

35 Thou also that art puffed up because of the shapeliness of thy body, and art

of an high look, shalt see the end of the promise thereof in the grave; and thou that rejoicest in adultery, know that both law and nature avenge it upon thee, and before these, conscience; and thou, adulteress, that art an adversary of the law, knowest not whither thou shalt come in the end. And thou that sharest not with the needy, but hast monies laid up, when thou departest out of this body and hast need of some mercy when thou burnest in fire, shalt have none to pity thee; and thou the wrathful and passionate, know that thy conversation is like the brute beasts; and thou, drunkard and quarreller, learn that thou losest thy senses by being enslaved to a shameful and dirty desire.

36 Thou that rejoicest in gold and delightest thyself with ivory and jewels, when night falleth, canst thou behold what thou lovest? thou that art vanquished by soft raiment, and then leavest life, will those things profit thee in the place whither thou goest? And let the murderer know that the condign punishment is laid up for him twofold after his departure hence. Likewise also thou poisoner, sorcerer, robber, defrauder, sodomite, thief, and as many as are of that band, ye shall come at last, as your works do lead you, unto unquenchable fire, and utter darkness, and the pit of punishment, and eternal threatenings. Wherefore, ye men of Ephesus, turn yourselves, knowing this also, that kings, rulers, tyrants, boasters, and they that have conquered in wars, stripped of all things when they depart hence, do suffer pain, lodged in eternal misery.

37 And having thus said, John by the power of God healed all the diseases.

[[This sentence must be an abridgement of a much longer narration. The manuscript indicates no break at this point: but we must suppose a not inconsiderable loss of text. For one thing, Andronicus, who is here an unbeliever, appears as a convert in the next few lines. Now he is, as we shall see later, the husband of an eminent believer, Drusiana; and his

and her conversion will have been told at some length; and I do not doubt that among other things there was a discourse of John persuading them to live in continence.]]

37 (continued.) Now the brethren from Miletus said unto John: We have continued a long time at Ephesus; if it seem good to thee, let us go also to Smyrna; for we hear already that the mighty works of God have reached it also. And Andronicus said to them: Whensoever the teacher willeth, then let us go. But John said: Let us first go unto the temple of Artemis, for perchance there also, if we show ourselves, the servants of the Lord will be found.

38 After two days, then, was the birthday of the idol temple. John therefore, when all were clad in white, alone put on black raiment and went up into the temple. And they took him and essayed to kill him. But John said: Ye are mad to set upon me, a man that is the servant of the only God. And he gat him up upon an high pedestal and said unto them:

39 Ye run hazard, men of Ephesus, of being like in character to the sea: every river that floweth in and every spring that runneth down, and the rains, and waves that press upon each other, and torrents full of rocks are made salt together by the bitter telementt (MS. promise!) that is therein. So ye also remaining unchanged unto this day toward true godliness are become corrupted by your ancient rites of worship. How many wonders and healings of diseases have ye seen wrought through me? And yet are ye blinded in your hearts and cannot recover sight. What is it, then, O men of Ephesus? I have adventured now and come up even into this your idol temple. I will convict you of being most godless, and dead from the understanding of mankind. Behold, I stand here: ye all say that ye have a goddess, even Artemis: pray then unto her that I alone may die; or else I only, if ye are not able to do this, will call upon mine own god, and for your unbelief I will cause every one of you to die.

40 But they who had beforetime made trial of him and had seen dead men raised up, cried out: Slay us not so, we beseech thee, John. We know that thou canst do it. And John said to them: If then ye desire not to die, let that which ye worship be confounded, and wherefore it is confounded, that ye also may depart from your ancient error. For now is it time that either ye be converted by my God, or I myself die by your goddess; for I will pray in your presence and entreat my God that mercy be shown unto you.

41 And having so said he prayed thus: O God that art God above all that are called gods, that until this day hast been set at nought in the city of the Ephesians; that didst put into my mind to come into this place, whereof I never thought; that dost convict every manner of worship by turning men unto thee; at whose name every idol fleeth and every evil spirit and every unclean power; now also by the flight of the evil spirit here at thy name, even of him that deceiveth this great multitude, show thou thy mercy in this place, for they have been made to err.

42 And as John spake these things, immediately the altar of Artemis was parted into many pieces, and all the things that were dedicated in the temple fell, and [MS. that which seemed good to him] was rent asunder, and likewise of the images of the gods more than seven. And the half of the temple fell down, so that the priest was slain at one blow by the falling of the (?roof, ? beam). The multitude of the Ephesians therefore cried out: One is the God of John, one is the God that hath pity on us, for thou only art God: now are we turned to thee, beholding thy marvellous works! have mercy on us, O God, according to thy will, and save us from our great error! And some of them, lying on their faces, made supplication, and some kneeled and besought, and some rent their clothes and wept, and others tried to escape.

43 But John spread forth his hands, and being uplifted in soul, said unto the Lord: Glory be to thee, my Jesus, the only God of truth, for that thou dost gain (receive) thy servants by divers devices. And having so said, he said to the people: Rise up from the floor, ye men of Ephesus, and pray to my God, and recognize the invisible power that cometh to manifestation, and the wonderful works which are wrought before your eyes. Artemis ought to have succoured herself: her servant ought to have been helped of her and not to have died. Where is the power of the evil spirit? where are her sacrifices? where her birthdays? where her festivals? where are the garlands? where is all that sorcery and the poisoning (witchcraft) that is sister thereto?

44 But the people rising up from off the floor went hastily and cast down the rest of the idol temple, crying: The God of John only do we know, and him hereafter do we worship, since he hath had mercy upon us! And as John came down from thence, much people took hold of him, saying: Help us, O John! Assist us that do perish in vain! Thou seest our purpose: thou seest the multitude following thee and hanging upon thee in hope toward thy God. We have seen the way wherein we went astray when we lost him: we have seen our gods that were set up in vain: we have seen the great and shameful derision that is come to them: but suffer us, we pray thee, to come unto thine house and to be succoured without hindrance. Receive us that are in bewilderment.

45 And John said to them: Men (of Ephesus), believe that for your sakes I have continued in Ephesus, and have put off my journey unto Smyrna and to the rest of the cities, that there also the servants of Christ may turn to him. But since I am not yet perfectly assured concerning you, I have continued praying to my God and beseeching him that I should then depart from Ephesus when I have confirmed you in the faith: and whereas I see that this is come to pass and yet more is being fulfilled, I will not leave you until I have weaned you like children from the nurse's milk, and have set you upon a firm rock.

46 John therefore continued with them, receiving them in the house of Andromeus. And one of them that were gathered laid down the dead body of the priest of Artemis before the door [of the temple], for he was his kinsman, and came in quickly with the rest, saying nothing of it. John, therefore, after the discourse to the brethren, and the prayer and the thanksgiving (eucharist) and the laying of hands upon every one of the congregation, said by the spirit: There is one here who moved by faith in God hath laid down the priest of Artemis before the gate and is come in, and in the yearning of his soul, taking care first for himself, hath thought thus in himself: It is better for me to take thought for the living than for my kinsman that is dead: for I know that if I turn to the Lord and save mine own soul, John will not deny to raise up the dead also. And John arising from his place went to that into which that kinsman of the priest who had so thought was entered, and took him by the hand and said: Hadst thou this thought when thou camest unto me, my child? And he, taken with trembling and affright, said: Yes, lord, and cast himself at his feet. And John said: Our Lord is Jesus Christ, who will show his power in thy dead kinsman by raising him up.

47 And he made the young man rise, and took his hand and said: It is no great matter for a man that is master of great mysteries to continue wearying himself over small things: or what great thing is it to rid men of diseases of the body? And yet holding the young man by the hand he said: I say unto thee, child, go and raise the dead thyself, saying nothing but this only: John the servant of God saith to thee, Arise. And the young man went to his kinsman and said this only -and much people was with him- and entered in unto John, bringing him alive. And John, when he saw him that was raised, said: Now that thou art raised, thou dost not truly live,

neither art partaker or heir of the true life: wilt thou belong unto him by whose name and power thou wast raised? And now believe, and thou shall live unto all ages. And he forthwith believed upon the Lord Jesus and thereafter clave unto John.

[[Another manuscript (Q. Paris Gr. 1468, of the eleventh century) has another form of this story. John destroys the temple of Artemis, and then 'we' go to Smyrna and all the idols are broken: Bucolus, Polycarp, and Andronicus are left to preside over the district. There were there two priests of Artemis, brothers, and one died. The raising is told much as in the older text, but more shortly.
'We' remained four years in the region, which was wholly converted, and then returned to Ephesus.]]

48 Now on the next day John, having seen in a dream that he must walk three miles outside the gates, neglected it not, but rose up early and set out upon the way, together with the brethren. And a certain countryman who was admonished by his father not to take to himself the wife of a fellow labourer of his who threatened to kill him -this young man would not endure the admonition of his father, but kicked him and left him without speech (sc. dead). And John, seeing what had befallen, said unto the Lord: Lord, was it on this account that thou didst bid me come out hither to-day?
49 But the young man, beholding the violence (sharpness) of death, and looking to be taken, drew out the sickle that was in his girdle and started to run to his own abode; and John met him and said: Stand still, thou most shameless devil, and tell me whither thou runnest bearing a sickle that thirsteth for blood. And the young man was troubled and cast the iron on the ground, and said to him: I have done a wretched and barbarous deed and I know it, and so I determined to do an evil yet worse and more cruel, even to die myself at once. For because my

father was alway curbing me to sobriety, that I should live without adultery, and chastely, I could not endure him to reprove me, and I kicked him and slew him, and when I saw what was done, I was hasting to the woman for whose sake I became my father's murderer, with intent to kill her and her husband, and myself last of all: for I could not bear to be seen of the husband of the woman, and undergo the judgement of death.
50 And John said to him: That I may not by going away and leaving you in danger give place to him that desireth to laugh and sport with thee, come thou with me and show me thy father, where he lieth. And if I raise him up for thee, wilt thou hereafter abstain from the woman that is become a snare to thee. And the young man said: If thou raisest up my father himself for me alive, and if I see him whole and continuing in life, I will hereafter abstain from her.
51 And while he was speaking, they came to the place where the old man lay dead, and many passers-by were standing near thereto. And John said to the youth: Thou wretched man, didst thou not spare even the old age of thy father? And he, weeping and tearing his hair, said that he repented thereof; and John the servant of the Lord said: Thou didst show me I was to set forth for this place, thou knewest that this would come to pass, from whom nothing can be hid of things done in life, that givest me power to work every cure and healing by thy will: now also give me this old man alive, for thou seest that his murderer is become his own judge: and spare him, thou only Lord, that spared not his father (because he) counselled him for the best.
52 And with these words he came near to the old man and said: My Lord will not be weak to spread out his kind pity and his condescending mercy even unto thee: rise up therefore and give glory to God for the work that is come to pass at this moment. And the old man said: I arise, Lord. And he rose and sat up and said: I was released from a terrible life and had to bear the insults of my son,

dreadful and many, and his want of natural affection, and to what end hast thou called me back, O man of the living God? (And John answered him: If) thou art raised only for the same end, it were better for thee to die; but raise thyself unto better things. And he took him and led him into the city, preaching unto him the grace of God, so that before he entered the gate the old man believed.

53 But the young man, when he beheld the unlooked-for raising of his father, and the saving of himself, took a sickle and mutilated himself, and ran to the house wherein he had his adulteress, and reproached her, saying: For thy sake I became the murderer of my father and of you two and of myself: there thou hast that which is alike guilty of all. For on me God hath had mercy, that I should know his power.

54 And he came back and told John in presence of the brethren what he had done. But John said to him: He that put it into thine heart, young man, to kill thy father and become the adulterer of another man's wife, the same made thee think it a right deed to take away also the unruly members. But thou shouldest have done away, not with the place of sin, but the thought which through those members showed itself harmful: for it is not the instruments that are injurious, but the unseen springs by which every shameful emotion is stirred and cometh to light. Repent therefore, my child, of this fault, and having learnt the wiles of Satan thou shalt have God to help thee in all the necessities of thy soul. And the young man kept silence and attended, having repented of his former sins, that he should obtain pardon from the goodness of God: and he did not separate from John.

55 When, then, these things had been done by him in the city of the Ephesians, they of Smyrna sent unto him saying: We hear that the God whom thou preachest is not envious, and hath charged thee not to show partiality by abiding in one place. Since, then, thou art a preacher of such a God, come unto Smyrna and unto the other cities, that we may come to know thy God, and having known him may have our hope in him.

[[Q has the above story also, and continues with an incident which is also quoted in a different form (and not as from these Acts) by John Cassian. Q has it thus:]]

Now one day as John was seated, a partridge flew by and came and played in the dust before him; and John looked on it and wondered. And a certain priest came, who was one of his hearers, and came to John and saw the partridge playing in the dust before him, and was offended in himself and said: Can such and so great a man take pleasure in a partridge playing in the dust? But John perceiving in the spirit the thought of him, said to him: It were better for thee also, my child, to look at a partridge playing in the dust and not to defile thyself with shameful and profane practices: for he who awaiteth the conversion and repentance of all men hath brought thee here on this account: for I have no need of a partridge playing in the dust. For the partridge is thine own soul.

Then the elder, hearing this and seeing that he was not bidden, but that the apostle of Christ had told him all that was in his heart, fell on his face on the earth and cried aloud, saying: Now know I that God dwelleth in thee, O blessed John! for he that tempteth thee tempteth him that cannot be tempted. And he entreated him to pray for him. And he instructed him and delivered him the rules (canons) and let him go to his house, glorifying God that is over all.

Cassian, Collation XXIV. 21, has it thus:

It is told that the most blessed Evangelist John, when he was gently stroking a partridge with his hands, suddenly saw one in the habit of a hunter coming to him. He wondered that a man of such repute and fame should demean himself to such small and humble amusements, and said: Art thou that John whose eminent and widespread fame hath enticed me also with great desire to know thee? Why then art thou taken up with such mean amusements? The blessed John said to him: What is that which thou carriest in thy hands? A bow, said he. And why, said he, dost thou not bear it about always stretched? He answered him: I must not, lest by constant bending the strength of its vigour be wrung and grow soft and perish, and when there is need that the arrows be shot with much strength at some beast, the strength being lost by excess of continual tension, a forcible blow cannot be dealt. Just so, said the blessed John, let not this little and brief relaxation of my mind offend thee, young man, for unless it doth sometimes ease and relax by some remission the force of its tension, it will grow slack through unbroken rigour and will not be able to obey the power of the Spirit.

[[The only common point of the two stories is that St. John amuses himself with a partridge, and a spectator thinks it unworthy of him. The two morals differ wholly. The amount of text lost here is of quite uncertain length. It must have told of the doings at Smyrna, and also, it appears, at Laodicca (see the title of the next section). One of the episodes must have been the conversion of a woman of evil life (see below, 'the harlot that was chaste')-]]

[[Our best manuscript prefixes a title to the next section:]]

From Laodicca to Ephesus the second time.

58 Now when some long time had passed, and none of the brethren had been at any time grieved by John, they were then grieved because he had said: Brethren, it is now time for me to go to Ephesus (for so have I agreed with them that dwell there) lest they become slack, now for a long time having no man to confirm them. But all of you must have your minds steadfast towards God, who never forsaketh us.

But when they heard this from him, the brethren lamented because they were to be parted from him. And John said: Even if I be parted from you, yet Christ is always with you: whom if ye love purely ye will have his fellowship without reproach, for if he be loved, he preventeth (anticipateth) them that love him.

59 And having so said, and bidden farewell to them, and left much money with the brethren for distribution, he went forth unto Ephesus, while all the brethren lamented and groaned. And there accompanied him, of Ephesus, both Andronicus and Drusiana and Lycomedes and Cleobius and their families. And there followed him Aristobula also, who had heard that her husband Tertullus had died on the way, and Aristippus with Xenophon, and the harlot that was chaste, and many others, whom he exhorted at all times to cleave to the Lord, and they would no more be parted from him.

60 Now on the first day we arrived at a deserted inn, and when we were at a loss for a bed for John, we saw a droll matter. There was one bedstead lying somewhere there without coverings, whereon we spread the cloaks which we were wearing, and we prayed him to lie down upon it and rest, while the rest of us all slept upon the floor. But he when he lay down was troubled by the bugs, and as they continued to become yet more troublesome to him, when it was now about the middle of the night, in the hearing of us all he said to them: I say unto you, O bugs, behave yourselves, one and all, and leave your abode for this night and remain quiet in one place, and keep your distance from the servants of God. And as we laughed, and went on talking for some time, John addressed himself to sleep; and we, talking low, gave him no disturbance (or, thanks to him we were not disturbed).

61 But when the day was now dawning I arose first, and with me Verus and Andronicus, and we saw at the door of the house which we had taken a great

number of bugs standing, and while we wondered at the great sight of them, and all the brethren were roused up because of them, John continued sleeping. And when he was awaked we declared to him what we had seen. And he sat up on the bed and looked at them and said: Since ye have well behaved yourselves in hearkening to my rebuke, come unto your place. And when he had said this, and risen from the bed, the bugs running from the door hasted to the bed and climbed up by the legs thereof and disappeared into the joints. And John said again: This creature hearkened unto the voice of a man, and abode by itself and was quiet and trespassed not; but we which hear the voice and commandments of God disobey and are light-minded: and for how long?

62 After these things we came to Ephesus: and the brethren there, who had for a long time known that John was coming, ran together to the house of Andronicus (where also he came to lodge), handling his feet and laying his hands upon their own faces and kissing them (and many rejoiced even to touch his vesture, and were healed by touching the clothes of the holy apostle. [So the Latin, which has this section; the Greek has: so that they even touched his garments).]

63 And whereas there was great love and joy unsurpassed among the brethren, a certain one, a messenger of Satan, became enamoured of Drusiana, though he saw and knew that she was the wife of Andronicus. To whom many said: It is not possible for thee to obtain that woman, seeing that for a long time she has even separated herself from her husband for godliness' sake. Art thou only ignorant that Andronicus, not being aforetime that which now he is, a God-fearing man, shut her up in a tomb, saying: Either I must have thee as the wife whom I had before, or thou shalt die. And she chose rather to die than to do that foulness. If, then, she would not consent, for godliness' sake, to cohabit with her lord and husband, but even persuaded him to be of the same mind as herself, will she consent to thee

desiring to be her seducer? depart from this madness which hath no rest in thee: give up this deed which thou canst not bring to accomplishment.

64 But his familiar friends saying these things to him did not convince him, but with shamelessness he courted her with messages; and when he learnt the insults and disgraces which she returned, he spent his life in melancholy (or better, she, when she learnt of this disgrace and insult at his hand, spent her life in heaviness). And after two days Drusiana took to her bed from heaviness, and was in a fever and said: Would that I had not now come home to my native place, I that have become an offence to a man ignorant of godliness! for if it were one who was filled with the word of God, he would not have gone to such a pitch of madness. But now (therefore) Lord, since I am become the occasion of a blow unto a soul devoid of knowledge, set me free from this chain and remove me unto thee quickly. And in the presence of John, who knew nothing at all of such a matter, Drusiana departed out of life not wholly happy, yea, even troubled because of the spiritual hurt of the man.

65 But Andronicus, grieved with a secret grief, mourned in his soul, and wept openly, so that John checked him often and said to him: Upon a better hope hath Drusiana removed out of this unrighteous life. And Andronicus answered him: Yea, I am persuaded of it, O John, and I doubt not at all in regard of trust in my God: but this very thing do I hold fast, that she departed out of life pure.

66 And when she was carried forth, John took hold on Andronicus, and now that he knew the cause, he mourned more than Andronicus. And he kept silence, considering the provocation of the adversary, and for a space sat still. Then, the brethren being gathered there to hear what word he would speak of her that was departed, he began to say:

67 When the pilot that voyageth, together with them that sail with him, and the ship herself, arriveth in a calm and stormless harbour, then let him say

that he is safe. And the husbandman that hath committed the seed to the earth, and toiled much in the care and protection of it, let him then take rest from his labours, when he layeth up the seed with manifold increase in his barns. Let him that enterpriseth to run in the course, then exult when he beareth home the prize. Let him that inscribeth his name for the boxing, then boast himself when he receiveth the crowns: and so in succession is it with all contests and crafts, when they do not fail in the end, but show themselves to be like that which they promised (corrupt).

68 And thus also I think is it with the faith which each one of us practiseth, that it is then discerned whether it be indeed true, when it continueth like itself even until the end of life. For many obstacles fall into the way, and prepare disturbance for the minds of men: care, children, parents, glory, poverty, flattery, prime of life, beauty, conceit, lust, wealth, anger, uplifting, slackness, envy, jealousy, neglect, fear, insolence, love, deceit, money, pretence, and other such obstacles, as many as there are in this life: as also the pilot sailing a prosperous course is opposed by the onset of contrary winds and a great storm and mighty waves out of calm, and the husbandman by untimely winter and blight and creeping things rising out of the earth, and they that strive in the games 'just do not win', and they that exercise crafts are hindered by the divers difficulties of them.

69 But before all things it is needful that the believer should look before at his ending and understand it in what manner it will come upon him, whether it will be vigorous and sober and without any obstacle, or disturbed and clinging to the things that are here, and bound down by desires. So is it right that a body should be praised as comely when it is wholly stripped, and a general as great when he hath accomplished every promise of the war, and a physician as excellent when he hath succeeded in every cure, and a soul as full of faith and worthy (or receptive) of God when it hath paid its promise in full: not that soul which began well and was dissolved into all the things of this life and fell away, nor that which is numb, having made an effort to attain to better things, and then is borne down to temporal things, nor that which hath longed after the things of time more than those of eternity, nor that which exchangeth those that endure not, nor that which hath honoured the works of dishonour that deserve shame, nor that which taketh pledges of Satan, nor that which hath received the serpent into its own house, nor that which suffereth reproach for God's sake and then is [not] ashamed, nor that which with the mouth saith yea, but indeed approveth not itself: but that which hath prevailed not to be made weak by foul pleasure, not to be overcome by light-mindedness, not to be caught by the bait of love of money, not to be betrayed by vigour of body or wrath.

70 And as John was discoursing yet further unto the brethren that they should despise temporal things in respect of the eternal, he that was enamoured of Drusiana, being inflamed with an horrible lust and possession of the many-shaped Satan, bribed the steward of Andronicus who was a lover of money with a great sum: and he opened the tomb and gave him opportunity to wreak the forbidden thing upon the dead body. Not having succeeded with her when alive, he was still importunate after her death to her body, and said: If thou wouldst not have to do with me while thou livedst, I will outrage thy corpse now thou art dead. With this design, and having managed for himself the wicked act by means of the abominable steward, he rushed with him to the sepulchre; they opened the door and began to strip the grave-clothes from the corpse, saying: What art thou profited, poor Drusiana? couldest thou not have done this in life, which perchance would not have grieved thee, hadst thou done it willingly?

71 And as these men were speaking

thus, and only the accustomed shift now remained on her body, a strange spectacle was seen, such as they deserve to suffer who do such deeds. A serpent appeared from some quarter and dealt the steward a single bite and slew him: but the young man it did not strike; but coiled about his feet, hissing terribly, and when he fell mounted on his body and sat upon him.

72 Now on the next day John came, accompanied by Andronicus and the brethren, to the sepulchre at dawn, it being now the third day from Drusiana's death, that we might break bread there. And first, when they set out, the keys were sought for and could not be found; but John said to Andronicus: It is quite right that they should be lost, for Drusiana is not in the sepulchre; nevertheless, let us go, that thou mayest not be neglectful, and the doors shall be opened of themselves, even as the Lord hath done for us many such things.

73 And when we were at the place, at the commandment of the master, the doors were opened, and we saw by the tomb of Drusiana a beautiful youth, smiling: and John, when he saw him, cried out and said: Art thou come before us hither too, beautiful one? and for what cause? And we heard a voice saying to him: For Drusiana's sake, whom thou art to raise up-for I was within a little of finding her -and for his sake that lieth dead beside her tomb. And when the beautiful one had said this unto John he went up into the heavens in the sight of us all. And John, turning to the other side of the sepulchre, saw a young man-even Callimachus, one of the chief of the Ephesians-and a huge serpent sleeping upon him, and the steward of Andronicus, Fortunatus by name, lying dead. And at the sight of the two he stood perplexed, saying to the brethren: What meaneth such a sight? or wherefore hath not the Lord declared unto me what was done here, he who hath never neglected me?

74 And Andronicus seeing those corpses, leapt up and went to Drusiana's tomb, and seeing her lying in her shift only, said to John: I understand what has happened, thou blessed servant of God, John. This Callimachus was enamoured of my sister; and because he never won her, though he often assayed it, he hath bribed this mine accursed steward with a great sum, perchance designing, as now we may see, to fulfil by his means the tragedy of his conspiracy, for indeed Callimachus avowed this to many, saying: If she will not consent to me when living, she shall be outraged when dead. And it may be, master, that the beautiful one knew it and suffered not her body to be insulted, and therefore have these died who made that attempt. And can it be that the voice that said unto thee, 'Raise up Drusiana', foreshowed this? because she departed out of this life in sorrow of mind. But I believe him that said that this is one of the men that have gone astray; for thou wast bidden to raise him up: for as to the other, I know that he is unworthy of salvation. But this one thing I beg of thee: raise up Callimachus first, and he will confess to us what is come about.

75 And John, looking upon the body, said to the venomous beast: Get thee away from him that is to be a servant of Jesus Christ; and stood up and prayed over him thus: O God whose name is glorified by us, as of right: O God who subduest every injurious force: O God whose will is accomplished, who alway hearest us: now also let thy gift be accomplished in this young man; and if there be any dispensation to be wrought through him, manifest it unto us when he is raised up. And straightway the young man rose up, and for a whole hour kept silence.

76 But when he came to his right senses, John asked of him about his entry into the sepulchre, what it meant, and learning from him that which Andronicus had told him, namely, that he was enamoured of Drusiana, John inquired of him again if he had fulfilled his foul intent, to insult a body full of holiness. And he answered him: How could I accomplish it when this fearful beast struck down Fortunatus at a blow

in my sight: and rightly, since he encouraged my frenzy, when I was already cured of that unreasonable and horrible madness: but me it stopped with affright, and brought me to that plight in which ye saw me before I arose. And another thing yet more wondrous I will tell thee, which yet went nigh to slay and was within a little of making me a corpse. When my soul was stirred up with folly and the uncontrollable malady was troubling me, and I had now torn away the grave-clothes in which she was clad, and I had then come out of the grave and laid them as thou seest, I went again to my unholy work: and I saw a beautiful youth covering her with his mantle, and from his eyes sparks of light came forth unto her eyes; and he uttered words to me, saying: Callimachus, die that thou mayest live. Now who he was I knew not, O servant of God; but that now thou hast appeared here, I recognize that he was an angel of God, that I know well; and this I know of a truth that it is a true God that is proclaimed by thee, and of it I am persuaded. But I beseech thee, be not slack to deliver me from this calamity and this fearful crime, and to present me unto thy God as a man deceived with a shameful and foul deceit. Beseeching help therefore of thee, I take hold on thy feet. I would become one of them that hope in Christ, that the voice may prove true which said to me, 'Die that thou mayest live': and that voice hath also fulfilled its effect, for he is dead, that faithless, disorderly, godless one, and I have been raised by thee, I who will be faithful, God-fearing, knowing the truth, which I entreat thee may be shown me by thee.

77 And John, filled with great gladness and perceiving the whole spectacle of the salvation of man, said: What thy power is, Lord Jesu Christ, I know not, bewildered as I am at thy much compassion and boundless long-suffering. O what a greatness that came down into bondage! O unspeakable liberty brought into slavery by us! O incomprehensible glory that is come unto us! thou that hast kept the dead tabernacle safe from insult; that hast redeemed the man that stained himself with blood and chastened the soul of him that would defile the corruptible body; Father that hast had pity and compassion on the man that cared not for thee; We glorify thee, and praise and bless and thank thy great goodness and long-suffering, O holy Jesu, for thou only art God, and none else: whose is the might that cannot be conspired against, now and world without end. Amen.

78 And when he had said this John took Callimachus and saluted (kissed) him, saying: Glory be to our God, my child, who hath had mercy on thee, and made me worthy to glorify his power, and thee also by a good course to depart from that thine abominable madness and drunkenness, and hath called thee unto his own rest and unto renewing of life.

79 But Andronicus, beholding the dead Callimachus raised, besought John, with the brethren, to raise up Drusiana also, saying: O John, let Drusiana arise and spend happily that short space (of life) which she gave up through grief about Callimachus, when she thought she had become a stumbling block to him: and when the Lord will, he shall take her again to himself. And John without delay went unto her tomb and took her hand and said: Upon thee that art the only God do I call, the more than great, the unutterable, the incomprehensible: unto whom every power of principalities is subjected: unto whom all authority boweth: before whom all pride falleth down and keepeth silence: whom devils hearing of tremble: whom all creation perceiving keepeth its bounds. Let thy name be glorified by us, and raise up Drusiana, that Callimachus may yet more be confirmed unto thee who dispensest that which unto men is without a way and impossible, but to thee only possible, even salvation and resurrection: and that Drusiana may now come forth in peace, having about her not any the least hindrance -now that the young man is turned unto thee-

in her course toward thee.

80 And after these words John said unto Drusiana: Drusiana, arise. And she arose and came out of the tomb; and when she saw herself in her shift only, she was perplexed at the thing, and learned the whole accurately from Andronicus, the while John lay upon his face, and Callimachus with voice and tears glorified God, and she also rejoiced, glorifying him in like manner.

81 And when she had clothed herself, she turned and saw Fortunatus lying, and said unto John: Father, let this man also rise, even if he did assay to become my betrayer. But Callimachus, when he heard her say that, said: Do not, I beseech thee, Drusiana, for the voice which I heard took no thought of him, but declared concerning thee only, and I saw and believed: for if he had been good, perchance God would have had mercy on him also and would have raised him by means of the blessed John: he knew therefore that the man was come to a bad end [Lat. he judged him worthy to die whom he did not declare worthy to rise again]. And John said to him: We have not learned, my child, to render evil for evil: for God, though we have done much ill and no good toward him, hath not given retribution unto us, but repentance, and though we were ignorant of his name he did not neglect us but had mercy on us, and when we blasphemed him, he did not punish but pitied us, and when we disbelieved him he bore us no grudge, and when we persecuted his brethren he did not recompense us evil but put into our minds repentance and abstinence from evil, and exhorted us to come unto him, as he hath thee also, my son Callimachus, and not remembering thy former evil hath made thee his servant, waiting upon his mercy. Wherefore if thou allowest not me to raise up Fortunatus, it is for Drusiana so to do.

82 And she, delaying not, went with rejoicing of spirit and soul unto the body of Fortunatus and said: Jesu Christ, God of the ages, God of truth, that hast granted me to see wonders and signs, and given to me to become

partaker of thy name; that didst breathe thyself into me with thy many-shaped countenance, and hadst mercy on me in many ways; that didst protect me by thy great goodness when I was oppressed by Andronicus that was of old my husband; that didst give me thy servant Andronicus to be my brother; that hast kept me thine handmaid pure unto this day; that didst raise me up by thy servant John, and when I was raised didst show me him that was made to stumble free from stumbling; that hast given me perfect rest in thee, and lightened me of the secret madness; whom I have loved and affectioned: I pray thee, O Christ, refuse not thy Drusiana that asketh thee to raise up Fortunatus, even though he assayed to become my betrayer.

83 And taking the hand of the dead man she said: Rise up, Fortunatus, in the name of our Lord Jesus Christ. And Fortunatus arose, and when he saw John in the sepulchre, and Andronicus, and Drusiana raised from the dead, and Callimachus a believer, and the rest of the brethren glorifying God, he said: O, to what have the powers of these clever men attained! I did not want to be raised, but would rather die, so as not to see them. And with these words he fled and went out of the sepulchre.

84 And John, when he saw the unchanged mind (soul) of Fortunatus, said: O nature that is not changed for the better! O fountain of the soul that abideth in foulness! O essence of corruption full of darkness! O death exulting in them that are thine! O fruitless tree full of fire! O tree that bearest coals for fruit! O matter that dwellest with the madness of matter (al. O wood of trees full of unwholesome shoots) and neighbour of unbelief! Thou hast proved who thou art, and thou art always convicted, with thy children. And thou knowest not how to praise the better things: for thou hast them not. Therefore, such as is thy way (?fruit), such also is thy root and thy nature. Be thou destroyed from among them that trust in the Lord: from their thoughts, from their mind, from their

souls, from their bodies, from their acts) their life, their conversation, from their business, their occupations, their counsel, from the resurrection unto (or rest in) God, from their sweet savour wherein thou wilt share, from their faith, their prayers, from the holy bath, from the eucharist, from the food of the flesh, from drink, from clothing, from love, from care, from abstinence, from righteousness: from all these, thou most unholy Satan, enemy of God, shall Jesus Christ our God and of all that are like thee and have thy character, make thee to perish.

85 And having thus said, John prayed, and took bread and bare it into the sepulchre to break it; and said: We glorify thy name, which converteth us from error and ruthless deceit: we glorify thee who hast shown before our eyes that which we have seen: we bear witness to thy loving-kindness which appeareth in divers ways: we praise thy merciful name, O Lord (we thank thee), who hast convicted them that are convicted of thee: we give thanks to thee, O Lord Jesu Christ, that we are persuaded of thy which is unchanging: we give thanks to thee who hadst need of our nature that should be saved: we give thanks to thee that hast given us this sure , for thou art alone, both now and ever. We thy servants give thee thanks, O holy one, who are assembled with intent and are gathered out of the world (or risen from death).

86 And having so prayed and given glory to God, he went out of the sepulchre after imparting unto all the brethren of the eucharist of the Lord. And when he was come unto Andronicus' house he said to the brethren: Brethren, a spirit within me hath divined that Fortunatus is about to die of blackness (poisoning of the blood) from the bite of the serpent; but let some one go quickly and learn if it is so indeed. And one of the young men ran and found him dead and the blackness spreading over him, and it had reached his heart: and came and told John that he had been dead three hours. And John said: Thou hast thy child, O devil.

'John therefore was with the brethren rejoicing in the Lord.' This sentence is in the best manuscript. In Bonnet's edition It introduces the last section of the Acts, which follows immediately in the manuscript. It may belong to either episode. The Latin has: And that day he spent joyfully with the brethren.

[[There cannot be much of a gap between this and the next section, which is perhaps the most interesting in the Acts.
The greater part of this episode is preserved only in one very corrupt fourteenth-century manuscript at Vienna. Two important passages (93-5 (part) and 97-8 (part)) were read at the Second Nicene Council and are preserved in the Acts thereof: a few lines of the Hymn are also cited in Latin by Augustine (Ep. 237 (253) to Ceretius): he found it current separately among the Priscillianists. The whole discourse is the best popular exposition we have of the Docetic view of our Lord's person.]]

87 Those that were present inquired the cause, and were especially perplexed, because Drusiana had said: The Lord appeared unto me in the tomb in the likeness of John, and in that of a youth. Forasmuch, therefore, as they were perplexed and were, in a manner, not yet stablished in the faith, so as to endure it steadfastly, John said (or John bearing it patiently, said):

88 Men and brethren, ye have suffered nothing strange or incredible as concerning your perception of the , inasmuch as we also, whom he chose for himself to be apostles, were tried in many ways: I, indeed, am neither able to set forth unto you nor to write the things which I both saw and heard: and now is it needful that I should fit them for your hearing; and according as each of you is able to contain it I will impart unto you those things whereof ye are able to become hearers, that ye may see the glory that is about him, which was and is, both now and for ever.

For when he had chosen Peter and Andrew, which were brethren, he cometh unto me and James my brother, saying: I have need of you, come unto me. And my brother hearing that, said: John, what would this child have that is upon the sea-shore and called us? And I said: What child? And he said to me again: That which beckoneth to us. And I answered: Because of our long watch we have kept at sea, thou seest not aright, my brother James; but seest thou not the man that standeth there, comely and fair and of a cheerful countenance? But he said to me: Him I see not, brother; but let us go forth and we shall see what he would have.

89 And so when we had brought the ship to land, we saw him also helping along with us to settle the ship: and when we departed from that place, being minded to follow him, again he was seen of me as having rather bald, but the beard thick and flowing, but of James as a youth whose beard was newly come. We were therefore perplexed, both of us, as to what that which we had seen should mean. And after that, as we followed him, both of us were by little and little perplexed as we considered the matter. Yet unto me there then appeared this yet more wonderful thing: for I would try to see him privily, and I never at any time saw his eyes closing (winking), but only open. And oft-times he would appear to me as a small man and uncomely, and then againt as one reaching unto heaven. Also there was in him another marvel: when I sat at meat he would take me upon his own breast; and sometimes his breast was felt of me to be smooth and tender, and sometimes hard like unto stones, so that I was perplexed in myself and said: Wherefore is this so unto me? And as I considered this, he . .

90 And at another time he taketh with him me and James and Peter unto the mountain where he was wont to pray, and we saw in him a light such as it is not possible for a man that useth corruptible (mortal) speech to describe what it was like. Again in like manner

he bringeth us three up into the mountain, saying: Come ye with me. And we went again: and we saw him at a distance praying. I, therefore, because he loved me, drew nigh unto him softly, as though he could not see me, and stood looking upon his hinder parts: and I saw that he was not in any wise clad with garments, but was seen of us naked, and not in any wise as a man, and that his feet were whiter than any snow, so that the earth there was lighted up by his feet, and that his head touched the heaven: so that I was afraid and cried out, and he, turning about, appeared as a man of small stature, and caught hold on my beard and pulled it and said to me: John, be not faithless but believing, and not curious. And I said unto him: But what have I done, Lord? And I say unto you, brethren, I suffered great pain in that place where he took hold on my beard for thirty days, that I said to him: Lord, if thy twitch when thou wast in sport hath given me so great pain, what were it if thou hadst given me a buffet? And he said unto me: Let it be thine henceforth not to tempt him that cannot be tempted.

91 But Peter and James were wroth because I spake with the Lord, and beckoned unto me that I should come unto them and leave the Lord alone. And I went, and they both said unto me: He (the old man) that was speaking with the Lord upon the top of the mount, who was he? for we heard both of them speaking. And I, having in mind his great grace, and his unity which hath many faces, and his wisdom which without ceasing looketh upon us, said: That shall ye learn if ye inquire of him.

92 Again, once when all we his disciples were at Gennesaret sleeping in one house, I alone having wrapped myself in my mantle, watched (or watched from beneath my mantle) what he should do: and first I heard him say: John, go thou to sleep. And I thereon feigning to sleep saw another like unto him [sleeping], whom also I heard say unto my Lord: Jesus, they whom thou

hast chosen believe not yet on thee (or do they not yet, &c.?). And my Lord said unto him: Thou sayest well: for they are men.

93 Another glory also will I tell you, brethren: Sometimes when I would lay hold on him, I met with a material and solid body, and at other times, again, when I felt him, the substance was immaterial and as if it existed not at all. And if at any time he were bidden by some one of the Pharisees and went to the bidding, we went with him, and there was set before each one of us a loaf by them that had bidden us, and with us he also received one; and his own he would bless and part it among us: and of that little every one was filled, and our own loaves were saved whole, so that they which bade him were amazed. And oftentimes when I walked with him, I desired to see the print of his foot, whether it appeared on the earth; for I saw him as it were lifting himself up from the earth: and I never saw it. And these things I speak unto you, brethren, for the encouragement of your faith toward him; for we must at the present keep silence concerning his mighty and wonderful works, inasmuch as they are unspeakable and, it may be, cannot at all be either uttered or heard.

94 Now before he was taken by the lawless Jews, who also were governed by (had their law from) the lawless serpent, he gathered all of us together and said: Before I am delivered up unto them let us sing an hymn to the Father, and so go forth to that which lieth before us. He bade us therefore make as it were a ring, holding one another's hands, and himself standing in the midst he said: Answer Amen unto me. He began, then, to sing an hymn and to say:

Glory be to thee, Father.
And we, going about in a ring, answered him: Amen.
Glory be to thee, Word: Glory be to thee, Grace. Amen.
Glory be to thee, Spirit: Glory be to thee, Holy One:
Glory be to thy glory. Amen.

We praise thee, O Father; we give thanks to thee, O Light, wherein darkness dwelleth not. Amen.

95 Now whereas (or wherefore) we give thanks, I say:
I would be saved, and I would save. Amen.
I would be loosed, and I would loose. Amen.
I would be wounded, and I would wound. Amen.
I would be born, and I would bear. Amen.
I would eat, and I would be eaten. Amen.
I would hear, and I would be heard. Amen.
I would be thought, being wholly thought. Amen.
I would be washed, and I would wash. Amen.
Grace danceth. I would pipe; dance ye all. Amen.
I would mourn: lament ye all. Amen.
The number Eight (lit. one ogdoad) singeth praise with us. Amen.
The number Twelve danceth on high. Amen.
The Whole on high hath part in our dancing. Amen.
Whoso danceth not, knoweth not what cometh to pass. Amen.
I would flee, and I would stay. Amen.
I would adorn, and I would be adorned. Amen.
I would be united, and I would unite. Amen.
A house I have not, and I have houses. Amen.
A place I have not, and I have places. Amen.
A temple I have not, and I have temples. Amen.
A lamp am I to thee that beholdest me. Amen.
A mirror am I to thee that perceivest me. Amen.
A door am I to thee that knockest at me. Amen.
A way am I to thee a wayfarer. .

96 Now answer thou (or as thou respondest) unto my dancing. Behold thyself in me who speak, and seeing

what I do, keep silence about my mysteries.

Thou that dancest, perceive what I do, for thine is this passion of the manhood, which I am about to suffer. For thou couldest not at all have understood what thou sufferest if I had not been sent unto thee, as the word of the Father. Thou that sawest what I suffer sawest me as suffering, and seeing it thou didst not abide but wert wholly moved, moved to make wise. Thou hast me as a bed, rest upon me. Who I am, thou shalt know when I depart. What now I am seen to be, that I am not. Thou shalt see when thou comest. If thou hadst known how to suffer, thou wouldest have been able not to suffer. Learn thou to suffer, and thou shalt be able not to suffer. What thou knowest not, I myself will teach thee. Thy God am I, not the God of the traitor. I would keep tune with holy souls. In me know thou the word of wisdom. Again with me say thou: Glory be to thee, Father; glory to thee, Word; glory to thee, Holy Ghost. And if thou wouldst know concerning me, what I was, know that with a word did I deceive all things and I was no whit deceived. I have leaped: but do thou understand the whole, and having understood it, say: Glory be to thee, Father. Amen.

97 Thus, my beloved, having danced with us the Lord went forth. And we as men gone astray or dazed with sleep fled this way and that. I, then, when I saw him suffer, did not even abide by his suffering, but fled unto the Mount of Olives, weeping at that which had befallen. And when he was crucified on the Friday, at the sixth hour of the day, darkness came upon all the earth. And my Lord standing in the midst of the cave and enlightening it, said: John, unto the multitude below in Jerusalem I am being crucified and pierced with lances and reeds, and gall and vinegar is given me to drink. But unto thee I speak, and what I speak hear thou. I put it into thy mind to come up into this mountain, that thou mightest hear those things which it behoveth a disciple to learn from his teacher and a man from

his God.

98 And having thus spoken, he showed me a cross of light fixed (set up), and about the cross a great multitude, not having one form: and in it (the cross) was one form and one likenesst [so the MS.; I would read: and therein was one form and one likeness: and in the cross another multitude, not having one form]. And the Lord himself I beheld above the cross, not having any shape, but only a voice: and a voice not such as was familiar to us, but one sweet and kind and truly of God, saying unto me: John, it is needful that one should hear these things from me, for I have need of one that will hear. This cross of light is sometimes called the (or a) word by me for your sakes, sometimes mind, sometimes Jesus, sometimes Christ, sometimes door, sometimes a way, sometimes bread, sometimes seed, sometimes resurrection, sometimes Son, sometimes Father, sometimes Spirit, sometimes life, sometimes truth, sometimes faith, sometimes grace. And by these names it is called as toward men: but that which it is in truth, as conceived of in itself and as spoken of unto you (MS. us), it is the marking-off of all things, and the firm uplifting of things fixed out of things unstable, and the harmony of wisdom, and indeed wisdom in harmony [this last clause in the MS. is joined to the next: 'and being wisdom in harmony']. There are of the right hand and the left, powers also, authorities, lordships and demons, workings, threatenings, wraths, devils, Satan, and the lower root whence the nature of the things that come into being proceeded.

99 This cross, then, is that which fixed all things apart (al. joined all things unto itself) by the (or a) word, and separate off the things that are from those that are below (lit. the things from birth and below it), and then also, being one, streamed forth into all things (or, made all flow forth. I suggested: compacted all into). But this is not the cross of wood which thou wilt see when thou goest down hence: neither am I he that is on the cross, whom now thou

seest not, but only hearest his (or a) voice. I was reckoned to be that which I am not, not being what I was unto many others: but they will call me (say of me) something else which is vile and not worthy of me. As, then, the place of rest is neither seen nor spoken of, much more shall I, the Lord thereof, be neither seen .

100 Now the multitude of one aspect (al. of one aspect) that is about the cross is the lower nature: and they whom thou seest in the cross, if they have not one form, it is because not yet hath every member of him that came down been comprehended. But when the human nature (or the upper nature) is taken up, and the race which draweth near unto me and obeyeth my voice, he that now heareth me shall be united therewith, and shall no more be that which now he is, but above them, as I also now am. For so long as thou callest not thyself mine, I am not that which I am (or was): but if thou hear me, thou, hearing, shalt be as I am, and I shall be that which I was, when I thee as I am with myself. For from me thou art that (which I am). Care not therefore for the many, and them that are outside the mystery despise; for know thou that I am wholly with the Father, and the Father with me.

101 Nothing, therefore, of the things which they will say of me have I suffered: nay, that suffering also which I showed unto thee and the rest in the dance, I will that it be called a mystery. For what thou art, thou seest, for I showed it thee; but what I am I alone know, and no man else. Suffer me then to keep that which is mine, and that which is thine behold thou through me, and behold me in truth, that I am, not what I said, but what thou art able to know, because thou art akin thereto. Thou hearest that I suffered, yet did I not suffer; that I suffered not, yet did I suffer; that I was pierced, yet I was not smitten; hanged, and I was not hanged; that blood flowed from me, and it flowed not; and, in a word, what they say of me, that befell me not, but what they say not, that did I suffer. Now what

those things are I signify unto thee, for I know that thou wilt understand. Perceive thou therefore in me the praising (al. slaying al. rest) of the (or a) Word (Logos), the piercing of the Word, the blood of the Word, the wound of the Word, the hanging up of the Word, the suffering of the Word, the nailing (fixing) of the Word, the death of the Word. And so speak I, separating off the manhood. Perceive thou therefore in the first place of the Word; then shalt thou perceive the Lord, and in the third place the man, and what he hath suffered.

102 When he had spoken unto me these things, and others which I know not how to say as he would have me, he was taken up, no one of the multitudes having beheld him. And when I went down I laughed them all to scorn, inasmuch as he had told me the things which they have said concerning him; holding fast this one thing in myself, that the Lord contrived all things symbolically and by a dispensation toward men, for their conversion and salvation.

103 Having therefore beheld, brethren, the grace of the Lord and his kindly affection toward us, let us worship him as those unto whom he hath shown mercy, not with our fingers, nor our mouth, nor our tongue, nor with any part whatsoever of our body, but with the disposition of our soul -even him who became a man apart from this body: and let us watch because (or we shall find that) now also he keepeth ward over prisons for our sake, and over tombs, in bonds and dungeons, in reproaches and insults, by sea and on dry land, in scourgings, condemnations, conspiracies, frauds, punishments, and in a word, he is with all of us, and himself suffereth with us when we suffer, brethren. When he is called upon by each one of us, he endureth not to shut his ears to us, but as being everywhere he hearkeneth to all of us; and now both to me and to Drusiana, -forasmuch as he is the God of them that are shut upbringing us help by his own compassion.

104 Be ye also persuaded, therefore, beloved, that it is not a man whom I preach unto you to worship, but God unchangeable, God invincible, God higher than all authority and all power, and elder and mightier than all angels and creatures that are named, and all aeons. If then ye abide in him, and are builded up in him, ye shall possess your soul indestructible.

105 And when he had delivered these things unto the brethren, John departed, with Andronicus, to walk. And Drusiana also followed afar off with all the brethren, that they might behold the acts that were done by him, and hear his speech at all times in the Lord.

[[The remaining episode which is extant in the Greek is the conclusion of the book, the Death or Assumption of John. Before it must be placed the stories which we have only in the Latin (of 'Abdias' and another text by 'Mellitus', i.e. Melito), and the two or three isolated fragments.]]

(Lat. XIV.)

Now on the next (or another) day Craton, a philosopher, had proclaimed in the market-place that he would give an example of the contempt of riches: and the spectacle was after this manner. He had persuaded two young men, the richest of the city, who were brothers, to spend their whole inheritance and buy each of them a jewel, and these they brake in pieces publicly in the sight of the people. And while they were doing this, it happened by chance that the apostle passed by. And calling Craton the philosopher to him, he said: That is a foolish despising of the world which is praised by the mouths of men, but long ago condemned by the judgement of God. For as that is a vain medicine whereby the disease is not extirpated, so is it a vain teaching by which the faults of souls and of conduct are not cured. But indeed my master taught a youth who desired to attain to eternal life, in these words; saying that if he would be perfect, he should sell all his goods and give to the poor, and so doing he would gain treasure in heaven and find the life that has no ending. And Craton said to him: Here the fruit of covetousness is set forth in the midst of men, and hath been broken to pieces. But if God is indeed thy master and willeth this to be, that the sum of the price of these jewels should be given to the poor, cause thou the gems to be restored whole, that what I have done for the praise of men, thou mayest do for the glory of him whom thou callest thy master. Then the blessed John gathered together the fragments of the gems, and holding them in his hands, lifted up his eyes to heaven and said: Lord Jesu Christ, unto whom nothing is impossible: who when the world was broken by the tree of concupiscence, didst restore it again in thy faithfulness by the tree of the cross: who didst give to one born blind the eyes which nature had denied him, who didst recall Lazarus, dead and buried, after the fourth day unto the light; and has subjected all diseases and all sicknesses unto the word of thy power: so also now do with these precious stones which these, not knowing the fruits of almsgiving, have broken in pieces for the praise of men: recover thou them, Lord, now by the hands of thine angels, that by their value the work of mercy may be fulfilled, and make these men believe in thee the unbegotten Father through thine only-begotten Son Jesus Christ our Lord, with the Holy Ghost the illuminator and sanctifier of the whole Church,

world without end. And when the faithful who were with the apostle had answered and said Amen, the fragments of the gems were forthwith so joined in one that no mark at all that they had been broken remained in them. And Craton the philosopher, with his disciples, seeing this, fell at the feet of the apostle and believed thenceforth (or immediately) and was baptized, with them all, and began himself publicly to preach the faith of our Lord Jesus Christ.

XV.

Those two brothers, therefore, of whom we spake, sold the gems which they had bought by the sale of their inheritance and gave the price to the poor; and thereafter a very great multitude of believers began to be joined to the apostle.

And when all this was done, it happened that after the same example, two honourable men of the city of the Ephesian sold all their goods and distributed them to the needy, and followed the apostle as he went through the cities preaching the word of God. But it came to pass, when they entered the city of Pergamum, that they saw their servants walking abroad arrayed in silken raiment and shining with the glory of this world: whence it happened that they were pierced with the arrow of the devil and became sad, seeing themselves poor and clad with a single cloak while their own servants were powerful and prosperous. But the apostle of Christ, perceiving these wiles of the devil, said: I see that ye have changed your minds and your countenances on this account, that, obeying the teaching of my Lord Jesus Christ, ye have given all ye had to the poor. Now, if ye desire to recover that which ye formerly possessed of gold, silver, and precious stones, bring me some straight rods, each of you a bundle. And when they had done so, he called upon the name of the Lord Jesus Christ, and they were turned into gold. And the apostle said to them: Bring me small stones from the seashore. And when they had done this also, he called upon the majesty of the Lord, and all the pebbles were turned into gems. Then the blessed John turned to those men and said to them: Go about to the goldsmiths and jewellers for seven days, and when ye have proved that these are true gold and true jewels, tell me. And they went, both of them, and after seven days returned to the apostle, saying: Lord, we have gone about the shops of all the goldsmiths, and they have all said that they never saw such pure gold. Likewise the jewellers have said the same, that they never saw such

excellent and precious gems.

XVI.

Then the holy John said unto them: Go, and redeem to you the lands which ye have sold, for ye have lost the estates of heaven. Buy yourselves silken raiment, that for a time ye may shine like the rose which showeth its fragrance and redness and suddenly fadeth away. For ye sighed at beholding your servants and groaned that ye were become poor. Flourish, therefore, that ye may fade: be rich for the time, that ye may be beggars for ever. Is not the Lord's hand able to make riches overflowing and unsurpassably glorious? but he hath appointed a conflict for souls, that they may believe that they shall have eternal riches, who for his name's sake have refused temporal wealth. Indeed, our master told us concerning a certain rich man who feasted every day and shone with gold and purple, at whose door lay a beggar, Lazarus, who desired to receive even the crumbs that fell from his table, and no man gave unto him. And it came to pass that on one day they died, both of them, and that beggar was taken into the rest which is in Abraham's bosom, but the rich man was cast into flaming fire: out of which he lifted up his eyes and saw Lazarus, and prayed him to dip his finger in water and cool his mouth for he was tormented in the flames. And Abraham answered him and said: Remember, son, that thou receivedst good things in thy life, but this Lazarus likewise evil things. Wherefore rightly is he now comforted while thou art tormented, and besides all this, a great gulf is fixed between you and us, so that neither can they come thence hither, nor hither thence. But he answered: I have five brethren: I pray that some one may go to warn them, that they come not into this flame. And Abraham said to him: They have Moses and the prophets, let them hear them. To that he answered: Lord, unless one rise up again, they will not believe. Abraham said to him: If they believe not Moses and the prophets, neither will they believe, if one rise again. And these words our Lord and Master confirmed by examples of mighty works: for when they said to him: Who hath come hither from thence, that we may believe him? he answered: Bring hither the dead whom ye have. And when they had brought unto him a young man which was dead (Ps.-Mellitus: three dead corpses), he was waked up by him as one that sleepeth, and confirmed all his words.

But wherefore should I speak of my Lord, when at this present there are those whom in his name and in your presence and sight I have raised from the dead: in whose name ye have seen palsied men healed, lepers cleansed, blind men enlightened, and many delivered from evil spirits ? But the riches of these mighty works they cannot have who have desired to have earthly wealth. Finally, when ye yourselves went unto the sick and called upon the name of Jesus Christ, they were healed: ye did drive out devils and restore light to the blind. Behold, this grace is taken from you, and ye are become wretched, who were mighty and great. And where as there was such fear of you upon the devils that at your bidding they left the men whom they possessed, now ye will be in fear of the devils. For he that loveth money is the servant of Mammon: and Mammon is the name of a devil who is set over carnal gains, and is the master of them that love the world. But even the lovers of the world do not possess riches, but are possessed of them. For it is out of reason that for one belly there should be laid up so much food as would suffice a thousand, and for one body so many garments as would furnish clothing for a thousand men. In vain, therefore, is that stored up which cometh not into use, and for whom it is kept, no man knoweth, as the Holy Ghost saith by the prophet: In vain is every man troubled who heapeth up riches and knoweth not for whom he gathereth them. Naked did our birth from women bring us into this light, destitute of food and drink: naked will the earth receive us which brought us forth. We possess in common the riches of the heaven, the brightness of the sun is equal for the rich and the poor, and likewise the light of the moon and the stars, the softness of the air and the drops of rain, and the gate of the church and the fount of sanctification and the forgiveness of sins, and the sharing in the altar, and the eating of the body and drinking of the blood of Christ, and the anointing of the chrism, and the grace of the giver, and the visitation of the Lord, and the pardon of sin: in all these the dispensing of the Creator is equal, without respect of persons. Neither doth the rich man use these gifts after one manner and the poor after another.

But wretched and unhappy is the man who would have something more than sufficeth him: for of this come heats of fevers rigours of cold, divers pains in all the members of the body, and he can neither be fed with food nor sated with drink, that covetousness may learn that money will not profit it, which being laid up bringeth to the keepers thereof anxiety by day and night, and suffereth them not even for an hour to be quiet and secure. For while they guard their houses against thieves, till their estate, ply the plough, pay taxes, build storehouses, strive for gain, try to baffle the attacks of the strong, and to strip the weak, exercise their wrath on whom they can, and hardly bear it from others, shrink not from playing at tables and from public shows, fear not to defile or to be defiled, suddenly do they depart out of this world, naked, bearing only their own sins with them, for which they shall suffer eternal punishment.

XVII.

While the apostle was thus speaking, behold there was brought to him by his mother, who was a widow, a young man who thirty days before had first married a vvife. And the people which were waiting upon the burial came with the widowed mother and cast themselves at the apostle's feet all together with groans, weeping, and mourning, and besought him that in the name of his

God, as he had done with Drusiana, so he would raise up this young man also. And there was so great weeping of them all that the apostle himself could hardly refrain from crying and tears. He cast himself down, therefore, in prayer, and wept a long time: and rising from prayer spread out his hands to heaven, and for a long space prayed within himself. And when he had so done thrice, he commanded the body which was swathed to be loosed, and said: Thou youth Stacteus, who for love of thy flesh hast quickly lost thy soul: thou youth which knewest not thy creator nor perceivedst the Saviour of men, and wast ignorant of thy true friend, and therefore didst fall into the snare of the worst enemy: behold, I have poured out tears and prayers unto my Lord for thine ignorance, that thou mayest rise from the dead, the bands of death being loosed, and declare unto these two, to Atticus and Eugenius, how great glory they have lost, and how great punishment they have incurred. Then Stacteus arose and worshipped the apostle, and began to reproach his disciples, saying: I beheld your angels vveeping, and the angels of Satan rejoicing at your overthrow. For now in a little time ye have lost the kingdom that was prepared for you, and the dwellingplaces builded of shining stones, full of joy, of feasting and delights, full of everlasting life and eternal light: and have gotten yourselves places of darkness, full of dragons, of roaring flames, of torments, and punishments unsurpassable, of pains and anguish, fear and horrible trembling. Ye have lost the places full of unfading flowers, shining, full of the sounds of instruments of music (organs), and have gotten on the other hand places wherein roaring and howling and mourning ceaseth not day nor night. Nothing else remaineth for you save to ask the apostle of the Lord that like as he hath raised me to life, he would raise you also from death unto salvation and bring back your souls which now are blotted out of the book of life.

XVIII. Then both he that had been raised and all the people together with Atticus and Eugenius, cast themselves at the apostle's feet and besought him to intercede for them with the Lord. Unto whom the holy apostle gave this answer: that for thirty days they should offer penitence to God, and in that space pray especially that the rods of gold might return to their nature and likewise the stones return to the meanness wherein they were made. And it came to pass that after thirty days were accomplished, and neither the rods were turncd into wood nor the gems into pebbles, Atticus and Eugenius came and said to the apostle: Thou hast always taught mercy, and preached forgiveness, and bidden that one man should spare another. And if God willeth that a man should forgive a man, how much more shall he, as he is God, both forgive and spare men. We are confounded for our sin: and whereas we have cried with our eyes which lusted after the world, we do now repent with eyes that weep. We pray thee, Lord, we pray thee, apostle of God, show in deed that mercy which in word thou hast always promised. Then the holy John said unto them as they wept and repented, and all interceded for them likewise: Our Lord God used these words when he spake concerning sinners: I will not the death of a sinner, but I will rather that he be converted and live. For when the Lord Jesus Christ taught us concerning the penitent, he said: Verily I say unto you, there is great joy in heaven over one sinner that repenteth and turneth himself from his sins: and there is more joy over him than over ninety and nine which have not sinned. Wherefore I would have you know that the Lord accepteth the repentance of these men. And he turned' unto Atticus and Eugenius and said: Go, carry back the rods unto the wood whence ye took them, for now are they returned to their own nature, and the stones unto the sea-shore, for they are become common stones as they were before. And when this was accomplished, they received again the grace which they had lost, so that again they cast out devils as before time and healed the sick and enlightened the blind, and daily the Lord did many mighty works by their means.

XIX

[[tells shortly the destruction oi the temple of Ephesus and the conversion of 12,000 people.
Then follows the episode of the poison-cup in a form which probably represents the story in the Leucian Acts. (We have seen that the late Greek texts place it at the beginning, in the presence of Domitian.)]]

XX

Now when Aristodemus, who was chief priest of all those idols, saw this, filled with a wicked spirit, he stirred up sedition among the people, so that one people prepared themselves to fight against the other. And John turned to him and said: Tell me, Aristodemus, what can I do to take away the anger from thy soul? And Aristodemus said: If thou wilt have me believe in thy God, I will give thee poison to drink, and if thou drink it, and die not, it will appear that thy God is true. The apostle answered: If thou give me poison to drink, when I call on the name of my Lord, it will not be able to harm me. Aristodemus said again: I will that thou first see others drink it and die straightway that so thy heart may recoil from that cup. And the blessed John said: I have told thee already that I am prepared to drink it that thou mayest believe on the Lord Jesus Christ when thou seest me whole after the cup of poison. Aristodemus therefore went to the proconsul and asked of him two men who were to undergo the sentence of death. And when he had set them in the midst of the market-place before all the people, in the sight of the apostle he made them drink the poison: and as soon as they had drunk it, they gave up the ghost. Then Aristodemus turned to John and said: Hearken to me and depart from thy teaching wherewith

thou callest away the people from the worship of the gods; or take and drink this, that thou mayest show that thy God is almighty, if after thou hast drunk, thou canst remain whole. Then the blessed Jolm, as they lay dead which had drunk the poison, like a fearless and brave man took the cup, and making the sign of the cross, spake thus: My God, and the Father of our Lord Jesus Christ, by whose word the heavens were established, unto whom all things are subject, whom all creation serveth, whom all power obeyeth, feareth, and trembleth, when we call on thee for succour: whose name the serpent hearing is still, the dragon fleeth, the viper is quiet, the toad (which is called a frog) is still and strengthless, the scorpion is quenched, the basilisk vanquished, and the phalangia (spider) doth no hurt -in a word, all venomous things, and the fiercest reptiles and noisome beasts, are pierced (or covered with darkness). [Ps.- Mellitus adds: and all roots hurtful to the health of men dry up.] Do thou, I say, quench the venom of this poison, put out the deadly workings thereof, and void it of the strength which it hath in it: and grant in thy sight unto all these whom thou hast created, eyes that they may see, and ears that they may hear and a heart that they may understand thy greatness. And when he had thus said, he armed his mouth and all his body with the sign of the cross and drank all that was in the cup. And after be had drunk, he said: I ask that they for whose sake I have drunk, be turned unto thee, O Lord, and by thine enlightening receive the salvation which is in thee. And when for the space of three hours the people saw that John was of a cheerful countenance, and that there was no sign at all of paleness or fear in him, they began to cry out with a loud voice: He is the one true God whom John worshippeth.

XXI.

But Aristodemus even so believed not, though the people reproached him: but turned unto John and said: This one thing I lack -if thou in the name of thy God raise up these that have died by this poison, my mind will be cleansed of all doubt. When he said that, the people rose against Aristodemus saying: We will burn thee and thine house if thou goest on to trouble the apostle further with thy words. John, therefore, seeing that there was a fierce sedition, asked for silence, and said in the hearing of all: The first of the virtues of God which we ought to imitate is patience, by which we are able to bear with the foolishness of unbelievers. Wherefore if Aristodemus is still held by unbelief, let us loose the knots of his unbelief. He shall be compelled, even though late, to acknowledge his creator -for I will not cease from this work until a remedy shall bring help to his wounds, and like physicians which have in their hands a sick man needing medicine, so also, if Aristodemus be not yet cured by that which hath now been done, he shall be cured by that which I will now do. And he called Aristodemus to him, and gave him his coat, and he himself stood clad only in his mantle. And Aristodemus said to him: Wherefore hast thou given me thy coat? John said to him: That thou mayest even so be put to shame and depart from thine unbelief. And Aristodemus said: And how shall thy coat make me to depart from unbelief? The apostle answered: Go and cast it upon the bodies of the dead, and thou shalt say thus: The apostle of our Lord Jesus Christ hath sent me that in his name may rise again, that all may know that life and death are servants of my Lord Jesus Christ. Which when Aristodemus had done, and had seen them rise, he worshipped John, and ran quickly to the proconsul and began to say with a loud voice: Hear me, hear me, thou proconsul; I think thou rememberest that I have often stirred up thy wrath against John and devised many things against him daily, wherefore I fear lest I feel his wrath: for he is a god hidden in the form of a man and hath drunk poison, and not only continueth whole, but them also which had died by the

poison he hath recalled to life by my means, by the touch of his coat, and they have no mark of death upon them. Which when the proconsul heard he said: And what wilt thou have me to do? Aristodemus answered: Let us go and fall at his feet and ask pardon, and whatever he commandeth us let us do. Then they came together and cast themselves down and besought forgiveness: and he received them and offered prayer and thanksgiving to God, and he ordained them a fast of a week, and when it was fulfilled he baptized them in the name of the Lord Jesus Christ and his Almighty Father and the Holy Ghost the illuminator. [And when they were baptized, with all their house and their servants and their kindred, they brake all their idols and built a church in the name of Saint John: wherein he himself was taken up, in manner following :]

[[This bracketed sentence, of late complexion, serves to introduce the last episode of the book.]]

[[James gives two additional fragments that do not fit in any other place. These fragments are very broken and are not of much use for this present project. However, if there is intrest in them, they can be found on pages 264-6 of the text.]]

[[The last episode of these Acts (as is the case with several others of the Apocryphal Acts) was preserved separately for reading in church on the Saint's day. We have it in at least nine Greek manuscripts, and in many versions: Latin, Syriac, Armenian, Coptic, Ethiopic, Slavonic.]]

106 John therefore continued with the brethren, rejoicing in the Lord. And on the morrow, being the Lord's day, and all the brethren being gathered together, he began to say unto them: Brethren and fellow-servants and coheirs and partakers with me in the kingdom of the Lord, ye know the Lord, hovv many mighty works he hath granted you by

my means, how many wonders, healings, signs, how great spirital gifts, teachings, governings, refreshings, ministries, knowledges, glories, graces, gifts, beliefs, communions, all which ye have seen given you by him in your sight, yet not seen by these eyes nor heard by these ears. Be ye therefore stablished in him, remembering him in your every deed, knowing the mystery of the dispensation which hath come to pass towards men, for what cause the Lord hath 1 accomplished it. He beseecheth you by me, brethren, and entreateth you, desiring to remain without grief, without insult, not conspired against, not chastened: for he knoweth even the insult that cometh of you, he knoweth even dishonour, he knoweth even conspiracy, he knoweth even chastisement, from them that hearken not to his commandments.

107 Let not then our good God be grieved, the compassionate, the merciful, the holy, the pure, the undefiled, the immaterial, the only, the one, the unchangeable, the simple, the guileless, the unwrathful, even our God Jesus Christ, who is above every name that we can utter or conceive, and more exalted. Let him rejoice with us because we walk aright, let him be glad because we live purely, let him be refreshed because our conversation is sober. Let him be without care because we live continently, let him be pleased because we communicate one with another, let him smile because we are chaste, let him be merry because we love him. These things I now speak unto you, brethren, because I am hasting unto the work set before me, and already being perfected by the Lord. For what else could I have to say unto you? Ye have the pledge of our God, ye have the earnest of his goodness, ye have his presence that cannot be shunned. If, then, ye sin no more, he forgiveth you that ye did in ignorance: but if after that ye have known him and he hath had mercy on you, ye walk again in the like deeds, both the former will be laid to your charge, and also ye will not have a part nor mercy before him.

108 And when he had spoken this unto them, he prayed thus: O Jesu who hast woven this crown with thy weaving, who hast joined together these many blossoms into the unfading flower of thy cormtenance, who hast sown in them these words: thou only tender of thy servants, and physician who healest freely: only doer of good and despiser of none, only merciful and lover of men, only saviour and righteous, only seer of all, who art in all and everywhere present and containing all things and filling all things: Christ Jesu, God, Lord, that with thy gifts and thy mercy shelterest them that trust in thee, that knowest clearly the wiles and the assaults of him that is everywhere our adversary, which he deviseth against us: do thou only, O Lord, succour thy servants by thy visitation. Even so, Lord.

109 And he asked for bread, and gave thanks thus: What praise or what offering or what thanksgiving shall we, breaking this bread, name save thee only, O Lord Jesu? We glorify thy name that was said by the Father: we glorify thy name that was said through the Son (or we glorify the name of Father that was said by thee . . . the name of Son that was said by thee): we glorify thine entering of the Door. We glorify the resurrection shown unto us by thee. We glorify thy way, we glorify of thee the seed, the word, the grace, the faith, the salt, the unspeakable (al. chosen) pearl, the treasure, the plough, the net, the greatness, the diadem, him that for us was called Son of man, that gave unto us truth, rest, knowledge, power, the commandment, the confidence, hope, love, liberty, refuge in thee. For thou, Lord, art alone the root of immortality, and the fount of incorruption, and the seat of the ages: called by all these names for us now that calling on thee by them we may make known thy greatness which at the present is invisible unto us, but visible only unto the pure, being portrayed in thy manhood only.

110 And he brake the bread and gave unto all of us, praying over each of the

brethren that he might be worthy of the grace of the Lord and of the most holy eucharist. And he partook also himself likewise, and said: Unto me also be there a part with you, and: Peace be with you, my beloved.

111 After that he said unto Verus: Take with thee some two men, with baskets and shovels, and follow me. And Verus without delay did as he was bidden by John the servant of God. The blessed John therefore went out of the house and walked forth of the gates, having told the more part to depart from him. And when he was come to the tomb of a certain brother of ours he said to the young men: Dig, my children. And they dug and he was instant with them yet more, saying: Let the trench be deeper. And as they dug he spoke unto them the word of God and exhorted them that were come with him out of the house, edifying and perfecting them unto the greatness of God, and praying over each one of us. And when the young men had finished the trench as he desired, we knowing nothing of it, he took off his garments wherein he was clad and laid them as it were for a pallet in the bottom of the trench: and standing in his shift only he stretched his hands upward and prayed thus:

112 O thou that didst choose us out for the apostleship of the Gentiles: O God that sentest us into the world: that didst reveal thyself by the law and the prophets: that didst never rest, but alway from the foundation of the world savedst them that were able to be saved: that madest thyself known through all nature: that proclaimedst thyself even among beasts: that didst make the desolate and savage soul tame and quiet: that gavest thyself to it when it was athirst for thy words: that didst appear to it in haste when it was dying: that didst show thyself to it as a law when it was sinking into lawlessness: that didst manifest thyself to it when it had been vanquished by Satan: that didst overcome its adversary when it fled unto thee: that avest it thine hand and didst raise it up from the things of Hades: that didst not leave it to walk after a bodily sort (in the body): that didst show to it its own enemy: that hast made for it a clear knowledge toward thee: O God, Jesu, the Father of them that are above the heavens, the Lord of them that are in the heavens, the law of them that are in the other, the course of them that are in the air, the keeper of them that are on the earth, the fear of them that are under the earth, the grace of them that are thine own: receive also the soul of thy John, which it may be is accounted worthy by thee.

113 O thou who hast kept me until this hour for thyself and untouched by union with a woman: who when in my youth I desired to marry didst appear unto me and say to me: John I have need of thee: who didst prepare for me also a sickness of the body: who when for the third time I would marry didst forthwith prevent me, and then at the third hour of the day saidst unto me on the sea: John, if thou hadst not been mine, I would have suffered thee to marry: who for two years didst blind me (or afflict mine eyes), and grant me to mourn and entreat thee: who in the third year didst open the eyes of my mind and also grant me my visible eyes: who when I saw clearly didst ordain that it should be grievous to me to look upon a woman: who didst save me from the temporal fantasy and lead me unto that which endureth always: who didst rid me of the foul madness that is in the flesh: who didst take me from the bitter death and establish me on thee alone: who didst muzzle the secret disease of my soul and cut off the open deed: who didst afflict and banish him that raised tumult in me: who didst make my love of thee spotless: who didst make my joining unto thee perfect and unbroken: who didst give me undoubting faith in thee, who didst order and make clear my inclination toward thee: thou who givest unto every man the due reward of his works, who didst put into my soul that I should have no possession save thee only: for what is more precious than thee? Now therefore Lord, whereas I have accomplished the dispensation wherewith I was entrusted, account

thou me worthy of thy rest, and grant me that end in thee which is salvation unspeakable and unutterable.

114 And as I come unto thee, let the fire go backward, let the darkness be overcome, let the gulf be without strength, let the furnace die out, let Gehenna be quenched. Let angels follow, let devils fear, let rulers be broken, let powers fall; let the places of the right hand stand fast, let them of the left hand not remain. Let the devil be muzzled, let Satan be derided, let his wrath be burned out, let his madness be stilled, let his vengeance be ashamed, let his assault be in pain, let his children be smitten and all his roots plucked up. And grant me to accomplish the journey unto thee without suffering insolence or provocation, and to receive that which thou hast promised unto them that live purely and have loved thee only.

115 And having sealed himself in every part, he stood and said: Thou art with me, O Lord Jesus Christ: and laid himself down in the trench where he had strewn his garments: and having said unto us: Peace be with you, brethren, he gave up his spirit rejoicing.

[[The less good Greek manuscripts and some versions are not content with this simple ending. The Latin says that after the prayer a great light appeared over the apostle for the space of an hour, so bright that no one could look at it. (Then he laid himself down and gave up the ghost.) We who were there rejoiced, some of us, and some mourned. . . . And forthwith manna issuing from the tomb was seen of all, which manna that place produceth even unto this day, &c. But perhaps the best conclusion is that of one Greek manuscript:]]

We brought a linen cloth and spread it upon him, and went into the city. And on the day following we went forth and found not his body, for it was translated by the power of our Lord Jesus Christ, unto whom be glory, &c.

[[Another says:]]

On the morrow we dug in the place, and him we found not, but only his sandals, and the earth moving (lit. springing up like a well), and after that we remembered that which was spoken by the Lord unto Peter, &c.

[[Augustine (on John xxi) reports the belief that in his time the earth over the grave was seen to move as if stirred by John's breathing.]]

THE ACTS OF PAUL

[[Large Portions of the texts are missing]]

.9. Paul went into (the house) at the place where the (dead) was. But Phila the wife of Panchares (Anchares, MS., see below) was very wroth and said to her husband in (great anger): Husband, thou hast gone . . . . the wild beasts, thou hast not begotten . . . . thy son . . . . where is mine?

p.10 (he hath not) desired food . . . to bury him. But (Panchares) stood in the sight of all and made his prayer at the ninth hour, until the people of the city came to bear the boy out. When he had prayed, Paul (came) and saw . . . and of Jesus Christ . . . . the boy . . . the prayer.

p.11 (a small piece only) . . . multitude . . . eight days . . . they thought that he raised up the (boy). But when Paul had remained

p.12. They asked? him? . . . the men listened to him . . . they sent for Panchares . . . and cried out, saying: We believe, Panchares, . . . but save the city from . . many things, which they said. Panchares said unto them: Judge ye whether your good deeds (?)

p.13 is not possible . . . but to (testify) . . . God who hath . . . his Son according to . . . salvation, and I also believe that, my brethren, there is no other God, save Jesus Christ the son of the Blessed, unto whom is glory for ever, Amen. But when they saw that he would not turn to them, they pursued Paul, and caught him, and brought him back into the city, ill-using (?) him, and cast stones at him and thrust him out of their city and out of their country. But Panchares would not return evil for evil: he shut the door of his house and went in with his wife . . . fasting . . . But when it was evening Paul came to him and said:

p.14. God hath . . . Jesus Christ.

[[These are the last words of the episode. The situation is a little cleared by a sentence in the Greek Acts of Titus ascribed to Zenas (not earlier than the fifth century?):]]

'They arrived at Antioch and found Barnabas the son of Panchares, whom Paul raised up.'

[[Barnabas may be a mistake, but Panchares is, I doubt not, right: for the Coptic definite article is p prefixed to the word, and the Coptic translator finding Panchares in his text has confused the initial of it with his own definite article, and cut it out. We have, then, a husband Panchares and wife Phila at Antioch (in Pisidia perhaps: this is disputed), and their son (possibly named Barnabas) is dead. Phila reproaches Panchares with want of parental affection. I take it that he is a believer, and has not mourned over his son, perhaps knowing that Paul was at hand and hoping for his help. Panchares prays till his fellow-townsmen come to carry out the body for burial. Paul arrives: at some point he raises the dead: but the people are irritated and some catastrophe threatens them at Paul's hands. Panchares makes a profession of faith, the result of which is Paul's ill-treatment and banishment. But Paul returns secretly and reassures Panchares.]]

II
[[The next episode is that of Paul and Thecla, in which the Greek text exists,
and will be followed. In the Coptic it has a title:
After the flight from Antioch, when he would go to Iconium.
It is possible that in this episode the author of the Acts may have used a local legend, current in his time, of a real Christian martyr Thecla. It is otherwise difficult to account for the very great popularity of the cult of St. Thecla, which spread over East and West, and made her the most famous of virgin martyrs. Moreover, one historical personage is introduced into the story, namely, Queen Tryphaena, who was the widow, it seems, of Cotys, King of Thrace, and the mother of Polemo II, King of Pontus. She was a great-niece of the Emperor Claudius. Professor W. M. Ramsay has contended that there was a written story of Thecla which was adapted by the author of the Acts: but his view is not generally accepted.]]

1 When Paul went up unto Iconium after he fled from Antioch, there journeyed with him Demas and Hermogenes the coppersmith, which were full of hypocrisy, and flattered Paul as though they loved him. But Paul, looking only unto the goodness of Christ, did them no evil, but loved them well, so that he assayed to make sweet unto them all the oracles of the Lord, and of the teaching and the interpretation (of the Gospel) and of the birth and resurrection of the Beloved, and related unto them word by word all the great works of Christ, how they were revealed unto him (Copt. adds: how that Christ was born of Mary the virgin, and of the seed of David).
2 And a certain man named Onesiphorus, when he heard that Paul was come to Iconium, went out with his children Simmias and Zeno and his wife Lectra to meet him, that he might receive him into his house: for Titus had told him what manner of man Paul was in appearance; for he had not seen him in the flesh, but only in the spirit.
3 And he went by the king's highway that leadeth unto Lystra and stood

expecting him, and looked upon them that came, according to tbe description of Titus. And he saw Paul coming, a man little of stature, thin-haired upon the head, crooked in the legs, of good state of body, with eyebrows joining, and nose somewhat hooked, full of grace: for sometimes he appeared like a man, and sometimes he had the face of an angel.

4 And when Paul saw Onesiphorus he smiled, and Onesiphorus said: Hail, thou servant of the blessed God. And he said: Grace be with thee and with thine house. But Demas and Hermogenes were envious, and stirred up their hypocrisy yet more, so that Demas said: Are we not servants of the Blessed, that thou didst not salute us so? And Onesiphorus said: I see not in you any fruit of righteousness, but if ye be such, come ye also into my house and refresh yourselves.

5 And when Paul entered into the house of Onesiphorus, there was great joy, and bowing of knees and breaking of bread, and the word of God concerning abstinence (or continence) and the resurrection; for Paul said:

Blessed are the pure in heart, for they shall see God.

Blessed are they that keep the flesh chaste, for they shall become the temple of God.

Blessed are they that abstain (or the continent), for unto them shall God speak.

Blessed are they that have renounced this world, for they shall be well-pleasing unto God.

Blessed are they that possess their wives as though they had them not, for they shall inherit God.

Blessed are they that have the fear of God, for they shall become angels of God.

6 Blessed are they that tremble at the oracles of God, for they shall be comforted.

Blessed are they that receive the wisdom of Jesus Christ, for they shall be called sons of the Most High.

Blessed are they that have kept their baptism pure, for they shall rest with the Father and with the Son.

Blessed are they that have compassed the understanding of Jesus Christ, for they shall be in light.

Blessed are they that for love of God have departed from the fashion of this world, for they shall judge angels, and shall be blessed at the right hand of the Father.

Blessed are the merciful, for they shall obtain mercy and shall not see the bitter day of judgement. Blessed are the bodies of the virgins, for they shall be well- pleasing unto God and shall not lose the reward of their continence (chastity), for the word of the Father shall be unto them a work of salvation in the day of his Son, and they shall have rest world Without end.

7 And as Paul was saying these things in the midst of the assembly (church) in the house of Onesiphorus, a certain virgin, Thecla, whose mother was Theocleia, which was betrothed to an husband, Thamyris, sat at the window hard by, and hearkened night and day unto the word concerning chastity which was spoken by Paul: and she stirred not from the window, but was led onward (or pressed onward) by faith, rejoicing exceedingly: and further, when she saw many women and virgins entering in to Paul, she also desired earnestly to be accounted worthy to stand before Paul's face and to hear the word of Christ; for she had not yet seen the appearance of Paul, but only heard his speech.

8 Now as she removed not from the window, her mother sent unto Thamyris, and he came with great joy as if he were already to take her to wife. Thamyris therefore said to Theocleia: Where is my Thecla? And Theocicia said: I have a new tale to tell thee, Thamyris: for for three days and three nights Thecla ariseth not from the window, neither to eat nor to drink, but looking earnestly as it were upon a joyful spectacle, she so attendeth to a stranger who teacheth deceitful and various words, that I marvel how the great modesty of the maiden is so hardly beset.

9 O Thamyris, this man upsetteth the whole city of the Iconians, and thy Thecla also, for all the women and the young men go in to him and are taught by him. Ye must, saith he, fear one only God and live chastely. And my daughter, too, like a spider at the window, bound by his words, is held by a new desire and a fearful passion: for she hangeth upon the things that he speaketh, and the maiden is captured. But go thou to her and speak to her; for she is betrothed unto thee.

10 And Thamyris went to her, alike loving her and fearing because of her disturbance (ecstasy), and said: Thecla, my betrothed, why sittest thou thus? and what passion is it that holdeth thee in amaze; turn unto thy Thamyris and be ashamed. And her mother also said the same: Thecla, why sittest thou thus, looking downward, and answering nothing, but as one stricken? And they wept sore, Thamyris because he failed of a wife, and Theocleia of a child, and the maidservants of a mistress; there was, therefore, great confusion of mourning in the house. And while all this was so, Thecla turned not away, but paid heed to the speech of Paul.

11 But Thamyris leapt up and went forth into the street and watched them that went in to Paul and came out. And he saw two men striving bitterly with one another, and said to them: Ye men, tell me who ye are, and who is he that is within with you, that maketh the souls of young men and maidens to err, deceiving them that there may be no marriages but they should live as they are. I promise therefore to give you much money if ye will tell me of him: for I am a chief man of the city.

12 And Demas and Hermogenes said unto him: Who this man is, we know not; but he defraudeth the young men of wives and the maidens of husbands, saying: Ye have no resurrection otherwise, except ye continue chaste, and defile not the flesh but keep it pure.

13 And Thamyris said to them: Come, ye men, into mine house and refresh yourselves with me. And they went to a costly banquet and much wine and great wealth and a brilliant table. And Thamyris made them drink, for he loved Thecla and desired to take her to wife: and at the dinner Thamyris said: Tell me, ye men, what is his teaching, that I also may know it: for I am not a little afflicted concerning Thecla because she so loveth the stranger, and I am defrauded of my marriage.

14 And Demas and Hermogenes said: Bring him before Castelius the governor as one that persuadeth the multitudes with the new doctrine of the Christians; and so will he destroy him and thou shalt have thy wife Thecla. And we will teach thee of that resurrection which he asserteth, that it is already come to pass in the children which we have, and we rise again when we have come to the knowledge of the true God.

15 But when Thamyris heard this of them, he was filled with envy and wrath, and rose up early and went to the house of Onesiphorus with the rulers and officers and a great crowd with staves, saying unto Paul: Thou hast destroyed the city of the Iconians and her that was espoused unto me, so that she will not have me: let us go unto Castelius the governor. And all the multitude said: Away with the wizard, for he hath corrupted all our wives. And the multitude rose up together against him.

16 And Thamyris, standing before the judgement seat, cried aloud and said: 0 proconsul, this is the man-we know not whence he is-who alloweth not maidens to marry: let him declare before thee wherefore he teacheth such things. And Demas and Hermogenes said to Thamyris: Say thou that he is a Christian, and so wilt thou destroy him. But the governor kept his mind steadfast and called Paul, saying unto him: Who art thou, and what teachest thou? for it is no light accusation that these bring against thee.

17 And Paul lifted up his voice and said: If I am this day examined what I teach, hearken, 0 proconsul. The living God, the God of vengeance, the jealous God, the God that hath need of nothing,

but desireth the salvation of men, hath sent me, that I may sever them from corruption and uncleanness and all pleasure and death, that they may sin no more. Wherefore God hath sent his own Child, whom I preach and teach that men should have hope in him who alone hath had compassion upon the world that was in error; that men may no more be under judgement but have faith and the fear of God and the knowledge of sobriety and the love of truth. If then I teach the things that have been revealed unto me of God, what wrong do I O proconsul? And the governor having heard that, commanded Paul to be bound and taken away to prison until he should have leisure to hear him more carefully.

18 But Thecla at night took off her bracelets and gave them to the doorkeeper, and when the door was opened for her she went into the prison, and gave the jailer a mirror of silver and so went in to Paul and sat by his feet and heard the wonderful works of God. And Paul feared not at all, but walked in the confidence of God: and her faith also was increased as she kissed his chains.

19 Now when Thecla was sought by her own people and by Thamyris, she was looked for through the streets as one lost; and one of the fellow-servants of the doorkeeper told that she went out by night. And they examined the doorkeeper and he told them that she was gone to the stranger unto the prison; and they went as he told them and found her as it were bound with him, in affection. And they went forth thence and gathered the multitude to them and showed it to the governor.

20 And he commanded Paul to be brought to the judgement seat; but Thecla rolled herself upon the place where Paul taught when he sat in the prison. And the governor commanded her also to be brought to the judgement seat, and she went exulting with joy. And when Paul was brought the second time the people cried out more vehemently: He is a sorcerer, away with him! But the governor heard Paul gladly concerning the holy works of Christ: and he took counsel, and called Thecla and said: Why wilt thou not marry Thamyris, according to the law of the Iconians? but she stood looking earnestly upon Paul, and when she answered not, her mother Theocleia cried out, saying: Burn the lawless one, burn her that is no bride in the midst of the theatre, that all the women which have been taught by this man may be affrighted.

21 And the governor was greatly moved: and he scourged Paul and sent him out of the city, but Thecla he condemned to be burned. And straightway the governor arose and went to the theatre: and all the multitude went forth unto the dreadful spectacle. But Thecla, as the lamb in the wilderness looketh about for the shepherd, so sought for Paul: and she looked upon the multitude and saw the Lord sitting, like unto Paul, and said: As if I were not able to endure, Paul is come to look upon me. And she earnestly paid heed to him: but he departed into the heavens.

22 Now the boys and the maidens brought wood and hay to burn Thecla: and when she was brought in naked, the governor wept and marvelled at the power that was in her. And they laid the wood, and the executioner bade her mount upon the pyre: and she, making the sign of the cross, went up upon the wood. And they lighted it, and though a great fire blazed forth, the fire took no hold on her; for God had compassion on her, and caused a sound under the earth, and a cloud overshadowed her above, full of rain and hail, and all the vessel of it was poured out so that many were in peril of death, and the fire was quenched, and Thecla was preserved.

23 Now Paul was fasting in Onesiphorus and his wife and their children in an open sepulchre on the way whereby they go from Iconium to Daphne. And when many days were past, as they fasted, the boys said unto Paul: We are anhungered. And they had not wherewith to buy bread, for Onesiphorus had left the goods of this

world, and followed Paul with all his house. But Paul took off his upper garment and said: Go, child, buy several loaves and bring them. And as the boy was buying, he saw his neighbour Thecla, and was astonished, and said: Thecla, whither goest thou? And she said: I seek Paul, for I was preserved from the fire. And the boy said: Come, I will bring thee unto him, for he mourneth for thee and prayeth and fasteth now these six days.

24 And when she came to the sepulchre unto Paul, who had bowed his knees and was praying and saying: O Father of Christ, let not the fire take hold on Thecla, but spare her, for she is thine: she standing behind him cried out: O Father that madest heaven and earth, the Father of thy beloved child Jesus Christ, I bless thee for that thou hast preserved me from the fire, that I might see Paul. And Paul arose and saw her and said: O God the knower of hearts, the Father of our Lord Jesus Christ, I bless thee that thou hast speedily accomplished that which I asked of thee, and hast hearkened unto me.

25 And there was much love within the sepulchre, for Paul rejoiced, and Onesiphorus, and all of them. And they had five loaves, and herbs, and water (and salt), and they rejoiced for the holy works of Christ. And Thecla said unto Paul: I will cut my hair round about and follow thee whithersoever thou goest. But he said: The time is ill-favoured and thou art comely: beware lest another temptation take thee, worse than the first, and thou endure it not but play the coward. And Thecla said: Only give me the seal in Christ, and temptation shall not touch me. And Paul said: Have patience, Thecla, and thou shalt receive the water.

26 And Paul sent away Onesiphorus with all his house unto Iconium, and so took Thecla and entered into Antioch: and as they entered in, a certain Syriarch, Alexander by name, saw Thecla and was enamoured of her, and would have bribed (flattered) Paul with money and gifts. But Paul said: I know not the woman of whom thou speakest, neither is she mine. But as he was of great power, he himself embraced her in the highway; and she endured it not, but sought after Paul and cried out bitterly, saying: Force not the stranger, force not the handmaid of God. I am of the first of the Iconians, and because I would not marry Thamyris, I am cast out of the city. And she caught at Alexander and rent his cloak and took the wreath from his head and made him a mocking-stock.

27 But he alike loving her and being ashamed of what had befallen him, brought her before the governor; and when she confessed that she had done this, he condemned her to the beasts; But the women were greatly amazed, and cried out at the judgement seat: An evil judgement, an impious judgement! And Thecla asked of the governor that she might remain a virgin until she should fight the beasts; and a certain rich queen, Tryphaena by name, whose daughter had died, took her into her keeping, and had her for a consolation.

28 Now when the beasts were led in procession, they bound her to a fierce lioness, and the queen Tryphaena followed after her: but the lioness, when Thecla was set upon her, licked her feet, and all the people marvelled. Now the writing (title) of her accusation was: Guilty of sacrilege. And the women with their children cried out from above: O God, an impious judgement cometh to pass in this city. And after the procession Tryphaena took her again. For her daughter Falconilla, which was dead, had said to her in a dream: Mother, thou shalt take in my stead Thecla the stranger that is desolate, that she may pray for me and I be translated into the place of the righteous.

29 When therefore Tryphaena received her after the procession, she alike bewailed her because she was to fight the beasts on the morrow, and also, loving her closely as her own daughter Falconilla; and said: Thecla, my second child, come, pray thou for my child that she may live for ever; for this have I seen in a dream. And she without delay

lifted up her voice and said: O my God, Son of the Most High that art in heaven, grant unto her according to her desire, that her daughter Faleonilla may live for ever. And after she had said this, Tryphaena bewailed her, considering that so great beauty was to be cast unto the beasts.

30 And when it was dawn, Alexander came to take her-for it was he that was giving the games-saying: The governor is set and the people troubleth us: give me her that is to fight the beasts, that I may take her away. But Tryphaena cried aloud so that he fled away, saying: A second mourning for my Falconilla cometh about in mine house, and there is none to help, neither child, for she is dead, nor kinsman, for I am a widow. O God of Thecla my child, help thou Thecla.

31 And the governor sent soldiers to fetch Thecla: and Tryphaena left her not, but herself took her hand and led her up, saying: I did bring my daughter Falconilla unto the sepulchre; but thee, Thecla, do I bring to fight the beasts. And Thecla wept bitterly and groaned unto the Lord, saying: Lord God in whom I believe, with whom I have taken refuge, that savedst me from the fire, reward thou Tryphaena who hath had pity on thine handmaid, and hath kept me pure.

32 There was therefore a tumult, and a voice of the beasts, and shouting of the people, and of the women which sat together, some saying: Bring in the sacrilegious one! and the women saying: Away with the city for this unlawful deed! away with all us, thou proconsul! it is a bitter sight, an evil judgement!

38 But Thecla, being taken out of the hand of Tryphaena, was stripped and a girdle put upon her, and was cast into the stadium: and lions and bears were set against her. And a fierce lioness running to her lay down at her feet, and the press of women cried aloud. And a bear ran upon her; but the lioness ran and met him, and tore the bear in sunder. And again a lion, trained against men, which was Alexander's, ran upon

her, and the lioness wrestled with him and was slain along with him. And the women bewailed yet more, seeing that the lioness also that succoured her was dead.

34 Then did they put in many beasts, while she stood and stretched out her hands and prayed. And when she had ended her prayer, she turned and saw a great tank full of water, and said: Now is it time that I should wash myself. And she cast herself in, saying: In the name of Jesus Christ do I baptize myself on the last day. And all the women seeing it and all the people wept, saying: Cast not thyself into the water: so that even the governor wept that so great beauty should be devoured by seals. So, then, she cast herself into the water in the name of Jesus Christ; and the seals, seeing the light of a flash of fire, floated dead on the top of the water. And there was about her a cloud of fire, so that neither did the beasts touch her, nor was she seen to be naked.

35 Now the women, when other more fearful beasts were put in, shrieked aloud, and some cast leaves, and others nard, others cassia, and some balsam, so that there was a multitude of odours; and all the beasts that were struck thereby were held as it were in sleep and touched her not; so that Alexander said to the governor: I have some bulls exceeding fearful, let us bind the criminal to them. And the governor frowning, allowed it, saying: Do that thou wilt. And they bound her by the feet between the bulls, and put hot irons under their bellies that they might be the more enraged and kill her. They then leaped forward; but the flame that burned about her, burned through the ropes, and she was as one not bound.

36 But Tryphaena, standing by the arena, fainted at the entry, so that her handmaids said: The queen Tryphaena is dead! And the governor stopped the games and all the city was frightened, and Alexander falling at the governor's feet said: Have mercy on me and on the city, and let the condemned go, lest the city perish with her; for if Caesar hear this, perchance he will destroy us and

the city, because his kinswoman the queen Tryphaena hath died at the entry. 37 And the governor called Thecla from among the beasts, and said to her: Who art thou? and what hast thou about thee that not one of the beasts hath touched thee? But she said: I am the handmaid of the living God; and what I have about me-it is that I have believed on that his Son in whom God is well pleased; for whose sake not one of the beasts hath touched me. For he alone is the goal (or way) of salvation and the substance of life immortal; for unto them that are tossed about he is a refuge, unto the oppressed relief, unto the despairing shelter, and in a word, whosoever believeth not on him, shall not live, but die everlastingly.

38 And when the governor heard this, he commanded garments to be brought and said: Put on these garments. And she said: He that clad me when I was naked among the beasts, the same in the day of judgement will clothe me with salvation. And she took the garments and put them on. And the governor forthwith issued out an act, saying: I release unto you Thecla the godly, the servant of God. And all the women cried out with a loud voice and as with one mouth gave praise to God, saying: One is the God who hath preserved Thecla: so that with their voice all the city shook.

39 And Tryphaena, when she was told the good tidings, met her with much people and embraced Thecla and said: Now do I believe that the dead are raised up: now do I believe that my child liveth: come within, and I will make thee heir of all my substance. Thecla therefore went in with her and rested in her house eight days, teaching her the word of God, so that the more part of the maid-servants also believed, and there was great joy in the house.

40 But Thecla yearned after Paul and sought him, sending about in all places; and it was told her that he was at Myra. And she took young men and maids, and girded herself, and sewed her mantle into a cloak after the fashion of a man, and departed into Myra, and found Paul speaking the word of God, and went to him. But he when he saw her and the people that were with her was amazed, thinking in himself: Hath some other temptation come upon her? But she perceived it, and said to him: I have received the washing, 0 Paul; for he that hath worked together with thee in the Gospel hath worked with me also unto my baptizing.

41 And Paul took her by the hand and brought her into the house of Hermias, and heard all things from her; so that Paul marvelled much, and they that heard were confirmed, and prayed for Tryphaena. And Thecla arose and said to Paul: I go unto Iconium. And Paul said: Go, and teach the word of God. Now Tryphaena had sent her much apparel and gold, so that she left of it with Paul for the ministry of the poor.

42 But she herself departed unto Iconium. And she entered into the house of Onesiphorus, and fell down upon the floor where Paul had sat and taught the oracles of God, and wept, saying: O God of me and of this house, where the light shone upon me, Jesu Christ the Son of God, my helper in prison, my helper before the governors, my helper in the fire, my helper among the beasts, thou art God, and unto thee be the glory for ever. Amen.

43 And she found Thamyris dead, but her mother living. And she saw her mother and said unto her: Theocleia my mother, canst thou believe that the Lord liveth in the heavens? for whether thou desirest money, the Lord will give it thee through me: or thy child, lo, I am here before thee. And when she had so testified, she departed unto Seleucia, and after she had enlightened many with the word of God, she slept a good sleep.

[[A good many manuscripts add that Theoeleia was not converted, but the Coptic does not support them: it ends the episode as above.

A long appendix is given by other Greek copies, telling how in Thecla's old age (she was ninety) she was living on Mount Calamon or Calameon, and

*some evil-disposed young men went up
to ill-treat her: and she prayed, and the
rock opened and she entered it, and it
closed after her. Some add that she
went underground to Rome: this, to
account for the presence of her body
there. Copt., p.38 of the MS.]]*

III

When he was departed from Antioch
and taught in Myra (Myrrha).
When Paul was teaching the word of
God in Myra, there was there a man,
Hermoerates by name, who had the
dropsy, and he put himself forward in
the sight of all, and said to Paul:
Nothing is impossible with God, but
especially with him whom thou
preachest; for when he came he healed
many, even that God whose servant
thou art. Lo, I and my wife and my
children, we cast ourselves at thy feet:
have pity on me that I also may believe
as thou hast believed on the living God.
Paul said unto him: I will restore thee
(thine health) not for reward, but
through the name of Jesus Christ thou
shalt become whole in the presence of
all these. (And he touched his body)
drawing his hand downwards: and his
belly opened and much water ran from
him and . . . he fell down like a dead
man, so that some said: It is better for
him to die than to continue in pain. But
when Paul had quieted the people, he
took his hand and raised him up and
asked him, saying: Hermocrates, ask for
what thou desirest. And he said: I would
eat. And he took a loaf and gave him to
eat. And in that hour he was whole, and
received the grace of the seal in the
Lord, he and his wife.
But Hermippus his son was angry with
Paul, and sought for a set time wherein
to rise up with them of his own age and
destroy him. For he wished that his
father should not be healed but should
die, that he might soon be master of his
goods. But Dion, his younger son,
heard Paul gladly.
Now all they that were with Hermippus
took counsel to fight against Paul so
that Hermippus . . . and sought to kill
him

Dion fell down and died: but
Hermippus watered Dion with his tears.
But Hermocrates mourned sore, for he
loved Dion more than his other son.
(Yet) he sat at Paul's feet, and forgat
that Dion was dead. But when Dion was
dead, his mother Nympha rent her
clothes and went unto Paul and set
herself before the face of Hermocrates
her husband and of Paul. And when
Paul saw her, he was aifrighted and
said: Wherefore art thou thus, Nympha?
But she said to him: Dion is dead; and
the whole multitude wept when they
beheld her. And Paul looked upon the
people that mourned and sent young
men, saying to them: Go and bring me
him hither. And they went: but
Hermippus caught hold of the body (of
Dion) in the street and cried out

[[A leaf lost.]]

the word in him (them?). But an angel
of the Lord had said unto him in the
night: Paul, thou hast to-day a great
conflict against thy body, but God, the
Father of his Son Jesus Christ, will
protect thee.
When Paul had arisen, he went unto his
brethren, and remained (sorrowful?)
saying: What meaneth this vision? And
while Paul thought upon this, he saw
Hermippus coming, having a sword
drawn in his hand, and with him many
other young men with staves. And Paul
said unto them: I am not a robber,
neither a murderer. The God of all
things, the Father of Christ, will turn
your hands backward, and your sword
into its sheath, and your strength into
weakness: for I am a servant of God,
though I be alone and a stranger, and
small and of no reputation (?) among
the Gentiles. But do thou, 0 God, look
down upon their counsel and suffer me
not to be brought to nought by them.
And when Hermippus ran upon Paul
with his sword drawn, straightway he
ceased to see, so that he cried out aloud,
saying: My dear comrades, forget not
your friend Hermippus. For I have
sinned, 0 Paul, I have pursued after
innocent blood. Learn, ye foolish and

ye of understanding, that this world is nought, gold is nought, all money is nought: I that glutted myself with all manner of goods am now a beggar and entreat of you all: Hearken to me all ye my companions, and every one that dwelleth in Myra. I have mocked at a man who hath saved my father: I have mocked at a man who hath raised up my brother Dion . . . I have mocked at a man who . . . without doing me any evil. But entreat ye of him: behold, he hath saved my father and raised up my brother; he is able therefore to save me also. But Paul stood there weeping alike before God, for that he heard him quickly, and before man, for that the proud was brought low. And he turned himself and went up . . . But the young men took the feet and bore Hermippus and brought him to the place where Paul was teaching and laid him down before the door and went unto their house. And when they were gone a great multitude came to the house of Hermocrates; and another great multitude entered in, to see whether Hermippus were shut up there. And Hermippus besought every one that went in, that they would entreat Paul, with him. But they that went in saw Hermocrates and Nympha, how they rejoiced greatly at the raising up of Dion, and distributed victuals and money unto the widows for his recovery. And they beheld Hermippus their son in the state of this second affliction, and how he took hold on the feet of every one, and on the feet of his parents also, and prayed them, as one of the strangers, that he might be healed. And his parents were troubled, and lamented to every one that came in, so that some said: Wherefore do these weep? for Dion is arisen. But Hermocrates possessed goods . . . and brought the value of the goods and took it and distributed it. And Hermocrates, troubled in mind and desiring that they might be satisfied, said: Brethren, let us leave the food . . . . and occupy ourselves . . . Hermocrates. And immediately Nympha cried out in great affliction unto Paul . . they said:

Nympha, Hermocrates calleth upon God that your son Hermippus may see and cease to grieve, for he hath resisted Christ and his minister. But they and Paul prayed to God. And when Hermippus recovered his sight, he turned himself to his mother Nympha, and said to her: Paul came unto me and laid his hand upon me while I wept, and in that hour I saw all things clearly. And she took his hand and led him unto the widows and Paul. But while Paul wept bitterly, Hermippus gave thanks, saying unto them: Every one that believeth, shall . . .

[[A leaf gone]]

. . . concord and peace . . . Amen. And when Paul had confirmed the brethren that were in Myra, he departed unto Sidon.

IV

When he was departed from Myra . Now when Paul was departed from Myra and would go unto Sidon there was great sadness of the brethren that were in Pisidia and Pamphylia, because they yearned after his word and his holy appearance in Christ; so that some from Perga followed Paul, namely Thrasymachus and Cleon with their wives Aline (?) and Chrysa, Cleon's wife. And on the way they nourished Paul: and they were eating their bread under a tree (?). And as he was about to say Amen, there came (five lines broken: the words 'the brethren' and 'idol' occur) . . . . table of devils . . . he dieth therefor, but every one that believeth on Jesus Christ who hath saved us from all defilement and all uncleanness and all evil thoughts, he shall be manifest. And they drew near unto the table (three lines broken. 'Idol' occurs) . . . . stood . . . a mighty idol. And an old man . . . . stood up among them, saying unto them: Ye men, (wait a little and see) what befalleth the priests which would draw near unto our gods: for verily when our fellow-citizen Charinus hearkened and would . . . . against the gods, there died he and his (father). And thereupon died Xanthus also, Chrysa (?), and (Hermocrates?) died, sick of the dropsy, and his wife Nympha.

[[Two leaves, at least, are gone.]]

(Paul is speaking)
after the manner of strange men. Wherefore presume ye to do that which is not seemly (?)? Or have ye not heard of that which came to pass, which God brought upon Sodom and Gomorrha, because they robbed . . . . after the manner of strangers and of women? God did not . . . . them but cast them down into hell. Now therefore we are not men of this fashion that ye say, nor such as ye think, but we are preachers of the living God and his Beloved. But that ye may not marvel, understand . . . the miracles (?) which bear witness for us. But they hearkened not unto him, but took the men and put them into the temple of Apollo, to keep them until the morrow, whereon they assembled the whole city. And many and costly were the victuals which they gave them. But Paul, who was fasting now the third day, testified all the night long, being troubled, and smote his face and said: O God, look down upon their threatenings and suffer us not to slide, and let not our adversaries cast us down, but save us and bring down quickly thy righteousness upon us. And as Paul cast himself down, with the brethren, Thrasymachus and Cleon, then the temple fell . . . . so that they that belonged to the temple and the magistrates that were set over it . . . . others of them in the . . . . for (the one part) fell down . . . . fell down . . . . round about, in the midst of the two parts. And they went in and beheld what had happened, and marvelled that . . . . in their . . . . and that the . . . . rejoiced over the falling of the temple (?). And they cried out, saying: Verily these are the works of the men of a mighty God! And they departed and proclaimed in the city: Apollo the god of the Sidonians is fallen, and the half of his temple. And all the dwellers in the city

ran to the temple and saw Paul and them that were with him, how they wept at this temptation, that they were made a spectacle for all men. But the multitude cried out: Bring them into the theatre. And the magistrates came to fetch them; and they groaned bitterly with one soul.
About two leaves gone.
(Paul speaking) through me.
Consider . . . . (nine lines much broken, 'the way of life (conversation) of Christ', 'not in the faith', occur) . . . . Egyptians . . . . and they . . . But the multitude . . . . and followed after Paul, crying: Praised be the God . . . . who hath sent Paul . . . that we should not . . . . of death. But Theudes . . . . and prayed at Paul's feet and embraced his feet, that he should give him the seal in the Lord. But he commanded them to go to Tyre . . . . in health (or farewell), and they put Paul (in a ship?) and went with him.

[[The purpose of confining Paul and his companions in the temple appears to have been connected with the sins of the cities of the plain of which Paul speaks.]]

[[The Acts of Titus, quoted before, have a sentence referring to this and the next episode: 'And Paul healed Aphphia the wife of Chrysippus who was possessed with a devil: and fasting for seven days he overthrew the idol of Apollo.' The Acts place this immediately after the conversion and preaching at Damascus, and put the Panehares episode later. They are not to be trusted, therefore, as a guide to the order of our book.]]

V
When he was departed out of Sidon and would go unto Tyre.
Now when Paul was entered unto Tyre there came a multitude of Jews . . . . in to him. These . . . . and they heard the mighty works . . . They marvelled . . . . Amphion (= Aphphia of the Acts of Titus) . . . . saying . . . . in . . . . Chrysippus . . . . devil with him . . . .

many . . . . When Paul came . . . . he said: He . . . . God and will not be an evil spirit (?) . . . . in (?) Amphion . . . . through the evil spirit . . . . without any one's having . . . . she said to him: Save me that I die not. And while the multitude . . . . then arose the other (?) evil spirit . . . . And forthwith the devils fled away. And when the multitude saw this, by the power of God, they praised him who had (given such power) unto Paul. And there was there one by name... rimus, who had a son born to him which was dumb.

[[On the next page is a proper name,]]

LIX

[[(or perhaps Kilix, a Cilician), and later the words,]]

'I preach the good tidings of the Saviour . . . . Son of God'.

[[On the next page. Lix perhaps occurs again,]]

and 'Moses'.

[[The next begins:]]

...for that which we say cometh to pass forthwith. Behold we will bring him hither unto thee that he may . . . . thee, to hear the truth of thy . . . .

[[Next page.]]

On God whose desire is come to pass in him, this is the wise man . . . . . . the Father and he hath sent Jesus Christ.

[[Next page,]]

turned toward the East. Moses . . .
. . . in Syria in Cyrene
Again I say unto you . . . I, that do the works . . .
that a man is not justifed by the Law, but that he is justified by the works of righteousness, and he . . .
Next page has the words 'liberty', 'and the yoke', 'all flesh'; and, 'and every one

confess that Jesus Christ is the glory of the Father'.

[[Next page, lower part:]]

is not water in him, but . . . being water, I am not hungry but I am thirsty; I am not but not to . . . . to suffer them, to be (devoured) by wild beasts, not to be able . . . . from the earth, but not to suffer them to be burnt by the fire, are these things of the present age testified, he which was a persecutor . . .

[[Next page, lower part,]]

(Cle)anthes. the law of God which is called . . . . who walketh here before them, hath he not followed us throughout all the cities . . . And when . . . . he turned himself toward the East after this (after two lines) such words, neither preacheth he as thou preachest them, 0 Paul, that thou mayest not . . . .
Next page begins: Thou art in the presence (sight, face) of Jerusalem, but I trust in the Lord that thou wilt . . .

[[The name 'Saul' is almost certain some lines later.]]

[[Next page begins:]]

whom they crucified.

[[And at the end:]]

raised up our flesh.

[[Next page, 7th line,]]

For since the day when . . . . persecuted the apostles which were (with me? se. Peter) out of Jerusalem, I hid myself that I might have comfort, and we nourish them which stand, through the word according to the promise (?) of his grace. I have fallen into many troubles and have subjected myself to the law, as for your sakes. But thought by night and by day in my trouble on Jesus Christ, waiting for him as a lamb . . . . when they crucified him he did not . . .

did not resist . . . . was not troubled.

[[The above may be a speech of Peter.
We have seen some indication that Paul
is now at Jerusalem, and the conjecture
is that a dialogue between him and
Peter occurred in this place.
The next page undoubtedly mentions
Peter.]]

[[Line 1 has 'Paul', line 3, 'twelve (?)
shepherds'.]]

[[Line 5.]]

through Paul. But . . . . was troubled
because of the questioning
(examination) that (was come) upon
Peter and he cried out, saying: Verily,
God is one, and there is no God beside
him: one also is Jesus Christ his Son,
whom we . . . this, whom thou
preachest, did we crucify, whom expect
in great glory, but ye say that he is God
and Judge of the living and the dead,
the King of the ages, for the in the form
of man.

VI
[[Paul is condemned to the mines in an
unknown place. Longinus and Firmilla
have a daughter, Frontina, who is to be
thrown down from a rock, and Paul
with her. It is my distinct opinion that
Fontina is already dead: her body is to
be thus contumeliously treated because
she has become a Christian.
The upper part of the page has
Longinus twice in lines 1, 2; 'Paul' in
1.7. Then:]]

For since . . . . the mine, there hath not .
. . nothing good hath befallen mine
house. And he advised that the men
which were to throw Frontina down,
should throw down Paul also with her,
alive. Now Paul knew these things, but
he worked fasting, in great
cheerfulness, for two days with the
prisoners. They commanded that on the
third day the men . . . . should bring
forth Frontina: and the whole city
followed after her. And Firmilla and
Longinus lamented and the soldiers . . .

But the prisoners carried the bed (bier).
And when Paul saw the great mourning
with the daughter and eight . . .

[[Next page, line 8.]]

Paul alive with the daughter. But when
Paul had taken the daughter in his arms,
he groaned unto the Lord Jesus Christ
because of the sorrow of Firmilla, and
cast himself on his knees in the mire . . .
. praying for Frontina with her in one
(a) prayer. In that hour Frontina rose up.
And the whole multitude was afraid,
and fled. Paul took the hand of the
daughter and led her through the city
unto the house of Longinus, and the
whole multitude said with one voice:
God is one, who hath made heaven and
earth, who hath granted the life of the
daughter in the presence of Paul . . . a
loaf. and he gave thanks to him.

[[Some lines later.]]
to Philippi (?).

VII
When he was departed from . . . and
would go .
Now when Paul was come to Philippi . .
. he entered into the house of . . . . and
there was great joy (among the
brethren) and to every one.

[[On the following pages begins the
episode of the correspondence with the
Corinthians, which was circulated
separately in Syriac, Latin, and
Armenian, and found a place in the
Syriac collection of Pauline epistles
(and is commented on with the rest by
Ephraem the Syrian), and in the
Armenian Bible. We have it in (a) many
Armenian MSS., (b) in Ephraem s
commentary-only extant in Armenian,
(c) in three Latin MSS., at Milan, Laon,
and Paris: as well as in the Coptic MS.,
which is here less fragmentary than in
the preceding pages.]]

[[We begin with a short narrative,
introducing the letter of the Corinthians
to Paul; then follows another short

piece of narrative, extant in Armenian only; then Paul's reply, commonly called the 'Third Epistle to the Corinthians'.

There are various phrases and whole sentences, especially in the Armenian and the Milan MS. of the Latin, which are absent from the Coptic and the Laon MS. and are regarded, rightly, as interpolations.

These will be distinguished by small capitals.

The page of the Coptic MS. on which the correspondence begins is fragmentary at the beginning.]]

1.1. the lawless one
1.2. the reward. They . . . . in
1.3. a prayer . . . . every
1.4. one, and every one (?)
1.6. Paul . . . . again (or together).
1.7. prayed that a messenger be sent to Philippi. For the Corinthians were in great trouble concerning Paul, that he would depart out of the world, before it was time. For there were certain men come to Corinth, Simon and Cleobius, saying: There is no resurrection of the flesh, but that of the spirit only: and that the body of man is not the creation of God; and also concerning the world, that God did not create it, and that God knoweth not the world, and that Jesus Christ was not crucified, but it was an appearance (i.e. but only in appearance), and that lie was not born of Mary, nor of the seed of David. And in a word, there were many things which they had taught in Corinth, deceiving many other men, (and deceiving also) themselves. When therefore the Corinthians heard that Paul was at Philippi, they sent a letter unto Paul to Macedonia by Threptus and Eutychus the deacons. And the letter was after this manner.

I.

1 Stephanus and the elders (presbyters) that are with him, even Daphnus and Eubulus and Theophilus and Zenon, unto Paul THEIR BROTHER ETERNAL greeting in the Lord.

2 There have come unto Corinth two men, Simon and Cleobius, which are overthrowing the faith of many with evil (CORRUPT) words,

3 which do thou prove AND EXAMINE:

4 for we have never heard such words from thee nor from the other apostles:

5 but all that we have received from thee or from them, that do we hold fast.

6 Since therefore the Lord hath had mercy on us, that while thou art still in the flesh we may hear these things again from thee,

7 If it be possible, either come unto us or write unto us.

8 For we believe, according as it hath been revealed unto Theonoe, that the Lord hath delivered thee out of the hand of the lawless one (enemy, Laon).

9 Now the things which these men say and teach are these:

10 They say that we must not use the prophets,

11 and that God is not Almighty,

12 and that there shall be no resurrection of the flesh,

13 and that man was not made by God,

14 and that Christ came not down (is not come, Copt.) in the flesh, neither was born of Mary,

15 and that the world is not of God, but of the angels.

16 Wherefore, brother, WE PRAY THEE use all diligence to come unto us, that the church of the Corinthians may remain without offence, and the madness of these men may be made plain. Farewell ALWAYS in the Lord.

II.

1 The deacons Threptus and Eutyches brought the letter unto Philippi,

2 so that Paul received it, being in bonds because of Stratonice the wife of Apollophanes, AND HE FORGAT HIS BONDS, and was sore afflicted,

3 and cried out, saying: It were better for me to die and to be with the Lord, than to continue in the flesh and to hear such things AND THE CALAMITIES OF FALSE DOCTRINE, so that trouble cometh upon trouble.

4 And over and above this so great

affliction I am in bonds and behold these evils whereby the devices of Satan are accomplished. (4 Harnack: may not the priests (intrigues) of Satan anticipate me while (or after) I suffer (have suffered) fetters for the sake (?) of men.)

5 Paul therefore, in great affliction, wrote a letter, answering thus:

III.

1 Paul, a prisoner of Jesus Christ, unto the brethren which are in Corinth, greeting.

2 Being in the midst of many tribulations, I marvel not if the teachings of the evil one run abroad apace.

3 For my Lord Jesus Christ will hasten his coming, and will set at nought (no longer endure the insolence of) them that falsify his words.

4 For I delivered unto you in the beginning the things which I received of the HOLY apostles which were before me, who were at all times with Jesus Christ:

5 namely, that our Lord Jesus Christ was born of Mary WHICH IS of the seed of David ACCORDING TO THE FLESH, the Holy Ghost being sent forth from heaven from the Father unto her BY THE ANGEL GABRIEL,

6 that he (JESUS) might come down into this world and redeem all flesh by his flesh, and raise us up from the dead in the flesh, like as he hath shown to us in himself for an ensample.

7 And because man was formed by his Father,

8 therefore was he sought when he was lost, that he might be quickened by adoption.

9 For to this end did God Almighty who made heaven and earth first send the prophets unto the Jews, that they might be drawn away from their sins.

10 For he designed to save the house of Israel: therefore he conferred a portion of the spirit of Christ upon the prophets and sent them unto the Jews first (or unto the first Jews), and they proclaimed the true worship of God for a long space of time.

11 But the prince of iniquity, desiring to be God, laid hands on them and slew them (banished them from God, Laon MS.), and bound all flesh by evil lusts (AND THE END OF THE WORLD BY JUDGEMENT DREW NEAR).

12 But God Almighty, who is righteous, would not cast away his own creation, BUT HAD COMPASSION ON THEM FROM HEAVEN,

13 and sent his spirit into Mary IN GALILEE,

[14 Milan MS. and Arm.: WHO BELIEVED WITH ALL HER HEART AND RECEIVED THE HOLY GHOST IN HER WOMB, THAT JESUS MIGHT COME INTO THE WORLD,]

15 that by that flesh whereby that wicked one had brought in death (had triumphed), by the same he should be shown to be overcome.

16 For by his own body Jesus Christ saved all flesh [AND RESTORED IT UNTO LIFE], 17 that he might show forth the temple of righteousness in his body.

18 In whom (or whereby) we are saved (Milan, Paris: in whom if we believe we are set free).

19 They therefore (Paris MS.; Arm. has: Know therefore that. Laon has: They therefore who agree with them) are not children of righteousness but children of wrath who reject the wisdom (providence?) of God, saying that the heaven and the earth and all that are in them are not the work of God.

20 THEY THEREFORE ARE CHILDREN OF WRATH, for cursed are they, following the teaching of the serpent,

21 whom do ye drive out from you and flee from their doctrine. [Arm., Milan, Paris:

22 FOR YE ARE NOT CHILDREN OF DISOBEDIENCE, BUT OF THE WELL-BELOVED CHURCH.

23 THEREFORE IS THE TIME OF THE RESURRECTION PROCLAIMED UNTO ALL.]

24 And as for that which they say, that there is no resurrection of the flesh, they indeed shall have no resurrection UNTO LIFE, BUT UNTO

JUDGEMENT,

25 because they believe not in him that is risen from the dead, NOT BELIEVING NOR UNDERSTANDING,

26 for they know not, O Corinthians, the seeds of wheat or of other seeds (grain), how they are cast bare into the earth and are corrupted and rise again by the will of God with bodies, and clothed.

27 And not only that [body] which is cast in riseth again, but manifold more blessing itself [i.e. fertile and prospering].

28 And if we must not take an example from seeds ONLY, BUT FROM MORE NOBLE BODIES,

29 ye know how Jonas the son of Amathi, when he would not preach to them of Nineve, BUT FLED, was swallowed by the sea-monster;

30 and after three days and three nights God heard the prayer of Jonas out of the lowest hell, and no part of him was consumed, not even an hair nor an eyelash.

31 How much more, O YE OF LITTLE FAITH, shall he raise up you that have believed in Christ Jesus, like as he himself arose.

32 Likewise also a dead man was cast upon the bones of the prophet Helisaetis by the children of Israel, and he arose, both body and soul and bones and spirit (Laon: arose in his body); how much more shall ye which have been cast upon the body and bones and spirit of the Lord [Milan, Paris: how much more, O ye of little faith, shall ye which have been cast on him] arise again in that day having your flesh whole, EVEN AS HE AROSE?

[33 Arm., Milan, Paris: LIKEWISE ALSO CONCERNING THE PROPHET HELIAS: HE RAISED UP THE WIDOW'S SON FROM DEATH: HOW MUCH MORE SHALL THE LORD JESUS RAISE YOU UP FROM DEATH AT THE SOUND OF THE TRUMPET, IN THE TWINKLING OF AN EYE? FOR HE HATH SHOWED US AN ENSAMPLE IN HIS OWN BODY.]

34 If, then, ye receive any other doctrine, GOD SHALL BE WITNESS AGAINST YOU; AND let no man trouble me,

35 for I bear these bonds that I may win Christ, and I therefore bear his marks in my body that I may attain unto the resurrection of the dead.

36 And whoso receiveth (abideth in) the rule which he hath received by the blessed prophets and the holy gospel, shall receive a recompense from the Lord, AND WHEN HE RISETH FROM THE DEAD SHALL OBTAIN ETERNAL LIFE.

37 But whoso trans- gresseth these things, with him is the fire, and with them that walk in like manner (Milan, Paris: with them that go before in the same way, WHO ARE MEN WITHOUT GOD),

38 which are a generation of vipers,

39 whom do ye reject in the power of the Lord,

40 and peace, GRACE, AND LOVE shall be with you.

[[Laon adds: This I found in an old book, entitled the third to the Corinthians, though it is not in the Canon.]]

VIII

AT EPHESUS

[[This episode is not traceable in the Coptic MS. but it undoubtedly formed part of the Acts, though its place is uncertain. It is preserved in an allusion by Hippolytus (early third century) and in an abstract by Nicephorus Callisti (fourteenth century) in his Ecclesiastical history (ii. 25). There is also a sentence in the Acts of Titus: 'They departed from Crete and came to Asia: and at Ephesus twelve thousand believed at the teaching of the holy Paul: there also he fought with beasts, being thrown to a lion.'

HIPPOLYTUS in his Commentary on Daniel, iii. 29, says:

For if we believe that when Paul was condemned to the beasts the lion that was set upon him lay down at his feet and licked him, how shall we not

believe that which happened in the case of Daniel?]]

NICEPHORUS:

Now they who drew up the travels of Paul have related that he did many other things, and among them this, which befell when he was at Ephesus. Hieronymus being governor, Paul used liberty of speech, and he (Hieronymus) said that he (Paul) was able to speak well, but that this was not the time for such words. But the people of the city, fiercely enraged, put Paul's feet into irons, and shut him up in the prison, till he should be exposed as a prey to the lions. But Eubula and Artemilla, wives of eminent men among the Ephesians, being his attached disciples, and visiting him by night, desired the grace of the divine washing. And by God's power, with angels to escort them and enlighten the gloom of night with the excess of the brightness that was in them, Paul, loosed from his iron fetters, went to the sea-shore and initiated them into holy baptism, and returning to his bonds without any of those in care of the prison perceiving it, was reserved as a prey for the lions.

A lion, then, of huge size and unmatched strength was let loose upon him, and it ran to him in the stadium and lay down at his feet. And when many other savage beasts, too, were let loose, it was permitted to none of them to touch the holy body, standing like a statue in prayer. At this juncture a violent and vast hailstorm poured down all at once with a great rush, and shattered the heads of many men and beasts as well, and shore off the ear of Hieronymus himself. And thereafter, with his followers, he came to the God of Paul and received the baptism of salvation. But the lion escaped to the mountains.

And thence Paul sailed to Macedonia and Greece, and thereafter through Macedonia came to Troas and to Miletus, and from there set out for Jerusalem.

Now it is not surprising that Luke has not narrated this fight with the beasts along with the other Acts: for it is not permitted to entertain doubt because (or seeing that) John alone of the evangelists has told of the raising of Lazarus: for we know that not every one writes, believes, or knows everything, but according as the Lord has imparted to each, as the spirit divides to each, so does he perceive and believe and write spiritually the things of the spirit.

Hippolytus is a voucher for the early date of the story, and Nicephorus for its source. It will be recognized, moreover, at once as being quite in the manner of our author. The anger of the Ephesians, it cannot be doubted, was roused by Paul's preaching of continence, to which Eubula and Artemilla had become converts. The episode is really little more than a repetition of Thecla, with Paul for the principal figure.

IX
FRAGMENTS: SCENES OF FAREWELL

(Paul speaking) . . . thanksgiving (?) The grace of the Lord will walk with me until I have fulfilled all the dispensations which shall come upon me with patience. But they were sorrowful, and fasted. And Cleobius was in the Spirit and said unto them: Brethren, (the Lord) will suffer Paul to fulfil every dispensation and thereafter will suffer him to go up (to Jerusalem). But thereafter shall be . . . . in much instruction and knowledge and sowing of the word, so that men shall envy him, and so he shall depart out of this world. But when Paul and the brethren heard this, they lifted up their voices, saying:

[[Next page, first extant line,]]

'beheld'.

[[Second]]

'shall say'.

[[Third,]]

But the Spirit came upon Myrte so that she said unto them: Brethren . . . and look upon this sign, that ye . . . For Paul the servant of the Lord shall save many in Rome, so that of them shall be no number, and he will manifest himself more than all the faithful. Thereafter shall . . . . of the Lord Jesus Christ come . . . . a great grace is . . . .at Rome. And this is the manner wherein the Spirit spake unto Myrte. And every one took the bread, and they were in joy, according to the custom of the fast, through . . . . and the psalms of David and . . . . he rejoiced.

[[On the next page the only significant words are 'to Rome'; 'the brethren'; 'grieved'; 'took the bread'; 'praised the Lord'; 'were very sorrowful'.
The next has ends of lines: 'the Lord'; 'risen'; 'Jesus'; 'Paul said to him'. The last is 'he (or they) greeted'.]]

[[Two more pages have nothing of moment. The next is concerned with the Martyrdom.]]

X
THE MARTYRDOM
[[This, preserved separately to be read on the day of Commemoration, exists in two Greek copies, an incomplete Latin version, and versions in Syriac, Coptic, Ethiopic, Slavonic, besides fragments in our Coptic MS.]]

I.
Now there were awaiting Paul at Rome Luke from Galatia (Gaul, Gk.) and Titus from Dalmatia: whom when Paul saw he was glad: and hired a grange outside Rome, wherein with the brethren he taught the word of truth, and he became noised abroad and many souls were added unto the Lord, so that there was a rumour throughout all Rome, and much people came unto him from the household of Caesar, believing, and there was great joy. And a certain Patroclus, a cup-bearer of Caesar, came at even unto the grange, and not being able because of the press to enter in to Paul, he sat in a high window and listened to him teaching the word of God. But whereas the evil devil envied the love of the brethren, Patroclus fell down from the window and died, and forthwith it was told unto Nero.

But Paul perceiving it by the spirit said: Men and brethren, the evil one hath gained occasion to tempt you: go out of the house and ye shall find a lad fallen from the height and now ready to give up the ghost; take him up and bring him hither to me. And they went and brought him; and when the people saw it they were troubled. But Paul said: Now, brethren, let your faith appear; come all of you and let us weep unto our Lord Jesus Christ, that this lad may live and we continue in quietness. And when all had lamented, the lad received his spirit again, and they set him on a beast and sent him back alive, together with the rest that were of Caesar's household.

II.
But Nero, when he heard of the death of Patroclus, was sore grieved, and when he came in from the bath he commanded another to be set over the wine. But his servants told him, saying: Caesar, Patroclus liveth and standeth at the table. And Caesar, hearing that Patroclus lived, was affrighted and would not go in. But when he went in, he saw Patroclus, and was beside himself, and said: Patroclus, livest thou? And he said: I live, Caesar. And he said: Who is he that made thee to live? And the lad, full of the mind of faith, said: Christ Jesus, the king of the ages. And Caesar was troubled and said: Shall he, then, be king of the ages and overthrow all kingdoms? Patroclus saith unto him: Yea, he overthroweth all kingdoms and he alone shall be for ever, and there shall be no kingdom that shall escape him. And he smote him on the face and said: Patroclus, art thou also a soldier of that king? And he said: Yea, Lord Caesar, for he raised me when I was dead. And Barsabas Justus of the broad feet, and Urion the Cappadocian, and Festus the Galatian,

Caesar's chief men, said: We also are soldiers of the king of the ages. And he shut them up in prison, having grievously tormented them, whom he loved much, and commanded the soldiers of the great king to be sought out, and set forth a decree to this effect, that all that were found to be Christians and soldiers of Christ should be slain.

III.

And among many others Paul also was brought, bound: unto whom all his fellow-prisoners gave heed; so that Caesar perceived that he was over the camp. And he said to him: Thou that art the great king's man, but my prisoner, how thoughtest thou well to come by stealth into the government of the Romans and levy soldiers out of my province? But Paul, filled with the Holy Ghost, said before them all: 0 Caesar, not only out of thy province do we levy soldiers, but out of the whole world. For so hath it been ordained unto us, that no man should be refused who wisheth to serve my king. And if it like thee also to serve him (Lat. thou wilt not repent thereof: but think not that the wealth, &c., which seems better), it is not wealth nor the splendour that is now in this life that shall save thee; but if thou submit and entreat him, thou shalt be saved; for in one day (or one day) he shall fight against the world with fire. And when Caesar heard that, he commanded all the prisoners to be burned with fire, but Paul to be beheaded after the law of the Romans. But Paul kept not silence concerning the word, but communicated with Longus the prefect and Cestus the centurion.

Nero therefore went on (was) (perhaps add 'raging') in Rome, slaying many Christians without a hearing, by the working of the evil one; so that the Romans stood before the palace and cried It sufficeth, Caesar! for the men are our own! thou destroyest the strength of the Romans! Then at that he was persuaded and ceased, and commanded that no man should touch any Christian, until he should learn throughly concerning them.

IV.

Then was Paul brought unto him after the decree; and he abode by his word that he should be beheaded. And Paul said: Caesar, it is not for a little space that I live unto my king; and if thou behead me, this will I do: I will arise and show myself unto thee that I am not dead but live unto my Lord Jesus Christ, who cometh to judge the world. But Longus and Cestus said unto Paul: Whence have ye this king, that ye believe in him and will not change your mind, even unto death? And Paul communicated unto them the word and said: Ye men that are in this ignorance and error, change your mind and be saved from the fire that cometh upon all the world: for we serve not, as ye suppose, a king that cometh from the earth, but from heaven, even the living God, who because of the iniquities that are done in this world, cometh as a judge; and blessed is that man who shall believe in him and shall live for ever when he cometh to burn the world and purge it throughly. Then they beseeching him said: We entreat thee, help us, and we will let thee go. But he answered and said: I am not a deserter of Christ, but a lawful soldier of the living God: if I had known that I should die, O Longus and Cestus, I would have done it, but seeing that I live unto God and love myself, I go unto the Lord, to come with him in the glory of his Father. They say unto him: How then shall we live when thou art beheaded?

V.

And while they yet spake thus, Nero sent one Parthenius and Pheres to see if Paul were already beheaded; and they found him yet alive. And he called them to him and said: Believe on the living God, which raiseth me and all them that believe on him from the dead. And they said: We go now unto Nero; but when thou diest and risest again, then will we believe on thy God. And as Longus and Cestus entreated him yet more concerning salvation, he saith to them:

Come quickly unto my grave in the morning and ye shall find two men praying, Titus and Luke. They shall give you the seal in the Lord.

Then Paul stood with his face to the east and lifted up his hands unto heaven and prayed a long time, and in his prayer he conversed in the Hebrew tongue with the fathers, and then stretched forth his neck without speaking. And when the executioner (speculator) struck off his head, milk spurted upon the cloak of the soldier. And the soldier and all that were there present when they saw it marvelled and glorified God which had given such glory unto Paul: and they went and told Caesar what was done.

VI.

And when he heard it, while he marvelled long and was in perplexity, Paul came about the niuth hour, when many philosophers and the centurion were standing with Caesar, and stood before them all and said: Caesar, behold, I, Paul, the soldier of God, am not dead, but live in my God. But unto thee shall many evils befall and great punishment, thou wretched man, because thou hast shed unjustly the blood of the righteous, not many days hence. And having so said Paul departed from him. But Nero hearing it and being greatly troubled commanded the prisoners to be loosed, and Patroclus also and Barsabas and them that were with him.

VII.

And as Paul charged them, Longus and Cestus the centurion went early in the morning and approached with fear unto the grave of Paul. And when they were come thither they saw two men praying, and Paul betwixt them, so that they beholding the wondrous marvel were amazed, but Titus and Luke being stricken with the fear of man when they saw Longus and Cestus coming toward them, turned to flight. But they pursued after them, saying: We pursue you not for death but for life, that ye may give it unto us, as Paul promised us, whom we

saw just now standing betwixt you and praying. And when they heard that, Titus and Luke rejoiced and gave them the seal in the Lord, glorifying the God and Father of our Lord Jesus Christ (Copt. and glorified the Lord Jesus Christ and all the saints). Unto whom be glory world without end. Amen.

THE ACTS OF PETER

I

The Act of Peter On the first day of the week, that is, on the Lord's day, a multitude gathered together, and they brought unto Peter many sick that he might heal them. And one of the multitude adventured to say unto Peter: Lo, Peter, in our presence thou hast made many blind to see and the deaf to hear and the lame to walk, and hast succoured the weak and given them strength: but wherefore hast thou not succoured thy daughter, the virgin, which grew up beautiful and hath believed in the name of God? For behold, her one side is wholly palsied, and she lieth there stretched out in the corner helpless. We see them that have been healed by thee: thine own daughter thou hast neglected.

But Peter smiled and said unto him: My son, it is manifest unto God alone wherefore her body is not whole. Know then that God is not weak nor powerless to grant his gift unto my daughter: but that thy soul may be convinced, and they that are here present may the more believe -then he looked unto his daughter and said to her: Raise thyself up from thy place, without any helping thee save Jesus only, and walk whole before all these, and come unto me. And she arose and came to him; and the multitude rejoiced at that which was come to pass. Then said Peter unto them: Behold, your heart is convinced that God is not without strength concerning all things that we ask of him. Then they rejoiced yet more and praised God. And Peter said to his daughter: Go unto thy place, and lay thee down and be again in thine infirmity, for this is expedient for me and for thee. And the maiden went back and lay down in her place and was as beforetime: and the whole multitude wept, and entreated Peter to make her whole.

But Peter said unto them: As the Lord liveth, this is expedient for her and for me. For on the day when she was born unto me I saw a vision, and the Lord said unto me: Peter, this day is a great temptation born unto thee, for this daughter will bring hurt unto many souls if her body continue whole. But I thought that the vision did mock me. Now when the maiden was ten years old, a stumbling-block was prepared for many by reason of her. And an exceeding rich man, by name Ptolemaeus, when he had seen the maiden with her mother bathing, sent unto her to take her to wife; but her mother consented not. And he sent oft-times to her, and could not wait.

[[Here a leaf is lost: the sense, however, is not hard to supply. Augustine speaks (quoting Apocryphal Acts) of a daughter of Peter struck with palsy at the prayer of her father. Ptolemaeus, unable to win the maiden by fair means, comes and carries her off. Peter hears of it and prays God to protect her. His prayer is heard. She is struck with palsy on one side of her body. Then the text resumes.]]

The servants of Ptolemaeus brought the maiden and laid her down before the door of the house and departed. But when I perceived it, I and her mother, we went down and found the maiden, that one whole side of her body from her toes even to her head was palsied and withered: and we bore her away, praising the Lord which had preserved his handmaid from defilement and shame and (corruption?). This is the cause of the matter, why the maiden continueth so unto this day.

Now, then, it is fitting for you to know the end of Ptolemaeus. He went home and sorrowed night and day over that which had befallen him, and by reason of the many tears which he shed, he became blind. And when he had resolved to rise up and hang himself, lo, about the ninth hour of the day, he saw a great light which enlightened the whole house, and heard a voice saying unto him: Ptolemaeus, God hath not given thee the vessels for corruption and shame, and yet more doth it not become thee which hast believed in me to defile my virgin, whom thou shalt know as thy sister, even as if I were unto you both one spirit (sic). But rise up and go quickly unto the house of the apostle Peter, and thou shalt see my glory; he shall make known unto thee what thou must do.

But Ptolemaeus was not negligent, and bade his servants show him the way and bring him unto me. And when they were come to me, he told me all that had befallen him by the power of our Lord Jesus Christ. Then did he see with the eyes of his flesh, and with the eyes of his soul, and much people believed (hoped) in Christ: and he did them good and gave them the gift of God. Thereafter Ptolemaeus died, departing out of this life, and went unto his Lord: and when he made his will he bequeathed a piece of land in the name of my daughter, because through her he had believed in God and was made whole. But I unto whom the disposition thereof fell, exercised it with great carefulness: I sold the land, and God alone knoweth neither I nor my daughter (received the price). I sold the land and kept nought back of the price, but gave all the money unto the poor. Know therefore, thou servant of Jesus Christ, that God directeth (?) them that are his, and prepareth good for every one of them, although we think that God hath forgotten us. Therefore now, brethren, let us be sorrowful and watch and pray, and so shall the goodness of God look upon us, whereon we wait.

And yet further discourse did Peter hold before them all, and glorified the name of Christ the Lord and gave them all of the bread: and when he had distributed it, he rose up and went unto his house.

[[The scene of this episode is probably Jerusalem. The subject of it was often used by later writers, most notably, perhaps, by the author of the late Acts of SS. Nereus and Achilleus (fifth or sixth century), who gives the daughter a name, Petronilla, which has passed into Kalendars, and as Perronelle, Pernel, or Parnell has become familiar.
A few critics have questioned whether this piece really belongs to the Acts of Peter: but the weight of probability and of opinion is against them. Nothing can be plainer than that it is an extract from a larger book, and that it is ancient (the manuscript may be of the fourth century). Moreover, Augustine, in dealing with apocryphal Acts, alludes to the story contained in it. What other large book of ancient date dealing with Peter's doings can we imagine save the Acts?]]

II

THE GARDENER'S DAUGHTER

[[Augustine (Against Adimantus, xvii. 5), says to his Manichaean opponent: the story of Peter killing Ananias and Sapphira by a word is very stupidly blamed by those who in the apocryphal Acts read and admire both the incident I mentioned about the apostle Thomas (the death of the cup-bearer at the feast in his Acts) 'and that the daughter of Peter himself was stricken with palsy at the prayer of her father, and that the daughter of a gardener died at the prayer of Peter. Their answer is that it was expedient for them, that the one should be disabled by palsy and the other should die: but they do not deny that it happened at the prayer of the apostle'.]]

[[This allusion to the gardener's daughter remained a puzzle until lately.

But a passage in the Epistle of Titus (already quoted) tells us the substance of the story.]]

A certain gardener had a daughter, a virgin, her father's only child: he begged Peter to pray for her. Upon his request, the apostle answered him that the Lord would give her that which was useful for her soul. Immediately the girl fell dead.

O worthy gain and suitable to God, to escape the insolence of the flesh and mortify the boastfulness of the blood! But that old man, faithless, and not knowing the greatness of the heavenly favour, ignorant of the divine benefit, entreated Peter that his only daughter might be raised again. And when she was raised, not many days after, as it might be to-day, the slave of a believer who lodged in the house ran upon her and ruined the girl, and both of them disappeared.

[[This was evidently a contrast to the story of Peter's daughter, and probably followed immediately upon it in the Acts. There is another sentence appropriate to the situation, which Dom de Bruyne found in a Cambrai MS. of the thirteenth century -a collection of apophthegms- and printed with the extracts from the Epistle of Titus.]]

That the dead are not to be mourned overmuch, Peter, speaking to one who lamented without patience the loss of his daughter, said: So many assaults of the devil, so many warrings of the body, so many disasters of the world hath she escaped, and thou sheddest tears as if thou knewest not what thou sufferest in thyself (what good hath befallen thee).

[[This might very well be part of Peter's address to the bereaved gardener.]]

III
THE VERCELLI ACTS

I. At the time when Paul was sojourning in Rome and confirming many in the faith, it came also to pass that one by name Candida, the wife of Quartus that was over the prisons, heard Paul and paid heed to his words and believed. And when she had instructed her husband also and he believed, Quartus suffered Paul to go whither he would away from the city: to whom Paul said: If it be the will of God, he will reveal it unto me. And after Paul had fasted three days and asked of the Lord that which should be profitable for him, he saw a vision, even the Lord saying unto him: Arise, Paul, and become a physician in thy body (i.e. by going thither in person) to them that are in Spain.

He therefore, having related to the brethren what God had commanded, nothing doubting, prepared himself to set forth from the city. But when Paul was about to depart, there was great weeping throughout all the brotherhood, because they thought that they should see Paul no more, so that they even rent their clothes. For they had in mind also how that Paul had oftentimes contended with the doctors of the Jews and confuted them, saying: Christ, upon whom your fathers laid hands, abolished their sabbaths and fasts and holy-days and circumcision, and the doctrines of men and the rest of the traditions he did abolish. But the brethren lamented (and adjured) Paul by the coming of our Lord Jesus Christ, that he should not be absent above a year, saying: We know thy love for thy brethren; forget not us when thou art come thither, neither begin to forsake us, as little children without a mother. And when they besought him long with tears, there came a sound from heaven, and a great voice saying: Paul the servant of God is chosen to minister all the days of his life: by the hands of Nero the ungodly and wicked man shall he be perfected before your eyes. And a very great fear fell upon the brethren because of the voice which came from heaven: and they were confirmed yet more in the faith.

II.

Now they brought unto Paul bread and water for the sacrifice, that he might make prayer and distribute it to every one. Among whom it befell that a woman named Rufina desired, she also, to receive the Eucharist at the hands of Paul: to whom Paul, filled with the spirit of God, said as she drew near: Rufina, thou comest not worthily unto the altar of God, arising from beside one that is not thine husband but an adulterer, and assayest to receive the Eucharist of God. For behold Satan shall trouble thine heart and cast thee down in the sight of all them that believe in the Lord, that they which see and believe may know that they have believed in the living God, the searcher of hearts. But if thou repent of thine act, he is faithful that is able to blot out thy sin and set thee free from this sin: but if thou repent not, while thou art yet in the body, devouring fire and outer darkness shall receive thee for ever. And immediately Rufina fell down, being stricken with palsy (?) from her head unto the nails of her feet, and she had no power to speak (given her) for her tongue was bound. And when both they that believed (in the faith) and the neophytes saw it, they beat their breasts, remembering their old sins, and mourned and said: We know not if God will forgive the former sins which we have committed. Then Paul called for silence and said: Men and brethren which now have begun to believe on Christ, if ye continue not in your former works of the tradition of your fathers, and keep yourselves from all guile and wrath and fierceness and adultery and defilement, and from pride and envy and contempt and enmity, Jesus the living God will forgive you that ye did in ignorance. Wherefore, ye servants of God, arm yourselves every one in your inner man with peace, patience, gentleness, faith, charity, knowledge, wisdom, love of the brethren, hospitality, mercy, abstinence, chastity, kindness, justice: then shall ye have for your guide everlastingly the first-begotten of all creation, and shall have strength in peace with our Lord. And when they had heard these things of Paul, they besought him to pray for them. And Paul lifted up his voice and said: O eternal God, God of the heavens, God of unspeakable majesty (divinity), who hast stablished all things by thy word, who hast bound upon all the world the chain of thy grace, Father of thine holy Son Jesus Christ, we together pray thee through thy Son Jesus Christ, strengthen the souls which were before unbelieving but now are faithful. Once I was a blasphemer, now I am blasphemed; once I was a persecutor, now do I suffer persecution of others; once I was the enemy of Christ, now I pray that I may be his friend: for I trust in his promise and in his mercy; I account myself faithful and that I have received forgiveness of my former sins. Wherefore I exhort you also, brethren, to believe in the Lord the Father Almighty, and to put all your trust in our Lord Jesus Christ his Son, believing in him, and no man shall be able to uproot you from his promise. Bow your knees therefore together and commend me unto the Lord, who am about to set forth unto another nation, that his grace may go before me and dispose my journey aright, that he may receive his vessels holy and believing, that they, giving thanks for my preaching of the word of the Lord, may be well grounded in the faith. But the brethren wept long and prayed unto the Lord with Paul, saying: Be thou, Lord Jesus Christ, with Paul and restore him unto us whole: for we know our weakness which is in us even to this day.

III.

And a great multitude of women were kneeling and praying and beseeching Paul; and they kissed his feet and accompanied him unto the harbour. But Dionysius and Balbus, of Asia, knights of Rome, and illustrious men, and a senator by name Demetrius abode by

Paul on his right hand and said: Paul, I would desire to leave the city if I were not a magistrate, that I might not depart from thee. Also from Caesar's house Cleobius and Iphitus and Lysimachus and Aristaeus and two matrons Berenice and Philostrate, with Narcissus the presbyter [after they had] accompanied him to the harbour: but whereas a storm of the sea came on, he (Narcissus?) sent the brethren back to Rome, that if any would, he might come down and hear Paul until he set sail: and hearing that, the brethren went up unto the city. And when they told the brethren that had remained in the city, and the report was spread abroad, some on beasts, and some on foot, and others by way of the Tiber came down to the harbour, and were confirmed in the faith for three days, and on the fourth day until the fifth hour, praying together with Paul, and making the offering: and they put all that was needful on the ship and delivered him two young men, believers, to sail with him, and bade him farewell in the Lord and returned to Rome.

[[There has been great dispute about these three chapters, whether they are not an excerpt from the Acts of Paul, or whether they are an addition made by the writer of the Greek original of the Vercelli Acts.

If they are from the Acts of Paul, it means that in those Acts Paul was represented as visiting Rome twice, and going to Spain between the visits. Evidently, if this was so, he did not return straight from Spain to Rome: at least the Coptic gives no indication that the prophecies of Cleobius and Myrte were uttered in Spain.

The question is a difficult one. All allow that the writer of the Acts of Peter knew and used the Acts of Paul: but there is strong opposition to the idea that Paul related two visits to Rome.

The writer of Paul obviously knew the canonical Acts very well and obviously took great liberties with them. Did he go so far, one wonders, as to suppress and ignore the whole story of the trial

before Felix and the shipwreck? If he told of but one visit to Rome -the final one- it appears that he did: for the conditions described in the Martyrdom -Paul quite free and martyred very shortly after his arrival- are totally irreconcilable with Luke (Paul arriving in custody and living two years at least in the city).]]

IV.

Now after a few days there was a great commotion in the midst of the church, for some said that they had seen wonderful works done by a certain man whose name was Simon, and that he was at Aricia, and they added further that he said he was a great power of God and without God he did nothing. Is not this the Christ? but we believe in him whom Paul preached unto us; for by him have we seen the dead raised, and men Delivered from divers infirmities: but this man seeketh contention, we know it (or, but what this contention is, we know not) for there is no small stir made among us. Perchance also he will now enter into Rome; for yesterday they besought him with great acclamations, saying unto him: Thou art God in Italy, thou art the saviour of the Romans: haste quickly unto Rome. But he spake to the people with a shrill voice, saying: Tomorrow about the seventh hour ye shall see me fly over the gate of the city in the form (habit) wherein ye now see me speaking unto you. Therefore, brethren, if it seem good unto you, let us go and await carefully the issue of the matter. They all therefore ran together and came unto the gate. And when it was the seventh hour, behold suddenly a dust was seen in the sky afar off, like a smoke shining with rays stretching far from it. And when he drew near to the gate, suddenly he was not seen: and thereafter he appeared, standing in the midst of the people; whom they all worshipped, and took knowledge that he was the same that was seen of them the day before. And the brethren were not a little offended among themselves, seeing,

moreover, that Paul was not at Rome, neither Timotheus nor Barnabas, for they had been sent into Macedonia by Paul, and that there was no man to comfort us, to speak nothing of them that had but just become catechumens. And as Simon exalted himself yet more by the works which he did, and many of them daily called Paul a sorcerer, and others a deceiver, of so great a multitude that had been stablished in the faith all fell away save Narcissus the presbyter and two women in the lodging of the Bithynians, and four that could no longer go out of their house, but were shut up (day and night): these gave themselves unto prayer (by day and night), beseeching the Lord that Paul might return quickly, or some other that should visit his servants, because the devil had made them fall by his wickedness.

V.

And as they prayed and fasted, God was already teaching Peter at Jerusalem of that which should come to pass. For whereas the twelve years which the Lord Christ had enjoined upon him were fulfilled, he showed him a vision after this manner, saying unto him: Peter, that Simon the sorcerer whom thou didst cast out of Judaea, convicting him, hath again come before thee (prevented thee) at Rome. And that shalt thou know shortly (or, and that thou mayest know in few words): for all that did believe in me hath Satan made to fall by his craft and working: whose Power Simon approveth himself to be. But delay thee not: set forth on the morrow, and there shalt thou find a ship ready, setting sail for Italy, and within few days I will show thee my grace which hath in it no grudging. Peter then, admonished by the vision, related it unto the brethren without delay, saying: It is necessary for me to go up unto Rome to fight with the enemy and adversary of the Lord and of our brethren.
And he went down to Caesarea and embarked quickly in the ship, whereof the ladder was already drawn up, not

taking any provision with him. But the governor of the ship whose name was Theon looked on Peter and said: Whatsoever we have, all is thine. For what thank have we, if we take in a man like unto ourselves who is in uncertain case (difficulty) and share not all that we have with thee? but only let us have a prosperous voyage. But Peter, giving him thanks for that which he offered, himself fasted while he was in the ship, sorrowful in mind and again consoling himself because God accounted him worthy to be a minister in his service. And after a few days the governor of the ship rose up at the hour of his dinner and asked Peter to eat with him, and said to him: O thou, whoever thou art, I know thee not, but as I reckon, I take thee for a servant of God. For as I was steering my ship at midnight I perceived the voice of a man from heaven saying to me: Theon, Theon! And twice it called me by my name and said to me: Among them that sail with thee let Peter be greatly honoured by thee, for by him shalt thou and the rest be preserved safe without any hurt after such a course as thou hopest not for. And Peter believed that God would vouchsafe to show his providence upon the sea unto them that were in the ship, and thenceforth began Peter to declare unto Theon the mighty works of God, and how the Lord had chosen him from among the apostles, and for what business he sailed unto Italy: and daily he communicated unto him the word of God. And considering him he perceived by his walk that he was of one mind in the faith and a worthy minister (deacon).

Now when there was a calm upon the ship in Hadria (the Adriatic), Theon showed it to Peter, saying unto him: If thou wilt account me worthy, whom thou mayest baptize with the seal of the Lord thou hast an opportunity. For all that were in the ship had fallen asleep, being drunken. And Peter went down by a rope and baptized Theon in the name of the Father and the Son and the Holy Ghost: and he came up out of the water rejoicing with great joy, and Peter also

was glad because God had accounted Theon worthy of his name. And it came to pass when Theon was baptized, there appeared in the same place a youth shining and beautiful, saying unto them: Peace be unto you. And immediately Peter and Theon went up and entered into the cabin; and Peter took bread and gave thanks unto the Lord which had accounted him worthy of his holy ministry, and for that the youth had appeared unto them, saying: Peace be unto you. And he said: Thou best and alone holy one, it is thou that hast appeared unto us, O God Jesu Christ, and in thy name hath this man now been washed and sealed with thy holy seal. Therefore in thy name do I impart unto him thine eucharist, that he may be thy perfect servant without blame for ever.

And as they feasted and rejoiced in the Lord, suddenly there came a wind, not vehement but moderate, at the ship's prow, and ceased not for six days and as many nights, until they came unto Puteoli.

VI.

And when they had touched at Puteoli, Theon leapt out of the ship and went unto the inn where he was wont to lodge, to prepare to receive Peter. Now he with whom he lodged was one by name Ariston, which alway feared the Lord, and because of the Name Theon entrusted himself with him (had dealings with him). And when he was come to the inn and saw Ariston, Theon said unto him: God who hath accounted thee worthy to serve him hath communicated his grace unto me also by his holy servant Peter, who hath now sailed with me from Judaea, being commanded by our Lord to come unto Italy. And when he heard that, Ariston fell upon Theon's neck and embraced him and besought him to bring him to the ship and show him Peter. For Ariston said that since Paul set forth unto Spain there was no man of the brethren with whom he could refresh himself, and, moreover, a certain Jew had broken into the city, named Simon, and with his charms of sorcery and his wickedness hath he made all the brotherhood fall away this way and that, so that I also fled from Rome, expecting the coming of Peter: for Paul had told us of him, and I also have seen many things in a vision. Now, therefore, I believe in my Lord that he will build up again his ministry, for all this deceit shall be rooted out from among his servants. For our Lord Jesus Christ is faithful, who is able to restore our minds. And when Theon heard these things from Ariston, who wept, his spirit was raised (increased) yet more and he was the more strengthened, because he perceived that he had believed on the living God.

But when they came together unto the ship, Peter looked upon them and smiled, being filled with the Spirit; so that Ariston falling on his face at Peter's feet, said thus: Brother and lord, that hast part in the holy mysteries and showest the right way which is in the Lord Jesus Christ our God, who by thee hath shown unto us his coming: we have lost all them whom Paul had delivered unto us, by the working of Satan; but now I trust in the Lord who hath commanded thee to come unto us, sending thee as his messenger, that he hath accounted us worthy to see his great and wonderful works by thy means. I pray thee therefore, make haste unto the city: for I left the brethren which have stumbled, whom I saw fall into the temptation of the devil, and fled hither, saying unto them: Brethren, stand fast in the faith, for it is of necessity that within these two months the mercy of our Lord bring his servant unto you. For I had seen a vision, even Paul, saying unto me: Ariston, flee thou out of the city. And when I heard it, I believed without delay and went forth in the Lord, although I had an infirmity in my flesh, and came hither; and day by day I stood upon the sea-shore asking the sailors: Hath Peter sailed with you? But now through the abundance of the grace of God I entreat thee, let us go up unto Rome without delay, lest the teaching of this wicked man prevail yet further.

And as Ariston said this with tears, Peter gave him his hand and raised him up from the earth, and Peter also groaning, said with tears: He hath prevented us which tempteth all the world by his angels; but he that hath power to save his servants from all temptations shall quench his deceits and put him beneath the feet of them that have believed in Christ whom we preach.

And, as they entered in at the gate, Theon entreated Peter, saying: Thou didst not refresh thyself on any day in so great a voyage (sea): and now after (before) so hard a journey wilt thou set out forthwith from the ship? tarry and refresh thyself, and so shalt thou set forth: for from hence to Rome upon a pavement of flint I fear lest thou be hurt by the shaking. But Peter answered and said to them: What if it come to pass that a millstone were hung upon me, and likewise upon the enemy of our Lord, even as my Lord said unto us of any that offended one of the brethren, and I were drowned in the sea? but it might be not only a millstone, but that which is far worse, even that I which am the enemy of this persecutor of his servants should die afar off from them that have believed on the Lord Jesus Christ (so Ficker: the sentence is corrupt; the sense is that Peter must at all costs be with his fellow-Christians, or he will incur even worse punishment than that threatened by our Lord's words). And by no exhortation could Theon prevail to persuade him to tarry there even one day.

But Theon himself delivered all that was in the ship to be sold for the price which he thought good, and followed Peter unto Rome; whom Ariston brought unto the abode of Narcissus the presbyter.

VII.

Now the report was noised through the city unto the brethren that were dispersed, because of Simon, that he might show him to be a deceiver and a persecutor of good men. All the multitude therefore ran together to see the apostle of the Lord stay (himself, or the brethren) on Christ. And on the first day of the week when the multitude was assembled to see Peter, Peter began to say with a loud voice: Ye men here present that trust in Christ, ye that for a little space have suffered temptation, learn for what cause God sent his Son into the world, and wherefore he made him to be born of the Virgin Mary; for would he so have done if not to procure us some grace or dispensation? even because he would take away all offence and all ignorance and all the contrivance of the devil, his attempts (beginnings) and his strength wherewith he prevailed aforetime, before our God shined forth in the world. And whereas men through ignorance fell into death by many and divers infirmities, Almighty God, moved with compassion, sent his Son into the world. With whom I was; and he (or I) walked upon the water, whereof I myself remain a witness, and do testify that he then worked in the world by signs and wonders, all of which he did. I do confess, dearly-beloved brethren, that I was with him: yet I denied him, even our Lord Jesus Christ, and that not once only, but thrice; for there were evil dogs that were come about me as they did unto the Lord's prophets. And the Lord imputed it not unto me, but turned unto me and had compassion on the infirmity of my flesh, when (or so that) afterward I bitterly bewailed myself, and lamented the weakness of my faith, because I was befooled by the devil and kept not in mind the word of my Lord. And now I say unto you, O men and brethren, which are gathered together in the name of Jesus Christ: against you also hath the deceiver Satan aimed his arrows, that ye might depart out of the way. But faint not, brethren, neither let your spirit fall, but be strong and persevere and doubt not: for if Satan caused me to stumble, whom the Lord had in great honour, so that I denied the light of mine hope, and if he overthrew me and persuaded me to flee as if I had put my trust in a man, what think ye will he do unto you which are but young in the faith? Did ye suppose that he would not turn you away to make you enemies of the kingdom of God, and cast you down into perdition by a new (or the last) deceit? For whomsoever he casteth out from the hope of our Lord Jesus Christ, he is a son of perdition for ever. Turn yourselves, therefore, brethren, chosen of the Lord, and be strong in God Almighty, the Father of our Lord Jesus Christ, whom no man hath seen at any time, neither can see, save he who hath believed in him. And be ye aware whence this temptation hath come upon you. For it is not only by words that I would convince you that this is Christ whom I preach, but also by deeds and exceeding great works of power do I exhort you by the faith that is in Christ Jesus, that none of you look for any other save him that was despised and mocked of the Jews, even this Nazarene which was crucified and died and the third day rose again.

VIII.

And the brethren repented and entreated Peter to fight against Simon: (who said that he was the power of God, and lodged in the house of Marcellus a senator, whom he had convinced by his charms) saying: Believe us, brother Peter: there was no man among men so wise as this Marcellus. All the widows that trusted in Christ had recourse unto him; all the fatherless were fed by him; and what more, brother? all the poor called Marcellus their patron, and his house was called the house of the strangers and of the poor, and the emperor said unto him: I will keep thee out of every office, lest thou despoil the provinces to give gifts unto the Christians. And Marcellus answered: All my goods are also thine. And Caesar said to him: Mine they would be if thou keptest them for me; but now they are not mine, for thou givest them to whom thou wilt, and I know not to what vile persons. Having this, then, before our eyes, brother Peter, we report it to thee, how the great mercy of this man is turned unto blasphemy; for if he had not turned, neither should we have departed from the holy faith of God our Lord. And now doth this Marcellus in anger repent him of his good deeds, saying: All this substance have I spent in all this time, vainly believing that I gave it for the knowledge of God! So that if any stranger cometh to the door of his house, he smiteth him with a staff and biddeth him be beaten, saying: Would God I had not spent so much money upon these impostors: and yet more doth he say, blaspheming. But if there abide in thee any mercy of our Lord and aught of the goodness of his commandments, do thou succour the error of this man who hath done so many alms-deeds unto the servants of God.

And Peter, when he perceived this, was smitten with sharp affliction and said: O the divers arts and temptations of the devil! O the contrivances and devices of the wicked! he that nourisheth up for himself a mighty fire in the day of wrath, the destruction of simple men, the ravening wolf, the devourer and scatterer of eternal life! Thou didst enmesh the first man in concupiscence and bind him with thine old iniquity and with the chain of the flesh: thou art wholly the exceeding bitter fruit of the tree of bitterness, who sendest divers lusts upon men. Thou didst compel Judas my fellow-disciple and fellow-apostle to do wickedly and deliver up our Lord Jesus Christ, who shall punish thee therefor. Thou didst harden the heart of Herod and didst inflame Pharaoh and compel him to fight against Moses the holy servant of God; thou didst give boldness unto Caiaphas, that he should deliver our Lord Jesus Christ unto the unrighteous multitude; and even until now thou shootest at innocent souls with thy poisonous arrows. Thou wicked one, enemy of all men, be thou accursed from the Church of him the Son of the holy God ommpotent and as a brand cast out of the fire shalt thou be quenched by the servants of our Lord Jesus Christ. Upon thee let thy blackness be turned and

upon thy children, an evil seed; upon thee be turned thy wickedness and thy threatenings; upon thee and thine angels be thy temptations, thou beginning of malice and bottomless pit of darkness! Let thy darkness that thou hast be with thee and with thy vessels which thou ownest! Depart from them that shall believe in God, depart from the servants of Christ and from them that desire to be his soldiers. Keep thou to thyself thy garments of darkness! Without cause knockest thou at other men's doors, which are not thine but of Christ Jesus that keepeth them. For thou, ravening wolf, wouldest carry off the sheep that are not thine but of Christ Jesus, who keepeth them with all care and diligence.

IX.

As Peter spake thus with great sorrow of mind, many were added unto them that believed on the Lord. But the brethren besought Peter to join battle with Simon and not suffer him any longer to vex the people. And without delay Peter went quickly out of the synagogue (assembly) and went unto the house of Marcellus, where Simon lodged: and much people followed him. And when he came to the door, he called the porter and said to him: Go, say unto Simon: Peter because of whom thou fleddest out of Judaea waiteth for thee at the door. The porter answered and said to Peter: Sir, whether thou be Peter, I know not: but I have a command; for he had knowledge that yesterday thou didst enter into the city, and said unto me: Whether it be by day or by night, at whatsoever hour he cometh, say that I am not within. And Peter said to the young man: Thou hast well said in reporting that which he compelled thee to say. And Peter turned unto the people that followed him and said: Ye shall now see a great and marvellous wonder. And Peter seeing a great dog bound with a strong chain, went to him and loosed him, and when he was loosed the dog received a man's voice and said unto Peter: What dost thou bid me to do, thou servant of the unspeakable and living God? Peter said unto him: Go in and say unto Simon in the midst of his company: Peter saith unto thee, Come forth abroad, for thy sake am I come to Rome, thou wicked one and deceiver of simple souls. And immediately the dog ran and entered in, and rushed into the midst of them that were with Simon, and lifted up his forefeet and in a loud voice said: Thou Simon, Peter the servant of Christ who standeth at the door saith unto thee: Come forth abroad, for thy sake am I come to Rome, thou most wicked one and deceiver of simple souls. And when Simon heard it, and beheld the incredible sight, he lost the words wherewith he was deceiving them that stood by, and all of them were amazed.

X.

But when Marcellus saw it he went out to the door and east himself at Peter's feet and said: Peter, I embrace thy feet, thou holy servant of the holy God; I have sinned greatly: but exact thou not my sins, if there be in thee the true faith of Christ, whom thou preachest, if thou remember his commandments, to hate no man, to be unkind to no man, as I learned from thy fellow apostle Paul; keep not in mind my faults, but pray for me unto the Lord, the holy Son of God whom I have provoked to wrath -for I have persecuted his servants- that I be not delivered with the sins of Simon unto eternal fire; who so persuaded me, that I set up a statue to him with this inscription: 'To Simon the new (young) God.' If I knew, O Peter, that thou couldest be won with money, I would give thee all my substance, yea I would give it and despise it, that I might gain my soul. If I had sons, I would account them as nothing, if only I might believe in the living God. But I confess that he would not have deceived me save that he said that he was the power of God; yet will I tell thee, O most gentle (sweet) Peter: I was not worthy to hear thee, thou servant of God, neither was I stablished in the faith of God which is in Christ; therefore was I made to stumble. I beseech thee, therefore, take

not ill that which I am about to say, that Christ our Lord whom thou preachest in truth said unto thy fellow-apostles in thy presence: If ye have faith as a grain of mustard seed, ye shall say unto this mountain: Remove thyself: and straightway it shall remove itself. But this Simon said that thou, Peter, wast without faith when thou didst doubt, in the waters. And I have heard that Christ said this also: They that are with me have not understood me. If, then, ye upon whom he laid his hands, whom also he chose, did doubt, I, therefore, having this witness, repent me, and take refuge in thy prayers. Receive my soul, who have fallen away from our Lord and from his promise. But I believe that he will have mercy upon me that repent. For the Almighty is faithful to forgive me my sins.

But Peter said with a loud voice: Unto thee, our Lord, be glory and splendour, O God Almighty, Father of our Lord Jesus Christ. Unto thee be praise and glory and honour, world without end. Amen. Because thou hast now fully strengthened and stablished us in thee in the sight of all, holy Lord, confirm thou Marcellus, and send thy peace upon him and upon his house this day: and whatsoever is lost or out of the way, thou alone canst turn them all again; we beseech thee, Lord, shepherd of the sheep that once were scattered, but now shall be gathered in one by thee. So also receive thou Marcellus as one of thy lambs and suffer him no longer to go astray (revel) in error or ignorance. Yea, Lord, receive him that with anguish and tears entreateth thee.

XI.

And as Peter spake thus and embraced Mareellus, Peter turned himself unto the multitude that stood by him and saw there one that laughed (smiled), in whom was a very evil spirit. And Peter said unto him: Whosoever thou art that didst laugh, show thyself openly unto all that are present. And hearing this the young man ran into the court of the house and cried out with a loud voice and dashed himself against the wall and said: Peter, there is a great contention between Simon and the dog whom thou sentest; for Simon saith to the dog: Say that I am not here. Unto whom the dog saith more than thou didst charge him; and when he hath accomplished the mystery which thou didst command him, he shall die at thy feet. But Peter said: And thou also, devil, whosoever thou art, in the name of our Lord Jesus Christ, go out of that young man and hurt him not at all: show thyself unto all that stand here. When the young man heard it, he ran forth and caught hold on a great statue of marble which was set in the court of the house, and brake it in pieces with his feet. Now it was a statue of Caesar. Which Marcellus beholding smote his forehead and said unto Peter: A great crime hath been committed; for if this be made known unto Caesar by some busybody, he will afflict us with sore punishments. And Peter said to him: I see thee not the same that thou wast a little while ago, for thou saidst that thou wast ready to spend all thy substance to save thy soul. But if thou indeed repentest, believing in Christ with thy whole heart, take in thine hands of the water that runneth down, and pray to the Lord, and in his name sprinkle it upon the broken pieces of the statue and it shall be whole as it was before. And Marcellus, nothing doubting, but believing with his whole heart, before he took the water lifted up his hands and said: I believe in thee, O Lord Jesu Christ: for I am now proved by thine apostle Peter, whether I believe aright in thine holy name. Therefore I take water in mine hands, and in thy name do I sprinkle these stones that the statue may become whole as it was before. If, therefore, Lord, it be thy will that I continue in the body and suffer nothing at Caesar's hand, let this stone be whole as it was before. And he sprinkled the water upon the stones, and the statue became whole, whereat Peter exulted that Marcellus had not doubted in asking of the Lord, and Marcellus was exalted in spirit for that such a sign was first wrought by his hands; and he therefore believed with his whole heart

in the name of Jesus Christ the Son of God, by whom all things impossible are made possible.

XII.

But Simon within the house said thus to the dog: Tell Peter that I am not within. Whom the dog answered in the presence of Marcellus: Thou exceeding wicked and shameless one, enemy of all that live and believe on Christ Jesus, here is a dumb animal sent unto thee which hath received a human voice to confound thee and show thee to be a deceiver and a liar. Hast thou taken thought so long, to say at last: 'Tell him that I am not within?' Art thou not ashamed to utter thy feeble and useless words against Peter the minister and apostle of Christ, as if thou couldst hide thee from him that hath commanded me to speak against thee to thy face: and that not for thy sake but for theirs whom thou wast deceiving and sending unto destruction? Cursed therefore shalt thou be, thou enemy and corrupter of the way of the truth of Christ, who shall prove by fire that dieth not and in outer darkness, thine iniquities that thou hast committed. And having thus said, the dog went forth and the people followed him, leaving Simon alone. And the dog came unto Peter as he sat with the multitude that was come to see Peter's face, and the dog related what he had done unto Simon. And thus spake the dog unto the angel and apostle of the true God: Peter, thou wilt have a great contest with the enemy of Christ and his servants, and many that have been deceived by him shalt thou turn unto the faith; wherefore thou shalt receive from God the reward of thy work. And when the dog had said this he fell down at the apostle Peter's feet and gave up the ghost. And when the great multitude saw with amazement the dog speaking, they began then, some to throw themselves down at Peter's feet, and some said: Show us another sign, that we may believe in thee as the minister of the living God, for Simon also did many signs in our presence and therefore did we follow him.

XIII.

And Peter turned and saw a herring (sardine) hung in a window, and took it and said to the people: If ye now see this swimming in the water like a fish, will ye be able to believe in him whom I preach? And they said with one voice: Verily we will believe thee. Then he said -now there was a bath for swimming at hand: In thy name, O Jesu Christ, forasmuch as hitherto it is not believed in, in the sight of all these live and swim like a fish. And he cast the herring into the bath, and it lived and began to swim. And all the people saw the fish swimming, and it did not so at that hour only, lest it should be said that it was a delusion (phantasm), but he made it to swim for a long time, so that they brought much people from all quarters and showed them the herring that was made a living fish, so that certain of the people even cast bread to it; and they saw that it was whole. And seeing this, many followed Peter and believed in the Lord.

And they assembled themselves day and night unto the house of Narcissus the presbyter. And Peter discoursed unto them of the scriptures of the prophets and of those things which our Lord Jesus Christ had wrought both in word and in deeds.

XIV.

But Marcellus was confirmed daily by the signs which he saw wrought by Peter through the grace of Jesus Christ which he granted unto him. And Mareellus ran upon Simon as he sat in his house in the dining chamber, and cursed him and said unto him: Thou most adverse and pestilent of men, corrupter of my soul and my house, who wouldest have made me fall away from my Lord and Saviour Christ! and laying hands on him he commanded him to be thrust out of his house. And the servants having received such licence, covered him with reproaches; some buffeted his face, others beat him with sticks, others cast stones, others emptied out vessels full of filth upon his head, even those who on his account had fled from their master and been a long time fettered; and other their fellowservants of whom he had spoken evil to their master reproached him. saying to him: Now by the will of God who hath had mercy on us and on our master, do we recompense thee with a fit reward. And Simon, shrewdly beaten and cast out of the house, ran unto the house where Peter lodged, even the house of Narcissus, and standing at the gate cried out: Lo, here am I, Simon: come thou down, Peter, and I will convict thee that thou hast believed on a man which is a Jew and a carpenter's son.

XV.

And when it was told Peter that Simon had said this, Peter sent unto him a woman which had a sucking child, saying to her: Go down quickly, and thou wilt find one that seeketh me. For thee there is no need that thou answer him at all, but keep silence and hear what the child whom thou holdest shall say unto him. The woman therefore went down. Now the child whom she suckled was seven months old; and it received a man's voice and said unto Simon: O thou abhorred of God and men, and destruction of truth, and evil seed of all corruption, O fruit by nature unprofitable! but only for a short and little season shalt thou be seen, and thereafter eternal punishment is laid up for thee. Thou son of a shameless father, that never puttest forth thy roots for good but for poison, faithless generation void of all hope! thou wast not confounded when a dog reproved thee; I a child am compelled of God to speak, and not even now art thou ashamed. But even against thy will, on the sabbath day that cometh, another shall bring thee into the forum of Julius that it may be shown what manner of man thou art. Depart therefore from the gate wherein walk the feet of the holy; for thou shalt no more corrupt the innocent souls whom thou didst turn out of the way and make sad; in Christ, therefore, shall be shown thine evil nature, and thy devices shall be cut in pieces. And now speak I this last word unto thee: Jesus Christ saith to thee: Be thou stricken dumb in my name, and depart out of Rome until the sabbath that cometh. And forthwith he became dumb and his speech was bound; and he went out of Rome until the sabbath and abode in a stable. But the woman returned with the child unto Peter and told him and the rest of the brethren what the child had said unto Simon: and they magnified the Lord which had shown these things unto men.

XVI.

Now when the night fell, Peter, while yet waking, beheld Jesus clad in a vesture of brightness, smiling and saying unto him: Already is much people of the brotherhood returned through me and through the signs which thou hast wrought in my name. But thou shalt have a contest of the faith upon the sabbath that cometh, and many more of the Gentiles and of the Jews shall be converted in my name unto me who was reproached and mocked and spat upon. For I will be present with thee when thou askest for signs and wonders, and thou shalt convert many: but thou shalt have Simon opposing thee by the works of his father; yet all his works shall be shown to be charms and contrivances of sorcery. But now slack thou not, and whomsoever I shall send unto thee thou shalt establish in my name. And when it was light, he told the brethren how the Lord had appeared unto him and what he had commanded him:

XVII.

[[This episode, inserted most abruptly, is believed by Vouaux to have been inserted here by the compiler of the Greek original of the Vercelli Acts: but it was not composed by him, but transferred with very slight additions from the earlier part of the Acts-now lost- of which the scene was laid in Judaea. I incline to favour this view.)]]

But believe ye me, men and brethren, I drove this Simon out of Judaea where he did many evils with his magical charms, lodging in Judaea with a certain woman Eubula, who was of honourable estate in this world, having store of gold and pearls of no small price. Here did Simon enter in by stealth with two others like unto himself, and none of the household saw them two, but Simon only, and by means of a spell they took away all the woman's gold, and disappeared. But Eubula, when she found what was done, began to torture her household, saying: Ye have taken occasion by this man of God and spoiled me, when ye saw him entering in to me to honour a mere woman; but his name is as the name of the Lord. As I fasted for three days and prayed that this matter should be made plain, I saw in a vision Italicus and Antulus (Antyllus?) whom I had instructed in the name of the Lord, and a boy naked and chained giving me a wheaten loaf and saying unto me: Peter, endure yet two days and thou shalt see the mighty works of God. As for all that is lost out of the house of Eubula, Simon hath used art magic and hath caused a delusion, and with two others hath stolen it away: whom thou shalt see on the third day at the ninth hour, at the gate which leadeth unto Neapolis, selling unto a goldsmith by name Agrippinus a young satyr of gold of two pound weight, having in it a precious stone. But for thee there is no need that thou touch it, lest thou be defiled; but let there be with thee some of the matron's servants, and thou shalt show them the shop of the goldsmith and depart from them. For by reason of this matter shall many believe on the name of the Lord, and all that which these men by their devices and wickedness have oft-times stolen shall be openly showed. When I heard that, I went unto Eubula and found her sitting with her clothes rent and her hair disordered, mourning; unto whom I said: Eubula, rise up from thy mourning and compose thy face and order thy hair and put on

THE ACTS OF PETER

raiment befitting thee, and pray unto the Lord Jesus Christ that judgeth every soul: for he is the invisible Son of God, by whom thou must be saved, if only thou repent with thine whole heart of thy former sins: and receive thou power from him; for behold, by me the Lord saith to thee: Thou shalt find all whatsoever thou hast lost. And after thou hast received them, take thou care that he find thee, that thou mayest renounce this present world and seek for everlasting refreshment. Hearken therefore unto this: Let certain of thy people keep watch at the gate that leadeth to Neapolis on the day after to-morrow at about the ninth hour, and they shall see two young men having a young satyr of gold, of two pound weight, set with gems, as a vision hath shown me: which thing they will offer for sale to one Agrippinus of the household of godliness and of the faith which is in the Lord Jesus Christ: by whom it shall be showed thee that thou shouldest believe in the living God and not on Simon the magician, the unstable devil, who hath desired that thou shouldest remain in sorrow, and thine innocent household be tormented; who by fair words and speech only hath deceived thee, and with his mouth only spake of godliness, whereas he is wholly possessed of ungodliness. For when thou didst think to keep holy-day, and settedst up thine idol and didst veil it and set out all thine ornaments upon a table (round three-legged table), he brought in two young men whom no man of yours saw, by a magic charm, and they stole away thine ornaments and were no more seen. But his device hath had no success (place); for my God hath manifested it unto me, to the end thou shouldest not be deceived, neither perish in hell, for those sins which thou hast committed ungodly and contrary to God, who is full of all truth, and the righteous judge of quick and dead; and there is none other hope of life unto men save through him, by whom those things which thou hast lost are recovered unto thee: and now do thou gain thine own soul.

But she cast herself down before my feet, saying: O man, who thou art I know not; but him I received as a servant of God, and whatsoever he asked of me to give it unto the poor, I gave much by his hands, and beside that I did give much unto him. What hurt did I do him, that he should contrive all this against mine house? Unto whom Peter said: There is no faith to be put in words, but in acts and deeds: but we must go on with that we have begun. So I left her and went with two stewards of Eubula and came to Agrippinus and said to him: See that thou take note of these men; for to-morrow two young men will come to thee, desiring to sell thee a young satyr of gold set with jewels, which belongeth to the mistress of these: and thou shalt take it as it were to look upon it, and praise the work of the craftsman, and then when these come in, God will bring the rest to the proof. And on the next day the stewards of the matron came about the ninth hour, and also those young men, willing to sell unto Agrippinus the young satyr of gold. And they being forthwith taken, it was reported unto the matron, and she in distress of mind came to the deputy, and with a loud voice declared all that had befallen her. And when Pompeius the deputy beheld her in distress of mind, who never had come forth abroad, he forthwith rose up from the judgement seat and went unto the praetorium, and bade those men to be brought and tortured; and while they were being tormented they confessed that they did it in the service of Simon, which, said they, persuaded us thereto with money. And being tortured a long time, they confessed that all that Eubula had lost was laid up under the earth in a cave on the other side of the gate, and many other things besides. And when Pompeius heard this, he rose up to go unto the gate, with those two men, each of them bound with two chains. And lo, Simon came in at the gate, seeking them because they tarried long. And he seeth a great multitude coming, and those two bound with chains; and he understood and betook him to flight,

302

and appeared no more in Judaea unto this day. But Eubula, when she had recovered all her goods, gave them for the service of the poor, and believed on the Lord Jesus Christ and was comforted; and despised and renounced this world, and gave unto the widows and fatherless, and clothed the poor. And after a long time she received her rest (sleep). Now these things, dearly beloved brethren, were done in Judaea, whereby he that is called the angel of Satan was driven out thence.

XVIII.

Brethren, dearest and most beloved, let us fast together and pray unto the Lord. For he that drove him out thence is able also to root him out of this place: and let him grant unto us power to withstand him and his magical charms, and to prove that he is the angel of Satan. For on the sabbath our Lord shall bring him, though he would not, unto the forum of Julius. Let us therefore bow our knees unto Christ, which heareth us, though we cry not; it is he that seeth us, though he be not seen with these eyes, yet is he in us: if we will, he will not forsake us. Let us therefore purify our souls of every evil temptation, and God will not depart from us. Yea, if we but wink with our eyes, he is present with us.

XIX.

Now after these things were spoken by Peter, Marcellus also came in, and said: Peter, I have for thee cleansed mine whole house from the footsteps (traces) of Simon, and wholly done away even his wicked dust. For I took water and called upon the holy name of Jesus Christ, together with mine other servants which belong unto him, and sprinkled all my house and all the dining chambers and all the porticoes, even unto the outer gate, and said: I know that thou, Lord Jesu Christ, art pure and untouched of any uncleanness: so let mine enemy and adversary be driven out from before thy face. And now, thou blessed one, have I bidden the widows and old women to assemble unto thee in my house which is purified (MS. common), that they may pray with us. And they shall receive every one a piece of gold in the name of the ministry (service), that they may be called indeed servants of Christ. And all else is now prepared for the service. I entreat thee, therefore, O blessed Peter, consent unto their request, so that thou also pay honour unto (ornament) their prayers in my stead; let us then go and take Narcissus also, and whosoever of the brethren are here. So then Peter consented unto his simplicity, to fulfil his desire, and went forth with him and the rest of the brethren.

XX.

But Peter entered in, and beheld one of the aged women, a widow, that was blind, and her daughter giving her her hand and leading her into Marcellus' house; and Peter said unto her: Come hither, mother: from this day forward Jesus giveth thee his right hand, by whom we have light unapproachable which no darkness hideth; who saith unto thee by me: Open thine eyes and see, and walk by thyself. And forthwith the widow saw Peter laying his hand upon her.

And Peter entered into the dining-hall and saw that the Gospel was being read, and he rolled up the book and said: Ye men that believe and hope in Christ, learn in what manner the holy Scripture of our Lord ought to be declared: whereof we by his grace wrote that which we could receive, though yet it appear unto you feeble, yet according to our power, even that which can be endured to be borne by (or instilled into) human flesh. We ought therefore first to know the will and the goodness of God, how that when error was everywhere spread abroad, and many thousands of men were being cast down into perdition, God was moved by his mercy to show himself in another form and in the likeness of man, concerning which neither the Jews nor we were able worthily to be enlightened. For every one of us according as he could contain the sight, saw, as he was able.

Now will I expound unto you that which was newly read unto you. Our Lord, willing that I should behold his majesty in the holy mount -I, when I with the sons of Zebedee saw the brightness of his light, fell as one dead and shut mine eyes, and heard such a voice from him as I am not able to describe, and thought myself to be blinded by his brightness. And when I recovered (breathed again) a little I said within myself: Peradventure my Lord hath brought me hither that he might blind me. And I said: If this also be thy will, Lord, I resist not. And he gave me his hand and raised me up; and when I arose I saw him again in such a form as I was able to take in. As, therefore, the merciful God, dearly beloved brethren, carried our infirmities and bare our sins (as the prophet saith: He beareth our sins and suffereth for us; but we did esteem him to be in affliction and smitten with plagues), for he is in the Father and the Father in him -he also is himself the fulness of all majesty, who hath shown unto us all his good things: he did eat and drink for our sakes, himself being neither an-hungered nor athirst; he carried and bare reproaches for our sakes, he died and rose again because of us; who both defended me when I sinned and comforted me by his greatness, and will comfort you also that ye may love him: this God who is great and small, fair and foul, young and old, seen in time and unto eternity invisible; whom the hand of man hath not held, yet is he held by his servants; whom no flesh hath seen, yet now seeth; who is the word proclaimed by the prophets and now appearing (so Gk.: Lat. not heard of but now known); not subject to suffering, but having now made trial of suffering for our sake (or like unto us); never chastised, yet now chastised; who was before the world and hath been comprehended in time; the great beginning of all principality, yet delivered over unto princes; beautiful, but among us lowly; seen of all yet foreseeing all (MS. foul of view, yet foreseeing). This Jesus ye have, brethren, the door, the light, the way,

the bread, the water, the life, the resurrection, the refreshment, the pearl, the treasure, the seed, the abundance (harvest), the mustard seed, the vine, the plough, the grace, the faith, the word: he is all things and there is none other greater than he. Unto him be praise, world without end. Amen.

XXI.
And when the ninth hour was fully come, they rose up to make prayer. And behold certain widows, of the aged, unknown to Peter, which sat there, being blind and not believing, cried out, saying unto Peter: We sit together here, O Peter, hoping and believing in Christ Jesus: as therefore thou hast made one of us to see, we entreat thee, lord Peter, grant unto us also his mercy and pity. But Peter said to them: If there be in you the faith that is in Christ, if it be firm in you, then perceive in your mind that which ye see not with your eyes, and though your ears are closed, yet let them be open in your mind within you. These eyes shall again be shut, seeing nought but men and oxen and dumb beasts and stones and sticks; but not every eye seeth Jesus Christ. Yet now, Lord, let thy sweet and holy name succour these persons; do thou touch their eyes; for thou art able -that these may see with their eyes.
And when all had prayed, the hall wherein they were shone as when it lighteneth, even with such a light as cometh in the clouds, yet not such a light as that of the daytime, but unspeakable, invisible, such as no man can describe, even such that we were beside ourselves with bewilderment, calling on the Lord and saying: Have mercy, Lord, upon us thy servants: what we are able to bear, that, Lord, give thou us; for this we can neither see nor endure. And as we lay there, only those widows stood up which were blind; and the bright light which appeared unto us entered into their eyes and made them to see. Unto whom Peter said: Tell us what ye saw. And they said: We saw an old man of such comeliness as we are not able to declare to thee; but others

said: We saw a young man; and others: We saw a boy touching our eyes delicately, and so were our eyes opened. Peter therefore magnified the Lord, saying: Thou only art the Lord God, and of what lips have we need to give thee due praise? and how can we give thee thanks according to thy mercy? Therefore, brethren, as I told you but a little while since, God that is constant is greater than our thoughts, even as we have learned of these aged widows, how that they beheld the Lord in divers forms.

XXII.

And having exhorted them all to think upon (understand) the Lord with their whole heart, he began together with Marcellus and the rest of the brethren to minister unto the virgins of the Lord, and to rest until the morning.
Unto whom Marcellus said: Ye holy and inviolate virgins of the Lord, hearken: Ye have a place to abide in, for these things that are called mine, whose are they save yours? depart not hence, but refresh yourselves: for upon the sabbath which cometh, even to-morrow, Simon hath a controversy with Peter the holy one of God: for as the Lord hath ever been with him, lo will Christ the Lord now stand for him as his apostle. For Peter hath continued tasting nothing, but fasting yet a day, that he may overcome the wicked adversary and persecutor of the Lord's truth. For lo, my young men are come announcing that they have seen scaffolds being set up in the forum, and much people saying: To-morrow at daybreak two Jews are to contend here concerning the teaching (?) of God. Now therefore let us watch until the morning, praying and beseeching our Lord Jesus Christ to hear our prayers on behalf of Peter. And Marcellus turned to sleep for a short space, and awoke and said unto Peter: O Peter, thou apostle of Christ, let us go boldly unto that which lieth before us. For just now when I turned myself to sleep for a little, I beheld thee sitting in a high place and before thee a great multitude, and a woman

exceeding foul, in sight like an Ethiopian, not an Egyptian, but altogether black and filthy, clothed in rags, and with an iron collar about her neck and chains upon her hands and feet, dancing. And when thou sawest me thou saidst to me with a loud voice: Marcellus the whole power of Simon and of his God is this woman that danceth; do thou behead her. And I said to thee: Brother Peter, I am a senator of a high race, and I have never defiled my hands, neither killed so much as a sparrow at any time. And thou hearing it didst begin to cry out yet more: Come thou, our true sword, Jesu Christ. and cut not off only the head of this devil, but hew all her limbs in pieces in the sight of all these Whom I have approved in thy service. And immediately one like unto thee, O Peter, having a sword, hewed her in pieces: so that I looked earnestly upon you both, both on thee and on him that cut in pieces that devil, and marvelled greatly to see how alike ye were. And I awaked, and have told unto thee these signs of Christ. And when Peter heard it he was the more filled with courage, for that Marcellus had seen these things, knowing that the Lord alway careth for his own. And being joyful and refreshed by these words, he rose up to go unto the forum.

XXIII.

Now the brethren were gathered together, and all that were in Rome, and took places every one for a piece of gold: there came together also the senators and the prefects and those in authority. And Peter came and stood in the midst, and all cried out: Show us, O Peter, who is thy God and what is his greatness which hath given thee confidence. Begrudge not the Romans; they are lovers of the gods. We have had proof of Simon, let us have it of thee; convince us, both of you, whom we ought truly to believe. And as they said these things, Simon also came in, and standing in trouble of mind at Peter's side, at first he looked at him. And after long silence Peter said: Ye men of Rome, be ye true judges unto us, for I say that I have believed on the living and true God; and I promise to give you proofs of him, which are known unto me, as many among you also can bear witness. For ye see that this man is now rebuked and silent, knowing that I drove him out of Judaea because of the deceits which he practised upon Eubula, an honourable and simple woman, by his art magic; and being driven out from thence, he is come hither, thinking to escape notice among you; and lo, he standeth face to face with me. Say now, Simon, didst thou not at Jerusalem fall at my feet and Paul's, when thou sawest the healings that were wrought by our hands, and say: I pray you take of me a payment as much as ye will, that I may be able to lay hands on men and do such mighty works? And we when we heard it cursed thee, saying: Dost thou think to tempt us as if we desired to possess money? And now, fearest thou not at all? My name is Peter, because the Lord Christ vouchsafed to call me 'prepared for all things': for I trust in the living God by whom I shall put down thy sorceries. Now let him do in your presence the wonders which he did aforetime: and what I have now said of him, will ye not believe it?

But Simon said: Thou presumest to speak of Jesus of Nazareth, the son of a carpenter, and a carpenter himself, whose birth is recorded (or whose race dwelleth) in Judaea. Hear thou, Peter: the Romans have understanding: they are no fools. And he turned to the people and said: Ye men of Rome, is God born? is he crucified? he that hath a master is no God. And when he so spake, many said: Thou sayest well, Simon.

XXIV.

But Peter said: Anathema upon thy words against (or in) Christ! Presumest thou to speak thus, whereas the prophet saith of him: Who shall declare his generation? And another prophet saith: And we saw him and he had no beauty nor comeliness. And: In the last times

shall a child be born of the Holy Ghost: his mother knoweth not a man, neither doth any man say that he is his father. And again he saith: She hath brought forth and not brought forth.[From the apocryphal Ezekiel (lost)] And again: Is it a small thing for you to weary men (lit. Is it a small thing that ye make a contest for men)? Behold, a virgin shall conceive in the womb. And another prophet saith, honouring the Father: Neither did we hear her voice, neither did a midwife come in.[From the Ascension of Isaiah, xi. 14] Another prophet saith: Born not of the womb of a woman, but from a heavenly place came he down. And: A stone was cut out without hands, and smote all the kingdoms. And: The stone which the builders rejected, the same is become the head of the corner; and he calleth him a stone elect, precious. And again a prophet saith concerning him: And behold, I saw one like the Son of man coming upon a cloud. And what more? O ye men of Rome, if ye knew the Scriptures of the prophets, I would expound all unto you: by which Scriptures it was necessary that this should be spoken in a mystery, and that the kingdom of God should be perfected. But these things shall be opened unto you hereafter. Now turn I unto thee, Simon: do thou some one thing of those wherewith thou didst before deceive them, and I will bring it to nought through my Lord Jesus Christ. And Simon plucked up his boldness and said: If the prefect allow it (prepare yourselves and delay not for my sake).

XXV.

But the prefect desired to show patience unto both, that he might not appear to do aught unjustly. And the prefect put forward one of his servants and said thus unto Simon: Take this man and deliver him to death. And to Peter he said: And do thou revive him. And unto the people the prefect said: It is now for you to judge whether of these two is acceptable unto God, he that killeth or he that maketh alive. And straightway

Simon spake in the ear of the lad and made him speechless, and he died. And as there began to be a murmuring among the people, one of the widows who were nourished (refreshed) in Marcellus' house, standing behind the multitude, cried out: O Peter, servant of God, my son is dead, the only one that I had. And the people made place for her and led her unto Peter: and she cast herself down at his feet, saying: I had one only son, which with his hands (shoulders) furnished me with nourishment: he raised me up, he carried me: now that he is dead, who shall reach me a hand? Unto whom Peter said: Go, with these for witness, and bring hither thy son, that they may see and be able to believe that by the power of God he is raised, and that this man (Simon) may behold it and fail (or, and she when she saw him, fell down). And Peter said to the young men: We have need of some young men, and, moreover, of such as will believe. And forthwith thirty young men arose, which were prepared to carry her or to bring thither her son that was dead. And whereas the widow was hardly returned to herself, the young men took her up; and she was crying out and saying: Lo, my son, the servant of Christ hath sent unto thee: tearing her hair and her face. Now the young men which were come examined (Gk. apparently, held) the lad's nostrils to see whether he were indeed dead; and seeing that he was dead of a truth, they had compassion on the old woman and said: If thou so will, mother, and hast confidence in the God of Peter, we will take him up and carry him thither that he may raise him up and restore him unto thee.

XXVI.

And as they said these things, the prefect (in the forum, Lat.), looking earnestly upon Peter (said: What sayest thou Peter?) Behold my lad is dead, who also is dear unto the emperor, and I spared him not, though I had with me other young men; but I desired rather to make trial (tempt) of thee and of the God whom thou (preachest), whether ye be true, and therefore I would have this lad die. And Peter said: God is not tempted nor proved, O Agrippa, but if he be loved and entreated he heareth them that are worthy. But since now my God and Lord Jesus Christ is tempted among you, who hath done so great signs and wonders by my hands to turn you from your sins -now also in the sight of all do thou, Lord, at my word, by thy power raise up him whom Simon hath slain by touching him. And Peter said unto the master of the lad: Go, take hold on his right hand, and thou shalt have him alive and walking with thee. And Agrippa the prefect ran and went to the lad and took his hand and raised him up. And all the multitude seeing it cried: One is the God, one is the God of Peter.

XXVII.

In the meanwhile the widow's son also was brought upon a bed by the young men, and the people made way for them and brought them unto Peter. And Peter lifted up his eyes unto heaven and stretched forth his hands and said: O holy Father of thy Son Jesus Christ. who hast granted us thy power, that we may through thee ask and obtain, and despise all that is in the world, and follow thee only, who art seen of few and wouldest be known of many: shine thou about us, Lord, enlighten us, appear thou, raise up the son of this aged widow, which cannot help herself without her son. And I, repeating the word of Christ my Lord, say unto thee: Young man, arise and walk with thy mother so long as thou canst do her good; and thereafter shalt thou serve me after a higher sort, ministering in the lot of a deacon of the bishop (or, and of a bishop). And immediately the dead man rose up, and the multitudes saw it and marvelled, and the people cried out: Thou art God the Saviour, thou, the God of Peter, the invisible God, the Saviour. And they spake among themselves, marvelling indeed at the power of a man that called upon his Lord with a word; and they received it unto sanctification.

XXVIII.

The fame of it therefore being spread throughout the city, there came the mother of a certain senator, and cast herself into the midst of the people, and fell at Peter's feet, saying: I have learned from my people that thou art a servant of the merciful God, and dost impart his grace unto all them that desire this light. Impart therefore the light unto my son, for I know that thou begrudgest none; turn not away from a matron that entreateth thee. Unto whom Peter said: Wilt thou believe on my God, by whom thy son shall be raised? And the mother said with a loud voice, weeping: I believe, O Peter, I believe! and all the people cried out: Grant the mother her son. But Peter said: Let him be brought hither before all these. And Peter turned himself to the people and said: Ye men of Rome, I also am one of yourselves, and bear a man's body and am a sinner, but have obtained mercy: look not therefore upon me as though I did by mine own power that which I do, but by the power of my Lord Jesus Christ, who is the judge of quick and dead. In him do I believe and by him am I sent, and have confidence when I call upon him to raise the dead. Go thou therefore also, O woman, and cause thy son to be brought hither and to rise again. And the woman passed through the midst of the people and went into the street, running, with great joy, and believing in her mind she came unto her house, and by means of her young men she took him up and came unto the forum. Now she bade the young men put caps [pilei, a sign that they were now freed.] on their heads, and to walk before the bier, and all that she had determined to burn upon the body of her son to be borne before his bier; and when Peter saw it he had compassion upon the dead body and upon her. And she came unto the multitude, while all bewailed her; and a great crowd of senators and matrons followed after, to behold the wonderful works of God: for this Nicostratus which was dead was exceeding noble and beloved of the senate. And they brought him and set him down before Peter. And Peter called for silence, and with a loud voice said: Ye men of Rome, let there now be a just judgement betwixt me and Simon; and judge ye whether of us two believeth in the living God, he or I. Let him raise up the body that lieth here, and believe in him as the angel of God. But if he be not able, and I call upon my God and restore the son alive unto his mother, then believe ye that this man is a sorcerer and a deceiver, which is entertained among you. And when all they heard these things, they thought that it was right which Peter had spoken, and they encouraged Simon, saying: Now, if there be aught in thee, show it openly! either overcome, or thou shall be overcome! (or, convince us, or thou shalt be convicted). Why standest thou still? Come, begin! But Simon, when he saw them all instant with him, stood silent; and thereafter, when he saw the people silent and looking upon him, Simon cried out, saying: Ye men of Rome, if ye behold the dead man arise, will ye cast Peter out of the city? And all the people said: We will not only cast him out, but on the very instant will we burn him with fire.

Then Simon went to the head of the dead man and stooped down and thrice raised himself up (or, and said thrice: Raise thyself), and showed the people that he (the dead) lifted his head and moved it, and opened his eyes and bowed himself a little unto Simon. And straightway they began to ask for wood and torches, wherewith to burn Peter. But Peter receiving strength of Christ, lifted up his voice and said unto them that cried out against him: Now see I, ye people of Rome, that ye are -I must not say fools and vain, so long as your eyes and your ears and your hearts are blinded. How long shall your understanding be darkened? see ye not that ye are bewitched, supposing that a dead man is raised, who hath not lifted himself up? It would have sufficed me, ye men of Rome, to hold my peace and die without speaking, and to leave you among the deceits of this world; but I have the chastisement of fire unquenchable before mine eyes. If therefore it seem good unto you, let the dead man speak, let him arise if he liveth, let him loose his jaw that is bound, with his hands, let him call upon his mother, let him say unto you that cry out: Wherefore cry ye? let him beckon unto us with his hand. If now ye would see that he is dead, and yourselves bewitched, let this man depart from the bier, who hath persuaded you to depart from Christ, and ye shall see that the dead man is such as ye saw him brought hither. But Agrippa the prefect had no longer patience, but thrust away Simon with his own hands, and again the dead man lay as he was before. And the people were enraged, and turned away from the sorcery of Simon and began to cry out: Hearken, O Caesar! if now the dead riseth not, let Simon burn instead of Peter, for verily he hath blinded us. But Peter stretched forth his hand and said: O men of Rome, have patience! I say not unto you that if the lad be raised Simon shall burn; for if I say it, ye will do it. The people cried out: Against thy will, Peter, we will do it. Unto whom Peter said: If ye continue in this mind the lad shall not arise: for we know not to render evil for evil, but we have learned to love our enemies and pray for our persecutors. For if even this man can repent, it were better; for God will not remember evil. Let him come, therefore, into the light of Christ; but if he cannot, let him possess the part of his father the devil, but let not your hands be defiled. And when he had thus spoken unto the people, he went unto the lad, and before he raised him, he said to his mother: These young men whom thou hast set free in the honour of thy son, can yet serve their God when he liveth, being free; for I know that the soul of some is hurt if they shall see thy son arise and know that these shall yet be in bondage: but let them all continue free and receive their sustenance as they did before, for thy son is about to rise again; and let them

be with him. And Peter looked long upon her, to see her thoughts. And the mother of the lad said: What other can I do? therefore before the prefect I say: whatsoever I was minded to burn upon the body of my son, let them possess it. And Peter said: Let the residue be distributed unto the widows. Then Peter rejoiced in soul and said in the spirit: O Lord that art merciful, Jesu Christ, show thyself unto thy Peter that calleth upon thee like as thou hast always shown him mercy and loving-kindness: and in the presence of all these which have obtained freedom, that these may become thy servants, let Nicostratus now arise. And Peter touched the lad's side and said: Arise. And the lad arose and put off his grave clothes and sat up and loosed his jaw, and asked for other raiment; and he came down from the bier and said unto Peter: I pray thee, O man of God, let us go unto our Lord Christ whom I saw speaking with me; who also showed me unto thee and said to thee: Bring him hither unto me, for he is mine. And when Peter heard this of the lad, he was strengthened yet more in soul by the help of the Lord; and Peter said unto the people: Ye men of Rome, it is thus that the dead are raised up, thus do they converse, thus do they arise and walk, and live so long time as God willeth. Now therefore, ye that have come together unto the sight, if ye turn not from these your evil ways, and from all your gods that are made with hands, and from all uncleanness and concupiscence, receive fellowship with Christ, believing, that ye may obtain everlasting life.

XXIX.

And in the same hour they worshipped him as a God, falling down at his feet, and the sick whom they had at home, that he might heal them.
But the prefect seeing that so great a multitude waited upon Peter, signified to Peter that he should withdraw himself: and Peter told the people to come unto Marcellus' house. But the mother of the lad besought Peter to set foot in her house. But Peter had

appointed to be with Marcellus on the Lord's day, to see the widows even as Marcellus had promised, to minister unto them with his own hands. The lad therefore that was risen again said: I depart not from Peter. And his mother, glad and rejoicing, went unto her own house. And on the next day after the sabbath she came to Marcellus' house bringing unto Peter two thousand pieces of gold, and saying unto Peter: Divide these among the virgins of Christ which serve him. But the lad that was risen from the dead, when he saw that he had given nothing to any man, went home and opened the press and himself offered four thousand pieces of gold, saying unto Peter: Lo, I also which was raised, offer a double offering, and myself also from this day forward as a speaking sacrifice unto God.

[[Here begins the original Greek text as preserved in one of our two manuscripts (that at Mt. Athos). The second (Patmos) manuscript begins, as do the versions, at ch. xxxiii. The Greek and not the Latin is followed in the translation.]]

XXX.

Now on the Lord's day as Peter discoursed unto the brethren and exhorted them unto the faith of Christ, there being present many of the senate and many knights and rich women and matrons, and being confirmed in the faith, one woman that was there, exceeding rich, which was surnamed Chryse because every vessel of hers was of gold -for from her birth she never used a vessel of silver or glass, but golden ones only- said unto Peter: Peter, thou servant of God, he whom thou callest God appeared unto me in a dream and said: Chryse, carry thou unto Peter my minister ten thousand pieces of gold; for thou owest them to him. I have therefore brought them, fearing lest some harm should be done me by him that appeared unto me, which also departed unto heaven. And so saying,

she laid down the money and departed. And Peter seeing it glorified the Lord, for that they that were in need should be refreshed. Certain, therefore, of them that were there said unto him: Peter, hast thou not done ill to receive the money of her? for she is ill spoken of throughout all Rome for fornication, and because she keepeth not to one husband, yea, she even hath to do with the young men of her house. Be not therefore a partner with the table of Chryse, but let that which came from her be returned unto her. But Peter hearing it laughed and said to the brethren: What this woman is in the rest of her way of life, I know not, but in that I have received this money, I did it not foolishly; for she did pay it as a debtor unto Christ, and giveth it unto the servants of Christ: for he himself hath provided for them.

XXXI.

And they brought unto him also the sick on the sabbath, beseeching that they might recover of their diseases. And many were healed that were sick of the palsy, and the gout, and fevers tertian and quartan, and of every disease of the body were they healed, believing in the name of Jesus Christ, and very many were added every day unto the grace of the Lord.

But Simon the magician, after a few days were past, promised the multitude to convict Peter that he believed not in the true God but was deceived. And when he did many lying wonders, they that were firm in the faith derided him. For in diningchambers he made certain spirits enter in, which were only an appearance, and not existing in truth. And what should I more say? though he had oft-times been convicted of sorcory, he made lame men seem whole for a little space, and blind likewise, and once he appeared to make many dead to live and move, as he did with Nicostratus (Gk. Stratonicus). But Peter followed him throughout and convicted him always unto the beholders: and when he now made a sorry figure and was derided by the people of Rome and disbelieved for that he never succeeded m the things which he promised to perform, being in such a plight at last he said to them: Men of Rome, ye think now that Peter hath prevailed over me, as more powerful, and ye pay more heed to him: ye are deceived. For to-morrow I shall forsake you, godless and impious that ye are, and fly up unto God whose Power I am, though I am become weak. Whereas, then, ye have fallen, I am He that standeth, and I shall go up to my Father and say unto him: Me also, even thy son that standeth, have they desired to pull down; but I consented not unto them, and am returned back unto myself.

XXXII.

And already on the morrow a great multitude assembled at the Sacred Way to see him flying. And Peter came unto the place, having seen a vision (or, to see the sight), that he might convict him in this also; for when Simon entered into Rome, he amazed the multitudes by flying: but Peter that convicted him was then not yet living at Rome: which city he thus deceived by illusion, so that some were carried away by him (amazed at him).

So then this man standing on an high place beheld Peter and began to say: Peter, at this time when I am going up before all this people that behold me, I say unto thee: If thy God is able, whom the Jews put to death, and stoned you that were chosen of him, let him show that faith in him is faith in God, and let it appear at this time, if it be worthy of God. For I, ascending up, will show myself unto all this multitude, who I am. And behold when he was lifted up on high, and all beheld him raised up above all Rome and the temples thereof and the mountains, the faithful looked toward Peter. And Peter seeing the strangeness of the sight cried unto the Lord Jesus Christ: If thou suffer this man to accomplish that which he hath set about, now will all they that have believed on thee be offended, and the signs and wonders which thou hast given them through me will not be

believed: hasten thy grace, O Lord, and let him fall from the height and be disabled; and let him not die but be brought to nought, and break his leg in three places. And he fell from the height and brake his leg in three places. Then every man cast stones at him and went away home, and thenceforth believed Peter.

But one of the friends of Simon came quickly out of the way (or arrived from a journey), Gemellus by name, of whom Simon had received much money, having a Greek woman to wife, and saw him that he had broken his leg, and said: O Simon, if the Power of God is broken to pieces, shall not that God whose Power thou art, himself be blinded? Gemellus therefore also ran and followed Peter, saying unto him: I also would be of them that believe on Christ. And Peter said: Is there any that grudgeth it, my brother? come thou and sit with us.

But Simon in his affliction found some to carry him by night on a bed from Rome unto Aricia; and he abode there a space, and was brought thence unto Terracina to one Castor that was banished from Rome upon an accusation of sorcery. And there he was sorely cut (Lat. by two physicians), and so Simon the angel of Satan came to his end.

[[Here the Martyrdom proper begins in the Patmos MS. and the versions.]]

XXXIII.

Now Peter was in Rome rejoicing in the Lord with the brethren, and giving thanks night and day for the multitude which was brought daily unto the holy name by the grace of the Lord. And there were gathered also unto Peter the concubines of Agrippa the prefect, being four, Agrippina and Nicaria and Euphemia and Doris; and they, hearing the word concerning chastity and all the oracles of the Lord, were smitten in their souls, and agreeing together to remain pure from the bed of Agrippa they were vexed by him.

Now as Agrippa was perplexed and grieved concerning them -and he loved them greatly- he observed and sent men privily to see whither they went, and found that they went unto Peter. He said therefore unto them when they returned: That Christian hath taught you to have no dealings with me: know ye that I will both destroy you, and burn him alive. They, then, endured to suffer all manner of evil at Agrippa's hand, if only they might not suffer the passion of love, being strengthened by the might of Jesus.

XXXIV.

And a certain woman which was exceeding beautiful, the wife of Albinus, Caesar's friend, by name Xanthippe, came, she also, unto Peter, with the rest of the matrons, and withdrew herself, she also, from Albinus. He therefore being mad, and loving Xanthippe, and marvelling that she would not sleep even upon the same bed with him, raged like a wild beast and would have dispatched Peter; for he knew that he was the cause of her separating from his bed. Many other women also, loving the word of chastity, separated themselves from their husbands, because they desired them to worship God in sobriety and cleanness. And whereas there was great trouble in Rome, Albinus made known his state unto Agrippa, saying to him: Either do thou avenge me of Peter that hath withdrawn my wife, or I will avenge myself. And Agrippa said: I have suffered the same at his hand, for he hath withdrawn my concubines. And Albinus said unto him: Why then tarriest thou, Agrippa? let us find him and put him to death for a dealer in curious arts, that we may have our wives again, and avenge them also which are not able to put him to death, whose wives also he hath parted from them.

XXXV.

And as they considered these things, Xanthippe took knowledge of the counsel of her husband with Agrippa, and sent and showed Peter, that he might depart from Rome. And the rest of the brethren, together with Marcellus, besought him to depart. But Peter said unto them: Shall we be runaways, brethren? and they said to him: Nay, but that thou mayest yet be able to serve the Lord. And he obeyed the brethren's voice and went forth alone, saying: Let none of you come forth with me, but I will go forth alone, having changed the fashion of mine apparel. And as he went forth of the city, he saw the Lord entering into Rome. And when he saw him, he said: Lord, whither goest thou thus (or here)? And the Lord said unto him: I go into Rome to be crucified. And Peter said unto him: Lord, art thou (being) crucified again? He said unto him: Yea, Peter, I am (being) crucified again. And Peter came to himself: and having beheld the Lord ascending up into heaven, he returned to Rome, rejoicing, and glorifying the Lord, for that he said: I am being crucified: the which was about to befall Peter.

XXXVI.

He went up therefore again unto the brethren, and told them that which had been seen by him: and they lamented in soul, weeping and saying: We beseech thee, Peter, take thought for us that are young. And Peter said unto them: If it be the Lord's will, it cometh to pass, even if we will it not; but for you, the Lord is able to stablish you in his faith, and will found you therein and make you spread abroad, whom he himself hath planted, that ye also may plant others through him. But I, so long as the Lord will that I be in the flesh, resist not; and again if he take me to him I rejoice and am glad.

And while Peter thus spake, and all the brethren wept, behold four soldiers took him and led him unto Agrippa. And he in his madness (disease) commanded him to be crucified on an accusation of godlessness.

The whole multitude of the brethren therefore ran together, both of rich and poor, orphans and widows, weak and strong, desiring to see and to rescue Peter, while the people shouted with one voice, and would not be silenced: What wrong hath Peter done, O Agrippa? Wherein hath he hurt thee? tell the Romans! And others said: We fear lest if this man die, his Lord destroy us all.

And Peter when he came unto the place stilled the people and said: Ye men that are soldiers of Christ! ye men that hope in Christ! remember the signs and wonders which ye have seen wrought through me, remember the compassion of God, how many cures he hath wrought for you. Wait for him that cometh and shall reward every man according to his doings. And now be ye not bitter against Agrippa; for he is the minister of his father's working. And this cometh to pass at all events, for the Lord hath manifested unto me that which befalleth. But why delay I and draw not near unto the cross?

XXXVII.

And having approached and standing by the cross he began to say: O name of the cross, thou hidden mystery! O grace ineffable that is pronounced in the name of the cross! O nature of man, that cannot be separated from God! O love (friendship) unspeakable and inseparable, that cannot be shown forth by unclean lips! I seize thee now, I that am at the end of my delivery hence (or, of my coming hither). I will declare thee, what thou art: I will not keep silence of the mystery of the cross which of old was shut and hidden from my soul. Let not the cross be unto you which hope in Christ, this which appeareth: for it is another thing, different from that which appeareth, even this passion which is according to that of Christ. And now above all, because ye that can hear are able to hear it of me, that am at the last and final hour of my life, hearken: Separate your souls from every thing that is of the senses, from every thing that appeareth, and does not exist in truth. Blind these eyes of yours, close these ears of yours,

put away your doings that are seen; and ye shall perceive that which concerneth Christ, and the whole mystery of your salvation: and let thus much be said unto you that hear, as if it had not been spoken. But now it is time for thee, Peter, to deliver up thy body unto them that take it. Receive it then, ye unto whom it belongeth. I beseech you the executioners, crucify me thus, with the head downward and not otherwise: and the reason wherefore, I will tell unto them that hear.

XXXVIII.

And when they had hanged him up after the manner he desired, he began again to say: Ye men unto whom it belongeth to hear, hearken to that which I shall declare unto you at this especial time as I hang here. Learn ye the mystery of all nature, and the beginning of all things, what it was. For the first man, whose race I bear in mine appearance (or, of the race of whom I bear the likeness), fell (was borne) head downwards, and showed forth a manner of birth such as was not heretofore: for it was dead, having no motion. He, then, being pulled down -who also cast his first state down upon the earth- established this whole disposition of all things, being hanged up an image of the creation (Gk. vocation) wherein he made the things of the right hand into left hand and the left hand into right hand, and changed about all the marks of their nature, so that he thought those things that were not fair to be fair, and those that were in truth evil, to be good. Concerning which the Lord saith in a mystery: Unless ye make the things of the right hand as those of the left, and those of the left as those of the right, and those that are above as those below, and those that are behind as those that are before, ye shall not have knowedge of the kingdom.

This thought, therefore, have I declared unto you; and the figure wherein ye now see me hanging is the representation of that man that first came unto birth. Ye therefore, my beloved, and ye that hear me and that shall hear, ought to cease from your former error and return back again. For it is right to mount upon the cross of Christ, who is the word stretched out, the one and only, of whom the spirit saith: For what else is Christ, but the word, the sound of God? So that the word is the upright beam whereon I am crucified. And the sound is that which crosseth it, the nature of man. And the nail which holdeth the cross-tree unto the upright in the midst thereof is the conversion and repentance of man.

XXXIX.

Now whereas thou hast made known and revealed these things unto me, O word of life, called now by me wood (or, word called now by me the tree of life), I give thee thanks, not with these lips that are nailed unto the cross, nor with this tongue by which truth and falsehood issue forth, nor with this word which cometh forth by means of art whose nature is material, but with that voice do I give thee thanks, O King, which is perceived (understood) in silence, which is not heard openly, which proceedeth not forth by organs of the body, which goeth not into ears of flesh, which is not heard of corruptible substance, which existeth not in the world, neither is sent forth upon earth, nor written in books, which is owned by one and not by another: but with this, O Jesu Christ, do I give thee thanks, with the silence of a voice, wherewith the spirit that is in me loveth thee, speaketh unto thee, seeth thee, and beseecheth thee. Thou art perceived of the spirit only, thou art unto me father, thou my mother, thou my brother, thou my friend, thou my bondsman, thou my steward: thou art the All and the All is in thee: and thou Art, and there is nought else that is save thee only. Unto him therefore do ye also, brethren, flee, and if ye learn that in him alone ye exist, ye shall obtain those things whereof he saith unto you: 'which neither eye hath seen nor ear heard, neither have they entered into the heart of man.' We ask, therefore, for that which thou hast promised to give unto us, O thou undefiled Jesu. We praise thee, we give thee thanks, and confess to thee, glorifying thee, even we men that are yet without strength, for thou art God alone, and none other: to whom be glory now and unto all ages. Amen.

XL.

And when the multitude that stood by pronounced the Amen with a great sound, together with the Amen Peter gave up his spirit unto the Lord.
And Marcellus not asking leave of any, for it was not possible, when he saw that Peter had given up the ghost, took him down from the cross with his own hands and washed him in milk and wine: and cut fine seven minae of mastic, and of myrrh and aloes and indian leaf other fifty, and perfumed (embalmed) his body and filled a coffin of marble of great price with Attic honey and laid it in his own tomb.
But Peter by night appeared unto Marcellus and said: Marcellus, hast thou heard that the Lord saith: Let the dead be buried of their own dead? And when Marcellus said: Yea, Peter said to him: That, then, which thou hast spent on the dead, thou hast lost: for thou being alive hast like a dead man cared for the dead. And Marcellus awoke and told the brethren of the appearing of Peter: and he was with them that had been stablished in the faith of Christ by Peter, himself also being stablished yet more until the coming of Paul unto Rome.

XLI.

[[This last chapter, and the last sentence of XL, are thought by Vouaux to be an addition by the author of i-iii, in other words by the compiler of the Greek original of the Vercelli Acts.]]

But Nero, learning thereafter that Peter was departed out of this life, blamed the prefect Agrippa, because he had been put to death without his knowledge; for he desired to punish him more sorely and with greater torment, because Peter had made disciples of certain of them that served him, and had caused them to depart from him: so that he was very wrathful and for a long season spake not unto Agrippa: for he sought to destroy all them that had been made disciples by Peter. And he beheld by night one that scourged him and said unto him: Nero, thou canst not now persecute nor destroy the servants of Christ: refrain therefore thine hands from them. And so Nero, being greatly affrighted by such a vision, abstained from harming the disciples at that time when Peter also departed this life. And thenceforth the brethren were rejoicing with one mind and exulting in the Lord, glorifying the God and Saviour (Father?) of our Lord Jesus Christ with the Holy Ghost, unto whom be glory, world without end. Amen.

THE ACTS OF ANDREW

CHAPTER 1

1 After the Ascension the apostles dispersed to preach in various countries. Andrew began in the province of Achaia, but Matthew went to the city of Mermidona.

2 Andrew left Mermidona and came back to his own allotted district. Walking with his disciples he met a blind man who said: 'Andrew, apostle of Christ, I know you can restore my sight, but I do not wish for that: only bid those with you to give me enough money to clothe and feed myself decently.' Andrew said: 'This is the devil's voice, who will not allow the man to recover his sight.' He touched his eyes and healed him. Then, as he had but a vile rough garment, Andrew said: 'Take the filthy garment off him and clothe him afresh.' All were ready to strip themselves, and Andrew said: 'Let him have what will suffice him.' He returned home thankful.

3 Demetrius of Amasea had an Egyptian boy of whom he was very fond, who died of a fever. Demetrius hearing of Andrew's miracles, came, fell at his feet, and besought help. Andrew pitied him, came to the house, held a very long discourse, turned to the bier, raised the boy, and restored him to his master. All believed and were baptized.

4 A Christian lad named Sostratus came to Andrew privately and told him: 'My mother cherishes a guilty passion for me: I have repulsed her, and she has gone to the proconsul to throw the guilt on me. I would rather die than expose her.' The officers came to fetch the boy, and Andrew prayed and went with him. The mother accused him. The proconsul bade him defend himself. He was silent, and so continued, until the proconsul retired to take counsel. The mother began to weep. Andrew said: 'Unhappy woman, that dost not fear to cast thine own guilt on thy son.' She said to the proconsul: 'Ever since my son entertained his wicked wish he has been in constant company with this man.' The proconsul was enraged, ordered the lad to be sewn into the leather bag of parricides and drowned in the river, and Andrew to be imprisoned till his punishment should be devised. Andrew prayed, there was an earthquake, the proconsul fell from his seat, every one was prostrated, and the mother withered up and died. The proconsul fell at Andrew's feet praying for mercy. The earthquake and thunder ceased, and he healed those who had been hurt. The proconsul and his house were baptized.

5 The son of Cratinus (Gratinus) of Sinope bathed in the women's bath and was seized by a demon. Cratinus wrote to Andrew for help: he himself had a fever and his wife dropsy. Andrew went there in a vehicle. The boy tormented by the evil spirit fell at his feet. He bade it depart and so it did, with outcries. He then went to Cratinus' bed and told him he well deserved to suffer because of his loose life, and bade him rise and sin no more. He was healed. The wife was rebuked for her infidelity. 'If she is to return to her former sin, let her not now be healed: if she can keep from it, let

her be healed.' The water broke out of her body and she was cured. The apostle brake bread and gave it her. She thanked God, believed with all her house, and relapsed no more into sin. Cratinus afterwards sent Andrew great gifts by his servants, and then, with his wife, asked him in person to accept them, but he refused saying: 'It is rather for you to give them to the needy.'

6 After this he went to Nicaea where were seven devils living among the tombs by the wayside, who at noon stoned passersby and had killed many. And all the city came out to meet Andrew with olive branches, crying: 'Our salvation is in thee, O man of God.' When they had told him all, he said: 'If you believe in Christ you shall be freed.' They cried: 'We will.' He thanked God and commanded the demons to appear; they came in the form of dogs. Said he: 'These are your enemies: if you profess your belief that I can drive them out in Jesus' name, I will do so.' They cried out: 'We believe that Jesus Christ whom thou preachest is the Son of God.' Then he bade the demons go into dry and barren places and hurt no man till the last day. They roared and vanished. The apostle baptized the people and made Callistus bishop.

7 At the gate of Nicomedia he met a dead man borne on a bier, and his old father supported by slaves, hardly able to walk, and his old mother with hair torn, bewailing. 'How has it happened ?' he asked. 'He was alone in his chamber and seven dogs rushed on him and killed him.' Andrew sighed and said: 'This is an ambush of the demons I banished from Nicaea. What will you do, father, if I restore your son ?' 'I have nothing more precious than him, I will give him.' He prayed: 'Let the spirit of this lad return.' The faithful responded, 'Amen'. Andrew bade the lad rise, and he rose, and all cried: 'Great is the God of Andrew.' The parents offered great gifts which he refused, but took the lad to Macedonia, instructing him.

8 Embarking in a ship he sailed into the Hellespont, on the way to Byzantium.

There was a great storm. Andrew prayed and there was calm. They reached Byzantium.

9 Thence proceeding through Thrace they met a troop of armed men who made as if to fall on them. Andrew made the sign of the cross against them, and prayed that they might be made powerless. A bright angel touched their swords and they all fell down, and Andrew and his company passed by while they worshipped him. And the angel departed in a great light.

10 At Perinthus he found a ship going to Macedonia, and an angel told him to go on board. As he preached the captain and the rest heard and were converted, and Andrew glorified God for making himself known on the sea.

11 At Philippi were two brothers, one of whom had two sons, the other two daughters. They were rich and noble, and said: 'There is no family as good as ours in the place: let us marry our sons to our daughters.' It was agreed and the earnest paid by the father of the sons. On the wedding-day a word from God came to them: 'Wait till my servant Andrew comes: he will tell you what you should do.' All preparations had been made, and guests bidden, but they waited. On the third day Andrew came: they went out to meet him with wreaths and told him how they had been charged to wait for him, and how things stood. His face was shining so that they marvelled at him. He said: 'Do not, my children, be deceived: rather repent, for you have sinned in thinking to join together those who are near of kin. We do not forbid or shun marriage It is a divine institution: but we condemn incestuous unions.' The parents were troubled and prayed for pardon. The young people saw Andrew's face like that of an angel, and said: 'We are sure that your teaching is true.' The apostle blessed them and departed.

12 At Thessalonica was a rich noble youth, Exoos, who came without his parents' knowledge and asked to be shown the way of truth. He was taught, and believed, and followed Andrew taking no care of his worldly estate. The

parents heard that he was at Philippi and tried to bribe him with gifts to leave Andrew. He said: 'Would that you had not these riches, then would you know the true God, and escape his wrath.' Andrew, too, came down from the third storey and preached to them, but in vain: he retired and shut the doors of the house. They gathered a band and came to burn the house, saying: 'Death to the son who has forsaken his parents': and brought torches, reeds, and faggots, and set the house on fire. It blazed up. Exoos took a bottle of water and prayed: 'Lord Jesu Christ, in whose hand is the nature of all the elements, who moistenest the dry and driest the moist, coolest the hot and kindlest the quenched, put out this fire that thy servants may not grow evil, but be more enkindled unto faith.' He sprinkled the flames and they died. 'He is become a sorcerer,' said the parents, and got ladders, to climb up and kill them, but God blinded them. They remained obstinate, but one Lysimachus, a citizen, said: 'Why persevere? God is fighting for these. Desist, lest heavenly fire consume you.' They were touched, and said: 'This is the true God.' It was now night, but a light shone out, and they received sight. They went up and fell before Andrew and asked pardon, and their repentance made Lysimachus say: 'Truly Christ whom Andrew preaches is the Son of God.' All were converted except the youth's parents, who cursed him and went home again, leaving all their money to public uses. Fifty days after they suddenly died, and the citizens, who loved the youth, returned the property to him. He did not leave Andrew, but spent his income on the poor.

13 The youth asked Andrew to go with him to Thessalonica. All assembled in the theatre, glad to see their favourite. The youth preached to them, Andrew remaining silent, and all wondered at his wisdom. The people cried out: 'Save the son of Carpianus who is ill, and we will believe.' Carpianus went to his house and said to the boy: 'You shall be cured to-day, Adimantus.' He said:

'Then my dream is come true: I saw this man in a vision healing me.' He rose up, dressed, and ran to the theatre, outstripping his father, and fell at Andrew's feet. The people seeing him walk after twenty-three years, cried: 'There is none like the God of Andrew.' 14 A citizen had a son possessed by an unclean spirit and asked for his cure. The demon, foreseeing that he would be cast out, took the son aside into a chamber and made him hang himself. The father said: 'Bring him to the theatre: I believe this stranger is able to raise him.' He said the same to Andrew. Andrew said to the people: 'What will it profit you if you see this accomplished and do not believe?' They said: 'Fear not, we will believe.' The lad was raised and they said: 'It is enough, we do believe.' And they escorted Andrew to the house with torches and lamps, for it was night, and he taught them for three days.

15 Medias of Philippi came and prayed for his sick son. Andrew wiped his cheeks and stroked his head, saying: 'Be comforted, only believe,' and went with him to Philippi. As they entered the city an old man met them and entreated for his sons, whom for an unspeakable crime Medias had imprisoned, and they were putrefied with sores. Andrew said: 'How can you ask help for your son when you keep these men bound? Loose their chains first, for your unkindness obstructs my prayers.' Medias, penitent, said: 'I will loose these two and seven others of whom you have not been told.' They were brought, tended for three days, cured, and freed. Then the apostle healed the son, Philomedes, who had been ill twenty-two years. The people cried: 'Heal our sick as well.' Andrew told Philomedes to visit them in their houses and bid them rise in the name of Jesus Christ, by which he had himself been healed. This was done, and all believed and offered gifts, which Andrew did not accept.

16 A citizen, Nicolaus, offered a gilt chariot and four white mules and four white horses as his most precious

possession for the cure of his daughter. Andrew smiled. 'I accept your gifts, but not these visible ones: if you offer this for your daughter, what will you for your soul? That is what I desire of you, that the inner man may recognize the true God, reject earthly things and desire eternal . . .' He persuaded all to forsake their idols, and healed the girl. His fame went through all Macedonia. 17 Next day as he taught, a youth cried out: 'What hast thou to do with us. Art thou come to turn us out of our own place?' Andrew summoned him: 'What is your work?' 'I have dwelt in this boy from his youth and thought never to leave him: but three days since I heard his father say, "I shall go to Andrew": and now I fear the torments thou bringest us and I shall depart.' The spirit left the boy. And many came and asked: 'In whose name dost thou cure our sick?'

Philosophers also came and disputed with him, and no one could resist his teaching.

18 At this time, one who opposed him went to the proconsul Virinus and said: 'A man is arisen in Thessalonica who says the temples should be destroyed and ceremonies done away, and all the ancient law abolished, and one God worshipped, whose servant he says he is.' The proconsul sent soldiers and knights to fetch Andrew. They found his dwelling: when they entered, his face so shone that they fell down in fear. Andrew told those present the proconsul's purpose. The people armed themselves against the soldiers, but Andrew stopped them. The proconsul arrived; not finding Andrew in the appointed place, he raged like a lion and sent twenty more men. They, on arrival, were confounded and said nothing. The proconsul sent a large troop to bring him by force. Andrew said: 'Have you come for me?' 'Yes, if you are the sorcerer who says the gods ought not to be worshipped.' 'I am no sorcerer, but the apostle of Jesus Christ whom I preach.' At this, one of the soldiers drew his sword and cried: 'What have I to do with thee, Virinus,

that thou sendest me to one who can not only cast me out of this vessel, but burn me by his power? Would that you would come yourself! you would do him no harm.' And the devil went out of the soldier and he fell dead. On this came the proconsul and stood before Andrew but could not see him. 'I am he whom thou seekest.' His eyes were opened, and he said in anger: 'What is this madness, that thou despisest us and our officers? Thou art certainly a sorcerer. Now will I throw thee to the beasts for contempt of our gods and us, and we shall see if the crucified whom thou preachest will help thee.' Andrew: 'Thou must believe, proconsul, in the true God and his Son whom he hath sent, specially now that one of thy men is dead.' And after long prayer he touched the soldier: 'Rise up: my God Jesus Christ raiseth thee.' He arose and stood whole. The people cried: 'Glory be to our God.' The proconsul: 'Believe not, O people, believe not the sorcerer.' They said: 'This is no sorcery but sound and true teaching.' The proconsul: 'I shall throw this man to the beasts and write about you to Caesar, that ye may perish for contemning his laws.' They would have stoned him, and said: 'Write to Caesar that the Macedonians have received the word of God, and forsaking their idols, worship the true God.'

Then the proconsul in wrath retired to the praetorium, and in the morning brought beasts to the stadium and had the Apostle dragged thither by the hair and beaten with clubs. First they sent in a fierce boar who went about him thrice and touched him not. The people praised God. A bull led by thirty soldiers and incited by two hunters, did not touch Andrew but tore the hunters to pieces, roared, and fell dead. 'Christ is the true God,' said the people. An angel was seen to descend and strengthen the apostle. The proconsul in rage sent in a fierce leopard, which left every one alone but seized and strangled the proconsul's son; but Virinus was so angry that he said nothing of it nor cared. Andrew said to the people: 'Recognize now that this is the true God, whose power subdues the beasts, though Virinus knows him not. But that ye may believe the more, I will raise the dead son, and confound the foolish father.' After long prayer, he raised him. The people would have slain Virinus, but Andrew restrained them, and Virinus went to the praetorium, confounded.

19 After this a youth who followed the apostle sent for his mother to meet Andrew. She came, and after being instructed, begged him to come to their house, which was devastated by a great serpent. As Andrew approached, it hissed loudly and with raised head came to meet him; it was fifty cubits long: every one fell down in fear. Andrew said: 'Hide thy head, foul one, which thou didst raise in the beginning for the hurt of mankind, and obey the servants of God, and die.' The serpent roared, and coiled about a great oak near by and vomited poison and blood and died.

Andrew went to the woman's farm, where a child killed by the serpent lay dead. He said to the parents: 'Our God who would have you saved hath sent me here that you may believe on him. Go and see the slayer slain.' They said: 'We care not so much for the child's death, if we be avenged.' They went, and Andrew said to the proconsul's wife 'Go and raise the boy.' She went, nothing doubting, and said: 'In the name of my God Jesus Christ, rise up whole.' The parents returned and found their child alive, and fell at Andrew's feet.

20 On the next night he saw a vision which he related. 'Hearken, beloved, to my vision. I beheld, and lo, a great mountain raised up on high, which had on it nothing earthly, but only shone with such light, that it seemed to enlighten all the world. And lo, there stood by me my beloved brethren the apostles Peter and John; and John reached his hand to Peter and raised him to the top of the mount, and turned to me and asked me to go up after Peter, saying: "Andrew, thou art to drink Peter's cup." And he stretched out his hands and said: "Draw near to me and stretch out thy hands so as to join them unto mine, and put thy head by my head." When I did so I found myself shorter than John. After that he said to me: "Wouldst thou know the image of that which thou seest, and who it is that speaketh to thee?" and I said: "I desire to know it." And he said to me: "I am the word of the cross whereon thou shalt hang shortly, for his name's sake whom thou preachest." And many other things said he unto me, of which I must now say nothing, but they shall be declared when I come unto the sacrifice. But now let all assemble that have received the word of God, and let me commend them unto the Lord Jesus Christ, that he may vouchsafe to keep them unblemished in his teaching. For I am now being loosed from the body, and go unto that promise which he hath vouchsafed to promise me, who is the Lord of heaven and earth, the Son of God Almighty, very God with the Holy Ghost, continuing for everlasting ages.'

All the brethren wept and smote their faces. When all were gathered, Andrew said: 'Know, beloved, that I am about to leave you, but I trust in Jesus whose word I preach, that he will keep you from evil, that this harvest which I have sown among you may not be plucked up by the enemy, that is, the knowledge and teaching of my Lord Jesus Christ. But do ye pray always and stand firm in the faith, that the Lord may root out all tares of offence and vouchsafe to gather you into his heavenly garner as pure wheat.' So for five days he taught and confirmed them: then he spread his hands and prayed: 'Keep, I beseech thee, O Lord, this flock which hath now known thy salvation, that the wicked one may not prevail against it, but that what by thy command and my means it hath received, it may be able to preserve inviolate for ever.' And all responded 'Amen'. He took bread, brake it with thanksgiving, gave it to all, saying: 'Receive the grace which Christ our Lord God giveth you by me his servant.' He kissed every one and commended them to the Lord, and departed to Thessalonica, and after teaching there two days, he left them.

21 Many faithful from Macedonia accompanied him in two ships. And all were desirous of being on Andrew's ship, to hear him. He said: 'I know your wish, but this ship is too small. Let the servants and baggage go in the larger ship, and you with me in this.' He gave them Anthimus to comfort them, and bade them go into another ship which he ordered to keep always near . . . that they might see him and hear the word of God. And as he slept a little, one fell overboard. Anthimus roused him, saying: 'Help us, good master; one of thy servants perisheth.' He rebuked the wind, there was a calm, and the man was borne by the waves to the ship. Anthimus helped him on board and all marvelled. On the twelfth day they reached Patrae in Achaia, disembarked, and went to an inn.

22 Many asked him to lodge with them, but he said he could only go where God bade him. That night he had no revelation, and the next night, being distressed at this, he heard a voice saying: 'Andrew, I am alway with thee and forsake thee not,' and was glad. Lesbius the proconsul was told in a vision to take him in, and sent a messenger for him. He came, and entering the proconsul's chamber found him lying as dead with closed eyes; he struck him on the side and said: 'Rise and tell us what hath befallen thee.' Lesbius said: 'I abominated the way which you teach and sent soldiers in ships to the proconsul of Macedonia to send you bound to me, but they were wrecked and could not reach their destination. As I continued in my purpose of destroying your Way, two black men (Ethiopes) appeared and scourged me, saying: "We can no longer prevail here, for the man is coming whom you mean to persecute. So to-night, while we still have the power, we will avenge ourselves on you." And they beat me sorely and left me. But now do you pray that I may be pardoned and healed.' Andrew preached the word and all believed, and the proconsul was healed and confirmed in the faith.

23 Now Trophima, once the proconsul's mistress, and now married to another, left her husband and clave to Andrew. Her husband came to her lady (Lesbius' wife) and said she was renewing her liaison with the proconsul. The wife, enraged, said: 'This is why my husband has left me these six months.' She called her steward (procurator) and had Trophima sentenced as a prostitute and sent to the brothel. Lesbius knew nothing, and was deceived by his wife, when he asked about her. Trophima in the brothel prayed continually, and had the Gospel on her bosom, and no one could approach her. One day one offered her violence, and the Gospel fell to the ground. She cried to God for help and an angel came, and the youth fell dead. After that, she raised him, and all the city ran to the sight.

Lesbius' wife went to the bath with the steward, and as they bathed an ugly demon came and killed them both. Andrew heard and said: 'It is the judgement of God for their usage of Trophima.' The lady's nurse, decrepit from age, was carried to the spot, and supplicated for her. Andrew said to Lesbius: 'Will you have her raised?' 'No, after all the ill she has done.' 'We ought not to be unmerciful.' Lesbius went to the praetorium; Andrew raised his wife, who remained shamefaced: he bade her go home and pray. 'First', she said, 'reconcile me to Trophima whom I have injured.' 'She bears you no malice.' He called her and they were reconciled. Callisto was the wife.

Lesbius, growing in faith, came one day to Andrew and confessed all his sins. Andrew said: 'I thank God, my son, that thou fearest the judgement to come. Be strong in the Lord in whom thou believest.' And he took his hand and walked with him on the shore.

24 They sat down, with others, on the sand, and he taught. A corpse was thrown up by the sea near them. 'We must learn', said Andrew, 'what the enemy has done to him.' So he raised him, gave him a garment, and bade him

tell his story. He said: 'I am the son of Sostratus, of Macedonia, lately come from Italy. On returning home I heard of a new teaching, and set forth to find out about it. On the way here we were wrecked and all drowned.' And after some thought, he realized that Andrew was the man he sought, and fell at his feet and said: 'I know that thou art the servant of the true God. I beseech thee for my companions, that they also may be raised and know him.' Then Andrew instructed him, and thereafter prayed God to show the bodies of the other drowned men: thirty-nine were washed ashore, and all there prayed for them to be raised. Philopator, the youth, said: 'My father sent me here with a great sum. Now he is blaspheming God and his teaching. Let it not be so.' Andrew ordered the bodies to be collected, and said: 'Whom will you have raised first?' He said: 'Warus my foster-brother.' So he was first raised and then the other thirty-eight. Andrew prayed over each, and then told the brethren each to take the hand of one and say: 'Jesus Christ the son of the living God raiseth thee.' Lesbius gave much money to Philopator to replace what he had lost, and he abode with Andrew.

25 A woman, Calliopa, married to a murderer, had an illegitimate child and suffered in travail. She told her sister to call on Diana for help; when she did so the devil appeared to her at night and said: 'Why do you trouble me with vain prayers? Go to Andrew in Achaia.' She came, and he accompanied her to Corinth, Lesbius with him. Andrew said to Calliopa: 'You deserve to suffer for your evil life: but believe in Christ, and you will be relieved, but the child will be born dead.' And so it was.

26 Andrew did many signs in Corinth. Sostratus the father of Philopator, warned in a vision to visit Andrew, came first to Achaia and then to Corinth. He met Andrew walking with Lesbius, recognized him by his vision, and fell at his feet. Philopator said: 'This is my father, who seeks to know what he must do.' Andrew: 'I know that he is come to learn the truth; we thank

God who reveals himself to believers.' Leontius the servant of Sostratus, said to him: 'Seest thou, sir, how this man's face shineth?' 'I see, my beloved,' said Sostratus; 'let us never leave him, but live with him and hear the words of eternal life.' Next day they offered Andrew many gifts, but he said: 'It is not for me to take aught of you but your own selves. Had I desired money, Lesbius is richer.'

27 After some days he bade them prepare him a bath; and going there saw an old man with a devil, trembling exceedingly. As he wondered at him, another, a youth, came out of the bath and fell at his feet, saying: 'What have we to do with thee, Andrew? Hast thou come here to turn us out of our abodes?' Andrew said to the people: 'Fear not,' and drove out both the devils. Then, as he bathed, he told them: 'The enemy of mankind lies in wait everywhere, in baths and in rivers; therefore we ought always to invoke the Lord's name, that he may have w power over us.' They brought their sick to him to be healed, and so they did from other cities.

28 An old man, Nicolaus, came with clothes rent and said: 'I am seventy-four years old and have always been a libertine. Three days ago I heard of your miracles and teaching. I thought I would turn over a new leaf, and then again that I would not. in this doubt, I took a Gospel and prayed God to make me forget my old devices. A few days after, I forgot the Gospel I had about me, and went to the brothel. The woman said: "Depart, old man, depart: thou art an angel of God, touch me not nor approach me, for I see in thee a great mystery." Then I remembered the Gospel, and am come to you for help and pardon.' Andrew discoursed long against incontinence, and prayed from the sixth to the ninth hour. He rose and washed his face and said: 'I will not eat till I know if God will have mercy on this man.' A second day he fasted, but had no revelation until the fifth day, when he wept vehemently and said: 'Lord, we obtain mercy for the dead,

and now this man that desireth to know thy greatness, wherefore should he not return and thou heal him?' A voice from heaven said: 'Thou hast prevailed for the old man; but like as thou art worn with fasting, let him also fast, that he may be saved.' And he called him and preached abstinence. On the sixth day he asked the brethren all to pray for Nicolaus, and they did. Andrew then took food and permitted the rest to eat. Nicolaus went home, gave away all his goods, and lived for six months on dry bread and water. Then he died. Andrew was not there, but in the place where he was he heard a voice: 'Andrew, Nicolaus for whom thou didst intercede, is become mine.' And he told the brethren that Nicolaus was dead, and prayed that he might rest in peace.

29 And while he abode in that place (probably Lacedaemon) Antiphanes of Megara came and said: 'If there be in thee any kindness, according to the command of the Saviour whom thou preachest, show it now.' Asked what his story was, he told it. Returning from a journey, I heard the porter of my house crying out. They told me that he and his wife and son were tormented of a devil. I went upstairs and found other servants gnashing their teeth, running at me, and laughing madly. I went further up and found they had beaten my wife: she lay with her hair over her face unable to recognize me. Cure her, and I care nothing for the others.' Andrew said: 'There is no respect of persons with God. Let us go there.' They went from Lacedaemon to Megara, and when they entered the house, all the devils cried out: 'What dost thou here, Andrew? Go where thou art permitted: this house is ours.' He healed the wife and all the possessed persons, and Antiphanes and his wife became firm adherents.

30 He returned to Patrae where Egeas was now proconsul, and one Iphidamia, who had been converted by a disciple, Sosias, came and embraced his feet and said: 'My lady Maximilla who is in a fever has sent for you. The proconsul is standing by her bed with his sword drawn, meaning to kill himself when

she expires.' He went to her, and said to Egeas: 'Do thyself no harm, but put up thy sword into his place. There will be a time when thou wilt draw it on me.' Egeas did not understand, but made way. Andrew took Maximilla's hand, she broke into a sweat, and was well: he bade them give her food. The proconsul sent him 100 pieces of silver, but he would not look at them.

31 Going thence he saw a sick man lying in the dirt begging, and healed him.

32 Elsewhere he saw a blind man with wife and son, and said: 'This is indeed the devil's work: he has blinded them in soul and body.' He opened their eyes and they believed.

33 One who saw this said: 'I beg thee come to the harbour; there is a man, the son of a sailor, sick fifty years, cast out of the house, lying on the shore, incurable, full of ulcers and worms.' They went to him. The sick man said: 'Perhaps you are the disciple of that God who alone can save.' Andrew said: 'I am he who in the name of my God can restore thee to health,' and added: 'In the name of Jesus Christ, rise and follow me.' He left his filthy rags and followed, the pus and worms flowing from him. They went into the sea, and the apostle washed him in the name of the Trinity and he was whole, and ran naked through the city proclaiming the true God.

34 At this time the proconsul's brother Stratocles arrived from Italy. One of his slaves, Alcman, whom he loved, was taken by a devil and lay foaming in the court. Stratocles hearing of it said: 'Would the sea had swallowed me before I saw this.' Maximilla and Iphidamia said: 'Be comforted: there is here a man of God, let us send for him.' When he came he took the boy's hand and raised him whole. Stratocles believed and clave to Andrew.

35 Maximilla went daily to the praetorium and sent for Andrew to teach there. Egeas was away in Macedonia, angry because Maximilla had left him since her conversion. As they were all assembled one day, he

returned, to their great terror. Andrew prayed that he might not be suffered to enter the place till all had dispersed. And Egeas was at once seized with indisposition, and in the interval the apostle signed them all and sent them away, himself last. But Maximilla on the first opportunity came to Andrew and received the word of God and went home.

36 After this Andrew was taken and imprisoned by Egeans, and all came to the prison to be taught. After a few days he was scourged and crucified; he hung for three days, preaching, and expired, as is fully set forth in his Passion. Maximilla embalmed and buried his body.

37 From the tomb comes manna like flour, and oil: the amount shows the barrenness or fertility of the coming season

CHAPTER 2

When, finally, Andrew also had come to a wedding, he too, to manifest the glory of God, disjoined certain who were intended to marry each other, men and women, and instructed them to continue holy in the single state.

There also is it written, that when this same Maximilla and Iphidamia were gone together to hear the apostle Andrew, a beautiful child, who, Leucius would have us understand, was either God or at least an angel, escorted them to the apostle Andrew and went to the praetorium of Egetes, and entering their chamber feigned a woman's voice, as of Maximilla, complaining of the sufferings of womankind, and of Iphidamia replying. When Egetes heard this dialogue, he went away.

1 . . . is there in you altogether slackness? are ye not yet convinced of yourselves that ye do not yet bear his goodness? let us be reverent, let us rejoice with ourselves in the bountiful (ungrudging) fellowship which cometh of him. Let us say unto ourselves: Blessed is our race! by whom hath it

been loved? blessed is our state! of whom hath it obtained mercy? we are not cast on the ground, we that have been recognized by so great highness: we are not the offspring of time, afterward to be dissolved by time; we are not a contrivance (product) of motion, made to be again destroyed by itself, nor things of earthly birth. ending again therein. We belong, then, to a greatness, unto which we aspire, of which we are the property, and peradventure to a greatness that hath mercy upon us. We belong to the better; therefore we flee from the worse: we belong to the beautiful, for whose sake we reject the foul; to the righteous, by whom we cast away the unrighteous, to the merciful, by whom we reject the unmerciful; to the Saviour, by whom we recognize the destroyer; to the light, by whom we have cast away the darkness; to the One, by whom we have turned away from the many; to the heavenly, by whom we have learned to know the earthly; to the abiding, by whom we have seen the transitory. If we desire to offer unto God that hath had mercy on us a worthy thanksgiving or confidence or hymn or boasting, what better cause (theme) have we than that we have been recognized by him?

2 And having discoursed thus to the brethren, he sent them away every one to his house, saying to them: Neither are ye ever forsaken of me, ye that are servants of Christ, because of the love that is in him: neither again shall I be forsaken of you because of his intercession (mediation). And every one departed unto his house: and there was among them rejoicing after this sort for many days, while Aegeates took not thought to prosecute the accusation against the Apostle. Every one of them then was confirmed at that time in hope toward the Lord, and they assembled without fear in the prison, with Maximilla, Iphidamia, and the rest, continually, being sheltered by the protection and grace of the Lord.

3 But one day Aegeates, as he was hearing causes, remembered the matter concerning Andrew: and as one seized

with madness, he left the cause which he had in hand, and rose up from the judgement seat and ran quickly to the praetorium, inflamed with love of Maximilla and desiring to persuade her with flatteries. And Maximilla was beforehand with him, coming from the prison and entering the house. And he went in and said to her:

4 Maximilla, thy parents counted me worthy of being thy consort, and gave me thine hand in marriage, not looking to wealth or descent or renown, but it may be to my good disposition of soul: and, that I may pass over much that I might utter in reproach of thee, both of that which I have enjoyed at thy parents' hands and thou from me during all our life, I am come, leaving the court, to learn of thee this one thing: answer me then reasonably, if thou wert as the wife of former days, living with me in the way we know, sleeping, conversing, bearing offspring with me, I would deal well with thee in all points; nay more, I would set free the stranger whom I hold in prison: but if thou wilt not to thee I would do nothing harsh, for indeed I cannot; but him, whom thou affectionest more than me, I will afflict yet more. Consider, then, Maximilla, to whether of the two thou inclinest, and answer me to-morrow; for I am wholly armed for this emergency.

5 And with these words he went out; but Maximilla again at the accustomed hour, with Iphidamia, went to Andrew: and putting his hands before her own eyes, and then putting them to her mouth, she began to declare to him the whole rmatter of the demand of Aegeates. And Andrew answered her: I know, Maximilla my child, that thou thyself art moved to resist the whole attraction (promise) of nuptial union, desiring to be quit of a foul and polluted way of life: and this hath long been firmly held in thine (MS. mine) intention; but now thou wishest for the further testimony of mine opinion. I testify, O Maximilla: do it not; be not vanquished by the threat of Aegeates: be not overcome by his discourse: fear not his shameful counsels: fall not to

his artful flatteries: consent not to surrender thyself to his impure spells, but endure all his torments looking unto us for a little space, and thou shalt see him wholly numbed and withering away from thee and from all that are akin to thee. But (For) that which I most needed to say to thee -for I rest not till I fulfil the business which is seen, and which cometh to pass in thy person- hath escaped me: and rightly in thee do I behold Eve repenting, and in myself Adam returning; for that which she suffered in ignorance, thou now (for whose soul I strive) settest right by returning: and that which the spirit suffered which was overthrown with her and slipped away from itself, is set right in me, with thee who seest thyself being brought back. For her defect thou hast remedied by not suffering like her; and his imperfection I have perfected by taking refuge with God, that which she disobeyed thou hast obeyed: that whereto he consented I flee from: and that which they both transgressed we have been aware of, for it is ordained that every one should correct (and raise up again) his own fall.

6 I, then, having said this as I have said it, would go on to speak as followeth: Well done, O nature that art being saved for thou hast been strong and hast not hidden thyself (from God like Adam)! Well done, O soul that criest out of what thou hast surfered, and returnest unto thyself ! Well done, O man that understandest what is thine and dost press on to what is thine! Well done, thou that hearest what is spoken, for I see thee to be greater than things that are thought or spoken! I recognize thee as more powerful than the things which seemed to overpower thee; as more beautiful than those which cast thee down into foulness, which brought thee down into captivity. Perceiving then, O man, all this in thyself, that thou art immaterial, holy light, akin to him that is unborn, that thou art intellectual, heavenly, translucent, pure, above the flesh, above the world, above rulers, above principalities, over whom thou art in truth, then comprehend thyself in

THE ACTS OF ANDREW

thy condition and receive full knowledge and understand wherein thou excellest: and beholding thine own face in thine essence, break asunder all bonds -I say not only those that are of thy birth, but those that are above birth, whereof we have set forth to thee the names which are execeding great -desire earnestly to see him that is revealed unto thee, him who doth not come into being, whom perchance thou alone shalt recognize with confidence.

7 These things have I spoken of thee, Maximilla, for in their meaning the things I have spoken reach unto thee. Like as Adam died in Eve because he consented unto her confession, so do I now live in thee that keepest the Lord's commandment and stablishest thyself in the rank (dignity) of thy being. But the threats of Aegeates do thou trample down, Maximilla, knowing that we have God that hath mercy on us. And let not his noise move thee, but continue chaste- and let him punish me not only with such torments as bonds, but let him cast me to the beasts or burn me with fire, and throw me from a precipice. And what need I say? there is but this one body; let him abuse that as he will, for it is akin to himself.

8 And yet again unto thee is my speech, Maximilla: I say unto thee, give not thyself over unto Aegeates: withstand his ambushes- for indeed, Maximilla, I have seen my Lord saying unto me: Andrew, Aegeates' father the devil will loose thee from this prison. Thine, therefore, let it be henceforth to keep thyself chaste and pure, holy, unspotted, sincere, free from adultery, not reconciled to the discourses of our enemy, unbent, unbroken, tearless, unwounded, not storm-tossed, undivided, not stumbling without fellow-feeling for the works of Cain. For if thou give not up thyself, Maximilla, to what is contrary to these, I also shall rest, though I be thus forced to leave this life for thy sake that is, for mine own. But if I were thrust out hence, even I, who, it may be, might avail through thee to profit others that are akin to me, and if thou wert

persuaded by the discourse of Aegeates and the flatteries of his father the serpent, so that thou didst turn unto thy former works, know thou that on thine account I should be tormented until thou thyself sawest that I had contemned life for the sake of a soul which was not worthy.

9 I entreat, therefore, the wise man that is in thee that thy mind continue clear seeing. I entreat thy mind that is not seen, that it be preserved whole: I beseech thee, love thy Jesus, and yield not unto the worse. Assist me, thou whom I entreat as a man, that I may become perfect: help me also, that thou mayest recognize thine own true nature: feel with me in my suffering, that thou mayest take knowledge of what I suffer, and escape suffering see that which I see, and thou shalt be blind to what thou seest: see that which thou shouldst, and thou shalt not see that thou shouldst not: hearken to what I say, and cast away that which thou hast heard.

10 These things have I spoken unto thee and unto every one that heareth, if he will hear. But thou, O Stratocles, said he, looking toward him, Why art thou so oppressed, with many tears and groanings to be heard afar off? what is the lowness of spirit that is on thee? why thy much pain and thy great anguish? dost thou take note of what is said, and wherefore I pray thee to be disposed in mind as my child? (or, my child, to be composed in mind): dost thou perceive unto whom my words are spoken? hath each of them taken hold on thine understanding? have they whetted (MS. touched) thine intellectual part? have I thee as one that hath hearkened to me? do I find myself in thee? is there in thee one that speaketh whom I see to be mine own? doth he love him that speaketh in me and desire to have fellowship with him? doth he wish to be made one with him? doth lie hasten to become his friend? doth he yearn to be joined with him? doth he find in him any rest? hath he where to lay his head? doth nought oppose him there? nought that is wroth with him, resisteth him, hateth him,

fleeth from him, is savage, avoideth, turneth away, starteth off, is burdened, maketh war, talketh with others, is flattered by others, agreeth with others? Doth nothing else disturb him? Is there one within that is strange to me? an adversary, a breaker of peace, an enemy, a cheat, a sorcerer, a crooked dealer, unsound, guileful, a hater of men, a hater of the word, one like a tyrant, boastful, puffed up, mad, akin to the serpent, a weapon of the devil, a friend of the fire, belonging to darkness? Is there in thee any one, Stratocles, that cannot endure my saying these things? Who is it? Answer: do I talk in vain? have I spoken in vain? Nay, saith the man in thee, Stratocles, who now again weepeth.

11 And Andrew took the band of Stratocles and said: I have him whom I loved; I shall rest on him whom I look for; for thy yet groaning, and weeping without restraint, is a sign unto me that I have already found rest, that I have not spoken to thee these words which are akin to me, in vain.

12 And Stratocles answered him: Think not, most blessed Andrew, that there is aught else that afflicteth me but thee; for the words that come forth of thee are like arrows of fire shot against me, and every one of them reacheth me and verily burneth me up. That part of my soul which inclineth to what I hear is tormented, divining the affliction that is to follow, for thou thyself departest, and, I know, nobly: but hereafter when I seek thy care and affection, where shall I find it, or in whom? I have received the seeds of the words of salvation, and thou wast the sower: but that they should sprout up and grow needs none other but thee, most blessed Andrew. And what else have I say to thee but this? I need much mercy and help from thee, to become worthy of the seed I have from thee, which will not otherwise increase perpetually or grow up into the light except thou willest it, and prayest for them and for the whole of me.

13 And Andrew answered him: This, my child, was what I beheld in thee myself. And I glorify my Lord that my thought of thee walked not on the void, but knew what it said. But that ye may know the truth, to-morrow doth Aegeates deliver me up to be crucified: for Maximilla the servant of the Lord will enrage the enemy that is in him, unto whom he belongeth, by not consenting to that which is hateful to her; and by turning against me he will think to console himself.

14 Now while the apostle spake these things, Maximilla was not there, for she having heard throughout the words wherewith he answered her, and being in part composed by them, and of such a mind as the words pointed out, set forth not inadvisedly nor without purpose and went to the praetorium. And she bade farewell to all the life of the flesh, and when Aegeates brought to her the same demand which he had told her to consider, whether she would lie with him, she rejected it- and thenceforth he bent himself to putting Andrew to death, and thought to what death he should expose him. And when of all deaths crucifixion alone prevailed with him, he went away with his like and dined; and Maximilla, the Lord going before her in the likeness of Andrew, with Iphidamia came back to the prison- and there being therein a great gathering of the brethren, she found Andrew discoursing thus:

15 I, brethren, was sent forth by the Lord as an apostle unto these regions whereof my Lord thought me worthy, not to teach any man, but to remind every man that is akin to such words that they live in evils which are temporal, delighting in their injurious delusions: wherefrom I have always exhorted you also to depart, and encouraged you to press toward things that endure, and to take flight from all that is transitory (flowing)- for ye see that none of you standeth, but that all things, even to the customs of men, are easily changeable. And this befalleth because the soul is untrained and erreth toward nature and holdeth pledges toft its error. I therefore account them blessed who have become obedient unto

the word preached, and thereby see the mysteries of their own nature; for whose sake all things have been builded up.

16 I enjoin you therefore, beloved children, build yourselves firmly upon the foundation that hath been laid for you, which is unshaken, and against which no evil- willer can conspire. Be then, rooted upon this foundation: be established, remembering what ye have seen (or heard) and all that hath come to pass while I walked with you all. Ye have seen works wrought through me which ye have no power to disbelieve, and such signs come to pass as perchance even dumb nature will proclaim aloud; I have delivered you words which I pray may so be received by you as the words themselves would have it. Be established then, beloved upon all that ye have seen, and heard, and partaken of. And God on whom ye have believed shall have mercy on you and present you lmto himself, giving you rest unto all ages.

17 Now as for that which is to befall me, let it not really trouble you as some strange spectacle, that the servant of God unto whom God himself hath granted much in deeds and words, should by an evil man be driven out of this temporal life: for not only unto me will this come to pass, but unto all them that have loved and believed on him and confess him. The devil that is wholly shameless will arm his own children against them, that they may consent unto him; and he will not have his desire. And wherefore he essayeth this I will tell you. From the beginning of all things, and if I may so say, since he that hath no beginning came down to be under his rule, the enemy that is a foe to peace driveth away from (God) such a one as doth not belong indeed to him, but is some one of the weaker sort and not fully enlightened (?), nor yet able to recognize himself. And because he knoweth him not, therefore must he be fought against by him (the devil). For he, thinking that he possesseth him and is his master for ever, opposeth him so much, that he maketh their enmity to

be a kind of friendship: for suggesting to him his own thoughts, he often portrayeth them as pleasurable and specious (MS. deceitful), by which he thinketh to prevail over him. He was not, then, openly shown to be an enemy, for he feigned a friendship that was worthy of him.

18 And this his work he carried on so long that he (man) forgat to recognize it, but he (the devil) knew it himself: that is, he, because of his gifts . But when the mystery of grace was lighted up, and the counsel of rest manifested, and the light of the word shown, and the race of them that were saved was proved, warring against many pleasures, the enemy himself despised, and himself, through the goodness of him that had mercy on us, derided because of his own gifts, by which he had thought to triumph over man- he began to plot against us with hatred and enmity and assaults; and this hath he dctcrmined, not to cease from us till he thinketh to separate us (from God). For before, our enemy was without care, and offered us a feigned friendship which was worthy of him, and was able not to fear that we, deceived by him, should depart from him. But when the light of dispensation was kindled, it made , I say not stronger, . For it exposed that part of his nature which was hidden and which thought to escape notice, and made it confess what it is.

Knowing therefore, brethren, that which shall be, let us be vigilant, not discontented, not making a proud figure, not carrying upon our souls marks of him which are not our own: but wholly lifted upward by the whole word, let us all gladly await the end, and take our flight away from him, that he may be henceforth shown as he is, who our nature unto (or against) our . . .

CHAPTER 3
THE MARTYRDOM
And after he had thus discoursed throughout the night to the brethren, and praved with them and committed them unto the Lord, early in the

morning Aegeates the proconsul sent for the apostle Andrew out of the prison and said to him: The end of thy judgement is at hand, thou stranger, enemy of this present life and foe of all mine house. Wherefore hast thou thought good to intrude into places that are not thine, and to corrupt my wife who was of old obedient unto me? why hast thou done this against me and against all Achaia ? Therefore shalt thou receive from me a gift in recompense of that thou hast wrought against me.

And he commanded him to be scourged by seven men and afterward to be crucified: and charged the executioners that his legs should be left unpierced, and so he should be hanged up: thinking by this means to torment him the more.

Now the report was noised throughout all Patrae that the stranger, the righteous man, the servant of Christ whom Aegeates held prisoner, was being crucified, having done nothing amiss: and they ran together with one accord unto the sight, being wroth with the proconsul because of his impious judgement.

And as the executioners led him unto the place to fulfil that which was commanded them, Stratocles heard what was come to pass, and ran hastily and overtook them, and beheld the blessed Andrew violently haled by the executioners like a malefactor. And he spared them not, but beating every one of them soundly and tearing their coats from top to bottom, he caught Andrew away from them, saying: Ye may thank the blessed man who hath instructed me and taught me to refrain from extremity of wrath: for else I would have showed you what Stratocles is able to do, and what is the power of the foul Aegeates. For we have learnt to endure that which others inflict upon us. And he took the hand of the apostle and went with him to the place by the sea-shore where he was to be crucified.

But the soldiers who had received him from the proconsul left him with Stratocles, and returned and told Aegeates, saying: As we went with Andrew Stratocles prevented us, and rent our coats and pulled him away from us and took him with him, and lo, here we are as thou seest. And Aegeates answered them: Put on other raiment and go and fulfil that which I commanded you, upon the condemned man: but be not seen of Stratocles, neither answer him again if he ask aught of you; for I know the rashness of his soul, what it is, and if he were provoked he would not even spare me. And they did as Aegeates said unto them.

But as Stratocles went with the apostle unto the place appointed, Andrew perceived that he was wroth with Aegeates and was reviling him in a low voice, and said unto him: My child Stratocles, I would have thee henceforth possess thy soul unmoved, and remove from thyself this temper, and neither be inwardly disposed thus toward the things that seem hard to thee, nor be inflamed outwardly: for it becometh the servant of Jesus to be worthy of Jesus. And another thing will I say unto thee and to the brethren that walk with me: that the man that is against us, when he dareth aught against us and findeth not one to consent unto him, is smitten and beaten and wholly deadened because he hath not accomplished that which he undertook; let us therefore, little children, have him alway before our eyes, lest if we fall asleep he slaughter us (you) like an adversary.

And as he spake this and yet more unto Stratocles and them that were with him, they came to the place where he was to be crucified: and (seeing the cross set up at the edge of the sand by the sea-shore) he left them all and went to the cross and spake unto it (as unto a living creature, with a loud voice):

Hail, O cross, yea be glad indeed! Well know I that thou shalt henceforth be at rest, thou that hast for a long time been wearied, being set up and awaiting me. I come unto thee whom I know to belong to me. I come unto thee that hast yearned after me. I know thy mystery, for the which thou art set up: for thou art planted in the world to establish the things that are unstable: and the one part of thee stretcheth up toward heaven that thou mayest signify the heavenly word (or, the word that is above) (the head of all things): and another part of thee is spread out to the right hand and the left that it may put to flight the envious and adverse power of the evil one, and gather into one the things that are scattered abroad (or, the world): And another part of thee is planted in the earth, and securely set in the depth, that thou mayest join the things that are in the earth and that are under the earth unto the heavenly things (Laud. that thou mayest draw up them that be under the earth and them that are held in the places beneath the earth, and join, &c.). O cross, device (contrivance) of the salvation of the Most High! O cross, trophy of the victory [of Christ] over the enemies! O cross, planted upon the earth and having thy fruit in the heavens! O name of the cross, filled with all things (lit. a thing filled with all).

Well done, O cross, that hast bound down the mobility of the world (or, the circumference)! Well done, O shape of understanding that hast shaped the shapeless (earth?)! Well done, O unseen chastisement that sorely chastisest the substance of the knowledge that hath many gods, and drivest out from among mankind him that devised it! Well done, thou that didst clothe thyself with the Lord, and didst bear the thief as a fruit, and didst call the apostle to repentance, and didst not refuse to accept us! But how long delay I, speaking thus, and embrace not the cross, that by the cross I may be made alive, and by the cross (win) the common death of all and depart out of life?

Come hitler ye ministers of joy unto me, ye servants of Aegeates: accomplish the desire of us both, and bind the lamb unto the wood of suffering, the man unto the maker, the soul unto the Saviour.

And the blessed Andrew having thus spoken, standing upon the earth, looked earnestly upon the cross, and bade the brethren that the executioners should come and do that which was commanded them; for they stood afar off.

And they came and bound his hands and his feet and nailed them not; for such a charge had they from Aegeates; for he wished to afflict him by hanging him up, and that in the night he might be devoured alive by dogs (Laud. that he might be wearied out and permit Maximilla to live with him). And they left him hanging and departed from him.

And when the multitudes that stood by of them that had been made disciples in Christ by him saw that they had done unto him none of the things accustomed with them that are crucified, they hoped to hear something again from him. For as he hung, he moved his head and smiled. And Stratocles asked him, saying: Wherefore smilest thou, servant of God? thy laughter maketh us to mourn and weep because we are bereaved of thee. And the blessed Andrew answered him: Shall I not laugh, my son Stratocles, at the vain assault (ambush) of Aegeates, whereby he thinketh to punish us? we are strangers unto him and his conspiracies. He hath not to hear; for if he had, he would have heard that the man of Jesus cannot be punished, because he is henceforth known of him.

And thereafter he spake unto them all in common, for the heathen also were come together, being wroth at the unjust judgement of Aegeates.

Ye men that are here present, and women and children, old and young, bond and free, and all that will hear, take ye no heed of the vain deceit of this present life, but heed us rather who hang here for the Lord's sake and are about to depart out of this body: and renounce all the lusts of the world and contemn (spit upon) the worship of the abominable idols, and run unto the true worshipping of our God that lieth not, and make yourselves a temple pure and ready to receive the word. (Narr. then becomes obviously late: Ep. Gr., which is far shorter, ends: And hasten to overtake my soul as it hasteneth toward heavenly things, and in a word despise all temporal things, and establish your minds as men believing in Christ.)

And the multitudes hearing the things which he spake departed not from the place; and Andrew continued speaking yet more unto them, for a day and a night. And on the day following, beholding his endurance and constancy of soul and wisdom of spirit and strength of mind, they were wroth, and hastened with one accord unto Aegeates, to the judgement-seat where he sat, and cried out against him, saying: What is this judgement of thine, O proconsul ? thou hast ill judged! thou hast condemned unjustly: thy court is against law! What evil hath this man done? wherein hath he offended? The city is troubled: thou injurest us all! destroy not Caesar's city! give us the righteous man! restore us the holy man! slay not a man dear to God! destroy not a man gentle and pious! lo, two days is he hanged up and yet liveth, and hath tasted nothing, and yet refresheth all us with his words, and lo, we believe in the God whom he preacheth. Take down the righteous man and we will all turn philosophers; loose the chaste man and all Patrae will be at peace, set free the wise man and all Achaia shall be set free by him! (or, obtain mercy.)

But when at the first Aegeates would not hear them, but beckoned with the hand to the people that they should depart, they were filled with rage and were at the point to do him violence, being in number about two thousand (Narr., Ep. Gr., Mart. II: 20,000). And when the proconsul saw them to be after a sort mad, he feared lest there should be a rising against him, and rose up from the judgement-seat and went with them, promising to release Andrew. And some went before and signified to the apostle and to the rest of the people that were there, wherefore the proconsul was coming. And all the multitude of the disciples rejoiced together with Maximilla and Iphidamia and Stratocles.

But when Andrew heard it, he began to say: O the dullness and disobedience and simplicity of them whom I have taught! how much have I spoken, and even to this day I have not persuaded them to flee from the love of earthly things! but they are yet bound unto them and continue in them, and will not depart from them. What meaneth this affection and love and sympathy with the flesh? how long heed ye worldly and temporal things? how long understand ye not the things that be above us, and press not to overtake them? leave me henceforth to be put to death in the manner which ye behold, and let no man by any means loose me from these bonds, for so is it appointed unto me to depart out of the body and be present with the Lord, with whom also I am crucified. And this shall be accomplished.

And he turned unto Aegeates and said with a loud voice: Wherefore art thou come, Aegeates, that art an alien unto me? what wilt thou dare afresh, what contrive, or what fetch? tell us that thou hast repented and art come to loose us? nay, not if thou repentest, indeed, Aegeates, will I now consent unto thee, not if thou promise me all thy substance will I depart from myself, not if thou say that thou art mine will I trust thee. And dost thou, proconsul, loose him that is bound? him that hath been set free? that hath been recognized by his kinsman? that hath obtained mercy and is beloved of him? dost thou loose him that is alien to thee? the stranger? that only appeareth to thee? I have one with whom I shall be for ever, with whom I shall converse for unnumbered ages. Unto him do I go, unto him do I hasten, who made thee also known unto me, who said to me: Understand thou Aegeates and his gifts let not that fearful one afright thee, nor think that he holdeth thee who art mine. He is thine enemy: he is pestilent, a deceiver, a corrupter, a madman, a sorcerer, a cheat, a murderer, wrathful, without compassion. Depart therefore from me, thou worker of all iniquity. (Ep. Gr. He is thine enemy. Therefore I know thee, through him that permitted me to know.

I depart from thee. For I and they that are akin to me hasten toward that which is ours, and leave thee to be what thou wast, and what thou knowest not thyself to be.)

And the Proconsul hearing this stood speechless and as it were beside himself; but as all the city made an e uproar that he should loose Andrew, he drew near to the cross to loose him and take him down. But the blessed Andrew cried out with a loud voice: Suffer not Lord, thine Andrew that hath been bound upon thy cross, to be loosed again; give not me that am upon thy mystery to the shameless devil; O Jesu Christ, let not thine adversary loose him that is hung upon thy grace; O Father, let not this mean (little) one humble any more him that hath known thy greatness. But do thou, Jesu Christ, whom I have seen, whom I hold, whom I love, in whom I am and shall be, receive me in peace into thine everlasting tabernacles, that by my going out there may be an entering in unto thee of many that are akin to me, and that they may rest in thy majesty. And having so said, and yet more glorified the Lord, he gave up the ghost, while we all wept and lamented at our parting from him.

And after the decease of the blessed Andrew, Maximilla together with Stratocles, caring nought for them that stood by, drew near and herself loosed his body: and when it was evening she paid it the accustomed care and buried it (hard by the sea-shore). And she continued separate from Aegeates because of his brutal soul and his wicked manner of life: and she led a reverend and quiet life, filled with the love of Christ, among the brethren. Whom Aegeates solicited much, and promised that she should have the rule over his affairs; but being unable to persuade her, he arose in the dead of night and unknown to them of his house cast himself down from a great height and perished.

But Stratocles, which was his brother after the flesh, would not touch aught of the things that were left of his

substance; for the wretched man died without offspring: but said: Let thy goods go with thee, Aegeates. For of these things we have no need, for they are polluted; but for me, let Christ be my friend and I his servant, and all my substance do I offer unto him in whom I have believed, and I pray that by worthy hearing of the blessed teaching of the apostle I may appear a partaker with him in the ageless and unending kingdom. And so the uproar of the people ceased, and all were glad at the amazing and untimely and sudden fall of the impious and lawless Aegeates.

THE ACTS OF THE HOLY APOSTLE THOMAS

THE FIRST ACT
when he went into India with Abbanes the merchant.

1 At that season all we the apostles were at Jerusalem, Simon which is called Peter and Andrew his brother, James the son of Zebedee and John his brother, Philip and Bartholomew, Thomas and Matthew the publican, James the son of Alphaeus and Simon the Canaanite, and Judas the brother of James: and we divided the regions of the world, that every one of us should go unto the region that fell to him and unto the nation whereunto the Lord sent him.

According to the lot, therefore, India fell unto Judas Thomas, which is also the twin: but he would not go, saying that by reason of the weakness of the flesh he could not travel, and 'I am an Hebrew man; how can I go amongst the Indians and preach the truth?' And as he thus reasoned and spake, the Saviour appeared unto him by night and saith to him: Fear not, Thomas, go thou unto India and preach the word there, for my grace is with thee. But he would not obey, saying: Whither thou wouldest send me, send me, but elsewhere, for unto the Indians I will not go.

2 And while he thus spake and thought, it chanced that there was there a certain merchant come from India whose name was Abbanes, sent from the King Gundaphorus and having commandment from him to buy a carpenter and bring him unto him. Now the Lord seeing him walking in the market-place at noon said unto him: Wouldest thou buy a carpenter? And he said to him: Yea. And the Lord said to him: I have a slave that is a carpenter and I desire to sell him. And so saying he showed him Thomas afar off, and agreed with him for three litrae of silver unstamped, and wrote a deed of sale, saying: I, Jesus, the son of Joseph the carpenter, acknowledge that I have sold my slave, Judas by name, unto thee Abbanes, a merchant of Gundaphorus, king of the Indians. And when the deed was finished, the Saviour took Judas Thomas and led him away to Abbanes the merchant, and when Abbanes saw him he said unto him: Is this thy master? And the apostle said: Yea, he is my Lord. And he said: I have bought thee of him. And thy apostle held his peace.

3 And on the day following the apostle arose early, and having prayed and besought the Lord he said: I will go whither thou wilt, Lord Jesus: thy will be done. And he departed unto Abbanes the merchant, taking with him nothing at all save only his price. For the Lord had given it unto him, saying: Let thy price also be with thee, together with my grace, wheresoever thou goest. And the apostle found Abbanes carrying his baggage on board the ship; so he also began to carry it aboard with him. And when they were embarked in the ship and were set down Abbanes questioned the apostle, saying: What craftsmanship knowest thou? And he said: In wood I can make ploughs and yokes and augers (ox-goads, Syr.), and

boats and oars for boats and masts and pulleys; and in stone, pillars and temples and court-houses for kings. And Abbanes the merchant said to him: Yea, it is of such a workman that we have need. They began then to sail homeward; and they had a favourable wind, and sailed prosperously till they reached Andrapolis, a royal city.

4 And they left the ship and entered into the city, and lo, there were noises of flutes and water-organs, and trumpets sounded about them; and the apostle inquired, saying: What is this festival that is in this city? And they that were there said to him: Thee also have the gods brought to make merry in this city. For the king hath an only daughter, and now he giveth her in marriage unto an husband: this rejoicing, therefore, and assembly of the wedding to-day is the festival which thou hast seen. And the king hath sent heralds to proclaim everywhere that all should come to the marriage, rich and poor, bond and free, strangers and citizens: and if any refuse and come not to the marriage he shall answer for it unto the king. And Abbanes hearing that, said to the apostle: Let us also go, lest we offend the king, especially seeing we are strangers. And he said: Let us go. And after they had put up in the inn and rested a little space they went to the marriage; and the apostle seeing them all set down (reclining), laid himself, he also, in the midst, and all looked upon him, as upon a stranger and one come from a foreign land: but Abbanes the merchant, being his master, laid himself in another place.

5 And as they dined and drank, the apostle tasted nothing; so they that were about him said unto him: Wherefore art thou come here, neither eating nor drinking? but he answered them, saying: I am come here for somewhat greater than the food or the drink, and that I may fulfil the king's will. For the heralds proclaim the king's message, and whoso hearkeneth not to the heralds shall be subject to the king's judgement. So when they had dined and drunken, and garlands and unguents were

THE ACTS OF THE HOLY APOSTLE THOMAS

brought to them, every man took of the unguent, and one anointed his face and another his beard and another other parts of his body; but the apostle anointed the top of his head and smeared a little upon his nostrils, and dropped it into his ears and touched his teeth with it, and carefully anointed the parts about his heart: and the wreath that was brought to him, woven of myrtle and other flowers, he took, and set it on his head, and took a branch of calamus and held it in his hand.

Now the flute-girl, holding her flute in her hand, went about to them all and played, but when she came to the place where the apostle was, she stood over him and played at his head for a long space: now this flute-girl was by race an Hebrew.

6 And as the apostle continued looking on the ground, one of the cup-bearers stretched forth his hand and gave him a buffet; and the apostle lifted up his eyes and looked upon him that smote him and said: My God will forgive thee in the life to come this iniquity, but in this world thou shalt show forth his wonders and even now shall I behold this hand that hath smitten me dragged by dogs. And having so said, he began to sing and to say this song:

The damsel is the daughter of light, in whom consisteth and dwelleth the proud brightness of kings, and the sight of her is delightful, she shineth with beauty and cheer. Her garments are like the flowers of spring, and from them a waft of fragrance is borne; and in the crown of her head the king is established which with his immortal food (ambrosia) nourisheth them that are founded upon him; and in her head is set truth, and with her feet she showeth forth joy. And her mouth is opened, and it becometh her well: thirty and two are they that sing praises to her. Her tongue is like the curtain of the door, which waveth to and fro for them that enter in: her neck is set in the fashion of steps which the first maker hath wrought, and her two hands signify and show, proclaiming the dance of the happy ages, and her fingers point out the gates of the city. Her chamber is bright with light and breatheth forth the odour of balsam and all spices, and giveth out a sweet smell of myrrh and Indian leaf, and within are myrtles strown on the floor, and of all manner of odorous flowers, and the door-posts(?) are adorned with freedst.

7 And surrounding her her groomsmen keep her, the number of whom is seven, whom she herself hath chosen. And her bridesmaids are seven, and they dance before her. And twelve in number are they that serve before her and are subject unto her, which have their aim and their look toward the bridegroom, that by the sight of him they may be enlightened; and for ever shall they be with her in that eternal joy, and shall be at that marriage whereto the princes are gathered together and shall attend at that banquet whereof the eternal ones are accounted worthy, and shall put on royal raiment and be clad in bright robes; and in joy and exultation shall they both be and shall glorify the Father of all, whose proud light they have received, and are enlightened by the sight of their lord; whose immortal food they have received, that hath no failing (excrementum, Syr.), and have drunk of the wine that giveth then neither thirst nor desire. And they have glorified and praised with the living spirit, the Father of truth and the mother of wisdom.

8 And when he had sung and ended this song, all that were there present gazed upon him; and he kept silence, and they saw that his likeness was changed, but that which was spoken by him they understood not, forasmuch as he was an Hebrew and that which he spake was said in the Hebrew tongue. But the flute-girl alone heard all of it, for she was by race an Hebrew and she went away from him and played to the rest, but for the most part she gazed and looked upon him, for she loved him well, as a man of her own nation; moreover he was comely to look upon beyond all that were there. And when the flute-girl had played to them all and ended, she sat down over against him, gazing and looking earnestly upon him.

But he looked upon no man at all, neither took heed of any but only kept his eyes looking toward the ground, waiting the time when he might depart thence.

But the cup-bearer that had buffeted him went down to the well to draw water; and there chanced to be a lion there, and it slew him and left him lying in that place, having torn his lirmbs in pieces, and forthwith dogs seized his members, and among them one black dog holding his right hand in his mouth bare it into the place of the banquet.

9 And all when they saw it were amazed and inquired which of them it was that was missing. And when it became manifest that it was the hand of the cup-bearer which had smitten the apostle, the flute-girl brake her flute and cast it away and went and sat down at the apostle's feet, saying: This is either a god or an apostle of God, for I heard him say in the Hebrew tongue: ' I shall now see the hand that hath smitten me dragged by dogs', which thing ye also have now beheld; for as he said, so hath it come about. And some believed her, and some not.

But when the king heard of it, he came and said to the apostle: Rise up and come with me, and pray for my daughter: for she is mine only-begotten, and to-day I give her in marriage. But the apostle was not willing to go with him, for the Lord was not yet revealed unto him in that place. But the king led him away against his will unto the bride-chamber that he might pray for them.

10 And the apostle stood, and began to pray and to speak thus: My Lord and mv God, that travellest with thy servants, that guidest and correctest them that believe in thee, the refuge and rest of the oppressed, the hope of the poor and ransomer of captives, the physician of the souls that lie sick and saviour of all creation, that givest life unto the world and strengthenest souls; thou knowest things to come, and by our means accomplishest them: thou Lord art he that revealeth hidden mysteries and maketh manifest words that are secret: thou Lord art the planter of the good tree, and of thine hands are all good works engendered: thou Lord art he that art in all things and passest through all, and art set in all thy works and manifested in the working of them all. Jesus Christ, Son of compassion and perfect saviour, Christ, Son of the living God, the undaunted power that hast overthrown the enemy, and the voice that was heard of the rulers, and made all their powers to quake, the ambassador that wast sent from the height and camest down even unto hell, who didst open the doors and bring up thence them that for many ages were shut up in the treasury of darkness, and showedst them the way that leadeth up unto the height: I beseech thee, Lord Jesu, and offer unto thce supplication for these young persons, that thou wouldest do for them the things that shall help them and be expedient and profitable for them. And he laid his hands on them and said: The Lord shall be with you, and left them in that place and departed.

11 And the king desired the groomsmen to depart out of the bride-chamber; and when all were gone out and the doors were shut, the bridegrroom lifted up the curtain of the bride-chamber to fetch the bride unto him. And he saw the Lord Jesus bearing the likeness of Judas Thomas and speaking with the bride; even of him that but now had blessed them and gone out from them, the apostle; and he saith unto him: Wentest thou not out in the sight of all? how then art thou found here? But the Lord said to him: I am not Judas which is also called Thomas but I am his brother. And the Lord sat down upon the bed and bade them also sit upon chairs, and began to say unto them:

12 Remember, my children, what my brother spake unto you and what he delivered before you: and know this, that if ye abstain from this foul intercourse, ye become holy temples, pure, being quit of impulses and pains, seen and unseen, and ye will acquire no cares of life or of children, whose end is destruction: and if indeed ye get many

children, for their sakes ye become grasping and covetous, stripping orphans and overreaching widows, and by so doing subject yourselves to grievous punishments. For the more part of children become useless oppressed of devils, some openly and some invisibly, for they become either lunatic or half withered or blind or deaf or dumb or paralytic or foolish; and if they be sound, again they will be vain, doing useless or abominable acts, for they will be caught either in adultery or murder or theft or fornication, and by all these vvill ye be afflicted.

But if ye be persuaded and keep your souls chaste before God, there will come unto you living children whom these blemishes touch not, and ye shall be without care, leading a tranquil life without grief or anxiety, looking to receive that incorruptible and true marriage, and ye shall be therein groomsmen entering into that bride-chamber which is full of immortality and light.

13 And when the young people heard these things, they believed the Lord and gave themselves up unto him, and abstained from foul desire and continued so, passing the night in that place. And the Lord departed from before them, saying thus: The grace of the Lord shall be with you.

And when the morning was come the king came to meet them and furnished a table and brought it in before the bridegroom and the bride. And he found them sitting over against each other and the face of the bride he found unveiled, and the bridegroom was right joyful. And the mother came unto the bride and said: Why sittest thou so, child, and art not ashamed, but art as if thou hadst lived with thine husband a long season? And her father said: Because of thy great love toward thine husband dost thou not even veil thyself?

14 And the bride answered and said: Verily, father, I am in great love, and I pray my Lord that the love which I have perceived this night may abide with me, and I will ask for that husband of whom I have learned to-day: and therefore I will no more veil myself, because the mirror (veil) of shame is removed from me; and therefore am I no more ashamed or abashed, because the deed of shame and confusion is departed far from me; and that I am not confounded, it is because my astonishment hath not continued with me; and that I am in cheerfulness and joy, it is because the day of my joy hath not been troubled; and that I have set at nought this husband and this marriage that passeth away from before mine eyes, it is because I am joined in another marriage; and that I have had no intercourse with a husband that is temporal, whereof the end is with lasciviousness and bitterness of soul, it is because I am yoked unto a true husband.

15 And while the bride was saying yet more than this, the bridegroom answered and said: I give thee thanks, O Lord, that hast been proclaimed by the stranger, and found in us; who hast removed me far from corruption and sown life in me; who hast rid me of this disease that is hard to be healed and cured and abideth for ever, and hast implanted sober health in me; who hast shown me thyself and revealed unto me all my state wherein I am; who hast redeemed me from falling and led me to that which is better, and set me free from temporal things and made me worthy of those that are immortal and everlasting; that hast made thyself lowly even down to me and my littleness, that thou mayest present me unto thy greatness and unite me unto thyself; who hast not withheld thine own bowels from me that was ready to perish, but hast shown me how to seek myself and know who I was, and who and in what manner I now am, that I may again become that which I was: whom I knew not, but thyself didst seek me out: of whom I was not aware, but thyself hast taken me to thee: whom I have perceived, and now am not able to be unmindful of him: whose love burneth within me, and I cannot speak it as is fit, but that which I am able to say of it is little and scanty, and not fitly

proportioned unto his glory: yet he blameth me not that presume to say unto him even that which I know not: for it is because of his love that I say even this much.

16 Now when the king heard these things from the bridegroom and the bride, he rent his clothes and said unto them that stood by him: Go forth quickly and go about the whole city, and take and bring me that man that is a sorcerer who by ill fortune came unto this city; for with mine own hands I brought him into this house, and I told him to pray over this mine ill-starred daugllter; and whoso findeth and bringeth him to me, I will give him whatsoever he asketh of me. They went, therefore and went about seeking him, and found him not; for he had set sail. They went also unto the inn where he had lodged and found there the flute-girl weeping and afflicted because he had not taken her with him. And when they told her the matter that had befallen with the young people she was exceeding glad at hearing it, and put away her grief and said: Now have I also found rest here. And she rose up and went unto them, and was with them a long time, until they had instructed the king also. And many of the brethren also gathered there until they heard the report of the apostle, that he was come unto the cities of India and was teaching there: and they departed and joined themselves unto him.

THE SECOND ACT
concerning his coming unto the king Gundaphorus.

17 Now when the apostle was come into the cities of India with Abbanes the merchant, Abbanes went to salute the king Gundaphorus, and reported to him of the carpenter whom he had brought with him. And the king was glad, and commanded him to come in to him. So when he was come in the king said unto him: What craft understandest thou? The apostle said unto him: The craft of carpentering and of building. The king saith unto him: What craftsmanship,

then, knowest thou in wood, and what in stone? The apostle saith: In wood: ploughs, yokes, goads, pulleys, and boats and oars and masts; and in stone: plllars, temples, and court-houses for kings. And the king said: Canst thou build me a palace? And he answered: Yea, I can both build and furnish it; for to this end am I come, to build and to do the work of a carpenter.

18 And the king took him and went out of the city gates and began to speak with him on the way concerning the building of the court-house, and of the foundations, how they should be laid, until they came to the place wherein he desired that the building should be; and he said: Here will I that the building should be. And the apostle said: Yea, for this place is suitable for the building. But the place was woody and there was much water there. So the king said: Begin to build. But he said: I cannot begin to build now at this season. And the king said: When canst thou begin? And he said: I will begin in the month Dius and finish in Xanthicus. But the king marvelled and said: Every building is builded in summer, and canst thou in this very winter build and make ready a palace? And the apostle said: Thus it must be, and no otherwise is it possible. And the king said: If, then, this seem good to thee, draw me a plan, how the work shall be, because I shall return hither after some long time. And the apostle took a reed and drew, measuring the place; and the doors he set toward the sunrising to look toward the light, and the windows toward the west to the breezes, and the bakehouse he appointed to be toward the south and the aqueduct for the service toward the north. And the king saw it and said to the apostle: Verily thou art a craftsman and it belitteth thee to be a servant of kings. And he left much money with him and departed from him.

19 And from time to time he sent money and provision, and victual for him and the rest of the workmen. But Thomas receiving it all dispensed it, going about the cities and the villages round about, distributing and giving

alms to the poor and afflicted, and relieving them, saying: The king knoweth how to obtain recompense fit for kings, but at this time it is needful that the poor should have refreshment. After these things the king sent an ambassador unto the apostle, and wrote thus: Signify unto me what thou hast done or what I shall send thee, or of what thou hast need. And the apostle sent unto him, saying: The palace (praetorium) is builded and only the roof remaineth. And the king hearing it sent him again gold and silver (lit. unstamped), and wrote unto him: Let the palace be roofed, if it is done. And the apostle said unto the Lord: I thank thee O Lord in all things, that thou didst die for a little space that I might live for ever in thee, and that thou hast sold me that by me thou mightest set free many. And he ceased not to teach and to refresh the afflicted, saying: This hath the Lord dispensed unto you, and he giveth unto every man his food: for he is the nourisher of orphans and steward of the widows, and unto all that are afflicted he is relief and rest.

20 Now when the king came to the city he inquired of his friends concerning the palace which Judas that is called Thomas was building for him. And they told him: Neither hath he built a palace nor done aught else of that he promised to perform, but he goeth about the cities and countries, and whatsoever he hath he giveth unto the poor, and teacheth of a new God, and healeth the sick, and driveth out devils, and doeth many other wonderful things; and we think him to be a sorcerer. Yet his compassions and his cures which are done of him freely, and moreover the simplicity and kindness of him and his faith, do declare that he is a righteous man or an apostle of the new God whom he preacheth; for he fasteth continually and prayeth, and eateth bread only, with salt, and his drink is water, and he weareth but one garment alike in fair weather and in winter, and receiveth nought of any man, and that he hath he giveth unto others. And when the king heard that, he rubbed his face with his hands, and shook his head for a long space.

21 And he sent for the merchant which had brought him, and for the apostle, and said unto him: Hast thou built me the palace? And he said: Yea. And the king said: When, then, shall we go and see it? but he answered him and said: Thou canst not see it now, but when thou departest this life, then thou shalt see it. And the king was exceeding wroth, and commanded both the merchant and Judas which is called Thomas to be put in bonds and cast into prison until he should inquire and learn unto whom the king's money had been given, and so destroy both him and the merchant.

And the apostle went unto the prison rejoicing, and said to the merchant: Fear thou nothing, only believe in the God that is preached by me, and thou shalt indeed be set free from this world, but from the world to come thou shalt receive life. And the king took thought with what death he should destroy them. And when he had determined to flay them alive and burn them with fire, in the same night Gad the king's brother fell sick, and by reason of his vexation and the deceit which the king had suffered he was greatly oppressed; and sent for the king and said unto him: O king my brother, I commit unto thee mine house and my children; for I am vexed by reason of the provocation that hath befallen thee, and lo, I die; and if thou visit not with vengeance upon the head of that sorcerer, thou wilt give my soul no rest in hell. And the king said to his brother: All this night have I considered how I should put him to death and this hath seemed good to me, to flay him and burn him with fire, both him and the merchant which brought him (Syr. Then the brother of the king said to him: And if there be anything else that is worse than this, do it to him; and I give thee charge of my house and my children).

22 And as they talked together, the soul of his brother Gad departed. And the king mourned sore for Gad, for he loved him much, and commanded that

he should be buried in royal and precious apparel (Syr. sepulchre). Now after this angels took the soul of Gad the king's brother and bore it up into heaven, showing unto him the places and dwellings that were there, and inquired of him: In which place wouldest thou dwell? And when they drew near unto the building of Thomas the apostle which he had built for the king, Gad saw it and said unto the angels: I beseech you, my lords, suffer me to dwell in one of the lowest rooms of these. And they said to him: Thou canst not dwell in this building. And he said: Wherefore ? And they say unto him: This is that palace which that Christian builded for thy brother. And he said: I beseech you, my lords, suffer me to go to my brother, that I may buy this palace of him, for my brother knoweth not of what sort it is, and he will sell it unto me.

23 Then the angels let the soul of Gad go. And as they were putting his grave clothes upon him, his soul entered into him and he said to them that stood about him: Call my brother unto me, that I may ask one petition of him. Straightway therefore they told the king, saying: Thy brother is revived. And the king ran forth with a great company and came unto his brother and entered in and stood by his bed as one amazed, not being able to speak to him. And his brother said: I know and am persuaded, my brother, that if any man had asked of thee the half of thy kingdom, thou wouldest have given it him for my sake; therefore I beg of thee to grant me one favour which I ask of thee, that thou wouldest sell me that which I ask of thee. And the king answered and said: And what is it which thou askest me to sell thee? And he said: Convince me by an oath that thou wilt grant it me. And the king sware unto him: One of my possessions, whatsoever thou shalt ask, I will give thee. And he saith to him: Sell me that palace which thou hast in the heavens ? And the king said: Whence should I have a palace in the heavens? And he said: Even that which

that Christian built for thee which is now in the prison, whom the merchant brought unto thee, having purchased him of one Jesus: I mean that Hebrew slave whom thou desiredst to punish as having suffered deceit at his hand: whereat I was grieved and died, and am now revived.

24 Then the king considering the matter, understood it of those eternal benefits which should come to him and which concerned him, and said: That palace I cannot sell thee, but I pray to enter into it and dwell therein and to be accounted worthy of the inhabiters of it, but if thou indeed desirest to buy such a palace, lo, the man liveth and shall build thee one better than it. And forthwith he sent and brought out of prison the apostle and the merchant that was shut up with him, saying: I entreat thee, as a man that entreateth the minister of God, that thou wouldest pray for me and beseech him whose minister thou art to forgive me and overlook that which I have done unto thee or thought to do, and that I may become a worthy inhabiter of that dwelling for the which I took no pains, but thou hast builded it for me, labouring alone, the grace of thy God working with thee, and that I also may become a servant and serve this God whom thou preachest. And his brother also fell down before the apostle and said: I entreat and supplicate thee before thy God that I may become worthy of his ministry and service, and that it may fall to me to be worthy of the things that were shown unto me by his angels.

25 And the apostle, filled with joy, said: I praise thee, O Lord Jesu, that thou hast revealed thy truth in these men; for thou only art the God of truth, and none other, and thou art he that knoweth all things that are unknown to the most; thou, Lord, art he that in all things showest compassion and sparest men. For men by reason of the error that is in them have overlooked thee but thou hast not overlooked them. And now at my supplication and request do thou receive the king and his brother and join

them unto thy fold, cleansing them with thy washing and anointing them with thine oil from the error that encompasseth them: and keep them also from the wolves, bearing them into thy meadows. And give them drink out of thine immortal fountain which is neither fouled nor drieth up; for they entreat and supplicate thee and desire to become thy servants and ministers, and for this they are content even to be persecuted of thine enemies, and for thy sake to be hated of them and to be mocked and to die, like as thou for our sake didst suffer all these things, that thou mightest preserve us, thou that art Lord and verily the good shepherd. And do thou grant them to have confidence in thee alone, and the succour that cometh of thee and the hope of their salvation which they look for from thee alone; and that they may be grounded in thy mysteries and receive the perfect good of thy graces and gifts, and flourish in thy ministry and come to perfection in thy Father.

26 Being therefore wholly set upon the apostle, both the king Gundaphorus and Gad his brother followed him and departed not from him at all, and they also relieved them that had need giving unto all and refreshing all. And they besought him that they also might henceforth receive the seal of the word, saying unto him: Seeing that our souls are at leisure and eager toward God, give thou us the seal; for we have heard thee say that the God whom thou preachest knoweth his own sheep by his seal. And the apostle said unto them: I also rejoice and entreat you to receive this seal, and to partake with me in this eucharist and blessing of the Lord, and to be made perfect therein. For this is the Lord and God of all, even Jesus Christ whom I preach, and he is the father of truth, in whom I have taught you to believe. And he commanded them to bring oil, that they might receive the seal by the oil. They brought the oil therefore, and lighted many lamps; for it was night (Syr. whom I preach: and the king gave orders that the bath should be closed for seven

days, and that no man should bathe in it: and when the seven days were done, on the eighth day they three entered into the bath by night that Judas might baptize them. And many lamps were lighted in the bath).

27 And the apostle arose and sealed them. And the Lord was revealed unto them by a voice, saying: Peace be unto you brethren. And they heard his voice only, but his likeness they saw not, for they had not yet received the added sealing of the seal (Syr. had not been baptized). And the apostle took the oil and poured it upon their heads and anointed and chrismed them, and began to say (Syr. And Judas went up and stood upon the edge of the cistern and poured oil upon their heads and said): Come, thou holy name of the Christ that is above every name.

Come, thou power of the Most High, and the compassion that is perfect.

Come, gift (charism) of the Most High.

Come, compassionate mother.

Come, communion of the male.

Come, she that revealeth the hidden mysteries.

Come, mother of the seven houses, that thy rest may be in the eighth house.

Come, elder of the five members, mind, thought, reflection, consideration, reason; communicate with these young men.

Come, holy spirit, and cleanse their reins and their heart, and give them the added seal, in the name of the Father and Son and Holy Ghost.

And when they were sealed, there appeared unto them a youth holding a lighted torch, so that their lamps became dim at the approach of the light thereof. And he went forth and was no more seen of them. And the apostle said unto the Lord: Thy light, O Lord, is not to be contained by us, and we are not able to bear it, for it is too great for our sight.

And when the dawn came and it was morning, he brake bread and made them partakers of the eucharist of the Christ. And they were glad and rejoiced. And many others also, believing, were added to them, and came into the refuge of the Saviour.

28 And the apostle ceased not to preach and to say unto them: Ye men and women, boys and girls, young men and maidens, strong men and aged, whether bond or free, abstain from fornication and covetousness and the service of the belly: for under these three heads all iniquity cometh about. For fornication blindeth the mind and darkeneth the eyes of the soul, and is an impediment to the life (conversation) of the body, turning the whole man unto weakness and casting the whole body into sickness. And greed putteth the soul into fear and shame; being within the body it seizeth upon the goods of others, and is under fear lest if it restore other men's goods to their owner it be put to shame. And the service of the belly casteth the soul into thoughts and cares and vexations, taking thought lest it come to be in want, and have need of those things that are far from it. If, then, ye be rid of these ye become free of care and grief and fear, and that abideth with you which was said by the Saviour: Take no thought for the morrow, for the morrow shall take thought for the things of itself. Remember also that word of him of whom I spake: Look at the ravens and see the fowls of the heaven, that they neither sow nor reap nor gather into barns, and God dispenseth unto them; how much more unto you, O ye of little faith? But look ye for his coming and have your hope in him and believe on his name. For he is the judge of quick and dead, and he giveth to every one according to their deeds, and at his coming and his latter appearing no man hath any word of excuse when he is to be judged by him, as though he had not heard. For his heralds do proclaim in the four quarters (climates) of the world. Repent ye, therefore, and believe the promise and receive the yoke of meekness and the light burden, that ye may live and not die. These things get, these keep. Come forth of the darkness that the light may receive you! Come unto him that is indeed good, that ye may receive grace of him and implant his sign in your souls.

29 And when he had thus spoken, some of them that stood by said: It is time for the creditor to receive the debt. And he said unto them: He that is lord of the debt desireth alway to receive more; but let us give him that which is due. And he blessed them, and took bread and oil and herbs and salt and blessed and gave unto them; but he himself continued his fast, for the Lord's day was coming on (Syr. And he himself ate, because the Sunday was dawning).

And when night fell and he slept, the Lord came and stood at his head, saying: Thomas, rise early, and having blessed them all, after the prayer and the ministry go by the eastern road two miles and there will I show thee my glory: for by thy going shall many take refuge with me, and thou shalt bring to light the nature and power of the enemy. And he rose up from sleep and said unto the brethren that were with him: Children, the Lord would accomplish somewhat by me to-day, but let us pray, and entreat of him that we may have no impediment toward him, but that as at all times, so now also it may be done according to his desire and will by us. And having so said, he laid his hands on them and blessed them, and brake the bread of the eucharist and gave it them, saying: This encharist shall be unto you for compassion and mercy, and not unto judgement and retribution. And they said Amen.

THE THIRD ACT
concerning the servent

30 And the apostle went forth to go where the Lord had bidden him; and when he was near to the second mile (stone) and had turned a little out of the way, he saw the body of a comely youth lying, and said: Lord, is it for this that thou hast brought me forth, to come hither that I might see this (trial) temptation? thy will therefore be done as thou desirest. And he began to pray and to say: O Lord, the judge of quick and dead, of the quick that stand by and the dead that lie here, and master and

father of all things; and father not only of the souls that are in bodies but of them that have gone forth of them, for of the souls also that are in pollutions (al. bodies) thou art lord and judge; come thou at this hour wherein I call upon thee and show forth thy glory upon him that lieth here. And he turned himself unto them that followed him and said: This thing is not come to pass without cause, but the enemy hath effected it and brought it about that he may assault (?) us thereby; and see ye that he hath not made use of another sort, nor wrought through any other creature save that which is his subjcct. 31 And when he had so said, a great (Syr. black) serpent (dragon) came out of a hole, beating with his head and shaking his tail upon the ground, and with (using) a loud voice said unto the apostle: I will tell before thee the cause wherefor I slew this man, since thou art come hither for that end, to reprove my works. And the apostle said: Yea, say on. And the serpent: There is a certain beautiful woman in this village over against us; and as she passed by me (or my place) I saw her and was enamoured of her, and I followed her and kept watch upon her; and I found this youth kissing her, and he had intercourse with her and did other shameful acts with her: and for me it was easy to declare them before thee, for I know that thou art the twin brother of the Christ and alway abolishest our nature (Syr. easy for me to say, but to thee I do not dare to utter them because I know that the ocean-flood of the Messiah will destroy our nature): but because I would not affright her, I slew him not at that time, but waited for him till he passed by in the evening and smote and slew him, and especially because he adventured to do this upon the Lord's day.
And the apostlc inquired of him, saying: Tell me of what seed and of what race thou art. 32 And he said unto him: I am a reptile of the reptile nature and noxious son of the noxious father: of him that hurt and smote the four brethren which stood upright (om. Syr.: the elerments or four cardinal points

may be meant) I am son to him that sitteth on a throne over all the earth that receiveth back his own from them that borrow: I am son to him that girdeth about the sphere: and I am kin to him that is outside the ocean, whose tail is set in his own mouth: I am he that entered through the barrier (fence) into paradise and spake with Eve the things which my father bade me speak unto her: I am he that kindled and inflamed Cain to kill his own brother, and on mine account did thorns and thistles grow up in the earth: I am he that cast down the angels from above and bound them in lusts after women, that children born of earth might come of them and I might work my will in them: I am he that hardened Pharaoh's heart that he should slay the children of Israel and enslave them with the yoke of cruelty: I am he that caused the multitude to err in the wilderness when they made the calf: I am he that inflamed Herod and enkindled Caiaphas unto false accusation of a lie before Pilate; for this was fitting to me: I am he that stirred up Judas and bribed him to deliver up the Christ: I am he that inhabiteth and holdeth the deep of hell (Tartarus), but the Son of God hath wronged rne, against my will, and taken (chosen) them that were his own from me: I am kin to him that is to come from the east, unto whom also power is given to do what he will upon the earth.
33 And wllen that serpent had spoken these things in the hearing of all the people, the apostle lifted up his voice on high and said: Cease thou henceforth, O most shameless one, and be put to confusion and die wholly, for the end of thy destruction is come, and dare not to tell of what thou hast done by them that have become subject unto thee. And I charge thee in the name of that Jesus who until now contendeth with you for the men that are his own, that thou suck out thy venom which thou hast put into this man, and draw it forth and take it from him. But the serpent said: Not yet is the end of our time come as thou hast said. Wherefore compellest thou me to take back that

which I have put into this man, and to die before my time? for mine own father, when he shall draw forth and suck out that which he hath cast into the creation, then shall his end come. And the apostle said unto him: Show, then, now the nature of thy father. And the serpent came near and set his mouth upon the wound of the young man and sucked forth the gall out of it. And by little and little the colour of the young man which was as purple, became white, but the serpent swelled up. And when the serpent had drawn up all the gall into himself, the young man leapt up and stood, and ran and fell at the apostle's feet: but the serpent being swelled up, burst and died, and his venom and gall were shed forth; and in the place where his venom was shed there came a great gulf, and that serpent was swallowed up therein. And the apostle said unto the king and his brother: Take workmen and fill up that place, and lay foundations and build houses upon them, that it may be a dwelling-place for strangers.

34 But the youth said unto the apostle with many tears: Wherein have I sinned against thee? for thou art a man that hast two forms, and wheresoever thou wilt, there thou art found, and art restrained of no man, as I behold. For I saw that man that stood by thee and said unto thee: I have many wonders to show forth by thy means and I have great works to accomplish by thee, for which thou shalt receive a reward; and thou shalt make many to live, and they shall be in rest in light eternal as children of God. Do thou then, saith he, speaking unto thee of me, quicken this youth that hath been stricken of the enemy and be at all times his overseer. Well, therefore, art thou come hither, and well shalt thou depart again unto him, and yet he never shall leave thee at any time. But I am become without care or reproach: and he hath enlightened me from the care of the night and I am at rest from the toil of the day: and I am set free from him that provoked me to do thus, sinning against him that taught me to do contrary thereto: and I have

lost him that is the kinsman of the night that compelled me to sin by his own deeds, and have found him that is of the light, and is my kinsman. I have lost him that darkeneth and blindeth his own subjects that they may not know what they do and, being ashamed at their own works, may depart from him, and their works come to an end; and have found him whose works are light and his deeds truth, which if a man doeth he repenteth not of them. And I have left him with whom lying abideth, and before whom darkness goeth as a veil, and behind him followeth shame, shameless in indolence; and I have found him that showeth me fair things that I may take hold on them, even the son of the truth that is akin unto concord, who scattereth away the mist and enlighteneth his own creation, and healeth the wounds thereof and overthroweth the enemies thereof. But I beseech thee, O man of God, cause me to behold him again, and to see him that is now become hidden from me, that I may also hear his voice whereof I am not able to express the wonder, for it belongeth not to the nature of this bodily organ.

35 And the apostle answered him, saying: If thou depart from these things whereof thou hast received knowledge, as thou hast said, and if thou know who it is that hath wrought this in thee, and learn and become a hearer of him whom now in thy fervent love thou seekest; thou shalt both see him and be with him for ever, and in his rest shalt thou rest, and shalt be in his joy. But if thou be slackly disposed toward him and turn again unto thy former deeds, and leave that beauty and that bright countenance which now was showed thee, and forget the shining of his light which now thou desirest, not only wilt thou be bereaved of this life but also of that which is to come and thou wilt depart unto him whom thou saidst thou hadst lost, and will no more behold him whom thou saidst thou hadst found.

36 And when the apostle had said this, he went into the city holding the hand of that youth, and saying unto him:

These things which thou hast seen, my child, are but a few of the many which God hath, for he doth not give us good tidings concerning these things that are seen, but greater things than these doth he promise us; but so long as we are in the body we are not able to speak and show forth those which he shall give unto our souls. If we say that he giveth us light, it is this which is seen, and we have it: and if we say it of wealth, which is and appeareth in the world, we name it (we speak of something which is in the world, Syr.), and we need it not, for it hath been said: Hardly shall a rich man enter into the kingdom of heaven: and if we speak of apparel of raiment wherewith they that are luxurious in this life are clad, it is named (we mention something that nobles wear, Syr.), and it hath been said: They that wear soft raiment are in the houses of kings. And if of costiy banquets, concerning these we have received a commandment to beware of them, not to be weighed down With revelling and drunkenness and cares of this life -speaking of things that are- and it hath been said: Take no thought for your life (soul), what ye shall eat or what ye shall drink, neither for your body, what ye shall put on, for the soul is more than the meat and the body than the raiment. And of rest, if we speak of this temporal rest, a judgement is appointed for this also. But we speak of the world which is above, of God and angels, of watchers and holy ones of the immortal (ambrosial) food and the drink of the true vine, of raiment that endureth and groweth not old, of things which eye hath not seen nor ear heard, neither have they entered into the heart of sinful men, the things which God hath prepared for them that love him. Of these things do we converse and of these do we bring good tidings. Do thou therefore also believe on him that thou mayest live, and put thy trust in him, and thou shalt not die. For he is not persuaded with gifts, that thou shouldest offer them to him, neither is he in need of sacrifices, that thou shouldest sacrifice unto him. But look

thou unto him, and he will not overlook thee; and turn unto him, and he will not forsake thee. For his comeliness and his beauty will make thee wholly desirous to love him: and indeed he permitteth thee not to turn thyself away.

37 And when the apostle had said these things unto that youth, a great multitude joined themselves unto them. And the apostle looked and saw them raising themselves on high that they might see him, and they were going up into high places; and the apostle said unto them: Ye men that are come unto the assembly of Christ, and would believe on Jesus, take example hereby, and see that if ye be not lifted up, ye cannot see me who am little, and are not able to spy me out who am like unto you. If, then, ye cannot see me who am like you unless ye lift yourselves up a little from the earth, how can ye see him that dwelleth in the height and now is found in the depth, unless ye first lift yourselves up out of your former conversation, and your unprofitable deeds, and your desires that abide not, and the wealth that is left here, and the possession of earth that groweth old, and the raiment that corrupteth, and the beauty that waxeth old and vanisheth away, and yet more out of the whole body wherein all these things are stored up, and which groweth old and becometh dust, returning unto its own nature? For it is the body which maintaineth all these things. But rather believe on our Lord Jesus Christ, vvhom we preach, that your hope may be in him and in him ye may have life world without end, that he may become your fellow traveller in this land of error, and may be to you an harbour in this troublous sea. And he shall be to you a fountain springing up in this thirsty land and a chamber fill of food in this place of them that hunger, and a rest unto your souls, yea, and a physician for your bodies.

38 Then the multitude of them that were gathered together hearing these things wept, and said unto the apostle: O man of God, the God whom thou preachest, we dare not say that we are his, for the

works which we have done are alien unto him and not pleasing to him; but if he will have compassion on us and pity us and save us, overlooking our former decds, and will set us free from the evils which we committed being in error, and not impute them unto us nor make remembrance of our former sins, we will become his servants and will accomplish his will unto the end. And the apostle answered them and said: He reckoneth not against you, neither taketh account of the sins which ye committed being in error, but overlooketh your transgressions which ye have done in ignorance.

THE FOURTH ACT
concerning the colt

39 And while the apostle yet stood in the highway and spake with the multitude, A she ass's colt came and stood before him (Syr. adds, And Judas said: It is not without the direction of God that this colt has come hither. But to thee I say, O colt that by the grace of our Lord there shall be given to thee speech before these multitudes who are standing here; and do thou say whatsoever thou wilt, that they may believe in the God of truth whom we preach. And the mouth of the colt was opened, and it spake by the power of our Lord and said to him) and opened its mouth and said: Thou twin of Christ, apostle of the Most High and initiate in the hidden word of Christ who receivest his secret oracles, fellow worker with the Son of God, who being free hast become a bondman, and being sold hast brought many into liberty. Thou kinsman of the great race that hath condemned the enemy and redeemed his own, that hast become an occasion of life unto man in the land of the Indians; for thou hast come (against thy will, Syr.) unto men that were in error, and by thy appearing and thy divine words they are now turning unto the God of truth which sent thee: mount and sit upon me and repose thyself until thou enter into the city. And the apostle answered and said: O Jesu Christ (Son)

that understandest the perfect mercy! O tranquillity and quiet that now art spoken of (speakest, Syr.) by (among) brute beasts! O hidden rest, that art manifested by thy working, Saviour of us and nourisher, keeping us and resting in alien bodies! O Saviour of our souls! spring that is sweet and unfailing; fountain secure and clear and never polluted; defender and helper in the fight of thine own servants, turning away and scaring the enemy from us, that fightest in many battles for us and makest us conquerors in all; our true and undefeated champion (athlete); our holy and victorious captain: glorious and giving unto thine own a joy that never passeth away, and a relief wherein is none affliction; good shepherd that givest thyself for thine own sheep, and hast vanquished the wolf and redeemed thine own lambs and led them into a good pasture: we glorify and praise thee and thine invisible Father and thine holy sipirit [and] the mother of all creation.
40 And when the apostle had said these things, all the multitude that were there looked upon him, expecting to hear what he would answer to the colt. And the apostle stood a long time as it were astonied, and looked up into heaven and said to the colt: Of whom art thou and to whom belongest thou? for marvellous are the things that are shown forth by thy mouth, and amazing and such as are hidden frorn the many. And the colt answered and said: I am of that stock that served Balaam, and thy lord also and teacher sat upon one that appertained unto me by race. And I also have now been sent to give thee rest by thy sitting upon me: and (that) I may receive (Syr. these may be confirmed in) faith, and unto me may be added that portion which now I shall receive by thy service wherewith I serve thee; and when I have ministered unto thee, it shall be taken from me. And the apostle said unto him: He is able who granted thee this gift, to cause it to be fulfilled unto the end in thee and in them that belong unto thee by race: for as to this mystery I am weak and powerless. And

he would not sit upon him. But the colt besought and entreated him that he might be blessed of him by ministering unto him. Then the apostic mounted him and sat upon him; and they followed him, some going before and some following after, and all of them ran, desiring to see the end, and how he would dismiss the colt.

41 But when he came near to the city gates he dismounted from him, saying: Depart, and be thou kept safe where thou wert. And straightway the colt fell to the ground at the apostle's feet and died. And all they that were present were sorry and said to the apostle: Bring him to life and raise him up. But he answered and said unto them: I indeed am able to raise him by the name of Jesus Christ: but this is by all means expedient (or, this is by any means expedient). For he that gave him speech that he might talk was able to cause that he should not die; and I raise him not, not as being unable, but because this is that which is expedient and profitable for him. And he bade them that were present to dig a trench and bury his body and they did as they were commanded.

THE FIFTH ACT
concerning the devil that took up his abode in the woman

42 And the apostle entered into the city and all the multitude followed him. And he thought to go unto the parents of the young man whom he had made alive when he was slain by the serpent: for they earnestly besought him to come unto them and enter into their house. But a very beautiful woman on a sudden uttered an exceeding loud cry, saying: O Apostle of the new God that art come into India, and servant of that holy and only good God; for by thee is he preached, the Saviour of the souls that come unto him, and by thee are healed the bodies of them that are tormented by the enemy, and thou art he that is become an occasion of life unto all that turn unto him: command me to be brought before thee that I may tell

thee what hath befallen me, and peradventure of thee I may have hope, and these that stand by thee may be more confident in the God whom thou preachest. For I am not a little tormented by the adversary now this five years' space [one Greek MS. And the apostle bade her come unto him, and the woman stood before him and said: I, O servant of him that is indeed God am a woman: the rest have, As a woman] I was sitting at the first in quiet, and peace encompassed me on every side and I had no care for anything, for I took no thought for any other. 43 And it fell out one day that as I came out from the bath there met me a man troubled and disturbed, and his voice and speech seemed to me exceeding faint and dim; and he stood before me and said: I and thou will be in one love and we will have intercourse together as a man with his wife; And I answered and said to him: I never had to do with my betrothed, for I refused to marry, and how shall I yield myself to thee that wouldest have intercourse with me in adulterous wise? And having so said, I passed on, and I said to rny handmaid that was with me: Sawest thou that youth and his shamelessness, how boldly he spake with me, and had no shame? but she said to me: I saw an old man speaking to thee. And when I was in mine house and had dined my soul suggested unto me some suspicion and especially because he was seen of me in two forms; and having this in my mind I fell asleep. He came, therefore, in that night and was joined unto me in his foul intercourse. And when it was day I saw him and fled from him, and on the night following that he came and abused me; and now as thou seest me I have spent five years being troubled by him, and he hath not departed from me. But I know and am persuaded that both devils and spirits and destroyers are subject unto thee and are filled with trembling at thy prayers: pray thou therefore for me and drive away from me the devil that ever troubleth me, that I also may be set free and be gathered unto the nature that is mine from the beginning, and receive the grace that hath been given unto my kindred.

44 And the apostle said: O evil that cannot be restrained! O shamelessness of the enemy! O envious one that art never at rest! O hideous one that subduest the comely! O thou of many forms! As he will he appeareth, but his essence cannot be changed. O the crafty and faithless one! O the bitter tree whose fruits are like unto him! O the devil that overcometh them that are alien to him! O the deceit that useth impudence! O the wickedness that creepeth like a serpent, and that is of his kindred! (Syr. adds a clause bidding the devil show himself.) And when the apostle said this, the malicious one came and stood before him, no man seeing him save the woman and the apostle, and with an exceeding loud voice said in the hearing of all:

45 What have we to do with thee, thou apostle of the Most High! What have we to do with thee, thou servant of Jesus Christ? What have we to do with thee, thou counsellor of the holy Son of God? Wherefore wilt thou destroy us, whereas our time is not yet come? Wherefore wilt thou take away our power? for unto this hour we had hope and time remaining to us. What have we to do with thee? Thou hast power over thine own, and we over ours. Wherefore wilt thou act tyrannously against us, when thou thyself teachest others not to act tyrannously? Wherefore dost thou crave other men's goods and not suffice thyself with thine own? Wherefore art thou made like unto the Son of God which hath done us wrong? for thou resemblest him altogether as if thou wert born of him. For we thought to have brought him under the yoke like as we have the rest, but he turned and made us subject unto him: for we knew him not; but he deceived us with his form of all uncomeliness and his poverty and his neediness: for seeing him to be such, we thought that he was a man wearing flesh, and knew not that it is he that giveth life unto men. And he gave us

power over our own, and that we should not in this present time leave them but have our walk in them: but thou wouldest get more than thy due and that which was given thee, and afflict us altogether.

46 And having said this the devil wept, saying: I leave thee, my fairest consort, whom long since I found and rested in thee; I forsake thee, my sure sister, my beloved in whom I was well pleased. What I shall do I know not, or on whom I shall call that he may hear me and help me. I know what I will do: I will depart unto some place where the report of this man hath not been heard, and peradventure I shall call thee, my beloved by another name (Syr. for thee my beloved I shall find a substitute). And he lifted up his voice and said: Abide in peace for thou hast taken refuge with one greater than I, but I will depart and seek for one like thee, and if I find her not, I will return unto thee again: for I know that whilst thou art near unto this man thou hast a refuge in him, but when he departeth thou wilt be such as thou wast before he appeared, and him thou wilt forget, and I shall have opportunity and confidence: but now I fear the name of him that hath saved thee. And having so said the devil vanished out of sight: only when he departed fire and smoke were seen there: and all that stood there were astonied.

47 And the apostle seeing it, said unto them: This devil hath shown nought that is alien or strange to him, but his own nature, wherein also he shall be consumed, for verily the fire shall destroy him utterly and the smoke of it shall be scattered abroad. And he began to say:

Jesu, the hidden mystery that hath been revealed unto us, thou art he that hast shown unto us many mysteries; thou that didst call me apart from all my fellows and spakest unto me three (one, Syr.) words wherewith I am inflamed, and am not able to speak them unto others. Jesu, man that wast slain, dead buried! Jesu, God of God, Saviour that quickenest the dead, and healest the sick! Jesu, that wert in need like and savest as one that hath no need, that didst catch the fish for the breakfast and the dinner and madest all satisfied with a little bread. Jesu, that didst rest from the weariness of wayfaring like a man, and walkedst on the waves like a God. 48 Jesu most high, voice arising from perfect mercy, Saviour of all, the right hand of the light, overthrowing the evil one in his own nature, and gathering all his nature into one place; thou of many forms, that art only begotten, first-born of many brethren God of the Most High God, man despised until now (Syr. and humble). Jesu Christ that neglectest us not when we call upon thee, that art become an occasion of life unto all mankind, that for us wast judged and shut up in prison, and loosest all that are in bonds, that wast called a deceiver and redeemest thine own from error: I beseech thee for these that stand here and believe on thee, for they entreat to obtain thy gifts, having good hope in thy help, and having their refuge in thy greatness; they hold their hearing ready to listen unto the words that are spoken by us. Let thy peace come and tabernacle in them and renew them from their former deeds, and let them put off the old man with his deeds, and put on the new that now is proclaimed unto them by me.

49 And he laid his hands on them and blessed them, saying: The grace of our Lord Jesus Christ shall be upon you for ever. And they said, Amen. And the woman besought him, saying: O apostle of the Most High, give me the seal, that that enemy return not again unto me. Then he caused her to come near unto him (Syr. went to a river which was close by there), and laid his hands upon her and sealed her in the name of the Father and the Son and the Holy Ghost; and many others also were sealed with her. And the apostle bade his minister (deacon) to set forth a table; and he set forth a stool which they found there, and spread a linen cloth upon it and set on the bread of blessing; and the apostle stood by it and said: Jesu, that hast accounted us worthy to partake of the eucharist of thine holy body and blood, lo, we are bold to draw near unto thine eucharist and to call upon thine holy name: come thou and communicate unto us (Syr. adds more).

50 And he began to say: Come, O perfect compassion, Come O communion of the male, Come, she that knoweth the mysteries of him that is chosen, Come, she that hath part in all the combats of the noble champion (athlete), Come, the silence that revealeth the great things of the whole greatness, Come, she that manifesteth the hidden things and maketh the unspeakable things plain, the holy dove that beareth the twin young, Come, the hidden mother, Come, she that is manifest in her deeds and giveth joy and rest unto them that are joined unto her: Come and communicate with us in this eucharist which we celebrate in thy name and in the love-feast wherein we are gathered together at thy calling. (Syr. has other clauses and not few variants.) And having so said he marked out the cross upon the bread, and brake it, and began to distribute it. And first he gave unto the woman, saying: This shall be unto thee for remission of sins and eternal transgressions (Syr. and for the everlasting resurrection). And after her he gave unto all the others also which had received the seal (Syr. and said to them: Let this eucharist be unto you for life and rest, and not for judgement and vengeance. And they said, Amen.).

THE SIXTH ACT
of the youth that murdered the Woman

51 Now there was a certain youth who had wrought an abominable deed, and he came near and received of the eucharist with his mouth: but his two hands withered up, so that he could no more put them unto his own mouth. And they that were there saw him and told the apostle what had befallen; and the apostle called him and said unto him: Tell me, my child, and be not ashamed, what was it that thou didst and camest hither? for the eucharist of

the Lord hath convicted thee. For this gift which passeth among many doth rather heal them that with faith and love draw near thereto, but thee it hath withered away; and that which is come to pass hath not befallen without some effectual cause. And the Youth, being convicted by the eucharist of the Lord, came and tell at the apostle's feet and besought him, saying: I have done an evil deed, yet I thought to do somewhat good. I was enamoured of a woman that dwelleth at an inn without the city, and she also loved me; and when I heard of thee and believed, that thou proclaimest a living God, I came and received of thee the seal with the rest; for thou saidst: Whosoever shall partake in the polluted union, and especially in adultery, he shall not have life with the God whom I preach. Whereas therefore I loved her much, I entreated her and would have persuaded her to become my consort in chastity and pure conversation, which thou also teachest: but she would not. When, therefore, she consented not, I took a sword and slew her: for I could not endure to see her commit adultery with another man.

52 When the apostle heard this he said: O insane union how ruinest thou unto shamelessness! O unrestrained lust, how hast thou stirred up this man to do this! O work of the serpent, how art thou enraged against thine own! And the apostle bade water to be brought to him in a bason; and when the water was brought, he said: Come, ye waters from the living waters, that were sent unto us, the true from the true, the rest that was sent unto us from the rest, the power of salvation that cometh from that power which conquereth all things and subdueth them unto its own will: come and dwell in these waters, that the gift of the Holy Ghost may be perfectly consummated in them. And he said unto the youth: Go, wash thy hands in these waters. And when he had washed they were restored; and the apostle said unto him: Believest thou in our Lord Jesus Christ that he is able to do all things? And he said: Though I be the least, yet I believe. But I committed this deed

thinking that I was doing somewhat good: for I besought her as I told thee, but she would not obey me, to keep herself chaste.

53 And the apostle said to him: Come, let us go unto the inn where thou didst commit this deed. And the youth went before the apostle in the way, and when they came to the inn they found her lying dead. And the apostle when he saw her was sorry, for she was a comely girl. And he commanded her to be brought into the midst of the inn: and they laid her on a bed and brought her forth and set her down in the midst of the court of the inn. And the apostle laid his hand upon her and began to say: Jesu, who alway showest thyself unto us; for this is thy will, that we should at all times seek thee, and thyself hast given us this power, to ask and to receive, and hast not only permitted this, but hast taught us to pray: who art not seen of our bodily eyes, but art never hidden from the eyes of our soul, and in thine aspect art concealed, but in thy works art manifested unto us: and in thy many acts we have known thee so far as we are able, and thyself hast given us thy gifts without measure, saying: Ask and it shall be given unto you, seek and ye shall find, knock and it shall be opened unto you: we beseech thee, therefore, having the fear (suspicion) of our sins; and we ask of thee, not riches, not gold, not silver, not possessions, not aught else of the things which come of the earth and return again unto the earth; but this we ask of thee and entreat, that in thine holy name thou wouldest raise up the woman that lieth here, by thy power, to the glory and faith of them that stand by.

54 And he said unto the youth (Syr. ' Stretch thy mind towards our Lord,' and he signed him with the cross), having signed (sealed) him: Go and take hold on her hand and say unto her: I with my hands slew thee with iron, and with my hands in the faith of Jesus I raise thee up. So the youth went to her and stood by her, saying: I have believed in thee, Christ Jesu. And he looked unto Judas Thomas the apostle and said to him:

Pray for me that my Lord may come to my help, whom I also call upon. And he laid his hand upon her hand and said: Come, Lord Jesu Christ: unto her grant thou life and unto me the earnest of faith in thee. And straightway as he drew her hand she sprang up and sat up, looking upon the great company that stood by. And she saw the apostle also standing over against her, and leaving the bed she leapt forth and fell at his feet and caught hold on his raiment, saying: I beseech thee, my lord where is that other that was with thee, who left me not to remain in that fearful and cruel place, but delivered me unto thee, saying: Take thou this woman, that she may be made perfect, and hereafter be gathered into her place?

55 And the apostle said unto her: Relate unto us where thou hast been. And she answered: Dost thou who wast with me and unto whom I was delivered desire to hear? And she began to say: [This description of hell-tourments is largely derived from the Apocalypse of Peter] A man took me who was hateful to look upon altogether black, and his raiment exceedingly foul, and took me away to a place wherein were many pits (chasms), and a great stench and hateful odour issued thence. And he caused me to look into every pit, and I saw in the (first) pit flaming fire, and wheels of fire ran round there, and souls were hanged upon those wheels, and were dashed (broken) against each other; and very great crying and howling was there, and there was none to deliver. And that man said to me: These souls are of thy tribe, and when the number of their days is accomplishcd (lit. in the days of the number) they are (were) delivered unto torment and affliction, and then are others brought in in their stead, and likewise these into another place. These are they that have reversed the intercourse of male and female. And I looked and saw infants heaped one upon another and struggling with each other as they lay on them. And he answered and said to me: These are the children of those others, and therefore are they set here for a testimony against them. (Syr. omits this clause of the children, and lengthens and dilutes the preceding speech.)

56 And he took me unto another pit, and I stooped and looked and saw mire and worms welling up, and souls wallowing there, and a great gnashing of teeth was heard thence from them. And that man said unto me: These are the souls of women which forsook their husbands and committed adultery with others, and are brought into this torment. Another pit he showed me whereinto I stooped and looked and saw souls hanging, some by the tongue, some by the hair, some by the hands, and some head downward by the feet, and tormented (smoked) with smoke and brimstone; concerning whom that man that was with me answered me: The souls which are hanged by the tongue are slanderers, that uttered lying and shameful words, and were not ashamed, and they that are hanged by the hair are unblushing ones which had no modesty and went about in the world bareheaded; and they that are hanged by the hands, these are they that took away and stole other men's goods, and never gave aught to the needy nor helped the afflicted, but did so, desiring to take all, and had no thought at all of justice or of the law; and they that hang upside down by the feet, these are they that lightly and readily ran in evil ways and disorderly paths, not visiting the sick nor escorting them that depart this life, and therefore each and every soul receiveth that which was done by it. (Syr. omits almost the whole section.)

57 Again he took me and showed me a cave exceeding dark, breathing out a great stench, and many souls were looking out desiring to get somewhat of the air, but their keepers suffered them not to look forth. And he that was with me said: This is the prison of those souls which thou sawest: for when they have fulfilled their torments for that which each did, thereafter do others succeed them: and there be some that are wholly consumed and (some, Syr.) that are delivered over unto other torments. And they that kept the souls

which were in the dark cave said unto the man that had taken me: Give her unto us that we may bring her in unto the rest until the time cometh for her to be delivered unto torment. But he answered them: I give her not unto you, for I fear him that delivered her to me: for I was not charged to leave her here, but I take her back with me until I shall receive order concerning her. And he took me and brought me unto another place wherein were men being sharply tormented (Syr. where men were). And he that was like unto thee took me and delivered me to thee, saying thus to thee: Take her, for she is one of the sheep that have gone astray. And I was taken by thee, and now am I before thee. I beseech thee, therefore, and supplicate that I may not depart unto those places of punishment which I have seen.

58 And the apostle said: Ye have heard what this woman hath related: and there are not these torments only, but others also, worse than these; and ye, if ye turn not unto this God whom I preach, and abstain from your former works and the deeds which ye committed without knowledge, shall have your end in those torments. Believe therefore on Christ Jesus, and he will forgive you the sins ye have committed hitherto, and will cleanse you from all your bodily lusts that abide on the earth, and will heal you of all your trespasses which follow you and depart with you and are found upon (before) you. Put off therefore every one of you the old man, and put on the new, and forsake your former walk and conversation; and let them that stole steal no more, but live by labouring and working; and let the adulterous no more fornicate, lest they deliver themselves unto eternal torment; for adultery is before God exceeding evil beyond other sins. And put away from you covetousness and lying and drunkenness and slandering, and render not evil for evil: for all these things are strange and alien unto the God who is preached by me: but rather walk ye in faith and meekness and holiness and hope, wherein God delighteth, that ye may become his own, expecting of him the gifts which some few only do receive.

59 All the people therefore believed and gave their souls obediently unto the living God and Christ Jesus, rejoicing in the blessed works of the Most High and in his holy service. And they brought much money for the service of the widows: for the apostle had them gathered together in the cities, and unto all of them he sent provision by his own ministers (deacons), both clothes and nourishment. And he himself ceased not preaching and speaking to them and showing that this is Jesus Christ whom the scriptures proclaimed, who is come and was crucified, and raised the third day from the dead. And next he showed them plainly, beginning from the prophets, the things concerning the Christ, that it was necessary that he should come, and that in him should be accomplished all things that were foretold of him. And the fame of him went forth into all the cities and countries, and all that had sick or them that were oppressed by unclean spirits brought them, and some they laid in the way whereby he should pass, and he healed them all by the power of the Lord. Then all that were healed by him said with one accord: Glory be to thee, Jesu, who hast granted us all alike healing through thy servant and apostle Thomas. And now being whole and rejoicing, we beseech thee that we may be of thy flock, and be numbered among thy sheep; receive us therefore, Lord, and impute not unto us our transgressions and our former faults which we committed being in ignorance.

60 And the apostle said: Glory be to the only-begotten of the Father! Glory be to the first-born of many brethren! Glory be to thee, the defender and helper of them that come unto thy refuge! that sleepest not, and awakest them that are asleep that livest and givest life to them that lie in death! O God Jesu Christ, Son of the living God, redeemer and helper, refuge and rest of all that are weary (labour) in thy work, giver of

healing to them that for thy name s sake bear the burden and heat of the day: we give thanks for (to) the gifts that are given us of thee and granted us by thy help and thy dispensation that cometh unto us from thee.

61 Perfect thou therefore these things in us unto the end that we may have the boldness that is in thee: look upon us for for thy sake have we forsaken our homes and our parents, and for thy sake have we gladly and willingly become strangers: look upon us, Lord, for we have forsaken our own possessions for thy sake, that we might gain thee the possession that cannot be taken away: look upon us, Lord, for we have forsaken them that belong unto us by race, that we might be joined unto thy kinship: look upon us, Lord, that have forsaken our fathers and mothers and fosters, that we might behold thy Father, and be satisfied with his divine food: look upon us, Lord, for for thy sake have we forsaken our bodily consorts and our earthly fruits, that we might be partakers in that enduring and true fellowship, and bring forth true fruits, whose nature is from above, which no man can take from us, with whom we shall abide and who shall abide with us.

THE SEVENTH ACT
of the Captain

62 Now while the apostle Thomas was proclaiming throughout all India the word of God, a certain captain of the king Misdaeus (Mazdai, Syr.) came to him and said unto him: I have heard of thee that thou takest no reward of any man, but even that thou hast thou givest to them that need. For if thou didst receive rewards, I would have sent thee a great sum, and would not have come myself, for the king doeth nought without me: for I have much substance and am rich, even one of the rich men of India. And I have never done wrong to any; but the contrary hath befallen me. I have a wife, and of her I had a daughter and I am well affectioned toward her, as also nature requireth and

have never made trial of another wife. Now it chanced that there was a wedding in our city, and they that made the marriage feast were well beloved of me: they came in therefore and bade me to it, bidding also my mife and her daughter. Forasmuch then as they were my good friends I could not refuse: I sent her therefore, though she desired not to go, and with them I sent also many servants: so they departed, both she and her daughter, decked with many ornaments.

63 And when it was evening and the time was come to depart from the wedding I sent lamps and torches to meet them: and I stood in the street to espy when she should come and I should see her with my daughter. And as I stood I heard a sound of lamentation. Woe for her! vvas heard out of every mouth. And my servants with their clothes rent came to me and told me what was done. We saw, said they, a man and a boy with him. And the man laid his hand upon thy wife, and the boy upon thy daughter: and they fled from them: and we smote (wounded) them with our swords, but our swords fell to the ground. And the same hour the womem fell down, gnashing their teeth and beating their heads upon the earth and seeing this we came to tell it thee. And when I heard this of my servants I rent my clothes and smote my face with my hands, and becoming like one mad I ran along the street, and came and found them cast in the market-place; and I took them and brought them to my house, and after a long space they awaked and stood up, and sat down.

64 I began therefore to inquire of my wife: What is it that hath befallen thee? And she said to me: Knowest thou not what thou hast done unto me? for I prayed thee that I might not go to the wedding, because I was not of even health in my body; and as I went on the way and came near to the aqueduct wherein the water floweth, I saw a black man standing over against me nodding at me with his head, and a boy like unto him standing by him; and I

said to my daughter: Look at those two hideous men, whose teeth are like milk and their lips like soot. And we left them and went towards the aqueduct; and when it was sunset and we departed from the wedding, as we passed by with the young men and drew near the aqueduct, my daughter saw them first, and was affrighted and fled towards me; and after her I also beheld them coming against us: and the servants that were with us fled from them (Syr.) and they struck us, and cast down both me and my daughter. And when she had told me these things, the devils came upon them again and threw them down: and from that hour they are not able to come forth, but are shut up in one room or a second (Syr. in a room within another): and on their account I suffer much, and am distressed: for the devils throw them down wheresoever they find them, and strip them naked. I beseech and supplicate thee before God, help me and have pity on me, for it is now three years that a table hath not been set in my house, and my wife and my daughter have not sat at a table: and especially for mine unhappy daughter, which hath not seen any good at all in this world.

65 And the apostle, hearing these things from the captain, was greatly grieved for him, and said unto him: Believest thou that Jesus will heal them? And the captain said: Yea. And the apostle said: Commit thyself then unto Jesus, and he will heal them and procure them succour. And the captain said: Show me him, that I may entreat him and believe in him. And the apostle said: He appeareth not unto these bodily eyes, but is found by the eyes of the mind. The captain therefore lifted up his voice and said: I believe thee, Jesu, and entreat and supplicate thee, help my little faith which I have in thee. And the apostle commanded Xenophon (Syr. Xanthippus) the deacon to assemble all the brethren; and when the whole multitude was gathered, the apostle stood in the midst and said:

66 Children and brethren that have believed on the Lord, abide in this faith, preaching Jesus who was proclaimed unto you by me, to bring you hope in him; and forsake not (be not forsaken of) him, and he will not forsake you. While ye sleep in this slumber that weigheth down the sleepers, he, sleeping not, keepeth watch over you; and when ye sail and are in peril and none can help, he walking upon the waters supporteth and aideth. For I am now departing from you, and it appeareth not if I shall again see you according to the flesh. Be ye not therefore like unto the people of Israel, who losing sight of their pastors for an hour, stumbled. But I leave unto you Xenophon the deacon in my stead; for he also like myself proclaimeth Jesus: for neither am I aught, nor he, but Jesus only; for I also am a man clothed with a body, a son of man like one of you; for neither have I riches as it is found with some, which also convict them that possess them, being wholly useless, and left behind upon the earth, whence also they came, and they bear away with them the transgressions and blemishes of sins which befall men by their means. And scantly are rich men found in almsgiving: but the merciful and lowly in heart, these shall inherit the kingdom of God: for it is not beauty that endureth with men, for they that trust in it, when age cometh upon them, shall suddenly be put to shame: all things therefore have their time; in their season are they loved and hated. Let your hope then be in Jesus Christ the Son of God, which is always loved, and always desired: and be mindful of us, as we of you: for we too, if we fulfil not the burden of the commandments are not worthy to be preachers of this name, and hereafter shall we pay the price (punishment) of our own head.

67 And he prayed with them and continued with them a long time in prayer and supplication, and committing them unto the Lord, he said: O Lord that rulest over every soul that is in the body; Lord, Father of the souls that have their hope in thee and expect thy mercies: that redeemest from error the men that are thine own and

settest free from bondage and corruption thy subjects that come unto thy refuge: be thou in the flock of Xenophon and anoint it with holy oil, and heal it of sores, and preserve it from the ravening wolves. And he laid his hand on them and said: The peace of the Lord shall be upon you and shall journey with us.

THE EIGHTH ACT
of the wild asses

68 The apostle therefore went forth to depart on the way: and they all escorted him, weeping and adjuring him to make remembrance of them in his prayers and not to forget them. He went up then and sat upon the chariot, leaving all the brethren, and the captain came and awaked the driver, saying: I entreat and pray that I may become worthy to sit beneath his feet, and I will be his driver upon this way, that he also may become my guide in that way whereby few go. 69 And when they had journeyed about two miles, the apostle begged of the captain and made him arise and caused him to sit by him, suffering the driver to sit in his own place. And as they went along the road, it came to pass that the beasts were wearied with the great heat and could not be stirred at all. And the captain was greatly vexed and wholly cast down, and thought to run on his own feet and bring other beasts for the use of the chariot; but the apostle said: Let not thine heart be troubled nor affrighted, but believe on Jesus Christ whom I have proclaimed unto thee, and thou shalt see great wonders. And he looked and saw a herd of wild asses feeding by the wayside, and said to the captain: If thou hast believed on Christ Jesus, go unto that herd of wild asses and say: Judas Thomas the apostle of Christ the new God saith unto you: Let four of you come, of whom we have need (or, of whom we may have use). 70 And the captain went in fear, for they were many; and as he went, they came to meet him; and when they were near, he said unto them: Judas Thomas the apostle of the new God commandeth you: Let four of you come, of whom I have need. And when the wild asses heard it, they ran with one accord and came to him, and when they came they did him reverence. [Syr. has a long prayer: And Judas Thomas the apostle of our Lord lifted up his voice in praise and said: Glorious art thou, God of truth and Lord of all natures, for thou didst will with thy will, and make all thy works and finish all thy creatures, and bring them to the rule of their nature, and lay upon them all thy fear that they might be subject to thy command. And thy will trod the path from thy secrecy to manifestation, and was caring for every soul that thou didst make, and was spoken of by the mouth of all the prophets, in all visions and sounds and voices; but Israel did not obey because of their evil inclination. And thou, because thou art Lord of all, hast a care for the creatures, so that thou spreadest over us thy mercy in him who came by thy will and put on the body, thy creature, which thou didst will and form according to thy glorious wisdom. He whom thou didst appoint in thy secrecy and establish in thy manifestation, to him thou hast given the name of Son, he who was thy will, the power of thy thought; so that ye are by various names, the Father and the Son and the Spirit, for the sake of the government of thy creatures, for the nourishing of all natures, and ye are one in glory and power and will; and ye are divided without being separated, and are one though divided, and all subsists in thee and is subject to thee, because all is thine. And I rely upon thee, Lord, and by thy command have subjected these dumb beasts, that thou mightest show thy ministering power upon us and upon them because it is needful, and that thy name might be glorified in us and in the beasts that cannot speak.] And the apostle said unto them: Peace be unto you. Yoke ye four of you in the stead of these beasts that have come to a stand. And every one of them came and pressed to be yoked: there were then four stronger than the rest, which also were yoked. And the rest, some

went before and some followed. And when they had journeyed a little way he dismissed the colts, saying: I say unto you the inhabiters of the desert, depart unto your pastures, for if I had had need of all, ye would all have gone with me; but now go unto your place wherein ye dwell. And they departed quietly until they were no more seen.

71 Now as the apostle and the captain and the driver went on, the wild asses drew the chariot quietly and evenly, lest they should disturb the apostle of God. And when they came near to the city gate they turned aside and stood still before the doors of the captain's house. And the captain said: It is not possible for me to relate what hath happened, but when I see the end I will tell it. The whole city therefore came to see the wild asses under the yoke; and they had heard also the report of the apostle that he was to come and visit them. And the apostle asked the captain: Where is thy dwelling, and whither dost thou bring us? And he said to him: Thou thyself knowest that we stand before the doors, and these which by thy commandment are come with thee know it better than I.

72 And having so said he came down from the chariot. The apostle therefore began to say: Jesu Christ, that art blasphemed by the ignorance of thee in this country; Jesu, the report of whom is strange in this city; Jesu, that receivest all (Syr. sendest on before the apostles in every country and in every city, and all thine that are worthy are glorified in thee; Jesu, that didst take a form and become as a man, and wert seen of all us that thou mightest not separate us from thine own love: thou, Lord, art he that gavest thyself for us, and with thy blood hast purchased us and gained us as a possession of great price: and what have we to give thee, Lord, in exchange for thy life which thou gavest for us? for that which we would give, thou gavest us: and this is, that we should entreat of thee and live.

73 And when he had so said, many assembled from every quarter to see the apostle of the new God. And again the apostle said: Why stand we idle? Jesu, Lord, the hour is come: what wilt thou have done? command therefore that that be fulfilled which needeth to be done. Now the captain's wife and her daughter were sore borne down by the devils, so that they of the house thought they would rise up no more: for they suffered them not to partake of aught, but cast them down upon their beds recognizing no man until that day when the apostle came thither. And the apostle said unto one of the wild asses that were yoked on the right hand: Enter thou within the gate, and stand there and call the devils and say to them: Judas Thomas the apostle and disciple of Jesus Christ saith unto you: Come forth hither: for on your account am I sent and unto them that pertain to you by race, to destroy you and chase you unto your place, until the time of the end come and ye go down into your own deep of darkness.

74 And that wild ass went in, a great multitude being with him, and said: Unto you I speak, the enemies of Jesus that is called Christ: unto you I speak that shut your eyes lest ye see the light: unto you I speak, children of Gehenna and of destruction, of him that ceaseth not from evil until now, that alway reneweth his workings and the things that befit his being: unto you I speak, most shameless, that shall perish by your own hands. And what I shall say of your destruction and end, and what I shall tell, I know not. For there are many things and innumerable to the hearing: and greater are your doings than the torment that is reserved for you (Syr. however great your bodies, they are too small for your retributions). But unto thee I speak, devil, and to thy son that followeth with thee: for now am I sent against you. And wherefore should I make many words concerning your nature and root, which yourselves know and are not ashamed? but Judas Thomas the apostle of Christ Jesus saith unto you, he that by much love and affection is sent hither: Before all this multitude that standeth here, come forth and tell me of what race ye are.

75 And straightway the woman came forth with her daughter, both like dead persons and dishonoured in aspect: and the apostle beholding them was grieved. especially for the girl, and saith unto the devils: God forbid that for you there should be sparing or propitiation, for ye know not to spare nor to have pity: but in the name of Jesus, depart from them and stand by their side. And when the apostle had so said, the women fell down and became as dead; for they neither had breath nor uttered speech: but the devil answered with a loud voice and said: Art thou come hither again, thou that deridest our nature and race? art thou come again, that blottest out our devices? and as I take it, thou wouldest not suffer us to be upon the earth at all: but this at this time thou canst not accomplish. And the apostle guessed that this devil was he that had been driven out from that other woman. 76 And the devil said: I beseech thee, give me leave to depart even whither thou wilt, and dwell there and take commandment from thee, and I will not fear the ruler that hath authority over me. For like as thou art come to preach good tidings, so I also am come to destroy; and like as, if thou fulfil not the will of him that sent thee, he will bring punishment upon thy head, so I also if I do not the will of him that sent me, before the season and time appointed, shall be sent unto mine own nature; and like as thy Christ helpeth thee in that thou doest, so also my father helpeth me in that I do; and like as for thee he prepareth vessels worthy of thine inhabiting, so also for me he seeketh out vessels whereby I may accomplish his deeds; and like as he nourisheth and provideth for his subjects, so also for me he prepareth chastisements and torments, with them that become my dwellingplaces (Syr. those in whom I dwell); and like as for a recompense of thy working he giveth thee eternal life, so also unto me he giveth for a reward of my works eternal destruction; and like as thou art refreshed by thy prayer and thy good works and spiritual thanksgivings, so I also am refreshed by murders and adulteries and sacrifices made with wine upon altars (Syr. sacrifices and libations of wine), and like as thou convertest men unto eternal life, so I also pervert them that obey me unto eternal destruction and torment: and thou receivest thine own and I mine. 77 And when the devil had said these things and yet more the apostle said: Jesus commandeth thee and thy son by me to enter no more into the habitation of man: but go ye forth and depart and dwell wholly apart from the habitation of men. And the devils said unto him: Thou hast laid on us a harsh commandment: but what wilt thou do unto them that now are concealed from thee? for they that have wrought all the images rejoice in them more than thee: and many of them do the more part worship, and perform their will, sacrificing to them and bringing them food, by libations and by wine and water and offering with oblations. And the apostle said: They also shall now be abolished, with their works. And suddenly the devils vanished away: but the women lay cast upon the earth as if were dead, and without speech. 78 And the wild asses stood together and parted not one from another; but he to whom speech was given by the power of the Lord -while all men kept silence, and looked to see what they would do- the wild ass said unto the apostle: Why standest thou idle, O apostle of Christ the Most High, who looketh that thou shouldest ask of him the best of learning? Wherefore then tarriest thou? (Syr. that thou shouldest ask him, and he would give thee? Why delayest thou, good disciple?) for lo, thy teacher desireth to show by thy hands his mighty works. Why standest thou still, O herald of the hidden one? for thy (Lord) willeth to manifest through thee his unspeakable things, which he reserveth for them that are worthy of him, to hear them. Why restest thou, O doer of mighty works in the name of the Lord? for thy Lord encourageth thee and engendereth boldness in thee. Fear not, therefore; for

he will not forsake the soul that belongeth unto thee by birth. Begin therefore to call upon him and he will readily hearken to thee. Why standest thou marvelling at all his acts and his workings? for these are small things which he hath shown by thy means. And what wilt thou tell concerning his great gifts? for thou wilt not be sufficient to declare them. And why marvellest thou at his cures of the body which he worketh? (Syr. which come to an end) especially when thou knowest that healing of his which is secure and lasting, which he bringeth forth by his own nature? And why lookest thou unto this temporal life, and hast no thought of that which is eternal (Syr. when thou canst every day think on that which is eternal)?

79 But unto you the multitudes that stand by and look to see these that are cast down raised up, I say, believe in the apostle of Jesus Christ: believe the teacher of truth, believe him that showeth vou the truth, believe Jesus, believe on the Christ that was born, that the born may live by his life: who also was raised up through infancy, that perfection might appear by his manhood (man). He did teach his own disciples: for he is the teacher of the truth and maketh wise men wise (Syr. who went to school that through him perfect wisdom might be known: he taught his teacher because he was the teacher of verity and the master of the wise). Who also offered the gift in the temple that he might show that all the (every) offering was sanctified. This is his apostle, the shewer-forth of truth: this is he that performeth the will of him that sent him. But there shall come false apostles and prophets of lawlessness, whose end shall be according to their deeds; preaching indeed and ordaining to flee from ungodliness, but themselves at all times detected in sins, clad indeed with sheep's clothing, but within, ravening wolves. Who suffice not themselves with one wife but corrupt many women; who, saying that they despise children, dcstroy many children (boys), for

whom they vvill pay the penalty; that content not themselves wiih their own possessions, but desire that all useless things should minister unto them only; professing to be his disciples; and with their mouth they utter one thing, but in their heart they think another; charging other men to beware of evil, but they themselves perform nought that is good; who are accounted temperate, and charge other men to abstain from fornication theft, and covetousness, but in all these things do they themselves walk secretly, teaching other men not to do them.

80 And when the wild ass had declared all these things, all men gazed upon him. And when he ceased the apostle said: What I shall think concerning thy beauty, O Jesu, and what I shall tell of thee, I know not, or rather I am not able, for I have no power to declare it, O Christ that art in rest, and only wise that only knowest the inward of the heart and understandest the thought. Glory be to thee, merciful and tranquil. Glory to thee, wise word. Glory to thy compassion that was born unto us. Glory to thy mercy that was spread out over us. Glory to thy greatness that was made small for us. Glory to thy most high kingship that was humbled for us. Glory to thy might which was enfeebled for us. Glory to thy Godhead that for us was seen in likeness of men. Glory to thy manhood that died for us that it might make us live. Glory to thy resurrection from the dead; for thereby rising and rest cometh unto our souls. Glory and praise (good report) to thine ascending into the heavens; for thereby thou hast shewed us the path of the height, and promised that we shall sit with thee on thy right hand and with thee judge the twelve tribes of Israel. Thou art the heavenly word of the Father: thou art the hidden light of the understanding, shewer of the way of truth, driver away of darkness, and blotter-out of error.

81 Having thus spoken, the apostle stood over the women, saying: My Lord and my God, I am not divided from thee (or doubt not concerning thee), nor

as one unbelieving do I call upon thee, who art always our helper and succourer and raiser-up; who breathest thine own power into us and encouragest us and givest confidence in love unto thine own servants. I beseech thee, let these souls be healed and rise up and become such as they were before they were smitten of the devils. And when he thus spake the women turned and sat up. And the apostle bade the captain that his servants should take them and bring them within (Syr. and give them food, for they had not eaten for many days). And when they were gone in, the apostle said unto the wild asses, Follow me. And they went after him until he had brought them without the gate. And when they had gone out, he said to them: Depart in peace unto your pastures. The wild asses therefore went away willingly; and the apostle stood and took heed to them lest they should be hurt of any, until they had gone afar off and were no more seen. And the apostle returned with the multitude into the house of the captain.

THE NINTH ACT
of the Wife of Charisius

82 Now it chanced that a certain woman, the wife of Charisius, that was next unto the king, whose name was Mygdonia, came to see and behold the new name and the new God who was being proclaimed, and the new apostle who had come to visit their country: and she was carried by her own servants; and because of the great crowd and the narrow way they were not able to bring her near unto him. And she sent unto her husband to send her more to minister to her; and they came and approached her, pressing upon the people and beating them. And the apostle saw it and said to them: Wherefore overthrow ye them that come to hear the word, and are eager for it? and ye desire to be near me but are far off, as it was said of the multitude that came unto the Lord: Having eyes ye see not, and having ears ye hear not; and he said to the multitudes: He that hath ears to hear, let him hear; and: Come unto me, all ye that labour and are heavy laden, and I will give you rest.

83 And looking upon them that carried her, he said unto them: This blessing and this admonition which was promised unto them is for you that are heavily burdened now. Ye are they that carry burdens grievous to be borne, and are borne about by her command. And though ye are men, they lay on you loads as on brute beasts, for they that have authority over you think that ye are not men such as themselves, whether bond or free. For neither shall possessions profit the rich, nor poverty save the poor from judgement; nor have we received a commandment which we are not able to perform, nor hath he laid on us burdens grievous to be borne which we are not able to carry; nor building which men build; nor to hew stones and prepare houses, as your craftsmen do by their own knowledge. But this commandment have we reccived of the Lord, that that which pleaseth not us when it is done by another this we should not do to any other man.

84 Abstain therefore first from adultery, for this is the beginning of all evils, and next from theft, which enticed Judas Iscariot, and brought him unto hanging; (and from covetousness,) for as many as yield unto covetousness see not that which they do; and from vainglory and from all foul deeds, especially them of the body, whereby cometh eternal condemnation. For this is the chief city of all evils; and likewise it bringeth them that hold their heads (necks) high unto tyranny, and draweth them down unto the deep, and subdueth them under its hands that they see not what they do; wherefore the things done of them are hidden from them.

85 But do ye become well-pleasing unto God in all good things, in meekness and quietness: for these doth God spare, and granteth eternal life and setteth death at nought. And in gentleness which followeth on all good things, and overcometh all enemies and

alone receiveth the crown of victory: with gentleness (Syr.), and stretching out of the hand to the poor, and supplying the want of the needy, and distributing to them that are in necessity, especially them that walk in holiness. For this is chosen before God and leadeth unto eternal life: for this is before God the chief city of all good: for they that strive not in the course (stadium) of Christ shall not obtain holiness. And holiness did appear from God, doing away fornication, overthrowing the enemy, well-pleasing unto God: for she is an invincible champion (athlete), having honour from God, glorified of many: she is an ambassador of peace, announcing peace: if any gain her he abideth without care, pleasing the Lord, expecting the time of redemption: for she doeth nothing amiss, but giveth life and rest and joy unto all that gain her. 86 But meekness hath overcome death and brought him under authority, meekness hath enslaved the enemy, meekness is the good yoke: meekness feareth not and opposeth not the many: meekness is peace and joy and exaltation of rest. Abide ye therefore in holiness and receive freedom from me, and be near unto meekness for in these three heads is portrayed the Christ whom I proclaim unto you. Holiness is the temple of Christ, and he that dwelleth in her getteth her for an habitation , because for forty days and forty nights he fasted, tasting nothing: and he that keepeth her shall dwell in her as on a mountain. And meekness is his boast: for he said unto Peter our fellow apostle: Turn back thy sword and put it again into the sheath thereof: for if I had willed so to do, could I not have brought more than twelve legions of angels from my Father?

87 And when the apostle had said these things in the hearing of all the multitude, they trode and pressed upon one another: and the wife of Charisius the king's kinsman leapt out of her chair and cast herself on the earth before the apostle, and caught his feet and besought and said: O disciple of the living God, thou art come into a desert country, for we live in the desert; being like to brute beasts in our conversation, but now shall we be saved by thy hands; I beseech thee, therefore, take thought of me, and pray for me, that the compassion of the God whom thou preachest may come upon me, and I may become his dwelling place and be joined in prayer and hope and faith in him, and I also may receive the seal and become an holy temple and he may dwell in me.

88 And the apostle said: I do pray and entreat for you all, brethren, that believe on the Lord, and for you, sisters, that hope in Christ, that in all of you the word of God may tabernacle and have his tabernacle therein: for we have no power over them (Syr. because ye are given power over your own souls). And he began to say unto the woman Mygdonia: Rise up from the earth and compose thyself (take off thine ornaments, P; be mindful of thyself, Syr.). For this attire that is put on shall not profit thee nor the beauty of thy body, nor thine apparel, neither yet the fame of thy rank, nor the authority of this world, nor the polluted intercourse with thine husband shall avail thee if thou be bereaved of the true fellowship: for the appearance (fantasy) of ornamenting cometh to nought, and the body waxeth old and changeth, and raiment weareth out, and authority and lordship pass away (U corrupt; P abridges; Syr. has: passeth away accompanied with punishment, according as each person hath conducted himself in it), and the fellowship of procreation also passeth away, and is as it were condemnation. Jesus only abideth ever, and they that hope in him. Thus he spake, and said unto the woman: Depart in peace, and the Lord shall make thee worthy of his own mysteries. But she said: I fear to go away, lest thou forsake me and depart unto another nation. But the apostle said to her: Even if I go, I shall not leave thee alone, but Jesus of his compassion will be with thee. And she fell down and did him reverence and

departed unto her house.

89 Now Charisius, the kinsman of Misdaeus the king, bathed himself and returned and laid him down to dine. And he inquired concerning his wife, where she was; for she had not come out of her own chamber to meet him as she was wont. And her handmaids said to him: She is not well. And he entered quickly into the chamber and found her lying on the bed and veiled: and he unveiled her and kissed her, saying: Wherefore art thou sorrowful to-day? And she said: I am not well. And he said unto her: Wherefore then didst thou not keep the guise of thy freedom (Syr. pay proper respect to thy position as a free woman) and remain in thy house, but didst go and listen unto vain speeches and look upon works of sorcery? but rise up and dine with me, for I cannot dine without thee. But she said to him: To-day I decline it, for I am greatly afeared.

90 And when Charisius heard this of Mygdonia, he would not go forth to dinner, but bade his servants bring her to dine with him (Syr. bring food to him that he might sup in her presence): when then they brought it in, he desired her to dine with him, but she excused herself; since then she would not, he dined alone, saying unto her: On thine account I refused to dine with Misdaeus the king, and thou, wast thou not willing to dine with me? but she said: It is because I am not well. Charisius therefore rose up as he was wont and would sleep with her, but she said: Did I not tell thee that for today I refused it?

91 When he heard that he went to another bed and slept; and awaking out of sleep he said: My lady Mygdonia, hearken to the dream which I have seen. I saw myself lie at meat near to Misdaeus the king, and a dish of all sorts was set before us: and I saw an eagle come down from heaven and carry off from before me and the king two partridges, which he set against his heart; and again he came over us and flew about above us, and the king bade a bow to be brought to him; and the eagle again caught away from before us a pigeon and a dove, and the king shot an arrow at him, and it passed through him from one side to the other and hurt him not; and he being unscathed rose up into his own nest. And I awoke, and I am full of fear and sore vexed, because I had tasted of the partridge, and he suffered me not to put it to my mouth again. And Mygdonia said unto him: Thy dream is good: for thou every day eatest partridges, but this eagle had not tasted of a partridge until now.

92 And when it was morning Charisius went and dressed himself and shod his right foot with his left shoe; and he stopped, and said to Mygdonia: What then is this matter? for look, the dream and this action of mine! But Mygdonia said to him: And this also is not evil, but seemeth to me very good; for from an unlucky act there will be a change unto the better. And he washed his hands and went to salute Misdaeus the king.

93 And likewise Mygdonia rose up early and went to salute Judas Thomas the apostle, and she found him discoursing with the captain and all the multitude, and he was advising them and speaking of the woman which had received the Lord in her soul, whose wife she was; and the captain said: She is the wife of Charisius the kinsman of Misdaeus the king. And: Her husband is a hard man, and in every thing that he saith to the king he obeyeth him: and he will not suffer her to continue in this mind which she hath promised; for often-times hath he praised her before the king, saying that there is none other like her in love: all things therefore that thou speakest unto her are strange unto her. And the apostle said: If verily and surely the Lord hath risen upon her soul and she hath received the seed that was cast on her, she will have no care of this temporal life, nor fear death, neither will Charisius be able to harm her at all: for greater is he whom she hath received into her soul, if she have received him indeed.

94 And Mygdonia hearing this said unto the apostle: In truth, my lord, I have received the seed of thy words, and I

will bear fruit like unto such seed. The apostle saith: Our souls give praise and thanks unto thee, O Lord, for they are thine: our bodies give thanks unto thee, which thou hast accounted worthy to become the dwelling-place of thy heavenly gift. And he said also to them that stood by: Blessed are the holy, whose souls have never condemned them, for they have gained them and are not divided against themselves: blessed are the spirits of the pure, and they that have received the heavenly crown whole from the world (age) which hath been appointed them: blessed are the bodies of the holy, for they have been made worthy to become temples of God, that Christ may dwell in them: blessed are ye, for ye have power to forgive sins: blessed are ye if ye lose not that which is committed unto you, but rejoicing and departing bear it away with you: blessed are ye the holy, for unto you it is given to ask and receive: blessed are ye meek for you hath God counted worthy to become heirs of the heavenly kingdom. Blessed are ye meek, for ye are they that have overcome the enemy: blessed are ye meek, for ye shall see the face of the Lord. Blessed are ye that hunger for the Lord's sake for for you is rest laid up, and your souls rejoice from henceforth. Blessed are ye that are quiet, (for ye have been counted worthy) to be set free from sin [and from the exchange of clean and unclean beasts]. And when the apostle had said these things in the hearing of all the multitude, Mygdonia was the more confirmed in the faith and glory and greatness of Christ.

95 But Charisius the kinsman and friend of Misdaeus the king came to his breakfast and found not his wife in the house; and he inquired of all that were in his house: Whither is your mistress oone? And one of them answered and said: She is gone unto that stranger. And when he heard this of his servant, he was wroth with the other servants because they had not straightway told him what was done: and he sat down and waited for her. And when it was evening and she was come into the house he said to her: Where wast thou? And she answered and said: With the physician. And he said: Is that stranger a physician? And she said: Yea, he is a physician of souls: for most physicians do heal bodies that are dissolved, but he souls that are not destroyed. Charisius, hearing this, was very angry in his mind with Mygdonia because of the apostle, but he answered her nothing, for he was afraid; for she was above him both in wealth and birth: but he departed to dinner, and she went into her chamber. And he said to the servants: Call her to dinner. But she would not come.

96 And when he heard that she would not come out of her chamber, he went in and said unto her: Wherefore wilt thou not dine with me and perchance not sleep with me as the wont is? yea, concerning this I have the greater suspicion, for I have heard that that sorcerer and deceiver teacheth that a man should not live with his wife, and that which nature requireth and the godhead hath ordained he overthroweth. When Charisius said these things, Mygdonia kept silence. He saith to her again: My lady and consort Mygdonia, be not led astray by deceitful and vain words, nor by the works of sorcery which I have heard that this man performeth in the name of Father, Son, and Holy Ghost; for it was never yet heard in the world that any raised the dead, and, as I hear, it is reported of this man that he raiseth dead men. And for that he neither eateth nor drinketh, think not that for righteousness sake he neither eateth nor drinketh but this he doth because he possesseth nought, for what should he do which hath not even his daily bread? And he hath one garment because he is poor, and as for his not receiving aught of any (he doth so, to be sure, because he knoweth in himself that he doth not verily heal any man, Syr.).

97 And when Charisius so said, Mygdonia was silent as any stone, but she prayed, asking when it should be day, that she might go to the apostle of Christ. And he withdrew from her and went to dinner heavy in mind, for he

thought to sleep with her according to the wont. And when he was gone out, she bowed her knees and prayed, saying: Lord God and Master, merciful Father, Saviour Christ, do thou give me strength to overcome the shamelessness of Charisius, and grant me to keep the holiness wherein thou delightest, that I also may by it find eternal life. And when she had so prayed she laid herself on her bed and veiled herself.

98 But Charisius having dined came upon her, and she cried out, saying: Thou hast no more any room by me: for my Lord Jesus is greater than thou, who is with me and resteth in me. And he laughed and said: Well dost thou mock, saying this of that sorcerer, and well dost thou deride him, who saith: Ye have no life with God unless ye purify yourselves. And when he had so said he essayed to sleep with her, but she endured it not and cried out bitterly and said: I call upon thee, Lord Jesu, forsake me not! for with thee have I made my refuge; for when I learned that thou art he that seekest out them that are veiled in ignorance and savest them that are held in error And now I entreat thee whose report I have heard and believed, come thou to my help and save me from the shamelessness of Charisius, that his foulness may not get the upper hand of me. And she smote her hands together (tied his hands, Syr.) and fled from him naked, and as she went forth she pulled down the curtain of the bed-chamber and wrapped it about her; and went to her nurse, and slept there with her.

99 But Charisius was in heaviness all night, and smote his face with his hands, and he was minded to go that very hour and tell the king concerning the violence that was done him, but he considered with himself, saying: If the great heaviness which is upon me compelleth me to go now unto the king, who will bring me in to him? for I know that my abuse hath overthrown me from my high looks and my vainglory and majesty, and hath cast me down into this vileness and separated my sister Mygonia from me. Yea, if the king himself stood before the dools at this hour, I could not have gone out and answered him. But I will wait until dawn, and I know that whatsoever I ask of the king, he granteth it me: and I will tell him of the madness of this stranger, how that it tyrannously casteth down the great and illustrious into the depth. For it is not this that grieveth me, that I am deprived of her companying, but for her am I grieved, because her greatness of soul is humbled: being an honourable lady in whom none of her house ever found fault (condemned), she hath fled away naked, running out of her own bedchamber, and I know not whither she is gone; and it may be that she is gone mad by the means of that sorcerer, and in her madness hath gone forth into the market-place to seek him; for there is nothing that appealeth unto her lovable except him and the things that are spoken by him.

100 And so saving he began to lament and say: Woe to me, O my consort, and to thee besides! for I am too quickly bereaved of thee. Woe is me, my most dear one, for thou excellest all my race: neither son nor daughter have I had of thee that I might find rest in them; neither hast thou yet dwelt with me a full year, and an evil eye hath caught thee from me. Would that the violence of death had taken thee, and I should yet have reckoned myself among kings and nobles: but that I should suffer this at the hands of a stranger, and belike he is a slave that hath run away, to mine ill fortune and the sorrow of mine unhappy soul! Let there be no impediment for me until I destroy him and avenge this night, and may I not be well-pleasing before Misdaeus the king if he avenge me not with the head of this stranger; (and I will also tell him) of Siphor the captain vvho hath been the occasion of this. For by his means did fhe stranger appear here, and lodgeth at his house: and many there be that go in and come out whom he teacheth a new doctrine; saying that none can live if he quit not all his substance and become a renouncer like himself: and he striveth to make many partakers with him.

101 And as Charisius thought on these things, the day dawned: and after the night (?) he put on a mean habit, and shod himself, and went downcast and in heaviness to salute the king. And when the king saw him he said: Wherefore art thou sorrowful, and comest in such garb? and I see that thy countenance is changed. And Charisius said unto the king: I have a new thing to tell thee and a new desolation which Siphor hath brought into India, even a certain Hebrew, a sorcerer, whom he hath sitting in his house and who departeth not from him: and many are there that go in to him: whom also he teacheth of a new God, and layeth on them new laws such as never yet were heard, saying: It is impossible for you to enter into that eternal life which I proclaim unto you, unless ye rid you of your wives, and likewise the wives of their husbands. And it chanced that mine unlucky wife also went to him and became a hearer of his words, and she believed them, and in the night she forsook me and ran unto the stranger. But send thou for both Siphor and that sorcerer that is hid with (in) him, and visit it (?) on their head, lest all that are of our nation perish.

102 And when Misdaeus his friend heard this he saith to him: Be not grieved nor heavy, for I will send for him and avenge thee, and thou shalt have thy wife again, and the others that cannot I will avenge. And the king went forth and sat on the judgement seat, and when he was set he commanded Siphor the captain to be called. They went therefore unto his house and found him sitting on the right hand of the apostle and Mygdonia at his feet, hearkening to him with all the multitude. And they that were sent from the king said unto Siphor: Sittest thou here listening to vain words, and Misdaeus the king in his wrath thinketh to destroy thee because of this sorcerer and deceiver whom thou hast brought into thine house? And Siphor hearing it was cast down, not because of the king's threat against him, but for the apostle, because the king was disposed contrary to him.

And he said to the apostle: I am grieved concerning thee: for I told thee at the first that that woman is the wife of Charisius the king's friend and kinsman, and he will not suffer her to perform that she hath promised, and all that he asketh of the king he granteth him. But the apostle said unto Siphor: Fear nothing, but believe in Jesus that pleadeth for us all, for unto his refuge are we gathered together. And Siphor, hearing that, put his garment about him and went unto Misdaeus the king,

103 And the apostle inquired of Mygdonia: What was the cause that thy husband was wroth with thee and devised this against us? And she said: Because I gave not myself up unto his corruption (destruction): for he desired last night to subdue me and subject me unto that passion which he serveth: and he to whom I have committed my soul delivered me out of his hands; and I fled away from him naked, and slept with my nurse: but that which befell him I know not, wherefore he hath contrived this. The apostle saith: These things will not hurt us; but believe thou on Jesus, and he shall overthrow the wrath of Charisius and his madness and his impulse; and he shall be a companion unto thee in the fearful way, and he shall guide thee into his kingdom, and shall bring thee unto eternal life giving thee that confidence which passeth not away nor changeth.

104 Now Siphor stood before the king, and he inquired of him: Who is that sorcerer and whence, and what teacheth he whom thou hast lurking in thine house? And Siphor answered the king: Thou art not ignorant, O king, what trouble and grief I, with my friends had concerning my wife, whom thou knowest and many others remember, and concerning my daughter, whom I value more than all my possessions, what a time and trial I suffered; for I became a laughing-stock and a curse in all our country. And I heard the report of this man and went to him and entreated him, and took him and brought him hither. And as I came by the way I saw wonderful and amazing

things: and here also many did hear the wild ass and concerning that devil whom he drove out, and healed my wife and daughter, and now are they whole; and he asked no reward but requireth faith and holiness, that men should become partakers with him in that which he doeth: and this he teacheth to worship and fear one God, the ruler of all things, and Jesus Christ his Son, that they may have eternal life. And that which he eateth is bread and salt, and his drink is water from evening unto evening, and he maketh many prayers; and whatsoever he asketh of his God, he giveth him. And he teacheth that this God is holy and mighty, and that Christ is living and maketh alive, wherefore also he chargeth them that are there present to come unto him in holiness and purity and love and faith.

105 And when Misdaeus the king heard these things of Siphor he sent many soldiers unto the house of Siphor the captain, to bring Thomas the apostle and all that were found there. And they that were sent entered in and found him teaching much people; and Mygdonia sat at his feet. And when they beheld the great multitude that were about him, they feared, and departed to their king and said: We durst not say aught unto him, for there was a great multitude about him, and Mygdonia sitting at his feet was listening to the things that were spoken by him. And when Misdaeus the king and Charisius heard these things, Charisius leaped out from before the king and drew much people with him and said: I will bring him, O king, and Mygdonia whose understanding he hath taken away. And he came to the house of Siphor the captain, greatly disturbed, and found him (Thomas) teaching: but Mygdonia he found not, for she had withdrawn herself unto her house, having learnt that it had been told her husband that she was there.

106 And Charisius said unto the apostle: Up, thou wicked one and destroyer and enemy of mine house: for me thy sorcery harmeth not, for I will visit thy sorcery on thine head. And when he so said, the apostle looked upon him and said unto him: Thy threatenings shall return upon thee, for me thou wilt not harm any whit: for greater than thee and thy king and all your army is the Lord Jesus Christ in whom I have my trust. And Chalisius took a kerchief (turban, Syr.) of one of his slaves and cast it about the neck of the apostle, saying: Hale him and bring him away; let me see if his God is able to deliver him out of my hands. And they haled him and led him away to Misdaeus the king. And the apostle stood before the king, and the king said to him: Tell me who thou art and by what power thou doest these things. But the apostle kept silence. And the king commanded his officers (subjects) that he should be scourged with an hundred and twenty-eight (hundred and fifty, Syr.) blows, and bound, and be cast into the prison; and they bound him and led him away. And the king and Charisius considered how they should put him to death, for the multitude worshipped him as God. And they had it in mind to say: The stranger hath reviled the king and is a deceiver.

107 But the apostle went unto the prison rejoicing and exulting, and said: I praise thee, Jesu, for that thou hast not only made me worthy of faith in thee, but also to endure much for thy sake. I give thee thanks therefore, Lord, that thou hast taken thought for me and given me patience: I thank thee Lord, that for thy sake I am called a sorcerer and a wizard. Receive thou me therefore with the blessing (Syr. let me receive of the blessing) of the poor, and of the rest of the weary, and of the blessings of them whom men hate and persecute and revile, and speak evil words of them. For lo, for thy sake I am hated: lo for thy sake I am cut off from the many, and for thy sake they call me such an one as I am not.

108 And as he prayed, all the prisoners looked on him, and besought him to pray for them: and when he had prayed and was set down, he began to utter a psalm in this wise:

THE ACTS OF THE HOLY APOSTLE THOMAS

*[[Here follows the Hymn of the Soul: a
most remarkable composition,
originally Syriac, and certainly older
than the Acts, with which it has no real
connection. We have it in Greek in one
manuscript, the Vallicellian, and in a
paraphrase by Nicetas of Thessalonica,
found and edited by Bonnet.]]*

1 When I was an infant child
in the palace of my Father
2 and resting in the wealth and luxury
of my nurturers,
out of the East, our native country, my
parents provisioned me and sent me.
4 And of the wealth of those their
treasures they put together a load
5 both great and light, that I might carry
it alone.
6 Gold is the load, of them that are
above (or of the land of the Ellaeans or
Gilaeans),
and silver of the great treasures (or of
Gazzak the great)
7 and stones, chalcedonies from the
Indians
and pearls from the Kosani (Kushan).
8 And they armed me with adamant
9 and they took off from me (Gr. put on
me) the garment set with gems,
spangled with gold, which they had
made for me because they loved me
10 and the robe that was yellow in hue,
made for my stature.
11 And they made a covenant with me,
and inscribed it on mine understanding,
that I should forget it, and said:
12 If thou go down into Egypt, and
bring back thence the one pearl
13 which is there girt about by the
devouring serpent
14 thou shalt put on the garment set
with gems, and that robe whereupon it
resteth (or which is thereon)
15 and become with thy brother that is
next unto us (Gr. of the well-
remembered) an heir (Gr. herald) in our
kingdom.

109.

16 And I came out of the East by a road
difficult and fearful, with two guides
17 and I was untried in travelling by it.
18 And I passed by the borders of the
Mosani (Maishan) where is the resort of
the merchants of the East,
19 and reached the land of the
Babylonians .
20 But when I entered into Egypt, the
guides left me which had journeyed
with me.
21 And I set forth by the quickest way
to the serpent, and by his hole I abode
22 watching for him to slumber and
sleep, that I might take my pearl from
him.
23 And forasmuch as I was alone I
made mine aspect strange, and appeared
as an alien to my people.
24 And there I saw my kinsman from
the East, the free-born
25 a lad of grace and beauty, a son of
princes (or an anointed one).
26 He came unto me and dwelt with
me,
27 and I had him for a companion, and
made him my friend and partaker in my
journey (or merchandise).
28 And I charged him to beware of the
Egyptians, and of partaking of those
unclean things (or consorting with those
unclean men).
29 And I put on their raiment, lest I
should seem strange, as one that had
come from without
30 to recover the pearl; and lest the
Egyptians should awake the serpent
against me.
31 But, I know not by what occasion,
they learned that I was not of their
country.
32 And with guile they mingled for me
a deceit, and I tasted of their food.
33 And I knew no more that I was a
king's son, and I became a servant unto
their king.
34 And I forgat also the pearl for which
my fathers had sent me,
35 and by means of the heaviness of
their food I fell into a deep sleep.

110.

36 But when this befell me, my fathers
also were ware of it, and grieved for me
37 and a proclamation was published in
our kingdom, that all should meet at our
doors.
38 And then the kings of Parthia and

they that bare office and the great ones of the East

39 made a resolve concerning me, that I should not be left in Egypt,

40 and the princes wrote unto me signifying thus (and every noble signed his name to it, Syr.):

41 From the (thy) Father the King of kings, and thy mother that ruleth the East,

42 and thy brother that is second unto us; unto our son that is in Egypt, peace.

43 Rise up and awake out of sleep, and hearken unto the words of the letter

44 and remember that thou art a son of kings; lo, thou hast come under the yoke of bondage.

45 Remember the pearl for the which thou wast sent into Egypt (Gr. puts this after 46).

46 Remember thy garment spangled with gold,

47 Thy name is named in the book of life,

48 and with thy brother whom thou hast received in our kingdom.

111.

49 and the King [as ambassador] sealed it

50 because of the evil ones, even the children of the Babylonians and the tyrannous demons of Labyrinthus (Sarbug, Syr.).

51

52 It flew and lighted down by me, and became all speech.>

53 And I at the voice of it and the feeling of it started up out of sleep

54 and I took it up and kissed it and read it.

55 And it was written concerning that which was recorded in mine heart.

56 And I remembered forthwith that I was a son of kings, and my freedom yearned (sought) after its kind.

57 I remembered also the pearl for the which I was sent down into Egypt

58 and I began (or came) with charms against the terrible serpent,

59 and I overcame him (or put him to sleep) by naming the name of my Father upon him,

60

61 And I caught away the pearl and turned back to bear it unto my fathers.

62 And I stripped off the filthy garment and left it in their land,

63 and directed my way forthwith to the light of my fatherland in the East.

64 And on the way I found my letter that had awakened me,

65 and it, like as it had taken a voice and raised me when I slept, so also guided me with the light that came from it.

66 For at times the royal garment of silk before mine eyes,

67

68 and with love leading me and drawing me onward,

69 I passed by Labyrinthus (Sarbug), and I left Babylon upon my left hand

70 and I came unto Meson (Mesene; Maishan) the great,

71 that lieth on the shore of the sea,

72

73 from the heights of Warkan (Hyrcania?) had my parents sent thither

74 by the hand of their treasurers, unto whom they committed it because of their faithfulness.

112.

75 But I remembered not the brightness of it; for I was yet a child and very young when I had left it in the palace ot my Father,

76 but suddenly, [when] I saw the garment made like unto me as it had been in a mirror.

77 And I beheld upon it all myself (or saw it wholly in myself) and I knew and saw myself through it,

78 that we were divided asunder, being of one; and again were one in one shape.

79 Yea, the treasurers also which brought me the garment

80 I beheld, that they were two, yet one shape was upon both, one royal sign was set upon both of them.

81 The money and the wealth had they in their hands, and paid me the due price,

82 and the lovely garment, which was variegated with bright colours

83 with gold and precious stones and

pearls of comely hue

84 they were fastened above (or in the height)

85

86 And the likeness of the King of kings was all in all of it.

87 Sapphire stones were fitly set in it above (or, like the sapphire stone also were its manifold hues).

113.

88 And again I saw that throughout it motions of knowledge were being sent forth,

89 and it was ready to utter speech.

90 And I heard it speak :

91 I am of him that is more valiant than all men, for whose sake I was reared up with the Father himself.

92 And I also perceived his stature (so Gr.- Syr. I perceived in myself that my stature grew in accordance with his working).

93 And all its royal motions rested upon me as it grew toward the impulse of it (And with its kingly motions it was spreading itself toward me).

94 And it hastened, reaching out from the hand of unto him that would receive it

95 and me also did yearning arouse to start forth and meet it and receive it.

96 And I stretched forth and received it, and adorned myself with the beauty of the colours thereof (mostly Syr.; Gr. corrupt)

97 and in my royal robe excelling in beauty I arrayed myself wholly.

98 And when I had put it on, I was lifted up unto the place of peace (sahltation) and homage

99 and I bowed my head and worshipped the brightness of the Father which had sent it unto me.

100 for I had performed his commandments, and he likewise that which he had promised,

101 and at the doors of his palace which was from the beginning I mingled among ,

102 and he rejoiced over me and received me with him into his palace,

103 and all his servants do praise him vvith sweet voices.

104 And he promised me that with him I shall be sent unto the gates of the king,

105 that with my gifts and my pearl we may appear together before the king.

114 And Charisius went home glad, thinking that his wife would be with him, and that she had become such as she was before, even before she heard the divine word and believed on Jesus. And he went, and found her with her hair dishevelled and her clothes rent, and when he saw it he said unto her: My lady Mygdonia, why doth this cruel disease keep hold on thee? and wherefore hast thou done this? I am thine husband from thy virginity, and both the gods and the law grant me to have rule over thee, what is this great madness of thine, that thou art become a derision in all our nation? but put thou away the care that cometh of that sorcerer; and I will remove his face from among us, that thou mayest see him no more.

115 But Mygdonia when she heard that gave herself up unto grief, groaning and lamenting and Charisius said again; Have I then so much wronged the gods that they have afflicted me with such a disease? what is my great offence that they have cast me into such humiliation? I beseech thee. Mvgdonia trangle my soul no more with the pitiful sight of thee and thy mean appearance and afflict not mine heart with care for thee I am Charisius thine husband, whom all the nation honoureth and feareth. What must I do? I know not whither to turn. What am I to think? shall I keep silence and endure? yet who can be patient when men take his treasure? and who can endure to lose thy sweet ways? and what is there for me? (Syr. thy beauties which are ever before me) the fragrance of thee is in my nostrils, and thy bright face is fixed in mine eyes. They are taking away my soul, and the fair body which I rejoiced to see they are destroying, and that sharpest of eyes they are blinding and cutting off my right hand: my joy is turning to grief and my life to death,

and the light of it is being dyed (?) with darkness. Let no man of you my kindred henceforth look on me; from you no help hath come to me, nor will I hereafter worship the gods of the east that have enwrapped me in such calamities, nor pray to them any more nor sacrifice to them, for I am bereaved of my spouse. And what else should I ask of them? for all my glory is taken away, yet am I a prince and next unto the king in power; but Mygdonia hath set me at nought, and taken away all these things. (Would that some one would blind one of my eyes, and that thine eyes would look upon me as they were wont, Syr. which has more clauses, to the same effect.)

116 And while Charisius spake thus with tears, Mygdonia sat silent and looking upon the ground; and again he came unto her and said: My lady Mygdonia, most desired of me, remember that out of all the women that are in India I chose and took thee as the most beautiful, though I might have joined to myself in marriage many more beautiful: but yet I lie, Mygdonia, for by the gods it would not have been possible to find another like thee in the land of India; but woe is me alway, for thou wilt not even answer me a word: but if thou wilt, revile me, so that I may only be vouchsafed a word from thee. Look at me, for I am more comely than that sorcerer: but thou art my wealth and honour: and all men know that there is none like me: and thou art my race and kindred; and lo, he taketh thee away from me.

117 And when Charisius had so said, Mygdonia saith unto him: He whom I love is better than thee and thy substance: for thy substance is of earth and returneth unto the earth; but he whom I love is of heaven and will take me with him unto heaven. Thy wealth shall pass away, and thy beauty shall vanish, and thy robes, and thy many works: and thou shalt be alone, naked, with thy transgressions. Call not to my remembrance thy deeds (unto me), for I pray the Lord that I may forget thee, so as to remember no more those former

pleasures and the custom of the body; which shall pass away as a shadow, but Jesus only endureth for ever, and the souls which hope in him. Jesus himself shall quit me of the shameful deeds which I did with thee. And when Charisius heard this, he turned him to sleep, vexed (dissolved) in soul, saying to her: Consider it by thyself all this night: and if thou wilt be with me such as thou wast before, and not see that sorcerer, I will do all according to thy mind, and if thou wilt remove thine affection from him I will take him out of the prison and let him go and remove into another country, and I will not vex thee, for I know that thou makest much of the stranger. And not with thee first did this matter come about, for many other women also hath he deceived with thee; and they have awaked sober and returned to themselves: do not thou then make nought of my words and cause me to be a reproach among the Indians.

118 And Charisius having thus spoken went to sleep: but she took ten denarii (20 zuze, Syr.), and went secretly to give them to the gaolers that she might enter in to the apostle. But on the way Judas Thomas came and met her, and she saw him and was afraid, for she thought that he was one of the rulers: for a great light went before him. And she said to herself as she fled: have lost thee, O my unhappy soul! for thou wilt not again see Judas the apostle of the living , and not yet hast thou received the holy seal. And she fled and ran into a narrow place and there hid herself, saying: I would rather choose to be killed (taken) by the poorer, whom it is possible to persuade, than to fall into the hand of this mighty ruler, who will despise gifts.

THE TENTH ACT
wherein Mygdonia receiveth baptism

119 And while Mygdonia thought thus with herself, Judas came and stood over her, and she saw him and was afraid, and fell down and became lifeless with terror. But he stood by her and took her by the hand and said unto her: Fear not,

Mygdonia: Jesus will not leave thee, neither will the Lord unto whom thou hast committed thy soul overlook thee. His compassionate rest will not forsake thee: he that is kind will not forsake thee, for his kindness' sake, nor he that is good for his goodness' sake. Rise up then from the earth, thou that art become wholly above it: look on the light, for the Lord leaveth not them that love him to walk in darkness: behold him that travelleth with his servants, that he is unto them a defender in perils. And Mygdonia arose and looked on him and said: Whither wentest thou, my lord? and who is he that brought thee out of prison to behold the sun? Judas Thomas saith unto her: My Lord Jesus is mightier than all powers and all kings and rulers.

120 And Mygdonia said: Give me the seal of Jesus Christ and I shall (let me) receive the gift at thy hands before thou departest out of life. And she took him with her and entered into the court and awaked her nurse, saying unto her: Narcia (Gr. Marcia), my mother and nurse, all thy service and refreshment thou hast done for me from my childhood until my present age are vain, and for them I owe thee thanks which are temporal; do for me now also a ravour, that thou mayest for ever receive a recompense from him that giveth great gifts. And Narcia in answer saith: What wilt thou, my daughter Mygdonia, and what is to be done for thy pleasure? for the honours which thou didst promise me before, the stranger hath not suffered thee to accomplish, and thou hast made me a reproach among all the nation. And now what is this new thing that thou commandest me? And Mygdonia saith: Become thou partaker with me in eternal life, that I may receive of thee perfect nurture: take bread and bring it me, and wine mingled with water, and spare my freedom (take pity on me a free-born woman, Syr.). And the nurse said: I will bring thee many loaves, and for water flagons of wine, and fulfil thy desire. But she saith to the nurse: Flagons I desire not, nor the many

loaves: but this only, bring wine mingled with water and one loaf, and oil .

121 And when Narcia had brought these things, Mygdonia stood before the apostle with her head bare; and he took the oil and poured it on her head, saying: Thou holy oil given unto us for sanctification, sccret mystery whereby the cross was shown unto us, thou art the straightener of the crooked limbs, thou art the humbler (softener) of hard things (works), thou art it that showeth the hidden treasures, thou art the sprout of goodness; let thy power come, let it be established upon thy servant Mygdonia, and heal thou her by this freedom. And when the oil was poured upon her he hade her nurse unclothe her and gird a linen cloth about her; and there was there a fountain of water upon which the apostle went up, and baptized Mygdonia in the name of the Father and the Son and the Holy Ghost. And when she was baptized and clad, he brake bread and took a cup of water and made her a partaker in the body of Christ and the cup of the Son of God, and said: Thou hast received thy seal, get for thyself eternal life. And immediately there was heard from above a voice saying: Yea, amen. And when Narcia heard that voice, she was amazed, and besought the apostle that she also might receive the seal; and the apostle gave it her and said: Let the care of the Lord be about thee as about the rest.

122 And having done these things the apostle returned unto the prison, and found the doors open and the guards still sleeping. And Thomas said: Who is like thee, O God? who withholdest not thy loving affection and care from any who is like thee, the merciful, who hast delivered thy creatures out of evil. Life that hath subdued death, rest that hath ended toil. Glory be to the only-begotten of the Father. Glory to the compassionate that was sent forth of his heart. And when he had said thus, the guards waked and beheld all the doors open, and the prisoners <+ asleep, Syr.>, and said in themselves: Did not we fasten the doors? and how are they

now open, and the prisoners within? 123 But at the dawn Charisius went unto Mygdonia , and found them praying and saying: O new God that by the stranger hast come hither unto us, hidden God of the dwellers in India (Syr. who art hidden from); God that hast shown thy glory by thine apostle Thomas, God whose report we have heard and believed on thee; God, unto whom we are come to be saved; God, who for love of man and for pity didst come down unto our littleness; God who didst seek us out when we knew him (thee) not; God that dwellest in the heights and from whom the depths are not hid: turn thou away from us the madness of Charisius. And Charisius hearing that said to Mygdonia: Rightly callest thou me evil and mad and foul I for if I had not borne with thy disobedience, and given thee liberty, thou wouldest not have called on God against me and made mention of my name before God. But believe me, Mygdonia that in that sorcerer there is no profit, and what he promiseth to perform he cannot: but I will perform before thy sight all that I promise, that thou mayest believe, and bear with my words and be to me as thou wast beforetime.

124 And he came near and besought her again, saying: If thou wilt be persuaded of me, I shall henceforth have no grief; remember that day when thou didst meet me first; tell the truth: was I more beautiful unto thee at that time, or Jesus at this? And Mygdonia said: That time required its own, and this time also; that was the time of the beginning, but this of the end; that was the time of temporal life, this of eternal; that of pleasure that passeth away, but this of pleasure that abideth for ever; that, of day and night, this of day without night. Thou sawest that marriage that was passing, and here, and single but this marriage continueth for ever; that was a partnership of corruption, but this of eternal life; those groomsmen (and maids) were men and women of time, but these abide unto the end. That marriage upon earth setteth up dropping dew of the love of men (Syr. That union was founded upon the earth where there is an unceasing press: this is founded upon the bridge of fire upon which is sprinkled grace: both corrupt); that bride-chamber is taken down again, but this remaineth always; that bed was strown with coverlets (that grow old), but this with love and faith. Thou art a bridegroom that passest away and art dissolved (changed), but Jesus is a true bridegroom, enduring for ever immortal, that dowry was of money and robes that grow old, but this is of living words which never pass away.

125 And when Charisius heard these things he went unto the king and told him all: and the king commanded Judas to be brought, that he might judge him and destroy him. But Charisius said: Have patience a little, O king, and first persuade the man making him afraid, that he may persuade Mygdonia to be unto me as formerly. And Misdaeus sent and fetched the apostle of Christ, and all the prisoners were grieved because the apostle departed from them, for they yearned after him, saying: Even the comfort which we had have they taken away from us.

126 And Misdaeus said unto Judas: Wherefore teachest thou this new doctrine, which both gods and men hate, and which hath nought of profit? And Judas said: What evil do I teach? And Misdaeus said: Thou teachest, saying that men with the God whom thou preachest. Judas saith: Thou sayest true, O king: thus do I teach. For tell me, art thou not wroth with thy soldiers if they wait on thee in filthy garments? if then thou, being a king of earth and returning unto earth, request thy subjects to be reverend in their doings, are ye wroth and said ye that I teach ill when I say that they who serve my king must be reverend and pure and free from all grief and care of children and unprofitable riches and vain trouble? For indeed thou wouldest have thy subjects follow thy conversation and thy manners, and thou punishest them if they despise thy commandments: how much more must they that believe on

him serve my God with much reverence and cleanness and security, and be quit of all pleasures of the body, adultery and prodigality and theft and drunkenness and belly-service and foul deeds?

127 And Misdaeus hearing these things said: Lo, I let thee go: go then and persuade Mygdonia, the wife of Charisius, not to desire to depart from him. Judas saith unto him: Delay not if thou hast aught to do: for her, if she hath rightly received what she hath learned, neither iron nor fire nor aught else stronger than these will avail to hurt or to root out him that is held in her soul. Misdaeus saith unto Judas: Some poisons do dissolve other poisons, and a theriac cureth the bites of the viper; and thou if thou wilt canst give a solvent of those diseases, and make peace and concord betwixt this couple: for by so doing thou wilt spare thyself, for not yet art thou sated with life; and know thou that if thou do not persuade her, I will catch thee away out of this life which is desirable unto all men. And Judas said: This life hath been given as a loan, and this time is one that changeth, but that life whereof I teach is incorruptible; and beauty and youth that are seen shall in a little cease to be. The king saith to him: I have counselled thee for the best, but thou knowest thine own alfairs.

128 And as the apostle went forth from before the king, Charisius came to him and entreated him and said: I beseech thee, O man: I have not sinned against thee or any other at any time, nor against the gods; wherefore hast thou stirred up this great calamity against me? and for what cause hast thou brought such disturbance upon mine house? and what profit hast thou of it? but if thou thinkest to gain somewhat, tell me the gain, what it is, and I will procure it for thee without labour. To what end dost thou make me mad, and cast thyself into destruction? for if thou persuade her not, I will both dispatch thee and finally take myself out of life. But if, as thou sayest, after our departing hence there is there life and death, and also condemnation and victory and a place of judgement, then will I also go in thither to be judged with thee: and if that God whom thou preachest is just and awardeth punishment justly, I know that I shall gain my cause against thee; for thou hast injured me, having suffered no wrong at my hands: for indeed even here I am able to avenge myself on thee and bring upon thee all that thou hast done unto me. Therefore be thou persuaded, and come home with me and persuade Mygdonia to be with me as she was at first, before she beheld thee. And Judas saith to him: Believe me, my child that if men loved God as much as they love one another, they would ask of him all things and receive them, and none would do them violence (there would be nothing which would not obey them, Syr.).

129 And as Thomas said this, they came unto the house of Charisius and found Mygdonia sitting and Narcia standing by her, and her hand supporting her cheek; and she was saying: Let the remainder of the days of my life, O mother, be cut off from me, and all the hours become as one hour, and let me depart out of life that I may go the sooner and behold that beautiful one, whose report I have heard, even that living one and giver of life unto them that believe on him, where is not day and night, nor light and darkness, nor good and evil, nor poor and rich, nor male and female, nor free and bond, nor proud that subjecteth the humble. And as she spake the apostle stood by her, and forthwith she rose up and did him reverence. Then Charisius said unto him: Seest thou how she feareth and honoureth thee and all that thou shalt bid her she will do willingly?

130 And as he so spake, Judas saith unto Mygdonia: My daughter Mygdonia, obey that which thy brother Charisius saith. And Mygdonia saith: If thou wast not able the deed in word wilt thou compel me to endure the act? for I have heard of thee that this life is of no profit, and this relief is for a time, and these possessions are transitory. And again thou saidst that whoso renounceth

this life shall receive the life eternal, and whoso hateth the light of day and night shall behold a light that is not overtaken, that whoso despiseth this money shall find other and eternal money. But now because thou art in fear. Who that hath done somewhat and is praised for the work changeth it? straightway overthroweth it from the foundation? who diggeth a spring water in a thirsty land and straightway filleth it in? who findeth a treasure and useth it not? And Charisius heard It and said: I will not imitate you, neither will I hasten to destroy you; nor though I may so do, will I put bonds about thee (but thee I will bind, Syr.); and I will not suffer thee to speak with this sorcerer; and if thou obey me, well, but if not, I know what I must do.

131 And Judas went out of Charisius' house and departed unto the house of Siphor and lodged there with him. And Siphor said: I will prepare for Judas a hall (triclinium) wherein he may teach (Syr. Siphor said to Judas: Prepare thyself an apartment, &c.). And he did so; and Siphor said : I and my wife and daughter will dwell henceforth in holiness, and in chastity, and in one affection. I beseech thee that we may receive of thee the seal, and become worshippers of the true God and numbered among his sheep and lambs. And Judas said: I am afraid to speak that which I think: yet I know somewhat, and what I know it is not possible for me to utter.

132 And he began to say concerning baptism: This baptism is remission of sins (the Greek MSS. U and P have divergent texts, both obscure): this bringeth forth again light that is shed about us: this bringeth to new birth the new man (this is the restorer of understandings Syr.): this mingleth the spirit (with the body), raiseth up in threefoldwise a new man and partaker of the remission of sins. Glory be to thee, hidden one, that art communicated in baptism. Glory to thee the unseen power that is in baptism. Glory to thee, renewal, whereby are renewed they that are baptized and with affection take

hold upon thee.

And having thus said, he poured oil over their heads and said: Glory be to thee the love of compassion (bowels). Glory to thee name of Christ. Glory to thee, power established in Christ. And he commanded a vessel to be brought, and baptized them in the name of the Father and the Son and the Holy Ghost. 133 And when they were baptized and clad, he set bread on the table and blessed it, and said: Bread of life, the which who eat abide incorruptible: Bread that filleth the hungry souls with the blessing thereof: thou art he that vouchsafest to receive a gift, that thou mayest become unto us remission of sins, and that they who eat thee may become immortal: we invoke upon thee the name of the mother, of the unspeakable mystery of the hidden powers and authorities (? we name the name of the unspeakable mystery, that is hidden from all &c.): we invoke upon thee the name of [thy?] Jesus. And he said: Let the powers of blessing come, and be established in this bread, that all the souls which partake of it may be washed from their sins. And he brake and gave unto Siphor and his wife and daughter.

THE ELEVENTH ACT
concerning the wife of Misdaeus

134 Now Misdaeus the king, when he had let Judas go, dined and went home, and told his wife what had befallen Charisius their kinsman, saying: See what hath come to pass to that unhappy man, and thou thyself knowest, my sister Tertia, that a man hath nought better than his own wife on whom he resteth; but it chanced that his wife went unto that sorcerer of whom thou hast heard that he is come to the land of the Indians, and fell into his charms and is parted from her own husband; and he knoweth not what he should do. And when I would have destroyed the malefactor, he would not have it. But do thou go and counsel her to incline unto her husband, and forsake the vain words of the sorcerer.

135 And as soon as she arose Tertia went to the house of Charisius her husband's , and found Mygdonia lying upon the earth in humiliation, and ashes and sackcloth were spread under her, and she was praying that the Lord would forgive her her former sins and she might soon depart out of life. And Tertia said unto her: Mygdonia, my dear sister and companion what is this hand (Syr. this folly)? what is the disease that hath overtaken thee? and why doest thou the deeds of madmen? Know thyself and come back unto thine own way, come near unto thy many kinsfolk, and spare thy true husband Charisius, and do not things unbefitting a free-woman. Mygdonia saith unto her: O Tertia, thou hast not yet heard the preacher of life: not yet hath he touched thine ears, not yet hast thou tasted the medicine of life nor art freed from corruptible mourning. Thou standest in the life of time, and the everlasting life and salvation thou knowest not, and perceivest not the incorruptible fellowship. Thou standest clad in robes that grow old and desirest not those that are eternal, and art proud of this beauty which vanisheth and hast no thought of the holiness of thy soul; and art rich in a multitude of servants, (and hast not freed thine own soul from servitude, Syr.) and pridest thyself in the glory that cometh of many, but redeemest not thyself from the condemnation of death. 136 And when Tertia heard this of Mygdonia she said: I pray thee, sister, bring me unto that stranger that teacheth these great things, that I also may go and hear him, and be taught to worship the God whom he preacheth, and become partaker of his prayers, and a sharer in all that thou hast told me of. And Mygdonia saith to her: He is in the house of Siphor the captain; for he is become the occasion of life unto all them that are being saved in India. And hearing that, Tertia went quickly to Siphor's house, that she might see the new apostle that was come thither. And when she entered in, Judas said unto her: What art thou come to see? a man that is a stranger and poor and contemptible and needy, having neither riches nor substance; yet one thing I possess which neither kings nor rulers can take away, that neither perisheth nor ceaseth, which is Jesus the Saviour of all mankind, the Son of the living God, who hath given life unto all that believe on him and take refuge with him and are known to be of the number of his servants (sheep, Syr.). Unto whom saith Tertia: May I become a partaker of this life which thou promisest that all they shall receive who come together unto the assembly of God. And the apostle said: The treasury of the holy king is opened wide, and they which worthily partake of the good things that are therein do rest, and resting do reign: but first, no man cometh unto him that is unclean and vile: for he knoweth our inmost hearts and the depths of our thought, and it is not possible for any to escape him. Thou, then, if verily thou believest in him, shalt be made worthy of his mysteries; and he will magnify thee and enrich thee, and make thee to be an heir of his hingdom.

137 And Tertia having heard this returned home rejoicing, and found her husband awaiting her, not having dined, and when Misdaeus saw her he said: Whence is it that thine entering in to-day is more beautiful? and wherefore art thou come walking, which beseemeth not free-born women like thee? And Tertia saith unto him: I owe thee the greatest of thanks for that thou didst send me unto Mygdonia, for I went and heard of a new life, and I saw the new apostle of the God that giveth life unto them that believe on him and fulfil his commandments; I ought therefore myself to recompense thee for this favour and admonition with good advice; for thou shalt be a great king in heaven if thou obey me and fear the God that is preached by the strangrer, and keep thyself holy unto the living God. For this kingdom passeth away, and thy comfort will be turned into affliction: but go thou to that man, and believe him, and thou shalt live unto the end. And when Misdaeus heard these things of his wife, he smote his face

with his hands and rent his clothes and said: May the soul of Charisius find no rest, for he hath hurt me to the soul; and may he have no hope, for he hath taken away my hope. And he went out greatly vexed.

138 And he found Charisius his friend in the market-place, and said unto him: Why hast thou cast me into hell to be another companion to thyself? why hast thou emptied and defrauded me to gain nought? why hast thou hurt me and profited thyself not at all? why hast thou slain me and thyself not lived? Why hast thou wronged me and thyself not got justice? why didst thou not suffer me to destroy that sorcerer before he corrupted my house with his wickedness? And he kept hold upon (was upbraiding, Syr.) Charisius. And Charisius saith: Why, what hath befallen thee? Misdaeus said: He hath bewitched Tertia. And they went both of them unto the house of Siphor the captain, and found Judas sitting and teaching. And all they that were there rose up before the king, but he arose not. And Misdaeus perceived that it was he, and took hold of the seat and overset it, and took up the seat with both his hands and smote his head so that he wounded it, and delivered him to his soldiers, saying: Take him away, and hale him with violence and not gently, that his shame may be manifest unto all men. And they haled him and took him to the place where Misdaeus judged, and he stood there, held of the soldiers of Misdaeus.

THE TWELFTH ACT
concerning Ouazanes (Iuzanes) the son of Misdaeus

139 And Ouazanes (Iuzanes, P; Vizan, Syr.) the son of Misdaeus came unto the soldiers and said: Give me him that I may speak with him until the king cometh. And they gave him up, and he brought him in where the king gave judgement. And Iuzanes saith: Knowest thou not that I am the son of Misdaeus the king, and I have power to say unto the king what I will, and he will sufier

thee to live? tell me then, who is thy God, and what power dost thou claim and glory in it? for if it be some power or art of magic, tell it me and teach me, and I will let thee go. Judas saith unto him: Thou art the son of Misdacus the king who is king for a time, but I am the servant of Jesus Christ the eternal king, and thou hast power to say to thy father to save whom thou wilt in the temporal life wherein men continue not, which thou and thy father grant, but I beseech my Lord and intercede for men, and he giveth them a new life which is altogether enduring. And thou boastest thyself of possessions and servants and robes and luxury and unclean chamberings, but I boast myself of povertv and philosophy and humility and lasting and prayer and the fellowship of the Holy Ghost and of my brethren that are worthy of God: and I boast myself of eternal life. And thou reliest on (hast taken refuge with) a man like unto thyself and not able to save his own soul from judgement and death, but I rely upon the living God, upon the saviour of kings and princes, who is the judge of all men. And ye indeed to-day perchance are, and to-morrow are no more, but I have taken refuge with him that abideth for ever and knoweth all our seasons and times. And if thou wilt become the servant of this God thou shalt soon do so; but show that thou wilt be a servant worthy of him hereby: first by holiness (puritv), which is the head of all good things, and then by fellowship with this God whom I preach, and philosophy and simplicity and love and faith and in him, and unity of pure food (simplicity of pure i e, Syr.).

140 And the young man was persuaded by the Lord and sought occasion how he might let Judas escape: but while he thought thereon, the king came, and the soldiers took Judas and led him forth. And Iuzanes went forth with him and stood beside him. And when the king was set he bade Judas be brought in, with his hands bound behind him; and he was brought into the midst and stood there. And the king saith: Tell me who

thou art and by what power thou doest these things. And Judas saith to him: I am a man like thee, and by the power of Jesus Christ I do these things. And Misdaeus saith: Tell me the truth before I destroy thee. And Judas saith: Thou hast no power against me, as thou supposest, and thou wilt not hurt me at all. And the king was wroth at his words, and commanded to heat iron plates and set him upon them barefoot; and as the soldiers took off his shoes he said: The wisdom of God is better than the wisdom of men. Thou Lord and King (do thou take counsel against them, Syr.) and let thy goodness resist his wrath. And they brought the plates which were like fire, and set the apostle upon them, and straightway water sprang up abundantly from the earth, so that the plates were swallowed up in it, and they that held him let him go and withdrew themselves.

141 And the king seeing the abundance of water said to Judas: Ask thy God that he deliver me from this death, that I perish not in the flood. And the apostle prayed and said: Thou that didst bind this element (nature) and gather it into one place and send it forth into divers lands; that didst bring disorder into order, that grantest mighty works and great wonders by the hands of Judas thy servant; that hast mercy on my soul, that I may alway receive thy brightness; that givest wages unto them that have laboured; thou saviour of my soul, restoring it unto its own nature that it may have no fellowship with hurtful things; that hast alway been the occasion of life: do thou restrain this element that it lift not up itself to destroy; for there are some of them that stand here who shall believe on thee and live. And when he had prayed, the water was swallowed up by little and little, and the place became dry. And when Misdaeus saw it he commanded him to be taken to the prison: Until I shall consider how he must be used. 142 And as Judas was led away to the prison they all followed him, and Iuzanes the king's son walked at his right hand, and Siphor at the left. And

he entered into the prison and sat down, and Iuzanes and Siphor, and he persuaded his wife and his daughter to sit down, for they also were come in to hear the word of life. For they knew that Misdaeus would slay him because of the excess of his anger. And Judas began to say: O liberator of my soul from the bondage of the many, because I gave myself to be sold ; behold, I rejoice and exult, knowing that the times are fulfilled for me to enter in and receive . Lo, I am to be set free from the cares that are on the earth; lo, I fulfil mine hope and receive truth; lo, I am set free from sorrow and put on joy alone; lo, I become careless and griefless and dwell in rest; lo, I am set free from bondage and am called unto liberty; lo, I have served times and seasons, and I am lifted up above times and seasons; lo, I receive my wages from my recompenser, who giveth without reckoning (number) because his wealth sufficeth for the gift; and I shall not put it on again; lo, I sleep and awake, and I shall no more go to sleep; lo, I die and live again, and I shall no more taste of death; lo, they rejoice and expect me, that I may come and be with their kindred and be set as a flower in their crown; lo, I reign in the kingdom whereon I set my hope, even frrom hence; lo, the rebellious fall before me, for I have escaped them; lo, (unto me) the peace hath come, whereunto all are gathered.

143 And as the apostle spake thus, all that were there hearkened, supposing that in that hour he would depart out of life. And again he said: Believe on the physician of all , both seen and unseen, and on the saviour of the souls that need help from him. This is the free-born of kings, this the physician of his creatures; this is he that was reproached of his own slaves; this is the Father of the height and the Lord of nature and the Judge (? Father of nature and Lord of the height and supreme Judge, Syr.): he came of the greatest, the only-begotten son of the deep; and he was called the son of (became visible through, Syr.) Mary the virgin, and was

termed the son of Joseph the carpenter: he whose littleness (we beheld) with the eyes of our body, but his greatness we received by faith, and saw it in his works whose human body we felt also with our hands, and his aspect we saw transfigured (changed) with our eyes, but his heavenly semblance on the mount we were not able to see: he that made the rulers stumble and did violence unto death: he, the truth that lieth not, that at the last paid the tribute for himself and his disciplcs: whom the prince beholding feared and the powers that were with him were troubled; and the prince bare witness (asked him, Syr.) who he was and from whence, and knew not the truth, because he is alien from truth: he that having authority over the world, and the pleasures therein, and the possessions and the comfort, all these things and turneth away his subjects, that they should not use them.

144 Alld having fulfilled these sayings, he arose and prayed thus: our Father, which art in heaven: hallowed be thy name: Thy kingdom come: Thy will be done, as in heaven so upon earth: and forgive us our debts as we also have forgiven our debtors. And lead us not into temptation, but deliver us from the evil one.

My Lord and God, hope and confidence and teacher, thou hast taught me to pray thus, behold, I pray this prayer and fulfil thy commandment: be thou with me unto the end; thou art he that from childhood hast sown life in me and kept me from corruption; thou art he that hast brought me unto the poverty of this world, and exhorted me unto the true riches; thou art he that hast made me known unto myself and showed me that I am thine; and I have kept myself pure from woman, that that which thou requirest be not found in defilement.

[At the words 'My Lord and God' begins the double text, represented on the one hand by the MS. U and on the other by the Paris MS. P, and three (partly four) others. These insert the prayer after ch. 167. Their text, I believe, may be the original Greek. I

follow it here, repeating the first paragraph.]

(144) My Lord and God, my hope and my confidence and my teacher, that hast implanted courage in me, thou didst teach me to pray thus; behold, I pray thy prayer and bring thy will to fulfilment: be thou with me unto the end. Thou art he that from my youth up didst give me patience in temptation and me life and preserve me from corruption; thou art he that didst bring me into the poverty of this world and fill me with the true riches; thou art he that didst show me that I was thine: wherefore I was never joined unto a wife, that the temple worthy of thee might not be found in pollution.

145 My mouth sufficeth not to praise thee, neither am I able to conceive the care and providence (carefulness) which hath been about me from thee which thou hast had for me). For I desired to gain riches, but thou by a vision didst show me that they are full of loss and iniury to them that gain them and I believed thy showing, and continued in the poverty of the world until thou, the true riches wert revealed unto me, who didst fill both me and the rest that were worthy of thee with thine own riches and set free thine own from care and anxiety. I have therefore fulfilled thy commandments, O Lord, and accomplished thy will, and become poor and needy and a stranger and a bondman and set at nought and a prisoner and hungry and thirsty and nalied and unshod, and I have toiled for thy sake, that my confidence might not perish and my hope that is in thee might not be confounded and my much labour might not be in vain and my weariness not be counted for nought: let not my prayers and rmy continual fastings perish, and my great zeal toward thee; let not my seed of wheat be changed for tares out of thy land, let not the enemy carry it away and mingle his own tares therewith; for thy land verily receiveth not his tares, neither indeed can they be laid up in thine houses.

146 I have planted thy vine in the earth, it hath sent down its roots into the depth

and its growth is spread out in the height, and the fruits of it are stretched forth upon the earth, and they that are worthy of thee are made glad by them, whom also thou hast gained. The money which thou hast from me I laid down upon the table (bank); this, when thou requirest it, restore unto me with usury, as thou hast promised. With thy one mind have I traded and have made ten, thou hast added rnore to me beside that I had, as thou didst covenant. I have forgiven my debtor the mine, require thou it not at my hands. I was bidden to the supper and I came: and I refused the land and the yoke of oxen and the wife, that I might not for their sake be rejected; I was bidden to the wedding, and I put on white raiment, that I might be worthy of it and not be bound hand and foot and cast into the outer darkness. My lamp with its bright light expecteth the master coming from the marriage, that it may receive him, and I may not (? he may not) see it dimmed because the oil is spent. Mine eyes, O Christ, look upon thee, and mine heart exulteth with joy because I have fulfilled thy will and perfected thy commandments; that I may be likened unto that watchful and careful servant who in his eagerness neglecteth not to keep vigil (other MSS.: I have not slumbered idly in keeping thy commandments: in the first sleep and at midnight and at cockcrow, that mine eyes may behold thee, &c.). All the night have I laboured to keep mine house from robbers, lest it be broken through.

147 My loins have I girt close with truth and bound my shoes on my feet, that I may never see them gaping: mine hands have I put unto the yoked plough and have not turned away backward, lest my furrows go crooked. The plough-land is become white and the harvest is come, that I may receive my wages. My garment that groweth old I have worn out, and the labour that hath brought me unto rest have I accomplished. I have kept the first watch and the second and the third, that I may behold thy face and adore thine

holy brightness. I have rooted out the worst (pulled down my barns, Syr.) and left thern desolate upon earth, that I may be filled full from thy treasures (Gr. MSS. add: all my substance have I sold, that I may gain thee the pearl). The moist spring that was in me have I dried up, that I may live and rest beside thine inexhaustible spring (al. and Syr.: rest beside thy living spring). The captive whom thou didst commit to me I have slain, that he which is set free in me may not fall from his confidence. Him that was inward have I made outward and the outward , and all thy fullness hath been fulfilled in me. I have not returned unto the things that are behind, but have gone forward unto the things that are before, that I become not a reproach. The dead man have I quickened, and the living one have I overcome, and that which was lacking have I filled up (Syr. Wright, not the older one, inserts negatives, ' not quickened ', &c.), that I may receive the crown of victory, and the power of Christ may be accomplished in me. I have received reproach upon earth, but give thou me the return and the recompense in the heavens. (U omits practically all this chapter.)

148 Let not the powers and the officers perceive me, and let them not have any thought concerning me; let not the publicans and exactors ply their calling upon me; let not the weak and the evil cry out against me that am valiant and humble, and when I am borne upward let them not rise up to stand before me, by thy power, O Jesu, which surroundeth me as a crown: for they do flee and hide themselves, they cannot look on thee: but (for) suddenly do they fall upon them that are subject to them, and the portion of tile sons of the evil one doth itself cry out and convict them; and it is not hid from them, nor their nature is made known: the children of the evil one are separated off. Do thou then grant me, Lord, that I may pass by in quietness and joy and peace, and pass over and stand before the judge, and let not the devil (or slanderer) look upon me; let his eyes be

blinded by thy light which thou hast made to dwell in me, close thou up (muzzle) his mouth: for he hath found nought against me.

149 And he said again unto them that were about him: believe in the Saviour of them that have laboured in his service: for my soul already flourisheth because my time is near to receive him; for he being beautiful draweth me on always to speak concerning his beauty, what it is though I be not able and suffice not to speak it worthily: thou that art the light (feeder, Syr.) of my poverty and the supplier of my defects and nurturer of my need: be thou with me until I come and receive thee for evermore.

THE THIRTEENTH ACT
wherein Iuzanes receiveth baptism with the rest

150 And Iuzanes the youth besought the apostle, saying: I pray thee, O man, apostle of God, suffer me to go, and I will persuade the gaoler to permit thee to come home with me, that by thee I may receive the seal, and become thy minister and a keeper of the commandments of the God whom thou preachest. For indeed, formerly I walked in those things which thou teachest, until my father compelled me and joined me unto a wife by name Mnesara; for I am in my one-and-twentieth year, and have now been seven years married, and before I was joined in marriage I knew no other woman, wherefore also I was accounted useless of my father, nor have I ever had son or daughter of this wife and also my wife herself hath lived with me in chastity all this time, and to-day, if she had been in health, and had listened to thee, I know well that both I should have been at rest and she would have received eternal life; but she is in peril and afflicted with much illness; I will therefore persuade the keeper that he promise to come with me, for I live by myself: and thou shalt also heal that unhappy one. And Judas the apostle of the Most High, hearing this, said to

Iuzanes: If thou believest, thou shalt see the marvels of God, and how he saveth his servants.

151 And as they spake thus together, Tertia and Mygdonia and Narcia stood at the door of the prison, and they gave the gaoler 363 staters of silver and entered in to Judas; and found Iuzanes and Siphor and his wife and daughter, and all the prisoners sitting and hearing the word. And when they stood by him he said to them: Who hath suffered you to come unto us? and who opened unto you the sealed door that ye came forth? Tertia saith unto him: Didst not thou open the door for us and tell us to come into the prison that we might take our brethren that were there, and then should the Lord show forth his glory in us? And when we came near the door, I know not how, thou wast parted from us and hid thyself and camest hither before us where also we heard the noise of the door, when thou didst shut us out. We gave money therefore to the keepers and came in and lo, we are here praying thee that we may persuade thee and let thee escape until the king's wrath against thee shall cease. Unto whom Judas said: Tell us first of all how ye were shut up.

152 And she saith to him: Thou wast with us, and didst never leave us for one hour, and askest thou how we were shut up? but if thou desirest to hear, hear. The king Misdaeus sent for me and said unto me: Not yet hath that sorcerer prevailed over thee, for, as I hear, he bewitcheth men with oil and water and bread, and hath not yet bewitched thee; but obey thou me, for if not, I will imprison thee and wear thee out, and him I will destroy; for I know that if he hath not yet given thee oil and water and bread, he hath not prevailed to get power over thee. And I said unto him: Over my body thou hast authority, and do thou all that thou wilt; but my soul I will not let perish with thee. And hearing that he shut me up in a chamber (beneath his dining-hall, Syr.): and Charisius brought Mygdonia and shut her up with me: and thou broughtest us out and didst bring us even hither; but

give thou us the seal quickly, that the hope of Misdacus who counselleth thus may be cut off.

153 And when the apostle heard this, he said: Glory be to thee, O Jesu of many forms, glory to thee that appearest in the guise of our poor manhood: glory to thee that encouragest us and makest us strong and givest grace and consolest and standest by us in all perils, and strengthenest our weakness. And as he thus spake, the gaoler came and said: Put out the lamps, lest any accuse you unto the king. And then they extinguished the lamps, and turned to sleep; but the apostle spake unto the Lord: It is the time now, O Jesu, for thee to make haste; for, lo the children of darkness sit (make us to sit, Syr.) in their own darkness, do thou therefore enlighten us with the light of thy nature. And on a sudden the whole prison was light as the day: and while all they that were in the prison slept a deep sleep, they only that had believed in the Lord continued waking.

154 Judas therefore saith to Iuzanes: Go thou before and make ready the things for our need. Iuzanes thererore saith: And who will open me the doors of the prison? for the gaolers shut them and are gone to sleep. And Judas saith: Believe in Jesus, and thou shalt find the doors open. And when he went forth and departed from them, all the rest followed after him. And as Iuzanes was gone on before, Mnesara his wife met him coming unto the prison. And she knew him and said: My brother Iuzanes, is it thou? and he saith, Yea, and art thou Mnesara? and she saith Yea. Iuzanes said unto her; Whither walkest thou, especiality at so untimely an hour? and how wast thou able to rise up? And she said: This youth laid his hand on me and raised me up, and in a dream I say that I should go where the stranger sitteth, and become perfectly whole. Iuzanes saith to her: What youth is with thee? And she said: Seest thou not him that is on my right hand, leading me by the hand?

155 And while they spake together thus, Judas, with Siphor and his wife and daughter and Tertia and Mygdonia and Narcia came unto Iuzanes' house. And Mnesara the wife of Iuzanes seeing him did reverence and said: Art thou come that savedst us from the sore disease? thou art he whom I saw in the night delivering unto me this youth to bring me to the prison. But thy goodness suffered me not to grow weary, but thou thyself art come unto me. And so saying she turned about and saw the youth no more; and finding him not, she saith to the apostle: I am not able to walk alone: for the youth whom thou gavest me is not here. And Judas said: Jesus will henceforth lead thee. And thereafter she came running unto him. And when they entered into the house of Iuzanes the son of Misdaeus the king though it was yet night, a great light shined and was shed about them.

156 And then Judas began to pray and to speak thus: O companion and defender (ally) and hope of the weak and confidence of the poor: refuge and lodging of the weary: voice that came forth of the height (sleep, Gr.): comforter dwelling in the midst: port and harbour of them that pass through the regions of the rulers: physician that healest without payment: who among men wast crucified for many: who didst go down into hell with great might: the sight of whom the princes of death endured not; and thou camest up with great glory, and gathering all them that fled unto thee didst prepare a way, and in thy footsteps all they journeyed whom thou didst redeem; and thou broughtest them into thine own fold and didst join them with thy sheep: son of mercy, the son that for love of man wast sent unto us from the perfect country (fatherland) that is above, the Lord of all possessions (undefiled possessions, Syr.): that servest thy servants that they may live: that fillest creation with thine own riches: the poor, that wast in need and didst hunger forty days: that satisfiest thirsty souls with thine own good things; be thou with Iuzanes the son of Misdaeus and with Tertia and Mnesara, and gather them into thy fold and mingle them with thy number; Be

unto them a guide in the land of error: be unto them a physician in the land of sickness: be unto them a rest in the land of the weary: sanctify them in a polluted land: be their physician both of bodies and souls: make them holy temples of thee, and let thine holy spirit dwell in them.

157 Having thus prayed over them, the apostle said unto Mygdonia: Unclothe thy sisters. And she took off their clothes and girded them with girdles and brought them: but Iuzanes had first gone before, and they came after him; and the apostle took oil in a cup of silver and spake thus over it: Fruit more beautifull than all other fruits, unto which none other whatsoever may be compared: altogether merciful: fervent with the force of the word: power of the tree which men putting upon them overcome their adversaries: crowner of the conquerors: help (symbol) and joy of the sick: that didst announce unto men their salvation that showest light to them that are in darkness; whose leaf is bitter, but in thy most sweet fruit thou art fair, that art rough to the sight but soft to the taste; seeming to be weak, but in the greatness of thy strength able to bear the power that beholdeth all things. Having thus said [a corrupt word follows]: Jesu: let his victorious might come and be established in this oil, like as it was established in the tree (wood) that was its kin, even his might at that time, whereof they that crucified thee could not endure the word: let the gift also come whereby breathing upon his (thine) enemies thou didst cause them to go backward and fall headlong and let it rest on this oil, whereupon we invoke thine holy name. And having thus said, he poured it first upon the head ol Iuzanes and then upon the women's heads, saying: In thy name, O Jesu Christ, let it be unto these souls for remission of sins and for turning back of the adversary and for salvation of their souls. And he commanded Mygdonia to anoint them but he himself anointed Iuzanes. And having anointed them he led them down into the water in the name of the Father and the Son and the Holy Ghost.

158 And when they were come up, he took bread and a cup, and blessed it and said: Thine holy body w}lich was crucified for us do we eat, and thy blood that was shed for us unto salvation do we drink; let therefore thy body be unto us salvation and thy blood for remission of sins. And for the gall which thou didst drink for our sakes let the gall of the devil be removed from us: and for the vinegar which thou hast drunk for us, let our weakness be made strong: and for the spitting which thou didst receive for us, let us receive the dew of thy goodness: and by (or for) the reed wherewith they smote thee for us, let us receive the perfect house: and whereas thou receivedst a crown of thorns for our sake, let us that have loved thee put on a crown that fadeth not away; and for the linen cloth wherein thou wast Wrapped, let us also be girt about with thy power that is not vanquished and for the new tomb and the burial let us receive renewing of soul and body: and for that thou didst rise up and revive, let us revive and live and stand before thee in righteous judgement. And he brake and gave the eucharist unto Iuzanes and Tertia and Mnesara and the wife and daughter of Siphor and said: Let this eucharist be unto you for salvation and joy and health of your souls. And they said: Amen. And a voice was heard, saying: Amen: fear ye not, but only believe.

[THE MARTYRDOM]

159 And after these things Judas departed to be imprisoned.
And Tertia with Mygdonia and Narcia also went to be imprisoned. And the apostle Thomas said unto them -the multitude of them that had believed being present: Daughters and sisters and fellow-servants which have believed in my Lord and God, ministers of my Jesus, hearken to me this day: for I do deliver my word unto you, and I shall no more speak with you in this flesh nor in this world; for I go up unto my Lord and God Jesus Christ, unto

him that sold me, unto that Lord that humbled himself even unto me the little, and brought me up unto eternal greatness, that vouchsafed to me to become his servant in truth and steadfastness: unto him do I depart, knowing that the time is fulfilled, and the day appointed hath drawn near for me to go and receive my recompense from my Lord and God: for my recompenser is righteous, who knoweth me, how I ought to receive my reward; for he is not grudging nor envious, but is rich in his gifts, he is not a lover of craft (OT sparing) in that he giveth, for he hath confidence in his possessions which cannot fail.

160 I am not Jesus, but I am his servant: I am not Christ, but I am his minister; I am not the Son of God, but I pray to become worthy of God. Continue ye in the faith of Christ: continue in the hope of the Son of God: faint not at affliction, neither be divided in mind if ye see me mocked or that I am shut up in prison ; for I do accomplish his will. For if I had willed not to die, I know in Christ that I am able thereto: but this which is called death, is not death, but a setting free from the body; wherefore I receive gladly this setting free from the body, that I may depart and see him that is beautiful and full of mercy, him that is to be loved: for I have endured much toil in his service, and have laboured for his grace that is come upon me, which departeth not from me. Let not Satan, then, enter you by stealth and catch away your thoughts: let there be in you no place for him: for he is mighty whom ye have received. Look for the coming of Christ, for he shall come and receive you, and this is he whom ye shall see when he cometh.

161 When the apostle had ended these sayings, they went into the house, and the apostle Thomas said: Saviour that didst suffer many things for us, let these doors be as they were and let seals be set on them. And he left them and went to be imprisoned: and they wept and were in heaviness, for they knew that Misdaeus would slay him (not knowing that, M. would release him, P.).

162 And the apostle found the keepers wrangling and saying: Wherein have we sinned against this wizard? for by his art magic he hath opened the doors and would have had all the prisoners escape: but let us go and report it unto the king, and tell him concerning his wife and his son. And as they disputed thus, Thomas held his peace. They rose up early, therefore, and went unto the king and said unto him: Our lord and king, do thou take away that sorcerer and cause him to be shut up elsewhere, for we are not able to keep him; for except thy good fortune had kept the prison, all the condemned persons would have escaped for now this second time have we found the doors open: and also thy wife, O king, and thy son and the rest depart not from him. And the king, hearing that, went, and found the seals that were set on the doors whole; and he took note of doors also, and said to the keepers: Wherefore lie ye? for the seals are whole. How said ye that Tertia and Mygdonia come unto him into the prison? And the keepers said: We have told thee the truth.

163 And Misdaeus went to the prison and took his seat, and sent for the apostle Thomas and stripped him (and girded him with a girdle) and set him before him and saith unto him: Art thou bond or free? Thomas said: I am the bondsman of one only, over whom thou hast no authority. And Misdaeus saith to him: How didst thou run away and come into this country? And Thomas said: I was sold hither by my master, that I might save many, and by thy hands depart out of this world. And Misdaeus said: Who is thy lord? and what is his name? and of what country is he? And Thomas said: My Lord is thy master and he is Lord of heaven and earth. And Misdaeus saith: What is his name? Thomas saith: Thou canst not hear his true name at this time: but the name that was given unto him is Jesus Christ. And Misdaeus saith unto him: I have not made haste to destroy thee, but have had long patience with thee: but thou hast added unto thine evil deeds,

and thy sorceries are dispersed abroad and heard of throughout all the country: but this I do that thy sorceries may depart with thee, and our land be cleansed from them. Thomas saith unto him; These sorceries depart with me when I set forth hence, and know thou this that I shall never forsake them that are here.

164 When the apostle had said these things, Misdaeus considered how he should put him to death; for he was afraid because of the much people that were subject unto him, for many also of the nobles and of them that were in authority believed on him. He took him therefore and went forth out of the city; and armed soldiers also went with him. And the people supposed that the king desired to learn somewhat of him, and they stood still and gave heed. And when they had walked one mile, he delivered him unto four soldiers and an offlcer, and commanded them to take him into the mountain and there pierce him with spears and put an end to him, and return again to the city. And saying thus unto the soldiers, he himself also returned unto the city.

165 But the men ran after Thomas, desiring to deliver him from death. And two soldiers went at the right hand of the apostle and two on his left, holding spears, and the officer held his hand and supported him. And the apostle Thomas said: O the hidden mysteries which even until our departure are accomplished in us! O riches of his glory, who will not suffer us to be swallowed up in this passion of the body! Four are they that cast me down, for of four am I made; and one is he that draweth me, for of one I am, and unto him I go. And this I now understand, that my Lord and God Jesus Christ being of one was pierced by one, but I, which am of four, am pierced by four.

166 And being come up into the mountain unto the place where he was to be slain, he said unto them that held him, and to the rest: Brethren, hearken unto me now at the last; for I am come to my departure out of the body. Let not

then the eyes of your heart be blinded, nor your ears be made deaf. Believe on the God whom I preach, and be not guides unto yourselves in the hardness of your heart, but walk in all your liberty, and in the glory that is toward men, and the life that is toward God.

167 And he said unto Iuzanes: Thou son (to the son, P) of the (earthly) king Misdaeus and minister (to the minister) of our Lord Jesus Christ: give unto the servants of Misdaeus their price that they may suffer me to go and pray. And Iuzanes persuaded the soldiers to let him pray. And the blessed Thomas went to pray, and kneeled down, and rose up and stretched forth his hands unto heaven, and spake thus:

[Here P and the rest give -rightly- the prayer of cc. 144-8. U and its companions give the following: He turned to his prayer; and it was this: My Lord and my God, and hope and redeemer and leader and guide in all countries, be thou with all them that serve thee, and guide me this day as I come unto thee. Let not any take my soul which I have committed unto thee: let not the publicans see me, and let not the exactors accuse me falsely (play the sycophant with me). Let not the serpent see me, and let not the children of the dragon hiss at me. Behold, Lord, I have accomplished thy work and perfected thy commandment. I have become a bondman; therefore to-day do I receive freedom. Do thou therefore give me this and perfect me: and this I say, not for that I doubt, but that they may hear for whom it is needful to hear.]

168 And when he had thus prayed he said unto the soldiers: Come hither and accomplish the commandments of him that sent you. And the four came and pierced him with their spears, and he fell down and died.

And all the brethren wept; and they brought beautiful robes and much and fair linen, and buried him in a royal sepulchre wherein the former (first) kings were laid.

169 But Siphor and Iuzanes would not go down to the city, but continued sitting by him all the day. And the

apostle Thomas appeared unto them and said: Why sit ye here and keep watch over me? I am not here, but I have gone up and received all that I was promised. But rise up and go down hence; for after a little time ye also shall be gathered unto me.

But Misdaeus and Charisius took away Mygdonia and Tertia and afflicted them sorely: howbeit they consented not unto their will. And the apostle appeared unto them and said: Be not deceived: Jesus the holy, the living one, shall quickly send help unto you. And Misdaeus and Charisius, when they perceived that Mygdonia and Tertia obeyed them not, suffered them to live according to their own desire.

And the brethren gathered together and rejoiced in the grace of the Holy Ghost: now the apostle Thomas when he departed out of the world made Siphor a presbyter and Iuzanes a deacon, when he went up into the mountain to die. And the Lord wrought with them, and many were added unto the faith.

170 Now it came to pass after a long time that one of the children of Misdaeus the king was smitten by a devil, and no man could cure him, for the devil was exceeding fierce. And Misdaeus the king took thought and sad: I will go and open the sepulchre, and take a bone of the apostle of God and hang it upon my son and he shall be healed. But while Misdaeus thought upon this, the apostle Thomas appeared to him and said unto him: Thou believedst not on a living man, and wilt thou believe on the dead? yet fear not, for my Lord Jesus Christ hath compassion on thee and pitieth thee of his goodness.

And he went and opened the scpulchre, but found not the apostle there, for one of the brethren had stolen him away and taken him unto Mesopotamia; but from that place where the bones of the apostle had lain Misdaeus took dust and put it about his son's neck, saying: I believe on thee, Jesu Christ, now that he hath left me which troubleth men and opposeth them lest they should see thee. And when he had hung it upon his son, the lad became whole.

Misdaeus the king therefore was also gathered among the brethren, and bowed his head under the hands of Siphor the priest; and Siphor said unto the bretbren: Pray ye for Misdaeus the king, that he may obtain mercy of Jesus Christ, and that he may no more remember evil against him. They all therefore, with one accord rejoicing, rmade prayer for him; and the Lord that loveth men, the King of Kings and Lord of lords, granted Misdaeus also to have hope in him; and he was gathered with the multitude of them that had believed in Christ, glorifying the Father and the Son and the Holy Ghost, whose is power and adoration, now and for ever and world without end. Amen.

[U (and Syr.) ends: The acts of Judas Thomas the apostle are completed, which he did in India, fulfilling the commandment of him that sent him. Unto whom be glory, world without end. Amen.]

THE ACTS OF THE HOLY APOSTLE AND EVANGELIST JOHN THE THEOLOGIAN OR,

THE ACTS OF JOHN THE THEOLOGIAN

About his exile and departure.

1 WHEN Agrippa, whom, on account of his plotting against Peace, they stoned and put to death, was king of the Jews, Vespasian Caesar, coming with a great army, invested Jerusalem;

2 And some prisoners of war he took and slew, others he destroyed by famine in the siege, and most he banished, and at length scattered up and down.

3 And having destroyed the temple, and

put the holy vessels on board a ship, he sent them to Rome, to make for himself a temple of peace, and adorned it with the spoils of war.

4 And when Vespasian was dead, his son Domitian, having got possession of the kingdom. along with his other wrongful acts, set himself also to make a persecution against the righteous men.

5 For, having learned that the city was filled with Jews, remembering the orders given by his father about them, he purposed casting them all out of the city of the Romans.

6 And some of the Jews took courage, and gave Domitian a book, in which was written as follows:

7 O Domitian, Caesar and king of all the world, as many of us as are Jews entreat thee, as suppliants we beseech of thy power not to banish us from thy divine and benignant countenance;

8 For we are obedient to thee, and the customs, and laws, and practices, and policy, doing wrong in nothing, but being of the same mind with the Romans.

9 But there is a new and strange nation, neither agreeing with other nations nor consenting to the religious observances of the Jews, uncircumcised, inhuman, lawless, subverting whole houses, proclaiming a man as God, all assembling together under a strange name, that of Christian.

10 These men reject God, paying no heed to the law given by Him, and proclaim to be the Son of God a man born of ourselves, Jesus by name, whose parents and brothers and all his family have been connected with the Hebrews;

11 Whom on account of his great blasphemy and his wicked fooleries we gave up to the cross.

12 And they add another blasphemous lie to their first one: him that was nailed up and buried, they glorify as having risen from the dead; and, more than this, they falsely assert that he has been taken up by clouds into the heavens.

13 At all this the king, being affected with rage ordered the senate to publish a decree that they should put to death all who confessed themselves to be Christians.

14 Those, then, who were found in the time of his rage, and who reaped the fruit of patience, and were crowned in the triumphant contest against the works of the devil, received the repose of incorruption.

15 And the fame of the teaching of John was spread abroad in Rome; and it came to the ears of Domitian that there was a certain Hebrew in Ephesus, John by name, who spread a report about the seat of empire of the Romans, saying that it would quickly be rooted out, and that the kingdom of the Romans would be given over to another.

16 And Domitian, troubled by what was said, sent a centurion with soldiers to seize John, and bring him. And having gone to Ephesus, they asked where John lived.

17 And having come up to his gate, they found him standing before the door; and, thinking that he was the porter, they inquired of him where John lived.

18 And he answered and said: I am he. And they, despising his common, and low, and poor appearance, were filled with threats, and said:

19 Tell us the truth. And when he declared again that he was the man they sought, the neighbours moreover bearing witness to it, they said that he was to go with them at once to the king in Rome.

20 And, urging them to take provisions for the journey, he turned and took a few dates, and straightway went forth.

21 And the soldiers, having taken the public conveyances, travelled fast, having seated him in the midst of them.

22 And when they came to the first change, it being the hour of breakfast, they entreated him to be of good courage, and to take bread, and eat with them.

23 And John said: I rejoice in soul indeed, but in the meantime I do not wish to take any food.

24 And they started, and were carried along quickly. And when it was evening they stopped at a certain inn; and as,

besides, it was the hour of supper, the centurion and the soldiers being most kindly disposed, entreated John to make use of what was set before them.

25 But he said that he was very tired, and in want of sleep more than any food.

26 And as he did this each day, all the soldiers were struck with amazement, and were afraid lest John should die, and involve them in danger.

27 But the Holy Spirit showed him to them as more cheerful.

28 And on the seventh day, it being the Lord's day, he said to them: Now it is time for me also to partake of food.

29 And having washed his hands and face, he prayed, and brought out the linen cloth, and took one of the dates, and ate it in the sight of all.

30 And when they had ridden a long time they came to the end of their journey, John thus fasting.

31 And they brought him before the king, and said: Worshipful king, we bring to thee John, a god, not a man; for, from the hour in which we apprehended him, to the present, he has not tasted bread.

32 At this Domitian being amazed, stretched out his mouth on account of the wonder, wishing to salute him with a kiss; but John bent down his head, and kissed his breast.

33 And Domitian said: Why hast thou done this? Didst thou not think me worthy to kiss thee?

34 And John said to him: It is right to adore the hand of God first of all, and in this way to kiss the mouth of the king; for it is written in the holy books, The heart of a king is in the hand of God.

35 And the king said to him: Art thou John, who said that my kingdom would speedily be uprooted, and that another king, Jesus, was going to reign instead of me?

36 And John answered and said to him: Thou also shalt reign for many years given thee by God, and after thee very many others; and when the times of the things upon earth have been fulfilled, out of heaven shall come a King, eternal, true, Judge of living and dead,

to whom every nation and tribe shall confess, through whom every earthly power and dominion shall be brought to nothing, and every mouth speaking great things shall be shut.

37 This is the mighty Lord and King of everything that hath breath and flesh, the Word and Son of the living One, who is Jesus Christ.

38 At this Domitian said to him: What is the proof of these things?

39 I am not persuaded by words only; words are a sight of the unseen.

40 What canst thou show in earth or heaven by the power of him who is destined to reign, as thou sayest?

41 For he will do it, if he is the Son of God. And immediately John asked for a deadly poison.

42 And the king having ordered poison to be given to him, they brought it on the instant.

43 John therefore, having taken it. put it into a large cup, and filled it with water, and mixed it, and cried out with a loud voice, and said:

44 In Thy name, Jesus Christ, Son of God, I drink the cup which Thou wilt sweeten; and the poison in it do Thou mingle with Thy Holy Spirit, and make it become a draught of life and salvation, for the healing of soul and body, for digestion and harmless assimilation, for faith not to be repented of, for an undeniable testimony of death as the cup of thanksgiving.

45 And when he had drunk the cup, those standing beside Domitian expected that he was going to fall to the ground in convulsions.

46 And when John stood, cheerful, and talked with them safe, Domitian was enraged against those who had given the poison, as having spared John.

47 But they swore by the fortune and health of the king, and said that there could not be a stronger poison than this.

48 And John, understanding what they were whispering to one another, said to the king:

49 Do not take it ill, O king, but let a trial be made, and thou shalt learn the power of the poison.

50 Make some condemned criminal be

brought from the prison. And when he had come, John put water into the cup, and swirled it round, and gave it with all the dregs to the condemned criminal. 51 And he, having taken it and drunk, immediately fell down and died.

52 And when all wondered at the signs that had been done, and when Domitian had retired and gone to his palace, John said to him: O Domitian, king of the Romans, didst thou contrive this, that, thou being present and bearing witness, I might to-day become a murderer?

53 What is to be done about the dead body which is lying?

54 And he ordered it to be taken and thrown away. But John, going up to the dead body, said: O God, Maker of the heavens, Lord and Master of angels, of glories, of powers, in the name of Jesus Christ, Thine only begotten Son, give to this man who has died for this occasion a renewal of life, and restore him his soul, that Domitian may learn that the Word is much more powerful than poison, and is the ruler of life.

55 And having taken him by the hand, he raised him up alive.

56 And when all were glorifying God, and wondering at the faith of John, Domitian said to him:

57 I have put forth a decree of the senate, that all such persons should be summarily dealt with, without trial; but since I find from thee that they are innocent, and that their religion is rather beneficial, I banish thee to an island, that I may not seem myself to do away with my own decrees.

58 He asked then that the condemned criminal should be let go; and when he was let go, John said: Depart, give thanks to God, who has this day delivered thee from prison and from death.

59 And while they were standing, a certain home-born slave of Domitian's, of those in the bed-chamber, was suddenly seized by the unclean demon, and lay dead; and word was brought to the king.

60 And the king was moved, and entreated John to help her.

61 And John said: It is not in man to do this; but since thou knowest how to reign, but dost not know from whom thou hast received it, learn who has the power over both thee and thy kingdom.

62 And he prayed thus: O Lord, the God of every kingdom, and master of every creature, give to this maiden the breath of life.

63 And having prayed, he raised her up. And Domitian, astonished at all the wonders, sent him away to an island, appointing for him a set time.

64 And straightway John sailed to Patmos, where also he was deemed worthy to see the revelation of the end.

65 And when Domitian was dead, Nerva succeeded to the kingdom, and recalled all who had been banished; and having kept the kingdom for a year, he made Trajan his successor in the kingdom.

66 And when he was king over the Romans, John went to Ephesus, and regulated all the teaching of the church, holding many conferences, anti reminding them of what the Lord had said to them, and what duty he had assigned to each.

67 And when he was old and changed, he ordered Polycarp to be bishop over the church.

68 And what like his end was, or his departure from men, who cannot give an account of?

69 For on the following day, which was the Lord's day, and in the presence of the brethren, he began to say to them:

70 Brethren, and fellow-servants, and co-heirs, and copartners of the kingdom of the Lord, know the Lord what miracles He hath shown you through me, what wonders, what cures, what signs, what gracious gifts, teachings, rulings, rests, services, glories, graces, gifts, faiths, communions; how many things you have seen with your eyes, that ear hath not heard.

71 Be strong, therefore, in Him, remembering Him in all your doings, knowing the mystery of the dispensation that has come to men, for the sake of which the Lord has worked.

72 He then, through me, exhorts you: Brethren, I wish to remain without

grief, without insult, without treachery, without punishment.

73 For He also knows insult from you, He knows also dishonour, He knows also treachery, He knows also punishment from those that disobey His commandments.

74 Let not therefore our God be grieved, the good, the compassionate, the merciful, the holy, the pure, the undefiled, the only, the one, the immutable, the sincere, the guileless, the slow to anger, He that is higher and more exalted than every name that we speak or think of--our God, Jesus Christ.

75 Let Him rejoice along with us because we conduct ourselves well; let Him be glad because we live in purity; let Him rest because we behave reverently; let Him be pleased because we live in fellowship; let Him smile because we are sober-minded; let Him be delighted because we love.

76 These things, brethren, I communicate to you, pressing on to the work set before me, already perfected for me by the Lord.

77 For what else have I to say to you? Keep the sureties of your God; keep His presence, that shall not be taken away from you.

78 And if then ye sin no more, He will forgive you what ye have done in ignorance; but if, after ye have known Him, and He has had compassion upon you, you return to the like courses, even your former offences will be laid to your charge, and ye shall have no portion or compassion before His face.

79 And when he had said this to them, he thus prayed: Jesus, who didst wreathe this crown by Thy twining, who hast inserted these many flowers into the everlasting flower of Thy countenance, who hast sown these words among them, be Thou Thyself the protector and healer of Thy people.

80 Thou alone art benignant and not haughty, alone merciful and kind, alone a Saviour, and just;

81 Thou who always seest what belongs to all, and art in all, and everywhere present, God Lord Jesus Christ;

82 Who with Thy gifts and Thy compassion coverest those that hope in Thee; who knowest intimately those that everywhere speak against us, and blaspheme Thy holy name, do Thou alone, O Lord, help Thy servants with Thy watchful care. So be it, Lord.

83 And having asked bread, he gave thanks thus, saying:

84 What praise, or what sort of offering, or what thanksgiving, shall we, breaking the bread, invoke, but Thee only?

85 We glorify the name by which Thou hast been called by the Father; we glorify the name by which Thou hast been called through the Son; we glorify the resurrection which has been manifested to us through Thee; of Thee we glorify the seed, the word, the grace, the true pearl, the treasure, the plough, the net, the majesty, the diadem, Him called Son of man for our sakes, the truth, the rest, the knowledge, the freedom, the place of refuge in Thee.

86 For Thou alone art Lord, the root of immortality, and the fountain of incorruption, and the seat of the ages;

87 Thou who hast been called all these for our sakes, that now we, calling upon Thee through these, may recognise Thine illimitable majesty, presented to us by Thy presence, that can be seen only by the pure, seen in Thine only Son.

88 And having broken the bread, he gave it to us, praying for each of the brethren, that he might be worthy of the Eucharist of the Lord.

89 He also therefore, having likewise tasted it, said: To me also let there be a portion with you, and peace, O beloved.

90 And having thus spoken, and confirmed the brethren, he said to Eutyches, also named Verus: Behold, I appoint thee a minister of the Church of Christ, and I entrust to thee the flock of Christ.

91 Be mindful, therefore, of the commandments of the Lord; and if thou shouldst fall into trails or dangers, be not afraid: for thou shall fall under many troubles, and thou shalt be shown to be an eminent witness of the Lord.

92 Thus, then, Verus, attend to the flock as a servant of God, until the time appointed for thy testimony.

93 And when John had spoken this, and more than this, having entrusted to him the flock of Christ, he says to him:

94 Take some brethren, with baskets and vessels, and follow me.

95 And Eutyches, without considering, did what he was bid. And the blessed John having gone forth from the house, went outside of the gates, having told the multitude to stand off from him.

96 And having come to the tomb of one of our brethren, he told them to dig. And they dug.

97 And he says: Let the trench be deeper. And as they dug, he conversed with those who had come out of the house with him, building them up, and furnishing them thoroughly into the majesty of the Lord.

98 And when the young men had finished the trench, as he had wished, while we knew nothing, he takes off the clothes he had on, and throws them, as if they were some bedding, into the depth of the trench; and, standing in only his drawers, stretched forth his hands, and prayed.

99 O God, who hast chosen us for the mission of the Gentiles, who hast sent us out into the world, who hast declared Thyself through the apostles;

100 who hast never rested, but always savest from the foundation of the world;

101 who hast made Thyself known through all nature;

102 who hast made our wild and savage nature quiet and peaceable;

103 who hast given Thyself to it when thirsting after knowledge;

104 who hast put to death its adversary, when it took refuge in Thee;

105 who hast given it Thy hand, and raised it from the things done in Hades;

106 who hast shown it its own enemy;

107 who hast in purity turned its thoughts upon Thee, O Christ Jesus, Lord of things in heaven, and law of things on earth, the course of things aerial, and guardian of things etherial, the fear of those under the earth, and grace of Thine own people, receive also the soul of Thy John, which has been certainly deemed worthy by Thee.

108 Thou who hast preserved me also till the present hour pure to Thyself, and free from intercourse with woman; who, when I wished in my youth to marry, didst appear to me, and say, I am in need of thee, John;

109 who didst strengthen for me beforehand my bodily weakness; who, when a third time I wished to marry, didst say to me at the third hour, in the sea, John, if thou wert not mine, I would let thee marry; who hast opened up the sight of my mind, and hast favoured my bodily eyes;

110 who, when I was looking about me, didst call even the gazing upon a woman hateful; who didst deliver me from temporary show, and preserve me for that which endureth for ever;

111 who didst separate me from the filthy madness of the flesh;

112 who didst stop up the secret disease of the soul, and cut out its open actions;

113 who didst afflict and banish him who rebelled in me;

114 who didst establish my love to Thee spotless and unimpaired;

115 who didst give me undoubting faith in Thee;

116 who hast drawn out for me pure thoughts towards Thee;

117 who hast given me the due reward of my works;

118 who hast set it in my soul to have no other possession than Thee alone: for what is more precious than Thou?

119 Now, O Lord, when I have accomplished Thy stewardship with which I was entrusted, make me worthy of Thy repose, having wrought that which is perfect in Thee, which is ineffable salvation.

120 And as I go to Thee, let the fire withdraw,

121 let darkness be overcome,

122 let the furnace be slackened,

123 let Gehenna be extinguished,

124 let the angels follow,

125 let the demons be afraid

126 let the princes be broken in pieces,

127 let the powers of darkness fall,

128 let the places on the right hand

stand firm,

129 let those on the left abide not,

130 let the devil be muzzled,

131 let Satan be laughed to scorn,

132 let his madness be tamed,

133 let his wrath be broken,

134 let his children be trodden under foot,

135 and let all his root he uprooted;

136 And grant to me to accomplish the journey to Thee, not insulted, not despitefully treated, and to receive what Thou hast promised to those that live in purity, and that have loved a holy life.

137 And gazing towards heaven, he glorified God; and having sealed himself altogether, he stood and said to us, Peace and grace be with you, brethren! and sent the brethren away.

138 And when they went on the morrow they did not find him, but his sandals, and a fountain welling up.

139 And after that they remembered what had been said to Peter by the Lord about him:

140 For what does it concern thee if I should wish him to remain until I come?

141 And they glorified God for the miracle that had happened.

142 And having thus believed, they retired praising and blessing the benignant God; because to Him is due glory now and ever, and to ages of ages. Amen.

THE ACTS OF BARNABAS

The Journeyings and Martyrdom of St. Barnabas the Apostle.

1 SINCE from the descent of the presence of our Saviour Jesus Christ, the unwearied and benevolent and mighty Shepherd and Teacher and Physician, I beheld and saw the ineffable and holy and unspotted mystery of the Christians, who hold the hope in holiness, and who have been sealed; and since I have zealously served Him, I have deemed it necessary to give account of the mysteries which I have heard and seen.

2 I John, accompanying the holy apostles Barnabas and Paul, being formerly a servant of Cyrillus the high priest of Jupiter, but now having received the gift of the Holy Spirit through Paul and Barnabas and Silos, who were worthy of the calling, and who baptized me in Iconium.

3 After I was baptized, then, I saw a certain man standing clothed in white raiment; and he said to me:

4 Be of good courage, John, for assuredly thy name shall be changed to Mark, and thy glory shall be proclaimed in all the world.

5 The darkness in thee has passed away from thee, and there has been given to thee understanding to know the mysteries of God.

6 And when I saw the vision, becoming greatly terrified, I went to the feet of Barnabas, and related to him the mysteries which I had seen and heard from that man.

7 And the Apostle Paul was not by when I disclosed the mysteries.

8 And Barnabas said to me: Tell no one the miracle which thou hast seen.

9 For by me also this night the Lord stood, saying, Be of good courage: for as thou hast given thy life for my name to death and banishment from thy nation, thus also shalt thou be made perfect.

10 Moreover, as for the servant who is with you, take him also with thyself; for he has certain mysteries.

11 Now then, my child, keep to thyself the things which thou hast seen and heard; for a time will come for thee to reveal them.

12 And I, having been instructed in these things by him, remained in Iconium many days; for there was there a holy man and a pious, who also entertained us, whose house also Paul had sanctified.

13 Thence, therefore, we came to Seleucia, and after staying three days sailed away to Cyprus; and I was

ministering to them until we had gone round all Cyprus.

14 And setting sail from Cyprus, we landed in Perga of Pamphylia.

15 And there I then stayed about two months, wishing to sail to the regions of the West; and the Holy Spirit did not allow me.

16 Turning, therefore, I again sought the apostles; and having learned that they were in Antioch, I went to them.

17 And I found Paul in bed in Antioch from the toil of the journey, who also seeing me, was exceedingly grieved on account of my delaying in Pamphylia.

18 And Barnabas coming, encouraged him, and tasted bread, and he took a little of it.

19 And they preached the word of the Lord, and enlightened many of the Jews and Greeks.

20 And I only attended to them, and was afraid of Paul to come near him, both because he held me as having spent much time in Pamphylia, and because be was quite enraged against me.

21 And I gave repentance on my knees upon the earth to Paul, and he would not endure it.

22 And when I remained for three Sabbaths in entreaty and prayer on my knees, I was unable to prevail upon him about myself; for his great grievance against me was on account of my keeping several parchments in Pamphylia.

23 And when it came to pass that they finished teaching in Antioch, on the first of the week they took counsel together to set out for the places of the East, and after that to go into Cyprus, and oversee all the churches in which they had spoken the word of God.

24 And Barnabas entreated Paul to go first to Cyprus, and oversee his own in his village; and Lucius entreated him to take the oversight of his city Cyrene.

25 And a vision was seen by Paul in sleep, that he should hasten to Jerusalem, because the brethren expected him there.

26 But Barnabas urged that they should go to Cyprus, and pass the winter, and then that they should go to Jerusalem at the feast.

27 Great contention, therefore, arose between them.

28 And Barnabas urged me also to accompany them, on account of my being their servant from the beginning, and on account of my having served them in all Cyprus until they came to Perga of Pamphylia; and I there had remained many days.

29 But Paul cried out against Barnabas, saying: It is impossible for him to go with us.

30 And those who were with us there urged me also to accompany them, because there was a vow upon me to follow them to the end.

31 So that Paul said to Barnabas: If thou wilt take John who also is surnamed Mark with thee, go another road; for he shall not come with us.

32 And Barnabas coming to himself, said: The grace of God does not desert him who has once served the Gospel and journeyed with us.

33 If, therefore, this be agreeable to thee, Father Paul, I take him and go.

34 And he said: Go thou in the grace of Christ, and we in the power of the Spirit.

35 Therefore, bending their knees, they prayed to God. And Paul, groaning aloud, wept, and in like manner also Barnabas, saying to one another:

36 It would have been good for us, as at first, so also at last, to work in common among men; but since it has thus seemed good to thee, Father Paul, pray for me that my labour may be made perfect to commendation: for thou knowest how I have served thee also to the grace of Christ that has been given to thee.

37 For I go to Cyprus, and hasten to be made perfect; for I know that I shall no more see thy face, O Father Paul.

38 And failing on the ground at his feet, he wept long. And Paul said to him:

39 The Lord stood by me also this night, saying, Do not force Barnabas not to go to Cyprus, for there it has been prepared for him to enlighten many; and do thou also, in the grace

that has been given to thee, go to Jerusalem to worship in the holy place, and there it shall be shown thee where thy martyrdom has been prepared.

40 And we saluted one another, and Barnabas took me to himself.

41 And having come down to Laodiceia, we sought to cross to Cyprus; and having found a ship going to Cyprus, we embarked.

42 And when we had set sail, the wind was found to be contrary.

43 And we came to Corasium; and having gone down to the shore where there was a fountain, we rested there, showing ourselves to no one, that no one might know that Barnabas had separated from Paul.

44 And having set sail from Corasium, we came to the regions of Isauria, and thence came to a certain island called Pityusa; and a storm having come on, we remained there three days; and a certain pious man entertained us, by name Euphemus, whom also Barnabas instructed in many things in the faith, with all his house.

45 And thence we sailed past the Aconesiae, and came to the city of Anemurium; and having gone into it, we found two Greeks.

46 And coming to us, they asked whence and who we were. And Barnabas said to them: If you wish to know whence and who we are, throw away the clothing which you have, and I shall put on you clothing which never becomes soiled; for neither is there in it anything filthy, but it is altogether splendid.

47 And being astonished at the saying, they asked us: What is that garment which you are going to give us?

48 And Barnabas said to them: If you shall confess your sins, and submit yourselves to our Lord Jesus Christ, you shall receive that garment which is incorruptible for ever.

49 And being pricked at heart by the Holy Spirit, they fell at his feet, entreating and saying:

50 We beseech thee, father, give us that garment; for we believe in the living and true God whom thou proclaimest.

51 And leading them down to the fountain, he baptized them into the name of Father, and Son, and Holy Ghost.

52 And they knew that they were clothed with power, and a holy robe. And having taken from me one robe, he put it on the one; and his own robe he put on the other.

53 And they brought money to him, and straightway Barnabas distributed it to the poor. And from them also the sailors were able to gain many things.

54 And they having come down to the shore, he spoke to them the word of God; and he having blessed them, we saluted them, and went on board the ship.

55 And the one of them who was named Stephanus wished to accompany us, and Barnabas did not permit him.

56 And we, having gone across, sailed down to Cyprus by night; and having come to the place called Crommyacita, we found Timon and Ariston the temple Servants, at whose house also we were entertained.

57 And Timon was afflicted by much fever. And having laid our hands upon him, we straightway removed his fever, having called upon the name of the Lord Jesus.

58 And Barnabas had received documents from Matthew, a book of the word of God, and a narrative of miracles and doctrines.

59 This Barnabas laid upon the sick in each place that we came to, and it immediately made a cure of their sufferings.

60 And when we had come to Lapithus, and an idol festival being celebrated in the theatre, they did not allow us to go into the city, but we rested a little at the gate.

61 And Timon, after he rose up from his disease, came with us. And having gone forth from Lapithus, we travelled through the mountains, and came to the city of Lampadistus, of which also Timon was a native; in addition to whom, having found also that Heracleius was there, we were entertained by him.

62 He was of the city of Tamasus, and had come to visit his relations; and Barnabas, looking stedfastly at him, recognised him, having met with him formerly at Citium with Paul; to whom also the Holy Spirit was given at baptism, and he changed his name to Heracleides.

63 And having ordained him bishop over Cyprus, and having confirmed the church in Tamasus, we left him in the house of his brethren that dwelt there.

64 And having crossed the mountain called Chionodes, we came to Old Paphos, and there found Rhodon, a temple servant, who also, having himself believed, accompanied us.

65 And we met a certain Jew, by name Barjesus, coming from Paphos, who also recognised Barnabas, as having been formerly with Paul.

66 He did not wish us to go into Paphos; but having turned away, we came to Curium.

67 And we found that a certain abominable race was being performed in the road near the city, where a multitude of women and men naked were performing the race.

68 And there was great deception and error in that place. And Barnabas turning, rebuked it; and the western part fell, so that many were wounded, and many of them also died and the rest fled to the temple of Apollo, which was close at hanoi in the city, which was called sacred.

69 And when we came near the temple, a great multitude of Jews who were there, having been put up to it by Barjesus. stood outside of the city, and did not allow us to go into the city; but we spent the evening under a tree near the city, and rested there.

70 And on the following day, we came to a certain village where Aristoclianus dwelt.

71 He being a leper, had been cleansed in Antioch, whom also Paul and Barnabas sealed to be a bishop, and sent to his village in Cyprus, because there were many Greeks there.

72 And we were entertained in the cave by him in the mountain, and there we remained one day.

73 And thence we came to Amathus and there was a great multitude of Greeks in the temple in the mountain, low women and men pouring libations.

74 There also Barjesus, getting the start of as, gained over the nation of the Jews, and did not allow us to enter into the city; but a certain widow woman. eighty years old. being outside of the city, and she also not worshipping the idols, coming forward to us, took us into her house one hour.

75 And when we came out we shook the dust off our feet over against that temple where the libation of the abominable took place.

76 And having gone out thence, we came through desert places, and Timon also accompanied us.

77 And having come to Citium, and there being a great uproar there also in their hippodrome, having learned this, we came forth out of the city, having all shaken the dust off our feet; for no one received us, except that we rested one hour in the gate near the aqueduct.

78 And having set sail in a ship from Citium, we came to Salamis, and landed in the so-called islands, where there was a place full of idols; and there there took place high festivals and libations.

79 And having found Heracleides there again, we instructed him to proclaim the Gospel of God, and to set up churches, and ministers in them.

80 And having gone into Salamis. we came to the synagogue near the place called Biblia; and when we had gone into it, Barnabas, having unrolled the Gospel which he had received from Matthew his fellow-labourer, began to teach the Jews.

81 And Barjesus, having arrived after two days, after not a few Jews had been instructed, was enraged, and brought together all the multitude of the Jews; and they having laid hold of Barnabas, wished to hand him over to Hypatius, the governor of Salamis.

82 And having bound him to take him away to the governor, and a pious Jebusite, a kinsman of Nero, having count to Cyprus, the Jews, learning this,

took Barnabas by night, and bound him with a rope by the neck; and having dragged him to the hippodrome from the synagogue, and having gone out of the city, standing round him, they burned him with fire, so that even his bones became dust.

83 And straightway that night, having taken his dust, they cast it into a cloth; and having secured it with lead they intended to throw it into the sea.

84 But I, finding an opportunity in the night, anti being able along with Timon and Rhodon to carry it we came to a certain place, and having found a cave, put it down there, where the nation of the Jebusites formerly dwelt.

85 And having found a secret place in it, we put it away, with the documents which he had received from Matthew.

86 And it was the fourth hour of the night of the second of the week.

87 And when we were hid in the place, the Jews made no little search after us; and having almost found us, they pursued us as far as the village of the Ledrians; and we, having found there also a cave near the village, took refuge in it, and thus escaped them.

88 And we were hid in the cave three days; and the Jews having gone away, we came forth and left the place by night.

89 And taking with us Ariston and Rhodon, we came to the village of Limnes.

90 And having come to the shore, we found an Egyptian ship; and having embarked in it, we landed at Alexandria.

91 And there I remained, teaching the brethren that came the word of the Lord, enlightening them, and preaching what I had been taught by the apostles of Christ, who also baptized me into the name of Father, and Son, and Holy Ghost;

92 Who also changed my name to Mark in the water of baptism, by which also I hope to bring many to the glory of God through His grace; because to Him is due honour and everlasting glory. Amen.

The journeyings and martyrdom of the holy apostle Barnabas have been fulfilled through God.

THE ACTS OF PHILIP

I.

When he came out of Galilee and raised the dead man.

1 When he was come out of Galilee, a widow was carrying out her only son to burial. Philip asked her about her grief: I have spent in vain much money on the gods, Ares, Apollo, Hermes, Artemis, Zeus, Athena, the Sun and Moon, and I think they are asleep as far as I am concerned. And I consulted a diviner to no purpose.

2 The apostle said: Thou hast suffered nothing strange, mother, for thus doth the devil deceive men. Assuage thy grief and I will raise thy son in the name of Jesus.

3 She said: It seems it were better for me not to marry, and to eat nothing but bread and water. Philip: You are right. Chastity is especially dear to God.

4 She said: I believe in Jesus whom thou preachest. He raised her son, who sat up and said: Whence is this light? and how comes it that an angel came and opened the prison of judgement where I was shut up? where I saw such torments as the tongue of man cannot describe.

5 So all were baptized. And the youth followed the apostle.

II.

When he went unto Greece of Athens

6 When he entered into the city of Athens which is called Hellas, 300 philosophers gathered and said: Let us go and see what his wisdom is, for they say of the wise men of Asia that their wisdom is great. For they supposed Philip to be a philosopher: he travelled

only in a cloak and an undergarment. So they assembled and looked into their books, lest he should get the better of them.

7 They said: If you have anything new to tell us, let us hear it, for we need nothing else but only to hear some new thing.

8 Philip: Then you must cast away the old man. The Lord said: Ye cannot put new wine into old bottles. I am glad to hear that you desire something new, for my Lord's teaching is new.

9 The philosophers: Who is thy Lord? Philip: Jesus Christ.

10 They: This is a new name to us. Give us three days to look into it.

11 They consulted, and said: Perhaps it will be best to send for the high priest of the Jews to discuss it with him.

12 So they wrote: The philosophers of Greece to Ananias the great high priest of the Jews at Jerusalem -and stated the case.

13 On reading the letter Ananias rent his clothes and said: Is that deceiver in Athens also? And Mansemat, that is, Satan entered into him. (This is another form of Mastema, the name of Satan in Jubilees and elsewhere.) And he consulted with the lawyers and Pharisees, and they said: Arm thyself and take 500 men and go and at all costs destroy Philip.

14 So he came in the high-priestly garments with great pomp and he and the philosophers went to Philip's lodging, and he came out, and Ananias said: Thou sorcerer and wizard, I know thee, that thy master the deceiver at Jerusalem called thee son of thunder; did not Judaea suffice you, but must you come here to deceive? Philip said: May the veil of unbelief be taken from thee, and thou learn who is the deceiver, thou or I.

15 Ananias' address: how Jesus destroyed the law and allowed all meats -was crucified, the disciples stole his body, and did many wonders, and were cast out of Jerusalem, and now go all about the world deceiving every one, like this Philip. But I will take him to Jerusalem, for the king Archelaus

seeketh him to kill him.

16 The people were not moved. Philip said: I will appeal to my God.

17 Ananias ran at him to smite him, his hand withered and he was blinded, and so were his 500 men: they cursed him, and prayed Philip for help.

18 Philip's prayer: O weak nature . . . O bitter sea. Come, Jesu, the holy light -thou overlookest us not when we cry to thee....

19 Ananias to Philip: Thinkest thou to turn us from the traditions of our fathers, and the God of the manna in the wilderness, and Moses, to follow the Nazarene, Jesus? Philip: I will ask my God to manifest himself to thee and to these -perchance thou wilt believe: but if not, a wonder shall befall thee. And he prayed God to send his Son.

20 The heavens opened and Jesus appeared in glory, his face seven times brighter than the sun, and his raiment whiter than snow. All the idols of Athens fell, and the devils in them fled crying out. Philip said: Hearest thou not the devils, and believest thou not him that is here? Ananias: I have no God save him that gave the manna in the wilderness.

21 Jesus went up into heaven, and there was a great earthquake, and the people fled to the apostle, crying for mercy.

22 Philip: There is no envy in us, and the grace of Christ shall restore your sight, but first let the high priest see. A voice from heaven: Philip, once son of thunder but now of meekness whatsoever thou askest my Father he will do for thee. The people were afraid at the voice. In the name of Christ, Philip made Ananias see. He said: How great is the art magic of Jesus! this Philip in a moment (or for a little) hath blinded me and in a moment restored my sight! I cannot be convinced by witchcraft. The 500 asked Philip to give back their sight that they might slay the unbelieving Ananias.

23 Philip: Render not evil for evil. To Ananias: There shall be a great sign shown in thee. Ananias: I know that thou art a sorcerer and disciple of Jesus;

thou canst not bewitch me. Philip to Jesus: Zabarthan, sabathabat, bramanouch, come quickly! The earth opened and swallowed Ananias to the knees. He cried: This is real magic, that the earth clave when Philip threatened it in Hebrew -and there are hooks below pulling at my legs to make me believe, but I will not, for I know his witchcraft from Jerusalem.

24 Philip, to the earth: Take him to the middle. And he sank further and said: One foot is frozen and the other hot -but I will not believe. The people wanted to stone him, but Philip checked them: This is for your salvation; if he repent, I will bring him up, but if not, he shall be swallowed into the deep.

25 He spread out his hand in the air over the 500, and their eyes were opened and they praised God. Philip, to Ananias: Confess now with a pure heart that Jesus is Lord, that thou mayest be saved like these. But he laughed at him.

26 Seeing him obstinate, Philip said to the earth: Open and swallow him to the neck. 27 And one of the first men of the city came and said: A devil has attacked my son, saying: As thou hast let a stranger come to the city, who destroys our idols what can I do but kill thine only son? and he has suffocated him help me, for I also believe.

28 Bring me thy son. And he ran, calling to his son, and bade the servants bring him: he was 23 years old. Philip seeing him grieved, and said to Ananias: This is through your folly: if I raise him will you believe? Ananias: I know you will raise him by your magic, but I will not believe. Philip was wroth and said: Catathema (cursed thing), go down into the abyss in the sight of all. And he was swallowed up: but the high-priestly robe flew away from him, and therefore no man knows where it is from that day.

Philip raised the lad and drove away the devil.

29 The people cried out, believing in God, and the 500 were baptized. And Philip stayed two years at Athens, and founded a church and ordained a bishop and a presbyter, and departed to Parthia to preach.

III.
Done in Parthia by Philip.

30 When Philip came to Parthia he found in a city the apostle Peter with disciples, and said: I pray you strengthen me, that I may go and preach like you.

31 And they prayed for him.

32 And John was there also, and said to Philip: Andrew is gone to Achaia and Thrace, and Thomas to India and the wicked flesh-eaters, and Matthew to the savage troglodytes. And do thou not be slack, for Jesus is with thee. And they let him depart.

33 And he came to the sea in the borders of the Candaci and found a ship going to Azotus, and agreed with the sailors for four staters, and sailed. A great wind came, and they began to cast out the tackle and say farewell to each other and lament.

34 Philip consoled them: Not even the ship shall be lost. He went up on the prow and said: Sea, sea, Jesus Christ by me his servant bids thee still thy wrath. There was calm, and the sailors thanked him and asked to become servants of Jesus. 35 And he instructed them to forsake the cares of this life. 36 And they believed, and Philip landed and baptized them all.

IV. Of the daughter of Nicocleides, whom he healed at Azotus.

37 There was great commotion in Azotus because of Philip's miracles, and many came and were healed, and devils were cast out and cried out against him. And people said divers things of him, some that he was good, and others that he was a wizard, and separated husbands and wives and preached chastity.

38 Evening came on and all dispersed. Philip sought a lodging, and went to the warehouses of one Nicocleides, a recorder (registrar), friend of the king, where many strangers lodged.

39 He stood in a corner and prayed for

blessing and healing on the house.

40 Charitine, daughter of Nicocleides, heard him and wept all night. She had a sore disease in her eye. In the morning she went to her father and said: I can no longer bear the taunts of my companions about my eye. He said: What can I do? have I not called in Leucius the king's physician and Elides the queen's eunuch and Solgia her attendant. She: I know it, but there is a strange physician come here last night: call him.

41 He went to the warehouses and found Philip: Art thou the physician lately come? Philip: Jesus is my physician. I will come with thee. They found the daughter weeping.

42 After reassuring words she fell at his feet: I sprinkle my chamber with pure water and lay my linen garments under thy feet, help me, for I know thou canst. To her father: Let us bring him in, and let him see my disease.

43 Philip comforted and instructed them, and bade her rise and put her right hand on her face and say: In the name of Jesus Christ let my eye be healed. And it was. 44 And both believed and were baptized, and a number of servants. And Charitine put on male attire and followed Philip.

V.

Done in the city Nicatera; and of Ireus.

45 Philip had in mind to go to Nicatera, a city of Greece, and many disciples accompanied him, and he taught continually.

46 And when he arrived there was great stir: What shall we do for his teaching will prevail . . . he separates husbands and wives. Let us cast him out before he begins to preach and our wives are deceived.

47 There were Jews, too, who spoke against him; but a chief of them, Ireus, said: Do not use force; let us test his teaching.

48 Ireus was wealthy. He was a just man and desired quietly to foil their counsel. He went to Philip and greeted him. And Philip saw there was no guile

in him, and promised him salvation, for having stood up for him.

49 Ireus was surprised at his knowing this. Philip exhorted him to faith and constancy.

50 Ireus: Lodge at my house. Philip: First cleanse it. Ireus: How? Philip: Do no wrong, and leave thy wife. And he went home.

51 His wife said: I hear you foiled the counsel of the Jews about a strange sorcerer. Ireus: Would that we might be worthy to have him lodge here. She: I will not have him here, for he separates husbands and wives. I will go home to my parents and take my dowry and servants; four years I have been your wife and never contradicted you.

52 Ireus mildly: Have patience, and you also will believe. She: Rise, eat, drink and be merry, for you cannot deceive me. Ireus: How can I eat while the man of God is hungry? Put away this folly: he is a man of God, of mildness and grace.

53 She: Is his God like those of this city, of gold, fixed in the temple? Ireus: No, but in heaven, almighty: the gods of this city are made by ungodly men. She: Bring him, that I may see the god in him.

54 He went to meet Philip, who told him what had passed, and Ireus was amazed at his knowledge, but asked him not to publish the reproach of his wife.

55 Philip's companions urged him to accept the refuge provided: and Ireus was glad. Philip consented to come, and followed Ireus.

56 The rulers and people saw it and determined not to allow it. Ireus arriving at his gate cried to the porter to open. Philip entered saying: Peace be to this house. Ireus found that his wife was in her chamber and went and asked her to come, and put off her gay robes. But she was angry and said: No one of the house has ever seen my face, and shall I show it to a stranger?

57 So he went out and set fine gilt chairs for Philip and the rest. But he said: Take them away. Ireus: Do not grieve me. Philip: I grieve no one, but I

have no use for gold, which passes away.

58 Ireus: Can I be saved? for my former sins trouble me Philip: Yes, Jesus is able to save you. And what of your wife who just now said to you: Depart from me. Ireus, surprised went to his wife and said: Come and see a man who has told me what passed between you and me. She was scornful, and said: What is to become of our children if we have to give up all our worldly wealth?

59 Artemela his daughter was listening. and said: If my father and mother are to enter a new life, may I not share it? She was very beautiful. Her mother Nerkela told her to rise and put off her gold-woven dress. Ireus said to Nerkela: Let us go out and see Philip (it seems Nerkela was converted, but the text does not show this clearly).

60 The women changed their attire for a sober one, and they all went out. And when they saw Philip, he shone with a great light, so that they were afraid.

61 But he saw it, and returned to his former likeness: and Nerkela asked pardon of him and made him welcome.

62, 63 And they professed belief and were instructed and baptized.

VI.

In Nicatera, a city of Greece.

64 The Jews and heathens were displeased at Ireus' conversion,

65 and sent seven men to his house. A handmaid told him of them; he came out smiling and asked their errand. 'The whole city wishes to see you.' He followed them.

66 And the assembly were surprised at his modest garb. One Onesimus asked him to explain about the sorcerer Philip.

67 Ireus: Why am I examined thus? do not trouble Philip.

68 But they said: Away with him. And Ireus went home and met Philip, who said: Are you afraid? No, he said.

69 The people now came with staves, crying out: Give us the deceiver.

70 Philip came forth and they took him to the assembly to scourge him, and said: Bind him hand and foot.

71 Ireus ran up the steps and cried: You shall not. But they would not hear, and Ireus pulled Philip away from them.

72 Philip said: If I choose, I can blind you; Aristarchus, son of Plegenes, a chief of the Jews, said: Do not be in a hurry to blind us: I know you can; but let us discuss I am powerful, and if I let the people, they will stone you;

73 And he caught Philip by the beard; he was rather angry, because of the people, and said: Your hand and your ears and your right eye shall suffer for threatening me and insulting God.

74 His eye became hollow as if absent, his ears pained him, his right hand dangled useless. He cried out for mercy.

75 They all said: Heal our chief.

76 Philip told Ireus to go sign him with the cross and heal him in Jesus' name, which was done, and he asked pardon and indulgence and leave to discuss the matter. And the people said: We will judge of it. 77 Philip smiled and bade him speak first. He said: Do you receive the prophets or no? Philip: Because of your unbelief there is need of the prophets. Aristarchus: It is written: Who shall declare thy might, O God? and, No man can know thy glory; and, Thy glory hath filled the earth; and, The Lord is judge of quick and dead; and God is a consuming fire and shall burn up his enemies on every side; and, One God hath made all these things. How then say you that Mary bore Jesus? . . . But you will say that he is the power and wisdom of God who was with him when he made the world. I do not deny that the first Scripture says: Let us make man.

78 Philip smiled and said: Hearken all: Isaiah said, Behold my servant (child) whom I have chosen . . . . And of the cross: He was led as a sheep to the slaughter . . . . And again: I gave my back to the scourger . . . . And another: I spread out my hands to a disobedient people. And: I was found of them that sought me not . . . . And David saith: Thou art my son . . . . And of his resurrection and Judas: Lord, why are they increased that trouble me . . . . And again David: I foresaw the Lord always

before me . . . . But David is dead. Take also of the twelve prophets: Say unto the daughter of Sion . . . . And: Out of Egypt have I called my son.

79 Aristarchus said: This Jesus is called Christ. Isaiah: Thus saith the Lord unto Christ my lord . . . . The Jews said: You are arguing for Christ. The people and rulers acclaimed Philip and said he should be received.

80 A bier was brought with a dead man, only son of a rich man: and with it ten slaves who were to be burnt with the corpse. The people said: Here is a great contest for the Christians. If theirs be God he will raise him and we will believe, and burn our idols.

81 Philip said to the parents: What will you do if I raise him? ' What you will.' The slaves made signs to him to remember them. There was this evil law of burning slaves, and sometimes even men's wives.

82 Philip said: Give me these slaves. Yes, and any more that you will.' He said to Aristarchus: Come, O Jew, raise him. And he touched his face and spat much on him and pulled his hand: in vain, and retired in confusion.

83 Nereus the father said: Raise my son and I will fight the Jews. Philip: If you will not promise not to hurt them, I will not raise him. Nerus: As you will.

84 Philip went to the bier and prayed, and breath entered into the lad Theophilus, and he opened his eyes and looked on Philip.

85 A second time Philip said: Young man, in the name of Jesus Christ who was crucified under Pontius Pilate, arise. And he leapt from the bier. All cried: One is the God of Philip . . . and the slaves were made free. All believed.

86 Philip taught, baptized, destroyed idols, ordained, gave canons and rules.

VII.
Of Nerkela (and) Ireus at Nicatera.

87 Nerkela and Artemela were blessed by Philip.

88 Ireus and Nereus consulted about building a church, and agreed to build it on Nereus' land.

89 Only the Jews were discontented and decided to withdraw.

90 Philip came to the new building and addressed the people,

91 and made Ireus bishop and prayed over him, and announced that he was going away.

92 All wept, but he consoled them.

93 They loaded camels with provisions and accompanied him 20 stadia. He dismissed them and would only take five loaves. They all saluted him thrice, and fell on their faces and prayed for his blessing, and watched him out of sight, and returned to the city.

VIII.
Wherein the kid and the leopard in the wilderness believed

94 It came to pass when the Saviour divided the apostles and each went forth according to his lot, that it fell to Philip to go to the country of the Greeks: and he thought it hard, and wept. And Mariamne his sister (it was she that made ready the bread and salt at the breaking of bread, but Martha was she that ministered to the multitudes and laboured much) seeing it, went to Jesus and said: Lord, seest thou not how my brother is vexed?

95 And he said: I know, thou chosen among women; but go with him and encourage him, for I know that he is a wrathful and rash man, and if we let him go alone he will bring many retributions on men. But lo, I will send Bartholomew and John to suffer hardships in the same city, because of the much wickedness of them that dwell there; for they worship the viper, the mother of snakes. And do thou change thy woman's aspect and go with Philip. And to Philip he said: Why art thou fearful? for I am always with thee.

96 So they all set out for the land of the Ophiani; and when they came to the wilderness of dragons, lo, a great leopard came out of a wood on the hill, and ran and cast himself at their feet and spoke with human voice: I worship you, servants of the divine greatness and apostles of the only-begotten Son

of God; command me to speak perfectly.

97 And Philip said: In the name of Jesus Christ, speak. And the leopard took perfect speech and said: Hear me Philip, groomsman of the divine word. Last night I passed through the flocks of goats over against the mount of the she-dragon, the mother of snakes, and seized a kid, and when I went into the wood to eat, after I had wounded it, it took a human voice and wept like a little child, saying to me: O leopard, put off thy fierce heart and the beast like part of thy nature, and put on mildness, for the apostles of the divine greatness are about to pass through this desert, to accomplish perfectly the promise of the glory of the only-begotten Son of God. At these words of the kid I was perplexed, and gradually my heart was changed, and my fierceness turned to mildness, and I did not eat it. And as I listened to its words, I lifted up my eyes and saw you coming, and knew that ye were the servants of the good God. So I left the kid and came to worship you. And now I beseech thee to give me liberty to go with thee everywhere and put off my beastlike nature.

98 And Philip said: Where is the kid? And he said: It is cast down under the oak opposite. Philip said to Bartholomew: Let us go and see him that was smitten, healed, and healing the smiter. And at Pllilip's bidding the leopard guided them to where the kid lay.

99 Philip and Bartholomew said: Now know we of a truth that there is none that surpasseth thy compassion, O Jesu lover of man; for thou preventest us and dost convince us by these creatures to believe more and earnestly fulfil our trust. Now therefore, Lord Jesu Christ, come and grant life and breath and secure footing (existence ?) to these creatures, that they may forsake their nature of beast and cattle and come unto tameness, and no longer eat flesh, nor the kid the food of cattle; but that men's hearts may be given them, and they may follow us wherever we go, and eat what we eat, to thy glory, and speak after the manner of men, glorifying thy name.

100 And in that hour the leopard and kid rose up and lifted up their forefeet and said: We glorify and bless thee that hast visited and remembered us in this desert, and changed our beastlike and wild nature into tameness, and granted us the divine word, and put in us a tongue and sense to speak and praise thy name, for great is thy glory. 101 And they fell and worshipped Philip and Bartholomew and Mariamne; and all set out together praising God.

IX.

Of the dragon that was slain.

102 They journeyed five days, and one morning after the midnight prayers a sudden wind arose, great and dark (misty), and out of it ran a great smoky (misty) dragon, with a black back, and a belly like coals of brass in sparkles of fire, and a body over 100 cubits long, and a multitude of snakes and their young followed it, and the desert quaked for a long distance.

103 And Philip said: Now is the time to remember the Lord's words: Fear nothing, neither persecution, nor the serpents of that land, nor the dark dragon. Let us stand fast and his power will fail; and pray and sprinkle the air from the cup and the smoke will scatter.

104 So they took the cup and prayed: Thou that sheddest dew on all pyres and bridlest darkness, putting a bit into the dragon's mouth, bringing to nought his anger, turning back the wickedness of the enemy and plunging him into his own fire, shutting his doors and stopping the exits and buffeting his pride: come and be with us in this desert, for we run by thy will and at thy bidding.

105 And he said: Now stand and raise your hands, with the cup you hold, and sprinkle the air in the form of the cross.

106 And there was as a flash of lightning which blinded the dragon and its brood; and they were withered up; and the rays of the sun entered the holes and broke the eggs. But the apostles

closed their eyes, unable to face the lightning, and remained unhurt.

Out of the Travels of Philip the Apostle: from the fifteenth Act to the end, wherein is the Martyrdom.

107 (Introductory.) In the days of Trajan, after the Martyrdom of Simon, son of Clopas, bishop of Jerusalem, successor to James, Philip the apostle was preaching through all the cities of Lydia and Asia.
108 And he came to the city Ophioryme (Snake street), which is called Hierapolis of Asia, and was received by Stachys, a believer. And with him were Bartholomew, one of the Seventy, and his sister Mariamne, and their disciples. And they assembled at Stachys' house.
109 And Mariamne sat and listened to Philip discoursing.
110-112 He spoke of the snares of the dragon, who has 'no shape' in creation, and is recognized and shunned by beasts and birds.
113 For the men of the place worshipped the snake and had images of it, and called Hierapolis Ophioryme. And many were converted.
114 And Nicanora the proconsul's wife believed, she was diseased, especially in her eyes, and had been healed. She now came in a silver litter.
115 And Mariamne said in Hebrew: Alikaman, ikasame, marmari, iachaman, mastranan, achaman, which means: O daughter of the father, my lady, who wast given as a pledge to the serpent, Christ is come to thee (and much more).
116 And Nicanora said: I am a Hebrew, speak to me in my fathers' tongue. I heard of your preaching and was healed.
117 And they prayed for her.
118 But her tyrant husband came and said: How is this? who has healed you?
119 And she said: Depart from me, and lead a chaste and sober life.
120 And he dragged her by the hair and threatened to kill her. And the apostles were arrested,
121 and scourged and dragged to the temple,
122 and shut up in it (with the leopard and the kid. These are omitted in the principal text, but constantly occur in another recension: rightly, of course).
123 The people and priests came and demanded vengeance on the sorcerers.
124 The proconsul was afraid of his wife, for he had been almost blinded by a wonderful light when he looked through the window at her when praying.
125 They stripped and searched the apostles for charms, and pierced Philip's ankles and thighs and hung him head downward, and Bartholomew they hung naked by the hair.
126 And they smiled on each other, as not being tormented. But Mariamne on being stripped became like an ark of glass full of light and fire and every one ran away.
127 And Philip and Bartholomew talked in Hebrew, and Philip said: Shall we call down fire from heaven?
128 And now John arrived, and asked what was happening, and the people told him.
129 And he was taken to the place. Philip said to Bartholomew in Hebrew: Here is John the son of Barega (or, he that is in Barek), that is (or, where is) the living water. And John said: The mystery of him that hanged between the heaven and the earth be with you.
130 Then John addressed the people, warning them against the serpent. Inter alia: When all matter was wrought and spread out throughout the system of heaven, the works of God entreated God that they might see his glory: and when they saw it, their desire became gall and bitterness, and the earth became the storehouse of that which went astray, and the result and the superfluity of the creation was gathered together and became like an egg: and the serpent was born.
131 The people said: We took you for a fellow citizen, but you are in league with these men. The priests are going to wring out your blood and mix it with wine and give it to the Viper. When they came to take John their hands were

paralysed. John said to Philip: Let us not render evil for evil. Philip said: I shall endure it no longer.

132 The three others dissuaded him; but he said: Abalo, arimouni, douthael, tharseleen, nachaoth, aeidounaph, teleteloein, which is (after many invocations descriptive of God): let the deep open and swallow these men: yea, Sabaoth.

133 It opened and the whole place was swallowed, about 7,000 men, save where the apostles were. And their voices came up, crying for mercy and saying: Lo, the cross enlighteneth us. And a voice was heard: I will have mercy on you in my cross of light.

134 But Stachys and his house, and Nicanora and 50 others, and 100 virgins remained safe.

135 Jesus appeared and rebuked Philip.

136 But he defended himself.

137 And the Lord said: Since you have been unforgiving and wrathful, you shall indeed die in glory and be taken by angels to paradise, but shall remain outside it forty days, in fear of the flaming sword, and then I will send Michael and he shall let you in. And Bartholomew shall go to Lycaonia and be crucified there, and Mariamne's body shall be laid up in the river Jordan. And I shall bring back those who have been swallowed up.

138 And he drew a cross in the air, reaching down into the abyss, and it was filled with light, and the cross was like a ladder. And Jesus called the people, and they all came up, save the proconsul and the Viper And seeing the apostles they mourned and repented.

139 And Philip, still hanging, spoke to them and told them of his offense

140 And some ran to take him down: but he refused and spoke to them . . . . " Be not grieved that I hang thus, for I bear the form (type) of the first man, who was brought upon earth head downwards, and again by the tree of the cross made alive from the death of his transgression. And now do I fulfil the precept. For the Lord said to me: Unless ye make that which is beneath to be above, and the left to be right (and the right left), ye shall not enter into my kingdom. Be like me in this: for all the world is turned the wrong way, and every soul that is in it."

141 Further he spoke to them of the incarnation,

142 and bade them loose Bartholomew, and told him and Mariamne of their destiny. Build a church in the place where I die, and let the leopard and kid be there, and let Nicanora look after them till they die, and then bury them at the church gate: and let your peace be in the house of Stachys: and he exhorted them to purity. "Therefore our brother Peter fled from every place where a woman was: and further, he had offense given by reason of his own daughter. And he prayed the Lord, and she had a palsy of the side that she might not be led astray."

143 Bury me not in linen like the Lord, but in papyrus, and pray for me forty days. Where my blood is dropping a vine will grow, and ye shall use the wine of it for the cup: and partake of it on the third day.

144 And he prayed the Lord to receive him, and protect him against all enemies. "Let not their dark air cover me, that I may pass the waters of fire and all the abyss. Clothe me in thy glorious robe and thy seal of light that ever shineth, until I have passed by all the rulers of the world and the evil dragon that opposeth us."

145 And he died.

146 And they buried him as he directed. And a heavenly voice said he had received the crown.

147 After three days the vine grew Up. And they made the offering daily for forty days, and built the church and made Stachys bishop. And all the city believed.

148 And at the end of forty days the Saviour appeared in the form of Philip and told Bartholomew and Mariamne that he had entered paradise, and bade them go their ways. And Bartholomew went to Lycaonia and Mariamne to Jordan, and Stachys and the brethren abode where they were.

THE ACTS OF PHILIP

[[The narrative of the Act preserved in Syriac is this.]]

1 Philip, at Jerusalem, had a vision of Jesus, who commanded him to go to the city of Carthage, ' which is in Azotus ', and drive out the ruler of Satan, and preach the kingdom.

2 He said: I know not Latin or Greek, and the people there do not know Aramaic. Jesus said:

3 Did I not create Adam and give him speech? Go, and I will be with thee.

4 He went to Samaria, thence to Caesarea, and to the harbour and found a ship waiting for a wind.

5 Asked to take Philip to Carthage, the captain said:

6 Do not annoy me, we have waited twenty days: fetch your baggage and perhaps we shall get a wind, for you look like a servant of God.

7 Philip: I have none; tell the passengers to come on board . . . . Let us pray for a fair wind.

8 Turning to the west he commanded the angel of peace who has charm of fair winds to send a wind to take him to Carthage in a single day.

9 On board was a Jew, Ananias, who blasphemed (sotto voce, it seems) and said:

10 May Adonai recompense thee, and the Christ on whom thou callest, who is become dust and lies in Jerusalem, while thou livest and leadest ignorant men astray by his name.

11 A wind came and filled the sail. The Jew rose to help to hoist the sail, and an angel bound him by the great toes and hung him head down on the top of the sail.

12 The ship flew onward and the Jew cried out. Philip said: You shall not come down till you confess.

13 He confessed his secret blasphemy. Philip: Dost thou now believe? Ananias confessed belief in a speech in which he enumerated Christ's (God's) mighty acts from creation to the deliverance of Susanna.

14 Philip asked that he might be pardoned, and the angel brought him down. And the 495 men on the ship feared.

15 They looked up and saw the pharos of Carthage, and said; Can this be true?

16 O fools, said Ananias, did ye not see what befell me for unbelief? If he commands that city in Christ's name, it will take all its inhabitants and go and stop in Egypt.

17 The ship came into harbour. Philip dismissed the passengers, and stayed on board to confirm the captain.

18 On the Sunday he went up to the city to drive out Satan, and as he entered the gates, signed himself with the cross.

19 He saw a black man on a throne with two serpents about his loins, and eyes like coals of fire, and flame coming from his mouth, there was a smell of smoke, and black men in troops were on his right and left.

20 When Philip crossed himself the ruler fell backward and all his troops. Philip said: Fall, and rise not . . . . The ruler said: Why curse me? I do not abide here, but my troops wander over the earth and come to me at the third hour of the day, but they do not touch a disciple of Jesus.

21 Woe is me! whither can I go? In all the four quarters of the world his gospel is preached. I am completely overthrown.

22 The whole city heard him, but saw him not. Philip bade him go, and he took his throne and his troops and flew away bewailing till they came to Babel, and he settled there.

23 The whole city was in fear and Philip bade them leave their idols and turn to God, They praised God, and Philip went back to the ship.

24 On the Sabbath the Jews assembled in their synagogue and summoned Ananias, and asked if his adventures were true.

25 He signed himself with the cross and said: It is true, and God forbid I should renounce Jesus the Christ.

26 He then addressed them in a long and very abusive speech, enumerating all their wicked acts.

27 Then arose Joshua, the son of Nun, and ye sought to kill him with deadly poison . . . .

28 Isaiah the prophet, and ye sawed him with a saw of boxwood . . .

29 Ezekiel, and ye dragged him by his feet until his brains were dashed out . . .

30 Habakkuk, and through your sins he went astray from his prophetic office.'

31 His face was like an angel. A priest arose and kicked him, and he died, and they buried him in the synagogue.

32 Next day Philip in the ship prayed and asked that Ananias might be delivered from the Jews.

33 God commanded the earth and it gave a passage like a water-pipe, and conveyed Ananias to the bottom of the sea, and a dolphin bore up the body.

34 Philip saw it, and after reassuring the people, bade it take the body back till he should go and convict the murderers.

35 Next day Philip went to the governor and got him to assemble all the Jews, and sit in judgement.

36 Philip, to the Jews: Where is Ananias?

37 They: Are we his keeper? Philip: Well are you called children of Cain, for.

38 Tell me where he is, and I will ask pardon for you. Jews: We have said we do not know. Philip: Do not lie.

39 Jews: If the spirit were in you, you would know that we do not lie.

40 Philip: If he is found with you, what do you deserve?

41 Jews: Death from God and Caesar. Philip: Swear to me. They swore they knew nothing.

42 He looked and saw a man leading a sick ox to sell.

43 He said to it: I command thee, go to the synagogue and call Ananias to rise and come and put these men to shame.

44 The ox dragged his owner along and ran and called Ananias. He rose and laid hold of the ox with his right hand, and they came to Philip and prostrated themselves.

45 Philip said: Whence comest thou?

46 Ananias said: From the synagogue of these Jews, who murdered me for confessing Jesus: do me justice.

47 Philip: The Lord has commanded us not to render evil for evil. The ox said:

Order me and I will kill these men with my horns.

48 Philip: Hurt no man, but go and serve thy master, and the Lord will heal thee. They went home in peace.

49 The governor said: These Jews deserve death. Philip: I am not come to kill but to give life. The Jews' mouths were closed.

50 Ananias spoke to the Jews and Philip also: but they did not ask pardon, so they were cast out. Three thousand Gentiles and fifteen hundred Jews believed; the unbelievers left the city, and before sunset an angel slew forty of the Jewish priests for shedding innocent blood: and all who saw it confessed and worshipped.

THE ACTS OF MATTHIAS AND ANDREW

1 At that time all the apostles were gathered together and divided the countries among themselves, casting lots. And it fell to Matthias to go to the land of the anthropophagi. Now the men of that city ate no bread nor drank wine, but ate the flesh and drank the blood of men; and every stranger who landed there they took, and put out his eyes, and gave him a magic drink which took away his understanding.

2 So when Matthias arrived he was so treated; but the drink had no effect on him, and he remained praying for help in the prison.

3 And a light came and a voice: Matthias, my beloved, receive sight. And he saw. And the voice continued: I will not forsake thee: abide twenty-seven days, and I will send Andrew to deliver thee and all the rest. And the Saviour went up into heaven. Matthias remained singing praises; when the executioners came to take victims, he kept his eyes closed. They came and looked at the ticket on his hand and

said: Three days more and we will slay him. For every victim had a ticket tied on his hand to show the date when his thirty days would be fulfilled.

4 When twenty-seven days had elapsed, the Lord appeared to Andrew in the country where he was teaching and said: In three days Matthias is to be slain by the man-eaters; go and deliver him. 'How is it possible for me to get there in time?' Early to-morrow go to the shore and you will find a ship.' And he left him.

5 They went, Andrew and his disciples, and found a little boat and three men. The pilot was the Lord, and the other two were angels. Andrew asked whither they were going. 'To the land of the man-eaters.' 'I would go there too.' 'Every man avoids that place; why will you go?' 'I have an errand to do; and if you can, take us.' He said: 'Come on board.'

6 Andrew said: 'I must tell you we have neither money nor victuals.' 'How then do you travel?' 'Our master forbade us to take money and provisions. If you will do us this kindness, tell us: if not, we will look for another ship.' 'If these are your orders, come on board and welcome, I desire truly to have disciples of Jesus on my ship.' So they embarked.

7 Jesus ordered three loaves to be brought and Andrew summoned his disciples to partake; but they could not answer him, for they were disturbed with the sea. So Andrew explained to the pilot, and he offered to set them ashore: but they refused to leave Andrew.

8 Jesus said: Tell your disciples some of the wonders your master did, to encourage them, for we are going to set sail: so they did, and Jesus steered. And Andrew told the disciples about the stilling of the storm, and prayed in himself that they might sleep: and they fell asleep.

9 Andrew said to Jesus: Tell me your art, sixteen years did I sail the sea, and this is the seventeenth, and I never saw such steering: the ship is as if on land. Jesus said: I, too, have often sailed the sea and been in danger; but because you are a disciple of Jesus, the sea knows you and is still. Andrew praised God that he had met such a man.

10 Jesus said: Tell me why the Jews did not believe on your master. Andrew enumerated the miracles: yet, he said, the Jews did not believe. 'Perhaps he did not do these signs before the high priests?'

11 'Yes, he did, both openly and privately, and they would not believe.' 'What were the signs he did in secret?' ' O man with the spirit of questioning, why do you tempt me thus?' 'I do not tempt you but my soul rejoices to hear his wonderful works.' ' I will tell you, then.

12 Once when we the twelve went with our Lord to a heathen temple that he might show us the ignorance of the devil, the high priests saw us and said: Why do you follow this man who says he is the Son of God? has God a son? Is not this Joseph and Mary's son, and his brothers are James and Simon? and our hearts were weakened. And Jesus perceived it, and took us apart into the wilderness and did mighty signs and strengthened our faith. And we said to the priests: Come and see; for he has convinced us.

13 'And the priests came to the heathen temple, and Jesus showed us the form of the heavens, "that we might learn whether it were true or no." Thirty men of the people and four priests were with us. On the right and left of the temple Jesus saw two sphinxes carved, and turned to us and said: Behold the form of the heaven: these are like the cherubim and seraphim in heaven. And he said to the sphinx on the right: You semblance of that which is in heaven, made by craftsmen, come down and convince these priests whether I be God or man.

14 It came down and spoke and said: O foolish sons of Israel. This is God who made man . . . . Tell me not that I am a stone image: better are the temples than your synagogue. Our priests purify themselves seven days from women, and approach not the temple but you

come straight from defilement. The temples will abolish your synagogues, and become churches of the only-begotten Son of God.

15 The priests said: It speaks by magic, ye heard it say that this man spake with Abraham. How is that possible? . . . Jesus said to the sphinx: Go to the cave of Mambre and call Abraham; bid him rise with Isaac and Jacob and come to the temples of the Jebusaeans to convict the priests. It went and called, and the twelve patriarchs rose and came out. "To which of us wast thou sent? " "Not to you, but to the three patriarchs: go back and rest." They went back, and the three patriarchs came and convicted the priests. Jesus bade them return, and sent the sphinx back to its place. But the priests did not believe. And many other wonders he did.'

16 Jesus seeing that they were near land, leaned his head on one of the angels and ceased speaking to Andrew: and Andrew went to sleep. Then Jesus bade the angels take the men and lay them outside the city of the man-eaters and return: and then all departed to heaven.

17 Andrew awoke and looked about him and realized what had happened, and roused his disciples. They told him their dream: eagles came and bore therm into paradise, and they saw the Lord on his throne, and angels, and the three patriarchs and David singing, "and you the twelve apostles and twelve angels by you, whom the Lord bade to obey you in everything."

18 Andrew rejoiced and prayed the Lord to show himself: and Jesus appeared in the form of a beautiful young child. Andrew asked pardon for his boldness on the ship. Jesus reassured him and told him what trials awaited him in the city, and encouraged him to endure them, and departed.

19 They entered the city, unseen, and went to the prison. The seven guards fell dead at his prayer: at the sign of the cross the doors opened. He found Matthias and they greeted each other.

20 Andrew looked at the victims, who were naked and eating grass, and smote his breast and reproached the devil: How long warrest thou with men? thou didst cause Adam to be cast out of paradise: thou didst cause his bread that was on the table to be turned to stones. Again, thou didst enter into the mind of the angels and cause them to be defiled with women and madest their savage sons the giants to devour men on the earth, so that God sent the flood . . . .

21 Then they both prayed, and they laid their hands on the prisoners and restored first their sight and then their sense, and Andrew bade them go out of the city and remain under a fig-tree and await him: there were 270 men and 49 women. And Andrew commanded a cloud, and it took Matthias and the disciples and brethren to the mount where Peter was teaching and there they remained.

22 Andrew went out and walked in the city, and sat down by a brazen pillar with a statue on it, to see what would happen. The executioners came and found the prison empty and the guards dead, and reported to the rulers. They said: Go and fetch the seven dead men for us to eat to-day, and assemble to-morrow, the old men, and we will cast lots for seven a day and eat them, till we can fit out ships and send and collect people to eat. So they fetched the seven corpses; there was a furnace in the midst of the city and a great vat for the blood: they put the men on the vat. A voice came: Andrew, look at this. Andrew prayed, and the men's swords fell and their hands turned to stone. The rulers cried: There are wizards in the city: go and gather the old men, for we are hungry.

23 They found 215, and lots were cast for 7. One of these said: Take my young son and kill him instead of me. They asked leave of the rulers, and it was granted, and the old man said: I have a daughter, take her too, and spare me. So the children were brought to the vat begging for their lives, but there was no pity. Andrew prayed, and again the swords fell from the men's hands, and there was much alarm.

24 Then came the devil in the guise of

an old man, and said: Woe to you, you will all die of hunger; but search now and look for a stranger named Andrew: he is the cause of your trouble. Andrew was looking at the devil, but the devil could not see him. And Andrew said: O Beliar, my lord will humble thee to the abyss. The devil said: I hear your voice and know it; but where you stand I see not. Andrew said: Art thou not called Amael because thou art blind? The devil said: Look for the man who spake to me, for it is he. And they shut the gates and looked everywhere, but could not find him. The Lord appeared and said to Andrew: Show thyself to them.

25 He rose and said I am Andrew whom ye seek. And they ran and took him, and debated how to kill him: If we cut off his head, it will not pain him enough; Let us put a rope round his neck and drag him through the streets every day till he dies, and divide his body and eat it. They did so, and his flesh was torn and his blood flowed, and they cast him into prison with his hands bound behind him.

26 And so they did next day, and he wept and cried to the Lord: and the devil told the people to smite his mouth that he might not speak; and they bound his hands behind him and left him in the prison. The devil took seven other devils, whom Andrew had driven out from places in the neighbourhood (this seems like a reference to the older Acts), and they came to Andrew, and the devil said: Now we will kill you like your master whom Herod slew.

27 And he said: Now my children, kill him. But they saw the seal on his forehead and were afraid, and said: Do you kill him, for we cannot. And one of them said: If we cannot kill him, let us mock him; and they stood before him and taunted him with his helplessness, and he wept. And a voice -the devil's voice disguised-said: Why weep? Andrew said: Because of our Lord's word: Have patience with them; otherwise I would have shown you! . . . But if the Lord grant me a visitation in this city, I will chastise you as you deserve. And they fled.

28 Next day the people dragged him again, and he cried out to the Lord: here are thy words: A hair of your heads shall not perish? lo, my flesh is torn from me. And a voice said in Hebrew: My words shall not pass away: look behind thee. And he saw great fruit-bearing trees growing up where his flesh and blood had fallen. And they took him back to prison, and said: Perhaps he will die to-morrow.

29 And the Lord came and took his hand and he rose up whole. And in the prison was a pillar, and on it a statue. Andrew went to it and spread out his hands seven times and said: Fear thou the sign of the cross, and let this statue pour forth water as a flood. And say not, I am but a stone for God made us of earth, but ye are clean, and therefore God gave his people the law on tables of stone. And the statue poured water out of its mouth as from a canal, and it was bitter and corroded men's flesh.

30 In the morning all the people began to flee. The water killed their cattle and their children. Andrew said: Let Michael wall the city about with fire. A cloud of fire came and surrounded it, and they could not escape. The water came up to their necks and consumed their flesh. They cried and lamented till he saw their spirit was crushed, and told the alabaster statue to cease. And Andrew went out of the prison, the water parting before him, and the people prayed for mercy.

31 The old man who had given up his children came and besought. But Andrew said: I wonder at you; you and the fourteen executioners shall be swallowed up and see the places of torment and of peace. And he went as far as the great vat, and prayed, and the earth opened and swallowed the water and the old man and the executioners. And all feared greatly, but he consoled them.

32 Then he bade them bring all who had been killed by the water, but there were too many, so he prayed and revived them. Then he drew out the plan of a church and baptized them and gave them the Lord's precepts. And they

begged him to stay with them a little; but he refused, saying I must first go to my disciples; and he set forth, and they lamented grievously.

33 And Jesus appeared in the form of a beautiful child and reproved him for leaving them, and told him to stay seven days; and then he should go with his disciples to the country of the barbarians, and then return and bring the men out of the abyss. And he returned and they all rejoiced greatly.

THE ACTS AND MARTYRDOM OF ST. MATTHEW THE APOSTLE

1 ABOUT that time Matthew, the holy apostle and evangelist of Christ, was abiding in the mountain resting, and praying in his tunic and apostolic robes without sandals; and, behold, Jesus came to Matthew in the likeness of the infants who sing in paradise, and said to him:

2 Peace to thee, Matthew! And Matthew having gazed upon Him, and not known who He was, said:

3 Grace to thee, and peace, O child highly favoured! And why hast thou come hither to me, having left those who sing in paradise, and the delights there?

4 Because here the place is desert; and what sort of a table I shall lay for thee, O child, I know not, because I have no bread nor oil in a jar.

5 Moreover, even the winds are at rest, so as not to cast down from the trees to the ground anything for food; because, for the accomplishing of my fast of forty days, I, partaking only of the fruits falling by the movement of the winds, am glorifying my Jesus.

6 Now, therefore, what shall I bring thee, beautiful boy? There is not even water near, that I may wash thy feet.

7 And the child said: Why sayest thou, O Matthew?

8 Understand and know that good discourse is better than a calf, and words of meekness better than every herb of the field, and a sweet saying as the perfume of love, and cheerfulness of countenance better that feeding, and a pleasant look is as the appearance of sweetness.

9 Understand, Matthew, and know that I am paradise, that I am the comforter, I am the power of the powers above, I the strength of those that restrain themselves, I the crown of the virgins, I the self-control of the once married, I the boast of the widowed, I the defence of the infants, I the foundation of the Church, I the kingdom of the bishops, I the glory of the presbyters, I the praise of the deacons.

10 Be a man, and be strong, Matthew, in, these words.

11 And Matthew said: The sight of thee hast altogether delighted me, O child; moreover also, thy words are full of life.

12 For assuredly thy face shines more than the lightning, and thy words are altogether most sweet.

13 And that indeed I saw thee in paradise when thou didst sing with the other infants who were killed in Bethlehem, I know right well; but how thou hast suddenly come hither, this altogether astonishes me.

14 But I shall ask thee one thing, O child: that impious Herod, where is he?

15 The child says to him: Since thou hast asked, hear his dwelling-place.

16 He dwells, indeed, in Hades; and there has been prepared for him fire unquenchable, Gehenna without end, bubbling mire, worm that sleeps not, because he cut off three thousand infants, wishing to slay the child Jesus, the ancient of the ages; but of all these ages I am father.

17 Now therefore, O Matthew, take this rod of mine, and go down from the mountain, and go into Myrna, the city of the man-eaters, and plant it by the

gate of the church which thou and Andrew founded;

18 And as soon as thou hast planted it, it shall be a tree, great and lofty and with many branches, and its branches shall extend to thirty cubits, and of each single branch the fruit shall be different both to the sight and the eating.

19 And from the top of the tree shall flow down much honey; and from its root there shall come forth a great fountain, giving drink to this country round about, and in it creatures that swim and creep; and in it the man-eaters shall wash themselves, and eat of the fruit of the trees of the vine and of the honey; and their bodies shall be changed, and their forms shall be altered so as to be like those of other men; and they shall be ashamed of the nakedness of their body, and they shall put on clothing of the rams of the sheep, and they shall no longer eat unclean things; and there shall be to them fire in superabundance, preparing the sacrifices for offerings, and they shall bake their bread with fire; and they shall see each other in the likeness of the rest of men, and they shall acknowledge me, and glorify my Father who is in the heavens.

20 Now therefore make haste, Matthew, and go down hence, because the departure from thy body through fire is at hand, and the crown of thy endurance.

21 And the child having said this, and given him the rod, was taken up into the heavens.

22 And Matthew went down from the mountain, hastening to the city.

23 And as he was about to enter into the city, there met him Fulvana the wife of the king, and his son Fulvanus and his wife Erva, who were possessed by an unclean spirit, and cried out shouting:

24 Who has brought thee here again, Matthew? or who has given thee the rod for our destruction? for we see also the child Jesus, the Son of God, who is with thee.

25 Do not go then, O Matthew, to plant the rod for the food, and for the transformation of the man-eaters: for I bare found what I shall do to thee.

26 For since thou didst drive me out of this city, and prevent me from fulfilling my wishes among the man-eaters, behold, I will raise up against thee the king of this city, and he will burn thee alive.

27 And Matthew, having laid his hands on each one of the demoniacs, put the demons to flight, and made the people whole; and they followed him.

28 And thus the affair being made manifest, Plato the bishop, having heard of the presence of the holy Apostle Matthew, met him with all the clergy; and having fallen to the ground, they kissed his feet.

29 And Matthew raised them, and went with them into the church, and the child Jesus was also with him. And Matthew, having come to the gate of the church, stood upon a certain lofty and immoveable stone; and when the whole city ran together, especially the brethren who had believed, began to say:

30 Men and women who appear in our sight, heretofore believing in the universe, but now knowing Him who has upheld and made the universe; until now worshipping the Satyr, and mocked by ten thousand false gods, but now through Jesus Christ acknowledging the one and only God, Lord, Judge; who have laid aside the immeasurable greatness of evil, and put on love, which is of like nature with affectionateness, towards men; once strangers to Christ, but now confessing Him Lord and God; formerly without form, but now transformed through Christ;--behold, the staff which you see in my hand, which Jesus, in whom you have believed and will believe, gave me; perceive now what comes to pass through me, and acknowledge the riches of the greatness which He will this day make for you.

31 For, behold, I shall plant this rod in this place, and it shall be a sign to your generations, and it shall become a tree,

great and lofty and flourishing, and its fruit beautiful to the view and good to the sight; and the fragrance of perfumes shall come forth from it, and there shall be a vine twining round it, full of clusters; and from the top of it honey coming down, and every flying creature shall find covert in its branches; and a fountain of water shall come forth from the root of it, having swimming and creeping things, giving drink to all the country round about.

32 And having said this, and called upon the name of the Lord Jesus, he fixed his rod in the ground, and straightway it sprung up to one cubit; and the sight was strange and wonderful.

33 For the rod having straightway shot up, increased in size, and grew into a great tree, as Matthew had said.

34 And the apostle said: Go into the fountain and wash your bodies in it, and then thus partake both of the fruits of the tree, and of the vine and the honey, and drink of the fountain, and you shall be transformed in your likeness to that of men; and after that, having gone into the church, you will clearly recognise that you have believed in the living and true God.

35 And having done all these things, they saw themselves changed into the likeness of Matthew; then, having thus gone into the church, they worshipped and glorified God.

36 And when they had been changed, they knew that they were naked; and they ran in haste each to his own house to cover their nakedness, because they were ashamed.

37 And Matthew and Plato remained in the church spending the night, and glorifying God.

38 And there remained also the king's wife, and his son and his wife, and they prayed the apostle to give them the seal in Christ.

39 And Matthew gave orders to Plato; and he, having gone forth, baptized them in the water of the fountain of the tree, in the name of the Father, and the Son, and the Holy Ghost.

40 And so thereafter, having one into the church, they communicated in the holy mysteries of Christ; and they exulted and passed the night, they also along with the apostle, many others having also come with them; and all in the church sang the whole night, glorifying God.

41 And when the dawn had fully come, the blessed Matthew, having gone along with the bishop Plato, stood in the place in which the rod had been planted, and he sees the rod grown into a great tree, and near it a vine twined round it, and honey coming down from above even to its root; and that tree was at once beautiful and flourishing, like the plants in paradise, and a river proceeded from its root watering all the land of the city of Myrna.

42 And all ran together, and ate of the fruit of the tree and the vine, just as any one wished.

43 And when what had come to pass was reported in the palace, the king Fulvanus, having learned what had been done by Matthew about his wife, and his son, and his daughter-in-law, rejoiced for a time at their purification;

44 But seeing that they were inseparable from Matthew, he was seized with rage and anger, and endeavoured to put him to death by fire.

45 And on that night in which the king intended to lay hands on Matthew, Matthew saw Jesus saying to him: I am with thee always to save thee, Matthew; be strong, and be a man.

46 And the blessed Matthew, having awoke, and sealed himself over all the body, rose up at dawn, and proceeded into the church; and having bent his knees, prayed earnestly.

47 Then the bishop having come, and the clergy, they stood in common in prayer, glorifying God.

48 And after they had ended the prayer, the bishop Plato said: Peace to thee, Matthew, apostle of Christ!

49 And the blessed Matthew said to him: Peace to you!

50 And when they had sat down, the apostle said to the bishop Plato, and to all the clergy: I wish you, children, to know, Jesus having declared it to me, that the king of this city is going to send soldiers against me, the devil having entered into him, and manifestly armed him against us.

51 But let us give ourselves up to Jesus, and He will deliver us from every trial, and all who have believed in Him.

52 And the king, plotting against the blessed Matthew how he should lay hands on him, and seeing also that the believers were very many, was very much at fault, and was in great difficulty.

53 Therefore the wicked and unclean devil who had come forth from the king's wife, and his son, and his daughter-in-law, put to flight by Matthew, having transformed himself into the likeness of a soldier, stood before the king, and said to him:

54 O king, why art thou thus put to the worse by this stranger and sorcerer?

55 Knowest thou not that he was a publican, but now he has been called an apostle by Jesus, who was crucified by the Jews?

56 For, behold, thy wife, and thy son, and thy daughter-in-law, instructed by him, have believed in him, and along with him sing in the church.

57 And now, behold, Matthew is going forth, and Plato with him, and they are going to the gate called Heavy; but make haste, and thou wilt find them, and thou shalt do to him all that may be pleasing in thine eyes.

58 The king having heard this, and being the more exasperated by the pretended soldier, sent against the blessed Matthew four soldiers, having threatened them, and said: Unless you bring Matthew to me, I shall burn you alive with fire; and the punishment which he is to undergo, you shall endure.

59 And the soldiers, having been thus threatened by the king, go in arms to where the Apostle Matthew and the bishop Plato are.

60 And when they came near them, they heard their speaking indeed, but saw no one.

61 And having come, they said to the king: We pray thee, O king, we went and found no one, but only heard the voices of persons talking.

62 And the king, being enraged, and having blazed up like fire, gave orders to send other ten soldiers--man-eaters--saying to them:

63 Go stealthily to the place, and tear them in pieces alive, and eat up Matthew, and Plato, who is with him.

64 And when they were about to come near the blessed Matthew, the Lord Jesus Christ, having come in the likeness of a most beautiful boy, holding a torch of fire, ran to meet them, burning out their eyes. And they, having cried out and thrown their arms from them, fled, and came to the king, being speechless.

65 And the demon who had before appeared to the king in the from of a soldier, being again transformed into the form of a soldier, stood before the king, and said to him: Thou seest, O king, this stranger has bewitched them all.

66 Learn, then, how thou shall take him.

67 The king says to him: Tell me first wherein his strength is, that I may know, and then I will draw up against him with a great force.

68 And the demon, compelled by an angel, says to the king: Since thou wishest to hear accurately about him, O king, I will tell thee all the truth.

69 Really, unless he shall be willing to be taken by thee of his own accord, thou labourest in vain, and thou wilt not be able to hurt him; but if thou wishest to lay hands on him, thou wilt be struck by him with blindness, and thou wilt be paralyzed.

70 And if thou send a multitude of soldiers against him, they also will be struck with blindness, and will be paralyzed.

71 And we shall go, even seven unclean demons, and immediately make away with thee and thy whole camp, and destroy all the city with lightning, except those naming that awful and holy name of Christ; for wherever a footstep of theirs has come, thence, pursued, we flee.

72 And even if thou shall apply fire to him, to him the fire will be dew; and if thou shalt shut him up in a furnace, to him the furnace will be a church; and if thou shalt put him in chains in prison, and seal up the floors, the doors will open to him of their own accord, and all who believe in that name will go in, even they, and say, This prison is a church of the living God, and a holy habitation of those that live alone.

73 Behold, O king, I have told thee all the truth. The king therefore says to the pretended soldier: Since I do not know Matthew, come with me, and point him out to me from a distance, and take from me gold, as much as thou mayst wish, or go thyself, and with thy sword kill him, and Plato his associate.

74 The demon says to him: I cannot kill him. I dare not even look into his face, seeing that he has destroyed all our generation through the name of Christ, proclaimed through him.

75 The king says to him: And who art thou? And he says: I am the demon who dwelt in thy wife, and in thy son, and in thy daughter-in-law; and my name is Asmodaeus; and this Matthew drove me out of them.

76 And now, behold, thy wife, and thy son, and thy daughter-in-law sing along with him in the church.

77 And I know, O king, that thou also after this wilt believe in him.

78 The king says to him: Whoever thou art, spirit of many shapes, I adjure thee by the God whom he whom thou callest Matthew proclaims, depart hence without doing hurt to any one.

79 And straightway the demon, no longer like a soldier, but like smoke, became invisible; and as he fled he cried out:

80 O secret name, armed against us, I pray thee, Matthew, servant of the holy God, pardon me, and I will no longer remain in this city.

81 Keep thou thine own; but I go away into the fire everlasting.

82 Then the king, affected with great fear at the answer of the demon, remained quiet that day.

83 And the night having come, and he not being able to sleep because lie was hungry, leaped up at dawn, and went into the church, with only two soldiers without arms, to take Matthew by craft, that he might kill him.

84 And having summoned two friends of Matthew, he said to them: Show to Matthew, says he, that I wish to be his disciple.

85 And Matthew hearing, and knowing the craft of the tyrant, and having been warned also by the vision of the Lord to him, went forth out of the church, led by the hand by Plato, and stood in the gate of the church.

86 And they say to the king: Behold Matthew in the gate!

87 And he says: Who he is, or where he is, I see not.

88 And they said to him: Behold, he is in sight of thee.

89 And he says: All the while I see nobody. For he had been blinded by the power of God.

90 And he began to cry out: Woe to me, miserable! what evil has come upon me, for my eyes have been blinded, and all my limbs paralyzed?

91 O Asmodaeus Beelzebul Satan! all that thou hast said to me has come upon me.

92 But I pray thee, Matthew, servant of God, forgive me as the herald of the good God; for assuredly the Jesus proclaimed by the three days ago through the night appeared to me altogether resplendent as with lightning, like a beautiful young man, and said to me, Since thou art entertaining evil counsels in the wickedness of thine heart in regard to my servant Matthew, know I have disclosed to him that

through thee will be the release of his body.

93 And straightway I saw him going up into heaven.

94 If therefore he is thy God, and if he wishes thy body to be buried in our city for a testimony of the salvation of the generations after this, and for the banishing of the demons, I shall know the truth for myself by this, by thee laying on hands upon me, and I shall receive my sight.

95 And the apostle having laid his hands upon his eyes, and saying EPHPHATHA, Jesus, he made him receive his sight instantly.

96 And straightway the king, laying hold of the apostle, and leading him by the right hand, brought him by craft into the palace; and Plato was on Matthew's left hand, going along with him, and keeping hold of him.

97 Then Matthew says: O crafty tyrant, how long dost thou not fulfil the works of thy father the devil?

98 And he was enraged at what had been said; for he perceived that he would inflict upon him a more bitter death.

99 For he resolved to put him to death by fire. And he commanded several executioners to come, and to lead him away to the place by the seashore, where the execution of malefactors was wont to take place, saying to the executioners:

100 I hear, says he, that the God whom he proclaims delivers from fire those who believe in him.

101 Having laid him, therefore, on the ground on his back, and stretched him out, pierce his hands and feet with iron nails, and cover him over with paper, having smeared it with dolphins' oil, and cover him up with brimstone and asphalt and pitch, and put tow and brushwood above.

102 Thus apply the fire to him; and if any of the same tribe with him rise up against you, he shall get the same punishment.

103 And the apostle exhorted the brethren to remain undismayed, and that they should rejoice, and accompany him with great meekness, singing and praising God, because they were deemed worthy to have the relics of the apostle.

104 Having therefore come to the place, the executioners, like most evil wild beasts, pinned down to the ground Matthew's hands and feet with long nails; and having done everything as they had been bid, applied the fire.

105 And they indeed laboured closely, kindling it all round; but all the fire was changed into dew, so that the brethren, rejoicing, cried out:

106 The only God is the Christians', who assists Matthew, in whom also we have believed: the only God is the Christians', who preserves His own apostle in the fire.

107 And by the voice the city was shaken.

108 And some of the executioners, having gone forth, said to the king:

109 We indeed, O king, by every contrivance of vengeance, have kindled the fire; but the sorcerer by a certain name puts it out, calling upon Christ, and invoking his cross; and the Christians surrounding him play with the fire, and walking in it with naked feet, laugh at us, and we have fled ashamed.

110 Then he ordered a multitude to carry coals of fire from the furnace of the bath in the palace, and the twelve gods of gold and silver; and place them, says he, in a circle round the sorcerer, lest he may even somehow bewitch the fire from the furnace of the palace.

111 And there being many executioners and soldiers, some carried the coals; and others, bearing the gods, brought them.

112 And the king accompanied them, watching lest any of the Christians should steal one of his gods, or bewitch the fire.

113 And when they came near the place where the apostle was nailed down, his face was looking towards heaven, and

all his body was covered over with the paper, and much brushwood over his body to the height of ten cubits.

114 And baring ordered the soldiers to set the gods in a circle round Matthew, five cubits off, securely fastened that they might not fall, again he ordered the coal to be thrown on, and to kindle the fire at all points.

115 And Matthew, having looked up to heaven, cried out, ADONAI ELOI SABAOTH MARMARI MARMUNTH; that is, O God the Father, O Lord Jesus Christ, deliver me, and burn down their gods which they worship; and let the fire also pursue the king even to his palace, but not to his destruction: for perhaps he will repent and be converted.

116 And when he saw the fire to be monstrous in height, the king, thinking that Matthew was burnt up, laughed aloud, and said:

117 Has thy magic been of any avail to thee, Matthew? Can thy Jesus now give thee any help?

118 And as he said this a dreadful wonder appeared; for all the fire along with the wood went away froth Matthew, and was poured round about their gods, so that nothing of the gold or the silver was any more seen; and the king fled, and said:

119 Woe's me, that my gods are destroyed by the rebuke of Matthew, of which the weight was a thousand talents of gold and a thousand talents of silver.

120 Better are the gods of stone and of earthenware, in that they are neither melted nor stolen.

121 And when the fire had thus utterly destroyed their gods, and burnt up many soldiers, there came to pass again another stranger wonder.

122 For the fire, in the likeness of a great and dreadful dragon, chased the tyrant as far as the palace, and ran hither and thither round the king, not letting him go into the palace.

123 And the king, chased by the fire, and not allowed to go into his palace, turned back to where Matthew was, and cried out, saying:

124 I beseech thee, whoever thou art, O mail, whether magician or sorcerer or god, or angel of God, whom so great a pyre has not touched, remove from me this dreadful and fiery dragon; forget the evil I have done, as also when thou madest me receive my sight.

125 And Matthew, having rebuked the fire, and the flames having been extinguished, and the dragon having become invisible, stretching his eyes to heaven, and praying in Hebrew, and commending his spirit to the Lord, said: Peace to you!

126 And having glorified the Lord, he went to his rest about the sixth hour.

127 Then the king, having ordered more soldiers to come, and the bed to be brought from the palace, which had a great show of gold, he ordered the apostle to be laid on it, and carried to the palace.

128 And the body of the apostle was lying as if in sleep, and his robe and his tunic unstained by the fire; and sometimes they saw him on the bed, and sometimes following, and sometimes going before the bed, and with his right hand put upon Plato's head, and singing along with the multitude, so that both the king and the soldiers, with the crowd, were struck with astonishment.

129 And many diseased persons and demoniacs, having only touched the bed, were made sound; and as many as were savage in appearance, in that same hour were changed into the likeness of other men.

130 And as the bed was going into the palace, we all saw Matthew rising up, as it were, from the bed, and going into heaven, led by the hand by a beautiful boy; and twelve men in shining garments came to meet him, having never-fading and golden crowns on their head; and we saw how that child crowned Matthew, so as to be like them, and in a flash of lightning they went away to heaven.

131 And the king stood at the gate of

the palace, and ordered that no one should come in but the soldiers carrying the bed.

132 And having shut the doors, he ordered an iron coffin to be made, put the body of Matthew into it, and sealed it up with lead; through the eastern gate of the palace at midnight put it into a boat, no one knowing of it, and threw it into the deep part of the sea.

133 And through the whole night the brethren remained before the gate of the palace, spending the night, and singing; and when the dawn rose there was a voice:

134 O bishop Plato, carry the Gospel and the Psalter of David; go along with the multitude of the brethren to the east of the palace, and sing the Alleluia, and read the Gospel, and bring as an offering the holy bread; and having pressed three clusters from the vine into a cup, communicate with me, as the Lord Jesus showed us how to offer up when He rose from the dead on the third day.

135 And the bishop having run into the church, and taken the Gospel and the Psalter of David, and having assembled the presbyters and the multitude of the brethren, came to the east of the palace at the hour of sunrise; and having ordered the one who was singing to go upon a certain lofty stone, he began to praise in singing of a song to God:

136 Precious in the sight of God is the death of His saints.

137 And again: I laid me down and slept; I arose: because the Lord will sustain me.

138 And they listened to the singing of a song of David:

139 Shall he that is dead not rise again?

140 Now I shall raise him up for myself, saith the Lord.

141 And all shouted out the Alleluia.

142 And the bishop read the Gospel, and all cried out:

143 Glory to Thee, Thou who hast been glorified in heaven and on earth.

144 And so then they offered the gift of the holy offering for Matthew; and

having partaken for thanksgiving of the undefiled and life-giving mysteries of Christ, they all glorified God.

145 And it was about the sixth hour, and Plato sees the sea opposite about seven furlongs off; and, behold, Matthew was standing on the sea, and two men, one on each side, in shining garments, and the beautiful boy in front of them.

146 And all the brethren saw these things, and they heard them saying Amen, Alleluia.

147 And one could see the sea fixed like a stone of crystal, and the beautiful boy its front of them, when out of the depth of the sea a cross came up, and at the end of the cross the coffin going up in which was the body of Matthew; and in the hour of the piercing on the cross, the boy placed the coffin on the ground, behind the palace towards the east, where the bishop had offered the offering for Matthew.

148 And the king having seen these things from the upper part of the house, and being terror-struck, went forth from the palace, and ran and worshipped towards the east at the coffin, and fell down before the bishop, and the presbyters, and the deacons, in repentance and confession, saying:

149 Truly I believe in the true God, Christ Jesus.

150 I entreat, give me the seal in Christ, and I will give you my palace, in testimony of Matthew, and you shall put the coffin upon my golden bed, in the great dining-room; only, having baptized me in it, communicate to me the Eucharist of Christ.

151 And the bishop having prayed, and ordered him to take off his clothes, and having examined him for a long time, and he having confessed and wept over what he had done, having sealed him, and anointed him with oil, put him down into the sea, in the name of Father, and Son, and Holy Ghost.

152 And when he came up from the water he ordered him to put on himself splendid garments, and so then having

given praise and thanks, communicating the holy bread and mixed cup, the bishop first gave them to the king, saying:

153 Let this body of Christ, and this cup, His blood shed for us, be to thee for the remission of sins unto life.

154 And a voice was heard from on high: Amen, amen, amen.

155 And when he had thus communicated in fear and joy, the apostle appeared and said:

156 King Fulvanus, thy name shall no longer be Fulvanus; but thou shall be called Matthew.

157 And thou, the son of the king, shall no longer be called Fulvanus, but Matthew also; and thou Ziphagia, the wife of the king, shall be called Sophia; and Erva, the wife of your son, shall be called Synesis.

158 And these names of yours shall be written in the heavens, and there shall not fail of your loins from generation to generation.

159 And in that same hour Matthew appointed the king a presbyter, and he was thirty-seven years old; and the king's son he appointed deacon, being seventeen years old; and the king's wife he appointed a presbyteress; and his son's wife he appointed a deaconess, and she also was seventeen years old.

160 And then he thus blessed them, saying:

161 The blessing and the grace of our Lord Jesus Christ shall be with you to time everlasting.

162 Then the king, having awakened out of sleep, and rejoiced with all his house at the vision of the holy Apostle Matthew, praised God.

163 And the king, having gone into his palace, broke all the idols to pieces, and gave a decree to those in his kingdom, writing thus:

164 King Matthew, to all those under my kingdom, greeting.

165 Christ having appeared upon earth, and having saved the human race, the so-called gods nave been found to be deceivers, and soul-destroyers, and plotters against the human race.

166 Whence, divine grace having shone abroad, and come even to us, and we having come to the knowledge of the deception of the idols, that it is vain anti false, it has seemed good to our divinity that there should not be many gods, but one, and one only, the God in the heavens.

167 And you, having received this our decree, keep to the purport of it, and break to pieces and destroy every idol; and if any one shall be detected from this time forth serving idols, or concealing them, let such an one be subjected to punishment by the sword.

168 Farewell all, because we also are well.

169 And when this order was given out, all, rejoicing and exulting, broke their idols to pieces, crying out and saying: There is one only God, He who is in the heavens, who does good to men.

170 And after all these things had come to pass, Matthew the apostle of Christ appeared to the bishop Plato, and said to him:

171 Plato, servant of God, and our brother, be it known unto thee, that after three years shall be thy rest in the Lord, and exultation to ages of ages.

172 And the king himself, whom after my own name I have called Matthew, shall receive the throne of thy bishopric, and after him his son.

173 And he, having said Peace to thee and all the saints, went to heaven.

174 And after three years the bishop Plato rested in the Lord.

175 And King Matthew succeeded him, having given up his kingdom willingly to another, whence there was given him grace against unclean demons, and he cured every affliction.

176 And he advanced his son to be a presbyter, and made him second to himself.

177 And Saint Matthew finished his course in the country of the man-eaters, in the city of Myrna, on the sixteenth of the month of November, our Lord Jesus Christ reigning, to whom be glory and

strength, now and ever, and to ages of ages. Amen.

THE ACTS AND MARTYRDOM OF THE HOLY APOSTLE ANDREW

1 WHAT we have all, both presbyters and deacons of the churches of Achaia, beheld with our eyes, we have written to all the churches established in the name of Christ Jesus, both in the east and west, north and south.

2 Peace to you, and to all who believe in one God, perfect Trinity, true Father unbegotten, true Son only-begotten, true Holy Spirit proceeding from the Father, and abiding in the Son, in order that there may be shown one Holy Spirit subsisting in the Father and Son in precious Godhead.

3 This faith we have learned from the blessed Andrew, the apostle of oar Lord Jesus Christ, whose passion also we, having seen it set forth before our eyes, have not hesitated to give an account of, according to the degree of ability we have.

4 Accordingly the proconsul AEgeates, having come into the city of Patras, began to compel those believing in Christ to worship the idols; to whom the blessed Andrew, running up, said:

5 It behoved thee, being a judge of men, to acknowledge thy Judge who is in the heaven, and having acknowledged Him, to worship Him; and worshipping Him who is the true God, to turn away thy thoughts from those which are not true gods.

6 To whom AEgeates said: Art thou Andrew, who destroyest the temples of the gods, and persuadest men about the religion which, having lately made its appearance, the emperors of the Romans have given orders to suppress?

7 The blessed Andrew said: The emperors of the Romans have never recognised the truth.

8 And this the Son of God, who came on account of the salvation of men, manifestly teaches--that these idols are not only not gods, but also most shameful demons, and hostile to the human race, teaching men to offend God, so that, by being offended, He turns away and will not hearken; that therefore, by His turning away and not hearkening, they may be held captive by the devil; and that they might work them to such a degree, that when they go out of the body they may be found deserted and naked, carrying nothing with them but sins.

9 AEgeates said: These are superfluous and vain words: as for your Jesus, for proclaiming these things to the Jews they nailed him to the tree of the cross.

10 The blessed Andrew answering, said: Oh, if thou wouldst recognise the mystery of the cross, with what reasonable love the Author of the life of the human race for our restoration endured this tree of the cross, not unwillingly, but willingly!

11 AEgeates said: Seeing that, betrayed by his own disciple, and seized by the Jews, he was brought before the procurator, and according to their request was nailed up by the procurator's soldiers, in what way dost thou say that he willingly endured the tree of the cross?

12 The holy Andrew said: For this reason I say willingly, since I was with Him when he was betrayed by His disciple.

13 For before He was betrayed, He spoke to us to the effect that He should be betrayed and crucified for the salvation of men, and foretold that He should rise again on the third day.

14 To whom my brother Peter said, Far be it from thee, Lord; let this by no means be.

15 And so, being angry, He said to Peter, Get thee behind me, Satan; for thou art not disposed to the things of God.

16 And in order that He might most fully explain that He willingly underwent the passion, He said to us, I have power to lay down my life, and I have power to take it again.

17 And, last of all, while He was supping with us, He said, One of you will betray me.

18 At these words, therefore, all becoming exceedingly grieved, in order that the surmise might be free from doubt, He made it clear, saying, To whomsoever I shall give the piece of bread out of my hand, he it is who betrays me.

19 When, therefore, He gave it to one of our fellow-disciples, and gave an account of things to come as if they were already present, He showed that He was to be willingly betrayed.

20 For neither did He run away, and leave His betrayer at fault; but remaining in the place in which He knew that he was, He awaited him.

21 AEgeates said: I wonder that thou, being a sensible man, shouldst wish to uphold him on any terms whatever; for, whether willingly or unwillingly, all the same, thou admittest that he was fastened to the cross.

22 The blessed Andrew said: This is what I said, if now thou apprehendest, that great is the mystery of the cross, which, if thou wishest, as is likely, to hear, attend to me.

23 AEgeates said: A mystery it cannot be called, but a punishment.

24 The blessed Andrew said: This punishment is the mystery of man's restoration. If thou wilt listen with any attention, thou wilt prove it.

25 AEgeates said: I indeed will hear patiently; but thou, unless thou submissively obey me, shalt receive the mystery of the cross in thyself.

26 The blessed Andrew answered: If I had been afraid of the tree of the cross, I should not have proclaimed the glory of the cross.

27 AEgeates said: Thy speech is foolish, because thou proclaimest that the cross is not a punishment, and through thy foolhardiness thou art not afraid of the punishment of death.

28 The holy Andrew said: It is not through foolhardiness, but through faith, that I am not afraid of the punishment of death; for the death of sins is hard.

29 And on this account I wish thee to hear the mystery of the cross, in order that thou perhaps, acknowledging it, mayst believe, and believing, mayst come somehow or other to the renewing of thy soul.

30 AEgeates said: That which is shown to have perished is for renewing.

31 Do you mean that my soul has perished, that thou makest me come to the renewing of it through the faith, I know not what, of which thou hast spoken?

32 The blessed Andrew answered: This it is which I desired time to learn, which also I shall teach and make manifest, that though the souls of men are destroyed, they shall be renewed through the mystery of the cross.

33 For the first man through the tree of transgression brought in death; and it was necessary for the human race, that through the suffering of the tree, death, which had come into the world, should be driven out.

34 And since the first man, who brought death into the world through the transgression of the tree, had been produced from the spotless earth, it was necessary that the Son of God should be begotten a perfect man from the spotless virgin, that He should restore eternal life, which men had lost through Adam, and should cut off the tree of carnal appetite through the tree of the cross.

35 Hanging upon the cross, He stretched out His blameless hands for the hands which had been incontinently stretched out; for the most sweet food of the forbidden tree He received gall

for food; and taking our mortality upon Himself, He made a gift of His immortality to us.

36 AEgeates said: With these words thou shalt be able to lead away those who shall believe in thee; but unless thou hast come to grant me this, that thou offer sacrifices to the almighty gods, I shall order thee, after having been scourged, to be fastened to that very cross which thou commendest.

37 The blessed Andrew said: To God Almighty, who alone is true, I bring sacrifice day by day not the smoke of incense, nor the flesh of bellowing bulls, nor the blood of goats, but sacrificing a spotless lamb day by day on the altar of the cross; and though all the people of the I faithful partake of His body and drink His blood, the Lamb that has been sacrificed remains after this entire and alive.

38 Truly, therefore, is He sacrificed, andtruly is His body eaten by the people, and His blood is likewise drunk; nevertheless, as I have said, He remains entire, and spotless, and alive.

39 AEgeates said: How can this be?

40 The blessed Andrew said: If thou wouldest know, take the form of a disciple, that thou mayst learn what thou art inquiring after.

41 AEgeates said: I will exact of thee through tortures the gift of this knowledge.

42 The blessed Andrew declared: I wonder that thou, being an intelligent man, shouldest fall into the folly of thinking that thou mayst be able to persuade me, through thy tortures, to disclose to thee the sacred things of God.

43 Thou hast heard the mystery of the cross, thou hast heard the mystery of the sacrifice.

44 If thou be lievest in Christ the Son of God, who was crucified, I shall altogether disclose to thee in what manner the Lamb that has been slain may live, after having been sacrificed and eaten, remaining in His kingdom entire and spotless.

45 AEgeates said: And by what means does the lamb remain in his kingdom after he has been slain and eaten by all the people, as thou hast said?

46 The blessed Andrew said: If thou believest with all thy heart, thou shalt be able to learn: but if thou believest not, thou shalt not by any means attain to the idea of such truth.

47 Then AEgeates, enraged, ordered him to be shut up in prison, where, when he was shut up, a multitude of the people came together to him from almost all the province, so that they wished to kill AEgeates, and by breaking down the doors of the prison to set free the blessed Andrew the apostle.

48 Them the blessed Andrew admonished in these words, saying: Do not stir up the peace of our Lord Jesus Christ into seditious and devilish uproar.

49 For my Lord, when He was betrayed, endured it with all patience; He did not strive, He did not cry out, nor in the streets did any one hear Him crying out.

50 Therefore do ye also keep silence, quietness, and peace; and hinder not my martyrdom, but rather get yourselves also ready beforehand as athletes to the Lord, in order that you may overcome threatenings by a soul that has no fear of man, and that you may get the better of injuries through the endurance of the body.

51 For this temporary fall is not to be feared; but that should be feared which has no end.

52 The fear of men, then, is like smoke which, while it is raised and gathered together, disappears.

53 And those torments ought to be feared which never have an end.

54 For these torments, which happen to be somewhat light, any one can bear; but if they are heavy, they soon destroy life.

55 But those torments are everlasting, where there are daily weepings, and mournings, and lamentations, and

never-ending torture, to which the proconsul AEgeates is not afraid to go.

56 Be ye therefore rather prepared for this, that through temporary afflictions ye may attain to everlasting rest, and may flourish for ever, and reign with Christ.

57 The holy Apostle Andrew having admonished the people with these and such like words through the whole night, when the light of day dawned,

58 AEgeates having sent for him, ordered the blessed Andrew to be brought to him; and having sat down upon the tribunal, he said:

59 I have thought that thou, by thy reflection during the night, hast turned away thy thoughts from folly, and given up thy commendation of Christ that thou mightst be able to be with us, and not throw away the pleasures of life; for it is folly to come for any purpose to the suffering of the cross, and to give oneself up to most shameful punishments and burnings.

60 The holy Andrew answered: I shall be able to have joy with thee, if thou wilt believe in Christ, and throw away the worship of idols; for Christ has sent me to this province, in which I have acquired for Christ a people not the smallest.

61 AEgeates said: For this reason I compel thee to make a libation, that these people who have been deceived by thee may forsake the vanity of thy teaching, and may themselves offer grateful libations to the gods; for not even one city has remained in Achaia in which their temples have not been forsaken and deserted.

62 And now, through thee, let them be again restored to the worship of the images, in order that the gods also, who have been enraged against thee, being pleased by this, may bring it about that thou mayst return to their friendship anti ours.

63 But if not, thou awaitest varied tortures, on account of the vengeance of the gods; and after these, fastened to the tree of the cross which thou commendest, thou shall die.

64 The holy Andrew said: Listen, O son of death and chaff made ready for eternal burnings, to me, the servant of God and apostle of Jesus Christ.

65 Until now I have conversed with thee kindly about the perfection of the faith, in order that thou, receiving the exposition of the truth, being made perfect as its vindicator, mightest despise vain idols, and worship God, who is in the heavens;

66 But since thou remainest in the same shamelessness at last, and thinkest me to be afraid because of thy threats, bring against me whatever may seem to thee greater in the way of tortures.

67 For the more shall I be well pleasing to my King, the more I shall endure in tortures for the confession of His name.

68 Then the proconsul AEgeates, being enraged, ordered the apostle of Christ to be afflicted by tortures.

69 Being stretched out, therefore, by seven times three soldiers, and beaten with violence, he was lifted up and brought before the impious AEgeates.

70 And he spoke to him thus: Listen to me, Andrew, and withdraw thy thoughts from the outpouring of thy blood; but if thou wilt not hearken to me, I shall cause thee to perish on the tree of the cross.

71 The holy Andrew said: I am a slave of the cross of Christ, and I ought rather to pray to attain to the trophy of the cross than to be afraid; but for thee is laid up eternal torment, which, however, thou mayst escape after thou hast tested my endurance, if thou wilt believe in my Christ.

72 For I am afflicted about thy destruction, and I am not disturbed about my own suffering. For my suffering takes up a space of one day, or two at most; but thy torment for endless ages shall never come to a close.

73 Wherefore henceforward cease from adding to thy miseries, and lighting up everlasting fire for thyself.

74 AEgeates then being enraged, ordered the blessed Andrew to be

fastened to the cross.

75 And he having left them all, goes up to the cross, and says to it with a clear voice: Rejoice, O cross, which has been consecrated by the body of Christ, and adorned by His limbs as if with pearls.

76 Assuredly before my Lord went up on thee, thou hadst much earthly fear; but now invested with heavenly longing, thou art fitted up according to my prayer.

77 For I know, from those who believe, how many graces thou hast in Him, how many gifts prepared beforehand.

78 Free from care, then, and with joy, I come to thee, that thou also exulting mayst receive me, the disciple of Him that was hanged upon thee; because thou hast been always faithful to me, and I have desired to embrace thee.

79 O good cross, which hast received comeliness and beauty from the limbs of the Lord; O much longed for, and earnestly desired, and fervently sought after, and already prepared beforehand for my soul longing for thee, take me away from men, and restore me to my Master, in order that through thee He may accept me who through thee has redeemed me.

80 And having thus spoken, the blessed Andrew, standing on the ground, and looking earnestly upon the cross, stripped himself and gave his clothes to the executioners, having urged the brethren that the executioners should come and do what had been commanded them; for they were standing at some distance.

81 And they having come up, lifted him on the cross; and having stretched his body across with ropes, they only bound his feet, but did not sever his joints, having received this order from the proconsul: for he wished him to be in distress while hanging, and in the night-time, as he was suspended, to be eaten up alive by dogs.

82 And a great multitude of the brethren stood by, nearly twenty thousand; and having beheld the executioners standing off, and that they had done to the

blessed one nothing of what those who were hanged up suffer, they thought that they would again hear something from him; for assuredly, as he was hanging, he moved his head smiling.

83 And Stratocles inquired of him: Why art thou smiling, Andrew, servant of God?

84 Thy laughter makes us mourn and weep, because we are deprived of thee.

85 And the blessed Andrew answered him: Shall I not laugh at all, my son Stratocles, at the empty stratagem of AEgeates, through which he thinks to take vengeance upon us?

86 We have nothing to do with him and his plans. He cannot hear; for if he could, he would be aware, having learned it by experience, that a man of Jesus is unpunished.

87 And having thus spoken, he discoursed to them all in common, for the people ran together enraged at the unjust judgment of AEgeates:

88 Ye men standing by me, and women, and children, and elders, bond and free, and as many as will hear; I beseech you, forsake all this life, ye who have for my sake assembled here; and hasten to take upon you my life, which leads to heavenly things, and once for all despise all temporary things, confirming the purposes of those who believe in Christ.

89 And he exhorted them all, teaching that the sufferings of this transitory life are not worthy to be compared with the future recompense of the eternal life.

90 And the multitude hearing what was said by him, did not stand off from the place, and the blessed Andrew continued the rather to say to them more than he had spoken.

91 And so much was said by him, that a space of three days and nights was taken up, and no one was tired and went away from him.

92 And when also on the fourth day they beheld his nobleness, and the unweariedness of his intellect, and the multitude of his words, and the serviceableness of his exhortations, and

the stedfastness of his soul, and the sobriety of his spirit, and the fixedness of his mind, and the perfection of his reason, they were enraged against AEgeates;

93 And all with one accord hastened to the tribunal, and cried out against AEgeates, who was sitting, saying:

94 What is thy judgment, O proconsul? Thou hast judged wickedly; thy awards are impious.

95 In what has the man done wrong; what evil has he done?

96 The city has been put in an uproar; thou grievest us all; do not betray Caesar's city.

97 Grant willingly to the Achaians a just man; grant willingly to us a God-fearing man; do not put to death a godly man.

98 Four days he has been hanging, and is alive; having eaten nothing, he has filled us all.

99 Take down the man from the cross, and we shall all seek after wisdom; release the man, and to all Achaia will mercy be shown.

100 It is not necessary that he should suffer this, because, though hanging, he does not cease proclaiming the truth.

101 And when the proconsul refused to listen to them, at first indeed signing with his hand to the crowd to take themselves off, they began to be emboldened against him, being in number about twenty thousand.

102 And the proconsul having beheld that they had somehow become maddened, afraid that something frightful would befall him, rose up from the tribunal and went away with them, having promised to set free the blessed Andrew.

103 And some went on before to tell the apostle the cause for which they came to the place.

104 While all the crowd, therefore, was exulting that the blessed Andrew was going to be set free, the proconsul having come up, and all the brethren rejoicing along with Maximilla, the blessed Andrew, having heard this, said

to the brethren standing by:

105 What is it necessary for me to say to him, when I am departing to the Lord, that will I also say.

106 For what reason hast thou again come to us, AEgeates?

107 On what account dost thou, being a stranger to us, come to us?

108 What wilt thou again dare to do, what to contrive? Tell us.

109 Hast thou come to release us, as having changed thy mind?

110 I would not agree with thee that thou hadst really changed thy mind.

111 Nor would I believe thee, saying that thou art my friend.

112 Dost thou, O proconsul, release him that has been bound? By no means.

113 For I have One with whom I shall be for ever; I have One with whom I shall live to countless ages.

114 To Him I go; to Him I hasten, who also having made thee known to me, has said to me, Let not that fearful man terrify thee; do not think that he will lay hold of thee, who art mine: for he is thine enemy.

115 Therefore, having known thee through him who has turned towards me, I am delivered from thee.

116 But if thou wishest to believe in Christ, there will be opened up for time, as I promised thee, a way of access; but if thou hast come only to release me, I shall not be able after this to be brought down from this cross alive in the body.

117 For I and my kinsmen depart to our own, allowing thee to be what thou art, and what thou dost not know about thyself.

118 For already I see my King, already I worship Him, already I stand before Him, where the fellowship of the angels is, where He reigns the only emperor, where there is light without night, where the flowers never fade, where trouble is never known, nor the name of grief heard, where there are cheerfulness and exultation that have no end.

119 O blessed cross! without the longing for thee, no one enters into that

place.

120 But I am distressed, AEgeates, about thine own miseries, because eternal perdition is ready to receive thee.

121 Run then, for thine own sake, O pitiable one, while yet thou canst, lest perchance thou shouldst wish then when thou canst not.

122 When, therefore, he attempted to come near the tree of the cross, so as to release the blessed Andrew, with all the city applauding him, the holy Andrew said with a loud voice:

123 Do not suffer Andrew, bound upon Thy tree, to be released, O Lord; do not give me who am in Thy mystery to the shameless devil.

124 O Jesus Christ, let not Thine adversary release me, who have been hanged by Thy favour; O Father, let this insignificant man no longer humble him who has known Thy greatness.

125 The executioners, therefore, putting out their hands, were not able at all to touch him.

126 Others, then, and others endeavoured to release him, and no one at all was able to come near him; for their arms were benumbed.

127 Then the blessed Andrew, having adjured the people, said: I entreat you earnestly, brethren, that I may first make one prayer to my Lord.

128 So then set about releasing me. All the people therefore kept quiet because of the adjuration.

129 Then the blessed Andrew, with a loud cry, said: Do not permit, O Lord, Thy servant at this time to be removed from Thee; for it is time that my body be committed to the earth, and Thou shalt order me to come to Thee.

130 Thou who givest eternal life, my Teacher whom I have loved, whom on this cross I confess, whom I know, whom I possess, receive me, O Lord; and as I have confessed Thee and obeyed Thee, so now in this word hearken to me; and, before my body come down from the cross, receive me to Thyself, that through my departure there may be access to Thee of many of my kindred, finding rest for themselves in Thy majesty.

131 When, therefore, he had said this, he became in the sight of all glad and exulting; for an exceeding splendour like lightning coming forth out of heaven shone down upon him, and so encircled him, that in consequence of such brightness mortal eyes could not look upon him at all.

132 And the dazzling light remained about the space of half an hour.

133 And when he had thus spoken and glorified the Lord still more, the light withdrew itself, and he gave up the ghost, and along with the brightness itself he departed to the Lord in giving Him thanks.

134 And after the decease of the most blessed Andrew the apostle, Maximilla being the most powerful of the notable women, and continuing among those who had come, as soon as she learned that the apostle had departed to the Lord, came up and turned her attention to the cross, along with Stratocles, taking no heed at all of those standing by, and with reverence took down the body of the most blessed apostle from the cross.

135 And when it was evening, bestowing upon him the necessary care, she prepared the body for burial with costly spices, and aid it in her own tomb.

136 For she had been parted from AEgeates on account of his brutal disposition and lawless conduct, having chosen for herself a holy and quiet life; and having been united to the love of Christ, she spent her life blessedly along with the brethren.

137 AEgeates had been very importunate with her, and promised that he would make her mistress of his wealth; but not having been able to persuade her, he was greatly enraged, and was determined to make a public charge against all the people, and to send to Caesar an accusation against both Maximilla and all the people.

138 And while he was arranging these things in the presence of his officers, at the dead of night he rose up, and unseen by all his people, having been tormented by the devil, he fell down from a great height, and rolling into the midst of the market-place of the city, breathed his last.

139 And this was reported to his brother Stratocles; and he sent his servants, having told them that they should bury him among those who had died a violent death.

140 But he sought nothing of his substance, saying: Let not my Lord Jesus Christ, in whom I have believed, suffer me to touch anything whatever of the goods of my brother, that the condemnation of him who dared to cut off the apostle of the Lord may not disgrace me.

141 These things were done in the province of Achaia, in the city of Patras on the day before the kalends of December, where his good deeds are kept in mind even to this day, to the glory and praise of our Lord Jesus Christ, to whom be glory for ever and ever. Amen.

THE ACTS OF THE HOLY APOSTLES PETER AND PAUL

1 IT came to pass, after Paul went out of the island Gaudomeleta, that he came to Italy; and it was heard of by the Jews who were in Rome, the elder of the cities, that Paul demanded to come to Caesar.

2 Having fallen, therefore, into great grief and much despondency, they said among themselves: It does not please him that he alone has afflicted all our brethren and parents in Judaea and Samaria, and in all Palestine; and he has not been pleased with these, but, behold, he comes here also, having through imposition asked Caesar to destroy us.

3 Having therefore made an assembly against Paul, and having considered many proposals, it seemed good to them to go to Nero the emperor, to ask him not to allow Paul to come to Rome.

4 Having therefore got in readiness not a few presents, and having carried them with them, with supplication they came before him, saying:

5 We beseech thee, O good emperor, send orders into all the governments of your worship, to the effect that Paul is not to come near these parts; because this Paul, having afflicted all the nation of our fathers, has been seeking to come hither to destroy us also.

6 And the affliction, O most worshipful emperor, which we have from Peter is enough for us.

7 And the Emperor Nero, having heard these things, answered them:

8 It is according to your wish. And we write to all our governments that he shall not on any account come to anchor in the parts of Italy.

9 And they also informed Simon the magician, having sent for him, that, as has been said, he should not come into the parts of Italy.

10 And while they were thus doing, some of those that had repented out of the nations, and that had been baptized at the preaching of Peter, sent elders to Paul with a letter to the following effect:

11 Paul, dear servant of our Lord Jesus Christ, and brother of Peter, the first of the apostles, we have heard from the rabbis of the Jews that are in this Rome, the greatest of the cities, that they have asked Caesar to send into all his governments, in order that, wherever thou mayst be found, thou mayst be put to death. But we have believed, and do believe, that as God does not separate

the two great lights which He has made, so He is not to part you from each other, that is, neither Peter from Paul, nor Paul from Peter; but we positively believe in our Lord Jesus Christ, into whom we have been baptized, that we have become worthy also of your teaching.

12 And Paul, having received the two men sent with the letter on the twentieth of the month of May, became eager to go, and gave thanks to the Lord and Master Jesus Christ.

13 And having sailed from Gaudomeleta, he did not now come through Africa to the parts of Italy, but ran to Sicily, until he came to the city of Syracuse with the two then who had been sent from Rome to him.

14 And having sailed thence, he came to Rhegium of Calabria, and from Rhegium he crossed to Mesina, and there ordained a bishop, Bacchylus by name.

15 And when he came out of Mesina he sailed to Didymus, and remained there one night. And having sailed thence, he came to Pontiole on the second day.

16 And Dioscorus the shipmaster, who brought him to Syracuse, sympathizing with Paul because he had delivered his son from death, having left his own ship in Syracuse, accompanied him to Pontiole.

17 And some of Peter's disciples having been found there, and having received Paul, exhorted him to stay with them.

18 And he stayed a week, in hiding, because of the command of Caesar.

19 And all the toparchs were watching to seize and kill him. But Dioscorus the shipmaster, being himself also bald, wearing his shipmaster's dress, and speaking boldly, on the first day went out into the city of Pontiole.

20 Thinking therefore that he was Paul, they seized him, and beheaded him, and sent his head to Caesar.

21 Caesar therefore, having summoned the first men of the Jews, announced to them, saying: Rejoice with great joy, for Paul your enemy is dead.

22 And he showed them the head. Having therefore made great rejoicing on that day, which was the fourteenth of the month of June, each of the Jews fully believed it.

23 And Paul, being in Pontiole, and having heard that Dioscorus had been beheaded, being grieved with great grief, gazing into the height of the heaven, said:

24 O Lord Almighty in heaven, who hast appeared to me in every place whither I have gone on account of Thine only-begotten Word, our Lord Jesus Christ, punish this city, and bring out all who have believed in God and followed His word.

25 He said to them therefore: Follow me: And going forth from Pontiole with those who Met believed in the word of God, they came to a place called Baias; and looking up with their eyes, they all see that city called Pontiole sunk into the sea-shore about one fathom; and there it is until this day, for a remembrance, under the sea.

26 And having gone forth from Baias, they went to Gaitas, and there he taught Timothy the word of God.

27 And he stayed there three days in the house of Erasmus, whom Peter sent from Rome to teach the Gospel of God.

28 And having come forth from Gaitas, he came to the castle called Taracinas, and stayed there seven days in the house of Caesarius the deacon, whom Peter had ordained by the laying on of hands.

29 And sailing thence, be came by the river to a place called Tribus Tabernes.

30 And those who bad been saved out of the city of Pontiole that had been swallowed up, reported to Caesar in Rome that Pontiole had been swallowed up, with all its multitude.

31 And the emperor, being in great grief on account of the city, having summoned the chief of the Jews, said to them:

32 Behold, on account of what I heard from you, I have caused Paul to be beheaded, and on account of this the city has been swallowed up.

33 And the chief of the Jews said to Caesar: Most worshipful emperor, did we not say to thee that he troubled all the country of the East, and perverted

our fathers?

34 It is better therefore, most worshipful emperor, that one city be destroyed, and not the seat of thine empire; for this had Rome to suffer.

35 And the emperor, having heard their words, was appeased.

36 And Paul stayed in Tribus Tabernes four days. And departing thence, he came to Appii Forum, which is called Vicusarape; and having slept there that night, he saw one sitting on a golden chair, and a multitude of blacks standing beside him, saying:

37 I have to-day made a son murder his father. Another said: And I have made a house fall, and kill parents with children.

38 And they reported to him many evil deeds--some of one kind, some of another.

39 And another coming, reported to him: I have managed that the bishop Juvenalius, whom Peter ordained, should sleep with the abbess Juliana.

40 And having heard all these things when sleeping in that Appii Forum, near Vicusarape, straightway and immediately be sent to Rome one of those who had followed him from Pontiole to the bishop Juvenalius, telling him this same thing which had just been done.

41 And on the following day, Juvenalius, running, threw himself at the feet of Peter, weeping and lamenting, and saying what had just befallen; and he recounted to him the matter, and said: I believe that this is the light which thou wast awaiting.

42 And Peter said to him: How is it possible that it is he when he is dead?

43 And Juvenalius the bishop took to Peter him that had been sent by Paul, and be reported to him that he was alive, and on his way, and that he was at Appii Forum.

44 And Peter thanked and glorified the God and Father of our Lord Jesus Christ.

45 Then having summoned his disciples that believed, he sent them to Paul as far as Tribus Tabernes. And the distance from Rome to Tribus Tabernes is thirty-eight miles.

46 And Paul seeing them, having given thanks to our Lord Jesus Christ, took courage; and departing thence, they slept in the city called Aricia.

47 And a report went about in the city of Rome that Paul the brother of Peter was coming.

48 And those that believed in God rejoiced with great joy. And there was great consternation among the Jews; and having gone to Simon the magian, they entreated him, saying:

49 Report to the emperor that Paul is not dead, but that he is alive, and has come.

50 And Simon said to the Jews: What head is it, then, which came to Caesar from Pontiole? Was it not bald also?

51 And Paul having come to Rome, great fear fell upon the Jews.

52 They came together therefore to him, and exhorted him, saying:

53 Vindicate the faith in which thou wast born; for it is not right that thou, being a Hebrew, and of the Hebrews, shouldst call thyself teacher of Gentiles, and vindicator of the uncircumcised; and, being thyself circumcised, that thou shouldst bring to nought the faith of the circumcision.

54 And when thou seest Peter, contend against his teaching, because be has destroyed all the bulwarks of our law; for he has prevented the keeping of Sabbaths and new moons, and the holidays appointed by the law.

55 And Paul, answering, said to them: That I am a true Jew, by this you can prove; because also you have been able to keep the Sabbath, and to observe the true circumcision; for assuredly on the day of the Sabbath God rested from all His works.

56 We have fathers, and patriarchs, and the law. What, then, does Peter preach in the kingdom of the Gentiles?

57 But if he shall wish to bring in any new teaching, without any tumult, and envy, and trouble, send him word, that we may see, and in your presence I shall convict him.

58 But if his teaching be true, supported by the book and testimony of the

Hebrews, it becomes all of us to submit to him.

59 Paul saying these and such like things, the Jews went and said to Peter: Paul of the Hebrews has come, and entreats thee to come to him, since those who have brought him say that he cannot meet whomsoever he may wish until he appear before Caesar.

60 And Peter having heard, rejoiced with great joy; and rising up, immediately went to him.

61 And seeing each other, they wept for joy; and long embracing each other, they bedewed each other with tears.

62 And when Paul had related to Peter the substance of all his doings, and how, through the disasters of the ship, he had come, Peter also told him what he had suffered from Simon the magician, and all his plots. And having told these things, he went away towards evening.

63 And in the morning of the following day, at dawn, behold, Peter coming, finds a multitude of the Jews before Paul's door. And there was a great uproar between the Christian Jews and the Gentiles. For, on the one hand, the Jews said:

64 We are a chosen race, a royal priesthood, the friends of Abraham, and Isaac, and Jacob, and all the prophets, with whom God spake, to whom He showed His own mysteries and His great wonders.

65 But you of the Gentiles are no great thing in your lineage; if otherwise, you have become polluted and abominable by idols and graven images.

66 While the Jews were saying such things, and such-like, those of the Gentiles answered, saying:

67 We, when we heard the truth, straightway followed it, having abandoned our errors.

68 But you, both knowing the mighty deeds of your fathers, and seeing the signs of the prophets, and having received the law, and gone through the sea with dry feet, and seen your enemies sunk in its depths, and the pillar of fire by night and of cloud by day shining upon you, and manna having been given to you out of heaven, and water flowing to you out of a rock,--after all these things you fashioned to yourselves the idol of a calf, and worshipped the graven image.

69 But we, having seen none of the signs, believe to be a Saviour the God whom you have forsaken in unbelief.

70 While they were contending in these and such-like words, the Apostle Paul said that they ought not to make such attacks upon each other, but that they should rather give heed to this, that God had fulfilled His promises which He swore to Abraham our father, that in his seed he should inherit all the nations.

71 For there is no respect of persons with God. As many as have sinned in law shall be judged according to law, and as many as have sinned without law shall perish without law.

72 But we, brethren, ought to thank God that, according to His mercy, He has chosen us to be a holy people to Himself: so that in this we ought to boast, whether Jews or Greeks; for you are all one in the belief of His name.

73 And Paul having thus spoken, both the Jews and they of the Gentiles were appeased.

74 But the rulers of the Jews assailed Peter. And Peter, when they accused him of having renounced their synagogues, said:

75 Hear, brethren, the holy Spirit about the patriarch David, promising, Of the fruit of thy womb shall He set upon thy throne.

76 Him therefore to whom the Father said, Thou art my Son, this day have I begotten Thee, the chief priests through envy crucified; but that He might accomplish the salvation of the world, it was allowed that He should suffer all these things.

77 Just as, therefore, from the side of Adam Eve was created, so also from the side of Christ was created the Church, which has no spot nor blemish.

78 In Him, therefore, God has opened an entrance to all the sons of Abraham, and Isaac, and Jacob, in order that they may be in the faith of profession towards Him, and have life and salvation in His name.

79 Turn, therefore, and enter into the joy of your father Abraham, because God hath fulfilled what He promised to him.

80 Whence also the prophet says, The Lord hath sworn, and will not repent: Thou art a priest for ever, after the order of Melchizedec.

81 For a priest He became upon the cross, when He offered the whole burnt-offering of His own body and blood as a sacrifice for all the world.

82 And Peter saying this and such-like, the most part of the people believed.

83 And it happened also that Nero's wife Libia, and the yoke-fellow of Agrippa the prefect, Agrippina by name, thus believed, so that also they went away from beside their own husbands.

84 And on account of the teaching of Paul, many, despising military life, clung to God; so that even from the emperor's bed-chamber some came to him, and having become Christians, were no longer willing to return to the army or the palace.

85 When, consequently, the people were making a seditious murmuring, Simon, moved with zeal, rouses himself, and began to say many evil things about Peter, saying that he was a wizard and a cheat.

86 And they believed him, wondering at his miracles; for he made a brazen serpent move itself, and stone statues to laugh and move themselves, and himself to run and suddenly to be raised into the air.

87 But as a set-off to these, Peter healed the sick by a word, by praying made the blind to see, put demons to flight by a command; sometimes he even raised the dead.

88 And he said to the people that they should not only flee from Simon's deceit, but also that they should expose him, that they might not seem to be slaves to the devil.

89 And thus it happened that all pious men abhorred Simon the magian, and proclaimed him impious.

90 But those who adhered to Simon strongly affirmed Peter to be a magian, bearing false witness as many of them as were with Simon the magian; so that the matter came even to the ears of Nero the Caesar, and he gave order to bring Simon the magian before him.

91 And he, coming in, stood before him, and began suddenly to assume different forms, so that on a sudden he became a child, and after a little an old man, and at other times a young man; for he changed himself both in face and stature into different forms, and was in a frenzy, having the devil as his servant.

92 And Nero beholding this, supposed him to be truly the son of God; but the Apostle Peter showed him to be both a liar and a wizard, base and impious and apostate, and in all things opposed to the truth of God, and that nothing yet remained except that his wickedness, being made apparent by the command of God, might be made manifest to them all.

93 Then Simon, having gone in to Nero, said: Hear, O good emperor: I am the son of God come down from heaven.

94 Until now I have endured Peter only calling himself an apostle; but now he has doubled the evil: for Paul also himself teaches the same things, and having his mind turned against me, is said to preach along with him; in reference to whom, if thou shalt not contrive their destruction, it is very plain that thy kingdom cannot stand.

95 Then Nero, filled with concern, ordered to bring them speedily before him.

96 And on the following day Simon the magian, and Peter and Paul the apostles of Christ, having come in to Nero, Simon said:

97 These are the disciples of the Nazarene, and it is not at all well that they should be of the people of the Jews, Nero said: What is a Nazarene?

98 Simon said: There is a city of Judah which has always been opposed to us, called Nazareth, and to it the teacher of these men belonged.

99 Nero said: God commands us to love every man; why, then, dost thou persecute them? Simon said: This is a

race of men who have turned aside all Judaea from believing in me.

100 Nero said to Peter: Why are you thus unbelieving, according to your race? Then Peter said to Simon: Thou hast been able to impose upon all, but upon me never; and those who have been deceived, God has through me recalled from their error.

101 And since thou hast learned by experience that thou canst not get the better of me, I wonder with what face thou boastest thyself before the emperor, and supposest that through thy magic art thou shalt overcome the disciples of Christ.

102 Nero said: Who is Christ? Peter said: He is what this Simon the magian affirms himself to be; but this is a most wicked man, and his works are of the devil.

103 But if thou wishest to know, O good emperor, the things that have been done in Judaea about Christ, take the writings of Pontius Pilate sent to Claudius, and thus thou wilt know all.

104 And Nero ordered them to be brought, and to he read in their presence; and they were to the following effect:

105 Pontius Pilate to Claudius, greeting. There has lately happened an event which I myself was concerned in.

106 For the Jews through envy have inflicted on themselves, and those coming after them, dreadful judgments.

107 Their fathers had promises that their God would send them his holy one from heaven, who according to reason should be called their king, and he had promised to send him to the earth by means of a virgin.

108 He, then, when I was procurator, came into Judaea. And they saw him enlightening the blind, cleansing lepers, healing paralytics, expelling demons from men, raising the dead, subduing the winds, walking upon the waves of the sea, and doing many other wonders, and all the people of the Jews calling him Son of God.

109 Then the chief priests, moved with envy against him, seized him, and delivered him to me; and telling one lie after another, they said that he was a wizard, and did contrary to their law.

110 And I, having believed that these things were so, gave him up, after scourging him, to their will; and they crucified him, and after he was buried set guards over him.

111 But he, while my soldiers were guarding him, rose on the third day.

112 And to such a degree was the wickedness of the Jews inflamed against him, that they gave money to the soldiers, saying, Say his disciples have stolen his body.

113 But they, having taken the money, were not able to keep silence as to what had happened; for they have testified that they have seen him (After he was) risen, and that they have received money from the Jews.

114 These things, therefore, have I reported, that no one should falsely speak otherwise, and that thou shouldest not suppose that the falsehoods of the Jews are to be believed.

115 And the letter having been read, Nero said: Tell me, Peter, were all these things thus done by him?

116 Peter said: They were, with your permission, O good emperor.

117 For this Simon is full of lies and deceit, even if it should seem that he is what he is not--a god.

118 And in Christ there is all excellent victory through God and through man, which that incomprehensible glory assumed which through man deigned to come to the assistance of men.

119 But in this Simon there are two essences, of man and of devil, who through man endeavours to ensnare men.

120 Simon said: I wonder, O good emperor, that you reckon this man of any consequence--a man uneducated, a fisherman of the poorest, and endowed with power neither in word nor by rank.

121 But, that I may not long endure him as an enemy, I shall forthwith order my angels to come and avenge me upon him.

122 Peter said: I am not afraid of thy angels; but they shall be much more

afraid of me in the power and trust of my Lord Jesus Christ, whom thou falsely declarest thyself to be.

123 Nero said: Art thou not afraid, Peter, of Simon, who confirms is godhead by deeds?

124 Peter said: Godhead is in Him who searcheth the hidden things of the heart.

125 Now then, tell me what I am thinking about, or what I am doing.

126 I disclose to thy servants who are here what my thought is, before he tells lies about it, in order that he may not dare to lie as to what I am thinking about.

127 Nero said: Come hither, and tell me what thou art thinking about. Peter said: Order a barley loaf to be brought, and to be given to me secretly.

128 And when he ordered it to be brought, and secretly given to Peter, Peter said: Now tell us, Simon, what has been thought about, or what said, or what done.

129 Nero said: Do you mean me to believe that Simon does not know these things, who both raised a dead man, and presented himself on the third day after he had been beheaded, and who has done whatever he said he would do?

130 Peter said: But he did not do it before me, Nero said: But he did all these before me.

131 For assuredly he ordered angels to come to him, and they came.

132 Peter said: If he has done what is very great, why does he not do what is very small?

133 Let him tell what I had in my mind, and what I have done.

134 Nero said: Between you, I do not know myself. Simon said: Let Peter say what I am thinking of, or what I am doing.

135 Peter said: What Simon has in his mind I shall show that I know, by my doing what he is thinking about.

136 Simon said: Know this, O emperor, that no one knows the thoughts of men, but God alone. Is not, therefore, Peter lying?

137 Peter said: Do thou, then, who sayest that thou art the Son of God, tell what I have in my mind; disclose, if

thou canst, what I have just done in secret.

138 For Peter, having blessed the barley loaf which he had received, and hawing broken it with his right hand and his left, had heaped it up in his sleeves.

139 Then Simon, enraged that he was not able to tell the secret of the apostle, cried out, saying: Let great dogs come forth, and eat him up before Caesar.

140 And suddenly there appeared great dogs, and rushed at Peter.

141 But Peter, stretching forth his hands to pray, showed to the dogs the loaf which he had blessed; which the dogs seeing, no longer appeared.

142 Then Peter said to Nero: Behold, I have shown thee that I knew what Simon was thinking of, not by words, but by deeds; for he, having promised that he would bring angels against me, has brought dogs, in order that he might show that he had not god-like but dog-like angels.

143 Then Nero said to Simon: What is it, Simon?

144 I think we have got the worst of it. Simon said: This man, both in Judaea and in all Palestine and Caesarea, has done the same to me; and from very often striving with me, he has learned that this is adverse to them.

145 This, then, he has learned how to escape from me; for the thoughts of men no one knows but God alone.

146 And Peter said to Simon: Certainly thou feignest thyself to be a god; why, then, dost thou not reveal the thoughts of every man?

147 Then Nero, turning to Paul, said: Why dost thou say nothing, Paul?

148 Paul answered and said: Know this, O emperor, that if thou permittest this magician to do such things, it will bring an access of the greatest mischief to thy country, and will bring down thine empire from its position.

149 Nero said to Simon: What sayest thou?

150 Simon said: If I do not manifestly hold myself out to be a god, no one will bestow upon me due reverence.

151 Nero said: And now, why dost thou delay, and not show thyself to be a god,

in order that these men may be punished?

152 Simon said: Give orders to build for me a lofty tower of wood, and I, going up upon it, will call my angels, and order them to take me, in the sight of all, to my father in heaven; and these men, not being able to do this, are put to shame as uneducated men.

153 And Nero said to Peter: Hast thou heard, Peter, what has been said by Simon? From this will appear how much power either he or thy god has. Peter said: O most mighty emperor, it thou wert willing, thou mightst perceive that he is full of demons. Nero said: Why do you make to me roundabouts of circumlocutions? To-morrow will prove you.

154 Simon said: Dost thou believe, O good emperor, that I who was dead, and rose again, am a magician?

155 For it had been brought about by his own cleverness that the unbelieving Simon had said to Nero:

156 Order me to be beheaded in a dark place, and there to be left slain; and if I do not rise on the third day, know that I am a magician; but if I rise again, know that I am the Son of God.

157 And Nero having ordered this, in the dark, by his magic art be managed that a ram should be beheaded.

158 And for so long did the ram appear to be Simon until he was beheaded. And when he had been beheaded in the dark, he that had beheaded him, taking the head, found it to be that of a ram; hut he would not say anything to the emperor, lest be should scourge him, having ordered this to be done in secret.

159 Thereafter, accordingly. Simon said that he bad risen on the third day, because he took away the head of the ram and the limbs--but the blood had been there congealed--and on the third day he showed himself to Nero, and said:

160 Cause to be wiped away my blood that has been poured out; for, behold, having been beheaded, as I promised, I have risen again on the third day.

161 And when Nero said, To-morrow will prove yon, turning to Paul, he says:

162 Thou Paul, why dost thou say nothing? Either who taught thee, or whom thou hast for a master, or how thou hast taught in the cities, or what things have happened through thy teaching?

163 For I think that thou hast not any wisdom, and art not able to accomplish any work of power.

164 Paul answered: Dost thou suppose that I ought to speak against a desperate man, a magician, who has given his soul up to death, whose destruction and perdition will come speedily?

165 For he ought to speak who pretends to be what he is not, and deceives men by magic art.

166 If thou consentest to hear his words, and to shield him, thou shalt destroy thy soul and thy kingdom, for he is a most base man.

167 And as the Egyptians Jannes and Jambres led Pharaoh and his army astray until they were swallowed up in the sea, so also he, through the instruction of his father the devil, persuades men to do many evils to themselves, and thus deceives many of the innocent, to the peril of thy kingdom.

168 But as for the word of the devil, which I see has been poured out through this man, with groanings of my heart am dealing with the Holy Spirit, that it may clearly shown what it is; for as far as he seems to raise himself towards heaven, so far will he be sunk down into the depth of Hades, where there is weeping and gnashing of teeth.

169 But about the teaching of my Master, of which thou didst ask me, none attain it except the pure, who allow faith to come into their heart.

170 For as many things as belong to peace and love, these have I taught.

171 Round about from Jerusalem, and as far as Illyricum, I have fulfilled the word of peace.

172 For I have taught that in honour they should prefer one another; I have taught those that are eminent and rich not to be lifted up, and hope in uncertainty of riches, but to place their hope in God;

173 I have taught those in a middle station to be content with food and covering; I have taught the poor to rejoice in their own poverty; I have taught fathers to teach their children instruction in the fear of the Lord, children to obey their parents in wholesome admonition;

174 I have taught wives to love their own husbands, and to fear them as masters, and husbands to observe fidelity to their wives; I have taught masters to treat their slaves with clemency, and slaves to serve their own masters faithfully;

175 I have taught the churches of the believers to reverence one almighty, invisible, and incomprehensible God.

176 And this teaching has been given me, not from men, nor through men, but through Jesus Christ, who spoke to me out of heaven, who also has sent me to preach, saying to me, Go forth, for I will be with thee; and all things, as many as thou shalt say or do, I shall make just.

177 Nero said: What sayest thou, Peter?

178 He answered and said: All that Paul has said is true. For when he was a persecutor of the faith of Christ, a voice called him out of heaven, and taught him the truth; for he was not an adversary of our faith from hatred, but from ignorance.

179 For there were before us false Christs, like Simon, false apostles, and false prophets, who, contrary to the sacred writings, set themselves to make void the truth; and against these it was necessary to have in readiness this man, who from his youth up set himself to no other thing than to search out the mysteries of the divine law, by which he might become a vindicator of truth and a persecutor of falsehood.

180 Since, then, his persecution was not on account of hatred, but on account of the vindication of the law, the very truth out of heaven held intercourse with him, saying, I am the truth which you persecutest; cease persecuting me.

181 When, therefore, he knew that this was so, leaving off that which he was vindicating, he began to vindicate this way of Christ which he was persecuting.

182 Simon said: O good emperor, take notice that these two have conspired against me; for I am the truth, and they purpose evil against me.

183 Peter said: There is no truth in thee; but all thou sayest is false.

184 Nero said: Paul, what sayest thou? Paul said: Those things which thou hast heard from Peter, believe to have been spoken by me also; for we purpose the same thing, for we have the same Lord Jesus the Christ.

185 Simon said: Dost thou expect me, O good emperor, to hold an argument with these men, who have come to an agreement against me?

186 And having turned to the apostles of Christ, he said: Listen, Peter and Paul: if I can do nothing for you here, we are going to the place where I must judge you.

187 Paul said: O good emperor, see what threats he holds out against us.

188 Peter said: Why was it necessary to keep from laughing outright at a foolish man, made the sport of demons, so as to suppose that he cannot be made manifest?

189 Simon said: I spare you until I shall receive my power.

190 Paul said: See if you will go out hence safe.

191 Peter said: If thou do not see, Simon, the power of our Lord Jesus Christ, thou wilt not believe thyself not to be Christ.

192 Simon said: Most sacred emperor, do not believe them, for they are circumcised knaves.

193 Paul said: Before we knew the truth. we had the circumcision of the flesh; but when the truth appeared, in the circumcision of the heart we both are circumcised, and circumcise.

194 Peter said: If circumcision be a disgrace, why hast thou been circumcised, Simon?

195 Nero said: Has, then, Simon also been circumcised?

196 Peter said: For not otherwise could he have deceived souls, unless he reigned himself to be a Jew, and made a

show of teaching the law of God.

197 Nero said: Simon, thou, as I see, being carried away with envy, persecutest these men.

198 For, as it seems, there is great hatred between thee anti their Christ; and I am afraid that thou wilt be worsted by them, and involved in great evils.

199 Simon said: Thou art led astray, O emperor.

200 Nero said: How am I led astray? What I see in thee, I say.

201 I see that thou art manifestly an enemy of Peter anti Paul and their master.

202 Simon said: Christ was not Paul's master.

203 Paul said: Yes; through revelation He taught me also.

204 But tell me what I asked thee--Why wast thou circumcised?

205 Simon said: Why have you asked me this?

206 Paul said: We have a reason for asking you this.

207 Nero said: Why art thou afraid to answer them?

208 Simon said: Listen, O emperor. At that time circumcision was enjoined by God when I received it. For this reason was I circumcised.

209 Paul said: Hearest thou, O good emperor, what has been said by Simon? If, therefore, circumcision be a good thing, why hast thou, Simon, given up those who have been circumcised, and forced them, after being condemned, to be put to death?

210 Nero said: Neither about you do I perceive anything good.

211 Peter and Paul said: Whether this thought about us be good or evil has no reference to the matter; but to us it was necessary that what our Master promised should come to pass.

212 Nero said: If I should not be willing? Peter said: Not as thou willest, but as He promised to us.

213 Simon said: O good emperor, these men have reckoned upon thy clemency, and have bound thee.

214 Nero said: But neither hast thou yet made me sure about thyself.

215 Simon said: Since so many excellent deeds and signs have been shown to thee by me, I wonder how thou shouldst be in doubt.

216 Nero said: I neither doubt nor favour any of you; but answer me rather what I ask.

217 Simon said: Henceforward I answer thee nothing.

218 Nero said: Seeing that thou liest, therefore thou sayest this.

219 But if even I can do nothing to thee, God, who can, will do it.

220 Simon said: I no longer answer thee.

221 Nero said: Nor do I consider thee to be anything: for, as I perceive, thou art a liar in everything.

222 But why do I say so much? The three of you show that your reasoning is uncertain; and thus in all things you have made me doubt, so that I find that I can give credit to none of you.

223 Peter said: We preach one God and Father of our Lord Jesus Christ, that has made the heaven and the earth and the sea, and all that therein is, who is the true King; and of His kingdom there shall be no end.

224 Nero said: What king is lord?

225 Paul said: The Saviour of all the nations.

226 Simon said: I am he whom you speak of.

227 Peter and Paul said: May it never be well with thee, Simon, magician, and full of bitterness.

228 Simon said: Listen, O Caesar Nero, that thou mayst know that these men are liars, and that I have been sent from the heavens: to-morrow I go up into the heavens, that I may make those who believe in me blessed, and show my wrath upon those who have denied me.

229 Peter and Paul said: Us long ago God called to His own glory; but thou, called by the devil, hastenest to punishment.

230 Simon said: Caesar Nero, listen to me. Separate these madmen from thee, in order that when I go into heaven to my father, I may be very merciful to thee.

231 Nero said: And whence shall we

prove this, that thou goest away into heaven? Simon said: Order a lofty tower to be made of wood, and of great beams, that I may go up upon it, and that my angels may find me in the air; for they cannot come to me upon earth among the sinners.

232 Nero said: I will see whether thou wilt fulfil what thou sayest.

233 Then Nero ordered a lofty tower to be made in the Campus Martins, and all the people and the dignities to be present at the spectacle. And on the following day, all the multitude having come together, Nero ordered Peter and Paul to he present, to whom also he said: Now the truth has to be made manifest.

234 Peter and Paul said: We do not expose him, but our Lord Jesus Christ, the Son of God, whom he has falsely declared himself to be.

235 And Paul, having turned to Peter, said: It is my part to bend the knee, and to pray to God; and thine to produce the effect, if thou shouldst see him attempting anything, because thou wast first taken in hand by the Lord.

236 And Paul, bending his knees, prayed. And Peter, looking stedfastly upon Simon, said: Accomplish what thou hast begun; for both thy exposure and our call is at hand: for I see my Christ calling both me and Paul.

237 Nero said: And where will you go to against my will?

238 Peter said: Whithersoever our Lord has called us.

239 Nero said: And who is your lord?

240 Peter said: Jesus the Christ, whom I see calling us to Himself.

241 Nero said: Do you also then intend to go away to heaven?

242 Peter said: If it shall seem good to Him that calls us.

243 Simon said: In order that thou mayst know, O emperor, that these are deceivers, as soon as ever I ascend into heaven, I will send my angels to thee, and will make thee come to me.

244 Nero said: Do at once what thou sayest.

245 Then Simon went up upon the tower in the face of all, and, crowned with laurels, he stretched forth his hands, and began to fly.

246 And when Nero saw him flying, he said to Peter: This Simon is true; hut thou and Paul are deceivers.

247 To whom Peter said: Immediately shalt thou know that we are true disciples of Christ; but that he is not Christ, but a magician, and a malefactor.

248 Nero said: Do you still persist? Behold, you see him going up into heaven.

249 Then Peter, looking stedfastly upon Paul, said: Paul, look up and see.

250 And Paul, having looked up, full of tears, and seeing Simon flying, said: Peter, why art thou idle? finish what thou hast begun; for already our Lord Jesus Christ is calling us.

251 And Nero hearing them, smiled a little, and said: These men see themselves worsted already, and are gone mad.

252 Peter said: Now thou shalt know that we are not mad.

253 Paul said to Peter: Do at once what thou doest.

254 And Peter, looking stedfastly against Simon, said: I adjure you, ye angels of Satan, who are carrying him into the air, to deceive the hearts of the unbelievers, by the God that created all things, and by Jesus Christ, whom on the third day He raised from the dead, no longer from this hour to keep him up, but to let him go.

255 And immediately, being let go, he fell into a place called Sacra Via, that is, Holy Way, and was divided into four parts, having perished by an evil fate.

256 Then Nero ordered Peter and Paul to be put in irons, and the body of Simon to be carefully kept three days, thinking that he would rise on the third day.

257 To whom Peter said: He will no longer rise, since he is truly dead, being condemned to everlasting punishment.

258 And Nero said to him: Who commanded thee to do such a dreadful deed?

259 Peter said: His reflections and blasphemy against my Lord Jesus

Christ have brought him into this gulf of destruction.

260 Nero said: I will destroy you by an evil taking off.

261 Peter said: This is not in thy power, even if it should seem good to thee to destroy us; but it is necessary that what our Master promised to us should he fulfilled.

262 Then Nero, having summoned Agrippa the propraetor, said to him: It is necessary that men introducing mischievous religious observances should die. Wherefore I order them to take iron clubs, and to be killed in the sea-fight.

263 Agrippa the propraetor said: Most sacred emperor, what thou hast ordered is not fitting for these men,since Paul seems innocent beside Peter.

264 Nero said: By what fate, then, shall they die?

265 Agrippa answered and said: As seems to me, it is just that Paul's head should be cut off, and that Peter should be raised on a cross as the cause of the murder.

266 Nero said: Thou hast most excellently judged.

267 Then both Peter and Paul were led away from the presence of Nero.

268 And Paul was beheaded on the Ostesian road.

269 And Peter, having come to the cross, said: Since my Lord Jesus Christ, who came down from the heaven upon the earth, was raised upon the cross upright, and He has deigned to call to heaven me, who am of the earth, my cross ought to be fixed head downmost, so as to direct my feet towards heaven; for I am not worthy to be crucified like my Lord.

270 Then, having reversed the cross, they nailed his feet up.

271 And the multitude was assembled reviling Caesar, and wishing to kill him.

272 But Peter restrained them, saying: A few days ago, being exhorted by the brethren, I was going away; and my Lord Jesus Christ met me, and having adored Him, I said, Lord, whither art Thou going?

273 And He said to me, I am going to Rome to be crucified. And I said to Him, Lord, wast Thou not crucified once for all?

274 And the Lord answering, said, I saw thee fleeing from death, and I wish to be crucified instead of thee. And I said, Lord, I go; I fulfil Thy command.

275 And He said to me, Fear not, for am with thee. On this account, then, children, do not hinder my going; for already my feet are going on the road to heaven. Do not grieve, therefore, but rather rejoice with me, for to-day I receive the fruit of my labours.

276 And thus: speaking, he said: I thank Thee, good Shepherd, that the sheep which Thou hast entrusted to me, sympathize with me; I ask, then, that with me they may have a part in Thy kingdom.

277 And having thus spoken, he gave up the ghost.

278 And immediately there appeared men glorious and strange in appearance; and they said:

279 We are here, on account of the holy and chief apostles, from Jerusalem.

280 And they, along with Marcellus, an illustrious man, who, having left Simon, had believed in Peter, took up his body secretly, and put it under the terebinth near the place for the exhibition of sea-fights in the place called the Vatican.

281 And the men who had said that they came from Jerusalem said to the people:

282 Rejoice, and be exceeding glad, because you have been deemed worthy to have great champions.

283 And know that Nero himself, after these not many days, will be utterly destroyed, and his kingdom shall be given to another.

284 And after these things the people revolted against him; and when he knew of it, he fled into desert places, and through hunger and cold he gave up the ghost, and his body became food for the wild beasts.

285 And some devout men of the regions of the East wished to carry off the relics of the saints, and immediately there was a great earthquake in the city; and those that dwelt in the city having

become aware of it, ran and seized the men, but they fled.

286 But the Romans having taken them, put them in a place three miles froth the city, and there they were guarded a year and seven months, until they had built the place in which they intended to put them.

287 And after these things, all having assembled with glory and singing of praise, they put them in the place built for them.

288 And the consummation of the holy glorious Apostles Peter and Paul was on the 29th of the month of June--in Christ Jesus our Lord, to whom be glory and strength.

THE STORY OF PERPETUA

1 AND as Paul was being led away to be beheaded at a place about three miles from the city, he was in irons. And there were three soldiers guarding him who were of a great family.

2 And when they had gone out of the gate about the length of a bow-shot, there met them a God-fearing woman; and she, seeing Paul dragged along in irons, had compassion on him, and wept bitterly.

3 And the name of the woman was called Perpetua; and she was one-eyed. And Paul, seeing her weeping, says to her:

4 Give me thy handkerchief, and when I turn back I shall give it to thee.

5 And she, having taken the handkerchief, gave it to him willingly.

6 And the soldiers laughed, and said to the woman: Why dost thou wish, woman, to lose thy handkerchief?

7 Knowest thou not that he is going away to be beheaded?

8 And Perpetua said to them: I adjure you by the health of Caesar to bind his eyes with this handkerchief when you cut off his head. Which also was done.

9 And they beheaded him at the place called Aquae Salviae, near the pine tree. And as God had willed, before the soldiers came back, the handkerchief, having on it drops of blood, was restored to the woman.

10 And as she was carrying it, straightway and immediately her eye was opened.

CONTINUATION OF THE STORY OF PERPETUA

11 And the three soldiers who had cut off the head of Saint Paul, when after three hours they came on the same day with the BULLA bringing it to Nero, having met Perpetua, they said to her:

12 What is it, woman? Behold, by thy confidence thou hast lost thy handkerchief.

13 But she said to them: I have both got my handkerchief, and my eye has recovered its sight. And as the Lord, the God of Paul, liveth, I also have entreated him that I may be deemed worthy to become the slave of his Lord.

14 Then the soldiers who had the BULLA, recognising the handkerchief, and seeing that her eye had been opened, cried out with a loud voice, as if from one mouth, and said:

15 We too are the slaves of Paul's master. Perpetua therefore having gone away, reported in the palace of the Emperor Nero that the soldiers who had beheaded Paul said:

16 We shall no longer go into the city, for we believe in Christ whom Paul preached, and we are Christians.

17 Then Nero, filled with rage, ordered Perpetua, who had informed him of the soldiers, to be kept fast in irons; and as to the soldiers, he ordered one to be beheaded outside of the gate about one mile from the city, another to be cut in two, and the third to be stoned.

18 And Perpetua was in the prison; and in this prison there was kept Potentiana, a noble maiden, because she had said: I forsake my parents and all the substance of my father, and I wish to become a Christian.

19 She therefore joined herself to Perpetua, and ascertained from her everything about Paul, and was in much anxiety about the faith in Christ.

20 And the wife of Nero was Potentiana's sister; and she secretly informed her about Christ, that those who believe in Him see everlasting joy, and that everything here is temporary,

but there eternal: so that also she fled out of the palace, and some of the senators' wives with her.

21 Then Nero, having inflicted many tortures upon Perpetua, at last tied a great stone to her neck, and ordered her to be throw over a precipice. And her remains lie at the Momentan gate.

22 And Potentiana also underwent many torments; and at last, having made a furnace one day, they burned her.

THE ACTS OF PAUL AND THECLA

CHAPTER 1

1 Demas and Hermogenes become Paul's companions. 4 Paul visits Onesiphorus. 8 Invited by Demas and Hermogenes. 11 Preaches to the household of Onesiphorus. 12 His sermon.

WHEN Paul went up to Iconium, after his flight from Antioch, Demas and Hermogenes became his companions, who were then full of hypocrisy.

2 But Paul looking only at the goodness of God, did them no harm, but loved them greatly.

3 Accordingly he endeavoured to make agreeable to them, all the oracles and doctrines of Christ, and the design of the Gospel of God's well-beloved Son, instructing them in the knowledge of Christ, as it was revealed to him.

4 ¶ And a certain man named Onesiphorus, hearing that Paul was come to Iconium, went out speedily to meet him, together with his wife Lectra, and his sons Simmia and Zeno, to invite him to their house.

5 For Titus had given them a description of Paul's personage, they as yet not knowing him in person, but only

being acquainted with his character.

6 They went in the king's highway to Lystra, and stood there waiting for him, comparing all who passed by, with that description which Titus had given them.

7 At length they saw a man coming (namely Paul), of a low stature, bald (or shaved) on the head, crooked thighs, handsome legs, hollow-eyed; had a crooked nose; full of grace; for sometimes he appeared as a man, sometimes he had the countenance of an angel. And Paul saw Onesiphorus, and was glad.

8 ¶ And Onesiphorus said: Hail, thou servant of the blessed God. Paul replied, The grace of God be with thee and thy family.

9 But Demos and Hermogenes were moved with envy, and, under a show of great religion, Demas said, And are not we also servants of the blessed God? Why didst thou not salute us?

10 Onesiphorus replied, Because I have not perceived in, you the fruits of righteousness; nevertheless, if ye are of that sort, ye shall be welcome to my house also.

11 Then Paul went into the house of Onesiphorus, and there was great joy among the family on that account: and they employed themselves in prayer, breaking of bread, and hearing Paul preach the word of God concerning temperance and the resurrection, in the following manner:

12 ¶ Blessed are the pure in heart; for they shall see God.

13 Blessed are they who keep their flesh undefiled (or pure); for they shall be the temple of God.

14 Blessed are the temperate (or chaste); for God will reveal himself to them.

15 ¶ Blessed are they who abandon their secular enjoyments; for they shall be accepted of God.

16 Blessed are they who have wives, as though they had them not; for they shall be made angels of God.

17 Blessed are they who tremble at the word of God; for they shall be comforted.

18 Blessed are they who keep their

baptism pure; for they shall find peace with the Father, Son, and Holy Ghost.

19 ¶ Blessed are they who pursue the wisdom (or doctrine) of Jesus Christ; for they shall be called the sons of the Most High.

20 Blessed are they who observe the instructions of Jesus Christ; for they shall dwell in eternal light.

21 Blessed are they, who for the love of Christ abandon the glories of the world; for they shall judge angels, and be placed at the right hand of Christ, and shall not suffer the bitterness of the last judgment.

22 ¶ Blessed are the bodies and souls of virgins; for they are acceptable to God, and shall not lose the reward of their virginity; for the word of their (heavenly) Father shall prove effectual to their salvation in the day of his Son, and they shall enjoy rest for evermore.

CHAPTER 2

1 Thecla listens anxiously to Paul's preaching. 5 Thamyris, her admirer, concerts with Theoclia her mother to dissuade her, 12 in vain. 14 Demos and Hermogenes viler Paul to Thamyria.

WHILE Paul was preaching this sermon in the church which was in the house of Onesiphorus, a certain virgin, named Thecla (whose mother's name was Theoclia, and who was betrothed to a man named Thamyris) sat at a certain window in her house.

2 From whence, by the advantage of a window in the house where Paul was, she both night and day heard Paul's sermons concerning God, concerning charity, concerning faith in Christ, and concerning prayer;

3 Nor would she depart from the window, till with exceeding joy she was subdued to the doctrines of faith.

4 At length, when she saw many women and virgins going in to Paul, she earnestly desired that she might be thought worthy to appear in his presence, and hear the word of Christ; for she had not yet seen Paul's person, but only heard his sermons, and that alone.

5 ¶ But when she would not be prevailed upon to depart from the window, her mother sent to Thamyris, who came with the greatest pleasure, as hoping now to marry her. Accordingly he said to Theoclia, Where is my Thecla?

6 Theoclia replied, Thamyris, I have something very strange to tell you; for Thecla, for the space of three days, will not move from the window not so much as to eat or drink, but is so intent in hearing the artful and delusive discourses of a certain foreigner, that I perfectly admire, Thamyris, that a young woman of her known modesty, will suffer herself to be so prevailed upon.

7 For that man has disturbed the whole city of Iconium, and even your Thecla, among others, All the women and young men flock to him to receive his doctrine; who, besides all the rest, tells them that there is but one God, who alone is to be worshipped, and that we ought to live in chastity.

8 ¶ Notwithstanding this, my daughter Thecla, like a spider's web fastened to the window, is captivated by the discourses of Paul, and attends upon them with prodigious eagerness, and vast delight; and thus, by attending on what he says, the young woman is seduced. Now then do you go, and speak to her, for she is betrothed to you.

9 Accordingly Thamyris went, and having saluted her, and taking care not to surprise her, he said, Thecla, my spouse, why sittest thou in this melancholy posture? What strange impressions are made upon thee? Turn to Thamyris, and blush.

10 Her mother also spake to her after the same manner, and said, Child, why dost thou sit so melancholy, and, like one astonished, makest no reply?

11 Then they wept exceedingly, Thamyria, that he had lost his spouse; Theoclia, that she had lost her daughter; and the maids, that they had lost their mistress; and there was an universal mourning in the family.

12 But all these things made no impression upon Thecla, so as to incline

her so much as to turn to them, and take notice of them; for she still regarded the discourses of Paul.

13 Then Thamyris ran forth into the street to observe who they were who went into Paul, and came out from him; and he saw two men engaged in a very warm dispute, and said to them;

14 ¶ Sirs, what business have you here? and who is that man within, belonging to you, who deludes the minds of men, both young men and virgins, persuading them, that they ought not to marry, but continue as they are?

15 I promise to give you a considerable sum, if you will give me a just account of him; for I am the chief person of this city.

16 Demas and Hermogenes replied, We cannot so exactly tell who he is; but this we know, that he deprives young men of their (intended) wives, and virgins of their (intended) husbands, by teaching, There can be no future resurrection, unless ye continue in chastity, and do not defile your flesh.

CHAPTER 3

1 They betray Paul. 7 Thamyris arrests him with officers.

THEN said Thamyris, Come along with me to my house, and refresh yourselves. So they went to a very splendid entertainment, where there was wine in abundance, and very rich provision.

2 They were brought to a table richly spread, and made to drink plentifully by Thamyris, on account of the love he had for Thecla and his desire to marry her.

3 Then Thamyris said, I desire ye would inform me what the doctrines of this Paul are, that I may understand them; for I am under no small concern about Thecla, seeing she so delights in that stranger's discourses, that I am in danger of losing my intended wife.

4 ¶ Then Demas and Hermogenes answered both together, and said, Let him be brought before the governor Castellius, as one who endeavours to persuade the people into the new religion of the Christians, and he, according to the order of Cæsar, will

put him to death, by which means you will obtain your wife;

5 While we at the same time will teach her, that the resurrection which he speaks of is already come, and consists in our having children; and that we then arose again, when we came to the knowledge of God.

6 Thamyris having this account from them, was filled with hot resentment:

7 And rising early in the morning he went to the house of Onesiphorus, attended by the magistrates, the jailor, and a great multitude of people with staves, and said to Paul;

8 Thou hast perverted the city of Iconium, and among the rest, Thecla, who is betrothed to me, so that now she will not marry me. Thou shalt therefore go with us to the governor Castellius.

9 And all the multitude cried out, Away with this impostor
(magician), for he has perverted the minds of our wives, and all the people hearken to him.

CHAPTER 4

1 Paul accused before the governor by Thamyris. 5 Defends himself. 9 Is committed to Prison, 10 and visited by Thecla.

THEN Thamyris standing before the governor's judgment-seat, spake with a loud voice in the following manner.

2 O governor, I know not whence this man cometh; but he is one who teaches that matrimony is unlawful. Command him therefore to declare before you for what reason he publishes such doctrines.

3 While he was saying thus, Demas and Hermogenes (whispered to Thamyris, and) said; Say that he is a Christian, and he will presently be put to death.

4 But the governor was more deliberate, and calling to Paul, he said, Who art thou? What dost thou teach? They seem to lay gross crimes to thy charge.

5 Paul then spake with a loud voice, saying, As I am now called to give an account, O governor, of my doctrines, I desire your audience.

6 That God, who is a God of

vengeance, and who stands in need of nothing but the salvation of his creatures, has sent me to reclaim them from their wickedness and corruptions, from all (sinful) pleasures, and from death; and to persuade them to sin no more.

7 On this account, God sent his Son Jesus Christ, whom I preach, and in whom I instruct men to place their hopes as that I person who only had such compassion on the deluded world, that it might not, O governor, be condemned, but have faith, the fear of God, the knowledge of religion, and the love of truth.

8 So that if I only teach those things which I have received by revelation from God, where is my crime?

9 When the governor heard this, he ordered Paul to be bound, and to be put in prison, till he should be more at leisure to hear him more fully.

10 But in the night, Thecla taking off her ear-rings, gave them to the turnkey of the prison, who then opened the doors to her, and let her in;

11 And when she made a present of a silver looking-glass to the jailor, was allowed to go into the room where Paul was; then she sat down at his feet, and heard from him the great things of God.

12 And as she perceived Paul not to be afraid of suffering, but that by divine assistance he behaved himself with courage, her faith so far increased that she kissed his chains.

CHAPTER 5

1 Thecla sought and found by her relations. 4 Brought with Paul before the governor. 9 Ordered to be burnt, and Paul to be whipt. 15 Thecla miraculously saved.

AT length Thecla was missed, and sought for by the family and by Thamyris in every street, as though she had been lost, but one of the porter's fellow-servants told them, that she had gone out in the night-time.

2 Then they examined the porter, and he told them, that she was gone to the prison to the strange man.

3 They went therefore according to his direction, and there found her; and when they came out, they got a mob together, and went and told the governor all that happened.

4 Upon which he ordered Paul to be brought before his judgment seat.

5 Thecla in the mean time lay wallowing on the ground in the prison, in that same place where Paul had sat to teach her; upon which the governor also ordered her to be brought before his judgment-seat; which summons she received with joy, and went.

6 When Paul was brought thither, the mob with more vehemence cried out, He is a magician, let him die.

7 Nevertheless the governor attended with pleasure upon Paul's discourses of the holy works of Christ; and, after a council called, he summoned Thecla, and said to her, Why do you not, according to the law of the Iconians, marry Thamyris?

8 She stood still, with her eyes fixed upon Paul; and finding she made no reply, Theoclia, her mother, cried out, saying, Let the unjust creature be burnt; let her be burnt in the midst of the theatre, for refusing Thamyris, that all women may learn from her to avoid such practices.

9 Then the governor was exceedingly concerned, and ordered Paul to be whipt out of the city, and Thecla to be burnt.

10 So the governor arose, and went immediately into the theatre; and all the people went forth to see the dismal sight.

11 But Thecla, just as a lamb in the wilderness looks every way to see his shepherd, looked around for Paul;

12 And as she was looking upon the multitude, she saw the Lord Jesus in the likeness of Paul, and said to herself, Paul is come to see me in my distressed circumstances. And she fixed her eyes upon him; but he instantly ascended up to heaven, while she looked on him.

13 Then the young men and women brought wood and straw for the burning of Thecla; who, being brought naked to the stake, extorted tears from the governor, with surprise beholding the

greatness of her beauty.

14 And when they had placed the wood in order, the people commanded her to go upon it; which she did, first making the sign of the cross.

15 Then the people set fire to the pile; though the flame was exceeding large, it did not touch her, for God took compassion on her, and caused a great eruption from the earth beneath, and a cloud from above to pour down great quantities of rain and hail;

16 Insomuch that by the rupture of the earth, very many were in great danger, and some were killed, the fire was extinguished, and Thecla preserved.

CHAPTER 6

1 Paul with Onesiphorus in a cave. 7 Thecla discovers Paul; 12 proffers to follow him: 13 he exhorts her not for fear of fornication.

IN the mean time Paul, together with Onesiphorus, his wife and children, was keeping a fast in a certain cave, which was in the road from Iconium to Daphne.

2 And when they had fasted for several days, the children said to Paul, Father, we are hungry, and have not wherewithal to buy bread; for Onesiphorus had left all his substance to follow Paul with his family.

3 Then Paul, taking off his coat, said to the boy, Go, child, and buy bread, and bring it hither.

4 But while the boy was buying the bread, he saw his neighbour Thecla and was surprised, and said to her, Thecla, where are you going?

5 She replied, I am in pursuit of Paul, having been delivered from the flames.

6 The boy then said, I will bring you to him, for he is under great concern on your account, and has been in prayer and fasting these six days.

7 ¶ When Thecla came to the cave, she found Paul upon his knees praying and saying, O holy Father, O Lord Jesus Christ, grant that the fire may not touch Thecla; but be her helper, for she is thy servant.

8 Thecla then standing behind him,

cried out in the following words: O sovereign Lord, Creator of heaven and earth, the Father of thy beloved and holy Son, I praise thee that thou hast preserved me from the fire, to see Paul again.

9 Paul then arose, and when he saw her, said, O God, who searchest the heart, Father of my Lord Jesus Christ, I praise thee that thou hast answered my prayer.

10 ¶ And there prevailed among them in the cave an entire affection to each other; Paul, Onesiphorus, and all that were with them being filled with joy.

11 They had five loaves, some herbs and water, and they solaced each other in reflections upon the holy works of Christ.

12 Then said Thecla to Paul, If you be pleased with it, I will follow you whithersoever you go.

13 He replied to her, Persons are now much given to fornication, and you being handsome, I am afraid lest you should meet with greater temptation than the former, and should not withstand, but be overcome by it.

14 Thecla replied, Grant me only the seal of Christ, and no temptation shall affect me.

15 Paul answered, Thecla, wait with patience, and you shall receive the gift of Christ.

CHAPTER 7

1 Paul and Thecla go to Antioch. 2 Alexander, a magistrate, falls in love with Thecla: kisses her by force: 5 she resists him: 6 is carried before the governor, and condemned to be thrown to wild beasts.

THEN Paul sent back Onesiphorus and his family to their own home, and taking Thecla along with him, went for Antioch;

2 And as soon as they came into the city, a certain Syrian, named Alexander, a magistrate, in the city, who had done many considerable services for the city during his magistracy, saw Thecla and fell in love with her, and endeavoured by many rich presents to engage Paul m his interest.

3 But Paul told him, I know not the woman of whom you speak, nor does she belong to me.

4 But he being a person of great power in Antioch, seized her in the street and kissed her; which Thecla would not bear, but looking about for Paul, cried out in a distressed loud tone, Force me not, who am a stranger; force me not, who am a servant of God; I am one of the principal persons of Iconium, and was obliged to leave that city because I would not be married to Thamyris.

5 Then she laid hold on Alexander, tore his coat, and took his crown off his head, and made him appear ridiculous before all the people.

6 But Alexander, partly as he loved her, and partly being ashamed of what had been done, I led her to the governor, and upon her confession of what she had done,' he condemned her to be thrown among the beasts.

CHAPTER 8

2 Thecla entertained by Trifina; 3 brought out to the wild beasts; a she-lion licks her feet. 5 Trifina upon a vision of her deceased daughter, adopts Thecla, 11 who is taken to the amphitheatre again.

WHICH when the people saw, they said: The judgments passed in this city are unjust. But Thecla desired the favour of the governor, that her chastity might not be attacked, but preserved till she should be cast to the beasts.

2 The governor then inquired, Who would entertain her; upon which a certain very rich widow, named Trifina, whose daughter was lately dead, desired that she might have the keeping of her; and she began to treat her in her house as her own daughter.

3 At length a day came, when the beasts were to be brought forth to be seen; and Thecla was brought to the amphitheatre, and put into a den in which was an exceeding fierce she-lion, in the presence of a multitude of spectators.

4 Trifina, without any surprise, accompanied Thecla, and the she-lion licked the feet of Thecla. The title written which denotes her crime, was, Sacrilege. Then the woman cried out, O God, the judgments of this city are unrighteous.

5 After the beasts had been shewn, Trifina took Thecla home with her, and they went to bed; and behold, the daughter of Trifina, who was dead, appeared to her mother, and said; Mother, let the young woman, Thecla, be reputed by you as your daughter in my stead; and desire her that she should pray for me, that I may be translated to a state of happiness.

6 Upon which Trifina, with a mournful air, said, My daughter Falconilla has appeared to me, and ordered me to receive you in her room; wherefore I desire, Thecla, that you would pray for my daughter, that she may be translated into a state of happiness, and to life eternal.

7 When Thecla heard this, she immediately prayed to the Lord, and said: O Lord God of heaven and earth, Jesus Christ, thou Son of the Most High, grant that her daughter Falconilla may live forever. Trifina hearing this groaned again, and said: O unrighteous judgments! O unreasonable wickedness! that such a creature should (again) be cast to the beasts!

8 ¶ On the morrow, at break of day, Alexander came to Trifina's house, and said: The governor and the people are waiting; bring the criminal forth.

9 But Trifina ran in so violently upon him, that he was affrighted, and ran away. Trifina was one of the royal family; and she thus expressed her sorrow, and said; Alas! I have trouble in my house' nn two accounts, and there is no one who will relieve me, either under the loss of my daughter, or my being unable to save Thecla. But now, O Lord God, be thou the helper of Thecla thy servant.

10 While she was thus engaged, the governor sent one of his own officers to bring Thecla. Trifina took her by the hand, and, going with her, said: I went with Falconilla to her grave, and. now must go with Thecla to the beasts.

11 When Thecla heard this, she

weeping prayed, and said: O Lord God, whom I have made my confidence and refuge, reward Trifina for her compassion to me, and preserving my chastity.

12 Upon this there was a great noise in the amphitheatre; the beasts roared, and the people cried out, Bring in the criminal.

13 But the woman cried out, and said: Let the whole city suffer for such crimes; and order all of us, O governor, to the same punishment. O unjust judgment! O cruel sight!

14 Others said, Let the whole city be destroyed for this vile action. Kill us all, O governor. O cruel sight! O unrighteous judgment.

CHAPTER 9

1 Thecla thrown naked to the wild beasts; 2 they all refuse to attack her; 8 throws herself into a pit of water. 10 other wild beasts refuse her. 11 Tied to wild bulls. 13 Miraculously saved. 15 Released. 24 Entertained by Trifina.

THEN Thecla was taken out of the hand of Trifina, stripped naked, had a girdle put on, and thrown into the place appointed for fighting with the beasts: and the lions and the bears were let loose upon her.

2 But a she-lion, which was of all the most fierce, ran to Thecla, and fell down at her feet. Upon which the multitude of women shouted aloud.

3 Then a she-bear ran fiercely towards her; but the she-lion met the bear, and tore it to pieces.

4 Again, a he-lion, who had been wont to devour men, and which belonged to Alexander, ran towards her; but the she-lion encountered the he-lion, and they killed each other.

5 Then the women were under a greater concern, because the she-lion, which had helped Thecla, was dead.

6 Afterwards they brought out many other wild beasts; but Thecla stood with her hands stretched towards heaven, and prayed; and when she had done praying, she turned about, and saw a pit of water, and said, Now it is a proper time for me to be baptized.

7 Accordingly she threw herself into the water, and said, In thy name, O my Lord Jesus Christ, I am this last day baptized. The women and the people seeing this, cried out, and said, Do not throw yourself into the water. And the governor himself cried out, to think that the fish (sea-calves) were like to devour so much beauty.

8 ¶ Notwithstanding all this, Thecla threw herself into the water, in the name of our Lord Jesus Christ.

9 But the fish (sea-calves,) when they saw the lighting and fire, were killed, and swam dead upon the surface of the water, and a cloud of fire surrounded Thecla, so that as the beasts could not come near her, so the people could not see her nakedness.

10 Yet they turned other wild beasts upon her; upon which they made a very mournful outcry; and some of them scattered spikenard, others cassia, others amomus (a sort of spikenard, or the herb of Jerusalem, or ladies-rose) others ointment; so that the quantity of ointment was large, in proportion to the number of people; and upon this all the beasts lay as though they had been fast asleep, and did not touch Thecla.

11 Whereupon Alexander said to the Governor, I have some very terrible bulls; let us bind her to them. To which the governor, with concern, replied, You may do what you think fit.

12 Then they put a cord round Thecla's waist, which bound also her feet, and with it tied her to the bulls, to whose privy-parts they applied red-hot irons, that so they being the more tormented, might more violently drag Thecla about, till they had killed her.

13 The bulls accordingly tore about, making a most hideous noise; but the flame which was about Thecla, burnt off the cords which were fastened to the members of the bulls, and she stood in the middle of the stage, as unconcerned as if she had not been bound.

14 But in the mean time Trifina, who sat upon one of the benches, fainted away and died; upon which the whole city was under a very great concern.

15 And Alexander himself was afraid, and desired the governor, saying: I entreat you, take compassion on me and the city, and release this woman, who has fought with the beasts; lest, both you and I, and the whole city be destroyed

16 For if Cæsar should have any account of what has passed now, he will certainly immediately destroy the city, because Trifina, a person of royal extract, and a relation of his, is dead upon her seat.

17 Upon this the governor called Thecla from among the beasts to him, and said to her, Who art thou? and what are thy circumstances, that not one of the beasts will touch thee?

18 Thecla replied to him; I am a servant of the living God; and as to my state, I am a believer on Jesus Christ his Son, in whom God is well pleased; and for that reason none of the beasts could touch me.

19 He alone is the way to eternal salvation, and the foundation of eternal life. He is a refuge to those who are in distress; a support to the afflicted, hope and defence to those who are hopeless; and, in a word, all those who do not believe on him, shall not live, but suffer eternal death.

20 When the govern or heard these things, he ordered her clothes to be brought, and said to her put on your clothes.

21 Thecla replied: May that God who clothed me when I was naked among the beasts, in the day of judgment clothe your soul with the robe of salvation. Then she took her clothes, and put them on; and the governor immediately published an order in these words; I release to you Thecla the servant of God.

22 Upon which the women cried out together with a loud voice, and with one accord gave praise unto God, and said; There is but one God, who is the God of Thecla; the one God who delivered Thecla.

23 So loud were their voices that the whole city seemed to be shaken; and Trifina herself heard the glad tidings, and arose again, and ran with the multitude to meet Thecla; and embracing her, said: Now I believe there shall be a resurrection of the dead; now I am persuaded that my daughter is alive. Come therefore home with me, my daughter Thecla, and I will make over all that I have to you.

24 So Thecla went with Trifina, and was entertained there a few days, teaching her the word of the Lord, whereby many young women were converted; and there was great joy in the family of Trifina.

25 But Thecla longed to see Paul, and inquired and sent everywhere to find him; and when at length she was informed that he was at Myra, in Lycia, she took with her many young men and women; and putting on a girdle, and dressing herself in the habit of a man, she went to him to Myra in Lycia, and there found Paul preaching the word of God; and she stood by him among the throng.

CHAPTER 10

1 Thecla visits Paul. 8 Visits Onesiphorus. 8 Visits her mother. 9 Who repulses her. 12 Is tempted by the devil. Works miracles.

BUT it was no small surprise to Paul when he saw her and the people with her; for he imagined some fresh trial was coining upon them;

2 Which when Thecla perceived, she said to him: I have been baptized, O Paul; for he who assists you in preaching, has assisted me to baptize.

3 Then Paul took her, and led her to the house of Hermes; and Thecla related to Paul all that had befallen her in Antioch, insomuch that Paul exceedingly wondered, and all who heard were confirmed in the faith, and prayed for Trifina's happiness.

4 Then Thecla arose, and said to Paul, I am going to Iconium. Paul replied to her: Go, and teach the word of the Lord.

5 But Trifina had sent large sums of money to Paul, and also clothing by the hands of Thecla, for the relief of the poor.

6 ¶ So Thecla went to Iconium. And when she came to the house of Onesiphorus, she fell down upon the floor where Paul had sat and preached, and, mixing tears with her prayers, she praised and glorified God in the following words:

7 O Lord the God of this house, in which I was first enlightened by thee; O Jesus, son of the living God, who wast my helper before the governor, my helper in the fire, and my helper among the beasts; thou alone art God forever and ever. Amen.

8 ¶ Thecla now (on her return) found Thamyris dead, but her mother living. So calling her mother, she said to her: Theoclia, my mother, is it possible for you to be brought to a belief, that there is but one Lord God, who dwells in the heavens? If you desire great riches, God will give them to you by me; if you want your daughter again, here I am.

9 These and many other things she represented to her mother, (endeavouring) to persuade her (to her own opinion). But her mother Theoclia gave no credit to the things which were said by the martyr Thecla.

10 So that Thecla perceiving she discoursed to no purpose, signing her whole body with the sign (of the cross), left the house and went to Daphine; and when she came there, she went to the cave, where she had found Paul with Onesiphorus, and fell down on the ground; and wept before God.

11 When she departed thence, she went to Seleucia, and enlightened many in the knowledge of Christ.

12 ¶ And a bright cloud conducted her in her journey.

13 And after she had arrived at Seleucia she went to a place out of the city, about the distance of a furlong, being afraid of the inhabitants, because they were worshippers of idols.

14 And she was led (by the cloud) into a mountain called Calamon, or Rodeon. There she abode many years, and underwent a great many grievous temptations of the devil, which she bore in a becoming manner, by the assistance which she had from Christ.

15 At length certain gentlewomen hearing of the virgin Thecla, went to her, and were instructed by her in the oracles of God, and many of them abandoned this world, and led a monastic life with her.

16 Hereby a good report was spread everywhere of Thecla, and she wrought several (miraculous) cures, so that all the city and adjacent countries brought their sick to that mountain, and before they came as far as the door of the cave, they were instantly cured of whatsoever distemper they had.

17 The unclean spirits were cast out, making a noise; all received their sick made whole, and glorified God, who had bestowed such power on the virgin Thecla;

18 Insomuch that the physicians of Seleucia were now of no more account, and lost all the profit of their trade, because no one regarded them; upon which they were filled with envy, and began to contrive what methods to take with this servant of Christ.

CHAPTER 11
1 Is attempted to be ravished, 12 escapes by a rock opening, 17 and closing miraculously.

THE devil then suggested bad advice to their minds; and being on a certain day met together to consult, they reasoned among each other thus: The virgin is a priestess of the great goddess Diana, and whatsoever she requests from her, is granted, because she is a virgin, and so is beloved by all the gods.

2 Now then let us procure some rakish fellows, and after we have made them sufficiently drunk, and given them a good sum of money, let us order them to go and debauch this virgin, promising them, if they do it, a larger reward.

3 (For they thus concluded among themselves, that if they be able to debauch her, the gods will no more regard her, nor Diana cure the sick for her.)

4 They proceeded according to this resolution, and the fellows went to the

mountain, and as fierce as lions to the cave, knocking at the door.

5 The holy martyr Thecla, relying upon the God in whom she believed, opened the door, although she was before apprized of their design, and said to them, Young men, what is your business?

6 They replied, Is there any one within, whose name is Thecla? She answered, What would you have with her? They said, We have a mind to lie with her.

7 The blessed Thecla answered: Though I am a mean old woman, I am the servant of my Lord Jesus Christ; and though you have a vile design against me, ye shall not be able to accomplish it. They replied: It is impossible but we must be able to do with you what we have a mind.

8 And while they were saying this, they laid hold on her by main force, and would have ravished her. Then she with the (greatest) mildness said to them: Young men have patience, and see the glory of the Lord.

9 And while they held her, she looked up to heaven and said; O God most reverend, to whom none can be likened; who makest thyself glorious over thine enemies; who didst deliver me from the fire, and didst not give me up to Thamyris, didst not give me up to Alexander; who deliveredst me from the wild beasts; who didst preserve me in the deep waters; who hast everywhere been my helper, and hast glorified thy name in me;

10 Now also deliver me from the hands of these wicked and unreasonable men, nor suffer them to debauch my chastity which I have hitherto preserved for thy honour; for I love thee and long for thee, and worship thee, O Father, Son, and Holy Ghost, for evermore. Amen.

11 Then came a voice from heaven, saying, Fear not, Thecla, my faithful servant, for I am with thee. Look and see the place which is opened for thee: there thy eternal abode shall be; there thou shalt receive the beatific vision.

12 The blessed Thecla observing, saw the rock opened to as large a degree as that a man might enter in; she did as she was commanded, bravely fled from the vile crew, and went into the rock, which instantly so closed, that there was not any crack visible where it had opened.

13 The men stood perfectly astonished at so prodigious a miracle, and had no power to detain the servant of God; but only, catching hold of her veil, or hood, they tore off a piece of it;

14 And even that was by the permission of God, for the confirmation of their faith who should come to see this venerable place, and to convey blessings to those in succeeding ages, who should believe on our Lord Jesus Christ from a pure heart.

15 Thus suffered that first martyr and apostle of God, and virgin, Thecla; who came from Iconium at eighteen years of age; afterwards, partly in journeys and travels, and partly in a monastic life in the cave, she lived seventy-two years; so that she was ninety years old when the Lord translated her.

16 Thus ends her life.

17 The day which is kept sacred to her memory, is the twenty-fourth of September, to the glory of the Father, and the Son, and the Holy Ghost, now and for evermore. Amen.

THE ACTS OF PETER AND THE TWELVE APOSTLES

[[Parts of the text are fragmented]]

1 [...] which [...] purpose [... after ...] us [...] apostles [...]. We sailed [...] of the body.

2 Others were not anxious in their hearts.

3 And in our hearts, we were united.

4 We agreed to fulfill the ministry to which the Lord appointed us.

5 And we made a covenant with each other.

6 We went down to the sea at an opportune moment, which came to us from the Lord.

7 We found a ship moored at the shore ready to embark, and we spoke with the sailors of the ship about our coming aboard with them.

8 They showed great kindliness toward us as was ordained by the Lord.

9 And after we had embarked, we sailed a day and a night.

10 After that, a wind came up behind the ship and brought us to a small city in the midst of the sea.

11 And I, Peter, inquired about the name of this city from residents who were standing on the dock.

12 A man among them answered, saying, "The name of this city is Habitation, that is, Foundation [...] endurance."

13 And the leader among them holding the palm branch at the edge of the dock.

14 And after we had gone ashore with the baggage, I went into the city, to seek advice about lodging.

15 A man came out wearing a cloth bound around his waist, and a gold belt girded it.

16 Also a napkin was tied over his chest, extending over his shoulders and covering his head and his hands.

17 I was staring at the man, because he was beautiful in his form and stature.

18 There were four parts of his body that I saw: the soles of his feet and a part of his chest and the palms of his hands and his visage.

19 These things I was able to see.

20 A book cover like (those of) my books was in his left hand.

21 A staff of styrax wood was in his right hand.

22 His voice was resounding as he slowly spoke, crying out in the city, "Pearls! Pearls!"

23 I, indeed, thought he was a man of that city. I said to him, "My brother and my friend!"

24 He answered me, then, saying, "Rightly did you say, 'My brother and my friend.' What is it you seek from me?"

25 I said to him, "I ask you about lodging for me and the brothers also, because we are strangers here."

26 He said to me, "For this reason have I myself just said, 'My brother and my friend,' because I also am a fellow stranger like you."

27 And having said these things, he cried out, "Pearls! Pearls!" The rich men of that city heard his voice.

28 They came out of their hidden storerooms. And some were looking out from the storerooms of their houses.

29 Others looked out from their upper windows. And they did not see (that they could gain) anything from him, because there was no pouch on his back nor bundle inside his cloth and napkin.

30 And because of their disdain they did not even acknowledge him.

31 He, for his part, did not reveal himself to them.

32 They returned to their storerooms, saying, "This man is mocking us."

33 And the poor of that city heard his voice, and they came to the man who sells this pearl.

34 They said, "Please take the trouble to show us the pearl so that we may, then, see it with our (own) eyes.

35 For we are the poor. And we do not have this [...] price to pay for it.

36 But show us that we might say to our friends that we saw a pearl with our (own) eyes."

37 He answered, saying to them, "If it is possible, come to my city, so that I may not only show it before your (very) eyes, but give it to you for nothing."

38 And indeed they, the poor of that city, heard and said, "Since we are beggars, we surely know that a man does not give a pearl to a beggar, but (it is) bread and money that is usually received.

39 Now then, the kindness which we want to receive from you (is) that you show us the pearl before our eyes.

40 And we will say to our friends proudly that we saw a pearl with our (own) eyes" - because it is not found among the poor, especially such beggars (as these).

41 He answered (and) said to them, "If it is possible, you yourselves come to

my city, so that I may not only show you it, but give it to you for nothing." The poor and the beggars rejoiced because of the man who gives for nothing.

42 The men asked Peter about the hardships.

43 Peter answered and told those things that he had heard about the hardships of the way.

44 Because they are interpreters of the hardships in their ministry.

45 He said to the man who sells this pearl, "I want to know your name and the hardships of the way to your city because we are strangers and servants of God.

46 It is necessary for us to spread the word of God in every city harmoniously."

47 He answered and said, "If you seek my name, Lithargoel is my name, the interpretation of which is, the light, gazelle-like stone.

48 "And also (concerning) the road to the city, which you asked me about, I will tell you about it.

49 No man is able to go on that road, except one who has forsaken everything that he has and has fasted daily from stage to stage.

50 For many are the robbers and wild beasts on that road.

51 The one who carries bread with him on the road, the black dogs kill because of the bread.

52 The one who carries a costly garment of the world with him, the robbers kill because of the garment.

53 The one who carries water with him, the wolves kill because of the water, since they were thirsty for it.

54 The one who is anxious about meat and green vegetables, the lions eat because of the meat.

55 If he evades the lions, the bulls devour him because of the green vegetables."

56 When he had said these things to me, I sighed within myself, saying, "Great hardships are on the road! If only Jesus would give us power to walk it!"

57 He looked at me since my face was sad, and I sighed.

58 He said to me, "Why do you sigh, if you, indeed, know this name "Jesus" and believe him? He is a great power for giving strength. For I too believe in the Father who sent him."

59 I replied, asking him, "What is the name of the place to which you go, your city?"

60 He said to me, "This is the name of my city, 'Nine Gates.'

61 Let us praise God as we are mindful that the tenth is the head."

62 After this I went away from him in peace.

63 As I was about to go and call my friends, I saw waves and large high walls surrounding the bounds of the city.

64 I marveled at the great things I saw.

65 I saw an old man sitting and I asked him if the name of the city was really Habitation.

66 He [...], "Habitation [...]."

67 He said to me, "You speak truly, for we inhabit here because we endure."

68 I responded, saying, "Justly [...] have men named it [...], because (by) everyone who endures his trials, cities are inhabited, and a precious kingdom comes from them, because they endure in the midst of the apostasies and the difficulties of the storms.

69 So that in this way, the city of everyone who endures the burden of his yoke of faith will be inhabited, and he will be included in the kingdom of heaven."

70 I hurried and went and called my friends so that we might go to the city that he, Lithargoel, appointed for us.

71 In a bond of faith we forsook everything as he had said (to do).

72 We evaded the robbers, because they did not find their garments with us.

73 We evaded the wolves, because they did not find the water with us for which they thirsted.

74 We evaded the lions, because they did not find the desire for meat with us.

75 We evaded the bulls [...] they did not find green vegetables.

76 A great joy came upon us and a peaceful carefreeness like that of our

Lord.

77 We rested ourselves in front of the gate, and we talked with each other about that which is not a distraction of this world.

78 Rather we continued in contemplation of the faith.

79 As we discussed the robbers on the road, whom we evaded, behold Lithargoel, having changed, came out to us.

80 He had the appearance of a physician, since an unguent box was under his arm, and a young disciple was following him carrying a pouch full of medicine. We did not recognize him.

81 Peter responded and said to him, "We want you to do us a favor, because we are strangers, and take us to the house of Lithargoel before evening comes."

82 He said, "In uprightness of heart I will show it to you. But I am amazed at how you knew this good man. For he does not reveal himself to every man, because he himself is the son of a great king.

83 Rest yourselves a little so that I may go and heal this man and come (back)." He hurried and came (back) quickly.

84 He said to Peter, "Peter!" And Peter was frightened, for how did he know that his name was Peter?

85 Peter responded to the Savior, "How do you know me, for you called my name?" Lithargoel answered, "I want to ask you who gave the name Peter to you?" He said to him, "It was Jesus Christ, the son of the living God. He gave this name to me."

86 He answered and said, "It is I! Recognize me, Peter."

87 He loosened the garment, which clothed him - the one into which he had changed himself because of us - revealing to us in truth that it was he.

88 We prostrated ourselves on the ground and worshipped him.

89 We comprised eleven disciples.

90 He stretched forth his hand and caused us to stand.

91 We spoke with him humbly.

92 Our heads were bowed down in unworthiness as we said, "What you

wish we will do. But give us power to do what you wish at all times."

93 He gave them the unguent box and the pouch that was in the hand of the young disciple.

94 He commanded them like this, saying, "Go into the city from which you came, which is called Habitation. Continue in endurance as you teach all those who have believed in my name, because I have endured in hardships of the faith.

95 I will give you your reward. To the poor of that city give what they need in order to live until I give them what is better, which I told you that I will give you for nothing."

96 Peter answered and said to him, "Lord, you have taught us to forsake the world and everything in it.

97 We have renounced them for your sake. What we are concerned about (now) is the food for a single day.

98 Where will we be able to find the needs that you ask us to provide for the poor?"

99 The Lord answered and said, "O Peter, it was necessary that you understand the parable that I told you! Do you not understand that my name, which you teach, surpasses all riches, and the wisdom of God surpasses gold, and silver and precious stone(s)?"

100 He gave them the pouch of medicine and said, "Heal all the sick of the city who believe in my name."

101 Peter was afraid to reply to him for the second time.

102 He signaled to the one who was beside him, who was John: "You talk this time."

103 John answered and said, "Lord, before you we are afraid to say many words.

104 But it is you who asks us to practice this skill.

105 We have not been taught to be physicians.

106 How then will we know how to heal bodies as you have told us?"

107 He answered them, "Rightly have you spoken, John, for I know that the physicians of this world heal what belongs to the world. The physicians of

souls, however, heal the heart.

108 Heal the bodies first, therefore, so that through the real powers of healing for their bodies, without medicine of the world, they may believe in you, that you have power to heal the illnesses of the heart also.

109 "The rich men of the city, however, those who did not see fit even to acknowledge me, but who reveled in their wealth and pride - with such as these, therefore, do not dine in their houses nor be friends with them, lest their partiality influence you.

110 For many in the churches have shown partiality to the rich, because they also are sinful, and they give occasion for others to sin.

111 But judge them with uprightness, so that your ministry may be glorified, and that my name also, may be glorified in the churches."

112 The disciples answered and said, "Yes, truly this is what is fitting to do."

113 They prostrated themselves on the ground and worshipped him.

114 He caused them to stand and departed from them in peace. Amen.

The Acts of Peter and the Twelve Apostles

THE EPISTLE OF PAUL THE APOSTLE
TO THE
LAODICEANS

1 Paul, an apostle not of men nor by man, but by Jesus Christ, unto the brethren that are at Laodicea.

2 Grace be unto you and peace from God the Father and the Lord Jesus Christ.

3 I give thanks unto Christ in all my prayers, that ye continue in him and persevere in his works, looking for the promise at the day of judgement.

4 Neither do the vain talkings of some overset you, which creep in, that they may turn you away from the truth of the Gospel which is preached by me.

5 And now shall God cause that they that are of me shall continue ministering unto the increase of the truth of the Gospel and accomplishing goodness, and the work of salvation, even eternal life.

6 And now are my bonds seen of all men, which I suffer in Christ, wherein I rejoice and am glad.

7 And unto me this is for everlasting salvation, which also is brought about by your prayers, and the ministry of the Holy Ghost, whether by life or by death.

8 For verily to me life is in Christ, and to die is joy.

9 And unto him shall he work his mercy in you that ye may have the same love, and be of one mind.

10 Therefore, dearly beloved, as ye have heard in my presence so hold fast and work in the fear of God, and it shall be unto you for life eternal.

11 For it is God that worketh in you.

12 And do ye without afterthought whatsoever ye do.

13 And for the rest, dearly beloved, rejoice in Christ, and beware of them that are filthy in lucre.

14 Let all your petitions be made openly before God, and be ye steadfast in the mind of Christ.

15 And what things are sound and true and sober and just and to be loved, do ye.

16 And what ye have heard and received, keep fast in your heart.

17 And peace shall be unto you.

18 The saints salute you.

19 The grace of the Lord Jesus be with your spirit.

20 And cause this epistle to be read unto them of Colossae, and the epistle of the Colossians to be read unto you.

THE EPISTLES OF CORINTH AND THE APOSTLE PAUL
OR,
THIRD CORINTHIANS

From Corinth to Paul

Stephanus and the presbyters who are with him, Daphnus, Eubulus, Theophilus and Xenon, to Paul their brother in the Lord, greeting.

Two men have come to Corinth, Simon and Cleobius, who pervert the faith of many through pernicious words we want you to respond to. We have never heard such things from you or the other apostles. What ever you and the other apostles teach we will believe. The Lord has shown mercy to us, since you are still alive we wish to hear from you again. Please do write or come to us. We believe, what has been revealed to Theonoe, that the Lord delivered you out of the hand of the lawless one. What they teach is as follows:

1. We must not appeal to the prophets
2. God is not Almighty
3. There is no resurrection of the flesh
4. Creation is not God's work
5. The Lord did not come in the flesh
6. The Lord was not born of Mary
7. The world is not of God but the Angels

So brother, hurry and come here, that the church here in Corinth may remain pure, and the foolishness of these men may be made known to all. Farewell in the Lord.

From Paul to Corinth

Paul, the prisoner of Jesus Christ, to the brothers in Corinth, greeting!

Since I am in prison, I am not surprised that the teachings of the evil one are quickly gaining ground. My Lord Jesus Christ will quickly come, since he is rejected by those who falsify His words. I delivered to you from the beginning what I received from the apostles who were before me, who were at all times together with the Lord Jesus Christ.

Our Lord Jesus Christ was born of Mary of the seed of David. The Holy Spirit was sent from Heaven by the Father into her, that he might come into this world to redeem all flesh through his own flesh, and that he might raise up from the dead we who are fleshly, just as He has shown Himself as our example.

Since man was molded by his Father, man was sought for when he was lost, that he might be quickened by adoption into sonship. The almighty God, who made heaven and earth, first sent the prophets to the Jews, that they might turn from their sins; for he had determined how to save the house of Israel, therefore he sent a portion of the spirit of Christ into the prophets, who at many times proclaimed the faultless worship of God. But since the prince who was unrighteous wished to be God, he laid hands on them and killed them, and so all the flesh of men were bound to passions. But God, the almighty, who is righteous and would not repudiate his own creation, sent the Holy Spirit to Mary the Galilean, who believed with all her heart, and she received the Holy Spirit into her womb that Jesus might enter the world, in order that the evil one might be conquered by the same flesh which he held sway, and be convinced that he was not God.

For by his own body Jesus Christ saved all flesh and brought it to eternal life through faith, that he might present a temple of righteousness in his own body, through whom we are redeemed. These are not children of righteousness but of wrath, who reject the providence of God, saying that heaven and earth and all that is in them are not the works of the Father. They are themselves therefore children of wrath, for they have the accursed faith of the serpent. From them turn away, and flee from there teaching! For you are not sons of disobedience but of the church most dearly beloved. This is why the time of the resurrection is proclaimed.

As for those who tell you there is no resurrection of the flesh, for them there is no resurrection, who do not believe in Him who has risen. You men of Corinth must understand that they don't know about the sowing of wheat or other seeds. That they are cast naked to the ground and when they have perished below are raised again by the will of God in a body and clothed. The body is not only raised up, but abundantly blessed. And consider not only the seeds, but nobler bodies.

You know how Jonah the son of Amathios, when he would not preach in Nineveh but fled, was swallowed by a whale and after three days and three nights God heard Jonah's prayer out of the deepest hell, and no part of him was corrupted, not even an eyelid. How much more, you of so little faith, will he raise up you who have believed in Christ Jesus, as he himself rose up? And if, when a corpse was thrown by the children of Israel on the bones of the prophet Elisha, the man's body rose up, so you also who have been cast upon the body and bones and spirit of the Lord will rise up on that day with your flesh whole.

But if you receive anything else, do not cause me trouble; for I have these fetters on my hands that I may gain Christ, and his marks on my body that I may attain to the resurrection form the dead. And whoever abides by the rule which he received by the prophets and the holy Gospel, he shall receive a reward and when he has risen form the dead shall obtain eternal life. But to him that turns aside form them – there is fire with him and those who go before him in the way, since they are men without God, a generation of vipers; from these turn away in the power of the Lord May peace, grace and love be with you. Amen.

THE EPISTLE OF THE APOSTLES

1 The book which Jesus Christ revealed unto his disciples: and how that Jesus Christ revealed the book for the company of the apostles, the disciples of Jesus Christ, even the book *which is* for all men. Simon and Cerinthus, the false apostles, concerning whom it is written that no man shall cleave unto them, for there is in them deceit wherewith they bring men to destruction. (The book hath been written) that ye may be not flinch nor be troubled, and depart not from the word of the Gospel which ye have heard. Like as we heard it, we keep it in remembrance and have written it for the whole world. We commend you our sons and our daughters in joy <in the grace of God in the name of God the Father the Lord of the world, and of Jesus Christ. Let grace be multiplied upon you.

2 *We*, John, Thomas, Peter, Andrew, James, Philip, Batholomew, Matthew, Nathanael, Judas Zelotes, and Cephas, write unto the churches of the east and the west, of the north and the south, the declaring and imparting unto you that which concerneth our Lord Jesus Christ: we do write according as we have seen and heard and touched him, after that he was risen from the dead: and how that he revealed unto us things mighty and wonderful and true.

3 This know we: that our Lord and Redeemer Jesus Christ is God the Son of God, who was sent of God the Lord of the whole world, the maker and creator *of it*, who is named by all names, and high above all powers, Lord of lords, King of kings, Ruler of rulers, the heavenly one, that sitteth above the cherubim and seraphim at the right hand of the throne of the Father: who by his word *made* the heavens, and formed the earth and that which is in it,

and set bounds to the sea that it should not pass: the deeps also and fountains, that they should spring forth and flow over the earth: the day and the night, the sun and the moon, did he establish, and the stars in the heaven: that did separate the light from the darkness: that called forth hell, and in the twinkling of an eye ordained the rain of the winter, the snow (cloud), the hail, and the ice, and the days in their several seasons: that maketh the earth to quake and again establisheth it: that created man in his own image, after his likeness, and by the fathers of old and the prophets is it declared (*or*, and spake in parables with the fathers of old and the prophets in verity), of whom the apostles preached, and whom the disciples did touch. In God, the Lord, the Son of God, do we believe, that he is the word become flesh: that of Mary the holy virgin took a body, begotten of the Holy Ghost, not of the will (lust) of the flesh, but by the will of God: that he was wrapped in swaddling clothes in Bethlehem and made manifest, and grew up and came to ripe age, when *also* we beheld *it*.

4 This did our Lord Jesus Christ, who was sent by Joseph and Mary his mother to be taught. [And] when he that taught him said unto him: Say Alpha: then answered he and said: Tell thou me first what is Beta.

This thing which then came to pass is to true and of verity.

5 Thereafter was there a marriage in Cana of Galilee; and they bade him with his mother and his brethren, and he changed water into wine. He raised the dead, he caused the lame to walk: him whose hand was withered he caused to stretch it out, and the woman which had suffered an issue of blood twelve years touched the hem of his garment and was healed in the same hour. And when we marvelled at the miracle which was done, he said: Who touched me? Then said we: Lord, the press of men hath touched thee. But he answered and said unto us: I perceive that a virtue is gone out of me. Straightway that woman came before him, and answered and said unto him: Lord, I touched thee. And he answered and said unto her: Go, thy faith hath made thee whole.

Thereafter he made the deaf to hear and the blind to see; out of them that were possessed he cast out the unclean spirits, and cleansed the lepers. The spirit which dwelt in a man, whereof the name was Legion, cried out against Jesus, saying: Before the time of our destruction is come, thou art come to drive us out. But the Lord Jesus rebuked him, saying: Go out of this man and do him no hurt. And he entered into the swine and drowned them in the water and they were choked.

Thereafter he did walk upon the sea, and the winds blew, and he cried out against them (rebuked them), and the waves of the sea were made calm. And when we his disciples had no money, we asked him: What shall we do because of the tax-gatherer? And he answered and told us: Let one of you cast an hook into the deep, and take out a fish, and he shall find therein a penny: that give unto the tax-gatherer for me and you. And thereafter when we had no bread, but only five loaves and two fishes, he commanded the people to sit them down, and the number of them was five thousand, besides children and women. We did set pieces of bread before them, and they ate and were filled, and there remained over, and we filled twelve baskets full of the fragments, asking one another and saying: What *mean* these five loaves? They are the symbol of our faith in the Lord of the Christians (in the great Christendom), *even* in the Father, the Lord Almighty, and in Jesus Christ our redeemer, in the Holy Ghost the comforter, in the holy church, and in the remission of sins.

6 These things did our Lord and Saviour reveal unto us and teach us. And we do even as he, that ye may become partakers in the grace of our Lord and in our ministry and our giving of thanks (glory), and think upon life eternal. Be ye steadfast and waver not in the knowledge and confidence of our Lord Jesus Christ, and he will have

mercy on you and save you everlastingly, world without end.

[[Here begins the Coptic text.]]

7 Cerinthus and Simon are come to go to and fro in the world, but they are enemies of our Lord Jesus Christ, for they do pervert the word and the true thing, even (faith in) Jesus Christ. Keep yourselves therefore far from them, for death is in them, and great pollution and corruption, even in these on whom shall come judgement and the end and everlasting destruction.

8 Therefore have we not shrunk from writing unto you concerning the testimony of Christ our Saviour, of what he did, when we followed with him, how he enlightened our understanding...

9 Concerning whom we testify that the Lord is he who was crucified by Pontius Pilate and Archelaus between the two thieves (and with them he was taken down from the tree of the cross, *Eth.*), and was buried in a place which is called the place of a skull (*Kranion*). And thither went three women, Mary, she that was kin to Martha, and Mary Magdalene (Sarrha, Martha, and Mary, *Eth.*), and took ointments to pour upon the body, weeping and mourning over that which was come to pass. And when they drew near to the sepulchre, they looked in and found not the body (*Eth.* they found the stone rolled away and opened the entrance).

10 And as they mourned and wept, the Lord showed himself unto them and said to them: For whom weep ye? weep no more. I am he whom ye seek. But let one of you go to your brethren and say: Come ye, the Master is risen from the dead. Martha (Mary, *Eth.*) came and told us. We said unto her: What haw we to do with thee, woman ? He that is dead and buried, is it possible that he should live? And we believed her not that the Saviour was risen from the dead. Then she returned unto the Lord and said unto him: None of them hath believed me, that thou livest. He said: Let another of you go unto them and tell them again. Mary (Sarrha, *Eth.*) came and told us again, and we believed her not; and she returned unto the Lord and she also told him.

11 Then said the Lord unto Mary and her sisters: Let us go unto them. And he came and found us within (sitting veiled or fishing, *Eth.*), and called us out; but we thought that it was a phantom and believed not that it was the Lord. Then said he unto us: Come, fear ye not. I am your master, even he, O Peter, whom thou didst deny thrice; and dost thou now deny again? And we came unto him, doubting in our hearts whether it were he. Then said he unto us: Wherefore doubt ye still, and are unbelieving? I am he that spake unto you of my flesh and my death and my resurrection. But that ye may know that I am he, do thou, Peter, put thy finger into the print of the nails in mine hands, and thou also, Thomas, put thy finger into the wound of the spear in my side; but thou, Andrew, look on my feet and see whether they press the earth; for it is written in the prophet: A phantom of a devil maketh no footprint on the earth.

12 And we touched him, that we might learn of a truth whether he were risen in the flesh; and we fell on our faces (and worshipped him) confessing our sin, that we had been unbelieving. Then said our Lord and Saviour unto us: Rise up, and I will reveal unto you that which is above the heaven and in the heaven, and your rest which is in the kingdom of heaven. For my Father hath given me power (sent me, *Eth.*) to take you up thither, and them also that believe on me.

13 Now that which he revealed unto us is this, which he spake: It came to pass when I was about (minded) to come hither from the Father of all things, and passed through the heavens, then did I put on the wisdom of the Father, and I put on the power of his might. I was in heaven, and I passed by the archangels and the angels in their likeness, like as if I were one of them, among the princedoms and powers. I passed through them because I possessed the wisdom of him that had sent me. Now

the chief captain of the angels, [is] Michael, and Gabriel and Uriel and Raphael followed me unto the fifth firmament (heaven), for they thought in their heart that I was one of them; such power was given me of my Father. And on that day did I adorn the archangels with a wonderful voice (so *Copt.: Eth., Lat.,* I made them quake--amazed them), so that they should go unto the altar of the Father and serve and fulfil the ministry until I should return unto him. And so wrought I the likeness by my wisdom; for I became all things in all, that I might praise the dispensation of the Father and fulfil the glory of him that sent me (*the verbs might well be transposed*) and return unto him. (*Here the Latin omits a considerable portion of text without notice, to near the beginning of c.* 17.)

14 For ye know that the angel Gabriel brought the message unto Mary. And we answered: Yea, Lord. He answered and said unto us: Remember ye not, then, that I said unto you a little while ago: I became an angel among the angels, and I became all things in all? We said unto him: Yea, Lord. Then answered he and said unto us: On that day whereon I took the form of the angel Gabriel, I appeared unto Mary and spake with her. Her heart accepted me, and she believed (She believed and laughed, *Eth.*), and I formed myself and entered into her body. I became flesh, for I alone was a minister unto myself in that which concerned Mary (I was mine own messenger, *Eth.*) in the appearance of the shape of an angel. For so must I needs (or, was I wont to) do. Thereafter did I return to my Father (*Copt.* After my return to the Father, *and run on*).

15 But do ye commemorate my death. Now when the Passover (Easter, pascha) cometh, one of you shall be cast into prison for my name's sake; and he will be in grief and sorrow, because ye keep the Easter while he is in prison and separated from you, for he will be sorrowful because he keepeth not Easter with you. And I will send my power in the form of mine angel Gabriel, and the

doors of the prison shall open. And he shall come forth and come unto you and keep the night-watch with you until the cock crow. And when ye have accomplished the memorial which is made of me, and the Agape (love-feast), he shall again be cast into prison for a testimony, until he shall come out thence and preach that which I have delivered unto you.

And we said unto him: Lord, is it then needful that we should again take the cup and drink? (Lord, didst not thou thyself fulfil the drinking of the Passover? is it then needful that we should accomplish it again? *Eth.*) He said unto us: Yea, it is needful, until the day when I come again, with them that have been put to death for my sake (come with my wounds, *Eth.*).

16 Then said we to him: Lord, that which thou hast revealed unto us (revealest, *Eth.*) is great. Wilt thou come in the power of any creature or in an appearance of any kind ? (In what power or form wilt thou come? *Eth.*) He answered and said unto us: Verily I say unto you, I shall come like the sun when it is risen, and my brightness will be seven times the brightness thereof! The wings of the clouds shall bear me in brightness, and the sign of the cross shall go before me, and I shall come upon earth to judge the quick and the dead.

17 We said unto him: Lord, after how many years shall this come to pass ? He said unto us: When the hundredth part and the twentieth part is fulfilled, between the Pentecost and the feast of unleavened bread, then shall the coming of my Father be (*so Copt.*: When an hundred and fifty years are past, in the days of the feast of Passover and Pentecost, &c., *Eth.*: . . . (*imperfect word*) year is fulfilled, between the unleavened bread and Pentecost shall be the coming of my Father, *Lat.*).

We said unto him: Now sayest thou unto us: I will come; and how sayest thou: He that sent me is he that shall come? Then said he to us: I am wholly in the Father and my Father is in me. Then said we to him: Wilt thou indeed forsake us until thy coming? Where can we find a master? But he answered and said unto us: Know ye not, then, that like as until now I have been here, so also was I there, with him that sent me? And we said to him: Lord, is it then possible that thou shouldest be both here and there? But he answered us: I am wholly in the Father and the Father in me, because of (in regard of) the likeness of the form and the power and the fullness and the light and the full measure and the voice. I am the word, I am become unto him a thing, that is to say (*word gone*) of the thought, fulfilled in the type (likeness); I have into the Ogdoad (eighth number), which is the Lord's day. (*In place of these sentences Eth. has*: I am of his resemblance and form, of his power and completeness, and of his light. I am his complete (fulfilled, entire) Word.

18 But it came to pass after he was crucified, and dead and arisen again, *when* the work *was fulfilled* which was accomplished in the flesh, and he was crucified and the ascension come to pass at the end of the days, then said he thus, &c. *It is an interpolation, in place of words which the translator did not understand, or found heretical.*) But the whole fulfilment of the fulfilment shall ye see after the redemption which hath come to pass by me, and ye shall see me, how I go up unto my Father which is in heaven. But behold, now, I give unto you a new commandment: Love one another and [*a leaf lost in Copt.*] obey one another, that peace may rule alway among you. Love your enemies, and what ye would not that man do unto you, that do unto no man.

19 And this preach ye also and teach them that believe on me, and preach the kingdom of heaven of my Father, and how my Father hath given me the power, that ye may bring near the children of my heavenly Father. Preach ye, and they shall obtain faith, that ye may be they for whom it is ordained that they shall bring his children unto heaven.

And we said unto him: Lord, unto thee it is possible to accomplish that whereof thou tellest us; but how shall we be able to do it? He said to us: Verily I say unto you, preach and proclaim as I *command you*, for I will be with you, for it is my good pleasure to be with you, that ye may be heirs with me in the kingdom of heaven, *even the kingdom* of him that sent me. Verily I say unto you, ye shall be my brethren and my friends, for my Father hath found pleasure in you: and so also shall they be that believe on me by your means. Verily I say unto you, such and so great joy hath my Father prepared for you that the angels and the powers desired and do desire to see it and look upon it; but it is not given unto them to behold the glory of my Father. We said unto him: Lord, what is this whereof thou speakest to us?

Copt. begins again: words are missing. He answered us: Ye shall behold a light, more excellent than that which shineth... (shineth more brightly than the light, and is more perfect than perfection. And the Son shall become perfect through the Father who is Light, for the Father is perfect which bringeth to pass death and resurrection, and ye shall see a perfection more perfect than the perfect. And I am wholly at the right hand of the Father, even in him that maketh perfect. (*So Eth.: Copt. has gaps*).

And we said unto him: Lord, in all things art thou become salvation and life unto us, for that thou makest known such a hope unto us. And he said to us: Be of good courage and rest in me. Verily I say unto you, your rest shall be above (?), in the place where is neither eating nor drinking, nor care (*Copt.* joy) nor sorrow, nor passing away of them that are therein: for ye *shall* have no part in (the things of earth, *Eth.*) but ye shall be received in the everlastingness of my Father. Like as I am in him, so shall ye also be in me.

Again we said unto him: In what form? in the fashion of angels, or in flesh ? And he answered and said unto us: Lo, I have put on your flesh, wherein I was born and crucified, and am risen again through my Father which is in heaven, that the prophecy of David the prophet

might be fulfilled, in regard of that
which was declared concerning me and
my death and resurrection, saying:
Lord, they are increased that fight with
me, and many are they that are risen up
against me.
Many there be that say to my soul:
There is no help for him in his God.
But thou, O Lord, art my defender: thou
art my worship, and the lifter up of my
head.
I did call upon the Lord with my voice
and he heard me (out of the high place
of his temple, *Eth.*).
I laid me down and slept, and rose up
again: for thou, O Lord, art my
defender.
I will not be afraid for ten thousands of
the people, that have set themselves
against me round about.
Up, Lord, and help me, O my God: for
thou hast smitten down all them that
without cause are mine enemies: thou
hast broken the teeth of the ungodly.
Salvation belongeth unto the Lord, and
his good pleasure is upon his people
(Ps. iii. 1-8).
If, therefore, all the words which were
spoken by the prophets have been
fulfilled in me (for I myself was in
them), how much more shall that which
I say unto you come to pass indeed, that
he which sent me may be glorified by
you and by them that believe on me?
20 And when he had said this unto us,
we said to him: In all things hast thou
had mercy on us and saved us, and hast
revealed all things unto us; but yet
would we ask of thee somewhat if thou
give us leave. And he said unto us: I
know that ye pay heed, and that your
heart is well-pleased when ye hear me:
now concerning that which ye desire, I
will speak good words unto you. 21 For
verily I say unto you: Like as my Father
hath raised me from the dead, so shall
ye also rise (in the flesh, *Eth.*) and be
taken up into the highest heaven, unto
the place whereof I have told you from
the beginning, unto the place which he
who sent me hath prepared for you. And
so will I accomplish all dispensations
(all grace, *Eth.*), even I who am
unbegotten and yet begotten of

mankind, who am without flesh and yet
have borne flesh <and have grown up
like unto you that were born in flesh,
Eth.>: for to that end am I come, that
(*gap in Copt.: Eth. continues*) ye might
rise from the dead in your flesh, in the
second birth, even a vesture that shall
not decay, together with all them that
hope and believe in him that sent me:
for so is the will of my Father, that I
should give unto you, and unto them
whom it pleaseth me, the hope of the
kingdom.
Then said we unto him: Great is that
which thou sufferest us to hope, and
tellest us. And he answered and said:
Believe ye that everything that I tell you
shall come to pass ? We answered and
said: Yea, Lord. (*Copt. resumes for a
few lines: then another gap. I follow
Eth.*) He said unto us: Verily I say unto
you, that I have obtained the whole
power of my Father, that I may bring
back into light them that dwell in
darkness, them that are in corruption
into incorruption, them that are in death
into life, and that I may loose them that
are in fetters. For that which is
impossible with men, is possible with
the Father. I am the hope of them that
despair, the helper of them that have no
saviour, the wealth of the poor, the
health of the sick, and the resurrection
of the dead.
22 When he had thus said, we said unto
him: Lord, is it true that the flesh shall
be judged together with the soul and the
spirit, and that the one part shall rest in
heaven and the other part be punished
everlastingly yet living? And he said
unto us: (*Copt. resumes*) How long will
ye inquire and doubt?
23 Again we said unto him: Lord, there
is necessity upon us to inquire of thee--
because thou hast commanded us to
preach--that we ourselves may learn
assuredly of thee and be profitable
preachers, and that they which are
instructed by us may believe in thee.
Therefore must we needs inquire of
thee.
24 He answered us and said: Verily I
say unto you, the resurrection of the
flesh shall come to pass with the soul

therein and the spirit. And we said unto him: Lord, is it then possible that that which is dissolved and brought to nought should become whole? and we ask thee not as unbelieving, neither as if it were impossible unto thee; but verily we believe that that which thou sayest shall come to pass. And he was wroth with us and said: O ye of little faith, how long will ye ask questions? But what ye will, tell it me, and I myself will tell you without grudging: only keep ye my commandments and do that which I bid you, and turn not away your face from any man, that I turn not my face away from you, but without shrinking and fear and without respect of persons, minister ye in the way that is direct and narrow and strait. So shall my Father himself rejoice over you.

25 Again we said unto him: Lord, already are we ashamed that we question thee oft-times and burden thee. And he answered and said unto us: I know that in faith and with your whole heart ye do question me; therefore do I rejoice over you, for verily I say unto you: I rejoice, and my Father that is in me, because ye question me; and your importunity (shamelessness) is unto me rejoicing and unto you it giveth life. And when he had so said unto us, we were glad that we had questioned him, and we said to him: Lord, in all things thou makest us alive and hast mercy on us. Wilt thou now declare unto us that which we shall ask thee? Then said he unto us: Is it the flesh that passeth away, or is it the spirit? We said unto him: The flesh is it that passeth away. Then said he unto us: That which hath fallen shall rise again, and that which was lost shall be found, and that which was weak shall recover, that in these things that are so created the glory of my Father may be revealed. As he hath done unto me, so will I do unto all that believe in me.

26 Verily I say unto you: the flesh shall arise, and the soul, alive, that their defence may come to pass on that day in regard of that that they have done, whether it be good or evil: that there may be a choosing-out of the faithful who have kept the commandments of my Father that sent me; and so shall the judgement be accomplished with strictness. For my Father said unto me: My Son, in the day of judgement thou shalt have no respect for the rich, neither pity for the poor, but according to the sins of every man shalt thou deliver him unto everlasting torment. But unto my beloved that have done the commandments of my Father that sent me will I give the rest of life in the kingdom of my Father which is in heaven, and they shall behold that which he hath given me. And he hath given me authority to do that which I will, and to give that which I have promised and determined to give and grant unto them.

27 For to that end went I down unto the place of Lazarus, and preached unto the righteous and the prophets, that they might come out of the rest which is below and come up into that which is above; and I poured out upon them with my right hand the water (?) (baptism, *Eth.*) of life and forgiveness and salvation from all evil, as I have done unto you and unto them that believe on me. But if any man believe on me and do not my commandments, although he have confessed my name, he hath no profit therefrom but runneth a vain race: for such will find themselves in perdition and destruction, because they have despised my commandments.

28 But so much the more have I redeemed you, the children of light, from all evil and from the authority of the rulers (archons), and every one that believeth on me by your means. For that which I have promised unto you will I give unto them also, that they may come out of the prison-house and the fetters of the rulers. We answered and said: Lord, thou hast given unto us the rest of life and hast given us <joy?> by wonders, unto the confirmation of faith: wilt thou now preach the same unto us, seeing that thou hast preached it unto the <righteous> and the prophets? Then said he unto us: Verily I say unto you, all that have believed on me and that believe in him that sent me

will I take up into the heaven, unto the place which my Father hath prepared for the elect, and I will give you the kingdom, the chosen kingdom, in rest, and everlasting life.

29 But all they that have offended against my commandments and have taught other doctrine, (perverting) the Scripture and adding thereto, striving after their own glory, and that teach with other words them that believe on me in uprightness, if they make them fall thereby, shall receive everlasting punishment. We said unto him: Lord, shall there then be teaching by others, diverse from that which thou hast spoken unto us ? He said unto us: It must needs be, that the evil and the good may be made manifest; and the judgement shall be manifest upon them that do these things, and according to their works shall they be judged and shall be delivered unto death.

Again we said unto him: Lord, blessed are we in that we see thee and hear thee declaring such things, for our eyes have beheld these great wonders that thou hast done. He answered and said unto us: Yea, rather blessed are they that have not seen and yet have believed, for they shall be called children of the kingdom, and they shall be perfect among the perfect, and I will be unto them life in the kingdom of my Father. Again we said unto him: Lord, how shall men be able to believe that thou wilt depart and leave us; for thou sayest unto us: There shall come a day and an hour when I shall ascend unto my Father?

30 But he said unto us: Go ye and preach unto the twelve tribes, and preach also unto the heathen, and to all the land of Israel from the east to the west and from the south unto the north, and many shall believe on <me> the Son of God. But we said unto him: Lord, who will believe us, or hearken unto us, or (how shall we be able, *Eth.*) to teach the powers and signs and wonders which thou hast done ? Then answered he and said to us: Go ye and preach the mercifulness of my Father, and that which he hath done through me

will I myself do through you, for I am in you, and I will give you my peace, and I will give you a power of my spirit, that ye may prophesy to them unto life eternal. And unto the others also will I give my power, that they may teach the residue of the peoples.

[[(Six leaves lost in Copt.: Eth. continues.)]]

31 And behold a man shall meet you, whose name is Saul, which being interpreted is Paul: he is a Jew, circumcised according to the law, and he shall receive my voice from heaven with fear and terror and trembling. And his eyes shall be blinded, and by your hands by the sign of the cross shall they be protected (healed: *other Eth. MSS.* with spittle by your hands shall his eyes, &c.). Do ye unto him all that I have done unto you. Deliver it (? the word of God) unto the other. And at the same time that man shall open his eyes and praise the Lord, even my Father which is in heaven. He shall obtain power among the people and shall preach and instruct; and many that hear him shall obtain glory and be redeemed. But thereafter shall men be wroth with him and deliver him into the hands of his enemies, and he shall bear witness before kings that are mortal, and his end shall be that he shall turn unto me, whereas he persecuted me *at the first.* He shall preach and teach and abide with the elect, as a chosen vessel and a wall that shall not be overthrown, *yea,* the last of the last shall become a preacher unto the Gentiles, made perfect by the will of my Father. Like as ye have learned from the Scripture that your fathers the prophets spake of me, and in me it is indeed fulfilled.

And he said unto us: Be ye also therefore guides unto them; and all things that I said unto you, and that ye write concerning me (tell ye them), that I am the word of the Father and that the Father is in me. Such also shall ye be unto that man, as becometh you. Instruct him and bring to his mind that which is spoken of me in the Scripture

and is fulfilled, and thereafter shall he become the salvation of the Gentiles.
32 And we asked him: Lord, is there for us and for them the self-same expectation of the inheritance? He answered and said unto us: Are then the fingers of the hand like unto each other, or the ears of corn in the field, or do *all* fruit-trees bear the same fruit? Doth not every one bear fruit according to its nature? And we said unto him: Lord, wilt thou again speak unto us in parables? Then said he unto us: Lament not. Verily I say unto you, ye are my brethren, and my companions in the kingdom of heaven unto my Father, for so is his good pleasure. Verily I say unto you, unto them also whom ye teach and who believe on me will I give that expectation.
33 And we asked him again: When shall we meet with that man, and when wilt thou depart unto thy Father and our God and Lord? He answered and said unto us: That man will come out of the land of Cilicia unto Damascus of Syria, to root up the church which ye must found there. It is I that speak through you; and he shall come quickly: and he shall become strong in the faith, that the word of the prophet may be fulfilled, which saith: Behold, out of Syria will I begin to call together a new Jerusalem, and Sion will I subdue unto me, and it shall be taken, and the place which is childless shall be called the son and daughter of my Father, and my bride. For so hath it pleased him that sent me. But that man will I turn back, that he accomplish not his evil desire, and the praise of my Father shall be perfected in him, and after that I am gone home and abide with my Father, I will speak unto him from heaven, and all things shall be accomplished which I have told you before concerning him.
34 And we said unto him again: Lord, so many great things hast thou told us and revealed unto us as never yet were spoken, and in all hast thou given us rest and been gracious unto us. After thy resurrection thou didst reveal unto us all things that we might be saved indeed; but thou saidst unto us only:

There shall be wonders and strange appearances in heaven and on earth before the end of the world come. Tell us now, how shall we perceive it? And he answered us: I will teach it you; and not that which shall befall you only, but them also whom ye shall teach and who shall believe, as well as them who shall hear that man and believe on me. In those years and days shall it come to pass.

And we said again unto him: Lord, what shall come to pass? And he said unto us: Then shall they that believe and they that believe not hear (see, *Eth.*) a trumpet in the heaven, a vision of great stars which shall be seen in the day, wonderful sights in heaven reaching down to the earth; stars which fall upon the earth like fire, and a great and mighty hail of fire (a star shining from the east unto this place, like unto fire, *Eth.* 2). The sun and the moon fighting one with the other, a continual rolling and noise of thunders and lightnings, thunder and earthquake; cities falling and men perishing in their overthrow, a continual dearth for lack of rain, a terrible pestilence and great mortality, mighty and untimely, so that they that die lack burial: and the bearing forth of brethren and sisters and kinsfolk shall be upon one bier. The kinsman shall show no favour to his kinsman, nor any man to his neighbour. And they that were overthrown shall rise up and behold them that overthrew them, that they lack burial, for the pestilence shall be full of hatred and pain and envy: and men shall take from one and give to another. And thereafter shall it wax yet worse than before. (Bewail ye them that have not hearkened unto my commandments, *Eth.* 2.)
85 Then shall my Father be wroth at the wickedness of men, for many are their transgressions, and the abomination of their uncleanness weigheth heavy upon them in the corruption of their life. And we asked him: What of them that trust in thee? He answered and said unto us: Ye are yet slow of heart; and how long? Verily I say unto you, as the

prophet David spake of me and of my people, so shall it be (?) for them also that believe on me. But they that are deceivers in the world and enemies of righteousness, upon them shall come the fulfilment of the prophecy of David, who said: Their feet are swift to shed blood, their tongue uttereth slander, adders' poison is under their lips. I behold thee companying with thieves, and partaking with adulterers, thou continuest speaking against thy brother and puttest stumbling-blocks before thine own mother's son. What thinkest thou, that I shall be like unto thee? Behold now how the prophet of God hath spoken of all, that all things may be fulfilled which he said aforetime.

36 And again we said unto him: Lord, will not then the nations say: Where is their God? And he answered and said unto us: Thereby shall the elect be known, that they, being plagued with such afflictions, come forth. We said: Will then their departure out of the world be by a pestilence which giveth them pain? He answered us: Nay, but if they suffer such affliction, it will be a proving of them, whether they have faith and remember these my sayings, and fulfil my commandments. These shall arise, and short will be their expectation, that he may be glorified that sent me, and I with him. For he hath sent me unto you to tell you these things; and that ye may impart them unto Israel and the Gentiles and they may hear, and they also be redeemed and believe on me and escape the woe of the destruction. But whoso escapeth from the destruction of death, him will they take and hold him fast in the prison-house in torments like the torments of a thief.

And we said unto him: Lord, will they *that believe* be *treated* like the unbelievers, and wilt thou punish them that have escaped from the pestilence? And he said unto us: If they that believe in my name deal like the sinners, then have they done as though they had not believed. And we said again to him: Lord, have they on whom this lot hath fallen no life? He answered and said

unto us: Whoso hath accomplished the praise of my Father, he *shall abide in* the resting-place of my Father.

37 Then said we unto him: Lord, teach us what shall come to pass thereafter? And he answered us: In those years and days shall war be kindled upon war; the four ends of the earth shall be in commotion and fight against each other. Thereafter shall be quakings of clouds (*or*, clouds of locusts), darkness, and dearth, and persecutions of them that believe on me and against the elect. Thereupon shall come doubt and strife and transgressions against one another. And there shall be many that believe on my name and yet follow after evil and spread vain doctrine. And men shall follow after them and their riches, and be subject unto their pride, and lust for drink, and bribery, and there shall be respect of persons among them.

38 But they that desire to behold the face of God and respect not the persons of the rich sinners, and are not ashamed before the people that lead them astray, but rebuke (?) them, they shall be crowned by the Father. And they also shall be saved that rebuke their neighbours, for they are sons of wisdom and of faith. But if they become not children of wisdom, whoso hateth his brother and persecuteth him and showeth him no favour, him will God despise and reject.

[[(Copt. resumes.)]]

But they that walk in truth and in the knowledge of the faith, and have love towards me--for they have endured insult--they shall be praised for that they walk in poverty and endure them that hate them and put them to shame. Men have stripped them naked, for they despised them because they continued in hunger and thirst, but after they have endured patiently, they shall have the blessedness of heaven, and they shall be with me for ever. But woe unto them that walk in pride and boasting, for their end is perdition.

39 And we said unto him: Lord, is this thy purpose, that thou leavest us, to

come upon them? (Will all this come to pass, *Eth.*) He answered and said unto us: After what manner shall the judgement be? whether righteous or unrighteous? (In *Copt.* and *Eth.* the general sense is the same: but the answer of Jesus in the form of a question is odd, and there is probably a corruption.)

We said unto him: Lord, in that day they will say unto thee: Thou hast not distinguished between (*probably*: will they not say unto thee: Thou hast distinguished between) righteousness and unrighteousness, between the light and the darkness, and evil and good? Then said he: I will answer them and say: Unto Adam was power given to choose one of the two: he chose the light and laid his hand thereon, but the darkness he left behind him and cast away from him. Therefore have all men power to believe in the light which is life, and which is the Father that hath sent me. And every one that believeth and doeth the works of the light shall live in them; but if there be any that confesseth that he belongeth unto the light, and doeth the works of darkness, such an one hath no defence to utter, neither can he lift up his face to look upon the Son of God, which Son am I. For I will say unto him: As thou soughtest, so hast thou found, and as thou askedst, so hast thou received. Therefore condemnest thou me, O man? Wherefore hast thou departed from me and denied me? And wherefore hast thou confessed me and yet denied me? hath not every man power to live and to die? Whoso then hath kept my commandments shall be a son of the light, that is, of the Father that is in me. But because of them that corrupt my words am I come down from heaven. I am the word: I became flesh, and I wearied myself (or, suffered) and taught, saying: The heavy laden shall be saved, and they that are gone astray shall go astray for ever. They shall be chastised and tormented in their flesh and in their soul.

40 And we said unto him: O Lord, verily we are sorrowful for their sake.

And he said unto us: Ye do rightly, for the righteous are sorry for the sinners, and pray for them, making prayer unto my Father. Again we said unto him: Lord, is there none that maketh intercession unto thee (*so Eth.*)? And he said unto us: Yea, and I will hearken unto the prayer of the righteous which they make for them.

When he had so said unto us, we said to him: Lord, in all things hast thou taught us and had mercy on us and saved us, that we might preach unto them that are worthy to be saved, and that we might obtain a recompense with thee. (Shall we be partakers of a recompense from thee? *Eth.*) 41 He answered and said unto us: Go and preach, and ye shall be labourers, and fathers, and ministers. We said unto him: Thou art he (or, Art thou he) that shalt preach by us. (Lord, thou art our father. *Eth.*) Then answered he us, saying: Be not (*or*, Are not ye) all fathers or all masters. (Are then all fathers, or all servants, or all masters? *Eth.*) We said unto him: Lord, thou art he that saidst unto us: Call no man your father upon earth, for one is your Father, which is in heaven, and your master. Wherefore sayest thou now unto us: Ye shall be fathers of many children, and servants and masters? He answered and said unto us: According as ye have said (Ye have rightly said, *Eth.*). For verily I say unto you: whosoever shall hear you and believe on me, shall receive of you the light of the seal through me, and baptism through me: ye shall be fathers and servants and masters.

42 But we said unto him: Lord, how may it be that every one of us should be these three? He said unto us: Verily I say unto you: Ye shall be called fathers, because with praiseworthy heart and in love ye have revealed unto them the things of the kingdom of heaven. And ye shall be called servants, because they shall receive the baptism of life and the remission of their sins at my hand through you. And ye shall be called masters, because ye have given them the word without grudging, and have admonished them, and when ye

admonished them, they turned themselves (were converted). Ye were not afraid of their riches, nor ashamed before their face, but ye kept the commandments of my Father and fulfilled them. And ye shall have a great reward with my Father which is in heaven, and they shall have forgiveness of sins and everlasting life, and be partakers in the kingdom of heaven. And we said unto him: Lord, even if every one of us had ten thousand tongues to speak withal, we could not thank thee, for that thou promisest such things unto us. Then answered he us, saying: Only do ye that which I say unto you, even as I myself also have done it. 43 And ye shall be like the wise virgins which watched and slept not, but went forth unto the lord into the bridechamber: but the foolish *virgins* were not able to watch, but slumbered. And we said unto him: Lord, who are the wise and who are the foolish? He said unto us: Five wise and five foolish; for these are they of whom the prophet hath spoken: Sons of God are they. Hear now their names.

But we wept and were troubled for them that slumbered. He said unto us: The five wise are Faith and Love and Grace and Peace and Hope. Now they of the faithful which possess this (these) shall be guides unto them that have believed on me and on him that sent me. For I am the Lord and I am the bridegroom whom they have received, and they have entered in to the house of the bridegroom and are laid down with me in the bridal chamber rejoicing. But the five foolish, when they had slept and had awaked, came unto the door of the bridal chamber and knocked, for the doors were shut. Then did they weep and lament that no man opened unto them.

We said unto him: Lord, and their wise sisters that were within in the bridegroom's house, did they continue without opening unto them, and did they not sorrow for their sakes nor entreat the bridegroom to open unto them? He answered us, saying: They were not yet able to obtain favour for them. We said unto him: Lord, on what day shall they enter in for their sisters' sake? Then said he unto us: He that is shut out, is shut out. And we said unto him: Lord, is this word (determined?). Who then are the foolish? He said unto us: Hear their names. They are Knowledge, Understanding (Perception), Obedience, Patience, and Compassion. These are they that slumbered in them that have believed and confessed me but have not fulfilled my commandments. 44 On account of them that have slumbered, on they shall remain outside the kingdom and the fold of the shepherd and his sheep. But whoso shall abide outside the sheepfold, him will the wolves devour, and he shall be (condemned?) and die in much affliction: in him shall be no rest nor endurance, and (*Eth.*) although he be hardly punished, and rent in pieces and devoured in long and evil torment, yet shall he not be able to obtain death quickly.

45 And we said unto him: Lord, well hast thou revealed all this unto us. Then answered he us, saying: Understand ye not (*or*, Ye understand not) these words? We said unto him: Yea, Lord. By five shall men enter into thy kingdom <and by five shall men remain without>: notwithstanding, they that watched were with thee the Lord and bridegroom, even though they rejoiced not because of them that slumbered (yet will they have no pleasure, because of, *Eth.*). He said unto us: They will indeed rejoice that they have entered in with the bridegroom, the Lord; and they are sorrowful because of them that slumbered, for they are their sisters. For all ten are daughters of God, even the Father. Then said we unto him: Lord, is it then for thee to show them favour on account of their sisters? (It becometh thy majesty to show them favour, *Eth.*) He said unto us: <It is not mine,> but his that sent me, and I am consenting with him (It is not yours, &c., *Eth.*).

46 But be ye upright and preach rightly and teach, and be not abashed by any man and fear not any man, and especially the rich, for they do not my

commandments, but boast themselves (swell) in their riches. And we said unto him: Lord, tell us if it be the rich only. He answered, saying unto us: If any man who is not rich and possesseth a small livelihood giveth unto the poor and needy, men will call him a benefactor.

47 But if any man fall under the load <because> of sin that he hath committed, then shall his neighbour correct him because of the good that he hath done unto his neighbour. And if his neighbour correct him and he return, he shall be saved, and he that corrected him shall receive a reward and live for ever. For a needy man, if he see him that hath done him good sin, and correct him not, shall be judged with severe judgement. Now if a blind man lead a blind, they both fall into a ditch: and whoso respecteth persons for their sake, shall be as the two <blind>, as the prophet hath said: Woe unto them that respect persons and justify the ungodly for reward, even they whose God is their belly. Behold that judgement shall be their portion. For verily I say unto you: On that day will I neither have respect unto the rich nor pity for the poor.

48 If thou behold a sinner, admonish him betwixt him and thee: (if he hear thee, thou hast gained thy brother, *Eth.*) and if he hear thee not, then take to thee another, as many as three, and instruct thy brother: again, if he hear thee not, let him be unto thee...

[[(Copt. defective from this point.)]]

as an heathen man or a publican.

49 If thou hear aught against thy brother, give it no credence; slander not, and delight not in hearing slander. For thus it is written: Suffer not thine ear to receive aught against thy brother: but if thou seest aught, correct him, rebuke him, and convert him.

And we said unto him: Lord, thou hast in all things taught us and warned us. But, Lord, concerning the believers, even them to whom it belongeth to believe in the preaching of thy name: is it determined that among them also

there shall be doubt and division, jealousy, confusion, hatred, and envy? For thou sayest: They shall find fault with one another and respect the person of them that sin, and hate them that rebuke them. And he answered and said unto us: How then shall the judgement come about, that the corn should be gathered into the garner and the chaff thereof cast into the fire?

50 They that hate such things, and love me and rebuke them that fulfil not my commandments, shall be hated and persecuted and despised and mocked. Men will of purpose speak of them that which is not true, and will band themselves together against them that love me. But these will rebuke them, that they may be saved. But them that will rebuke and chasten and warn them, them will they (the others) hate, and thrust them aside, and despise them, and hold themselves far from them that wish them good. But they that endure such things shall be like unto the martyrs with the Father, because they have striven for righteousness, and have not striven for corruption.

And we asked him: Lord, shall such things be among us? And he answered us: Fear not; it shall not be in many, but in a few. We said unto him: Yet tell us, in what manner it shall come to pass. And he said unto us: There shall come forth another doctrine, and a confusion, and because they shall strive after their own advancement, they shall bring forth an unprofitable doctrine. And therein shall be a deadly corruption (of uncleanness), and they shall teach it, and shall turn away them that believe on me from my commandments and cut them off from eternal life. But woe unto them that falsify this my word and commandment, and draw away them that hearken to them from the life of the doctrine and separate themselves from the commandment of life: *for* together with them they shall come into everlasting judgement.

51 And when he had said this, and had finished his discourse with us, he said unto us again: Behold, on the third day and at the third hour shall he come

which hath sent me, that I may depart with him. And as he so spake, there was thunder and lightning and an earthquake, and the heavens parted asunder, and there appeared a light (bright) cloud which bore him up. And *there came* voices of many angels, rejoicing and singing praises and saying: Gather us, O Priest, unto the light of the majesty. And when they drew nigh unto the firmament, we heard his voice *saying unto us*: Depart hence in peace.

THE APOCALYPSE OF PETER

CHAPTER 1

THE Second Coming of Christ and Resurrection of the Dead which Christ revealed unto Peter of those who died because of their sins, for that they kept not the commandment of God their creator.

2 And Peter pondered thereon, that he might perceive the mystery of the Son of God, the merciful and lover of mercy.

3 And when the Lord was seated upon the Mount of Olives, his disciples came unto him.

4 And we besought and entreated him severally and prayed him, saying unto him: Declare unto us what are the signs of thy coming and of the end of the world, that we may perceive and mark the time of thy coming and instruct them that come after us, unto whom we preach the word of thy gospel, and whom we set over thy church, that they when they hear it may take heed to themselves and mark the time of thy coming.

5 And our Lord answered us, saying: Take heed that no man deceive you, and that ye be not doubters and serve other gods.

6 Many shall come in my name, saying:

I am the Christ. Believe them not, neither draw near unto them.

7 For the coming of the Son of God shall not be plain; but as the lightning that shineth from the east unto the west, so will I come upon the clouds of heaven with a great host in my majesty;

8 With my cross going before my face will I come in my majesty, shining sevenfold more than the sun will I come in my majesty with all my saints, mine holy angels.

9 And my Father shall set a crown upon mine head, that I may judge the quick and the dead and recompense every man according to his works.

10 And ye, take ye the likeness thereof and learn a parable from the fig-tree: so soon as the shoot thereof is come forth and the twigs grown, the end of the world shall come.

11 And I, Peter, answered and said unto him: Interpret unto me concerning the fig-tree, whereby we shall perceive it; for throughout all its days doth the fig-tree send forth shoots, and every year it bringeth forth its fruit for its master.

12 What then meaneth the parable of the fig-tree? We know it not.

13 And the Master (Lord) answered and said unto me: Understandest thou not that the fig-tree is the house of Israel?

14 Even as a man that planted a fig-tree in his garden, and it brought forth no fruit. And he sought the fruit thereof many years and when he found it not, he said to the keeper of his garden:

15 Root up this fig-tree that it make not our ground to be unfruitful. And the gardener said unto God:

16 Suffer us to rid it of weeds and dig the ground round about it and water it. If then it bear not fruit, we will straightway remove its roots out of the garden and plant another in place of it.

17 Hast thou not understood that the fig-tree is the house of Israel?

18 Verily I say unto thee, when the twigs thereof have sprouted forth in the last days, then shall the antichrist come and awake expectation saying: I am the Christ, that am now come into the world.

19 And when Israel shall perceive the

wickedness of their deeds they shall turn away after them and deny him; even the Christ whom they crucified and therein sinned a great sin.

21 But the deceiver is not the Christ but the antichrist.

22 And when they reject him he shall slay with the sword, and there shall be many martyrs.

23 Then shall the twigs of the fig-tree, that is, the house of Israel, shoot forth: many shall become martyrs at his hand.

24 Enoch and Elias shall be sent to teach them that this is the deceiver which must come into the world and do signs and wonders to deceive.

25 And therefore shall they that die by his hand be martyrs, and shall be reckoned among the good and righteous martyrs who have pleased God in their life.

26 And he showed me in his right hand the souls of all men, And on the palm of his right hand the image of that which shall be accomplished at the last day:

27 And how the righteous and the sinners shall be separated, and how they do that are upright in heart, and how the evil-doers shall be rooted out unto all eternity.

28 We beheld how the sinners wept in great affliction and sorrow, until all that saw it with their eyes wept, whether righteous or angels, and he himself also.

29 And I asked him and said unto him: Lord, suffer me to speak thy word concerning the sinners: It were better for them if they had not been created.

30 And the Saviour answered and said unto me: Peter, wherefore speakest thou thus, that not to have been created were better for them? Thou resistest God.

31 Thou wouldest not have more compassion than he for his image: for he hath created them and brought them forth out of not being.

32 Now because thou hast seen the lamentation which shall come upon the sinners in the last days, therefore is thine heart troubled; but I will show thee their works, whereby they have sinned against the Most High.

33 Behold now what shall come upon them in the last days, when the day of God and the day of the decision of the judgement of God cometh.

34 From the east unto the west shall all the children of men be gathered together before my Father that liveth for ever.

35 And he shall command hell to open its bars of adamant and give up all that is therein.

36 And the wild beasts and the fowls shall he command to restore all the flesh that they have devoured, because he willeth that men should appear; for nothing perisheth before God, and nothing is impossible with him, because all things are his.

37 For all things come to pass on the day of decision, on the day of judgement, at the word of God: and as all things were done when he created the world and commanded all that is therein and it was done.

38 Even so shall it be in the last days; for all things are possible with God. And therefore saith he in the scripture: Son of man, prophesy upon the several bones and say unto the bones: bone unto bone in joints, sinew. nerves, flesh and skin and hair thereon.

39 And soul and spirit shall the great Uriel give them at the commandment of God; for him hath God set over the rising again of the dead at the day of judgement.

40 Behold and consider the corns of wheat that are sown in the earth. As things dry and without soul do men sow them in the earth: and they live again and bear fruit, and the earth restoreth them as a pledge entrusted unto it.

41 And this that dieth, that is sown as seed in the earth, and shall become alive and be restored unto life, is man.

42 How much more shall God raise up on the day of decision them that believe in him and are chosen of him, for whose sake he made the world?

43 And all things shall the earth restore on the day of decision, for it also shall be judged with them, and the heaven with it.

CHAPTER 2

AND this shall come at the day of

judgement upon them that have fallen away from faith in God and that have committed sin:

2 Floods of fire shall be let loose; and darkness and obscurity shall come up and clothe and veil the whole world and the waters shall be changed and turned into coals of fire and all that is in them shall burn, and the sea shall become fire.

3 Under the heaven shall be a sharp fire that cannot be quenched and floweth to fulfil the judgement of wrath.

4 And the stars shall fly in pieces by flames of fire, as if they had not been created and the firmaments of the heaven shall pass away for lack of water and shall be as though they had not been.

5 The heaven shall turn to lightning and the lightnings thereof shall affright the world.

6 The spirits also of the dead bodies shall be like unto them and shall become fire at the commandment of God.

7 And so soon as the whole creation dissolveth, the men that are in the east shall flee unto the west, unto the east; they that are in the south shall flee to the north, and they that are in the south.

8 And in all places shall the wrath of a fearful fire overtake them and an unquenchable flame driving them shall bring them unto the judgement of wrath, unto the stream of unquenchable fire that floweth, flaming with fire.

9 And when the waves thereof part themselves one from another, burning, there shall be a great gnashing of teeth among the children of men.

10 Then shall they all behold me coming upon an eternal cloud of brightness: and the angels of God that are with me.

11 I shall sit upon the throne of my glory at the right hand of my Heavenly Father; and he shall set a crown upon mine head.

12 And when the nations behold it, they shall weep, every nation apart.

13 Then shall he command them to enter into the river of fire while the works of every one of them shall stand before them; to every man according to his deeds.

14 As for the elect that have done good, they shall come unto me and not see death by the devouring fire.

15 But the unrighteous, the sinners, and the hypocrites shall stand in the depths of darkness that shall not pass away, and their chastisement is the fire, and angels bring forward their sins and prepare for them a place wherein they shall be punished for ever every one according to his transgression.

16 And Uriel, the angel of God, shall bring forth the souls of those sinners; every one according to his transgression who perished in the flood.

17 And of all that dwelt in all idols, in every molten image, in every object of love, and in pictures, and of those that dwelt on all hills and in stones and by the wayside, whom men called gods: they shall burn them with them in everlasting fire;

18 And after that all of them with their dwelling places are destroyed, they shall be punished eternally.

CHAPTER 3

1 Then many false prophets shall come, and shall teach ways and diverse doctrines of perdition.

2 And they shall become sons of perdition.

3 And then shall God come unto my faithful ones that hunger and thirst and are afflicted and prove their souls in this life, and shall judge the sons of iniquity.

4 And the Lord added and said: Let us go unto the mountain (and) pray.

5 And going with him, we the twelve disciples besought him that he would show us one of our righteous brethren that had departed out of the world, that we might see what manner of men they are in their form, and take courage, and encourage also the men that should hear us.

6 And as we prayed, suddenly there appeared two men standing before the Lord (perhaps add, to the east) upon whom we were not able to look.

7 For there issued from their countenance a ray as of the sun, and

their raiment was shining so as the eye of man never saw the like: for no mouth is able to declare nor heart to conceive the glory wherewith they were clad and the beauty of their countenance.

8 Whom when we saw we were astonied, for their bodies were whiter than any snow and redder than any rose.

9 And the redness of them was mingled with the whiteness, and, in a word, I am not able to declare their beauty.

10 For their hair was curling and flourishing (flowery), and fell comely about their countenance and their shoulders like a garland woven of nard and various flowers, or like a rainbow in the air: such was their comeliness.

11 We, then, seeing the beauty of them were astonied at them, for they appeared suddenly.

12 And I drew near to the Lord and said: Who are these?

13 He saith to me: These are your (our) righteous brethren whose appearance ye did desire to see.

14 And I said unto him: And where are all the righteous? or of what sort is the world wherein they are, and possess this glory?

15 And the Lord showed me a very great region outside this world exceeding bright with light, and the air of that place illuminated with the beams of the sun, and the earth of itself flowering with blossoms that fade not, and full of spices and plants, fair-flowering and incorruptible, and bearing blessed fruit.

16 And so great was the blossom that the odour thereof was borne thence even unto us.

17 And the dwellers in that place were clad with the raiment of shining angels, and their raiment was like unto their land.

18 And angels ran round about them there.

19 And the glory of them that dwelt there was all equal, and with one voice they praised the Lord God, rejoicing in that place.

20 The Lord saith unto us: This is the place of your leaders (or, high priests), the righteous men.

21 And I saw also another place over against that one, very squalid; and it was a place of punishment, and they that were punished and the angels that punished them had their raiment dark, according to the air of the place.

22 And some there were there hanging by their tongues; and these were they that blasphemed the way of righteousness, and under them was laid fire flaming and tormenting them.

23 And there was a great lake full of flaming mire, wherein were certain men that turned away from righteousness; and angels, tormentors, were set over them.

24 And there were also others, women, hanged by their hair above that mire which boiled up; and these were they that adorned themselves for adultery. And the men that were joined with them in the defilement of adultery were hanging by their feet, and had their heads hidden in the mire, and said: We believed not that we should come unto this place.

25 And I saw the murderers and them that were consenting to them cast into a strait place full of evil, creeping things, and smitten by those beasts, and so turning themselves about in that torment. And upon them were set worms like clouds of darkness. And the souls of them that were murdered stood and looked upon the torment of those murderers and said: O God, righteous is thy judgement.

26 And hard by that place I saw another strait place wherein the discharge and the stench of them that were in torment ran down, and there was as it were a lake there. And there sat women up to their necks in that liquor, and over against them many children which were born out of due time sat crying: and from them went forth rays of fire and smote the women in the eyes: and these were they that conceived out of wedlock (?) and caused abortion.

27 And other men and women were being burned up to their middle and cast down in a dark place and scourged by evil spirits, and having their entrails devoured by worms that rested not. And

these were they that had persecuted the righteous and delivered them up.

28 And near to them again were women and men gnawing their lips and in torment, and having iron heated in the fire set against their eyes. And these were they that did blaspheme and speak evil of the way of righteousness.

29 And over against these were yet others, men and women, gnawing their tongues and having flaming fire in their mouths. And these were the false witnesses.

30 And in another place were gravel-stones sharper than swords or any spit, heated with fire, and men and women clad in filthy rags rolled upon them in torment. And these were they that were rich and trusted in their riches, and had no pity upon orphans and widows but neglected the commandments of God.

31 And in another great lake full of foul matter and blood and boiling mire stood men and women up to their knees And these were they that lent money and demanded usury upon usury.

32 And other men and women being cast down from a great rock fell to the bottom, and again were driven by them that were set over them, to go up upon the rock, and thence were cast down to the bottom and had no rest from this torment. And these were they that did defile their bodies behaving as women: and the women that were with them were they that lay with one another as a man with a woman.

33 And beside that rock was a place full of much fire, and there stood men which with their own hands had made images for themselves instead of God, [And beside them other men and women] having rods of fire and smiting one another and never resting from this manner of torment.

34 And yet others near unto them, men and women, burning and turning themselves about and roasted as in a pan. And these were they that forsook the way of God.

CHAPTER 4

THEN shall men and women come unto the place prepared for them. By their tongues wherewith they have blasphemed the way of righteousness shall they be hanged up.

2 There is spread under them unquenchable fire, that they escape it not.

3 Behold, another place: therein is a pit, great and full. In it are they that have denied righteousness:

4 And angels of punishment chastise them and there do they kindle upon them the fire of their torment.

5 And again behold two corrupt women: they hang them up by their neck and by their hair; they shall cast them into the pit.

6 These are they which plaited their hair, not for good but to turn them to fornication, that they might ensnare the souls of men unto perdition.

7 And the men that lay with them in fornication shall be hung by their loins in that place of fire; and they shall say one to another: We knew not that we should come unto everlasting punishment.

8 And the murderers and them that have made common cause with them shall they cast into the fire, in a place full of venomous beasts, and they shall be tormented without rest, feeling their pains; and their worms shall be as many in number as a dark cloud.

9 And the angel Ezrael shall bring forth the souls of them that have been slain, and they shall behold the torment of them that slew them, and say one to another: Righteousness and justice is the judgement of God.

10 For we heard, but we believed not, that we should come into this place of eternal judgement.

11 And near by this flame shall be a pit, great and very deep, and into it floweth from above all manner of torment, foulness, and issue.

12 And women are swallowed up therein up to their necks and tormented with great pain. These are they that have caused their children to be born untimely, and have corrupted the work of God that created them.

13 Over against them shall be another place where sit their children [both]

alive, and they cry unto God.

14 And flashes (lightnings) go forth from those children and pierce the eyes of them that for fornication's sake have caused their destruction.

15 Other men and women shall stand above them, naked; and their children stand over against them in a place of delight, and sigh and cry unto God because of their parents, saying:

16 These are they that have despised and cursed and transgressed thy commandments and delivered us unto death: they have cursed the angel that formed us, and have hanged us up, and withheld from us (or, begrudged us) the light which thou hast given unto all creatures.

17 And the milk of their mothers flowing from their breasts shall congeal, and from it shall come beasts devouring flesh, which shall come forth and turn and torment them for ever with their husbands, because they forsook the commandments of God and slew their children.

18 As for their children, they shall be delivered unto the angel Temlakos.

19 And they that slew them shall be tormented eternally, for God willeth it so.

20 Ezrael the angel of wrath shall bring men and women, the half of their bodies burning, and cast them into a place of darkness, even the hell of men; and a spirit of wrath shall chastise them with all manner of torment, and a worm that sleepeth not shall devour their entrails: and these are the persecutors and betrayers of my righteous ones.

21 And beside them that are there, shall be other men and women, gnawing their tongues; and they shall torment them with red-hot iron and burn their eyes.

22 These are they that slander and doubt of my righteousness. Other men and women whose works were done in deceitfulness shall have their lips cut off, and fire entereth into their mouth and their entrails.

23 These are the false witnesses (al. these are they that caused the martyrs to die by their lying).

24 And beside them, in a place near at hand, upon the stone shall be a pillar of fire, and the pillar is sharper than swords.

25 And there shall be men and women clad in rags and filthy garments, and they shall be cast thereon, to suffer the judgement of a torment that ceaseth not: these are they that trusted in their riches and despised the widows and the woman with fatherless children before God.

26 And into another place hard by, full of filth, do they cast men and women up to the knees. These are they that lent money and took usury.

27 And other men and women cast themselves down from an high place and return again and run, and devils drive them. [These are the worshippers of idols] and they put them to the end of their wits (drive them up to the top of the height) and they cast themselves down.

28 And thus do they continually, and are tormented for ever. These are they which have cut their flesh as [apostles] of a man: and the women that were with them and these are the men that defiled themselves together as women.

29 And beside them shall be a fire burning and beneath them shall the angel Ezrael prepare a place of much fire: and all the idols of gold and silver, all idols, the work of men's hands, and the semblances of images of cats and lions, of creeping things and wild beasts, and the men and women that have prepared the images thereof, shall be in chains of fire and shall be chastised because of their error before the idols, and this is their judgement for ever.

30 And beside them shall be other men and women, burning in the fire of the judgement, and their torment is everlasting. These are they that have forsaken the commandment of God and followed the (persuasions ?) of devils.

31 And there shall be another place, very high.

32 There shall be a furnace and a brazier wherein shall burn fire. The fire that shall burn shall come from one end of the brazier).

33 The men and women whose feet slip, shall go rolling down into a place where is fear. And again while the fire that is prepared floweth, they mount up and fall down again and continue to roll down.

34 Thus shall they be tormented for ever. These are they that honoured not their father and mother and of their own accord withheld (withdrew) themselves from them. Therefore shall they be chastised eternally.

35 Furthermore the angel Ezrael shall bring children and maidens to show them those that are tormented.

36 They shall be chastised with pains, with hanging up (?) and with a multitude of wounds which flesh-devouring birds shall inflict upon them.

37 These are they that boast themselves (trust) in their sins, and obey not their parents and follow not the instruction of their fathers, and honour not them that are more aged than they.

38 Beside them shall be girls clad in darkness for a garment and they shall be sore chastised and their flesh shall be torn in pieces.

39 These are they that kept not their virginity until they were given in marriage, and with these torments shall they be punished, and shall feel them.

40 And again, other men and women, gnawing their tongues without ceasing, and being tormented with everlasting fire. These are the servants (slaves) which were not obedient unto their masters; and this then is their judgement for ever.

41 And hard by this place of torment shall be men and women dumb and blind, whose raiment is white.

42 They shall crowd one upon another, and fall upon coals of unquenchable fire. These are they that give alms and say:

43 We are righteous before God: whereas they have not sought after righteousness.

Ezrael the angel of God shall bring them forth out of this fire and establish a judgement of decision.

44 This then is their judgement. A river of fire shall flow and all judgement (they that are judged) shall be drawn down into the middle of the river.

45 And Uriel shall set them there. And there are wheels of fire and men and women hung thereon by the strength of the whirling thereof.

46 And they that are in the pit shall burn: now these are the sorcerers and sorceresses. Those wheels shall be in a decision (judgement, punishment) by fire without number.

47 Thereafter shall the angels bring mine elect and righteous which are perfect in all uprightness, and bear them in their hands, and clothe them with the raiment of the life that is above.

48 They shall see their desire on them that hated them, when he punisheth them, and the torment of every one shall be for ever according to his works.

49 And all they that are in torment shall say with one voice: have mercy upon us, for now know we the judgement of God, which he declared unto us aforetime, and we believed not.

50 And the angel Tatirokos (Tartaruchus, keeper of hell: a word corresponding in formation to Temeluchus) shall come and chastise them with yet greater torment, and say unto them:

51 Now do ye repent, when it is no longer the time for repentance, and nought of life remaineth.

52 And they shall say: Righteous is the judgement of God, for we have heard and perceived that his judgement is good; for we are recompensed according to our deeds.

CHAPTER 5

1 Then will I give unto mine elect and righteous the washing (baptism) and the salvation for which they have besought me, in the field of Akrosja which is called Aneslasleja (Elysium).

2 They shall adorn with flowers the portion of the righteous, and I shall go and I shall rejoice with them.

3 I will cause the peoples to enter in to mine everlasting kingdom, and show them that eternal thing (life ?) whereon I have made them to set their hope, even I and my Father which is in

heaven.

4 I have spoken this unto thee, Peter, and declared it unto thee. Go forth therefore and go unto the land (or city) of the west.

5 And enter into the vineyard which I shall tell thee of, in order that by the sickness (sufferings) of the Son who is without sin the deeds of corruption may be sanctified.

6 As for thee, thou art chosen according to the promise which I have given thee. Spread thou therefore my gospel throughout all the world in peace.

7 Verily men shall rejoice: my words shall be the source of hope and of life, and suddenly shall the world be ravished.

8 And my Lord Jesus Christ our King said unto me: Let us go unto the holy mountain. 9 And his disciples went with him, praying.

9 And behold there were two men there, and we could not look upon their faces, for a light came from them, shining more than the sun, and their rairment also was shining, and cannot be described, and nothing is sufficient to be compared unto them in this world.

10 And the sweetness of them was so that no mouth is able to utter the beauty of their appearance (or, the mouth hath not sweetness to express, &c.), for their aspect was astonishing and wonderful.

11 And the other, great, I say (probably: and, in a word, I cannot describe it), shineth in his aspect above crystal.

12 Like the flower of roses is the appearance of the colour of his aspect and of his body . . . his head (al. their head was a marvel).

13 And upon his (their) shoulders (evidently something about their hair has dropped out) and on their foreheads was a crown of nard woven of fair flowers.

14 As the rainbow in the water, [Probably: in the time of rain. From the LXX of Ezek.i.28.] so was their hair.

15 And such was the comeliness of their countenance, adorned with all manner of ornament.

16 And when we saw them on a sudden, we marvelled.

17 And I drew near unto the Lord (God) Jesus Christ and said unto him:

18 O my Lord, who are these? And he said unto me: They are Moses and Elias.

19 And I said unto him: Abraham and Isaac and Jacob and the rest of the righteous fathers?

20 And he showed us a great garden, open, full of fair trees and blessed fruits, and of the odour of perfumes.

21 The fragrance thereof was pleasant and came even unto us. And thereof (al. of that tree) . . . saw I much fruit. And my Lord and God Jesus Christ said unto me: Hast thou seen the companies of the fathers?

22 As is their rest, such also is the honour and the glory of them that are persecuted for my righteousness' sake. And I rejoiced and believed [and believed] and understood that which is written in the book of my Lord Jesus Christ.

23 And I said unto him: O my Lord, wilt thou that I make here three tabernacles, one for thee, and one for Moses, and one for Elias?

24 And he said unto me in wrath: Satan maketh war against thee, and hath veiled thine understanding; and the good things of this world prevail against thee.

25 Thine eyes therefore must be opened and thine ears unstopped that a tabernacle, not made with men's hands, which my heavenly Father hath made for me and for the elect.

26 And we beheld it and were full of gladness.

27 And behold, suddenly there came a voice from heaven, saying: This is my beloved Son in whom I am well pleased.

28 And then came a great and exceeding white cloud over our heads and bare away our Lord and Moses and Elias.

29 And I trembled and was afraid: and we looked up and the heaven opened and we beheld men in the flesh, and they came and greeted our Lord and Moses and Elias and went into another heaven.

30 And the word of the scripture was fulfilled: This is the generation that seeketh him and seeketh the face of the God of Jacob.

31 And great fear and commotion was there in heaven and the angels pressed one upon another that the word of the scripture might be fulfilled which saith: Open the gates, ye princes.

32 Thereafter was the heaven shut, that had been open.

33 And we prayed and went down from the mountain, glorifying God, which hath written the names of the righteous in heaven in the book of life.

34 And the Lord opened my mouth and I said 'God created all things for his glory,'

35 'The Son at his coming will raise the dead and will make my righteous ones shine seven times more than the sun, and will make their crowns shine like crystal and like the rainbow in the time of rain (crowns) which are perfumed with nard and cannot be contemplated (adorned) with rubies, with the colour of emeralds shining brightly, with topazes, gems, and yellow pearls that shine like the stars of heaven, and like the rays of the sun, sparkling which cannot be gazed upon.'

36 Their eyes shall shine like the morning star. The beauty of their appearance cannot be expressed....
Their raiment is not woven, but white as that of the fuller, according as I saw on the mountain where Moses and Elias were.

37 Our Lord showed at the transfiguration the apparel of the last days, of the day of resurrection, unto Peter, James and John the sons of Zebedee, and a bright cloud overshadowed us, and we heard the voice of the Father saying unto us:

38 This is my Son whom I love and in whom I am well pleased: hear him. And being afraid we forgat all the things of this life and of the flesh, and knew not what we said because of the greatness of the wonder of that day, and of the mountain whereon he showed us the second coming in the kingdom that passeth not away.

39 For the Father hath committed all judgement unto the Son.'

40 And my Lord answered me and said to me: 'Hast thou understood that which I said unto thee before?

41 It is permitted unto thee to know that concerning which thou askest: but thou must not tell that which thou hearest unto the sinners lest they transgress the more, and sin.'

42 'My Father will give unto them all the life, the glory, and the kingdom that passeth not away,' . . . 'It is because of them that have believed in me that I am come. It is also because of them that have believed in me, that, at their word, I shall have pity on men.'

THE APOCALYPSE OF PAUL

Here Begins the Vision of Saint Paul the Apostle.
"But I will come to visions and revelations of the Lord: I know a man in Christ fourteen years ago (whether in the body, I know not; or out of the body, I know not, God knoweth) snatched up in this manner to the third heaven: and I know such a man, whether in the body or out of the body I know not, God knoweth; how that he was snatched up into Paradise and heard secret words which it is not lawful for men to speak; on behalf of such a one will I glory; but on mine own behalf I will not glory, save in my infirmities."
-2 Corinthians 12:1-5

1 At what time was this revelation made? In the consulship of Theodosius Augustus the Younger and Cynegius, a certain nobleman then living in Tarsus, in the house which was that of Saint Paul, an angel appearing in the night revealed to him, saying that he should open the foundations of the house and

should publish what he found, but he thought that these things were dreams. 2 But the angel coming for the third time forced him to open the foundation. And digging he found a marble box, inscribed on the sides; there was the revelation of Saint Paul, and his shoes in which he walked teaching the word of God. But he feared to open that box and brought it to the judge; when he had received it, the judge, because it was sealed with lead, sent it to the Emperor Theodosius, fearing lest it might be something else; which when he had received the emperor opened it, and found the revelation of Saint Paul; a copy of it he sent to Jerusalem, and retained the original himself.

3 While I was in the body in which I was snatched up to the third heaven, the word of the Lord came to me saying: speak to the people: until when will you transgress, and heap sin upon sin, and tempt the Lord who made you? You are the sons of God, doing the works of the devil in the faith of Christ, on account of the impediments of the world. Remember therefore and know that while every creature serves God, the human race alone sins. But it reigns over every creature and sins more than all nature.

4 For indeed the sun, the great light, often addressed the Lord saying: Lord God Almighty, I look out upon the impieties and injustices of men; permit me and I shall do unto them what are my powers, that they may know that you are God alone. And there came a voice saying to him: I know all these things, for my eye sees and ear hears, but my patience bears them until they shall be converted and repent. But if they do not return to me I will judge them all.

5 For sometimes the moon and stars addressed the Lord saying: Lord God Almighty, to us you have given the power of the night; till when shall we look down upon the impieties and fornications and homicides done by the sons of men? Permit us to do unto them according to our powers, that they may know that you are God alone. And there

came a voice unto them saying: I know all these things, and my eye looks forth and ear hears, but my patience bears with them until they shall be converted and repent. But if they do not return unto me I will judge them.

6 And frequently also the sea exclaimed saying: Lord God Almighty, men have defiled your holy name in me; permit me to arise and cover every wood and orchard and the whole world, until I blot out all the sons of men from before your face, that they may know that you are God alone. And the voice came again and said: I know all things; my eye sees everything, and mine ear hears, but my patience bears with them until they be converted and repent. But if they do not return, I will judge them. Sometimes the waters also spoke against the sins of men saying: Lord God Almighty, all the sons of men have defiled your holy name. And there came a voice saying: I know all things before they come to pass, for my eye sees and mine ear hears all things, but my patience bears with them until they be converted. But if not I will judge them. Frequently also the earth too exclaimed to the Lord against the sons of men saying: Lord God Almighty, I above every other creature of yours am harmed, supporting the fornications, adulteries, homicides, thefts, perjuries and magic and ill-doings of men and all the evil they do, so that the father rises up against the son, and the son upon the father, the alien against the alien, so that each one defiles his neighbour's wife. The father ascends upon the bed of his own son, and the son likewise ascends the couch of his own father; and in all these evils, they who offer the sacrifice to your name have defiled your holy place. Therefore I am injured above every creature, desiring not to show my power to myself, and my fruits to the sons of men. Permit me and I will destroy the virtue of my fruits. And there came a voice and said: I know all things, and there is none who can hide himself from his sin. Moreover I know their impieties, but my holiness suffers them until they be converted and repent.

But if they do not return unto me I will judge them.

7 Behold, you sons of men, the creature is subject to God, but the human race alone sins. For this cause, therefore, you sons of men, bless the Lord God unceasingly, every hour and every day: but more especially when the sun has set: for at that hour all the angels proceed to the Lord to worship him and to present the works of men, which every man has wrought from the morning till the evening, whether good or evil. And there is a certain angel who proceeds rejoicing concerning the man in whom he dwells. When therefore the sun has set in the first hour of night, in the same hour the angel of every people and every man and woman, who protect and preserve them, because man is the image of God: similarly also in the matin hour which is the twelfth of the night, all the angels of men and women, go up to God to worship God, and present every work which each man has wrought, whether good or evil. Moreover every day and night the angels show to God an account of all the acts of the human race. To you, therefore, I say, you sons of men, bless the Lord God without fail all the days of your life.

8 Therefore at the appointed hour all the angels whatever, rejoicing at once together, proceed before God that they may meet to worship at the hour determined. And behold suddenly it became the hour of meeting, and the angels came to worship in the presence of God, and the spirit proceeded to meet them: and there came a voice and said: Whence come ye, our angels, bearing the burdens of tidings?

9 They answered and said: We come from those who have renounced this world for the sake of your holy name, wandering as pilgrims, and in caves of the rocks, and weeping every hour in which they inhabited the earth, and hungering and thirsting because of your name, with their loins girded, having in their hands the incense of their hearts, and praying and blessing every hour, and restraining and overcoming

themselves, weeping and wailing above the rest that inhabit the earth. And we indeed, their angels, mourn along with them: whither therefore it shall please you, command us to go and minister, lest others also do it, but the destitute above the rest who are on earth. And there came the voice of God to them saying: Know ye that now henceforward my grace is appointed unto you, and my help, who is my well-beloved Son, shall be present with them, guiding them every hour; ministering also to them, never deserting them, since their place is his habitation.

10 When therefore these angels had retired, behold other angels came to adore in the presence of honour, in the assembly, who wept; and the spirit of God proceeded to meet them, and there came the voice of God and said: Whence come ye, our angels, bearing the burdens of the ministry of the tidings of the world? They answered and said in the presence of God: We have arrived from those who called upon your name, and the impediments of the world made them wretched, devising many occasions every hour, not even making one pure prayer, nor out of their whole heart, in all the time of their life; what need, therefore, is there to be present with men who are sinners? And there came the voice of God to them: It is necessary that you should minister to them, until they be converted and repent: but if they do not return to me I will judge them. Know therefore, sons of men, that whatever things are wrought by you, these angels relate to God, whether good or evil.

11 And the angel answered and said unto me: Follow me, and I will show you the place of the just where they are led when they are deceased, and after these things taking you into the abyss, I will show you the souls of sinners and what sort of place they are led into when they have deceased. And I proceeded back after the angel, and he led me into heaven, and I looked back upon the firmament, and I saw in the same place power, and there was there

oblivion which deceives and draws down to itself the hearts of men, and the spirit of detraction, and the spirit of fornication, and the spirit of madness, and the spirit of insolence, and there were there the princes of vices: these I saw under the firmament of heaven: and again I looked back, and I saw angels without mercy, having no pity, whose countenance was full of madness, and their teeth sticking out beyond the mouth: their eyes shone like the morning star of the east, and from the hairs of their head sparks of fire went out, or from their mouth. And I asked the angel saying: Sir, who are those? And the angel answered and said unto me: These are those who are destined to the souls of the impious in the hour of need, who did not believe that they had the Lord for their helper, nor hoped in him.

12 And I looked on high and I saw other angels whose countenance shone as the sun, their loins girded with golden girdles, having palms in their hands, and the sign of God, clothed with garments in which was written the name of the Son of God, filled moreover with all meekness and pity; and I asked the angels saying: Who are these, Lord, in so great beauty and pity? And the angel answered and said unto me: These are the angels of justice who are sent to lead up the souls of the just, in the hour of need, who believed that they had the Lord for their helper. And I said to him: Do the just and sinners necessarily meet witnesses when they have died? And the angel answered and said to me: There is one way by which all pass over to God, but the just having their helper with them are not confounded when they go to appear in the sight of God.

13 And I said to the angel: I wished to see the souls of the just and of sinners going out of the world. And the angel answered and said unto me: Look down upon the earth. And I looked down from heaven upon the earth, and saw the whole world, and it was nothing in my sight and I saw the sons of men as though they were naught, and a-

wanting, and I wondered and said to the angel: Is this the greatness of men? And the angel answered and said unto me: It is, and these are they who do evil from morning till evening. And I looked and saw a great cloud of fire spread over the whole world, and I said to the angel: What is this, my Lord? And he said to me: This is injustice stirred up by the princes of sinners.

14 I indeed when I had heard this sighed and wept, and said to the angel: I wished to see the souls of the just and of sinners, and to see in what manner they go out of the body. And the angel answered and said unto me: Look again upon the earth. And I looked and saw all the world, and men were as naught and a-wanting: and I looked carefully and saw a certain man about to die, and the angel said to me: This one whom you see is a just man. And I looked again and saw all his works, whatever he had done for the sake of God's name, and all his desires, both what he remembered, and what he did not remember; they all stood in his sight in the hour of need; and I saw the just man advance and find refreshment and confidence, and before he went out of the world the holy and the impious angels both attended: and I saw them all, but the impious found no place of habitation in him, but the holy took possession of his soul, guiding it till it went out of the body: and they roused the soul saying: Soul, know your body whence you go out, for it is necessary that you should return to the same body on the day of the resurrection, that you may receive the things promised to all the just. Receiving therefore the soul from the body, they immediately kissed it as familiarly known to them, saying to it: Do manfully, for you have done the will of God while placed in the earth. And there came to meet him the angel who watched him every day, and said to him: Do manfully, soul; for I rejoice in you, because you have done the will of God on earth: for I related to God all your works, such as they were. Similarly also the spirit proceeded to meet him and said: Soul, fear not, nor

be disturbed, until you come into a place which you have never known, but I will be a helper unto you: for I found in you a place of refreshment in the time when I dwelt in you, while I was on earth. And his spirit strengthened him, and his angel received him, and led him into heaven: and an angel said: Whither do you run, O soul, and do you dare to enter into heaven? Wait and let us see if there is anything of ours in you: and behold we find nothing in you. I see also your divine helper and angel, and the spirit is rejoicing along with you, because you have done the will of God on earth. And they led him along till he should worship in the sight of God. And when they had ceased, immediately Michael and all the army of angels, with one voice, adored the footstool of his feet, and his doom, saying at the same time to the soul: This is your God of all things, who made you in his own image and likeness. Moreover the angel returns and points him out saying: God, remember his labours: for this is the soul, whose works I related to you, doing according to your judgment. And the spirit said likewise: I am the spirit of vivification inspiring him: for I had refreshment in him, in the time when I dwelt in him, doing according to your judgment. And there came the voice of God and said: In as much as this man did not vex me, neither will I vex him; for according as he had pity, I also will have pity. Let him therefore be handed over to Michael, the angel of the Covenant, and let him lead him into the Paradise of joy, that he himself may become co-heir with all the saints. And after these things I heard the voices of a thousand thousand angels, and archangels, and cherubim, and twenty-four elders saying hymns, and glorifying the Lord and crying: you are just, O Lord, and just are your judgments, and there is no acceptance of persons with you, but you reward unto every man according to your judgment. And the angel answered and said unto me: Have you believed and known, that whatever each man of you has done, he sees in the hour of

need? And I said: Yes, sir.

15 And he says to me: Look again down on the earth, and watch the soul of an impious man going out of the body, which vexed the Lord day and night, saying: I know nothing else in this world, I eat and drink, and enjoy what is in the world; for who is there who has descended into hell, and ascending has declared to us that there is judgment there! And again I looked carefully, and saw all the scorn of the sinner, and all that he did, and they stood together before him in the hour of need: and it was done to him in that hour, in which he was threatened about his body at the judgment, and I said: It were better for him if he had not been born. And after these things, there came at the same time, the holy angels, and the malign, and the soul of the sinner and the holy angels did not find a place in it. Moreover the malign angels cursed it; and when they had drawn it out of the body, the angels admonished it a third time, saying: O wretched soul, look upon your flesh, whence you came out: for it is necessary that you should return to your flesh in the day of resurrection, that you may receive the due for your sins and your impieties.

16 And when they had led it forth, the customary angel preceded it, and said to it: O wretched soul, I am the angel belonging to you, relating daily to the Lord your malign works, whatever you did by night or day: and if it were in my power, not for one day would I minister to you, but none of these things was I able to do: the judge is pitiful and just, and he himself commanded us that we should not cease to minister to the soul, till you should repent, but you have lost the time of repentance. I indeed was strange to you and you to me. Let us go on then to the just judge: I will not dismiss you, before I know from today why I was strange to you. And the spirit confounded him, and the angel troubled him. When, therefore, they had arrived at the power, when he started to enter heaven, a labour was imposed upon him, above all other labour: error and oblivion and murmuring met him, and

the spirit of fornication, and the rest of the powers, and said to him: Where are you going, wretched soul, and do you dare to rush into heaven? Hold, that we may see if we have our qualities in you, since we do not see that you have a holy helper. And after that I heard voices in the height of heaven saying: Present that wretched soul to God, that it may know that it is God that it despised. When, therefore, it had entered heaven, all the angels saw it, a thousand thousand exclaimed with one voice, all saying: Woe to you, wretched soul, for the sake of your works which you did on earth; what answer are you about to give to God when you shall have approached to adore him? The angel who was with it answered and said: Weep with me, my beloved, for I have not found rest in this soul. And the angels answered him and said: Let such a soul be taken away from the midst of ours, for from the time he entered, the stink of him crosses to us angels. And after these things it was presented, that it might worship in the sight of God, and an angel of God showed him God who made him after his own image and likeness. Moreover his angel ran before him saying: Lord God Almighty, I am the angel of this soul, whose works I presented to you day and night, not doing according to your judgment. And the spirit likewise said: I am the spirit who dwelt in it from the time it was made, in itself moreover I know it, and it has not followed my will: judge it, Lord, according to your judgment. And there came the voice of God to it and said: Where is your fruit which you have made worthy of the goods which you have received? Have I put a distance of one day between you and the just man? Did I not make the sun to arise upon you as upon the just? But the soul was silent, having nothing to answer: and again there came a voice saying: Just is the judgment of God, and there is no acceptance of persons with God, for whoever shall have done mercy, on them shall he have mercy, and whoever shall not have pitied neither shall God pity him. Let him

therefore be handed over to the angel Tartaruch, who is set over the punishments, and let him place him in outer darkness, where there is weeping and gnashing of teeth, and let him be there till the great day of judgment. And after these things I heard the voice of angels and archangels saying: You are just, Lord, and your judgment is just. 17 And again I saw, and behold a soul which was led forward by two angels, weeping and saying: Have pity on me, just God, God the judge, for today is seven days since I went out of my body, and I was handed over to these two angels, and they led me through to those places, which I had never seen. And God, the just judge, says to him: What have you done? For you never did mercy, wherefore you were handed over to such angels as have no mercy, and because you did not do uprightly, so neither did they act piously with you in the hour of your need. Confess therefore your sins which you committed when placed in the world. And he answered and said: Lord, I did not sin. And the Lord, the just Lord, was angered in fury when it said: I did not sin, because it lied; and God said: Do you think you are still in the world? If any one of you, sinning there, conceal and hide his sin from his neighbour, here indeed nothing whatever shall be hid: for when the souls come to adore in sight of the throne, both the good works and the sins of each one are made manifest. And hearing these things the soul was silent, having no answer. And I heard the Lord God, the just judge, again saying: Come, angel of this soul, and stand in the midst. And the angel of the sinful soul came, having in his hands a manuscript, and said: These, Lord, in my hands, are all the sins of this soul from his youth till today, from the tenth year of his birth: and if you command, Lord, I will also relate his acts from the beginning of his fifteenth year. And the Lord God, the just judge, said: I say unto you, angel, I do not expect of you an account of him since he began to be fifteen years old, but state his sins for five years before he died and before he came hither. And again God, the just judge, said: For by myself I swear, and by my holy angels, and by my virtue, that if he had repented five years before he died, on account of one year's life, oblivion would now be thrown over all the evils which he sinned before, and he would have indulgence and remission of sins: now indeed he shall perish. And the angel of the sinful soul answered and said: Lord, command that angel to exhibit those souls.

18 And in that same hour the souls were exhibited in the midst, and the soul of the sinner knew them; and the Lord said to the soul of the sinner: I say unto you, soul, confess your work which you wrought in these souls, whom you see, when they were in the world. And he answered and said: Lord, it is not yet a full year since I slew this one and poured his blood upon the ground, and with another (a woman) I committed fornication: not this alone, but I also greatly harmed her in taking away her goods. And the Lord God, the just judge, said: Either you did not know that he who does violence to another, if he dies first who sustains the violence, is kept in this place until the doer of hurt dies, and then both stand in the presence of the judge, and now each receives according to his deed. And I heard a voice of one saying: Let that soul be delivered into the hands of Tartarus, and led down into hell: he shall lead him into the lower prison and he shall be put in torments, and left there till the great day of judgment. And again I heard a thousand thousand angels saying hymns to the Lord, and crying: You are just, O Lord, and just are your judgments.

19 The angel answered and said unto me: Have you perceived all these things? And I said, Yes, sir. And he said to me: Follow me again, and I will take you, and show you the places of the just. And I followed the angel, and he raised me to the third heaven, and placed me at the entry of the door: and looking carefully I saw, and the door was of gold, and two columns of gold, full above of golden letters, and the angel tuned again to me and said: Blessed were you, if you had entered into these doors, for it is not allowed to any to enter except only to those who have goodness and innocence of body in all things. And I asked the angel about everything and said: Sir, tell me on what account these letters are put upon those tables? The angel answered and said unto me: These are the names of the just, serving God with their whole heart, who dwell on the earth. And again I said: Sir, therefore their names and countenance and the likeness of these who serve God are in heaven, and are known to the angels: for they know who are the servants of God with all their heart, before they go out of the world.

20 And when I had entered the interior of the gate of Paradise, there came out to meet me an old man whose countenance shone as the sun; and when he had embraced me he said: Hail, Paul, beloved of God. And he kissed me with a cheerful countenance. He wept, and I said to him: Brother, why do you weep? And again sighing and lamenting he said: We are hurt by men, and they vex us greatly; for many are the good things which the Lord has prepared, and great is his promise, but many do not perceive them. And I asked the angel, and said: Sir, who is this? And he said to me: This is Enoch, the scribe of righteousness. And I entered into the interior of that place, and immediately I saw the sun, and coming it saluted me laughing and rejoicing. And when it had seen (me), it turned away and wept, and said to me: Paul, would that you should receive your labours which you have done in the human race. For me, indeed, I have seen the great and many good things, which God has prepared for the just, and the promises of God are great, but many do not perceive them; but even by many labours scarcely one or two enters into these places.

21 And the angel answered and said to me, Whatever I now show you here,

and whatever you shall hear, tell it not to any one in the earth. And he led me and showed me: and there I heard words which it is not lawful for a man to speak. And again he said, For now follow me, and I will show you what you ought to narrate in public and relate.

And he took me down from the third heaven, and led me into the second heaven, and again he led me on to the firmament and from the firmament he led me over the doors of heaven: the beginning of its foundation was on the river which waters all the earth. And I asked the angel and said, Lord, what is this river of water? And he said to me, This is Oceanus! And suddenly I went out of heaven, and I understood that it is the light of heaven which lightens all the earth. For the land there is seven times brighter than silver. And I said, Lord, what is this place? And he said to me, This is the land of promise. Have you never heard what is written: Blessed are the meek: for they shall inherit the earth? The souls therefore of the just, when they have gone out of the body, are meanwhile dismissed to this place. And I said to the angel, Then this land will be manifested before the time? The angel answered and said to me, When Christ, whom you preach, shall come to reign, then, by the sentence of God, the first earth will be dissolved and this land of promise will then be revealed, and it will be like dew or cloud, and then the Lord Jesus Christ, the King Eternal, will be manifested and will come with all his saints to dwell in it, and he will reign over them a thousand years, and they will eat of the good things which I shall now show unto you.

22 And I looked around upon that land and I saw a river flowing of milk and honey, and there were trees planted by the bank of that river, full of fruit: moreover each single tree bore twelve fruits in the year, having various and diverse fruits: and I saw the created things which are in that place and all the work of God, and I saw there palms of twenty cubits, but others of ten

cubits: and that land was seven times brighter than silver. And there were trees full of fruits from the roots to the highest branches, of ten thousand fruits of palms upon ten thousand fruits. The grape-vines moreover had ten thousand plants. Moreover in the single vines there were ten thousand thousand bunches and in each of these a thousand single grapes: moreover these single trees bore a thousand fruits. And I said to the angel, Why does each tree bear a thousand fruits? The angel answered and said unto me, Because the Lord God gives an abounding flood of gifts to the worthy, because they also of their own will afflicted themselves when they were placed in the world doing all things on account of his holy name. And again I said to the angel, Sir, are these the only promises which the Most Holy God makes? And he answered and said to me: No! There are seven times greater than these. But I say unto you that when the just go out of the body they shall see the promises and the good things which God has prepared for them. Till then, they shall sigh, and lament saying: Have we emitted any word from our mouth to vex our neighbour even on one day? I asked and said again: Are these alone the promises of God? And the angel answered and said unto me: These whom you now see are the souls of the married and those who kept the chastity of their nuptials, containing themselves. But to the virgins and those who hunger and thirst after righteousness and those who afflicted themselves for the sake of the name of God, God will give seven times greater than these, which I shall now show you.

And then he took me up from that place where I saw these things and behold, a river, and its waters were greatly whiter than milk, and I said to the angel, What is this? And he said to me: This is the Acherousian Lake where is the City of Christ, but not every man is permitted to enter that city; for this is the journey which leads to God, and if anyone is a fornicator and impious, and is converted and shall repent and do fruits worthy of repentance, at first indeed when he shall have gone out of the body, he is led and adores God, and thence by command of the Lord he is delivered to the angel Michael and he baptizes him in the Acherousian Lake—thus he leads them into the City of Christ alongside of those who have never sinned. But I wondered and blessed the Lord God for all the things which I saw.

23 And the angel answered and said unto me: Follow me and I will lead you into the City of Christ. And he was standing on the Acherousian Lake and he put me into a golden ship and angels as it were three thousand were saying hymns before me till I arrived at the City of Christ. Moreover those who inhabited the City of Christ greatly rejoiced over me as I went to them, and I entered and saw the City of Christ, and it was all of gold, and twelve walls encircled it, and twelve interior towers, and each wall had between them single stadia in the circuit: And I said to the angel, Sir, how much is a stadium? The angel answered and said to me: As much as there is between the Lord God and the men who are on the earth, for the City of Christ is alone great. And there were twelve gates in the circuit of the city, of great beauty, and four rivers which encircled it. There was, moreover, a river of honey and a river of milk, and a river of wine and a river of oil. And I said to the angel: What are these rivers surrounding that city? And he says to me: These are the four rivers which flow sufficiently for those who are in this land of promise, of which the names are: the river of honey is called Fison, and the river of milk Euphrates, and the river of oil Gion, and the river of wine Tigris, such therefore they are for those who when placed in the world did not use the power of these things, but they hungered for these things and afflicted themselves for the sake of the Lord God: so that when these enter into this city, the Lord will assign them these things on high above all measure. 24 I indeed entering the gates saw trees great and very high before the doors of the city, having no fruit but leaves only, and I saw a few men scattered in the midst of the trees, and they lamented greatly when they saw anyone enter the city. And those trees were sorry for them and humbled themselves and bowed down and again erected themselves. And I saw and wept with them and I asked the angel and said: Sir, who are these who are not admitted to enter into the City of Christ? And he said to me: These are they who zealously abstained day and night in fasts, but they had a proud heart above other men, glorifying and praising themselves and doing nothing for their neighbours. For they gave some friendly greeting, but to others they did not even say hail! And indeed they showed hospitality to those only whom they wished, and if they did anything whatever for their neighbour they were immoderately puffed up. And I said: What then, Sir? Did their pride prevent them from entering into the City of Christ? And the angel answered and said unto me: Pride is the root of all evils. Are they better than the Son of God who came to the Jews with much humility? And I asked him and said: Why is it that the trees humble themselves and erect themselves again? And the angel answered and said to me: The whole time which these men passed on earth zealously serving God, on account of the confusion and reproaches of men at the time, they blushed and humiliated themselves, but they were not saddened. nor did they repent that they should recede from their pride which was in them. This is why the trees humble themselves, and again are raised up. And I asked and said: For what cause were they admitted to the doors of the city? The angel answered and said unto me: Because of the great goodness of God, and because there is the entry of his holy men entering into this city: for this cause they are left in this place, but when Christ the King Eternal enters with his saints, as he enters just men may pray for these, and then they may enter into the city along with them: but yet none

of them is able to have assurance such as they have who humbled themselves, serving the Lord God all their lives.
25 But I went on while the angel instructed me, and he carried me to the river of honey, and I saw there Isaiah and Jeremiah and Ezekiel and Amos, and Micah and Zechariah, the minor and major prophets, and they saluted me in the city. I said to the angel: What way is this? And he said to me: This is the way of the prophets, every one who shall have afflicted his soul and not done his own will because of God, when he shall have gone out of the world and have been led to the Lord God and adored him, then by the command of God he is handed over to Michael, and he leads him into the city to this place of the prophets, and they salute him as their friend and neighbour because he did the will of God.
26 Again he led me where there is a river of milk, and I saw in that place all the infants whom Herod slew because of the name of Christ, and they saluted me, and the angel said to me: All who keep their chastity with purity, when they shall have come out of the body, after they adore the Lord God are delivered to Michael and are led to the infants and they salute them, saying that they are our brothers and friends and members; in themselves they shall inherit the promises of God.
27 Again he took me up and carried me to the north of the city and led me where there was a river of wine, and there I saw Abraham and Isaac and Jacob, Lot and Job and other saints, and they saluted me: and I asked and said: What is this place, my Lord? The angel answered and said to me: All who are receivers of pilgrims, when they go out of the world, first adore the Lord God, and are delivered to Michael and by this way are led into the city, and all the just salute him as son and brother, and say unto him: Because you have observed humanity and the receiving of pilgrims, come, have an inheritance in the city of the Lord our God: every just man shall receive good things of God in the city, according to his own action.

28 And again he carried me near the river of oil on the east of the city. And I saw there men rejoicing and singing psalms, and I said: Who are those, my Lord? And the angel says to me: Those are they who devoted themselves to God with their whole heart and had no pride in themselves. For all those who rejoice in the Lord God and sing psalms to the Lord with their whole heart are here led into this city.
29 And he carried me into the midst of the city near the twelve walls. But there was in this place a higher wall, and I asked and said: Is there in the City of Christ a wall which in honour exceeds this place? And the angel answering said to me: There is a second better than the first, and similarly a third than the second, as each exceeds the other, unto the twelfth wall. And I said: Tell me, Sir, why one exceeds another in glory? And the angel answered and said unto me: All who have in themselves even a little detraction or zeal or pride, something of his glory would be made void even if he were in the city of Christ: look backward!
And turning round I saw golden thrones placed in each gate, and on them men having golden diadems and gems: and I looked carefully and I saw inside between the twelve men thrones placed in another rank which appeared of much glory, so that no one is able to recount their praise. And I asked the angel and said: My lord, who is on the throne? And the angel answered and said unto me: Those thrones belong to those who had goodness and understanding of heart and made themselves fools for the sake of the Lord God, nor knew new Scriptures nor psalms, but, mindful of one chapter of the commands of God, and hearing what it contained they wrought thereby in much diligence and had a right zeal before the Lord God, and the admiration of them will seize all the saints in presence of the Lord God, for talking with one another they say, Wait and see the unlearned who know nothing more: by which means they merited so great and such a garment and

so great glory on account of their innocence.

And I saw in the midst of this city a great altar, very high, and there was one standing near the altar whose countenance shone as the sun, and he held in his hands a psaltery and harp, and he sang psalms, saying Halleluia! And his voice filled the whole city: at the same time when all they who were on the towers and gates heard him they responded Halleluia! so that the foundations of the city were shaken: and I asked the angel and said, Sir, who is this of so great power? And the angel said to me: This is David: this is the city of Jerusalem, for when Christ the King of Eternity shall come with the assurance of His kingdom, he again shall go before him that he may sing psalms, and all the just at the same time shall sing psalms responding Halleluia! And I said, Sir, how did David alone above the other saints make a beginning of psalm-singing? And the angel answered and said unto me: Because Christ the Son of God sits at the right hand of His Father, and this David sings psalms before him in the seventh heaven, and as is done in the heavens so also below, because the host may not be offered to God without David, but it is necessary that David should sing psalms in the hour of the oblation of the body and blood of Christ: as it is performed in heaven so also on earth.

30 And I said to the angel: Sir, what is Alleluia? And the angel answered and said to me: You ask questions about everything. And he said to me, Alleluia is said in the Hebrew language of God and angels, for the meaning of Alleluia is this: tecel cat. marith macha. And I said, Sir, what is tecel cat. marith macha? And the angel answered and said unto me: Tecel cat. marith macha is: Let us all bless him together. I asked the angel and said, Sir, do all who say Alleluia bless the Lord? And the angel answered and said to me: It is so, and again, therefore, if any one sing Alleluia and those who are present do not sing at the same time, they commit sin because

they do not sing along with him. And I said: My lord, does he also sin if he be hesitating or very old? The angel answered and said unto me: Not so, but he who is able and does not join in the singing, know such as a despiser of the Word, and it would be proud and unworthy that he should not bless the Lord God his maker.

31 Moreover when he had ceased speaking to me, he led me outside the city through the midst of the trees and far from the places of the land of the good, and put me across the river of milk and honey: and after that he led me over the ocean which supports the foundations of heaven.

The angel answered and said unto me: Do you understand why you go hence? And I said: Yes, sir. And he said to me: Come and follow me, and I will show you the souls of the impious and sinners, that you may know what manner of place it is. And I proceeded with the angel and he carried me by the setting of the sun, and I saw the beginning of heaven founded on a great river of water, and I asked: What is this river of water? And he said to me: This is Ocean which surrounds all the Earth. And when I was at the outer limit of Ocean I looked, and there was no light in that place, but darkness and sorrow and sadness: and I sighed.

And I saw there a fervent river of fire, and in it a multitude of men and women immersed up to the knees, and other men up to the navel, others even up to the lips, others moreover up to the hair. And I asked the angel and said: Sir, who are those in the fiery river? And the angel answered and said to me: They are neither hot nor cold, because they were found neither in the number of the just nor in the number of the impious. For those spent the time of their life on earth passing some days in prayer, but others in sins and fornications, until their death. And I asked him and said: Who are these, Sir, immersed up to their knees in fire? He answered and said to me: These are they who when they have gone out of church throw themselves into strange conversations to dispute. Those indeed who are immersed up to the navel are those who, when they have taken the body and blood of Christ go and fornicate and did not cease from their sins till they died. Those who are immersed up to the lips are the detractors of each other when they assemble in the church of God: those up to the eyebrows are those who nod approval of themselves and plot spite against their neighbour.

32 And I saw on the north a place of various and diverse punishments full of men and women, and a river of fire ran down into it. Moreover I observed and I saw pits great in depth, and in them several souls together, and the depth of that place was as it were three thousand cubits, and I saw them groaning and weeping and saying: Have pity on us, O Lord! And none had pity on them. And I asked the angel and said: Who are these, Sir? And the angel answered and said unto me: These are they who did not hope in the Lord, that they would be able to have him as their helper. And I asked and said: Sir, if these souls remain for thirty or forty generations thus one upon another, if they were sent deeper, the pits I believe would not hold them. And he said to me: The Abyss has no measure, for beyond this it stretches down below him who is down in it: and so it is, that if perchance anyone should take a stone and throw it into a very deep well and after many hours it should reach the bottom, such is the abyss. For when the souls are thrown in there, they hardly reach the bottom in fifty years.

33 I, indeed, when I heard this, wept and groaned over the human race. The angel answered and said unto me: Why do you weep? Are you more pitiful than God? For though God is good, He knows also that there are punishments, and He patiently bears with the human race, dismissing each one to work his own will in the time in which he dwells on the earth.

34 I further observed the fiery river and saw there a man being tortured by Tartaruchian angels having in their hands an iron with three hooks with which they pierced the bowels of that old man: and I asked the angel, and said: Sir, who is that old man on whom such torments are imposed? And the angel answered and said to me: He whom you see was a presbyter who did not perform well his ministry: when he had been eating and drinking and committing fornication he offered the host to the Lord at his holy altar.

35 And I saw not far away another old man led on by malign angels running with speed, and they pushed him into the fire up to his knees, and they struck him with stones and wounded his face like a storm, and did not allow him to say: Have pity on me! And I asked the angel and he said to me: He whom you see was a bishop, and did not perform well his episcopate, who indeed accepted the great name but did not enter into the witness of him who gave him the name in all his life, seeing that he did not do just judgment, and did not pity widows and orphans, but now he receives retribution according to his iniquity and his works.

36 And I saw another man in the fiery river up to his knees. Moreover his hands were stretched out and bloody, and worms proceeded from his mouth and nostrils and he was groaning and weeping, and crying he said: Have pity on me! For I am hurt above the rest who are in this punishment. And I asked, Sir, who is this? And he said to me: This man whom you see was a deacon who devoured the oblations and committed fornications and did not right in the sight of God, for this cause he unceasingly pays this penalty. And I looked closely and saw alongside of him another man whom they delivered up with haste and cast into the fiery river, and he was (in it) up to the knees: and there came the angel who was set over the punishments having a great fiery razor, and with it he cut the lips of that man and the tongue likewise. And sighing, I lamented and asked: Who is that, sir. And he said to me, He whom you see was a reader and read to the people, but he himself did

not keep the precepts of God: now he also pays the proper penalty.

37 And I saw another multitude of pits in the same place, and in the midst of it a river full of a multitude of men and women, and worms consumed them. But I lamented and sighing asked the angel and said: Sir, who are these? And he said to me: These are those who exacted interest on interest and trusted in their riches and did not hope in God that He was their helper.

And after that I looked and saw another place, very narrow, and it was like a wall, and fire round about it. And I saw inside men and women gnawing their tongues, and I asked: Sir, who are these. And he said to me: These are they who in church disparage the Word of God, not attending to it, but as it were make naught of God and His angels: for that cause they now likewise pay the proper penalty.

38 And I observed and saw another old man down in a pit and his countenance was like blood, and I asked and said, Sir, what is this place? And he said to me: Into that pit stream all the punishments. And I saw men and women immersed up to the lips and I asked, Sir, who are these? And he said to me: These are the magicians who prepared for men and women evil magic arts and did not find how to stop them till they died.

And again I saw men and women with very black faces in a pit of fire, and I sighed and lamented and asked, Sir, who are these? And he said to me: These are fornicators and adulterers who committed adultery having wives of their own: likewise also the women committed adultery having husbands of their own: therefore they uneasingly suffer penalties.

39 And I saw there girls having black raiment, and four terrible angels having in their hands burning chains, and they put them on the necks of the girls and led them into darkness: and I, again weeping, asked the angel: Who are these, Sir? And he said to me: These are they who, when they were virgins, defiled their virginity unknown to their parents; for which cause they unceasingly pay the proper penalties.

And again I observed there men and women with hands cut and their feet placed naked in a place of ice and snow, and worms devoured them. But seeing them I lamented and asked: Sir, who are these? And he said to me: These are they who harmed orphans and widows and the poor, and did not hope in the Lord, for which cause they unceasingly pay the proper penalties.

And I observed and saw others hanging over a channel of water, and their tongues were very dry, and many fruits were placed in their sight, and they were not permitted to take of them, and I asked: Sir, who are these? And he said to me: These are they who break their fast before the appointed hour, for this cause they unceasingly pay these penalties.

And I saw other men and women hanging by their eyebrows and their hair, and a fiery river drew them, and I said: Who are these, my Lord? And he said to me: These are they who join themselves not to their own husbands and wives but to whores, and therefore they unceasingly pay the proper penalties.

And I saw other men and women covered with dust, and their countenance was like blood, and they were in a pit of pitch and sulphur and running down into a fiery river, and I asked: Sir, who are these? And he said to me: These are they who committed the iniquity of Sodom and Gomorrha, the male with the male, for which reason they unceasingly pay the penalties.

40 And I observed and saw men and women clothed in bright garments, having their eyes blind, placed in a pit, and I asked: Sir, who are these? And he said to me: These are of the people who did alms, and knew not the Lord God, for which reason they unceasingly pay the proper penalties. And I observed and saw other men and women on an obelisk of fire, and beasts tearing them in pieces, and they were not allowed to say, Lord have pity on us! And I saw

the angel of penalties putting heavy punishments on them and saying: Acknowledge the Son of God; for this was predicted to you, when the divine Scriptures were read to you, and you did not attend; for which cause God's judgment is just, for your actions have apprehended you and brought you into these penalties. But I sighed and wept, and I asked and said: Who are these men and women who are strangled in fire and pay their penalties? And he answered me: These are women who defiled the image of God when bringing forth infants out of the womb, and these are the men who lay with them. And their infants addressed the Lord God and the angels who were set over the punishments, saying: Cursed be the hour to our parents, for they defiled the image of God, having the name of God but not observing His precepts: they gave us for food to dogs and to be trodden down of swine: others they threw into the river. But their infants were handed over to the angels of Tartarus who were set over the punishments, that they might lead them to a wide place of mercy: but their fathers and mothers were tortured in a perpetual punishment.

And after that I saw men and women clothed with rags full of pitch and fiery sulphur, and dragons were coiled about their necks and shoulders and feet, and angels having fiery horns restrained them and smote them, and closed their nostrils, saying to them: Why did ye not know the time in which it was right to repent and serve God, and did not do it? And I asked: Sir, who are these? And he said to me: These are they who seem to give up the world for God, putting on our garb, but the impediments of the world made them wretched, not maintaining agapæ, and they did not pity widows and orphans: they did not receive the stranger and the pilgrim, nor did they offer the oblations, and they did not pity their neighbour. Moreover their prayer did not even on one day ascend pure to the Lord God, but many impediments of the world detained them, and they were not able to do right

in the sight of God, and the angels enclosed them in the place of punishments. Moreover they saw those who were in punishments and said to them: We indeed when we lived in the world neglected God, and you also did likewise: as we also truly when we were in the world knew that you were sinners. But ye said: These are just and servants of God, now we know why you were called by the name of the Lord: for which cause they also pay their own penalties.

And sighing I wept and said: Woe unto men, woe unto sinners! Why were they born? And the angel answered and said unto me: Why do you lament? Are you more pitiful than the Lord God who is blessed forever, who established judgment and sent forth every man to choose good and evil in his own will and do what pleases him? Then I lamented again very greatly, and he said to me: Do you lament when as yet you have not seen greater punishments? Follow me and you shall see seven times greater than these.

41 And he carried me south and placed me above a well, and I found it sealed with seven seals: and answering, the angel who was with me said to the angel of that place: Open the mouth of the well that Paul, the well-beloved of God, may see, for authority is given him that he may see all the pains of hell. And the angel said to me: Stand afar off that you may be able to bear the stench of this place. When therefore the well was opened, immediately there arose from it a certain hard and malign stench, which surpasses all punishments: and I looked into the well and I saw fiery masses glowing in every part, and narrow places, and the mouth of the well was narrow so as to admit one man only. And the angel answered and said unto me: If any man shall have been put into this well of the abyss and it shall have been sealed over him, no remembrance of him shall ever be made in the sight of the Father and His Son and the holy angels. And I said: Who are these, Sir, who are put into this well? And he said to me: They are

whoever shall not confess that Christ has come in the flesh and that the Virgin Mary brought him forth, and whoever says that the bread and cup of the Eucharist of blessing are not this body and blood of Christ.

42 And I looked to the south in the west and I saw there a restless worm and in that place there was gnashing of teeth: moreover the worms were one cubit long, and had two heads, and there I saw men and women in cold and gnashing of teeth. And I asked and said, Sir, who are these in this place? And he said to me: These are they who say that Christ did not rise from the dead and that this flesh will not rise again. And I asked and said: Sir, is there no fire nor heat in this place? And he said to me: In this place there is nothing else but cold and snow: and again he said to me: Even if the sun should rise upon them, they do not become warm on account of the superabundant cold of that place and the snow.

But hearing these things I stretched out my hands and wept, and sighing again, I said: It were better for us if we had not been born, all of us who are sinners.

43 But when those who were in the same place saw me weeping with the angel, they themselves cried out and wept saying, Lord God have mercy upon us! And after these things I saw the heavens open, and Michael the archangel descending from heaven, and with him was the whole army of angels, and they came to those who were placed in punishment and seeing him, again weeping, they cried out and said, Have pity on us! Michael the archangel, have pity on us and on the human race, for on account of your prayers the earth stands. We now see the judgment and acknowledge the Son of God! It was impossible for us before these things to pray for this, before we entered into this place: for we heard that there was a judgment before we went out of the world, but impediments and the life of the world did not allow us to repent. And Michael answered and said: Hear Michael speaking! I am he who stands in the sight of God every hour: As the Lord lives, in whose sight I stand, I do not intermit one day or one night praying incessantly for the human race, and I indeed pray for those who are on the earth: but they do not cease doing iniquity and fornications, and they do not bring to me any good while they are placed on earth: and you have consumed in vanity the time in which you ought to have repented. But I have always prayed thus and I now beseech that God may send dew and send forth rains upon the earth, and now I desire until the earth produce its fruits and verily I say, that if any have done but a little good, I will agonise for him, protecting him till he have escaped the judgment of penalties. Where therefore are your prayers? Where are your penances? You have lost your time contemptuously. But now weep and I will weep with you and the angels who are with me with the well-beloved Paul, if perchance the merciful God will have pity and give you refreshment. But hearing these words they cried out and wept greatly, and all said with one voice: Have pity on us, Son of God! And I, Paul, sighed and said: O Lord God! Have pity on your creature, have pity on the sons of men, have pity on your image.

44 And I looked and saw the heaven move like a tree shaken by the wind. Suddenly, moreover, they threw themselves on their faces in the sight of the throne. And I saw twenty-four elders and twenty-four thousand adoring God, and I saw an altar and veil and throne, and all were rejoicing; and the smoke of a good odour was raised near the altar of the throne of God, and I heard the voice of one saying: For the sake of what do ye our angels and ministers intercede? And they cried out saying: We intercede seeing your many kindnesses to the human race. And after these things I saw the Son of God descending from heaven, and a diadem was on his head. And seeing him those who were placed in punishment exclaimed all with one voice saying: Have pity, Son of the High God! You are He who shows refreshment for all in

the heavens and on earth, and on us likewise have pity, for since we have seen You, we have refreshment. And a voice went out from the Son of God through all the punishments saying: And what work have ye done that you demand refreshment from me? My blood was poured out for your sakes, and not even so did ye repent: for your sakes I wore the crown of thorns on my head: for you I received buffets on my cheeks, and not even so did ye repent. I asked water when hanging on the cross and they gave me vinegar mixed with gall, with a spear they opened my right side, for my name's sake they slew my prophets and just men, and in all these things I gave you a place of repentance and you would not. Now, however, for the sake of Michael the archangel of my covenant and the angels who are with him, and because of Paul the well-beloved, whom I would not vex, for the sake of your brethren who are in the world and offer oblations, and for the sake of your sons, because my precepts are in them, and more for the sake of my own kindness, on the day on which I rose from the dead, I give to you all who are in punishment a night and a day of refreshment forever. And they all cried out and said, We bless you, Son of God, that You have given us a night and a day of respite. For better to us is a refreshment of one day above all the time of our life which we were on earth, and if we had plainly known that this was intended for those who sin, we would have worked no other work, we would have done no business, and we would have done no iniquity: what need had we for pride in the world? For here our pride is crushed which ascended from our mouth against our neighbour: our plagues and excessive straitness and the tears and the worms which are under us, these are much worse to us than the pains which we have left behind us. When they said thus, the malign angels of the penalties were angered with them, saying: How long do ye lament and sigh? For you had no pity. For this is the judgment of God who had no pity. But ye received this great grace of a day and a night's refreshment on the Lord's Day for the sake of Paul the well-beloved of God who descended to you.

45 And after that the angel said to me: Have you seen all these things? And I said: Yes, Sir. And he said to me: Follow me and I will lead you into Paradise, that the just who are there may see you, for lo! They hope to see you, and they are ready to come to meet you in joy and gladness. And I followed the angel by the impulse of the Holy Spirit, and he placed me in Paradise and said to me: This is Paradise in which Adam and his wife erred. Moreover I entered Paradise and saw the beginning of waters, and there was an angel making a sign to me and he said to me: Observe, said he, the waters, for this is the river of Physon which surrounds all the land of Evilla, and the second is Geon which surrounds all the land of Egypt and Ethiopia, and the third is Thigris which is over against the Assyrians, and another is Eufrates which waters all the land of Mesopotamia. And when I had gone inside I saw a tree planted from whose roots water flowed out, and from this beginning there were four rivers. And the spirit of God rested on that tree, and when the Spirit blew, the waters flowed forth, and I said: My Lord, is it this tree itself which makes the waters flow? And he said to me: That from the beginning, before the heavens and earth were manifested, and all things here invisible, the Spirit of God was borne upon the waters, but from the time when the command of God made the heavens and earth to appear, the Spirit rested upon this tree: wherefore whenever the Spirit blows, the waters flow forth from the tree. And he held me by the hand and led me near the tree of knowledge of good and evil, and he said: This is the tree by which death entered into the world, and receiving of it through his wife Adam ate and death entered into the world. And he showed me another tree in the midst of Paradise, and says to me: This is the tree of life.

46 While I was yet looking upon the tree, I saw a virgin coming from afar and two hundred angels before her saying hymns, and I asked and said: Sir, who is she who comes in so great glory? And he said to me: This is Mary the Virgin, the Mother of the Lord. And coming near she saluted me and said: Hail, Paul! Well-beloved of God and angels and men. For all the saints prayed my Son Jesus who is my Lord that you might come hither in the body that they might see you before you go out of the world. And the Lord said to them: Bear and be patient: yet a little and you shall see him and he shall be with you for ever: and again they all said to him together: Do not vex us, for we desire to see him in the flesh, for by him Your name was greatly glorified in the world, and we have seen that he endured all the labours whether of the greater or of the less. This we learn from those who come hither. For when we say: Who is he who directed you in the world? They reply to us: There is one in the world whose name is Paul, he preaches and announces Christ, and we believe that many have entered into the kingdom through the virtue and sweetness of his speeches. Behold all the just men are behind me coming to meet you, Paul, and I first come for this cause to meet them who did the will of my Son and my Lord Jesus Christ, I first advance to meet them and do not send them away to be as wanderers until they meet in peace.

47 When she had thus spoken, I saw three coming from afar, very beautiful in the likeness of Christ, and their forms were shining, and their angels, and I asked: Sir, who are these? And he said to me: Do you not know those? And I said: No, Sir. And he answered: These are the fathers of the people, Abraham, Isaac, and Jacob. And coming near they saluted me, and said: Hail, Paul, well-beloved of God and men; blessed is he who suffers violence for the Lord's sake. And Abraham answered me and said: This is my son Isaac, and Jacob my well-beloved, and we have known the Lord and followed him; blessed are all they who believed in your word, that they may be able to inherit the Kingdom of God by labour, by renunciation, and sanctification, and humility, and charity, and meekness, and right faith in the Lord; and we also have had devotion to the Lord whom you preach in the testament, that we might assist those who believed in him with their whole soul, and might minister unto them as fathers minister to their children.

When they had thus spoken, I saw other twelve coming from afar in honour, and I asked: Sir, who are these? And he said: These are the patriarchs. And coming near they saluted me and said: Hail, Paul, well-beloved of God and men: the Lord did not vex us, that we might see you yet in the body, before you go out of the world. And each one of them reminded me of his name in order, from Ruben to Benjamin: and Joseph said to me: I am he who was sold; but I say to you, Paul, that all the things, whatever my brothers did to me, in nothing did I act maliciously with them, nor in all the labour which they imposed on me, nor in any point was I hurt by them on that account from morning till evening: blessed is he who receives some hurt on account of the Lord, and bears it, for the Lord will repay it to him manifold, when he shall have gone out of the world.

48 When he had spoken thus far, I saw another beautiful one coming from afar, and his angels saying hymns, and I asked: Sir, who is this that is beautiful of countenance? And he says to me: Do you not know him? And I said: No, Sir. And he said to me: This is Moses the law-giver, to whom God gave the law. And when he had come near me, he immediately wept, and after that he saluted me: and I said to him: What do you lament? For I have heard that you excel every man in meekness. And he answered saying: I weep for those whom I planted with toil, because they did not bear fruit, nor did any profit by them; and I saw all the sheep whom I fed, that they were scattered and become as if they had no shepherd, and

because all the toils which I endured for the sake of the sons of Israel were accounted as naught, and how greatsoever virtues I did in the midst of them these they did not understand, and I wonder that strangers and uncircumcised and idol-worshippers have been converted and have entered into the promises of God, but Israel has not entered; and now I say unto you, brother Paul, that in that hour when the people hanged Jesus whom you preach, that the Father, the God of all, who gave me the law, and Michael and all the angels and archangels, and Abraham and Isaac, and Jacob, and all the just wept over the Son of God hanging on the cross. In that hour all the saints attended on me looking (upon me) and they said to me: See, Moses, what men of your people have done to the Son of God. Wherefore you are blessed, Paul, and blessed the generation and race which believed in your word.

49 When he had spoken thus far, there came other twelve, and seeing me said: Are you Paul the glorified in heaven and on earth? And I answered and said: What are you? The first answered and said: I am Esaias whom Manasses cut asunder with a wooden saw. And the second said likewise: I am Jeremias who was stoned by the children of Israel and slain. And the third said: I am Ezekiel whom the children of Israel dragged by the feet over a rock in a mountain till they knocked out my brains, and we endured all these toils, wishing to save the children of Israel: and I say unto you that after the toils which they laid upon me, I cast myself on my face in the sight of the Lord praying for them, bending my knees until the second hour of the Lord's day, till Michael came and lifted me up from the earth. Blessed are you, Paul, and blessed the nation which believed through you.

And as these passed by, I saw another, beautiful of countenance, and I asked: Sir, Who is this? Who when he had seen me, rejoiced and said to me: This is Lot who was found just in Sodom. And approaching he saluted me and said:

Blessed are you, Paul, and blessed the generation to which you ministered. And I answered and said to him: Are you Lot who wast found just in Sodom? And he said: I entertained angels, as travellers, and when they of the city wished to violate them, I offered them my two virgin daughters who had not yet known men, and gave them to them saying: use them as you will, but only to these men you shall do no evil; for this cause they entered under the roof of my house. For this cause, therefore, we ought to be confident and know that if anyone shall have done anything, God shall repay him manifold when they shall come to him. Blessed are you, Paul, and blessed the nation which believed in your word.

When, therefore, he had ceased talking to me, I saw another coming from a distance, very beautiful of countenance, and smiling, and his angels saying hymns: and I said to the angel who was with me: Has then each of the just an angel for companion? And he said to me: Each one of the saints has his own (angel) assisting him, and saying a hymn, and the one does not depart from the other. And I said: Who is this, Sir? And he said: This is Job. And approaching, he saluted me and said: Brother Paul, you have great praise with God and men. And I am Job, who laboured much for a period of thirty years from a plague in the blood; and verily in the beginning, the wounds which went forth from my body were like grains of wheat. But on the third day, they became as the foot of an ass; worms moreover which fell four digits in length: and on the third (day) the devil appeared and said to me: Say something against God and die. I said to him: If such be the will of God that I should remain under a plague all the time of my life till I die, I shall not cease from blessing the Lord, and I shall receive more reward. For I know that the labours of that world are nothing to the refreshment which is afterwards: for which cause blessed are you, Paul, and blessed the nation which believed through you.

50 When he had spoken thus far, another came calling from afar and saying: Blessed are you, Paul, and blessed am I because I saw you, the beloved of the Lord. And I asked the angel: Sir, who is this? And he answered and said unto me: This is Noe in the time of the deluge. And immediately we saluted each other: and greatly rejoicing he said to me: You are Paul the most beloved of God. And I asked him: Who are you? And he said: I am Noe, who was in the time of the deluge. And I say to you, Paul, that working for a hundred years, I made the ark, not putting off the tunic with which I was clad, nor did I cut the hair of my head. Till then also I cherished continence, not approaching my own wife: in those hundred years not a hair of my head grew in length, nor did my garments become soiled: and I besought men at all times saying: Repent, for a deluge of waters will come upon you. But they laughed at me, and mocked my words; and again they said to me: But this is the time of those who are able to play and sin freely, desiring her with whom it is possible to commit fornication frequently: for God does not regard this, and does not know what things are done by us men, and there is no flood of waters straightway coming upon this world. And they did not cease from their sins, till God destroyed all flesh which had the breath of life in it. Know then that God loves one just man more than all the world of the impious. Wherefore, blessed are you, Paul, and blessed is the nation which believes through you.

51 And turning round, I saw other just ones coming from afar, and I asked the angel: Sir, who are those? And he answered me: These are Elias and Eliseus. And they saluted me: and I said to them: Who are you? And one of them answered and said: I am Elias, the prophet of God; I am Elias who prayed, and because of my word, the heaven did not rain for three years and six months, on account of the unrighteousness of men. God is just and true, who does the will of his servants: for the angels often besought the Lord for rain, and he said: Be patient till my servant Elias shall pray and petition for this and I will send rain on the earth.

THE APOCALYPSE OF THOMAS

Here beginneth the epistle of the Lord unto Thomas.

VERSION 1

1 Hear thou, Thomas, the things which must come to pass in the last times: there shall be famine and war and earthquakes in divers places, snow and ice and great drought shall there be and many dissensions among the peoples, blasphemy, iniquity, envy and villainy, indolence, pride and intemperance, so that every man shall speak that which pleaseth him.

2 And my priests shall not have peace among themselves, but shall sacrifice unto me with deceitful mind: therefore will I not look upon them.

3 Then shall the priests behold the people departing from the house of the Lord and turning unto the world and setting up (or, transgressing) landmarks in the house of God.

4 And they shall claim (vindicate) for themselves many things and places that were lost and that shall be subject unto Caesar as also they were aforetime: giving poll-taxes of (for) the cities, even gold and silver and the chief men of the cities shall be condemned and their substance brought into the treasury of the kings, and they shall be filled.

5 For there shall be great disturbance throughout all the people, and death.

6 The house of the Lord shall be desolate, and their altars shall be abhorred, so that spiders weave their webs therein. The place of holiness shall be corrupted, the priesthood polluted, distress (agony) shall increase,

virtue shall be overcome, joy perish, and gladness depart.

7 In those days evil shall abound: there shall be respecters of persons, hymns shall cease out of the house of the Lord, truth shall be no more, covetousness shall abound among the priests; an upright man (al. an upright priesthood) shall not be found.

8 On a sudden there shall arise near the last time a king, a lover of the law, who shall hold rule not for long: he shall leave two sons.

9 The first is named of the first letter A, the second of the eighth H. The first shall die before the second.

10 Thereafter shall arise two princes to oppress the nations under whose hands there shall be a very great famine in the right-hand part of the east, so that nation shall rise up against nation and be driven out from their own borders.

11 Again another king shall arise, a crafty man , and shall command a golden image of Caesar to be made (al. to be worshipped in the house of God), wherefore martyrdoms shall abound.

12 Then shall faith return unto the servants of the Lord, and holiness shall be multiplied and distress (agony) increase.

13 The mountains shall the comforted and shall drop down sweetness of fire from the facet, that the number of the saints may be accomplished.

14 After a little space there shall arise a king out of the east, a lover of the law, who shall cause all good things and necessary to abound in the house of the Lord: he shall show mercy unto the widows and to the needy, and command a royal gift to be given unto the priests: in his days shall be abundance of all things.

15 And after that again a king shall arise in the south part of the world, and shall hold rule a little space: in whose days the treasury shall fail because of the wages of the Roman soldiers so that the substance of all the aged shall be commanded (to be taken) and given to the king to distribute.

16 Thereafter shall be plenty of corn and wine and oil, but great dearness of money, so that the substance of gold and silver shall be given for corn, and there shall be great dearth.

17 At that time shall be very great rising of the sea, so that no man shall tell news to any man.

18 The kings of the earth and the princes and the captains shall be troubled, and no man shall speak freely (boldly).

19 Grey hairs shall be seen upon boys, and the young shall not give place unto the aged.

20 After that shall arise another king, a crafty man, who shall hold rule for a short space: in whose days there shall be all manner of evils, even the death of the race of men from the east even unto Babylon.

21 And thereafter death and famine and sword in the land of Chanaan even unto (Rome?).

22 Then shall all the fountains of waters and wells boil over and be turned into blood (or, into dust and blood).

23 The heaven shall be moved, the stars shall fall upon the earth, the sun shall be cut in half like the moon, and the moon shall not give her light.

24 There shall be great signs and wonders in those days when Antichrist draweth near.

25 These are the signs unto them that dwell in the earth. In those days the pains of great travail shall come upon them. (al. In those days, when Antichrist now draweth near, these are the signs. Woe unto them that dwell on the earth; in those days great pains of travail shall come upon them.)

26 Woe unto them that build, for they shall not inhabit.

27 Woe unto them that break up the fallow, for they shall labour without cause.

28 Woe unto them that make marriages, for unto famine and need shall they beget sons.

29 Woe unto them that join house to house or field to field, for all things shall be consumed with fire.

30 Woe unto them that look not unto themselves while time alloweth, for hereafter shall they be condemned for

ever.

31 Woe unto them that turn away from the poor when he asketh.

32 For I am of the high and powerful: I am the Father of all. (al. And know ye: I am the Father most high: I am the Father of all spirits.)

33 These are the seven signs the ending of this world.

34 There shall be in all the earth famine and great pestilences and much distress: then shall all men be led captive among all nations and shall fall by the edge of the sword.

35 On the first day of the judgement will be a great marvel (or, the beginning shall be).

36 At the third hour of the day shall be a great and mighty voice in the firmament of the heaven, and a great cloud of blood coming down out of the north, and great thunderings and mighty lightnings shall follow that cloud, and there shall be a rain of blood upon all the earth.

37 These are the signs of the first day.

38 And on the second day there shall be a great voice in the firmament of the heaven, and the earth shall be moved out of its place: and the gates of heaven shall be opened in the firmament of heaven toward the east, and a great power shall be sent belched) forth by the gates of heaven and shall cover all the heaven even until evening (al. and there shall be fears and tremblings in the world).

39 These are the signs of the second day.

40 And on the third day, about the second hour, shall be a voice in heaven, and the abysses of the earth shall utter their voice from the four corners of the world.

41 The first heaven shall be rolled up like a book and shall straightway vanish.

42 And because of the smoke and stench of the brimstone of the abyss the days shall be darkened unto the tenth hour.

43 Then shall all men say: I think that the end draweth near, that we shall perish. These are the signs of the third

day.

44 And on the fourth day at the first hour, the earth of the east shall speak, the abyss shall roar: then shall all the earth be moved by the strength of an earthquake.

45 In that day shall all the idols of the heathen fall, and all the buildings of the earth. These are the signs of the fourth day.

46 And on the fifth day, at the sixth hour, there shall be great thunderings suddenly in the heaven, and the powers of light and the wheel of the sun shall be caught away, and there shall be great darkness over the world until evening, and the stars shall be turned away from their ministry.

47 In that day all nations shall hate the world and despise the life of this world.

48 These are the signs of the fifth day.

49 And on the sixth day there shall be signs in heaven.

50 At the fourth hour the firmament of heaven shall be cloven from the east unto the west.

51 And the angels of the heavens shall be looking forth upon the earth the opening of the heavens.

52 And all men shall see above the earth the host of the angels looking forth out of heaven. Then shall all men flee...

[[Remaining Text is Lost]]

VERSION 2

1 Hear thou, O Thomas, for I am the Son of God the Father and I am the father of all spirits.

2 Hear thou of me the signs which shall come to pass at the end of this world, when the end of the world shall be fulfilled (Vienna: that it pass away) before mine elect depart out of the world.

3 I will tell thee that which shall come to pass openly unto men (or, will tell thee openly, &c.): but when these things shall be the princes of the angels know not, seeing it is now hidden from before them (Vienna adds: at what day the end shall be fulfilled).

4 Then shall there be in the world

sharings (participations) between king and king, and in all the earth shall be great famine great pestilences, and many distresses, and the sons of men shall be led captive among all nations and shall fall by the edge of the sword (and there shall be great commotion in the world: Vienna omits).

5 Then after that when the hour of the end draweth nigh there shall be for seven days great signs in heaven, and the powers of the heavens shall be moved.

6 Then shall there be on the first day the beginning: at the third hour of the day a great and mighty voice in the firmament of heaven and a bloody cloud coming up (down, Vienna) out of the north, and great thunderings and mighty lightnings shall follow it, and it shall cover the whole heaven, and there shall be a rain of blood upon all the earth.

7 These are the signs of the first day.

8 And on the second day there shall be a great voice in the firmament of heaven, and the earth shall be moved out of its place, and the gates of heaven shall be opened in the firmament of heaven toward the east, and the (smoke of a great fire shall break forth through the gates of heaven and shall cover all the heaven until evening.

9 In that day there shall be fears and great terrors in the world.

10 These are the signs of the second day.

11 But on the third day about the third hour shall be a great voice in heaven, and the abysses of the earth (Vienna ends) shall roar from the four corners of the world; the pinnacles (so) of the firmament of heaven shall be opened, and all the air shall be filled with pillars of smoke.

12 There shall be a stench of brimstone, very evil, until the tenth hour, and men shall say: We think the time draweth nigh that we perish.

13 These are the signs of the third day.

14 And on the fourth day at the first hour, from the land of the east the abyss shall melt (so) and roar.

15 Then shall all the earth be shaken by the might of an earthquake.

16 In that day shall the ornaments of the heathen fall, and all the buildings of the earth, before the might of the earthquake.

17 These are the signs of the fourth day.

18 But on the fifth day at the sixth hour, suddenly there shall be a great thunder in heaven, and the powers of light and the wheel of the sun shall be caught away (MS. opened), and there shall be great darkness in the world until evening, and the air shall be gloomy (sad) without sun or moon, and the stars shall cease from their ministry.

19 In that day shall all nations behold as in a mirror (or, behold it as sackcloth) and shall despise the life of this world.

20 These are the signs of the fifth day.

21 And on the sixth day at the fourth hour there shall be a great voice in heaven, and the firmament of the heaven shall be cloven from the east unto the west, and the angels of the heavens shall be looking forth upon the earth by the openings of the heavens, and all these that are on the earth shall behold the host of the angels looking forth out of heaven.

22 Then shall all men flee unto the monuments (mountains ?) and hide themselves from the face of the righteous angels, and say:

23 Would that the earth would open and swallow us up! And such things shall come to pass as never were since this world was created.

24 Then shall they behold me coming from above in the light of my Father with the power and honour of the holy angels.

25 Then at my coming shall the fence of fire of paradise be done away -because paradise is girt round about with fire.

26 And this shall be that perpetual fire that shall consume the earth and all the elements of the world.

27 Then shall the spirits and souls of all men come forth from paradise and shall come upon all the earth: and every one of them shall go unto his own body, where it is laid up, and every one of them shall say:

28 Here lieth my body. And when the

great voice of those spirits shall be heard, then shall there be a great earthquake over all the world, and by the might thereof the mountains shall be cloven from above and the rocks from beneath.

29 Then shall every spirit return into his own vessel and the bodies of the saints which have fallen asleep shall arise.

30 Then shall their bodies be changed into the image and likeness and the honour of the holy angels, and into the power of the image of mine holy Father.

31 Then shall they be clothed with the vesture of life eternal, out of the cloud of light which hath never been seen in this world; for that cloud cometh down out of the highest realm of the heaven from the power of my Father.

32 And that cloud shall compass about with the beauty thereof all the spirits that have believed in me.

33 Then shall they be clothed, and shall be borne by the hand of the holy angels like as I have told you aforetime.

34 Then also shall they be lifted up into the air upon a cloud of light, and shall go with me rejoicing unto heaven, and then shall they continue in the light and honour of my Father.

35 Then shall there be unto them great gladness with my Father and before the holy angels.

36 These are the signs of the sixth day.

37 And on the seventh day at the eighth hour there shall be voices in the four corners of the heaven.

38 And all the air shall be shaken, and filled with holy angels, and they shall make war among them all the day long.

39 And in that day shall mine elect be sought out by the holy angels from the destruction of the world.

40 Then shall all men see that the hour of their destruction draweth near. These are the signs of the seventh day.

41 And when the seven days are passed by, on the eighth day at the sixth hour there shall be a sweet and tender voice in heaven from the east.

42 Then shall that angel be revealed which hath power over the holy angels: and all the angels shall go forth with him, sitting upon chariots of the clouds of mine holy Father (so) rejoicing and running upon the air beneath the heaven to deliver the elect that have believed in me.

43 And they shall rejoice that the destruction of this world hath come.

The words of the Saviour unto Thomas are ended, concerning the end of this world.

THE REVELATION OF STEPHEN

1 Two years after the Ascension there was a contest about Jesus. Many learned men had assembled at Jerusalem from Ethiopia, the Thebaid, Alexandria, Jerusalem, Asia, Mauretania and Babylon.

2 There was a great clamour among them like thunder, lasting till the fourth hour.

3 Stephen, a learned man of the tribe of Benjamin, stood on a high place and addressed the assembly. Why this tumult? said he.

4 Blessed is he who has not doubted concerning Jesus. Born of a pure virgin he filled the world with light.

5 By Satan's contrivances Herod slew 14,000 (144,000) children. He spoke of the miracles of Jesus.

6 Woe to the unbelievers when he shall come as judge, with angels, a fiery chariot, a mighty wind: the stars shall fall, the heavens open, the books be brought forward.

7 The twelve angels who are set over every soul shall unveil the deeds of men.

8 The sea shall move and give up what is in it.

9 The mountains fall, all the surface of the earth becomes smooth.

10 Great winged thrones are set.

11 The Lord, and Christ, and the Holy Spirit take their seats.

12 The Father bids Jesus sit on his right hand.

13 At this point the crowd cried out: Blasphemy! and took Stephen before Pilate.

14 Pilate stood on the steps and reproached them: You compelled me to crucify the Innocent; why rage against this man? Why gnash your teeth? Are ye yet foolish?

15 They led Stephen away. Caiaphas ordered him to be beaten till the blood ran. And he prayed: Lay not this sin to their charge. We saw how angels ministered to him.

16 In the morning Pilate called his wife and two children: they baptized themselves and praised God.

17 Three thousand men now assembled and disputed with Stephen for three days and three nights.

18 On the fourth day they took counsel and sent to Caesarea of Palestine for Saul of Tarsus, who had a commission to seize upon Christians.

19 He took his place on the judgement seat and said: I wonder that thou, a wise man, and my kinsman, believest all this.

20 None of the Sanhedrin have given up the Law. I have been through all Judaea, Galilee, Peraea, Damascus, and the city of the Jesitites to seek out believers.

21 Stephen lifted up his hands and said: Silence, persecutor! Recognize the Son of God.

22 Thou makest me doubt of my own descent. But I see that thou shalt ere long drink of the same cup as I. What thou doest, do quickly.

23 Saul rent his clothes and beat Stephen. Gamaliel, Saul's teacher, sprang forth and gave Saul a buffet, saying: Did I teach thee such conduct? know that what this man saith is acceptable and good.

24 Saul was yet more enraged, and looked fiercely on him, saying: I spare thine old age, but thou shalt reap a due reward for this.

25 Gamaliel answered: I ask nothing better than to suffer with Christ. The elders rent their clothes, cast dust on their heads, and cried: Crucify the blasphemers.

26 Saul said: Guard them until the morrow. Next day he sat on the judgement seat and had them brought before him, and they were led away to be crucified.

27 An angel came and cast away the cross, and Stephen's wounds were healed. Seven men came and poured molten lead into his mouth and pitch into his ears.

28 They drove nails into his breast and feet, and he prayed for their forgiveness. Again an angel came down and healed him, and a great multitude believed.

29 The next day all assembled and took him out of the city to judge him. He mounted upon a stone and addressed them: How long will ye harden your hearts?

30 The Law and the Prophets spake of Christ. In the first Law, and the second, and the other books it is written: When the year of the covenant cometh I will send my beloved angel, the good spirit of sonship, from a pure maiden, the fruit of truth, without ploughshare and without seed, and an image of sowing, and the fruit shall grow after the . . . of planting for ever from the word of my covenant, and signs shall come to pass.

31 And Isaiah saith: Unto us a child is born...

32 And again: Behold, a virgin shall conceive...

33 And the prophet Nathan said: I saw one, a maiden and without touch of man, and a man child in her arms, and that was the Lord of the earth unto the end of the earth.

34 And again the prophet Baruch saith: Christ the eternal appeareth as a stone from the mountain and breaketh in pieces the idol temples of the . . .

35 David also said: Arise, O Lord, unto thy resting place...

36 Understand then, O foolish ones, what the prophet saith: In this word shalt thou judge.

37 And he looked up to heaven and said: I see the heaven opened and the Son of man standing at the right hand of God.

38 Then they laid hands on him, saying:

He blasphemeth! Gamaliel said: Wherein? This righteous man hath seen the Son saying to the Father: Lo, the Jews rage against me and cease not to ill-treat them that confess my name.

39 And the Father said: Sit thou on my right hand until I make thine enemies thy footstool.

40 Then they bound Stephen and took him away to Alexander, the reader, who was a chief of the people, and of the troop in Tiberias.

41 In the fourth watch of the night, a light as of lightning shone round about him, and a voice said: Be strong.

42 Thou art my first martyr, and thine hour is nigh. I will write the record of thee in the book of everlasting life.

43 The Jews took counsel and decreed that he should be stoned. There were with him Abibas, Nicodemus, Gamaliel, Pilate, his wife and two children, and a multitude of believers.

44 Saul stood forth and beckoned, and said: It would have been better that this man should not be slain, because of his great wisdom: but forasmuch as he is an apostate, I condemn Stephen to be stoned.

45 The people said: He shall be stoned: but those who stood in the front rank with staves looked on each other and durst not lay hands on him: for he was renowned among the people.

46 Saul was wroth, and stripped those servants of their garments and laid them on the table; and commanded the men to stone Stephen.

47 Stephen looked round and said: Saul, Saul, that which thou doest unto me to-day, that same will the Jews do unto thee to-morrow. And when thou sufferest, thou shalt think on me.

48 The people cast stones upon him so thickly that the light of the sun was darkened. Nicodemus and Gamaliel put their arms about him and shielded him, and were slain, and gave up their souls to Christ.

49 Stephen prayed, saying: Forgive them that stone us, for by their means we trust to enter into thy kingdom.

50 And at the tenth hour he gave up the ghost. Then beautiful youths appeared, and fell upon the bodies and wept aloud: and the people beheld the souls borne up by angels into heaven, and saw the heavens open and the hosts coming to meet the souls.

51 And the people mourned for three days and three nights.

52 Pilate took the bodies and put each one into a silver coffin with his name upon it: but Stephen's coffin was gilt: and he laid them in his secret sepulchre.

53 But Stephen prayed: Let my body be buried in my land of Serasima in Kapogemala (Caphargamala) until the revealing, when the martyrs that follow me shall be gathered together.

54 And an angel came and removed the bodies thither. But Pilate rose early to burn incense before the bodies, and found them not; and rent his clothes, saying: Was I then not worthy to be thy servant?

55 On the night following, Stephen appeared and said to him: Weep not. I prayed God to hide our bodies.

56 In the time of our revealing one of thy seed shall find us after a vision, and thy desire shall be fulfilled.

57 But build a house of prayer and celebrate our feast in the month of April.

58 After seven months thou also shalt rest. And Pilate did so: and he died, and was buried at Kapartasala: and his wife also died in peace.

59 But the holy martyrs appeared thrice to venerable and believing men, speaking to them, and revealing divine words: for after their death many believed.

THE APOCALYPSE OF JOHN THE RIGHTEOUS

1 AFTER the taking up of our Lord Jesus Christ, I John was alone upon Mount Tabor, where also He showed us His undefiled Godhead; and as I was not able to stand, I fell upon the ground, and prayed to the Lord, and said:

2 O Lord my God, who hast deemed me worthy to be Thy servant, hear my voice, and teach me about Thy coming.

3 When Thou shall come to the earth, what will happen? The heaven and the earth, and the sun and the moon, what will happen to them in those times?

4 Reveal to me all; for I am emboldened, because Thou listenest to Thy servant.

5 And I spent seven days praying; and after this a cloud of light caught me up from the mountain, and set me before the face of the heaven.

6 And I heard a voice saying to me: Look up, John, servant of God, and know.

7 And having looked up, I saw the heaven opened, and there came forth from within the heaven a smell of perfumes of much sweet odour; and I saw an exceeding great flood of light, more resplendent than the sun.

8 And again I heard a voice saying to me: Behold, righteous John.

9 And I directed my sight, and saw a book lying, of the thickness, and I thought, of seven mountains; and the length of it the mind of man cannot comprehend, having seven seals.

10 And I said: O Lord my God, reveal to me what is written in this book.

11 And I heard a voice saying to me: Hear, righteous John. In this book which thou seest there have been written the things in the heaven, and the things in the earth, and the things in the abyss, and the judgments and righteousness of all the human race.

12 And I said: Lord, when shall these things come to pass? and what do those times bring? And I heard a voice saying to me: Hear, righteous John.

13 There shall be in that time abundance of corn and wine, such as there hath never been upon the earth, nor shall ever be until those times come.

14 Then the ear of corn shall produce a half choenix, and the bend of the branch shall produce a thousand clusters, and the cluster shall produce a half jar of wine; and in the following year there shall not be found upon the face of all the earth a half choenix of corn or a half jar of wine.

15 And again I said: Lord, thereafter what wilt Thou do?

16 And I heard a voice saying to me: Hear, righteous John.

17 Then shall appear the denier, and he who is set apart in the darkness, who is called Antichrist.

18 And again I said: Lord, reveal to me what he is like?

19 And I heard a voice saying to me: The appearance of his face is dusky; the hairs of his head are sharp, like darts; his eyebrows like a wild beast's; his right eye like the star which rises in the morning, and the other like a lion's; his mouth about one cubit; his teeth span long; his fingers like scythes; the print of his feet of two spans; and on his face an inscription, Antichrist.

20 He shall be exalted even to heaven, and shall be cast down even to Hades, making false displays.

21 And then will I make the heaven brazen, so that it shall not give moisture upon the earth; and I will hide the clouds in secret places, so that they shall not bring moisture upon the earth; and I will command the horns of the wind, so that the wind shall not blow upon the earth.

22 And again I said: Lord, and how many years will he do this upon the earth?

23 And I heard a voice saying to me:

Hear, righteous John.

24 Three years shall those times be; and I will make the three years like three months, and the three months like three weeks, and the three weeks like three days, and the three days like three hours, and the three hours like three seconds, as said the prophet David, His throne hast Thou broken down to the ground;

25 Thou hast shortened the days of his time; Thou hast poured shame upon him.

26 And then I shall send forth Enoch and Elias to convict him; and they shall show him to be a liar and a deceiver; and he shall kill them at the altar, as said the prophet, Then shall they offer calves upon Thine altar.

27 And again I said: Lord, and after that what will come to pass?

28 And I heard a voice saying to me: Hear, righteous John.

29 Then all the human race shall die, and there shall not be a living man upon all the earth.

30 And again I said: Lord, after that what wilt Thou do?

31 And I heard a voice saying to me: Hear, righteous John.

32 Then will I send forth mine angels, and they shall take the ram's horns that lie upon the cloud; and Michael and Gabriel shall go forth out of the heaven and sound with those horns, as the prophet David foretold, With the voice of a trumpet of horn.

33 And the voice of the trumpet shall be heard from the one quarter of the world to the other; and from the voice of that trumpet all the earth shall be shaken, as the prophet foretold, And at the voice of the bird every plant shall arise; that is, at the voice of the archangel all the human race shall arise.

34 And again I said: Lord, those who are dead froth Adam even to this day, and who dwell in Hades from the beginning of the world, and who die at the last ages, what like shall they arise?

35 And I heard a voice saying to me: Hear, righteous John.

36 All the human race shall arise thirty years old.

37 And again I said: Lord, they die male and female, and some old, and some young, and some infants. In the resurrection what like shall they arise?

38 And I heard a voice saying to me: Hear, righteous John.

39 Just as the bees are, and differ not one from another, but are all of one appearance and one size, so also shall every man be in the resurrection.

40 There is neither fair, nor ruddy, nor black, neither Ethiopian nor different countenances; but they shall all arise of one appearance and one stature.

41 All the human race shall arise without bodies, as I told you that in the resurrection they neither marry nor are given in marriage, but are as the angels of God.

42 And again I said: Lord, is it possible in that world to recognise each other, a brother his brother, or a friend his friend, or a father his own children, or the children their own parents?

43 And I heard a voice saying to me: Hear, John.

44 To the righteous there is recognition, but to the sinners not at all; they cannot in the resurrection recognise each other.

45 And again I John said: Lord, is there recollection of the things that are here, either fields or vineyards, or other things here?

46 And I heard a voice saying to me: Hear, righteous John.

47 The prophet David speaks, saying, I remembered that we are dust: as for man, his days are as grass; as a flower of the field, so he shall flourish: for a wind hath passed over it, and it shall be no more, and it shall not any longer know its place.

48 And again the same said: His spirit shall go forth, and he returns to his earth; in that day all his thoughts shall perish.

49 And again I said: Lord, and after that what wilt Thou do?

50 And I heard a voice saying to me: Hear, righteous John.

51 Then will I send forth mine angels over the face of all the earth, and they shall lift off the earth everything honourable, and everything precious,

and the venerable and holy images, and the glorious and precious crosses, and the sacred vessels of the churches, and the divine and sacred books; and all the precious and holy things shall be lifted up by clouds into the air.

52 And then will I order to be lifted up the great and venerable sceptre, on which I stretched forth my hands, and all the orders of my angels shall do reverence to it.

53 And then shall be lifted up all the race of men upon clouds, as the Apostle Paul foretold.

54 Along with them we shall be snatched up in clouds to meet the Lord in the air.

55 And then shall come forth every evil spirit, both in the earth and in the abyss, wherever they are on the face of all the earth, from the rising of the sun even to the setting, and they shall be united to him that is served by the devil, that is, Antichrist, and they shall be lifted up upon the clouds.

56 And again I said: Lord, and after that what wilt Thou do?

57 And I heard a voice saying to me: Hear, righteous John.

58 Then shall I send forth mine angels over the face of all the earth, and they shall burn up the earth eight thousand five hundred cubits.

59 And the great mountains shall be burnt up, and all the rocks shall be melted and shall become as dust, and every tree shall be burnt up, and every beast, and every creeping thing creeping upon the earth.

60 And every thing moving upon the face of the earth, and every flying thing flying in the air; and there shall no longer be upon the face of all the earth anything moving, and the earth shall be without motion.

61 And again I said: Lord, and after that what wilt Thou do?

62 And I heard a voice saying to me: Hear, righteous John.

63 Then shall I uncover the four parts of the east, and there shall come forth four great winds, and they shall sweep all the face of the earth from the one end of the earth to the other; and the Lord shall sweep sin from off the earth, and the earth shall be made white like snow, and it shall become as a leaf of paper, without cave, or mountain, or hill, or rock; but the face of the earth from the rising even to the setting of the sun shall be like a table, and white as snow; and the reins of the earth shall be consumed by fire, and it shall cry unto me, saying, I am a virgin before thee, O Lord, and there is no sin in me; as the prophet David said aforetime,

64 Thou shall sprinkle me with hyssop, and I shall be made pure; Thou shalt wash me, and I shall be made whiter than snow.

65 And again he said: Every chasm shall be filled up, and every mountain and hill brought low, and the crooked places shall be made straight, and the rough ways into smooth; and all flesh shall see the salvation of God.

66 And again I said: Lord, and after that what wilt Thou do?

67 And I heard a voice saying to me: Hear, righteous John.

68 Then shall the earth be cleansed from sin, and all the earth shall be filled with a sweet smell, because I am about to come down upon the earth; and then shall come forth the great and venerable sceptre, with thousands of angels worshipping it, as I said before; and then shall appear the sign of the Son of man from the heaven with power and great glory.

69 And then the worker of iniquity with his servants shall behold it, and gnash his teeth exceedingly, and all the unclean spirits shall be turned to flight. And then, seized by invisible power, having no means of flight, they shall gnash their teeth against him, saying to him:

70 Where is thy power? How hast thou led us astray? and we have fled away, and have fallen away from the glory which we had beside Him who is coming to judge us, and the whole human race.

71 Woe to us! because He banishes us into outer darkness.

72 And again I said: Lord, and after that what wilt Thou do?

73 And I heard a voice saying to me: Then will I send an angel out of heaven, and he shall cry with a loud voice, saying, Hear, O earth, and be strong, saith the Lord; for I am coming down to thee.

74 And the voice of the angel shall be heard from the one end of the world even to the other, and even to the remotest part of the abyss.

75 And then shall be shaken all the power of the angels and of the many-eyed ones, and there shall be a great noise in the heavens, and the nine regions of the heaven shall be shaken, and there shall be fear and astonishment upon all the angels.

76 And then the heavens shall be rent from the rising of the sun even to the setting, and an innumerable multitude of angels shall come down to the earth; and then the treasures of the heavens shall be opened, and they shall bring down every precious thing, and the perfume of incense, and they shall bring down to the earth Jerusalem robed like a bride.

77 And then there shall go before me myriads of angels and archangels, bearing my throne, crying out, Holy, holy, holy, Lord of Sabaoth; heaven and earth are full of Thy glory.

78 And then will I come forth with power and great glory, and every eye in the clouds shall see me; and then every knee shall bend, of things in heaven, and things on earth, and things under the earth.

79 And then the heaven shall remain empty; and I will come down upon the earth, and all that is in the air shall be brought down upon the earth, and all the human race and every evil spirit along with Antichrist, and they shall all be set before me naked, and chained by the neck.

80 And again I said: Lord, what will become of the heavens, and the sun, and the moon, along with the stars?

81 And I heard a voice saying to me: Behold, righteous John.

82 And I looked, and saw a Lamb having seven eyes and seven horns.

83 And again I heard a voice saying to me: I will bid the Lamb come before me, and will say, Who will open this book?

84 And all the multitudes of the angels will answer, Give this book to the Lamb to open it.

85 And then will I order the book to be opened. And when He shall open the first seal, the stars of the heaven shall fall, from the one end of it to the other.

86 And when He shall open the second seal, the moon shall be hidden, and there shall be no light in her.

87 And when He shall open the third seal, the light of the sun shall be withheld, and there shall not be light upon the earth.

88 And when He shall open the fourth seal, the heavens shall be dissolved, and the air shall be thrown into utter confusion, as saith the prophet:

89 And the heavens are the works of Thy hands; they shall perish, but Thou endurest, and they shall all wax old as a garment.

90 And when He shall open the fifth seal, the earth shall be rent, and all the tribunals upon the face of all the earth shall be revealed.

91 And when He shall open the sixth seal, the half of the sea shall disappear. And when He shall open the seventh seal, Hades shall be uncovered.

92 And I said: Lord, who will be the first to be questioned, and to receive judgment?

93 And I heard a voice saying to me, The unclean spirits, along with the adversary. I bid them go into outer darkness, where the depths are.

94 And I said: Lord, and in what place does it lie?

95 And I heard a voice saying to me: Hear, righteous John.

96 As big a stone as a man of thirty years old can roll, and let go down into the depth, even falling down for twenty years will not arrive at the bottom of Hades; as the prophet David said before, And He made darkness His secret place.

97 And I said: Lord, and after them what nation will be questioned?

98 And I heard a voice saying to me:

Hear, righteous John.

99 There will be questioned of Adam's race those nations, both the Greek and those who have believed in idols, and in the sun, and in the stars, and those who have defiled the faith by heresy, and who have not believed the holy resurrection, and who have not confessed the Father, and the Son, and the Holy Ghost: then will I send them away into Hades, as the prophet David foretold,

100 Let the sinners be turned into Hades, and all the nations that forget God. And again he said: They were put in Hades like sheep; death shall be their shepherd.

101 And again I said: Lord, and after them whom wilt Thou judge?

102 And I heard a voice saying to me: Hear, righteous John.

103 Then the race of the Hebrews shall be examined, who nailed me to the tree like a malefactor.

104 And I said: And what punishment will these get, and in what place, seeing that they did such things to Thee?

105 And I heard a voice saying to me: They shall go away into Tartarus, as the prophet David foretold,

106 They cried out, and there was none to save; to the Lord, and He did not hearken to them.

107 And again the Apostle Paul said: As many as have sinned without law shall also perish without law, and as many as have sinned in law shall be judged by means of law.

108 And again I said: Lord, and what of those who have received baptism?

109 And I heard a voice saying to me: Then the race of the Christians shall be examined, who have received baptism; and then the righteous shall come at my command, and the angels shall go and collect them from among the sinners, as the prophet David foretold:

110 The Lord will not suffer the rod of the sinners in the lot of the righteous; and all the righteous shall be placed on my right hand, and shall shine like the sun.

111 As thou seest, John, the stars of heaven, that they were all made together, but differ in light, so shall it be with the righteous and the sinners; for the righteous shall shine as lights and as the sun, but the sinners shall stand in darkness.

112 And again I said: Lord, and do all the Christians go into one punishment?--kings, high priests, priests, patriarchs, rich and poor, bond and free?

113 And I heard a voice saying to me: Hear, righteous John.

114 As the prophet David foretold, The expectation of the poor shall not perish for ever.

115 Now about kings: they shall be driven like slaves, and shall weep like infants; and about patriarchs, and priests, and Levites, of those that have sinned, they shall be separated in their punishments, according to the nature of the peculiar transgression of each,-some in the river of fire, and some to the worm that dieth not, and others in the seven-mouthed pit of punishment.

116 To these punishments the sinners will be apportioned.

117 And again I said: Lord, and where will the righteous dwell?

118 And I heard a voice saying to me: Then shall paradise be revealed; and the whole world and paradise shall be made one, and the righteous shall be on the face of all the earth with my angels, as the Holy Spirit foretold through the prophet David:

119 The righteous shall inherit the earth, and dwell therein for ever and ever.

120 And again I said: Lord, how great is the multitude of the angels? and which is the greater, that of angels or of men?

121 And I heard a voice saying to me: As great as is the multitude of the angels, so great is the race of men, as the prophet has said, He set bounds to the nations according to the number of the angels of God.

122 And again I said: Lord, and after that what wilt Thou do? and what is to become of the world? Reveal to me all.

123 And I heard a voice saying to me: Hear, righteous John.

124 After that there is no pain, there is no grief, there is no groaning; there is no recollection of evils, there are no tears, there is no envy, there is no hatred of brethren, there is no unrighteousness, there is no arrogance, there is no slander, there is no bitterness, there are none of the cares of life, there is no pain from parents or children, there is no pain from gold, there are no wicked thoughts, there is no devil, there is no death, there is no night, but all is day.

125 As I said before, And other sheep I have, which are not of this fold, that is, men who have been made like the angels through their excellent course of life; them also must I bring, and they will hear my voice, and there shall be one fold, one shepherd.

126 And again I heard a voice saying to me: Behold, thou hast heard all these things, righteous John; deliver them to faithful men, that they also may teach others, and not think lightly of them, nor cast our pearls before swine, lest perchance they should trample them with their feet.

127 And while I was still hearing this voice, the cloud brought me down, and put me on Mount Tabor.

128 And there came a voice to me, saying:

129 Blessed are those who keep judgment and do righteousness in all time.

130 And blessed is the house where this description lies, as the Lord said, He that loveth me keepeth my sayings in Christ Jesus our Lord; to Him be glory for ever. Amen.

Made in the USA
Middletown, DE
05 February 2017